The Rocky Mountain Journals of William Marshall Anderson

WILLIAM MARSHALL ANDERSON

(1807-1881)

The
Rocky Mountain Journals
of
William Marshall Anderson

THE WEST IN 1834

EDITED BY DALE L. MORGAN

AND ELEANOR TOWLES HARRIS

University of Nebraska Press
Lincoln and London

First Bison Book printing: 1987
Most recent printing indicated by the first digit below:
1   2   3   4   5   6   7   8   9   10

Library of Congress Cataloging-in-Publication Data
Anderson, William Marshall, 1807–1881.
   The Rocky Mountain journals of William Marshall Anderson.
   Reprint. Originally published: San Marino, Calif.:
Huntington Library, 1967.
   Bibliography: p.
   Includes index.
   1. West (U.S.)—Description and travel—To 1848.
2. Rocky Mountains Region—Description and travel.
3. Fur Trade—Rocky Mountains Region—History—19th
century. 4. Fur traders—Rocky Mountains Region—
Biography. 5. Anderson, William Marshall, 1807–1881—
Diaries. I. Morgan, Dale Lowell, 1914–1971.
II. Harris, Eleanor Towles. III. Title.
F592.A62 1987   917.8'042'0924 [B]   86-19304
ISBN 0-8032-5910-7 (pbk.)

Reprinted by arrangement with the Huntington Library

To Jim Holliday

FRIEND AND BOON COMPANION OF BOTH THE
AUTHOR AND THE EDITORS

Contents

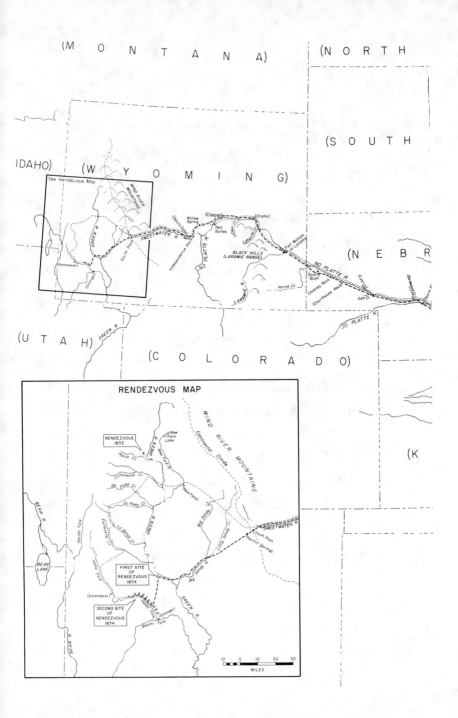

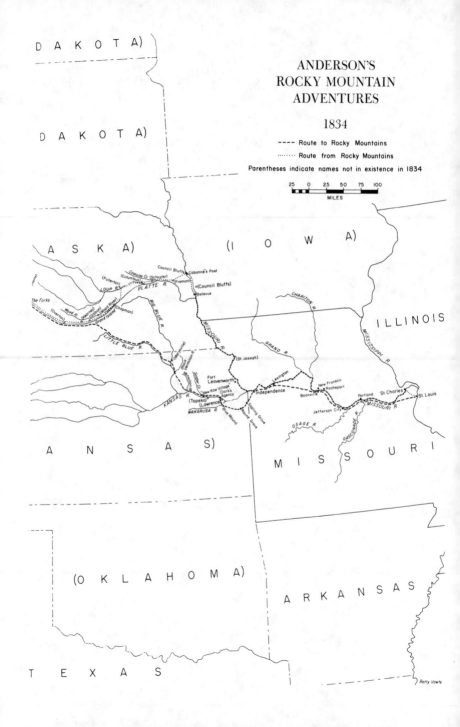

ANDERSON'S
ROCKY MOUNTAIN
ADVENTURES

1834

- - - - Route to Rocky Mountains
.... Route from Rocky Mountains

Parentheses indicate names not in existence in 1834

25 0 25 50 75 100
MILES

Anderson and His Times

Introduction

About to publish an account of a journey to the Rocky Mountains made in his young manhood, William Marshall Anderson was moved to preface it with a letter to Robert Campbell in St. Louis. Campbell had gone to the Rockies in one of General Ashley's parties, and there laid the foundations of his fortune; during a long life, he had known most of the major personalities of the American fur trade. On September 15, 1871, at his home in Circleville, Ohio, Anderson took up his pen:

Dear Sir:

If you will be kind enough to look over the accompanying notes, of a horseback journey, to and from the Rocky Mountains, in 1834, you will find, that through familiarity with identical scenes, and mutual friends, you and I, are not absolute strangers. My journal, though covered with the dust of nearly forty years, may, through the magic power of memory, bring before you, with all the lifelike vividness of yesterday, places and persons, almost forgotten. You and I have looked upon the same bold and beautiful scenery, the same noble and manly faces, with expressions too dear to die.

I am aware, in desiring your perusal of these, my old campfire records, that I am subjecting you to both pleasant and painful reminiscences. Such are the unaccountable, perhaps unavoidable, caprices of the mind. Of all that brave and hardy band of pioneers, companions of Ashley, successors of Sublette and Jackson, I know not how few are left, or how many are gone to the Spirit-land. Where is Fitzpatrick, "du main poc"? Where Fontenelle, Dripps, Vasquez and Bridger? Where are Chaboneau, Kit Carson, Black Harris and One-Eyed Emanuel? And, changing race and color, I would enquire, whether good old Insillah still lives? And can you tell me, whether the Coughing Snake, and the graceful and eloquent Bracelette-defer, yet follow the buffalo, and tell of the cruel and bloody devastation of the Blackfeet? Who are left? Who are gone? I know not, but it is certain that the survivors must follow their file-leaders. "Time is passing and we are passing with it." The question is, not when, but where we shall go. Let us be armed and prepared to march when the trumpet sounds.

And now, dear sir, I beg leave to subscribe myself,

Yours, with reverence and respect,

W. MARSHALL ANDERSON

3

To such a communication Robert Campbell could only have replied: "All are gone! All but Old Gabe." Jim Bridger had lately retired to a farm south of Westport, Missouri, to spend his last years in gathering darkness; he would survive Campbell and even Anderson, but only by a few months. The West the three had known was also gone. The Pacific Railroad was completed; miners' shacks speckled the Rocky Mountain gulches; hidehunters and cavalry were making an end of the buffalo and the plains tribes; and longhorns were plodding up from Texas to claim the short-grass country. The older West survived in memory alone.

Bridger's memory had the farthest reach, extending back to 1822, the morning of the world. Campbell had gone west in 1825, primarily in search of health, for in St. Louis he had begun to cough his lungs out. He had remained in the mountains four years, despite entreaties by his family that he come away from those "Black footed Black hearted & Blk headed savages" and lead a Christian life. Campbell had returned to the states in 1829, but after visiting his family in Ireland had spent parts of four more years in the mountains. William Drummond Stewart, who had been encountered by Anderson the day before he first laid eyes on Bridger, and who had died in April 1871, had gone to the Rockies with Campbell in 1833 and seen the next five rendezvous. From the vantage point of 1854, Sir William had concluded that 1833 was the last good year, for with 1834 came the spoilers—the idlers, the missionaries, the hard-fisted seekers after money. But 1834 is golden age enough, for William Marshall Anderson and for us.

Anderson left home, he tells us, "to accompany the dragoons on their escort of the traders to Santa Fe." Contradictorily, he also says he rode to St. Louis "to go with the dragoons on the Pawnee-Pic expedition." Had he accompanied either expedition, the young Kentuckian would never have seen the Rocky Mountains. The stars in their courses had determined that Anderson should go to the Rockies, but the dragoons induced him to leave home so that all the rest might follow.

In the winter of 1833 Congress had provided for the organization of a dragoon regiment. Officers tendered commissions included Henry Dodge, colonel, Stephen Watts Kearny, lieutenant colonel, R. B. Mason, major, Clifton Wharton and Edwin V. Sumner, captains, and Philip St. George Cooke, Jefferson Davis, and Lancaster P. Lupton, lieutenants. Officers traveled to nearly every state to enlist superior men. Through the fall of 1833 Anderson must have seen recruits passing down the Ohio en route to Jefferson Barracks near St. Louis. He might even have picked up some of the notions of the men, "that they would have nothing to do but to ride on horseback over the country, to explore the western prairies and forests, and, indeed, spend their time continually in delightful and inspiring occupations"—always a defective view of Army life.

Half of the regiment was ordered to Fort Gibson on the lower Arkansas. These five companies had a miserable time keeping themselves and their animals warm and fed until spring arrived. Men stationed at Jefferson Barracks seemed better off, but the rate of desertion was high. In the spring and summer of 1834, after Anderson gave up the idea of going along, most of the dragoons marched to the Red River under Colonel Dodge. After counciling with Pawnee-Pics, Comanches, and Kiowas, they got back to Fort Gibson in mid-August. Soon after, three companies were sent to take station at Fort Leavenworth. They arrived on September 22, a few hours after Anderson passed the fort homeward-bound.

Meanwhile Captain Wharton with Company A was escorting the Santa Fe traders as far as the Arkansas, an experience to set his teeth on edge since the traders were hardshelled individualists disposed to go their own way. On June 27 the caravan crossed the Arkansas. The farthest he could go, Wharton announced, was to the point where the Santa Fe road reached the Cimarron. The original commander, Josiah Gregg, having resigned, the new captain of the caravan, Ira G. Smith (younger brother of the lamented Jedediah, killed by Comanches in this vicinity three years earlier), declined further help. On the twenty-eighth the caravan started on for Santa Fe, and Wharton turned back to Fort Gibson. He arrived July 19, his horses nearly broken down, to report that no danger existed for traders east of Walnut Creek; the critical area was between the Arkansas and a point seventy miles out of Santa Fe. Over that stretch of trail, beyond the Mexican boundary, American troops could not go.

Had Anderson accompanied Wharton's command, he would have had an interesting time and witnessed a minor turning point in history. In the light of Wharton's experience, military escorts on the Santa Fe Trail were seen to serve no purpose. Next year Colonel Dodge led three companies of the dragoons on a grand tour of the West, north from Fort Leavenworth to the mouth of the Platte, up that river and the South Platte to the mountains, and home by way of the Arkansas and the Santa Fe Trail. But that was a parade to impress the plains Indians; after 1835, for ten years, no big dragoon expeditions were seen in the West.

* * *

Having thought better or worse of accompanying the dragoons, Anderson set off for the Rockies with William L. Sublette. He passes lightly over his journey across Missouri, and we shall do the same, except to pause with him at Lexington and Independence.

If Lexington was no longer the jumping-off place for wilderness-bound men, it retained a character all its own. Alphonso Wetmore commented a few years later:

Lexington is the seat of justice for Lafayette County, and a healthy, flourishing town. The location of the land-office at this place adds to the natural advantages . . . [which] consist in great salubrity of air, its vicinity to the richest lands of Missouri, and its elevated position. There is also a good landing opposite the town, and one lower down the river, at Webb's warehouse. . . . Lexington is one of the towns from which outfits are made in merchandise, mules, oxen, and wagons for the Santa Fé or New Mexican trade. The fur-traders who pass to the mountains by land make this town a place of rendezvous, and frequently are going out and coming in with their wagons and packed mules, at the same period of going and coming that is chosen by the Mexican traders. Lexington is therefore occasionally a thoroughfare of traders of great enterprise, and caravans of infinite value. The dress and arms of the traders, trappers, and hunters of these caravans, and caparison of the horses and mules they ride, present as great diversity as the general resurrection itself of all nations and ages can promise for the speculations of the curious.

After five days in Lexington "buying and branding horses, giving out and packing up goods for the mountain market," Sublette moved along to Independence, where he devoted four days to final arrangements. Anderson barely mentions Independence. John K. Townsend, who had arrived April 20, found the site beautiful, and very well selected, standing on a high point of land [3 miles back from the Missouri], and overlooking the surrounding country, but the town itself is very indifferent; the houses, (about fifty,) are very much scattered, composed of logs and clay, and are low and inconvenient. There are six or eight stores here, two taverns, and a few tipling houses. As we [himself and Thomas Nuttall] did not fancy the town, nor the society that we saw there, we concluded to take up our residence at the house on the landing until the time of starting on our journey. We were very much disappointed in not being able to purchase any mules here, all the saleable ones having been bought by the Santa Fee traders, several weeks since. Horses, also, are rather scarce, and are sold at higher prices than we had been taught to expect, the demand for them at this time being greater than usual.

The demand for mules and horses reflected the circumstance that all the mountain-bound companies (four of them in 1834) for the first time were making Independence their point of departure.

Independence became the seat of the new Jackson County in 1827; Joseph Reddeford Walker, as Jackson County's first sheriff, is said to have chosen the name. Alphonso Wetmore thought that the "regular and healthy growth" of Independence evidenced "the great value of the country around it, as well as its suitable location, with a view to the trade of the farming population." Independence having become the point of departure for the Santa Fe traders, "at this place much material for the outfit of the caravans is obtained. Here, likewise, the return trading-companies obtain supplies, when coming into port from a sea of prairie. The traders and their hands generally reach Independence destitute of every thing in the list of food and clothing. The necessities of these people bring to this frontier town singular advantages in a wide range of cash transactions."

The comings and goings of Santa Fe and Rocky Mountain traders were not the major preoccupation of the townsfolk as spring came on in 1834.

The little town of Independence [Townsend observed] has within a few weeks been the scene of a brawl, which at one time threatened to be attended with serious consequences. . . . It had been for a considerable time the stronghold of a sect of fanatics, called Mormons, or Mormonites, who, as their numbers increased, and they obtained power, showed an inclination to lord it over the less assuming inhabitants of the town. This was a source of irritation which they determined to rid themselves of in a summary manner, and accordingly the whole town rose, *en masse*, and the poor followers of the prophet were forcibly ejected from the community. They took refuge in the little town of Liberty, on the opposite side of the river, and the villagers here are now in a constant state of feverish alarm. Reports have been circulated that the Mormons are preparing to attack the town, and put the inhabitants to the sword, and they have therefore stationed sentries along the river for several miles, to prevent the landing of the enemy. The troops parade and study military tactics every day, and seem determined to repel, with spirit, the threatened invasion. . . .

Mormon missionaries to the Indians had made their way to Independence in 1830. Subsequently the Mormon prophet, Joseph Smith, pronounced Jackson County to be the promised land, and Mormon converts thronged westward, to the discomfiture of the Jacksonites. In July 1833 a mob of "old settlers" destroyed the Mormon press and tarred and feathered several prominent Mormons. They also forced nine leaders to agree that they would move out of Jackson County by the end of the year and induce their brethren to leave the county as soon as possible, half by January and all by April; the Mormons also agreed that no press should be set up. On the faith of assurances by the governor, the Mormons prepared to institute legal proceedings, but the Jackson mob rose again, and by mid-November the Mormons were fleeing across the Missouri into Clay County. In the spring of 1834 Joseph Smith mustered an army, "Zion's Camp," and set out from Ohio to "redeem Zion." Rumors concerning the coming of this force occasioned the defiant alarm described by Townsend. Cholera pounced upon the army after it crossed the Mississippi, and in June Zion's Camp gave up any idea of redeeming Zion by force. The Mormons agreed to take up lands north of the Missouri, and Joseph Smith made his disconsolate way back to Ohio. Passing through Missouri before the upshot could be known, William Marshall Anderson appears to have felt some sympathy for the Mormons, though William L. Sublette's associates and employees belonged to the class of Missourians who had driven out Smith's followers; to their viewpoint primarily Anderson would have been exposed in journeying across Missouri.

*   *   *

William Marshall Anderson's diary of his journey to and from the Rockies is one of the earliest documents of its kind. Down to this year there had been no Oregon Trail as such, only a "trace" used by fur traders carrying on their business in the Rockies. In 1830 William L. Sublette showed the capabilities of this trace by taking wagons to Wind River and back, and two years later Captain Bonneville brought wagons across South Pass to the Green River. That same year Nathaniel Wyeth went all the way to the Columbia, though not with wagons or by what could be called a road; he and the Methodist missionaries accompanying him in 1834 would be the first to travel what could reasonably be thought of as a road to Oregon. Whether to Oregon or only as far as the Rockies, few are the diaries of travel on this route antedating Anderson's.

In 1804-1806 Meriwether Lewis and William Clark went to the Pacific and back, but by way of the sources of the Missouri. In the spring of 1811 Wilson Price Hunt led his Astorians up the Missouri to the Arikara villages in present South Dakota. Obtaining horses from the Arikaras and Cheyennes, he rode west to the Wind River Mountains, and via Union Pass crossed over to the valley of the Green and went on over a divide to the Hoback River and Jackson Hole (Wyoming). His trail at its farthest south on Green River nearly touched that of Anderson, homeward-bound in 1834. Hunt went on to the Snake and, after many hardships, the Columbia.

In 1812 Robert Stuart led east some returning Astorians, his route from the Columbia to the Snake and the Bear in large part anticipating the eventually established Oregon Trail. Vainly hoping to evade Crow horse thieves, from Bear River Stuart made a long northern detour, regained Hunt's trail of the year before, and followed that trail to Jackson Hole and the upper Green. Here leaving Hunt's route, Stuart made for the southern end of the Wind River Mountains, and in October 1812 became the historic discoverer of South Pass. Continuing on, Stuart kept south of the Sweetwater, only striking this stream as he was approaching the North Platte. Stuart seems not to have understood the character of the Sweetwater, or the advantages it afforded travelers bound for Pacific waters, but he did comprehend the significance of South Pass for transcontinental travelers. He had to winter on the North Platte, but next spring resumed his journey down the Platte and reached St. Louis in April 1813.

John Jacob Astor's conception of a fur-trading empire based on the Columbia foundered under assorted disasters. Blackfoot hostility and the effect of the War of 1812 on the Missouri tribes hampered the fur trade based on St. Louis, and for seven years after Robert Stuart came home there was no travel to or from the northern Rockies.

In the summer of 1820 Major Stephen H. Long of the Topographical Engineers embarked upon a Western tour. The route he took, which kept north of the Platte as far as the Forks, was used by various fur traders over the next twenty years, especially by Lucien Fontenelle, who conducted Anderson over it in returning from the mountains in 1834; later the route became known as the Mormon Trail, one of the major branches of the Oregon Trail. Long rode up the South Platte to the Front Range of the Rockies, then south to the Arkansas. He sent a detachment under Captain John R. Bell down that river and took the rest of the party south in the expectation of falling upon the Red River. The river he reached was the Canadian, and he wound up on the lower Arkansas. Long's report represented the West as the Great American Desert, and for that it has been best remembered.

In the winter of 1824-1825 William H. Ashley followed Long's trail as far as the Rockies, then by way of the Cache la Poudre and the Laramie Plains made his way northwesterly to the Green River. Ashley's route, around the Medicine Bow Mountains to the upper North Platte, then on through the Great Divide Basin south of South Pass, brought him to the Green above the mouth of the Sandy. One of Ashley's diaries has survived, covering the period March 25-June 27, 1825, after he rounded the Medicine Bow Mountains and while he was making a voyage of discovery down the Green River. Ashley went far enough west to reach some of the streams draining into Great Salt Lake before he turned back for the first rendezvous of the fur trade. His diary has been edited by Dale L. Morgan in *The West of William H. Ashley, 1822-1838*.

The great Jedediah Smith, at the head of an Ashley party, made the effective discovery, or rediscovery, of South Pass early in 1824, by way of the Crow country. He accompanied Ashley back through South Pass in the summer of 1825 and became his partner. A year later with William L. Sublette and David E. Jackson, he founded a new partnership which bought out Ashley. Smith then embarked upon explorations farther south and west. William L. Sublette became the most important figure in the history of the trails between the Rockies and the Missouri. Unfortunately Sublette left no diaries for this trail-making. In the winter of 1827, to confirm a contract with Ashley for goods, Sublette journeyed down to St. Louis with a single companion, "Black" Harris. At this time he seems to have first traveled the road from the Platte via the Little Blue to the Kansas River, a road that became known as Sublette's Trace, and eventually as the Oregon Trail. Sublette traveled by this route to Bear Lake in the spring of 1827, back to Lexington in the fall; to the mountains again that same autumn; down from the Rockies in the late summer of 1828; out again next spring; and back to St. Louis by another winter journey early in 1830. That spring, to the Wind River rendezvous, he took ten wagons and two dearborns, which in the late summer he brought home laden with furs. Sublette again went to and from the mountains by this trail in 1832. Anderson in 1834 had the best of mentors in Sublette and repaid him by keeping the diary now published.

The earliest actual journal of a fur trader's travels to the northern Rockies from the Missouri is the narrative by Warren Angus Ferris. In the spring of 1830 Ferris went to the mountains with Lucien Fontenelle and Andrew Drips, taking the route north of the Platte which Fontenelle had used in going to the high country with Joshua Pilcher in 1827 and coming back to Council Bluffs next year. Ferris returned to the states with Fontenelle in 1835. His *Life in the Rocky Mountains*, serialized in a Buffalo periodical between 1842 and 1844, is extremely interesting but not a true diary, having been written with benefit of hindsight.

In 1831 a young Pennsylvanian, Zenas Leonard, journeyed to the Rockies in the Gantt-Blackwell party. After varied experiences, including two years in Captain Bonneville's service and a visit to California in Joseph Reddeford Walker's party, he came back to the states in 1835. Leonard's interesting, sometimes exasperating *Narrative*, published in 1839, was written without reference to a diary and therefore has the defects that are to be expected.

In 1832 Capt. B. L. E. Bonneville was first to leave the frontier for the mountains, departing from Fort Osage, near Independence, at the beginning of May. He kept a diary through three whole years until his return in the summer of 1835, but this diary and the narrative he afterward wrote have disappeared; we know Bonneville's experiences primarily from the book Washington Irving created from his manuscript. The hope of finding the Bonneville manuscripts perennially sustains students of Western history; meanwhile we fall back upon Washington Irving's *The Rocky Mountains* (as originally titled in 1837; retitled *The Adventures of Captain Bonneville* in later editions), though we cannot be sure that Irving did not write anachronisms into his narrative, and obviously he had failures of understanding. Bonneville traveled much the route taken by Anderson two years later, but there are frequent gaps in Irving's text and only a handful of dates.

William L. Sublette, journeying to the mountains that spring of 1832 to supply the Rocky Mountain Fur Company, was the dominant personality in a party that included Robert Campbell and Thomas Fitzpatrick. Campbell wrote a letter to his brother Hugh after reaching the Pierres Hole rendezvous, and Sublette wrote one to Ashley after getting back to Lexington in September. The net information is not extensive. But the green Nathaniel Wyeth accompanied Sublette to the mountains, and Wyeth enlightens us considerably.

Wyeth's 1832-1833 diary, a pioneer document for what became the main branch of the Oregon Trail, was edited, together with his 1834 diary and letters, by F. G. Young in 1899 as *The Correspondence and Journals of Captain Nathaniel J. Wyeth, 1831-6*. The diary has been maltreated by time; entries from May 12, when Wyeth left Independence, until June 7, when he reached the North Platte below Chimney Rock, are lost. Thereafter, as far as the Sweetwater, this diary is an authentic daily record of trail life. Its chronology is sometimes askew, and occasionally Wyeth let the diary lapse, slighting some parts when bringing it up to date, as in ascending the Sweetwater. Still, in the immediacy of its jottings, Wyeth's diary is unlike any trail record before Anderson's. From the rendezvous, Wyeth went on to the Columbia. Instead of taking the route through the valley of the Snake, he trapped southern tributaries of that river—the rugged country adjacent to the present Nevada-Idaho boundary—and only near the mouth of the Bruneau did he regain the Oregon Trail of later years. Wyeth arrived at Fort

Walla Walla on October 15 and continued on down the Columbia by boat to Fort Vancouver.

The deficiencies in Wyeth's record are rectified somewhat by one of his party, John Ball. The Oregon Historical Society has a copy of an itinerary by Ball that begins May 12, 1832, on leaving Independence, and continues until arrival at the rendezvous July 8. This itinerary resumes on departure from the rendezvous, July 24, and with only a few gaps continues until Ball reached Fort Walla Walla October 18. Sparse as this record may be, supplying only dates, miles traveled, courses, and place names, it corrects the chronology of Wyeth's diary and in skeletal fashion supplies the place of the missing first portion of that diary. Ball must have kept a more complete memorandum, for a later-written "journal" published in the Oregon Historical Society *Quarterly*, March 1902, has details scarcely dredged up from memory. Most dates seem trustworthy; and it is the only very full account of the journey of the Sublette-Wyeth party across Kansas and southern Nebraska to the Platte.

From the rendezvous, Ball wrote to Dr. T. C. Brinsmade a letter printed in the *Daily Troy* (N. Y.) *Press*, August 1833, with several other communications sent home from Oregon. These letters gave curious Americans an interesting picture of a transcontinental journey and of conditions on the Columbia. Ball came home by sea in 1834.

Another chronicle of Wyeth's first expedition was written by his young cousin, John B. Wyeth, who became dissatisfied and from Pierres Hole turned back to the states with Sublette. His account was ghostwritten in 1833 by a Cambridge physician and scientist who looked with a jaundiced eye on the Far West: *Oregon; or A Short History of a Long Journey from the Atlantic Ocean to the Region of the Pacific by Land*. The younger Wyeth thus anticipated Anderson in chronicling a summer's journey to the Rockies, but his *Oregon* is an extremely general narrative, its few dates almost uniformly incorrect.

Charles Larpenteur, who in 1833 accompanied Robert Campbell to the mountains and afterward went with him to build Fort William near the mouth of the Yellowstone, did not keep a diary on the trail, but commenced one at Fort Union on Sept. 8, 1834, at that time summarizing events of the previous year. Later Larpenteur wrote an autobiography, the basis of Elliott Coues' *Forty Years a Fur Trader on the Upper Missouri*. William Drummond Stewart, Sir William after 1838, also accompanied Campbell to the mountains in 1833. His anonymously published novel, *Edward Warren*, written from the vantage point of 1854, presents its hero as a man who traveled to the mountains some weeks in the rear of Campbell's party.

We must not take leave of 1833 without again noticing Nathaniel Wyeth. After wintering on the Columbia, the New Englander made his way to the Green River rendezvous in July 1833, joined the party of Campbell and Fitzpatrick, and traveled with them by way of South Pass to the Big Horn River, where he constructed a bullboat and voyaged back to the settlements, keeping a diary en route.

*　　*　　*

William Marshall Anderson in Sublette's party was not the first chronicler to leave Independence in 1834, Nathaniel Wyeth's second expedition having got the jump on the opposition. But because Sublette overtook Wyeth near the crossing of the Big Blue River and remained out in front the rest of the way to Green River, Anderson's journal stands first in the year's trail record.

The initial value of the journal is that it is the sole known account of Sublette's party en route to the mountains. For lack of an Anderson, we know next to nothing of the rival caravans taken to the Rockies by Michel S. Cerré and Etienne Provost. (More appears in this book than has ever before been published about either, which evidences the slimness of the record.) Anderson gives us a daily account of Sublette's company, details its size and strength, lists some of its personnel, and for good measure provides sidelights on the past, including Sublette's wagon caravan of 1830. His pocket Diaries are supplemented by more elaborate accounts written after his return home. The Anderson record is particularly valuable for the great landmarks of the trail, enabling us to see which had been named, like Scotts Bluff and Independence Rock, and which had yet to be named, like Courthouse Rock and Devils Gate.

Valuable as Anderson's complete trail record is, what it says of the

Rocky Mountain fur trade in a period of stress seems even more important. Anderson's is the only eyewitness account of the founding of Fort Laramie. He is also the first to provide a day-by-day record of a fur trade rendezvous—and this in a critical year. Only with Anderson's aid do we fully understand what happened in the mountains this summer; he was the sole chronicler on hand when Fitzpatrick, Sublette & Bridger (successor to the Rocky Mountain Fur Company, which had come to the end of the road a few weeks earlier) was merged with Fontenelle, Drips & Co. His contributions to the record persuaded the editors to portray the state of the fur trade in 1834, primarily by means of interconnected biographical sketches of the men Anderson met or mentioned; clearly we must think in new terms of the Rocky Mountain fur trade and its major personalities.

Anderson could not make up his mind whether to remain in the mountains with Fitzpatrick or to go back with Sublette. He elected to stay, but the unexpected union of the two fur companies made it necessary for Fitzpatrick as well as Fontenelle to go down to St. Louis. Because Anderson traveled the whole distance with Fitzpatrick, his diary fills in three months of the life of the "Broken Hand," and grants us a look at Fitzpatrick's Arapaho foster son, little Friday. If we except Wyeth's sparse diary of 1833, Anderson's is the only daily record of a descent of the Missouri by pirogue in this decade. When in his company we reach St. Louis, we have learned a great deal about the West in 1834.

William Marshall Anderson's personal record is made more interesting by reference to the diaries and letters that depict the westward passage of Nathaniel Wyeth's party in 1834. Wyeth kept a diary, as in 1832-1833, commenced at the crossing of the Kansas River on May 5. (His prior movements may be followed in the letters he wrote along the way.) Wyeth's chronology periodically became confused, and while he was at the rendezvous, June 18-July 3, he saved the news for the letters he was writing. Wyeth resumed his diary on taking the trail again, but laid it aside while building Fort Hall in present Idaho. On August 6, having "done as much as was requisite for safety to the Fort and drank a bale of liquor and named it Fort Hall in honor of the oldest partner of our concern," Wyeth set out once more, again making almost daily entries in his diary.

The New Englander's record is comparable in importance to Anderson's, varying in content and point of view.

If Wyeth's second-in-command, a one-time sea captain named Joseph Thing, kept a diary, it has never been found, but two *engagés* were eventually heard from. Osborne Russell kept memoranda written up in the 1840's as "Journal of a Trapper." Russell has a generally correct, though laconic, account of the journey to the rendezvous and on to Fort Hall. He remained at Fort Hall after Wyeth went on to the Columbia, and eventually became a free trapper. Russell's journal, from 1835 to 1842, when he moved on to the Willamette, is a priceless record of mountain life. One of Russell's associates, Isaac P. Rose, also ranged the mountains as a free trapper after leaving Wyeth's service. He returned home in 1838, and late in life gave his recollections to James B. Marsh; they were published in 1884 as *Four Years in the Rockies*. The book is not particularly valuable for its account of the 1834 journey to the mountains.

With Wyeth traveled two men of scientific bent. The naturalist Thomas Nuttall had ascended the Missouri with Wilson Price Hunt's Astorians in 1811, later pursued botanical researches in Arkansas, and was now having a look at the farther West. Unfortunately, Nuttall's journal has disappeared. His companion, a young Philadelphian with ornithological interests, was John Kirk Townsend, whose *Narrative of a Journey across the Rocky Mountains, to the Columbia River, and a Visit to the Sandwich Islands, Chili, &c.* ... (Philadelphia, 1839), republished in London, 1840, as *Sporting Excursion in the Rocky Mountains*, etc., is a superb personal narrative, as alive today as when written. Townsend admitted regretfully that in fording the Green River he lost the second volume of his diary, with his notes from the Black Hills onward (June 1-18), a gap he filled by recourse to Nuttall's (now lost) journal. Before Townsend's book was published, an excerpt from the diary sent his family from the Columbia on Oct. 6, 1834, containing almost daily notes from the time he reached the Blackfoot River on July 10 until his arrival at Fort Vancouver on September 16, was printed in *Waldies' Select Circulating Library*, 1835. (The installments thus sent home are preserved in the Academy of Natural Sciences of Philadelphia, consisting, the Academy says, of "141 pages of journal from 1834 to 1836, which are in effect distinct sections written to members of his family at various times and not a consecutive record of his travels. We also have fifteen letters, likewise written to members of his family, for the same period.")

Other diaries were kept by the Methodist missionaries who traveled with Wyeth to Oregon. The manuscript diary of Jason Lee is in the Oregon Historical Society Library, published in that Society's *Quarterly*, June-December 1916. Lee began this record on arrival at Liberty, Missouri, April 20, 1834, and kept it faithfully all across the continent.

In the course of his journey Lee wrote many letters, as noted in the Bibliography. Two of these, with an abstract of his journal, April 28-June 29, 1834, and July 2, 1834-Feb. 6, 1835, were printed in New York *Christian Advocate and Journal*, Oct. 3, 1834, Oct. 30, 1835. Small details in this printed version supplement the manuscript diary. Lee also left "The Mission Record Book of the Methodist Episcopal Church, Willamette Station, Oregon Territory, North America, Commenced 1834," of which a photocopy is owned by the Oregon Historical Society. This "Record Book" includes a dozen entries, April 25-Sept. 15, 1834, respecting the overland journey; it was printed in the Oregon Historical Society *Quarterly*, September 1922.

Jason Lee's nephew and fellow missionary, Daniel Lee, kept no diary so far as is known, but in 1844 joined with J. H. Frost in publishing *Ten Years in Oregon*. This book has only a slight account of the overland journey. A more important chronicler was the third missionary, Cyrus Shepard, whose manuscript diary, March 4, 1834-Dec. 20, 1835, is in the Coe Collection at Yale. In a religious sense, Shepard's diary is much more self-absorbed than is Lee's, setting a pattern for missionary diaries to come. An abstract, April 27-June 20, 1834, sent home from the rendezvous, was printed in *Zion's Herald*, as were a number of his letters (see Bibliography). Shepard died in the mission field, and his journals and letters provided the basis for an inspirational biography by Z. A. Mudge, *The Missionary Teacher: A Memorial of Cyrus Shepard*, which appeared in 1848.

The missionary party of 1834 also included a "non-professor," Courtney M. Walker, and a layman, Philip Leget Edwards. On June 23, 1834, Edwards addressed from the rendezvous a letter to the Liberty *Missouri Enquirer*, reprinted in *Niles' Register*, Oct. 11, 1834.

The Methodist contingent accompanied Wyeth only as far as Fort Hall. When Thomas McKay of the Hudson's Bay Company passed by with a small brigade, the missionaries and William Drummond Stewart decided to go on to the Columbia with him. Driving their cows, the first taken across the Rockies to Oregon, they pursued the road down the south bank of the Snake and across the Blue Mountains originally traveled by Robert Stuart eastbound in 1812.

*   *   *

Thus far we have been concerned with Anderson's journal primarily for its description of the Western trails in 1834. Another aspect of his record demands attention—what Anderson has to say about the Rocky Mountain fur trade and its distinctive institution, the rendezvous.

The annual summer rendezvous has become encrusted with fable. Ethnologists have tended to see the rendezvous as a conscious adaptation to white purposes of age-old intertribal trading fairs; fur trade historians have viewed it as a species of business convention— all fur companies being required to appear and all mountain men obliged to account for their doings of the past year. The image of rendezvous fostered by writers in too much of a hurry for mature judgment has been that of an orgy sustained over a period of several weeks, during which any Indians present were debauched and separated from their furs.

The rendezvous originated in economic necessity. William H. Ashley wrought an innovation in the fur trade by introducing into the mountains independent or "free" trappers, from whom he agreed to buy beaver at a stipulated price. Ashley had to carry goods to the mountains to trade for pelts, meeting the trappers at some predetermined point. The functional reality of rendezvous was this bringing together of merchandise from the states and beaver trapped in the mountains. Indians and their trading habits were irrelevant; Ashley had not even seen a mountain Indian when, in 1825, he designated the confluence of Henrys Fork and the Green as the site of the first rendezvous; and it is not established that Indians were present, other than Iroquois trappers who had deserted the Hudson's Bay Company service that spring.

Whether a rendezvous was originally contemplated for the summer of 1826 is doubtful. Ashley's new partner, Jedediah Smith, after accompanying the General to St. Louis in the summer of 1825, set out for the mountains at the end of October, hoping to get a new outfit to the Rockies that fall. Severe weather intervened; Smith lost many of his pack animals, was forced to winter with the Republican Pawnees, and had to send back for more mules. Ashley therefore made a second journey to the mountains in the spring of 1826, joining Smith in the valley of the Platte and going on to Cache Valley. The trappers traded with Ashley on the Bear River, as did a few curious Indians. Before returning home, Ashley sold out to a new partnership. Smith, Jackson & Sublette thereby acquired a monopoly, such as it was, of the mountain supply trade, but also hired men to hunt for them. That Smith, Jackson & Sublette would still be in business a year hence, they could not be sure, but they drew up an agreement by which Ashley should send up goods next year provided that the order was confirmed by March 1, 1827. Jedediah Smith went off to California, not to be heard from until the summer of 1827, but Sublette and Jackson did well during the fall hunt, and Sublette set out from Cache Valley on January 1. Accompanied only by Black Harris, he made it through to St. Louis by March 4.

Ashley meanwhile had invited the Chouteaus to join him in providing the indicated outfit. With Hiram Scott as captain and James Bruffee as business agent, the caravan of "Wm. H. Ashley & Co" started off to Bear Lake in April, accompanied by Sublette. Snakes and Utes, and possibly other Indians, were at Bear Lake when the pack party arrived in June; the idea of rendezvous was taking hold. After concluding the trade, Sublette and Jackson returned to the states with the caravan, were met by Ashley at Lexington, Missouri, with another outfit, and using the same pack animals, within a few days set out for the mountains again.

In consequence of an early and severe winter, Sublette and Jackson had to hole up en route and did not rendezvous at Bear Lake until June. (No caravan came up from the states in 1828; there was no necessity for one.) The partners had learned a lesson. There would be no more winter transport of supplies.

The 1828 rendezvous at Bear Lake had a certain novelty, for Joshua Pilcher & Co., successor to the Missouri Fur Company, appeared to provide some competition for Smith, Jackson & Sublette. The competition was feeble. Pilcher had set out from Council Bluffs the previous September, seen his horses run off by the Crows, and been so unlucky as to have the goods placed in cache badly damaged by seeping water. The free trappers, who had hoped for better things, sent emissaries to Kenneth Mackenzie, who was then building Fort Union near the mouth of the Yellowstone, asking that he send goods to the mountains. Mackenzie was not able to comply, though the next summer he sent William H. Vanderburgh with a small brigade to trap Yellowstone waters.

Sublette took Smith, Jackson & Sublette's returns down to Missouri in the summer of 1828 and brought a new outfit to the mountains the following spring. Robert Campbell, who had trapped the Crow country, met Sublette at the confluence of Wind River and the Popo Agie early in July. Jackson had gone far to the northwest, to the Kutenai country (where Jedediah Smith joined him after his varied experiences of 1827-1829 in California and along the Oregon coast). It would appear that Jackson sent Fitzpatrick on express to Campbell to advise of his returns, for Anderson records an incident related by Fitzpatrick, dating from this time. Sublette started Campbell back to the states with his own returns, launched a party down the Big Horn, then went on to Green River and Jackson Hole, and over the Tetons to Pierres Hole in present Idaho, where he met Jackson and Smith early in August. To the extent that there was a rendezvous in 1829 conforming to the pattern of the 1830's, it occurred in Pierres Hole.

Precariously situated, the partners gambled dangerously for a hunt in the fall of 1829. Jackson harvested in the heavily over-trapped Snake country again, but Smith and Sublette led toward the Blackfoot country a force large enough to look after itself, the first of the "fur brigades," so much a part of the mountain scene during the next decade. Smith and Sublette completely circled the future Yellowstone Park, and just before Christmas rendezvoused with Jackson on Wind River. Since the partners had done well enough to justify bringing up another outfit, on Christmas Day Sublette set out on the second of his winter treks to the states, Harris again his companion. He reached St. Louis Feb. 11, 1830, and by the second week of April was en route back to Wind River with an outfit carried in wagons. At the rendezvous in August, Smith, Jackson & Sublette sold out to the Rocky Mountain Fur Company (a famous name erroneously applied to the previous ventures of William H. Ashley, Ashley & Smith, and Smith, Jackson & Sublette). Five trappers joined to form this new concern, Thomas Fitzpatrick, Milton G. Sublette, James Bridger, Henry Fraeb, and Jean Baptiste Gervais.

The American Fur Company had managed to send a mountain expedition up from Council Bluffs, led by Lucien Fontenelle, Andrew Drips, and Michel Robidoux. This company was actually ahead of Sublette (the only time a party ever gained such an advantage), but that was their ill luck, for Sublette's wagon tracks would have led them to Wind River and the rendezvousing free trappers. They went on to Green River, Bear Lake, and Cache Valley, searching in vain for the free men. The A. F. Co. party trapped the country until the summer of 1831, when Drips and Fontenelle went below to get another outfit. Drips endeavored to return to the mountains that fall, but the third severe winter in six years forced him to hole up near the mouth of the Laramie. Thereafter all hands accepted the realities of mountain life; there were no more efforts to transport supplies out of season.

Etienne Provost delivered an outfit to William H. Vanderburgh on Green River, but otherwise the summer of 1831 was not a success in the mountains. Late in the winter Fitzpatrick had left Milton Sublette and Bridger in the Yellowstone country to go to St. Louis for supplies. He made slow progress down the blizzard-swept plains, not reaching Lexington until May. Learning that Jackson & Sublette had just set out on a Santa Fe trading venture, accompanied by their old partner, Jedediah Smith, Fitzpatrick spurred after the caravan. The traders agreed that if Fitzpatrick would journey out to New Mexico with them, Jackson & Sublette would furnish two-thirds of the outfit he wanted, Smith the rest. Fitzpatrick could pack his goods into the mountains from Taos.

Fitzpatrick's partners had converged on Cache Valley to meet him, but through August they waited in vain; this foregathering of the trappers lacked goods from the states to make it a true rendezvous. Fearing that Fitzpatrick had been killed, the partners started Fraeb down to St. Louis for the merchandise they must have. He met Fitzpatrick in the Black Hills. Accordingly Fraeb took over the outfit and turned back into the mountains, while Fitzpatrick made for the states. He reached Lexington before Sublette got back from New Mexico. (Jedediah Smith had been killed by Comanches on the journey out; Jackson had gone on to California on a star-crossed mule-buying venture.)

Sublette provided the R. M. F. Co. outfit for 1832, Fitzpatrick accompanying him back to the mountains as a supernumerary. Pierres Hole had been named as the place of rendezvous. The R. M. F. Co. parties assembled in that valley and were joined by W. H. Vanderburgh, expecting Etienne Provost from Fort Union, and Andrew Drips, looking for Lucien Fontenelle with goods from Council Bluffs. Free trappers straggled in, and there was a sizable representation from the mountain tribes, especially Flatheads and Nez Percés.

As it turned out, William Sublette was the only trader who delivered goods to the rendezvous of 1832. The American Fur Company had combined its two mountain ventures under the authority of Fontenelle; but because his merchandise had to be transported up the Missouri in the steamboat the American Fur Company was now using to supply its river posts, Fontenelle was slow getting away and did not reach even Green River until after the rendezvous in Pierres Hole had broken up. Captain Bonneville had made a slow passage with his wagons to Green River and was also too late for the rendezvous.

The rendezvous of 1833, regarded by William Drummond Stewart as the last great one, in a sense was the first. Never before had all mountain companies assembled in one place, and for the first time there was real competition. Traders and trappers gathered in the vicinity of Horse Creek and the Green, where Bonneville had built his first post. On hand were Bonneville's parties, the A. F. Co. party under Drips (Vanderburgh having been killed by Blackfeet the previous autumn), two of the R. M. F. Co. partners, various small operators, and any number of free trappers and Indians.

The camps were set up at intervals of several miles so that the various caballadas could be kept apart with sufficient pasturage. Drips confidently awaited Fontenelle, who was coming up from Fort Pierre. Bonneville was standing pat on goods brought up the year before. But the Rocky Mountain Fur Company had made no arrangements for an outfit this summer, evidence of the continuously shaky finances of this firm. Only Gervais and Milton Sublette originally represented the company in this gathering; they had trapped the Snake lands in the course of the spring hunt. Fitzpatrick, Bridger, and Fraeb during the spring had trapped to the southeast, as far as the Black Hills, and with such success that they had decided to send Fraeb to St. Louis for an outfit.

As it happened, Sublette & Campbell, a new partnership organized in St. Louis in December 1832, had decided on a speculation. While Sublette went up the Missouri by keelboat, establishing posts in opposition to the A. F. Co., Campbell took an outfit to the mountains, hoping to dispose of it to the R. M. F. Co. or the free trappers. Meeting Fraeb at the Laramie River, Campbell sent an express to summon Fitzpatrick, who agreed to purchase Campbell's goods. Fraeb rode off to join Bridger in a summer hunt through the Laramie Plains and the Three Parks of the Rockies (neither, in consequence, appearing at the rendezvous), while Fitzpatrick wheeled around to accompany Campbell to Green River. They got there about eight days ahead of Fontenelle, to the chagrin of the American Fur Company.

After the rendezvous broke up, Fitzpatrick escorted Campbell and the furs to the Big Horn River, prior to floating them down to the mouth of the Yellowstone, where Campbell expected to meet his partner. Bonneville also marched to the Big Horn, escorting M. S. Cerré, who took this route to the states because Arikaras in the valley of the Platte were plundering trappers right and left. Only Etienne Provost risked land transport of furs this summer; he left Green River about the first of August, a week after the departure of the others, and in due course delivered Fontenelle's furs at Fort Pierre.

En route home from Oregon, Nathaniel Wyeth also took the water route. If he had lost financially from his first mountain year, he had profited in experience. While returning east, he had discussed with Bonneville a project by which he would take a joint trapping expedition to California. When this idea fell through, perhaps because Bonneville wanted to send Joe Walker there on his own account, Wyeth made a proposition to the Rocky Mountain Fur Company. The agreement reached was shaky on both sides. The R. M. F. Co. could not be sure that they would be able to pay for an outfit the next summer, and Wyeth could not be sure of finding backing. The contract for goods provided for a five-hundred-dollar forfeit should either party fail to carry out its undertaking.

The Rocky Mountain Fur Company was near the end of its tether. Its financial condition had always been painful, and the country was now badly overtrapped, with more and more fur seekers entering the field. In 1832 Fitzpatrick had tried to reach an accommodation with the American Fur Company, and since then the two concerns had been feeling each other out. An "arrangement" would involve a division of the country and an agreement on the part of the R. M. F. Co. to market furs and obtain supplies through the A. F. Co. Fitzpatrick's hope was that through Wyeth he could obtain goods at better prices and that the market price of beaver would continue at a high level.

For Wyeth, supplying the R. M. F. Co. was small potatoes but would cover the cost of transporting his own goods to the mountains. Wyeth contemplated a base on Snake waters, tied to one on the Columbia, which would be supplied by sea. He also thought he could inaugurate a salmon-packing business. Wyeth went home, and he found men to back him. In the course of the winter Milton Sublette joined him in Boston to help pick out goods. Wyeth let no grass grow under his feet and was first to get away from the frontier in the spring of 1834.

Meanwhile Sublette & Campbell had been involved in grandiose maneuvers. Their project for establishing a large-scale Indian trade on the Missouri may have had the ultimate object of forcing the A. F. Co. into an accommodation. Robert Campbell, wintering at the new fort built at the mouth of the Yellowstone, made overtures to Kenneth Mackenzie, which were brusquely rejected, but down in the states Sublette was more successful. The A. F. Co. had never been convinced that the mountain trade was worth the trouble, and had a healthy respect for Sublette, with his unbroken record of success and his possession of a powerful ally in Ashley, now the Congressman from Missouri. Besides, the A. F. Co. was in serious difficulties with the government. This past year Mackenzie had flouted the liquor laws by constructing a distillery at Fort Union, and earlier J. P. Cabanné had engaged in a piece of high-handedness farther down the Missouri; for a time it seemed likely the Company would be ordered out of the Indian country.

Toward the end of January, Sublette and Astor's people agreed in New York upon a division of the fur country. Sublette & Campbell would withdraw from the Missouri, the A. F. Co. buying all their property along the river. In turn, Astor's firm would concede the mountain trade. Fontenelle and Drips had already contracted for goods Provost would be taking out to them in the spring, but henceforth they would have to deal with Sublette & Campbell or find a new supplier. There would no longer be any intermeddling by Mackenzie in R. M. F. Co. affairs. No one thought Bonneville could keep afloat much longer. Consequently, Wyeth was the only cloud on Sublette's horizon as spring arrived in 1834.

Sublette must reach the mountains first; he could not allow Wyeth to beat him as Campbell had beaten Fontenelle in the past. A paper victory only had been won in New York; possession of their fur empire Sublette & Campbell would have to win on the ground. They would need a permanent base in the high country; even before he left St. Louis, Sublette had decided to build a post near the mouth of the Laramie, as evidenced by the trading license he obtained from General Clark.

Accordingly Sublette sent his brother Andrew up the Missouri with the papers Campbell required to transfer the property. (Campbell abandoned the fort on the Yellowstone in July and descended the Missouri to St. Louis, sending Andrew overland to the new post on the Laramie.) And with great energy Sublette himself got together the mountain party that William Marshall Anderson joined.

We can now appreciate the haste and jockeying for position by Sublette and Wyeth en route to the mountains. Sublette did indeed arrive first at the rendezvous, on the Green near the mouth of the Sandy. On June 15 Anderson witnessed the warm welcome Sublette received from such old comrades as Louis Vasquez and Thomas Fitzpatrick, to say nothing of his Indian friends. But Anderson was not Sublette's business confidant. Wyeth, coming into camp on June 18, brings the scene into sharp focus: "found rendezvous . . . and much to my astonishment the goods which I had contracted to bring up to the Rocky Mountain fur Co. were refused by those honorable gentlemen."

There was more to the story, much more than one can garner from the bitter Wyeth. This had been the most disastrous year since the mountain trade began. During the fall Fitzpatrick had been robbed by the Crows—at the instigation of the A. F. Co., he was sure. Bridger and Fraeb had made a fairly successful summer hunt, but a copartnership venture with Edmund Christy west into the Snake country—Gervais going along—had been a failure; Fraeb had accomplished little in a southern hunt during the winter; and though Bridger was not yet back from another hunt in the Parks, Fitzpatrick may have had an express from him detailing his lack of success. The free trappers had done no better, and Bonneville had had a catastrophic year, with no more creditable returns from his own parties in the Snake country than from Joe Walker's California venture. (Bonneville and Walker, off to the west, would have no part in this rendezvous; Cerré would deliver on Bear River the goods he had brought out this spring.) Drips and Fontenelle had probably made the best hunt of any of the parties, though this had been accomplished, Fontenelle observed, by splitting their force into "thirty different parties at least," and some of the scattered men "traded their fall's hunt with other companies during the winter."

Anderson tells us that on June 19 the Sublette and Fitzpatrick camps moved from Green River over to Hams Fork. They were seeking better pasturage. Wyeth followed on June 20, and ere long Drips and Fontenelle set up at the confluence of Hams Fork and Blacks Fork. Thus the parties were scattered along Hams Fork during the rendezvous.

On June 20 Fraeb and Gervais sold their interest in the Rocky Mountain Fur Company, opening the way for organization of a new firm, Fitzpatrick, Sublette & Bridger. Fitzpatrick was running the show, for Bridger would not reach camp for another five days, and Milton Sublette was under medical care in St. Louis. The understanding that William Sublette reached with Thomas Fitzpatrick is not at all clear, but Fitzpatrick handed over what furs he had—some forty packs—in exchange for Sublette's goods.

*　　*　　*

Let us look at this scene over Wyeth's shoulder. On June 20-21 he wrote to friends, relatives, and business associates letters colored by disappointment. To James W. Fenno: "Our route hither has been attended with success so far as travelling but not otherwise. We have had no fighting and seen few Indians and what horses we have lost have been worn out and not stolen. The companies here have all failed of making hunts, some from quareling among themselves some from having been defeated by the Indians and some from want of horses, and what few furs have been taken have been paid to the men for their services leaving none for me. I shall build a fort on Lewis River about a hundred and fifty miles west of this . . . and there deposite my goods for sale when there is Beaver to pay for them." To Leonard Jarvis: "So far this buisness looks black. The companys here have not complied with their contracts with me and in consequence I am obliged to make a fort on Lewis River to dispose of the goods I have with me. I think I can in a little time realize good returns, but in the meantime the concern at home may get discouraged and if they do the whole is spoiled, and I shall be obliged to give up the buisness." To Leonard Wyeth: "Affairs in this region are going bad Murder is rife and distrust among themselves makes the whites an easy prey to Indians. There has been little Beaver caught and of that little I get less than I ought. As yet there is no positive indication of the event of this buisness. I shall do all I can and if those at home do not get discouraged it will yet turn out well but of this I am afraid."

Wyeth's lieutenant, Captain Thing, wrote on June 29 to Tucker & Williams, who had principally financed the venture: "The mountain men are all assembled on this river this season for Rendezvous and as crazy a set of men as I ever saw, drinking is the order of the day and trade is then best effected as it seems, two or three glasses of grog is the best introduction to trade for that is the time men feel the richest and can buy all the world in thirty minutes, in particular if you will trust them."

Wyeth on July 1 wrote Milton G. Sublette:

I arrived at Rendesvous at the mouth of Sandy on the 17th June. Fitzpatric refused to receive the goods he paid however, the forfieit and the cash advance I made to you this however is no satisfaction to me. I do not accuse you or him of any intention of injuring me in this manner when you made the contract but I think he has been bribed to sacrifice my interests by better offers from your brother. Now Milton, buisness is closed between us, but you will find that you have only bound yourself over to receive your supplies at such price as may be inflicted and that all that you will ever make in the country will go to pay for your goods, you will be kept as you have been a mere slave to catch Beaver for others.

I sincerly wish you well and believe had you been here these things would not have been done. I hope that your leg is better and that you will yet be able to go whole footed in all respects.

The most difficult letter Wyeth wrote the same day to Tucker & Williams:

Gent. I arrived here on the 17th inst. and Wm Sublette arrived two days before me. This he was enabled to do by leaving one half of his goods and horses on the route, which of course I could not do. On arrival the Rocky Mountain Fur Co. refused to receive the goods alledging that they were unable to continue buisness longer, and that they had disolved, but offered to pay the advances made to M. G. Sublette and the Forfeit. These terms I have been obliged to accept altho they would not even pay the interest on cash advances for there is no Law here. I have also sold a few goods at low prices. The proceeds of the Forfeit &c and Sales after deducting a small amt. for payment of wages of men who have gone home, from this place, I have forwarded to Mess. Von Phull & McGill of Saint Louis subject to your order, in one draft Four months from date July 1st 1834 for $864.12½ and for $1002.81 same date 12 months both by Fitzpatric Sublette & Bridger, accepted by Sublette & Campbell of St. Louis.

In addition to not fullfilling their agreement with me every exertion is made to debauch my men in which they have had some success, but I have hired enough of theirs to make up, and do not fear falling short of troops. These circumstances induce me to quit their neighborhood as soon as possible.

I shall proceed about 150 miles west of this and establish a fort in order to make sales of the goods which remain on my hands. I have sent out messengers to the Pawnacks, Shoshonees, Snakes, Nez Perces and Flatheads to make robes and come and trade them at this Post. I am under the impression that these Indians will make a good quantity of Robes whenever they find they can sell them and I believe the Transportation will not be too expensive for the value of the article besides which I have no doubt that tolerable good returns of Beaver may be made at this post. I propose to establish it on a river called Portneuf on Snake or Lewis River.

I feel much disappointed that the contract was not complied with. Had M. G. Sublette been able to come I think it would have been. I much fear that the gentlemen at home will get discouraged if no returns are made the first year. I shall do the best I can but cannot now promise anything immediate. . . .

Bonneville & Co. I have not seen, but he is not far from me on my proposed route. I fear that he has done nothing of consequence. I shall endeavour to take home his Beaver what there is of it if I can get an adequate price. I think his concern is finished. . . .

I have now with me 126 horses and mules in good order and 41 persons all told that are in the employ, and can hire as many more as I want. The amount due for wages is trifling. Almost all the men take up as fast as they earn, and would faster if I would let them, in goods at about 500 per ct. on the original cost. Our expenses after this year will be very small, and I have strong hopes as ever of success notwithstanding appearances so far.

So passed Wyeth from the rendezvous of 1834. On July 10 Sublette departed for the states, accompanied by Christy and Cerré, the latter with Bonneville's returns. The brigades were in no hurry to take the field, and on July 19 Anderson noted that Fitzpatrick and Bridger "visited the A. F C.s camp . . . to transact some business which is as yet sub rosa." The parties were now moving north and east toward the site of last year's rendezvous, but conferences continued. Anderson knew more than he wrote in his Journal, for at last on August 3 he recorded: "The arrangement some time contemplated between the two neighboring camps, has been this day effected. They are now, una anima, uno corpore." Fontenelle, Fitzpatrick & Co. had come into being, Fontenelle, Drips & Co. having merged with Fitzpatrick, Sublette & Bridger. As Fontenelle wrote Pierre Chouteau six weeks later, the arrangements between Sublette "and Messrs. Fitzpatrick, Milton Sublette and others having expired last spring, they concluded not to have anything more to do with William Sublette. . . . I have entered into a partnership with the others and the whole of the beaver caught by them is to be turned over to us. . . ." (This letter is printed in full on pp. 214-215.)

For the new concern Drips could lead a brigade in one direction, Bridger in the other. But a large question remained. Astor having decided to withdraw from the fur business, Pratte, Chouteau & Co. in St. Louis was resuming suzerainty over the Western trade. Yet the company was bound by the January agreement with Sublette; it could not supply firms competing with Sublette & Campbell. That was the problem Fontenelle and Fitzpatrick had to work out, the reason Fitzpatrick came down with Fontenelle.

During the winter, the necessary "accommodation" was reached. Fontenelle, Fitzpatrick & Co. purchased the fort on the Laramie, but more to the point they bought territorial rights and the privilege of dealing with Pratte, Chouteau & Co. For their part, Sublette & Campbell agreed not to supply any competitors. In the spring of 1835 Campbell went up to the Laramie to transfer the property and bring down accumulated robes and beaver. Thereafter Sublette & Campbell would be St. Louis merchants, primarily. They renewed their partnership in 1836 and 1839, and let it lapse in 1842. Three years later Sublette died. Campbell lived to become a millionaire.

We can now better appreciate the events of 1834, which Anderson brings home to us. Fables of fur trade history will have to be dispensed with: Astor's "trust" did not bring the Rocky Mountain Fur Company to its knees by unrelenting competition, to remain in victorious possession of the mountain scene; and Sublette did not throw away the Rocky Mountain Fur Company like an orange squeezed dry, no longer of any use to him. The play of cause and effect was much more subtle.

It would go on being subtle as the mountain fur trade spiraled inexorably downward. By the summer of 1836 Fontenelle, Fitzpatrick & Co. had reached such a pass that Pratte, Chouteau & Co. sent Joshua Pilcher to the mountains to buy out the partners. For the next three years the Chouteaus carried on the trade through their "Rocky Mountain Outfit." Meanwhile the price of fur plummeted, though ever less beaver was being trapped. By 1838, the Panic of '37 having further stricken the market, P. Chouteau Jr. & Co. was weighing complete withdrawal from mountain operations. The trappers cursed Chouteau for "being so hard," having little appreciation of economic realities and feeling themselves exploited; they were less prepared for a new price and credit structure in consequence of the fantastic inflation of 1833-1834, when beaver and mountain wages had been bid up to impossible heights.

The Rocky Mountain Outfit kept a brigade in the field in 1838-1839, but returns fell off still more badly, and at the rendezvous of 1839 the company announced that it was withdrawing from the mountains. On speculation, Chouteau sent Andrew Drips to Green River with a small stock of goods in 1840, but that was the end. The pale shadow of the rendezvous in 1840 marks the death of a famous institution of mountain life.

It is not our purpose to develop in detail the history of the rendezvous. Except in 1838, when the site was the confluence of Wind River and the Popo Agie, from 1835 to 1840 the rendezvous was held in the valley of the Green near the mouth of Horse Creek, where the rendezvous of 1833 had been held. Only in Anderson's year was Hams Fork the place of gathering. Something should be said of the viewpoint of others respecting this rendezvous. Diary entries by Lee and Shepard, and Townsend's narrative, we have quoted in the notes, but some letters also merit attention.

Jason Lee wrote the *Christian Advocate* on July 1, 1834:

Mr. Wm. Sublette is building a trading fort at Laramies Fork, on the Platte, about thirty days' march from Independence, Mo. Here I think is a very favorable location for a missionary establishment.—Mr. Sublette mentioned it to me, of his own accord, as a favorable place. The Sous Indians, which are a powerful and numerous tribe, range along near this place, and will in future, no doubt, often frequent his place, as well as many other tribes. A party will pass up from the settlements yearly, connected with the fort, and many others on their way to the Rocky Mountains. I hope you will investigate this subject; and perhaps your board may see fit to establish a mission there immediately. There are government agents among them [the Sioux], who have already or are about to commence agricultural operations; and I think this is the most favorable opening that this country presents at present.

The Crow Indians range along the Missouri and Yellow Stone, and far up toward this country. They have 400 lodges, and about 4,000 souls—no agents; but there are traders among them. They are friendly to whites, who are in their camp; and I have no doubt that missionaries would be well received among them, if the traders did not oppose; and even if they did, I think their opposition might be overcome.—Way of approach, up the Yellow Stone.

We are now in the Snake country. They are a large nation consisting, according to my information, of various tribes, such as Snakes, Pawnocks, Eutaws, Root-diggers, &c. Whites in their camp are perfectly safe; and here too I think a mission might be established. There are few Snakes here at rendezvous, and some from various other tribes. The Black Feet are the most numerous tribe in the mountains; and though they are hostile to most other tribes, and to whites that are not connected with themselves, yet all who are with them are treated in the most hospitable manner; and I should not hesitate in the least to go among them to establish a mission, if Providence opens the way. . . .

In sending down an abstract of his journal, Lee further commented:

The traders here, some of them, and perhaps all, are opposed to our enterprise. Some have told me that they were opposed from principle, but perhaps they would come nigher to it if they had said from interest. But I must say they have treated me with the greatest politeness.

There are Indians of various tribes here, some Flat Heads and some Na Pierce. We conversed a little with them through an indifferent interpreter, and they seemed very much pleased that we were going to their country; asked if we intended to cultivate the earth, and if we could build houses, and said if we could build one at Wollawollah that the Indians would catch plenty of beaver for us, which we think is a favorable omen, indicating that they have a desire to adopt the customs of civilized man. One said he had three children, and he would give them to us that we might learn them to read and write and be good. Some of the Na Pierces have worship in their tents, and respect the ordinances of religion far more than the white men. One went from this company to purchase meat from them, and wanted them to bring it to our camp, but they refused, saying, "It is the Sabbath."

P. L. Edwards, a layman in Lee's party, took more interest in the mountain men than did his missionary companions, as shown in his letter of June 23:

Here is the hardy mountain veteran who has ranged these wilds for more than thirty years. Pecuniary emolument was perhaps his first inducement, but now he is as poor as at first. Reckless of all provision for the future, his great solicitude is to fill up his mental insanity by animal gratification. Here is the man, now past the meridian of life, who has been in the country from his youth, whose connections and associations with the natives have identified his interests and habits with theirs.

To form an adequate conception of their apparel, you must see it. A suit of clothes is seldom washed or turned from the time it is first worn until it is laid aside. Caps and hats are made of beaver and otter skins, the skins of buffalo calves, &c. Some of these are fantastically ornamented with tails and horns. These ornaments may be badges of distinction, for aught that I know, but being a stranger in the country, I am not able to speak decidedly. You will perhaps recollect to have seen in the "far west" of our own United States, the buckskin hunting shirt and leggins gracefully hung with fringes along the arms and sides. But I am sure you have never seen the tasty fashion of fringes carried to perfection. Here they are six or seven inches long, and hung densely on every seam, I believe, both of the hunting shirt and leggins. Indeed their weight is a great burden. But it is perhaps advisable, under existing circumstances, that I should leave your imagination to supply the picture. . . .

In taking leave of the rendezvous, let us say a word respecting the spree-loving mountain men and the scenes of drunkenness and carousal that shocked missionaries. It must be remembered that there were no kegs of applejack stowed away under mountain roof beams for the long winter nights, no taverns for convivial tippling, no opportunities for Saturday night or county fair blow-outs. If a mountain man was going to treat his comrades, show himself a good fellow and generous withal, he had to do it at the rendezvous. The excesses of a whole year were compacted into a few weeks; and the mountain men took a perverse pleasure in shocking onlookers. Indians at the rendezvous were their friends, and as friends might be treated. Over the whole history of the rendezvous, no red visitors were debauched or impoverished by alcohol. Such incidents rather attended the trade for buffalo robes, especially on the High Plains, after the fort-building epoch began.

* * *

Though Fort William on the Laramie was one of the earliest among the interior posts, it was by no means the first. Captain Bonneville erected Fort Bonneville on the plains of Horse Creek in the summer of 1832. When visiting Taos the previous February, John Gantt had informed the New Mexican government that he intended to establish at "the junction of Las Animas and Napeste [Arkansas] Rivers," and on the bank of the latter, "a provisional fort and a warehouse for commerce," but not until the winter of 1832-1833 did he build on the Arkansas near the mouth of Fountain Creek the post he called Fort Cass. Farther down the Arkansas, Bent & St. Vrain erected the adobe citadel that became known as Bent's Fort; this firm also built a log establishment called Fort William in the immediate vicinity of Gantt's post. (This log fort may have preceded the adobe structure. After it was abandoned, the name Fort William was transferred to Bent's Fort.) A great many posts had meanwhile been commenced on Missouri and Yellowstone waters, including another Fort Cass near the mouth of the Big Horn founded by the American Fur Company in 1832, and Sublette & Campbell's first post, also called Fort William, erected at the mouth of the Yellowstone; however, these were river-supplied. Nathaniel Wyeth's Fort Hall, near the confluence of the Snake and the Portneuf, founded a few weeks after Sublette's post on the Laramie, led to the building by the Hudson's Bay Company's Thomas McKay of a fort on the Boise River. (Both of these posts were maintained after 1837 by the British concern.)

33

The site of Fort Laramie had commended itself to mountain men from earliest times. Men had wintered there at intervals at least from 1831, and Bonneville in 1832 found the site attractive. "Laramie's fork" he described as "a clear and beautiful stream, rising in the west-southwest, maintaining an average width of twenty yards, and winding through broad meadows abounding in currants and gooseberries, and adorned with groves and clumps of trees." As seen in the notes, William Drummond Stewart found the locality no less appealing.

Anderson's Diary says on May 30: "This evening we are encamped on the banks of the aforesaid fork. Tis here that Mr S. designs erecting a small fort. In a day or two he will recommence his march to the rocky mountains with such of his men as he does not leave for the erection of the fort."[1] On June 1 Anderson adds: "we remained all the day yesterday in our previous days encampment making arrangements for the fort builders. Mr Patton was left behind with 12 men, which reduces us to 23, *to erect* the works. . . . The fort on Laramy's fork is called f. William, in honour of its founder Mr S."

In his Journal, written after reaching home, Anderson rendered the entry respecting Fort William as follows: "This evening we arrived at Laramie's fork, where Mr Sublettes designs erecting a trading fort—This is a very pretty clear rapid stream running out of the black hills from the south— As soon as the fort is planed & commenced, we shall resume our mountainward march. . . . June 1st Mr. Sublette left his clerk Mr Patton [*interlined*: and 14 men] to build the fort[2] reducing our number to twenty-three, with which we recommence our still westward march—"

In his Narrative of 1871 Anderson provides a much fuller account. Under the date we have found to be May 30 he writes: "This evening we arrived at the mouth of Laramee's Fork, where Capt. Sublette intends to erect a trader's fort. . . ." And on May 31: "This day we laid the foundation *log* of a fort, on Laramee's fork. A friendly dispute arose between our leader and myself, as to the name. He proposed to

---

[1] Anderson's chronology in his Diary became confused, so that both in this record and in his later Journal he mistakenly gave May 31 as the date of arrival at the Laramie River and June 1 as the date of the founding of Fort William. We have corrected his dates, as will appear hereafter in the notes.

[2] In pencil, and probably at a much later date, Anderson here amended his original text to note that this fort "is to be called fort William, in honor Sublette & myself."

34

call it Fort Anderson, I insisted upon baptising it Fort Sublette, and holding the trump card in my hand, (a bottle of champagne) was about to claim the trick. Sublette stood by, cup reversed, still objecting, when Patton offered a compromise which was accepted, and the foam flew, in honor of Fort William, which contained the triad prenames of clerk, leader and friend." (As appears elsewhere in this book, there is reason to regard as incorrect Anderson's conception of 1871, that Patton also bore the name William.) The Narrative says further, on June 1, "Leaving Patton and fourteen men to finish the job, we started upwards."

Down to the present the natal date for Fort Laramie has been given as June 1, 1834, but close study of the Anderson record makes it evident that May 31 must be celebrated as the birthday of this famous post.

On August 20, when homeward-bound, Anderson wrote in his Diary: "This is Fort William where we drank the champaigne a few weeks ago—now there is enclosed one hundred feet, which gives protection to men and animals." His Journal enlarges the entry: "here I am, at, and in Fort William—here a month or two ago, I aided in emptying a bottle of good, genuine, New York imported champaigne, to the 'to be built['] fort, now, here she stands, defying wind, rain & Indians." He told of the welcome by Patton, without giving his first name, which opened the way for a possible mistake in 1871.

Anderson may have been speaking in general terms in saying that the fort "enclosed one hundred feet," but F. A. Wislizenus approximately agreed with him in 1839. Alfred Jacob Miller described the fort in 1837 as "of a quadrangular form, with bastions at the diagonal corners to sweep the fronts in case of attack; over the ground entrance is a large block house, or tower, in which is placed a cannon. The interior is possibly 150 feet square, a range of houses built against the palisades overlooking the interior court. Tribes of Indians encamp here 3 or 4 times a year, bringing with them peltries to be traded or exchanged for dry-goods, tobacco, vermillion, brass, and diluted alcohol."

On June 14, 1839, Wislizenus observed that at a distance the post

resembles a great blockhouse; and lies in a narrow valley, enclosed by grassy hills, near by the left bank of the Laramie, which empties into the

North Platte about a mile below. . . . We crossed the Laramie toward noon, and encamped outside the fort. The fort itself first attracted my attention. It lies on a slight elevation, and is built in a rectangle of about eighty by a hundred feet. The outside is made of cottonwood logs, about fifteen feet high, hewed off, and wedged closely together. On three sides there are little towers on the wall that seem designed for watch and defense. In the middle a strong gate, built of blocks, constitutes the entrance. Within, little buildings with flat roofs are plastered all around against the wall, like swallows' nests. One is the store house; another the smithy; the others are dwellings not unlike monks' cells. A special portion of the court yard is occupied by the so-called horse-pen, in which the horses are confined at night. The middle space is free, with a tall tree [liberty pole] in it, on which the flag is raised on occasions of state.

The exact site of Fort William has not been determined by archaeological means. Because the fort had begun to decay by 1840, next year P. Chouteau Jr. & Co. replaced it—possibly on the same site— with an adobe structure formally christened Fort John, but known in its turn as Fort Laramie. The name Fort William persisted, even after Sublette & Campbell sold the establishment to Fontenelle, Fitzpatrick & Co. in 1835. The latter firm renamed the post Fort Lucien in honor of Fontenelle, and various trade licenses employ that name down to 1840. Notwithstanding, the name Fort William continued in familiar use, which has led to confusion in the literature, the very identity of Fort Lucien sometimes being questioned.

Reproduced on the opposite page is the painting by Alfred Jacob Miller of Fort William in 1837, from a watercolor in the Thomas Gilcrease Institute of American History and Art at Tulsa, Oklahoma. A notation on the verso indicates that this copy was made by Miller in 1851. This version has a different foreground from two others that are extant, the Porter copy now in the Joslyn Museum at Omaha, Nebraska (reproduced in Bernard DeVoto's *Across the Wide Missouri*), and the Walters copy at Baltimore (reproduced in Marvin G. Ross's *The West of Alfred Jacob Miller*); neither of these shows the Laramie River in the foreground. From the three versions, it would appear that the longer dimension of Fort William (if Wislizenus is correct) was from north to south. DeVoto reproduces a distant view, "Scene near Fort Laramie," which is not included in the Ross book; in it the fort appears on a slight elevation, which

Courtesy of Thomas Gilcrease Institute of American History and Art

Fort William in 1837, by Alfred Jacob Miller

would go to support the Wislizenus description, and gives added interest to our illustration. Interior views of the fort are reproduced by DeVoto in color and by Ross in black and white, but the fort could not have been finished to that extent when Anderson passed by.

* * *

Soon after Anderson returned to Kentucky, he expanded the two volumes we describe as his Diary into the record we call his Journal. The Diary is bound in sheep. Volume I, labeled "Rocky Mountains," and with entries from March 13 to July 9, 1834, measures 14.8 by 9 cm. Both sides of the leaves have been written in ink, with some pencil revisions. The back leaves are blank, and pages with writing are numbered from 2 to 79. Paper is of nineteenth-century mat finish, with light-blue horizontal lines.

Volume II, with entries dated from July 10 to Sept. 29, 1834, measures 18.2 by 10.5 cm. This volume was given to Anderson by Sublette at the rendezvous, having been used in 1831-1832 as an account book. (The accounts are not printed here but are incorporated by Dale L. Morgan in a work on Robert Campbell.) It is vertically lined, contains a front pocket, and at the back a thumb-index alphabet. Half of the book was written in reverse, progressing toward the middle from each end. The handwriting is mainly in ink, with occasional pencil notations reinforced in ink. Pages are not numbered but total 106.

The rewritten version we term the Journal covers the whole Western journey, with entries dated from March 11 to Sept. 29, 1834, and is bound in boards with leather spine, measuring 19 by 15.7 cm. The early leaves, some of which are loose, are written in pencil, and the balance in ink, with revisions in both pencil and ink. Page numbers, from 1 to 139, appear only on recto pages, though verso pages have been included in the count. In all three volumes, the handwriting is reasonably legible.

In 1837 Anderson contributed three articles to the *American Turf Register and Sporting Magazine*, a monthly periodical published in New York; they appeared in the May, July, and November issues (VIII, 409-412, 454-457, 549-552). Under the title *Adventures in the Rocky Mountains in 1834*, these articles were reprinted in an edition of one hundred copies by Edward Eberstadt & Sons, New York, 1951; we have again reprinted them.

Many years later, on Feb. 16, 1860, Anderson addressed a letter to the *National Intelligencer*, Washington, D. C., protesting the claims of Louis Vasquez to be the discoverer of Great Salt Lake, and recalling his 1837 contribution to the *American Turf Register*. This letter, first published Feb. 25, 1860, and also now reprinted, came to the attention of James H. Simpson, who at the time was preparing a report on his Great Basin explorations, not published until 1876 in consequence of the Civil War. We may attribute to Simpson's republication of the letter the comment of 2nd Lt. C. C. Miner, Post Adjutant, when preparing a history of Fort Bridger for H. H. Bancroft in 1885: "The vicinity of the post appears to have been a rendezvous for trappers as early as 1834, the neighboring branches of Green River abounding in Beaver at that time. During the summer of that year a number of trappers, in the employ of the North American and Rocky Mountain Fur Companies (then consolidated), assembled here and, dividing into parties, proceeded in various directions on Beaver-trapping expeditions. Among these trappers may be mentioned: Wm Sublette, Fitzpatrick Fentenelle, Basil La Jeunesse, W. M. Anderson, James Bridger and Jack Robinson." Anderson would no doubt have been pleased to be thus made a mountain man in good standing.

Not until 1871 was William Marshall Anderson impelled to make further literary capital out of his mountain jaunt of 1834. He described his experiences from the time of leaving home to June 20, shortly after reaching the rendezvous, in four issues of the Circleville, Ohio, *Democrat and Watchman*, Sept. 15, 22, 29, and Oct. 13, 1871. The third and fourth of these articles came to the attention of Albert J. Partoll, who edited them as "Anderson's Narrative of a Ride to the Rocky Mountains in 1834," *Frontier and Midland* (Autumn 1938); they were subsequently reprinted as *Sources of Northwest History*, *No. 27* (Missoula, 1938), and again in John W. Hakola, ed., *Frontier Omnibus* (Missoula and Helena, 1962).

The existence of Anderson's original journals was announced by his great-grandson, Charles Anderson Gauld III (then a student of history at the University of Washington), in a communication printed under the somewhat misleading title, "A Trip to Yellowstone and the Oregon Country in 1834," in *Washington Historical Quarterly*, January 1935, reprinted in *Annals of Wyoming*, January 1940. Robert S. Ellison, Oklahoma oil man and collector of Americana, obtained a copy of one of the Anderson manuscripts, and began to prepare it for publication, but died before he had advanced far.

Thus the manuscripts slumbered until 1948, when Jacquelin S. (Jim) Holliday unearthed them in Circleville, Ohio, a story he has related with characteristic enthusiasm in a foreword to Anderson's Mexican diaries, *An American in Maximilian's Mexico*, published in 1959. The Anderson manuscripts were purchased by the Huntington Library in 1954 at the W. J. Holliday auction in the Parke-Bernet Galleries in New York. California historian Robert Glass Cleland began transcription. Again death intervened, and it has fallen to the present editors to dress William Marshall Anderson's record of the West for publication in book form.

Impressed with the unique viewpoint and detail of the Anderson journals, the editors have elected to present his trail Diary and his later version with comparable entries on facing pages, so that the similarities and differences of the two records may be readily compared. Nothing quite like this has ever been attempted in preparing a Western trail record for publication, and it is our hope that students will not only benefit from but much enjoy this pioneering approach.

With the conviction that Anderson had the right to participate in a definitive presentation of his journals, we have reprinted his Narrative of 1871, with a few of his emendations, as far as this version extends—that is, to the entry for June 20. (Additional details found in the Journal have been inserted in brackets.) The Journal itself supplies the secondary text printed from June 21 to September 29, when Anderson arrived back in St. Louis.

At the back of the second volume of his trail Diary, Anderson kept a separate log of the homeward journey; because the text was already sufficiently complex, we have added each day's log at the end of the entry for that date. We have assembled on pages 231-236 various ethnological notes found in the end pages of Diary and Journal. A few random geographical observations we have placed at appropriate points in the text of the Diary, as remarked in the notes.

So important is the Anderson record—the more one knows of the Western trails and the fur trade, the more one finds in it—that the editors have made it a vehicle for investigating the names of the great landmarks along the Oregon Trail. Despite all that has been published about overland trails, no one has thought to develop the history of these place names with critical attention to chronology.

Anderson's plea of 1871 to be informed what had become of Fitzpatrick, Fontenelle, Drips, Vasquez, Bridger, Charbonneau, One-Eyed Emanuel, and a good many more has not gone unanswered. We have supplied biographical sketches of all the mountain personalties to whom Anderson refers. For many, no sketches have existed, not even for such commanding figures as Andrew Drips and Lucien Fontenelle. Our primary purpose has been to determine where each man was, each year of the fur trade era. Such is the bulk of this book that it has not been feasible to document every statement. The files of the senior editor, built up over a long period of time, especially through research in the Missouri Historical Society's fur trade collections, have provided a foundation for many of these sketches. Together, the sketches offer a new view of the American fur trade during the 1820's and 1830's, and we hope that they will serve as points of departure for further studies.

Our biography of William Marshall Anderson is based on numerous contributions by individuals, and letters and documents from the Huntington Library's Anderson collection. At the invitation of the Library, in 1954 Charles Anderson Gauld of Vancouver, Washington, wrote a seven-page monograph on his great-grandfather's life. Mr. Gauld's continued interest has been of great encouragement and profit to the editors. Miss Mabel C. Weaks, archivist of The Filson Club, Louisville, Kentucky, kindly supplied microfilm copies of letters from the Club's Anderson-Latham collection. Part of this collection is missing; there are tantalizing records of letters no longer in the possession of the Club. Miss Weaks next referred us to Miss Marie Dickoré, of the Historical and Philosophical Society of Ohio, who had had previous occasion to study the collection. Miss Dickoré went to considerable pains to help locate the lost papers, and put us in touch with libraries and historical societies all over the Midwest.

Anderson's Catholicism did not endear him to his predominantly Protestant family, and their reminiscences are sometimes colored by personal dislike. Information gleaned from county histories, newspaper notices, and obituaries has been carefully weighed for accuracy. One common error, perpetuated by Anderson's son Thomas McArthur Anderson in his monograph of the Anderson, Clark, Marshall, and McArthur connection, was that he went to the Great Salt Lake with a party of trappers in 1832. Another is that he was a Confederate and abandoned his country in the time of crisis.

Helpful was a five-page biography by Robert S. Ellison, intended to preface his publication of the Journal and reportedly written with the help of Robert M. Anderson, one member of Anderson's family who recognized the value of his father's papers. Also of value was Kitty Anderson's history of Soldiers' Retreat. Charles Anderson's unsigned pamphlet, *Ye Andersons of Virginia*, contains the fullest printed account of his grandfather's life and, despite errors, affords one of the few sympathetic pictures of Anderson by a member of his family. Publication of the present book, we hope, will bring to light additional material on Anderson and those he met in the West in 1834.

* * *

To those who have helped us gather material, performed research, and given counsel, we are very grateful. Space does not permit us to list individual and institutional contributions, but there are few pages in this volume that do not reflect the encouragement and interest of those listed below.

Individuals: James Anderson, Mrs. Juanita Brooks, Charles L. Camp, Richard M. Clokey, Joseph G. Colgan, Edward F. Corson, Rev. W. L. Davis, Glen Dawson, Miss Marie Dickoré, Clifford M. Drury, Charles and Lindley Eberstadt, Charles Anderson Gauld, the late Everett D. Graff, Mr. and Mrs. Meldrum Gray, the late Kate L. Gregg, Mrs. Ann W. Hafen, LeRoy R. Hafen, J. Wayne Harris, Mrs. Richard B. Hershey, Jacquelin S. (Jim) Holliday, Donald Jackson, the late Perry W. Jenkins, Alvin M. Josephy, Jr., Charles Kelly, the late J. Roderic Korns, Mrs. Janet Lecompte, Mrs. Luella C. Lowie,

Walter McCausland, Paul O. McGrew, Mrs. Mary Anderson Matheson, Harold P. Morgan, Doyce B. Nunis, Jr., the late Miss Effie Olds, Albert J. Partoll, Mrs. Carol Pearson, Mrs. Mae Reed Porter, the late Clyde H. Porter, Miss Madeline Reeder, Floyd E. Risvold, Fred A. Rosenstock, Mrs. Agnes Wright Spring, John E. Sunder, Harvey E. Tobie, Betty Vawter, Ann Wells, and the late Carl I. Wheat.

Institutions: Mrs. Venia T. Phillips, Academy of Natural Sciences of Philadelphia; Miss Mary Walker, American Board of Commissioners for Foreign Missions; George P. Hammond, Robert H. Becker, Mrs. Helen Harding Bretnor, Miss Marie Byrne, Mrs. Vivian Fisher, Mrs. Julia H. Macleod, Miss Estelle Rebec, John Barr Tompkins, Bancroft Library, Berkeley; Allan R. Ottley, California State Library, Sacramento; Miss Mabel C. Weaks, The Filson Club, Louisville, Ky.; David L. Hieb, Fort Laramie National Monument; Thomas Gilcrease Institute of American History and Art, Tulsa; Miss Caroline Jakeman, Harvard University Library; Hudson's Bay Company, London; John E. Pomfret, Miss Mary Jane Bragg, Mrs. Nancy C. Moll, Miss Haydée Noya, and Miss Mary Alice Slater, The Huntington Library; Mrs. Theodore C. Pease, Illinois Historical Survey; Miss Mildred Goosman, Joslyn Museum and Art Gallery, Omaha; Mrs. Lela Barnes, Nyle Miller, Miss Louise Barry, and Mrs. Lorene Hawley, Kansas State Historical Society; Library of Congress, Washington, D. C.; Miss Lucile Kane, Minnesota Historical Society; Mrs. Frances Biese, George R. Brooks, Mrs. Brenda R. Gieseker, Mrs. Frances H. Stadler, and Charles van Ravenswaay, Missouri Historical Society; Mrs. Janet White, State Historical Society of Missouri; Miss Jane Smith, The National Archives, Washington, D. C.; Miss Frances L. Goudy and Mrs. S. Winifred Smith, The Ohio Historical Society; Kenneth W. Duckett and Miss Priscilla Knuth, Oregon Historical Society; St. Joseph Public Library, St. Joseph, Mo.; St. Louis Probate Court; Frank H. Anderson, Scotts Bluff (Neb.) National Monument; Frank H. H. Roberts and F. M. Seltzler, Smithsonian Institution, Washington, D. C.; Haruo Aoki and Harry Hoijer, University of California at Los Angeles; John James, Utah State Historical Society; Miss Gertrude Hassler, The Western Reserve Historical Society; Miss Josephine L. Harper, State Historical Society of Wisconsin; and Archibald Hanna, Jr., Yale University Library.

Biography of William Marshall Anderson

On a morning in July 1789 the neighbors assembled in arms at Soldiers' Retreat. This fortress-like house, located ten miles east of what is now downtown Louisville, Kentucky, was the home of the Andersons and the community stronghold. The Colonel, William Marshall Anderson's father, prepared to lead the last armed party against the Indians in Jefferson County. He had been informed of a raid upon the Chenoweth station and, reaching the smoldering house, beheld a small four-year-old girl warming her hands over the dying ashes in the fireplace.

"We are all dead here, Colonel Anderson," she said. Three of her brothers and a servant lay at her feet. The Indians had looted the house, but had not seen her in the bed they emptied on the floor. Outside, in the dark, her mother and an older brother had been severely tortured and left on the ground as dead. It was too late to capture the marauders, but the survivors were brought back to Soldiers' Retreat. As a youth William Marshall Anderson heard Mrs. Chenoweth's account, as she uncovered her bald head, of how it had been "peeled like an onion by the Indian's bluntest scalping knife."

This was the wilderness Col. Richard Clough Anderson had reached following the Buffalo Trail with his new wife, a babe, four slaves, and seven pack animals. His nearest neighbors were five miles away at Linn's station, and even farther off lived Captain Chenoweth and his family. The stations, or villages as they were later called, consisted of two or three houses and a stable surrounded by a high log structure, which had to be periodically defended against raids by Indian parties, forcing the settlers to rally under the commander.

Colonel Anderson was eminently qualified for this perilous task. During the Revolution he was with General Washington at the Battle of Assunpink Bridge. He was wounded and after a smallpox attack in the hospital had gained the reputation of being one of the three ugliest men in the Army. He was in the leading brigade that stopped Lord Cornwallis at Brandywine, took part in the foggy battle at Germantown, and the mortally wounded Count Pulaski gave him his sword at the Battle of Savannah. In 1780 he was taken prisoner with General Lincoln for nine months. As aide-de-camp to General Lafayette, Lt. Col. Anderson attended the surrender of Cornwallis.

On Dec. 17, 1783, the Society of the Cincinnati appointed Richard Clough Anderson surveyor general of lands in present Ohio and Kentucky to be distributed as wartime pay to soldiers from Virginia. Claims were weighed in terms of service and rank, but choice of land was individual, and the number of cases involving tedious litigation and the activities of wily land speculators complicated Anderson's task.[1]

Colonel Anderson's first wife, Elizabeth, was the sister of Generals George Rogers Clark and William Clark. Their son, Richard Clough Anderson, Jr., achieved prominence as an orator.[2] Two years after his wife's death in 1795, Anderson married Sarah Marshall, first cousin of Chief Justice John Marshall and a relative of the Clarks on her mother's side. To them were born seven sons and five daughters. Several of William Marshall Anderson's brothers became leaders in their generation.[3]

[1]Edward Lowell Anderson later wrote: "As surveyor-general my grandfather was compelled to remain almost constantly in his office, for assistants made the actual surveys and reported them to him. . . . This office-life was not to my grandfather's liking, and, whenever he could lay aside his pen, he would seize his gun and seek the woods. In these excursions he was often accompanied by George Rogers Clark. . . . These two would consider themselves happy when they could leave the safety of the fort, and without shelter, and exposed to many perils, wander in the grim forest." *Soldier and Pioneer: A Biographical Sketch of Lt.-Col. Richard C. Anderson of the Continental Army*, p. 44.

[2]Richard Clough Anderson, Jr. (1788-1826), graduated from William and Mary, became a representative in the Kentucky legislature from 1815 to 1817, a member of Congress from 1817 to 1821, speaker of the Kentucky House of Representatives in 1822, and from 1823 to 1826 minister to Colombia, where he negotiated the first treaty between the United States and a South American country. He died of yellow fever at Cartagena en route to the Congress of Panama of 1826. See "Cartagena to Bogatá, 1825-1826: The Diary of Richard Clough Anderson, Jr.," *Hispanic American Historical Review*, XLII (May 1962), 217-231, or his *Diary and Journal, 1814-1826*, Durham, N. C., 1964.

[3]Larz Anderson (1803-1878) graduated from Harvard Law School and moved to Cincinnati when he married into the Nicholas Longworth family. He amassed a considerable fortune on his own as well as that inherited through his wife, and his nine sons all married Cincinnati heiresses.
Robert Anderson (1805-1871), a graduate of West Point, may be said to have started the Civil War by defending Fort Sumter instead of surrendering it to the rebels as they expected. He was promoted to brigadier general and placed in command of the Department of Kentucky. His bravery and loyalty to the Union were commended by President Lincoln.
Charles Anderson (1814-1891) became a prominent Dayton lawyer and was one of the few Americans, other than his friend Sam Houston, to be governor of two states, Ohio and Kentucky.

With the turn of the century the "dense wood and dreary cane-brakes filled with wild beasts and savage men were now smiling farms and peaceful friends," and the city of Louisville flourished. Colonel Anderson was widely known for his hospitality, and to his table came old Army comrades, pioneers looking for homes, wandering hunters, and even Indians.

It was at the 800-acre Soldiers' Retreat that William Marshall Anderson was born on June 24, 1807. The magnificent fortress home, with stone walls five feet thick, stood two stories high, with wings of one story. The entrance from the road was a mile long and bordered with forest trees. Behind the main building were quarters for twenty or more slaves and the overseer's office, forming a court planted in gardens. Both in front and back, wide stone steps led into a spacious eighteen-foot wide hall with mahogany doors brought from Virginia. It was here that young Marshall, as his family called him, met such distinguished guests as Burr, Clay, Jackson, Monroe, and Chief Little Turtle of the Miamis. In 1825 General Lafayette was given a grand banquet and breakfast. Often the host would bring out his French violin and delight his guests. The "Doctrine" of his comrade of the Battle of Trenton, President Monroe, was proudly displayed in gold letters.

When Marshall was three years old, Mrs. Anderson wrote his sister Maria, who was in a private school:

The girls are all well and very busy making peach butter and I have dryed 7 bushels of peaches. . . . There is a barbacue today at Judge Crimsby's. It is supposed there will be a great number of gentlemen and Ladys at it. . . .

An anecdote from this period has been preserved by Miss Kitty Anderson:

We have a story in our family of one of the far-away cousins, a Carrington, who overtook a sturdy old figure riding from the city [Louisville] towards Soldiers' Retreat. Responding to inquiry as to the direction of the Anderson place, the rider offered to conduct the stranger to Soldiers' Retreat. The older man was dressed in buff vest, knee breeches, silken hose, silver buckles and wore his hair in a queue. Though it was long after the period when Jefferson had garbed the American male in sad colored clothes, this old timer continued to wear the dress of a Colonial gentleman. As they rode together young Carrington mentioned casually that he had been given to understand that the head of the house, to whom he referred as the "ugly old gentleman," had many broad acres and a number of beautiful daughters. He made inquiry as to these reports, also as to the possibility of his marrying some of these broad acres and incidentally, one of the pretty daughters. He guilelessly expatiated upon the variety of his wearing apparel in charge of his body servant, who was riding in the rear, and naïvely surmised that before he had exhausted the many changes of his gay raiment, he might make a conquest. His taciturn guide turned in at Soldiers' Retreat where a servant took charge of their horses. As they mounted the steps, a radiant young woman sprang out with arms extended and paused at the sight of a stranger. The old man who had served as a guide dropped back in his stately old school way and said: "Cousin Carrington, I am 'the ugly old gentleman' and this is one of my pretty daughters." Tradition has it that the surprised youth returned to Virginia.

Marshall's early schooling was with a tutor, a person of "education and correct habits." He was an eager student and early showed an interest in the classics. He wrote later:

Far back in my life, old Father Wilson, of Chillicothe, and parson Shannon of Shelbyville, Ky., were my instructors in Greek & Latin. The one was grave, dignified and solemn, the other was gentle, kind and almost sadly quiet. At that time, all my sources of knowledge & morality were Protestant. I drew Episcopalianism from my mother's breast. A Lutheran taught me my catechism. A Baptist taught me A B C and Latin grammar. Presbyterians taught me to parse glibly the galloping verses of Virgil.

On Sunday Marshall would attend the Lutheran Sabbath School at Brunerstown, three miles from home, and "With the exception of Jim Johnson, I believe no boy in the school came nearer committing whole chapters of the New Testament to memory."

This thorough study of the Bible and the classics is reflected in the Diary, where Marshall leans heavily on his literary background to draw allusions. In fact, his mind is so steeped with Biblical personages, Greek mythology, and Virgil, that his writing has the flare of romance, even extravagance. That he was well versed in American history and the democratic principles of freedom, for which his father had so recently been at war, is also revealed in the Diary, where he speaks of his country with a pride that is intensely personal. He refers to only two specific authors, Thomas Moore, the Irish poet, and the English Bishop Reginald Heber, a well-known hymnwriter.

The Diary also reflects a fluency in French, which he makes use of for an occasionally caustic comment.[4]

In 1822, at the age of fifteen, Marshall undertook his first horseback journey. He traveled through the unsettled wilderness of Ohio to Chillicothe, the home of his eldest sister, Maria, who had married one of his father's deputies, Allen Latham. For two years he studied at Chillicothe Academy and in 1823 was accepted as a freshman at Transylvania University in Lexington, Kentucky. His return to Kentucky was made by flatboat down the Scioto River to Portsmouth. As the river was very swift, the trip was considered hazardous, normally only to be undertaken in an emergency. From Portsmouth he proceeded to Louisville by steamboat.

On April 18, 1825, while at Transylvania, Marshall received a letter from his brother Larz at home. "You already know the result of our last application in your favour for a Cadet appointment. I regret its failure. However it is no great matter, as it is hoped that you will make the best of your present situation." Marshall was then obtaining a classical education, already contemplating a career in law. The situation at home was poor. The house had been damaged by an earthquake. Larz continues, "Be as economical as possible. Not only are the debts great, but the creditors pressing and much of our property is now under execution—some of it sold to satisfy judgements at a great sacrifice on our part! . . . My father . . . can now scarcely collect money enough to pay the interest of his debts. . . ."

In October 1826, when Marshall was starting his third and last year, his father lay dying. As Larz was studying at Harvard and Robert teaching at West Point, it was Marshall who was called home. He arrived by a relay of three horses to hold his father in his arms as he died.[5]

---

[4]When Marshall rewrote the Diary into the Narrative, he elaborated his notes by expanding the literary references. He refers to Buffon's *Histoire Naturelle*; one of James Baillie Fraser's works on Persia; and Wendell Phillips' speeches, which were not published until the 1860's. The narrative maintains the heroic style of the original diary by the numerous classical allusions.

[5]Richard Clough Anderson held the office of surveyor general until his death. At the time of Washington's second election, he was a member of the first electoral college in Kentucky and served in the legislature. He was the first Masonic Lodge Master west of the Appalachians—at Lexington about 1788. When Wilkinson and Sebastian attempted to declare Kentucky's independence and ally her with Spain, Anderson opposed their efforts at the Danville Convention. It is said that Wilkinson had advised the Spanish government to offer Anderson a bribe of a thousand dollars, he being a "man of ordinary ability but great influence." In 1795 the Colonel built the *Caroline*, first schooner to navigate the Ohio and to take Kentucky tobacco to London.

Despite his youth, Marshall was appointed executor of the estate and did not return to college. For the next three years he was involved in the management of the farm. The family had broken up, and Mrs. Anderson was anxious to remove to the home of her daughter Maria in Chillicothe, Ohio, at that time the social capital of "the West." On June 25, 1828, the following advertisement appeared in the *Louisville Public Advertiser:*

BEAR GRASS FARM FOR SALE

I will sell upon liberal terms, a tract of between 5 or 600 acres of land, in Jefferson county, owned by the late Col. Richard C. Anderson, and known by the name of "Soldier's Retreat. . . ." It is as healthy a situation as any in the State. There are nearly 200 acres cleared—and a fine, large and commodious stone house, with other convenient buildings upon the place; an extensive peach and apple orchard of most excellent fruit, and abundance of unfailing springs, in various parts. It is, perhaps, the best adapted for a stock farm of any place in the country. . . . The tract is susceptible of a convenient division into two farms.

LARZ ANDERSON

The farm was not sold till almost a year later, and then only in part, at seventeen dollars an acre.

By then Marshall was reading law in the office of Larz in Louisville. A letter of April 4, 1829, to Allen Latham in Chillicothe reveals his general discontent:

it had been my determination to move to Louisiana, that for that purpose I had some time since relinquished the study of common law, and been engaged after, in that of the Civil, For the purpose of more speedily improving myself in that branch of the professional science, it had been my desire to leave here for some southern point in January, and after in March, both of which I had put off from Larz's opposition, but that now I did not really know what to do. The season for removing to the south was passing. That I had no books suitable to their courts to study during the summer. And to your offer I felt inclined to accept it for the purpose of avoiding that dispicable thing of acting the gentleman, and feeding and clothing myself from the proceeds of my father's labour.[6]

He also complains that his social life is taken up with the weddings of his friends:

Anderson's contributions to his country during the Revolution and in private life reveal him as one of America's greatest patriots.

[6]This letter, and those of March 28 and April 9, 1832, and June 13, 1833, quoted below, are in the Anderson-Latham Papers, The Filson Club, Louisville, Ky.

I hope you will not form a bad opinion of my heart from this . . . that you will not think because I remain single and unengaged, in these general cooing and wooing times, that I am callous and unsusceptible to female charms. No! for it is not the case. But as the predestinarians say, "my time is not yet come."

This was a few weeks before he met Eliza McArthur, then thirteen years old, and already known as a brunette "Highland beauty."

In the next two years he managed a trip south, returning in March 1832 "all impatience" to resume the study of his profession. Under the instruction of Professor Mays of Lexington, he planned to take his examinations for a license and begin practice in the South. He needed a little money from his brother-in-law Allen for some debts "contracted in this place (in an honest way)," so on March 28 he offered to dispose of some property in Louisville. Twelve days later he was disillusioned:

I some times think that I have lost so much time in various ways and for various causes, since I have commenced the study of the law, that I ought, in justice to myself, and to those interested in my welfare, to redeem those precious lost moments, by the earliest possible commencement of my profession; at other times, I persuade myself that [I] should still delay my entree into business until I have better prepared myself to do credit to the honourable & responsible employment in which I hope to be engaged.

In May 1832 Marshall was awarded a license to practice law and received the title of colonel on the staff of Governor Breathitt of Kentucky. However, Eliza McArthur was in Chillicothe, and Marshall began to spend more than half of his time in Ohio. He took part in local affairs and was instrumental in the organization of the Ohio Importing Company of Ross County, a company formed to import Shorthorn Durham cattle from England to improve the local stock. In the summer of 1833 the worldwide epidemic of Asiatic cholera reached Ohio, and Marshall had what he described in a letter of June 13 as "a gentle visitation of his Oriental Mightiness."

The next word on Marshall comes early in 1834, when he visited his brother Robert, then a lieutenant at Baton Rouge. Upon his return to Louisville, Marshall suffered a brief attack of yellow fever. To regain his strength he decided on a trip to the Far West. His immediate family, on whom he seems to have been dependent both emotionally and financially, no doubt took a part in this decision. Already, Marshall was far overshadowed by his distinguished brothers. Arrangements were made with a relative, General Henry Atkinson,[7] for Marshall to accompany the Dragoons from St. Louis on a Pawnee-Pic expedition.

The droll figure Marshall cut as he rode off to St. Louis is described in his Narrative and in his 1837 communications to the *American Turf Register*. The General may have had doubts that Marshall was hardy enough to keep up with the Dragoons, for he recommended that he join the fur-trading party being taken to the Rocky Mountains by the Kentucky-born William L. Sublette.

The thirty-seven-man Sublette party represented a segment of society with which Marshall had had little experience in the urbane surroundings of Soldiers' Retreat. The party was made up of men with no formal education, men who existed by their wits, their physical strength, and their not inconsiderable skills. The qualities they most valued were courage and fortitude, as dictated by a philosophy of hard experience. In contrast, Marshall had adopted the philosophy of the ancients, being too inexperienced and impressionable to have formed one of his own. His polite society had conditioned him to value adventures of the mind rather than those of the body.

Marshall may have been as distasteful to the traders as many of them were to him, and his one friend on the long trip to the Rocky Mountains was William Sublette. Sublette was occupied leading the party, and Marshall turned to his journal to address those who would understand him—his "mother, sisters, little Dick and a pair of pretty blue eyes," those who embodied the traditions he held dear. "How unlike the first, and all intervening, is this last anniversary of my birth," he writes. "Far, far away from the grave of my father, the dear home of my mother, and the land of my countrymen, I am in a social waste, as soil-less and as desolate as the Desert in which I dwell."

The day-to-day notations in Marshall's journal reflect the interests of a gentleman farmer. "What better marks of good soil can

[7]General Atkinson's wife, Mary Anne Bullitt, was the granddaughter of Mrs. Owen Gwathmey, sister of Generals George Rogers Clark and William Clark and of Elizabeth Anderson (the first wife of Marshall's father). Marshall's own mother, Sarah Marshall, was also related to the Clark family. She was the granddaughter of Ann Clark McLeod, the aunt of the famous generals.

there be than black walnut, ash, sugartree, big paw paw, and bigger grapevines?" he asks as he rides through the settlements. The terrain is described in terms of its fertility, the prairie that changes from sandy to clear sand, and the moist green grass of the river shore that becomes a dry and yellow hay. In the mountains he notes the wild flax in bloom, but "being in the wrong season, I could procure no seed." Forest-born, he is oppressed by the treeless country of the Platte: "It is sand and nothing but sand. . . . How I long for a timbered country. . . . All that comes near to arborification is a fringe of cotton wood and willows along the banks of creeks and rivers." Wild animals are a constant source of pleasure to him and, as he meticulously records their appearance and habits, he often colors his observations with a literary or philosophical allusion—"that sly, old apple thief," the rattlesnake, with his "flattering tongue and caudal castanets." He is revolted at the view of an old bull buffalo with his "dirty, drunken beard"; but marvels at the speed of the ebon-footed antelope, the bighorns or Rocky Mountain sheep "peeping at us from their unapproachable towers"; the pine squirrels the size of the "old-fashion blue-rat"; and the gregarious prairie dogs in their subterranean cities.

Throughout the journal Marshall's curiosity is repeatedly aroused by Indians. Apprehension, anticipation, and awe—all contribute to his interest, which is surprisingly sympathetic, though he considers the Indian more of a savage than a man. "One of the finest specimens of the animal man I ever looked upon," he writes of an Indian chief. There is a certain admiration in his descriptions of their barbaric customs: the tree scaffold that bears the dead Sioux brave tightly wrapped in the honor robe with his implements of battle and chase and "left to the companionship of the birds of the air and his brothers of the Spirit land"; and the squaw mounted astride a most elegantly caparisoned horse, "whilst her proud head was turbaned with a most filthy and disgusting clout." His bookish notion of the "noble savage" is both dispelled and enhanced as he sees the "circle of blood-stained sticks, each bearing a lock of human hair" and the Indian chief "as graceful and dignified as a Roman Senator."

He listens intently to the anecdotes of the trappers and fur traders as they gather at night around the roasting buffalo ribs. Though he cannot condone their bravado, their drunken sports and rough manners, he develops a certain respect for their courage and humanity. "There are many brave, rough fellows among them, whom I do most heartily wish well. They have been kind and accomodating to me, a stranger. I have been hungry in the desert and they have given me elk and buffaloe meat. I doubt not that they would also have given me drink and raiment, if I had needed them." During the trip he is afraid of discomfort, of falling ill, and of losing his blond scalp, a coveted prize, but he learns not to voice his fears, and on the return journey he rides far ahead of the party as scout. Once back at the settlements, his encounter with a gentleman is "as unexpected and as agreeable as the song of the nightingale would be among the croaking bull frogs," but he has learned that fine clothes and polite conversation do not make the man: "I supped this minute at a tavern table, amidst village politicians, pedantic doctors, and wise *looking* lawyers—My dirty hunting shirt and greasy leather breeches seemed to offend their hypercritical eyes and too curious olfactories—God help them!"

During his absence, Anderson had written his brother Larz from the Kansas River on May 8 and a long letter to his mother from the rendezvous on July 6, not then knowing whether he would stay or return. Sublette tucked this letter into his saddlebags on leaving the rendezvous July 10.

Neither of these letters has been found, but there are echoes of the Rocky Mountain letter in the correspondence of Anderson's brother Robert with their mother, Sarah.[8] A letter dated Fort Constitution, New Hampshire, Sept. 7, 1834, says:

You have I hope by this time received letters from William. I did not understand whether he was to return this winter or not. When he returns, I think, we shall see him a different man. Such a life as he must lead in the Rocky Mountains will, if any thing can, restore a weak constitution to its proper vigor and a[c]tivity.

In a second letter dated Portsmouth, Oct. 26, 1834, Robert writes:

I am pleased with the extracts, you have given me, from Wm's letter—The trip to the Rocky Mountains, although ard[u]ous and not without dangers, is, I am confident, the best thing, which could have been recommended for

[8]Anderson Collection, Huntington Library.

the restoration of William's health. . . . He had designed, I believe, to accompany Colo. Dodge, and leaving Louisville with this intent, changed his plan after reaching St. Louis—The troops under Colo. D— were severely afflicted by the cholera and bilious fever—some of the officers, and many of the men, died—The journey taken by the Dragoons was so short, that, if Wm. could have escaped an attack of sickness, he would not, probably, have been much benefitted by the march—Now we may hope, that, on his return to us, he will be found more robust, than he has been for years —Health and a sound constitution, are blessings, I pray he may enjoy. My little favorite, "Black Hawk" should certainly give to the world a history of his travels— poor little fellow, he is with a kind master, one who, I am assured, will treat him well, and divide his scanty morcel with his faithful horse—He will, thank him, or, I will in his name, for all the kindnesses recd. . . .

His health restored, Anderson returned home in the fall of 1834 a full fifty pounds heavier. On Feb. 16, 1835, he was married to Eliza McArthur, a woman of both strong features and strong character. Eliza was known as a fine conversationalist, perhaps because she was a sympathetic listener. Her father, Duncan McArthur, was a former deputy surveyor with Anderson's own father. General McArthur had led an invasion near Windsor, Ontario, to burn flour mills supplying Indians who scalped Americans during the War of 1812. His long experience in public life included service in the legislature and in Congress. From 1830 to 1832 he was governor of Ohio. He ran for the U. S. House of Representatives in 1832 and by failing to vote personally lost the election by a single vote to his future son-in-law William Allen. In the next few years Anderson and Eliza spent much of their time at the McArthur mansion, Fruit Hill, outside Chillicothe.

On the death of Richard Clough Anderson in 1826, Allen Latham had been appointed deputy surveyor. The position no longer had its old importance, for most of the land had been distributed, and in 1838 Latham resigned. Anderson was temporarily appointed to the office on October 12, and on Jan. 21, 1839, became the permanent Surveyor General of the Virginia Military Land District in Ohio. The few duties allowed him time to pursue his studies and to practice law in Chillicothe.

At this time the Andersons were converted to Catholicism. Among the differing accounts of the conversion is one that tells of a distin-

guished priest who, on arriving at Chillicothe without accommoda-
tions, was invited to the home of the hospitable Andersons. The
family had just lost a child, and the priest reportedly so comforted
them that they embraced his faith. However, a granddaughter,
Miss Effie Anderson Olds[9] of Circleville, Ohio, stoutly maintained
as late as 1955: "My grandparents became Catholics through no
one's influence. They read about religions and decided that the
Catholic Church was the best one."

Anderson wrote later that he made his first communion Dec. 28,
1839, and received confirmation Jan. 1, 1840. Ten years later he as-
pired to a government mission to Rome but gave it up on the advice
of his brothers, who discouraged his seeking a diplomatic post without greater financial resources. His notes and newspaper articles indicate that he embraced Catholicism only after an intense period of
thought and study of various Protestant faiths. He was considered
in provincial Ohio an authority on religion and religious history. As
his family and friends were Protestant, he was involved in religious controversy during the rest of his life, especially with his sons,
who detested the strict Roman Catholic schools to which they were
sent. His daughters remained Catholic.

In 1838 the health of Governor McArthur was failing. Anderson
had been appointed McArthur's attorney and was occupied with
the management of the large Fruit Hill farm. A notebook in Anderson's hand shows him making out deeds, receiving payments for
land, renting houses, selling horses and cattle, and paying twenty
dollars for McArthur on subscription to buy a fire engine in Chillicothe. He was forced to resign as deputy surveyor. In May 1839 Governor McArthur died, leaving a will that precipitated one of the
most famous lawsuits in U. S. history. As McArthur's last attorney
Anderson was involved, but how far it is impossible to tell. He received a letter in May from Larz advising against his becoming executor of the McArthur estate because of the already apparent controversy within the family. By the terms of the will the extensive
farms were to be left in trust until the last grandchild was of age.
The will was immediately contested by McArthur's son Allen, who
argued that the testament was not only impracticable but written

[9]Miss Olds was the daughter of Mary Anderson (1846-1897) and Judge Joseph Olds of Cincinnati.

at a time when his father was not in possession of his faculties. The Ross County Court of Appeals was at that time presided over by Judge John H. Keith, a known suitor for the hand of one of the lovely McArthur girls, Effie, widow of Allen Coons. The will was broken and the property divided among the children. Ironically, Mrs. Coons passed up the judge, married her father's political rival William Allen, and moved into Fruit Hill. Most of the estate was disposed of at poor prices, because buyers feared that the will would be reinstated. On Feb. 7, 1858, Anderson wrote his brother Robert that his affairs had become so desperately involved, "my spirits sunk to such a depth of cowardly despondency that I gave up the attention to every thing but the endless endeavor to extricate myself from the McArthur injustice and iniquity. I set to work, to sell or exchange anything and every thing I had to pay off the $9000—which they claimed and secured against me."[10]

After the death of Allen McArthur, his widow and son Allen moved to Kentucky and in 1873 brought suit to reinstate the will. The case was fought to the U. S. Supreme Court, where it was decided that all lands must be given back to the McArthur grandchildren, including rents and profits. As the property alone was worth more than a million dollars, hundreds of people were affected by this decision. Allen McArthur, Jr., was sandbagged and almost killed in his attempt to carry out the court ruling and ended a very unhappy life by shooting himself.

Following the death of Governor McArthur, Anderson bought a small place near Chillicothe called Glen Mary, and devoted himself almost completely to his books. About 1840 he became interested in archaeology. The surrounding country was studded with Indian mounds, and with Dr. E. H. Davis and E. G. Squier, Anderson pioneered their exploration, and gathered a valuable collection of stone and copper artifacts. In the early 1850's he traced a line of fire signal stations up the Scioto Valley. He maintained a correspondence with archaeologists all over the world.

During the 1840's Anderson continued to expand his interests. A letter of Jan. 10, 1842, to Robert reports that their brother John had just returned from Columbus, where he had been to nominate a gov-

---

[10]Letter from Seven Oaks Farm, Ohio, to [Robert] Anderson, Anderson Collection, Huntington Library.

ernor. "He is almost as much a politician as Mr. Latham," Anderson writes. "Thank goodness . . . I am not troubled with that disease."[11] However, by December 29 of the next year, he writes Robert that he has joined Mr. Latham in his "editorial mania." "I lent him a helping hand as long as I thought it would benefit him politically. . . . And we did lash them, master & cur, most gloriously too; I thought it fine fun as long as there was any fight in them, but when it came to kicking a dead dog I desisted."

The letter continues:

I believe you have never been at old fort Moultrie. How delighted I should be, to go over the ground where our brave father endured so much danger and privation. Especially at Charleston & Savannah. Twas at the latter place, I believe that Count Pulaski presented him with his sword. I directed Campbell when he painted his likeness to represent a sword with a tiger's head and the date of the attack of Savannah on the blade. It would have commemorated his own gallant conduct on that occasion, as well as the death & friendship of the great Pole.

He asks about Robert's friend Muir, who has recently entered the field of historical painting, and tells of his acquisition of a fine Florentine miniature of Raphael's Madonna.[12]

In June 1844 Anderson was appointed secretary of "The American Art Union for the promotion of the Fine Arts in the United States." On Oct. 14-15, 1846, he attended an agricultural fair—especially notable for its exhibition of articles made by women—sponsored by the agricultural society of which he was president. In 1847 he is listed as one of the directors of the Marietta and Cincinnati Railroad. On December 14 of that year his brother Larz wrote to dissuade him from starting an apple orchard on river bottom land. Larz felt such land might be healthy for apples but not for people.

In the early 1850's Anderson became involved in a violent controversy over the visit of the anticlerical Louis Kossuth to the United States. The war of independence in Hungary had aroused American sympathy, and the U. S. Congress offered the Protestant Kossuth and his followers a new home. Groups that refused him a hearty welcome included Catholics and those who feared "embroiling their nation

---

[11]Letter from Chillicothe, Ohio, to Robert Anderson, Huntington Library.
[12]Letter from Glen Mary, Ohio, to Robert Anderson, Cincinnati, Ohio, Huntington Library.

in European contests." Anderson, in a letter dated March 26, 1852, to the *Scioto Gazette*, decried the Protestant divines with their cry of "Protestantism and Liberty!":

Where the carcass is there are the buzzards also. No sooner had the poetic Governor [Kossuth] landed on our shores, than he was surrounded by black coats and white cravats. . . . theological demagogues. . . . black-winged scavengers of war. . . . if their desires are fulfilled, we shall see rivers of blood pouring down the beautiful hills and overflowing the lovely valleys of Hungary.

The next day both the Chillicothe editor and his contributors rallied to attack Anderson: "Outrageous charges made by Mr. A. in such abusive language"; "one of the grossest slanders against the Protestant clergy of the country." One irate writer called on him "as a man of honor, as a professing Christian, as an American lawyer, and as a Democrat to prove what he has said . . . or retract with due apology; or sit down a dishonored man."

On Sept. 16, 1853, the *Scioto Gazette* carried the following notice:

Mr. Editor: You will please announce the name of w. MARSHALL ANDERSON, as an Independent candidate for the Senate of Ohio, in the District composed of the counties of Ross and Highland and oblige

MANY VOTERS.

Anderson's platform was based on his opposition to prohibition, an issue that soon came before the General Assembly. Maine had recently prohibited liquor and this had spurred temperance movements in other states. Party leaders in Ohio were reluctant to antagonize reformers, and as much attention was paid to the Maine law as to the slavery question.

On September 23 the *Gazette* printed a vituperative attack by Anderson on Horace Greeley, who had recommended impeaching the use of wine in the Sacrament. These words foreshadow the arguments of later antiprohibitionists against morality by legislation:

. . . Is it not incredible, is it not lamentable, that ministers of the gospel, and teachers of religion, have joined with these political philanthropists, these fanatics and fools, in urging on their silly mania, with almost drunken haste and fury? What blind, though perhaps honest zeal, impels them in this course? Are they really convinced that they have no spiritual remedy for this moral sickness? . . . Drunkenness is so disgusting, and so beastly a vice, that no sane man can look upon it with pleasure or approval. We need no picture of a father contemplating an only son, in hopeless, slavering idiocy; or wife, suffering a martyrdom of agony, as she watches the husband of her heart reeling home, bruised, bloated and covered with filth. All will concede that it is desirable to remedy the evil as far as possible. But how can this be done? Not, certainly, by this spawn of folly, which is the same curse to temperance, that abolitionism is to the cause of emancipation. As to the effect of this law ask Boston and Portland, and what answer will they return? At this very moment, bottles of brandy, rum and wine are marshalled on the public tables, as if in open defiance of the law. Let us not, then, pass a law which would fall dead-born from the press. Such a law would be mocked and scorned, and might not unaptly be styled "An act to represent Don Quixote's battle with the wine bags."

Anderson was not elected, but the "Maine law" was defeated by an overwhelming majority in the Ohio legislature.

In 1853 the Andersons moved from Chillicothe to Circleville, Ohio. Here they stayed for a year before settling down in their new house at Seven Oaks Farm in Pickaway County. This farm was included in the inheritance of over two thousand acres Eliza had received from her father. It was remarkable for a giant oak tree that appeared to have grown from one acorn, seven large and symmetrical trees springing from a common trunk.

Eliza had not long to enjoy the comforts of her new home, for she died on Sept. 2, 1855. She left four children (six more had died in infancy): three boys, Thomas McArthur, Henry (Harry) Reuben, and Charles; and a girl, Mary. All of the sons had Army careers. Thomas McArthur (1836-1917) abandoned the bar in 1861 and by 1865 became a major in the regular Army. In 1886-1898 he commanded Vancouver Barracks, then—on the outbreak of the Spanish-American War—led the first American expedition to the Philippines, capturing Manila as a brigadier and major general of volunteers. In 1900 he retired and for three years headed the Ohio Soldiers and Sailors Home in Sandusky before settling in Oregon. Among his several publications are *Conspiracies preceding the Revolution* and *What Are American Principles?* He is the author of a two-hundred-page unpublished history of Fort Vancouver, 1853-1893, now in the Coe Collection, Yale University.

Harry (1844-1918) entered gunboat service at the outbreak of the Civil War and served in the Army for forty years, campaigning in the West against the Cheyennes and Sioux.

Charles (1850-1913) was an Army doctor in the 1880's and 1890's and settled in Santa Barbara, California.

Mary, born in 1846, married Judge Joseph Olds of Cincinnati. It was in the home of their daughters Effie Olds and Eleanor (Mrs. Meldrum) Gray at 611 Guilford Road, Circleville, Ohio, that the Rocky Mountain Diary and Journal of 1834 and the Mexican diaries of 1865-1866[13] were discovered in 1948 by J. S. Holliday.

William Marshall Anderson became not only prosperous but prominent in the community. Though never known as a man of business, he successfully managed his farm for twenty-five years. His nature inclined him more to cultural pursuits. He is reported to have had one of the most discriminating book collections in the country. In the end pages of the Journal is a list of a 154-volume library, presumably belonging to Anderson and perhaps compiled while he was preparing the Journal. The list comprises books in the fields of history, philosophy, the classics, literature, and languages. (Scientific texts are noticeably in the minority; perhaps Anderson did not choose to list them.)

For many years Anderson devoted himself to the study of art and to the encouragement of young artists. They were his friends and companions, and he never missed an opportunity to entertain those who came to Ohio. Always an admirer of nature, as is shown in this work, he became well informed on ornithology, botany, horticulture, and floriculture. He took a great interest in welfare projects in his community and was a member and president of the Circleville Board of Education as well as one of the organizers and president of the Board of Managers of the Circleville Public Library. Through all his life he remained a Southern gentleman. His fondness for company gave him an opportunity to display his gift of conversation. He could speak with authority on a great variety of topics, was rich in reminiscences, and was known for his charming anecdotes.

It was to this prominent widower that the bishop of the local Catholic diocese, playing Cupid, introduced Ellen Columba Ryan. Miss Ryan and her two sisters had been known in their youth as "The Three Graces" because of their great beauty and charm. Ellen had come with her parents from Londonderry, Ireland, at the age of

[13]*An American in Maximilian's Mexico 1865-1866: The Diaries of William Marshall Anderson*, ed. Ramón Eduardo Ruiz.

61

twelve, to settle on a farm near Urbana, Ohio. She had been educated at the Nazareth (Kentucky) Convent and at Sacred Heart in New Orleans and had traveled extensively in this country and in Europe. A woman of firm conviction, she shared with Anderson a devout Catholic faith, a great interest in reading, and a rare conversational gift. When Anderson married her on April 21, 1857, she had already inherited a considerable fortune.

The couple had four children, only one of whom survived to adulthood—Robert Marshall Anderson (1862-1939), who preserved his father's diaries and papers. Robert was graduated from Notre Dame University in 1883. He spent twelve years at Stevens Institute, Hoboken, New Jersey. An expert civil engineer, he left Stevens to become vice-president of a New York engineering company. His several scrapbooks, placed in the Huntington Library, reveal his interest in Anderson family history.

On Jan. 1, 1860, William Marshall Anderson was elected president of "The Pickaway-co Horse Association for the Improvement of the Horse." A number of fine Canadian stallions were imported to improve the local stock. During these years Anderson kept up an active correspondence with his nephew Richard Clough Anderson, Jr.,[14] on such topics as farm equipment, the problems of freed slaves in farming, and the training of thoroughbreds and race horses. They exchanged colts and trainers as frequently as letters.

The outbreak of the Civil War proved difficult to those Ohioans who maintained family and traditional ties with the South. Shortly after the Battle of Antietam, September 1862, Anderson had a visit from an old Virginia friend and neighbor.

"Colonel Anderson," said McNemara with some feeling, "I hate all this tyranny, of Stanton and Seward and his little bell. I would rather see this Union smashed than that any man should lay violent hands on our beloved Constitution."

"Mr. McNemara, of what use would our Constitution be without the Union?" Anderson asked. "If the Union is destroyed the country

---

[14]Richard Clough Anderson (1829-1878), the "little Dick" of the Journal, was the only child of Larz and Cynthia Ann (Pope) Anderson (1808-1829). A graduate of Kenyon College, he was elected to the Kentucky House of Representatives, where he helped save the state to the Union. A "rare modesty" that seems to have been common to several of the Anderson family prevented him from pursuing a career in public life, but not from being a frequent anonymous contributor to the press. His sudden death from a stroke of apoplexy was a profound shock to Anderson, who loved him as his own son.

is destroyed so far as government is concerned. And without a country of what use is a Constitution?"

"Perhaps you are right in your way of looking at it, but it is hard to know that your blood relations are being shot down in their homes and that the fields over which I have hunted as boy and man are devastated and drenched with the blood of my family and neighbors." He added bitterly, "I am disappointed in finding that your sympathies are not all with us for I understood that you were against the Lincolnites, soul and body."

"I am thoroughly opposed to the ways of Seward and Stanton and many of their military underlings and always shall be, but it is futile to speak of upholding the Constitution and destroying the Union," replied Anderson.[15]

Anderson remained at Seven Oaks, largely removed from the war itself, until the summer of 1863, when southern Ohio was invaded by Morgan's raiders. Nearly fifty thousand men then responded to the Governor's call to arms. Anderson was unanimously chosen Company Captain of the Home Guards of Pickaway County, which was ordered to report to General Mason at Camp Chase, near Columbus. Because of his age, Anderson felt he could not learn to drill well enough to handle the company, and he resigned his commission after a few days, but he held the rank of sergeant until the company returned home about a month later.

Though a firm Unionist, Anderson saw the follies of the Republicans, and his zealous nature led him into several bitter controversies after the war. His eloquent speeches and letters were in demand with many Ohio newspapers, where the debates raged. These articles prove beyond doubt Anderson's allegiance to the Union, but the fervency of his language no doubt was often misunderstood. After his death an old enemy stirred the dying embers of this controversy, and Anderson's position was eloquently defended by a Cincinnati editor:

The regular correspondent of Cincinnati *Gazette*, in this city, who is the echo of a little clique of narrow partisans, in noticing the death of W. Marshall Anderson, Esq., said "during the war Mr. Anderson sympathized with the rebels" . . . mean and cowardly reference to Mr. Anderson, after he was beyond human aid or injury. . . . Mr. Anderson did not sympathize

[15]Charles Anderson, *Ye Andersons of Virginia*, pp. 30-32.

with the rebels or the rebellion. While he favored the suppression of the rebellion and was offered a position of prominence in the Federal army, he could not tolerate the wrongs and outrages perpetrated by the dominant party, calling itself Republican, to perpetuate its power, and he strongly opposed the attempt to Africanize the South and make the whites the serfs and vassals of the negro population. He loved his country, the Union, and free government, but he detested with all the ardor of his nature the Republican party and its arrogance. He was a true patriot, and came of a race of patriots, than whom none have served their country better.[16]

Anderson's dissatisfaction with the Reconstruction played a large part in his enigmatic trip to Mexico in 1865-1866.[17] Ostensibly on an archaeological expedition, he spent six months in a subtropical zone near Veracruz assisting in the establishment of a small Confederate colony. In December of that year he received a commission from Maximilian to survey lands in northeastern Mexico for possible colonization by defeated Confederates anxious to quit the ruined South.

In northern Mexico Anderson was in a dangerous situation. As an agent of the Emperor, he could not depend on his American citizenship to protect him from Juárez, "the Lincoln of Mexico." Alone and speaking little Spanish, he turned to his diaries as his confidant. These diaries were dedicated to Frances Ketchum, Ellen Anderson's sister.[18] Written on scraps of paper and in pencil, these journals were evidently the only personal effects he managed to save in his escape

[16]Newspaper clipping, Anderson Collection, Huntington Library.

[17]In his preface to the Mexican diaries, Professor Ruiz presents Anderson as an "incurable romanticist," longing for an opportunity that would give him a place in history. However, in leaving for Mexico, Anderson virtually abandoned his country and renounced home and fortune, all seeming to point to a stronger motivation than a romantic spirit of adventure in a fifty-eight-year-old man. Perhaps the answer is better found in his profound disgust with the political course of the Civil War, added to his desire to live in a Catholic state. The following note signed by Anderson and dated May 1, 1868, was found in 1961 by Charles Anderson Gauld: "Whereas on the sale of my personal property after I left home on a trip to Mexico, there was sold certain horses cattle and other effects which I had given to my wife Ellen C. Anderson and the money therefrom amounting to the sum of Seventeen Hundred and sixteen dollars $1716.00/100 including a then unascertained sum to be deducted from the sale of lands in Clinton County, all of which money having been appropriated and used by my agent on this farm and for the use and benefit of the estate, now therefore I acknowledge myself to be indebted to my wife in the above mentioned sum, and I obligate myself my heirs and representatives will and duty to pay the said sum of Seventeen hundred and sixteen dollars with legal interest from [blank] until paid." It is doubtful whether Anderson would have returned to the states had Maximilian not been killed. He had contracted to buy land to settle outside Córdoba when his plans were arrested by lack of money. After the downfall of Maximilian, he had no choice but to return home.

[18]Professor Ruiz bases his contention that the diaries were dedicated to Anderson's sister-in-law rather than his wife on a question of personality, Frances being gay and Ellen austere. However, it also seems unlikely that a man would address diaries to a wife he had just deserted.

from the soldiers of Juárez. His youngest son, Robert Marshall, has left the following account, preserved in the Huntington Library, as he heard it in his youth from his father:

The [Anderson] party fell into the hands of a company of Liberals near Hermanas, where they were relieved of their horses and other possessions. The members of his party were allowed to go, but he was retained a prisoner, holding a commission from Maximillian, and was taken deeper into the country prior to being shot. He had concluded to take a chance for liberty, and fortunately he was aided by an overardent celebration by his guards of a fiesta. During the day he had made friends of the children and dogs of the hacienda and that night, despite the bright moonlight, two sides of the patio being in deep shadow with but a short distance to the exit in full light, gave him a chance of escaping unseen. He had been gone but a short time when he heard the hoof beats of the horses of the pursuing guards, and crawling under a cactus thicket he waited for them to pass, sitting tailor fashion facing the opening and holding a bowie knife for an emergency. He had not long to wait to hear them pass, voluble with those rich rolling Mexican-Spanish oaths, when two of the dogs appeared at the opening through which he had crept, and after seeming ages, they wagged their tails and trotted off. After a continuous tramp throughout the night, scaling the Saltillo Mountains, and continuing the following morning until nearly noon, without seeing anyone or being seen, when climbing out of an arroyo he found himself in full sight of laborers harvesting tobacco. He had no alternative but to go forward, come what may; however, to his great relief, he was informed that he was then within the French lines. After a good rest and a sound sleep on the baled tobacco in the warehouse, he proceeded to the City of Mexico, then to Vera Cruz and home by the way of Havana.

The day after he left Veracruz Anderson suffered a severe attack of yellow fever[19] and was forced to disembark in Cuba. He did not reach home until the summer of 1866, by which time his family had moved into Circleville. Though he remained in Circleville, till his death he made almost daily visits to Seven Oaks Farm.

His continuing interest in archaeology led him in the winter of 1871 to visit the Lake George area of Mississippi to study the mound

[19]According to his own statements, this would be the second time Anderson was infected with yellow fever. The first attack, it will be recalled, occurred in Louisville, 1834, following a visit to his brother Robert at Baton Rouge, and led Anderson to undertake the trip to the Rocky Mountains. Charles Anderson Gauld has forwarded us a letter from P. S. Hench, M.D., of the Mayo Clinic to the effect that it is highly improbable that a person could contract yellow fever twice. We surmise that on one of the two occasions Anderson was taken ill the disease was not yellow fever.

builders. He was successful in uncovering a valuable collection of pottery, identical in many respects to the Toltec remains found in Mexico. A calendar stone, with feathered serpent figures, indicated that this lost race was culturally advanced over the later Indians of the Mississippi area. The Huntington Library preserves his short but very interesting account of uncovering the mound.

Anderson's last years were troubled with illness and family dissension. In 1878 he suffered severe injuries in a railroad accident, from which he never fully recovered. His sons had withdrawn from him in rejecting Catholicism. Letters from his sister Louisa and his son Thomas reveal the bitterness aroused by his continued efforts to convert them. Those who knew him best perhaps had a greater measure of understanding. His youngest brother Charles wrote in 1879:

You were always endowed with that spirit of veneration and faith in and towards men and God, which has made you religious and a Christian. I must confess . . . that I believe myself, by nature, possessed of such a *minus* quantity of that spirit, as to make it impossible, for me to become a believer. . . . I really believe your faith has made you a happier and a better man, than I have been.

In his weakened condition Anderson died of double pneumonia in Circleville on Jan. 7, 1881, receiving the final sacraments of his Catholic faith. As with so many other men of a generation that has now passed on, William Marshall Anderson's diaries and letters have outlived him. They come forth in another day to evoke his young manhood and a West that will never exist again.

The Anderson Journals

WILLIAM MARSHALL ANDERSON's *original Diary, as written on the trail, is printed on left-hand pages. The text on right-hand pages is taken from two rewrites of the trail Diary, which we describe as the Narrative and the Journal. The Narrative, covering the period March 11 to June 20, 1834, was printed during Anderson's lifetime in the Circleville, Ohio,* DEMOCRAT AND WATCHMAN *in 1871. The Journal, a complete version on which the Narrative was based, covers the entire period March 11 to September 29, 1834, and has furnished the complementary text after June 20, when the Narrative breaks off. We have also extracted from the Journal prior to June 21 some passages of special interest, incorporating them into the text of the Narrative by means of brackets.*

Printing the text of Diary and Narrative (or Journal) in juxtaposition has presented the editors with novel problems of annotation, for the differences between the two basic records are as pronounced as the similarities, and notes applying to one text may or may not apply to the other. Instead of conventionally keyed footnotes, a running commentary on the unfolding Anderson text seemed most useful, and this commentary will be found at the bottom of pertinent pages.

Diary

MARCH 13, 1834—*left Louisville to accompany the dragoons on their escort of the traders to Santa Fe.*

Thinking better, or worse of the matter as time will show, I changed my mind and determined to accompany Mr W. L. Sublette to the Rocky Mountains. With that view, I started with Mr Sublette from St. Louis April 20 to his rendezvous in Lexington [Mo.] which we reached in 5 days.

MARCH 11/13—In the Diary Anderson gave March 13 as the date of departure, but in Journal and Narrative the date became March 11. The Diary and Narrative vary in describing Anderson's plans on leaving home. This confusion perhaps reflects the double duties assigned the newly organized U. S. Dragoons. The Narrative affords a more extended account than the Diary of the journey to St. Louis, and some things in it are worthy of remark. The Salt River flows northerly into the Ohio at West Point, below Louisville. During the 1830's it had a remarkable impact on the American vernacular. The boisterous "half-horse, half-alligator" type was known as the Salt River "roarer" or "screamer"; and the expression going or being "up" Salt River implied reverses, especially political. Shawneetown, Illinois, at which Anderson duly arrived, was settled soon after 1800, laid out in 1808, and incorporated in 1814; it was an important port and trading center that declined in the era of the railroad. Thomas Posey, to whose family at Shawneetown Anderson refers, was born in Virginia in 1750, served in the militia against the Indians in 1774, was an officer in the Seventh Virginia Regiment during the Revolutionary War, and retired in 1783 with the rank of lieutenant colonel. Later a brigadier general under Anthony Wayne, Posey settled in Kentucky, was elected to the legislature, and served ex officio as lieutenant governor. A resident of Louisiana when the War of 1812 broke out, he was appointed U. S. Senator from that state. He served as governor of Indiana Territory from 1814 until Indiana attained statehood in 1816. Owing to impaired health, he lived at Jeffersonville rather than at Corydon, the territorial capital. He was U. S. Indian Agent for Illinois Territory from 1816 until his death in 1818 at Shawneetown. Posey's large family was born of successive marriages to Martha Matthews and Mary (Alexander) Thornton. See the sketch in *Dictionary of American Biography*. Alexander and Thomas were sons by his second wife.

Narrative

MARCH 11, 1834—Louisville, Ky. Well, I am off at last, but who can say when or where I shall stop? This day I begin too, to scribble down such incidents, accidents and observations, as may occur, during the horseback journey I am now undertaking. The object of this equestration, is to regain the health and strength lost in a late severe illness. Had I started from home expressly in search of adventures, I surely made a good beginning. I do not believe I had gone twenty miles, or reached Salt River, when I found myself stumbling in the rapids. Passing a wagon, the driver called out:

"Look! Look Bet! Quick! Ain't that the tightest fit you ever saw—horse, man and gun! I say, mister, you have forgot one thing."

"What is that?" I asked.

"Why, a coffee-pot, to put the whole works in when it rains."

Roars of laughter followed this speech. The man laughed, the woman laughed, the children laughed, and I am not sure I did not hear a horse laugh. Confound the fools; what do they find so funny in that? Kicking and spurring poor Blackhawk, I tried to get out of word-shot as soon as possible; and foaming and fretting, I endeavored to ease myself by muttering, "beasts" "blackguards;" and heartily wishing the whole crew in a very warm place.

I crossed the Ohio River at Shawneetown, where I rested one day. Here I met Gen. Alexander Posey, who introduced himself to me as the friend and companion of my brother Robert in the Blackhawk campaign. In twenty minutes as warm a friendship existed as if we had been acquainted for many years. And how could it be otherwise? A few years before, I had camped out with his brother, Col. Thomas Posey, of Corydon, on the headwaters of White River, hunting deer. Here was brother for brother; besides which, and above all, his father, Gen. Thomas Posey, and my father, Col. Richard C. Ander-

DIARY

APRIL 30, 1834—*left the camp ground near Lexington, La Fayette county. I saw nothing remarkable on the road from St Louis to Lex., but most remarkably fertile, strong soil, the best land I ever beheld in so large a body. Saline, Jackson & La Fayette counties are very fertile and beautiful. The first and last, principally prairie, the second, prairie & timbered. My first essay, in tent sleeping, produced a singular result, cured me of a very bad cold the first night.*

APRIL 20—In his Diary, under the entry for March 13, Anderson gave April 20 as the date of leaving St. Louis. Because the date was imperfectly written, in both the Journal and the Narrative it was transcribed as April 26, an obvious mistake which we have corrected. Concerning Lexington, see the Introduction and Anderson's brief remarks on September 23.

APRIL 30—Anderson's date for the departure from Lexington is confirmed by a letter written May 1, 1834, by James Aull: "Sublette and his party started from this place yesterday. The Santa Fé men are beginning to arrive and I suppose the party will start 15 inst" (Ralph P. Bieber, ed., "Letters of James and Robert Aull," p. 281). Josiah Gregg captained the Santa Fe caravan as far as the Arkansas River, where he gave way to Ira G. Smith, a younger brother of Jedediah Smith. This caravan was escorted by Company A of the U. S. Dragoons.

See Introduction with regard to Independence and the Mormons, not mentioned in the Diary. Anderson's Narrative may not have expressed the point of view of his Journal, which says simply: "Here was the scene of civil bloodshed—Here the Mormonites and the Jacksonites met in deadly conflict—More unholy redemptionless villains I do not believe ever disgraced our country—except the Charlestown rioters. . . ." By analogy, this would be a reflection on "the Jacksonites," rather than on "the Mormonites." The Charlestown riots occurred shortly before Anderson's return to the states. A rumor spread in Boston that a young woman had fled from a convent of Ursuline nuns at Charlestown, Massachusetts, only to be inveigled back, and that she had then disappeared. A mob gathered on the night of August 11, stoned the convent, and fired the building. At a mass meeting held at Faneuil Hall "a most respectable committee was appointed . . . to assist in bringing the offenders to justice, and expressing, in the severest terms, the public indignation at the outrage committed" (*Niles' Register*, Aug. 16, 1834, XLVI, 413).

son, had gone through the great Revolution together. To show how intimate, how free and easy we had become, I told him my adventure with the wagoner, and having had time to cool, he made me see and feel that there really was some wit in it. "Why, Will, just consider. Blackhawk is not over fourteen hands high; you, about feather weight for a scrub race, and your little Tryon rifle, not much larger or heavier than a common fowling-piece." Then there was another good, hearty laugh, but to confess the truth, I think he enjoyed it more than I did.

My next pause was at St Louis. I had come on here to go with the dragoons on the Pawnee-Pic expedition. As my relative, Gen. Atkinson, was to command, and my new made friend, Posey, had given me a letter to Gen. Dodge, I esteemed my self pretty well backed up for a supernumerary. But, "circumstances alter cases," and I did not go with the military. By the advice of Atkinson, I accepted an invitation from Capt. Wm. S. [L.] Sublette to accompany him to the Rocky Mountains.

APRIL 20, 1834—This day, bright and early, we started, "all on horses, gee up and gee O," for his rendezvous near Lexington, Mo. Here we tarried until the 30th, buying and branding horses, giving out and packing up goods for the mountain market.

APRIL 30, 1834—We are finally up and off for the west, the far west. Where is that? I had always believed I had been born in the West; but no, here we go in search of it, farther on, farther on. The land between Lexington and Independence is similar in quality to the very fertile soil of the counties of La Mine and Saline, through which we passed in our outward march from St. Louis. I am inclined to think these four counties contain the richest body of land for their extent I ever saw. Being forest-born, I rather prefer La Fayette and Jackson to the other two, as better timbered. [The two first have too much prairie.] And what better marks of good soil can there be than black walnut, ash, sugartree, big paw paw, and bigger grapevines?

Late in the evening, we reached the town of Independence. This is now the very verge of civilization, and what civilization? Here was the scene of bloodshed, of civil bloodshed. Here the Mormons and the Jacksonites met in deadly conflict. If the statements made

DIARY

MAY 5, 1834—*we are encamped at the Sapling grove, about 20 miles from Indepen[den]ce." We are about 37 men strong—[deleted: 86 or 7] 95 horses. I am now out of the US. for the first time.*

MAY 6, 1834—*Breakfasted at a small clump of trees called the round grove. Leaving which I saw an eminence in the prairie which seemed but a mile or two distant, a day & halfs travel however, proved it to be 30 miles or more. The night of the 6th we encamped on the waters of the Kansas or Kaw.*

MAY 5—Sapling Grove, on the old Santa Fe Trail from Independence, was situated on Indian Creek, a western tributary of the Big Blue River of Missouri (west of present Dallas, Missouri). Anderson's being beyond the bounds of the United States shows that Sapling Grove was in Indian territory. The name had only brief currency; we have not found it used before Anderson, or after 1841, when the Bartleson party rendezvoused at the grove before starting for California. On April 25, 1838, William H. Gray commented that the name came "from a few scattered trees lining the water course running N. West [N. East] into the Big Blue." F. A. Wislizenus and Asahel Munger, en route to the Rockies in 1839, used the name familiarly. Wislizenus described Sapling Grove as a "little hickory wood, with fresh spring water." It was here that Anderson remarked the next day the presence of Etienne Provost and Michel Sylvestre Cerré.

MAY 6—Round Grove, so called in 1825 by the commissioners appointed to mark the Santa Fe Trail, also became known as Caravan Grove, Elm Grove, and finally Lone Elm. It was situated on the head of Cedar Creek, 4 miles south of present Olathe, Kansas, and some 15 miles southwest of Sapling Grove. As early as 1841 Richard L. Wilson found that "nothing remained but the name—Elm Grove, and one solitary Logan of a stricken tree 'To mark where an Elm Grove had been' " (*Short Ravelings*, p. 9). Yet the name Round Grove persisted in the diaries of the 1840's, notably in that of William L. Sublette (*Mississippi Valley Historical Review*, VI, 107). Sublette camped at "Round Grove" on May 27, 1843, after a 15-mile ride from Westport. Next day he "Left the Santafee Trace and took Sublette's Old Trace to the mountains." Anderson's Diary states that the 1834 party camped this night "on the waters of the Kansas or Kaw." The Journal more correctly speaks of camping "on a little stream which empties into the Kaw or Kansas river," but the Narrative says the camp was "on a bright, beautiful stream, bearing the double name of Kaw or Kansas." Probably the locale was Captain Creek, about 18 miles from Round Grove and 4 or 5 miles beyond the point of separation from the Santa Fe Trail, west of present Gardner, Kansas.

to me are true, more unholy, redemptionless villains than said Mormons never disgraced our country, always saving and excepting the Charlestown rioters. This last affair has more than counterbalanced the battle of Bunker Hill. Defenceless women and children, driven from their beds and burning homes, at the hour of midnight; a convent rased to the ground, [bibles burnt] and even tombs, those mansions of the mouldering dead, torn open and desecrated. And by whom? By the degenerate sons of patriots and heroes. Spirits of Warren, Hancock and Putnam, look down with shame and sorrow on this atrocious act of the bastard sons of New England!

MAY 1, 2, 3, 4, 1834—In camp near Independence.

MAY 5, 1834—To-day we have left the settlements. After a twenty-mile horse-walk we have reached and made our camp in Sapling Grove. We are a mighty band to meet and contend with a whole village of red-skins. We count thirty-seven, in all, with ninety-five horses and mules. I presume I am not [now] out of the United States, and in the territory of our good Uncle Sam. But does his law, or power, still protect me? Shall I say to the redman, "Take care what you do! If you strike me, I will sue you for assault and battery; if you steal my horse, I will send you to the penitentiary."

MAY 6, 1834—Provost and Cere are here, [each] with a company of men, having the same destination as ourselves. Left the grove this morning [before sunrise] and breakfasted at the Round grove, which does not contain more than seven or eight trees. At night, camped on a bright, beautiful stream, bearing the double name of the Kaw or Kansas. [I shot a fox squirrel to sup on.] This evening, one monsieur wolf and I gave each other a mutual scare. He, however, tucked his tail between his legs, and put off at a great rate of speed. Had I been able, I have no doubt I should have done the same thing, tail and all.

There is a large mound in sight all day. Though apparently near, we have not reached it at nightfall. What causes this occular delusion on the plains? Do prairies and broad land-levels produce the same deception of sight, as wide expanses of water? To-night, we rest again on the Kaw.

MAY 7, 1834.—*In the morning we reachd the hill before seen &
spoken of, & which is named, Wausaroosa or Black-bear hill. The
view from the top of the twin hills, for there are two of them, is the
most beautiful I ever have had the satisfaction of beholding. To the
east, from its eminence of near 300 feet above the prairie, is seen a
boundless extent of country—boundless at least to the sight—A waste
of fertility—unused pastures, unenjoyed gardens. To the west, and
towards the Kansas (distant about 8 miles) rich bottoms covered
with timber. I consider the spectacle from Wausaroosa more beautiful & gratifying than that of Monticello near Chillicothe, O. To night,
we shall cross the river, leaving the Shawnee territory, and entering
upon the Kaws, Who call themselves Kawsies.*

MAY 7—Blue Mound (1,052 feet) is about 5 miles south-southeast of present Lawrence, Kansas.
The second mound is half a mile southeast of the first and about thirty feet lower. When Frémont's
Second Expedition passed by on May 31, 1843, says Theodore Talbot, "We placed our signal as
agreed on the 'Blue Mound', an elevation in sight of the residence of our Indian hunters, to let them
know that we had passed" (*Journal*, p. 9). Blue Mound was used for signal purposes during the era
of "bleeding Kansas," flags being flown from its summit to warn Free-staters of approaching
enemies. Jacob R. Snyder, California-bound in 1845, noted the dual character of the mounds:
"They stand alone without any other hills about them, each about 300 yards in length at top and
about 700 at the base, one running N & S the other E & W" (Society of California Pioneers, *Quarterly*, VIII, 225). The Blue Mound as a single eminence is represented on the maps of Charles
Preuss (1846) and T. H. Jefferson (1849).

Wakarusa, which Anderson interprets as meaning Black Bear, was spelled many ways. Lewis
and Clark wrote "Wor-rah-ru-za"; Thomas Say of Long's party, "Warreruza"; and Isaac McCoy,
"Warhusa." Few travelers agreed on the meaning. On April 25, 1838, W. H. Gray observed that the
"WaKorusah" was so called "from a root found in abundance on its banks made use of for food by
the Natives." Father P. J. De Smet in May 1840 echoed Gray's explanation of the name, referring
to the *"wakarusa*, or cottonwood [in his original French, *Waggere-rousse, ou la fleur de cotonnier*],
a plant which is abundant in this region, and on which the Indians feed. It is found along a river
that bears the same name, and which flows into the Kansas" (Chittenden and Richardson, eds., *Life
of De Smet*, I, 202). On May 24, 1843, Pierson B. Reading said the creek was "called by the Indians
—'Walka Rocha', which signifies 'to surround'" (Society of California Pioneers, *Quarterly*, VII,
149). Matthew Field, returning from the mountains in Sir William Drummond Stewart's party,
on Oct. 18, 1843, alluded to "the *Wakaroosi*—Wahka-Roosi—Wahkaroosi, or 'Big Elk'" (*Prairie
and Mountain Sketches*, p. 212). Anderson does not mention the Wakarusa itself, which flows
northeasterly into the Kansas River beyond Blue Mound.

The Shawnee Indians, originally living in South Carolina, Tennessee, Pennsylvania, and Ohio,
were one of the greatest obstacles to the westward expansion of the American people. For fifty
years after the onset of the French and Indian War, they warred against the English and Americans; and more than any other tribe the Shawnees made Kentucky the "dark and bloody ground"
recalled in Anderson's Journal on July 27. During the 1790's, by Spanish invitation, tribesmen
began crossing the Mississippi into Missouri, where about half of the tribe finally settled. In 1825,
after the Osage and Kansa tribes ceded to the U. S. government most of their lands in present
Kansas, the Shawnees in Missouri began moving to a reservation created for them south of the
Kansas River and west of the Missouri line. About 1831 they were joined by Shawnees migrating
from Ohio. The tribe was considered semicivilized, and a few became mountain men, accepted as
equals by the whites as were no other Indians but the Delawares. About 1845 most of the tribe
moved to the Canadian River in present Oklahoma. The Kansa or Kaw Indians, of Siouan stock
and cousins of the Osages, had been a warlike people but by 1834 were much subdued. In 1825 they

MAY 7, 1834—This morning, we broke our fast at the base of two lovely mountlets—the same which all yesterday seemed but one, and so
singularly near. It, or they, are called, in the Kaw tongue, Wau-sa-
roo-sah, or Black Bear Hill. From their top—and the elevation is not
more than three hundred feet—the view is very extensive. All within eye-power is indeed most beautiful. Eastward, the sight floats over
a boundless sea of green. Broad meadows, with islands of flowers,
fill the air with sweets. To the west we see absolute wastes of fertility,
in the rich timber-covered bottoms of the Kaw. Inexperienced as I
am, in travel, I can find no words to express my admiration. [To me,
standing alone upon the height, the spectacle from Wausaroosa is
more lovely than that from Monticello.] I shall often think of, and
long remember, Wau-sa-roo-sah.

About five o'clock [p.m.], encamped again on the Kansas River,
opposite the agency of Gen. Marston G. Clark. Found here four old
buffalo-skin lodges, occupied by [Kansas] Kaws, or, as they call
themselves, Kawsies. The first syllable is sounded nasally, very
much as the crow makes it in his "kaw, kaw." They are a dirty, lousy-
looking set of rogues. After night, two chiefs, the senior and junior,
made a visit to Capt. Sublette, accompanied by their interpreter. This
latter was the oldest looking man I ever saw. He was as blind as a bat,
head white as newly fallen snow, and his face a perfect rasp of
wrinkles. He called himself Vieil, spoke a little French, which I
guessed into English. In due time, Sublette and myself returned their
call. This being the first lodge I ever entered, I will endeavor to describe it. The tent is [round topped, about 10 feet high in the centre]
made of tanned buffalo-skins, supported on poles drawn together at
top, funnel-fashion, and having near the ground an entrance, or flap
door, which can be lifted up or pulled aside at pleasure. The inmates,
though savages, were kind, natural and hospitable.

---

ceded their lands except a 30-mile-long strip beginning 20 leagues up the Kansas River, where they
dwelt until 1847. Attacks by Pawnees and other enemies having considerably reduced their numbers, they moved to a new reservation at Council Grove. In 1873 most of the survivors went to
present Oklahoma.

MAY 8, 1834.—*Reached the Kansas river opposite the agency of Gen.l Marston Clark last evening. Found four lodges on the banks, filled with a dirty, lousy looking set of Kawsies. A very old blind Indian, and an old, and a young chief, visited the captains tent. The aged blind sauvage spoke french & interpreted for the others. After dark Capt S. & myself return^d their call. The first lodge I ever entered— I found it truly savage & natural, rude & hospitable—apparent contradictions but reconcilable to those who are acquainted with Indian life.*

Left the agency and camped about 15 miles distant. Killed or shot an Indian dog for biting our sheep. I wrote a long letter to Larz which I left with Mastⁿ. Clark who promised to forward it. Placed out guards for the first time.

MAY 9, 1834.—*Breakfastd. on the bank of a creek called Soldier, tributary of the Kansas   Passed through a village, named the new Kansas village, The first I have seen. It is very, small. This night we encamp on a small creek about 10 miles from the village. We met a brother of Mr W. Sublettes's returning on account of indisposition—from an excursion begun to the mountains. All this evening I have had a severe pain in the side. I am fearing the pleurisy. Four hundred miles from St Louis. Seven do. from Louisville the anticipation of illness is no pleasant thought.*

MAY 7/8—As seen in the Diary, Anderson described under May 8 the events of the previous evening and inadvertently made this description a separate day. He then entered the date "May 9" before the words "Left the agency. . . ." In consequence of this mistake, his dates to May 31 are one day ahead of the correct dates. He rewrote the Diary twice but never found the original error, although he was aware of it. (He omitted the date May 8 from the Narrative but failed to combine entries and thus continued the error.) To keep the record clear, and after careful study of other 1834 trail diaries, we have combined Anderson's entries in the Diary for May 8 and 9 under May 8, corrected as May 8 his entry for May 9 in the Narrative, and continuously corrected his dates down to May 31.

The Kansas Agency was located on the north bank of the Kansas River at present Williamstown, 7 miles west of Lawrence. It was removed to this point in late 1826 or early 1827 from a site on the Missouri below the mouth of the Kansas by the subagent for the Iowas, A. F. (Baronet) Vasquez, who had been transferred to the new Kansas Subagency in April 1825. Vasquez died of cholera on Aug. 5, 1828, before the subagency was fully operative at the Kansas site. William Clark, Superintendent of Indian Affairs at St. Louis, appointed Daniel D. McNair as provisional subagent; but on recommendation of the Indiana delegation to Congress, Marston Greene Clark was named to the post. The old Indian interpreter mentioned by Anderson has not been identified. We have been unable to find Anderson's letter to Larz.

MAY 9—Soldier Creek enters the Kansas River opposite present Topeka. The name is first noted in the journal of Isaac McCoy on Sept. 4, 1830, being applied to a stream known earlier as Heart River. We are informed by Miss Louise Barry, on the authority of an account written by John C. McCoy in 1885, that when Maj. Angus L. Langham surveyed the Kansas River between August and October 1826, a small military escort accompanied him. "The name 'Soldier Creek' was adopted afterwards in honor of the flag that proudly waved over the Major's shanty and the war-

MAY 8, 1834.—Crossed our whole cavalcade, horses, cows and mules, to the west side by swimming. Had a long walk and talk, this morning, with Gen. Clark. After going some distance up the river, he turned around and said, "Now, kinsman, I will show you how I used to drink, out of your father's spring on Beargrass;" and extending himself on the pebbles, quenched his thirst from the waters of the Kaw. Supposing this my last opportunity, I wrote a long letter to my brother Larz, and left it with good old Marston Clark, who promised to forward it. This night find [s] us in the prairie, fifteen miles [west] from the agency. [In the sight of its master, I shot a Kawsie's dog for biting one of our sheep—I don't know which howled the loudest the dog or master.]

MAY 9, 1834.—This morning stopped for breakfast on the Soldier, a tributary of the Kaw. Last night, counted off, and divided our little company into watches. I am to be a sergeant, with three men in my guard. We are to have a three-hour turn every other night.

About noon passed through the new Kaw village. It is very small, and but few of the inhabitants were at home. At this place we met Capt. Sublette's brother, who had started to the mountains, but in consequence of lameness was obliged to return. He went back with us about ten miles, and camped for the night [on a small creek].

---

like aspect of the camp where the trophies secured during the winter were chiefly possums strung up by their tails curled over ropes and tugs stretched from tree to tree." As of May 19, 1846, J. Quinn Thornton erroneously explained that Soldier Creek owed its name to "the circumstance that several years before the time of our encamping there, a party of Indian traders and trappers had smuggled into the country a quantity of whisky. They were pursued by a company of U. S. dragoons, who overtook them at the place we were then at, and knocked in the heads of the barrels" (*Oregon and California in 1848*, p. 33). A similar tale was told by Edwin Bryant (who may have been Thornton's source). The incident involved Sibille & Adams and happened as late as August 1842.

The "new Kaw village" was that of Kah-he-gah-wa-ti-an-gah or Fool Chief, located about 6 miles west of the mouth of Soldier Creek, on the southeast quarter of Section 16, Township 11, Range 15 E, in Silver Lake township. (See George P. Morehouse, "History of the Kansa or Kaw Indians," p. 348.) Miss Barry is puzzled by Anderson's reference to the smallness of the Kansa town, for Fool Chief's village north of the Kansas River was the largest of the three then existing (the others were located south of the river). She quotes John Dougherty's letter of Jan. 30, 1830, as evidence that it was probably in late 1828 and early 1829 that the Kaw Indians moved down the Kansas River 40 miles from their long-established home near the mouth of the Big Blue. On Sept. 6, 1830, Isaac McCoy noted in his journal that "the village of Chachhaa hogeree, Prarie-village," contained "about 50 houses, with say three families to the house" (p. 352). The principal Kansa chief of this era, Wom-pa-wa-re ("he who scares all men"), better known to the whites as Plume Blanche or White Plume, lived not at the village but 2 miles west of the Kansas Agency. Much important now factual information respecting the Kaws is presented by Louise Barry in her "Kansas before 1854: A Revised Annals."

Forced by his lame leg to give up his journey to the Rockies with Nathaniel Wyeth, Milton G. Sublette had turned back from the Little Vermilion the previous morning.

MAY 10, 1834—*Travelled slowly through a very fertile and beautiful country. A glorious [interlined: charming] grazing region. No buffaloe—little game of any kind. I have thought that if our country should purchase it of the Indians, what a glorious [interlined: grand] state it would make. We are now in tents about 5 miles from Vermillion a beautiful little tributary of the Kansas. It is now getting to be a great relief to see timber. "Toujours, toujours, toujours" prairie is fatiguing. I have had the pain in my side all day. I have feared the pleurisy—God forbid! A thousand miles from home & pity,—poor encouragement to be sick.*

MAY 11, 1834—*Crossed a creek on Sublettes trace, which he made for ten wagons, 4 years past, called by some of his hands cannon ball creek. Camped nearly twenty five miles from our yestereens resting place, on a stream which empties in to the Blue river, of the Kanzas, which we call bee river, from finding a bee-tree near our tents— Accident, or some circumstance which has occurred to the trappers, has given names to all the points and streams of the country.—*

MAY 10—The Journal agrees with the Diary: "We are tented about 5 miles from the vermillion— a pretty tributary of the Kansas river." The Vermilion, also called Little or Red Vermilion, has often been confused with the Big or Black Vermilion, a tributary of the Blue River reached by Anderson a few days later. Sometimes the Little Vermilion, too, appears in early records as Black Vermilion. Beyond the Vermilion the trail veered northwest, away from the Kansas River. From here on, travelers guarded their camp and animals.

MAY 11—Cannon-ball Creek, now Rock Creek, is a name employed by Overton Johnson and William H. Winter (*Route across the Rocky Mountains*, p. 146) and also by James Clyman in his diary for June 23, 1844, and July 17, 1846. We first observe the modern name as "Rocky Fork" in the manuscript diaries of David Adams for September 1842 and September 1844. Anderson probably crossed the creek near present Westmoreland, Kansas. Interesting is his allusion in the Diary to the ten wagons (besides two dearborn carriages) that William L. Sublette took out to the Rockies in 1830—the first wagons to reach the mountains north of New Mexico. Thus Anderson contributes to the slender history of "Sublette's Trace." Clyman's diary for June 24, 1844, describing his travel from Rock Creek to the Big Vermilion, comments: "to day struck our old trail made on our return from the mountains in 1827 when I had the honorable post of being pilot." He had come down from the Rockies with Jackson and Sublette in 1827, in that year seemingly descending the Big Blue to the Kansas River. The cutoff Anderson was now following to the Big Blue may have been first used in 1830.

Bee River is the Big or Black Vermilion, called Burr Oak Creek by W. H. Gray in 1838 and James Clyman in 1844, also sometimes referred to as Black Paint Creek. Alfred Jacob Miller, who traveled this route three years after Anderson, painted "The Bee Hunter" as one of the characteristic scenes of the trail and supplied an excellent description of the technique of the hunt. For another account, see Washington Irving's work on Bonneville.

MAY 10, 1834.—I have passed the night in great pain. I fear it is an attack of pleurisy.

Four hundred miles from St. Louis and seven hundred from Louisville and home—the thought itself is misery. In spite of my suffering, I have admired exceedingly, the very beautiful and fertile country around us. Grass, grass, grass everywhere, but not a deer or buffalo in sight. We are tented to-night on the Vermilion, which sends its waters to the Kaw. The sight of timber begins to be a wish unsatisfied. "Toujours prairie," I feel will be tiresome after a while.

The pain in my side has continued all day. I believe the pleurisy is really coming. God forbid! So far from home and pity is poor encouragement to be sick.

MAY 11, 1834.—Crossed Cannon-ball creek, on a bridge, [in a wagon trail] made by Capt. Sublette, four years ago. Twenty [about twenty-five] miles from last night's resting place, we took up our lodgings on a little stream, which empties into the Blue, another tributary of the Kaw. Having found a tree, filled with honey, near the crossing, we determined to call this stream "The Bee." [Accident, or some circumstance which has happened to the trappers has given name to the points and streams of these regions and all west to the ocean.]

MAY 12, 1834—*We nooned about 10 miles on the north fork of Blue river. Thence to a small creek, which runs into the other fork of the Blue. Our general course since & even for several days before we passed the Kaw, has been west, and a little N. W., this day we have steered more to the north. This day killed my first rattle snake.*

MAY 13, 1834—*Made a long days march Crossed a creek called Raccoon creek, a branch of Blue. Stood guard for the first time. This is called Monday—The first elks I ever saw I saw dashing over the prairies to day. No Ottos have been seen, tho we have been three days in their territory.*

MAY 12—The Big Blue (called by Anderson the North Fork) was crossed between present Blue Rapids and Marysville, Kansas, 5 miles above the confluence of the Big and Little Blue. In reaching the Big Blue for nooning, Sublette got ahead of Wyeth's party, which had wandered too far north. Although disconcerted to learn that he had fallen behind, Wyeth was relieved to come upon Sublette's trail. In his party Townsend writes: "Our scouts came in this morning with the intelligence that they had found a large trail of white men, bearing N. W. We have no doubt that this is Wm. Sublette's party, and that it passed us last evening [rather, this very day]. They must have travelled very rapidly to overtake us so soon, and no doubt had men ahead watching our motions. It seems rather unfriendly, perhaps, to run by us in this furtive way, without even stopping to say good morning, but Sublette is attached to a rival company, and all stratagems are deemed allowable when interest is concerned. It is a matter of some moment to be the first at the mountain rendezvous, in order to obtain the furs brought every summer by the trappers." The Diary says Sublette's party went on to camp on a small creek running into the Little Blue. This may have been east of Hanover on Cottonwood Creek, some 10 miles northwest of the crossing of the Big Blue.

MAY 13—Possibly Raccoon Creek is Walnut Creek, which joins the Little Blue northwest of modern Fairbury, Nebraska. The Oto Indians, like the Kansa, were of Siouan stock. Migrants from east of the Mississippi, they settled on the Platte 80 miles above its mouth, but later moved closer to the Missouri River, from 1817 to 1841 dwelling near the confluence. Anderson's expectation of meeting Otos was not unreasonable. The previous night Wyeth's horses had stampeded, two not being recovered, and on the 13th three Oto Indians came into camp. "These were men of rather short stature," Townsend says, "but strong and firmly built. Their countenances resemble in general expression those of the Kanzas, and their dresses are very similar. We are all of opinion, that it is to these Indians we owe our difficulties of last night . . . but as we cannot prove it upon them, and cannot even converse with them, (having no interpreters,) we are compelled to submit to our loss in silence." Cyrus Shepard admits the injustice of these suspicions; the missing horses were subsequently found by one of the parties coming along behind. Anderson himself later encountered some Otos; see his Diary for September 10.

In describing Sublette's manner of conducting a march in 1832, Ball gives us some conception of the daily routine Anderson followed two years later:

"We were kept in strict military order, and marched double file. Those first ready took their places next to the commander. We always camped in the form of a hollow square, making a river or stream the fourth side. The horses were hobbled (fore feet tied) and turned out of camp to feed. When brought into camp at night they were left hobbled, and were tied to stakes driven close to the ground, giving each horse as much room as could be spared him within the square. The watch changed every four hours. If found asleep, the watch was obliged to walk the next day for punishment. Captain Sublette's camp calls were as follows: 'Catch up; catch up,' which was at sunset. Then each man brought his horses into camp. At dawn the call was 'Turn out; turn out,' and then horses were turned out of camp to feed, while we breakfasted. Then the horses were saddled and packed. At noon a stop was always made for half an hour. The horses were unpacked to rest them,

MAY 12, 1834—Ten miles more, and we are on the North-fork of the Blue. For several days before, and since leaving the Kaw, our general course has been northwesterly, to day we are going nearly north. This evening killed my first rattle-snake. He and I met as representatives of our great first ancestors, and I bruised his head. This is a token of regard for mother Eve. Hereafter, when I war with that sly, old apple thief, it shall be out of reverence for father Adam, whose innocent sweet-heart had been decieved in the garden, by his flattering tongue, and caudal castanets.

MAY 13, 1834—A long day's march brought us to Raccoon Creek, a branch of the Blue. Stood guard last night, for the first time in my life, and felt this morning. "like big man me, Capt. John." The first wild Elks I ever saw, dashed over the plains before us to-day. What is their gait? It is neither trot, gallop, or pace. I can liken it to nothing but a lame shuffle, but they get over the ground, nevertheless.

Though we have been in the range of the Otoes, for several [four] days, we have seen no signs of them. To day, I shot at four antelopes as they whizzed by me. I do not know whether my aim was twisted, or whether they out ran my ball. Old traders and trappers tell marvelous things about their speed. They report them fleeter than greyhound or race horse. To this I say, "credat Jewsharp, non ego." With so short a stride it does not seem to be possible, that they can equal the race horse, or surpass the grey-hound. But then, if they did outrun my bullet I give it up, and confess "they are the fleetest of the fleet."

I will now describe them if I can. They are shorter and lower [by three or four inches] than our common deer, having the same general color, that is, a reddish dun, on the head, neck, bag [back] and leg. On each side, extending from near the shoulder to the hip, there

---

each horse carried one hundred and eighty pounds. Not being able to trot with this load, they soon formed the habit of walking fast.

"There was so little dew or rain that we did not need our tents, so we slept on the ground wrapped in our blankets, our saddles for pillows. I always wrapped myself first in my camlet [camelot] cloak, pulling the cape over my head to shut off the wind or moon. This was our camp routine until we reached the Rocky Mountains."

In an *Autobiography* published by his daughters in 1925, Ball adds: "Our order of march was always double file, the horses led, the first attached to the rider's and the third to him. So when under way our band was more than a hundred horses long—Mr. Sublette always giving all orders and leading the band, and Mr. Campbell as lieutenant bringing up the rear and seeing that all kept their places and the loose animals did not stray away." (In 1834 Sublette's clerk Patton doubtless had the place of responsibility at the rear.)

MAY 14, 1834.—*I saw and shot at an Antelope in full speed—missed of course. Shot at and missed, too, an elk. Gave chase to three on horse and found that my sorrel Sam can beat that beast—Camped on the main Blue. Made about 20 or 22 miles. Our direction, I think, has been more southerly than we have yet marched—*

MAY 15, 1834.—*on the Blue again—More antelopes—No shot—We went to day between 25 & 30 miles. One of Wyatts men came to us. He had been lost two or three days. Had been out to hunt Antelopes.*

MAY 16, 1834.—*At breakfast time, three Pawnees came to us. They say their camp is a very short distance above us on the Blue. They report the buffaloe to be within 2 days march of us. [*Interlined: In camp for the night.*] Leaving our camp to continue our journey; we saw a number of living things approaching, horses, buffaloes or men. They came in the greatest disorder, from the distant hills but were ranged in front of us in the prairie in battle array in less than fifteen minutes. The uncertainty of their intentions, produced an excitement by no means delightful. In front of us eighty or a hundred savages—mounted on swift but shabby horses, armed with guns, spears and bows; the odds were largely against us, perhaps three times our number, and in the neighbourhood of their village.*

MAY 14—By "Blue" and "main Blue" Anderson refers to the Little Blue. That river was occasionally miscalled Big Blue, as by Cyrus Shepard, and sometimes also masqueraded as "Republican Fork."

MAY 15—There is more than meets the eye in the appearance of Wyeth's "lost" man in Sublette's camp. On May 12, the day Wyeth discovered that Sublette had passed him, he wrote "To Thos Fitzpatric or Co. In the Rocky Mountains": "Wm Sublette having passed me here, I am induced to write to you by this opportunity and hope you will get it. You may expect me by the 1st July at the rendesvous named in your letter to Milton which you sent by Dr. [Benjamin] Harrison who opened it and I presume told Wm Sublette of the place. I am not heavily loaded and shall travell as fast as possible and have a sufficient equipment of goods for you according to contract. Cerre will be much later than me and also the Am. Fur Co. Milton left me a few days since on account of his leg which is very bad. . . . P. S. I have sent a vessell around the Horn with such goods as you want and would like to give you a supply for winter rendesvous for next year on such terms as I know would suit you."

The expression "this opportunity" shows that Wyeth hoped to send his letter by someone accompanying Sublette. Sublette himself could not be expected to carry such a missive. Townsend supplies the missing detail on May 15: "This morning a man was sent ahead to see W. Sublette's camp, and bear a message to him, who returned in the evening with the information that the company is only one day's journey beyond, and consists of about thirty-five men. We see his deserted camps every day, and, in some cases, the fires are not yet extinguished."

MAY 16—In the Journal Anderson relates: "While breakfasting three Pawnees came to us. They said their camp was a very short distance above us on the Blue. They also informed us that the buffaloe is within 2 or 3 days march. After leaving our breakfast place, to continue our journey, we beheld at a great distance, approaching us in rapid confusion, living beings. We could not at first is a large white spot, and another covering the entire rear, from tail to hocks; which last gives them the appearance of white animals, when moving from you. [The hair is like hair much swollen in water, spongy & soft.] The bucks have short, black, in-turning horns [from eight to ten inches in length], with no distinct prong, but a bud, or semblance of one, about two inches from the tip. The females are alike in all respects, except that they have less weight, and no horns. I had more than half believed that the "bug [buck] ague" was an imaginary complaint—but to-day I was staggered—to test the thing fairly, with a good [Kentucky] rifle, on level ground, a steady rest and first-rate "death dust." I shot at and missed an elk and an antelope, at a distance that a Kentucky girl would have bored a squirrel's eye out. I am disgusted with theories. I will thank any doctor to tell me whether I was standing on my head or my heels. [From an experiment today, I am persuaded that with a commonly active horse and good rider, the elk may be overtaken & killed.]

[MAY 14, 1834.]—On the Blue again, after a ride of some twenty [or 22] miles. Course a little southerly to-day.

MAY 15, 1834—[More antelopes—very wild—no shot.] Whilst nooning, on the Blue, one of Wyatt's men came to us looking half-starved. He went out to hunt antelopes, got tangled in his mind, and has been lost for [two or] three days. Poor fellow! I suspect his track has been as crooked as the streets of Boston, or a Yankee's conscience. About twenty [25] miles to day.

MAY 16, 1834—Three Pawnees surprised us to-day, when at breakfast. They report their camp a short distance above us, on the Blue. They also say that we are within [2 or] three days [march] of the buffalo. We had scarcely got fairly under way, when Sublette's quick eye saw a cloud of dust far off in the South. It seemed to move rapidly, though there was no wind. In a remarkably short time our leader found a gully deep enough to hide our horses. We had not more than time to drive down pickets, throw up side and top bales on the brink, as a breastwork, when Charley Lajeunnesse, flag in hand, had stopped the dust raisers, some two hundred yards off. There they stood, about one hundred devils, "in a string of fight." The odds were fearfully against us—nearly three to one—and as there is always doubt and uncertainty as to Indian intentions where the power is

DIARY

Our leader, sent one of his men who speaks their tongue, to demand that their chief or chiefs should approach. They came four in number—one a fine looking fellow. To sum up the story, we gratified their cupidity by giving them presents. They grunted their approbation and told us we might go. I stand guard again to night. Perhaps they will visit me to take possession of Black hawk who has mightily stricken the fancy of every Indian I have met. After amicable arrangements were made one of the many who came up shook hands with Mr S. and then did me the same favour with the addition of an embrace on horseback, at the same time rubbing his hand over his left breast which meant, as I am informed, that his heart was made glad by seeing me. Finding that his compliments did not open mine sufficiently to bestow multitudes of gifts upon him, he rode churlis[h]ly off, and took no further notice of me. We leave the Blue to morrow morning and shall reach the Platte by 12 m. upon which we shall tent, & content ourselves, for the next 20 days. Our visiters were the Grand and Republican Pawnees. I was amused at their savage cunning, or ingenuity, when the presents were put upon the ground and we in waiting, to see when they were satisfied. They gravely observed that it was very good, & stepping apart, two & two, he said we are two bands, which meant, we wish as much again; twas given & recievd.

distinguish whether they were humans, horses, or buffaloes. They came in the greatest disorder from the distant hills beyond the Blue, & were ranged before us in an inconcievably short time in battle array. The doubt & uncertainty of indian intentions, when brute force is with them, produced a sensation, vivid, but by no means delightful. In front of us, who stood by our unpacked & picketed animals, eighty or a hundred savages, mounted on shabby, yet hardy, & swift horses, armed with guns, spears and bows. The odds were against us, perhaps three to one, and they in the neighbourhood of their village. 'Twas enough to make one feel a little tremulous about the corners of the mouth. I confess 'that for my single self' I would rather have had a few more to share the honours, provided we were to gain any—It may be said, I think, that I was a little scared, but ready—One of Mr Sublette's 'engagées' fortunately spoke the Pawnee tongue, & was sent out to direct the gentlemen redskins, to halt at a short distance, & let only their chiefs come to hold a talk. Four representatives of the band presented themselves. One, a very remarkably fine looking fellow —To sum up the story, We made smooth our outward path by making them presents, of tobacco, powder, balls, beads, paint & &c.—They condescendingly grunted out their approbation and told us we might go—To night is my guard again—Possibly I may watch to some effect, as many of the savages have manifested a desire to get my little Black hawk. After amicable arrangements were made, one, of the many, who came up, shook hands with Mr. S. and then did me the same honour, with the additional favour of a hug on horseback, at the same time rubbing his hand over his left breast, which meant, as I was informed, that his heart was glad at seeing me. Finding that his compliments did not open my pack, he rode off as churlish as a bear and took no further notice of me. We shall leave the Blue tomorrow, and perhaps reach the Platte at 12 M., upon which we shall tent & *con*tent ourselves for the next twenty days—Our visitors were the Grand & Republican Pawnees—This name arises from their former residence on the Republican fork of the Kaw—Their savage cunning and ingenuity, amused me. When the presents were placed out before them, on with them, I began to soliloquize thus: I said to myself. "Well, little fellow, how do you feel? Ain't you scared? And the little fellow answered yes, I am, and I don't care a d____n if *you* do know it." And with true Spartan courage I assert, that if then and there, I wished for "that coffee-pot," it was no body's business but my own. A glance down the line, and oh, fortunate glance! brought us up, all standing —no more shifting from right foot to left—no more forced smiles. Orders had been given that none but the chiefs should come down to parley. Contrary to expectations, four representatives stood before us. To shorten the matter, and as I then thought, to bring things to a head, Sublette asked, "What do you want?" Tobacco, powder, balls, paint, beads, &c., &c. The various articles were soon placed in a pile, and when we supposed they were satisfied, the four paired off, saying here is one village, and there is another. A good hearty "d____n the rascals," came from Sublette, but the things were duplicated and they grunted out their approval. One of the chiefs was, I think, the finest specimen of the animal man, I ever looked upon. He was tall, straight, broad-shouldered and tapering; had a well formed head and a remarkably thoughtful countenance. Examining Sublette carefully, during the short time he was before us, he pointed down at

the ground, having with unmoved countenances watched us whilst disposing of them, they gravely observed 'that it was good; but, there were two bands—The hint was understood and the identical articles in quantity & quality was laid down to them.'

This encounter with the Pawnees was the first incident Anderson wrote up at length in his letters to the *American Turf Register*. There were four principal subdivisions of the Pawnees, a people of Caddoan stock continuously at war with the neighboring Sioux. The Skidis, also known as the Wolf or Loup Pawnees, gave name to a northern fork of the Platte. The Chauis or Grand Pawnees long dwelt on the Platte; the Kitkehahkis or Republican Pawnees, an offshoot of the Chauis, lived for extended periods on the Republican Fork of the Kansas River (most recently from about 1823 to 1832); and the Pitahauerats or Tapages, sometimes called the Noisy Pawnees, usually lived in close association with the Chauis. (See the entries for September 7–8.) The Pawnee-Pics, whom Anderson mentions in the opening pages of his Narrative, are now better known as the Wichitas; they dwelt on Red River far to the south, having become separated from their kinsmen many generations before. (See George E. Hyde, *Pawnee Indians*, passim.) The Pawnees were a notorious scourge of the New Mexican frontier. The trails they beat out were mapped by Frémont and others. Wyeth, who arrived at night where Sublette's party had breakfasted this day, mentions coming upon "the pawnee trail to the head of the Arkansas" and finding that "a very large party had passed it about 10 days before and a smaller one this morning." Jason Lee says: "Came about 20 m. to day. Saw an Indian trail about a week old where a large party had passed. Crossed the Pawnee trail just before we camped   it is worn by travel so that it appears like a wagon road. They had just passed and I perc[e]ive our camp is arranged with more care than usual."

In his third letter to the *American Turf Register*, Anderson says "Arra-raish, . . . the straight walking cane," was a name given to Sublette by the Crow Indians. But Matthew Field mentions on July 13, 1843, "the thunder storms that sometimes drive horizontally over this region, flooding all the hollows in [their] path, and, perhaps, leaving a creek 20 yards distant dry. . . . The Crow Indians call this 'straight walking rain' (*Harah–ereshe*) a name they have given to Col. Wm. L. Sublette" (*Prairie and Mountain Sketches*, p. 96). But p. 87 implies that the name is Pawnee.

MAY 17, 1834—*We are taking breakfast in the prairie about 5 miles from the Platte, which we have not reached in consequence of making an offset, from our course, in order to mislead a small party of Pawnees, who came upon us, like spirits from the grave. unheard, unexpected & undesired. They also recieved their small pieces of tobacco and departed. The devil speed them! We arrived on the banks of the Platte 3 o'clock p M. This river, is, what the Indian name Nebraska indicates, the flat river. It appears like the Mississippi, to be a resistless, bold, muddy stream. Except in mud, it belies its looks. It is, here, nearly three miles wide, spread around Grand Island. Where you might imagine a seventy four would float with ease, you could walk without wetting your knees. The earth here is whitened with a salts called glaber—but I do not know. I never before regretted my ignorance of chemistry, botany, mineralogy &c, not that I would take great pleasure in the investigations but because I could gratify the desires of the scientific portion of my friends by a description of what I see.*

MAY 17—On this day, which was Saturday, not Friday, Sublette must have continued up the Platte some distance after reaching it, for Wyeth did not overtake him. The New Englander writes: "17th. Made 3 miles up the stream [Little Blue] crossing a very small run course W. by N. then struck out N.W 3 miles and crossed a little run the same as passed in the morning then same course 6 mil[e]s . . . then 5 mil[e]s more same course and got sight of the Platte then W.N.W. 5 mil[e]s to the river and camped." In somewhat more detail, Jason Lee says: "Started this morning at 7 O'clock. Made a severe march of 9 hours from the Blue to the Platte. Left the main Blue on the left hand crossed a small branch or brook and having left the trail on the right we came by compass N. W. till we found the trail of Mr W^m. Sublet after marching say 15 m. We then took nearly a W. course   soon found the old waggon trail [of 1830 and 1832]   saw some small sand Hills a mile distant and as we approched them saw the timber on the banks of Platte. Came a few m. up and encamped the first place where we could find good grass and wood. . . . We came to day 15 *m.* N. W. and 10 *m.* W. Total 25 m." Cyrus Shepard mentions traveling all day without the usual noon halt, "passing through a delightful and highly divirsified country till about five o'clock P.M. when to our no small comfort a long stretch of cotton wood trees made their appearance some miles ahead indicating the vicinity of water—Soon the course of the Platte was distinctly seen which waas quite an agreable sight after a long, tedious and wearisome march."

The Platte was known to the French at least as early as 1714, when Etienne Veniard de Bourgmont ascended the Missouri to a point beyond its mouth. The name Platte ("flat" or "shallow," the meaning also of the Spanish "Chato" and the Oto term "Nebraska") came into general use soon after. See A. P. Nasatir, *Before Lewis and Clark*, I, 12-13.

Anderson gives a fuller account of Grand Island on September 6. Estimates of its length varied widely, depending on the state of the river and what islands were considered to be part of it. (In mapping the Platte in the 1890's, the U. S. Geological Survey scarcely admitted the existence of Grand Island as such.) The name became current at a very early date. Robert Stuart knew of it as "Big Island," and it helped to orient him when he was descending the Platte in the spring of 1813.

him, saying A-ra-rashe. It was so, indeed. A term I shall explain hereafter, perhaps.

This is my guard night, and I think I shall keep vigilant watch, as several of the red rogues expressed great admiration for my little Blackhawk. Touching their own horses, and pointing at mine, they would pass one hand rapidly over the other, which meant, I was told, "swop." After we had gone some distance a skulker rode up, shook hands with Sublette, gave me a shake, with the additional honor of a hug on horseback, then rubbing his right hand over his left breast, as much as to say, "my heart is glad when my eyes see you." Finding that his compliments did not open my pack, he rode off, looking as surly as a bear.

We shall leave the Blue to-morrow, and hope to reach the Platte by noon. On that stream we will have to tent, and content ourselves for the next twenty-five or thirty days. I forgot to say that our late visitors were of the Grand and Republican Pawnees. The latter derive their name from a late residence, on the Republican fork of the Kaw.

MAY 17, 1834—Friday. We breakfasted in the prairie, about five miles from the river. We did not arrive at the Platte at the appointed time, in consequence of an offset, made to mislead a small party of reds who dropped down upon us, out of the clouds. Like ghosts from the grave, they came unheard, uninvited and undesired. About 3 o'clock, P.M. this day, I saw one of the greatest lies in the world, if a lie can be seen, the Platte. The name is not a lie, for the outward seeming is always in French, Indian, or English, *platte, nebraska flat,* but there it ends. In appearance, it is like the Mississippi, broad, boisterous and deep; in appearance, capable of bearing the navies of the world, and yet the infernal liar is hardly able to float a canoe. This fussy, foaming, seething thing is like some big bragging men I have seen, all blubber and belly.

The ground hereabouts is covered with a white efflorescence, a feathery substance, which at a short distance resembles snow. How lovely is this pure, this heavenly looking vegetation! Stems, flowers, and leaves, spotless as an angel's wing, and yet it is nothing but the very bitterness of beauty—the unfulfilled promise of earthly happiness.

MAY 18, 1834.—*This morning we met a small war party on foot. They were too week to be saucy. I saw upon the way side a human skull. This reflection came into my mind as I passed by it, that perhaps he had like myself been rejoicing in the beauties of nature, that impelled by the spirit of adventure, he had sought to behold the wonders of the mountains and the savage forest, but cruel fate had cut the thread of his existence & his head once the domicil of mind, was a loom-house for the spider to weave his curious silk in or a nest, for the field-mouse to dwell & engender in. We passed by a spot to day, where sixty or seventy lodges of Indians had been fixed. I remarked a great many red painted twigs stuck into the ground in a circle. This is called a medicine—some barbarian incantation. An Indian told our interpreter that there had been recently a battle in the vicinity, and that this was a charm consequent upon that event. Many of the sticks were stained with blood, & had locks of hair fastened on the end. This night we are on the Platte, near twenty five miles from our last nights lodgement.*

MAY 18—Sunday, May 18, was a wet day according to the journals of the Wyeth party. Jason Lee wrote at 7:30 A.M.: "The rain has been falling gently since about mid-night which is the [first] we have had since the 6th except occasionally [a] few drops though we have been traveling over what is considered a rainy country. This seems more like Sabbath than any we have passed since we left the settlements. The rain prevents the men from being out hallooing cursing and shooting. . . .While writing the above orders were given to prepare for marching. We packed in the rain and marched 5 hours and encamped in a small spot of wood   plenty of grass for the animals."

Shepard says they traveled till 4 P.M., going 15 miles: "Rainy most of the morning so that we came into camp wet, cold, weary and hungry." Wyeth writes briefly: "Raining in morning   caught some Cat fish   found fresh track of Indians a small party."

The Pawnees Anderson encountered this day were perhaps the ones whom Wyeth met on May 19 (misdated in his diary as May 20). Wyeth says the company had just raised camp when they discovered "two Indians who were shy of coming to us but after a while suffered us to approach them   they said they were Pawnees but as we did not know the Pawnees this might be so or not   perhaps Ricarees [who in 1833 had made the vicinity of the Platte hazardous]   afterward saw several more on the blufs who did not come to us." Cyrus Shepard elucidates: "Two indians appeared on horseback soon after we commenced our journey   Capt. W. went to meet them and ascertained that they were Pawnees. they informed him that their village was near by & that they would sleep with him tomorrow night—Capt. W. now determined to move forward with as much celerity as possible to avoid if he could the intended visit by making longer journeys than the indians as they would probably endeavour to steal our horses." And Wyeth adds: "this night doubled guard." His company made 26 miles in all on the 19th, he says. Townsend's is the best report: ". . . we perceived two men on horseback, at a great distance; and upon looking at them with our telescope, discovered them to be Indians, and that they were approaching us. When they arrived within three or four hundred yards, they halted, and appeared to wish to communicate with us, but feared to approach too nearly. Captain W. rode out alone and joined them, while the party proceeded slowly on its way. In about fifteen minutes he returned with the information that they were of the tribe called Grand Pawnees. They told him that a war party of their people, consisting of fifteen hundred warriors, was encamped about thirty miles below; and the captain inferred that these men had been sent to watch our motions, and ascertain our place of encampment; he was therefore careful to impress upon them that we intended to go but a few miles further, and pitch our tents upon a little stream near the main river. When we were satisfied that the messen-

Opposite Grand Island, and the question arises, whether, in the sense of magnitude, there is a grander fresh water island in the world. It is variously estimated at eighty, one hundred, and one hundred and twenty miles in length. Though this may be guess measure, yet, if we settle upon the shorter distance, the man who undertakes to walk it under a hot sun will find it long enough—as long as a sleepless night.

MAY 18, 1834—This morning, we met a small party of dirty Pawnees. They tried to look big, and called themselves warriors. [They were too few to be saucy.] One of them was a grey young man. [I should suppose from his features and figure, about 27 or 8 years of age.] He looked healthy, active and strong, and yet he was perfectly gray. Granting these "braves" a little time to swagger, lie and beg, we passed on. I picked up to-day a human skull, and carried it for many miles. My companions had passed it by, without comment, perhaps without reflection, but I could not help feeling saddened at the sight. I built it up as a living being, as a companion, invested with flesh, vivified with spirit. It told me, that, impelled by the love of adventure, he had, years gone by, bade adieu to his kin and country, and sought to behold the wonders of these unknown wilds; that he had

---

gers were out of sight of us, on their return to their camp, our whole caravan was urged into a brisk trot, and we determined to steal a march upon our neighbors. The little stream was soon passed, and we went on, and on, without slackening our pace, until 12 o'clock at night. We then called a halt on the bank of the river, made a hasty meal, threw ourselves down in our blankets, without pitching the tents, and slept soundly for three hours. We were then aroused, and off we went again, travelling steadily the whole day, making about thirty-five miles, and so got quite clear of the Grand Pawnees."

Anderson says in the Journal: "We passed by a spot where there had recently been sixty or seventy lodges. The demi-devils had not long previous been successful in some engagement. There was, at this spot, a circle of red painted twigs stuck into the ground. This was a great medicine—i.e. some barbarian incantation—This term, is certainly a french misapplication, as there is nothing in the matters so called, to which the savages attribute any physical or spiritual medical quality—From my own observation or information I should think it something correspondent to a phylactery or amulet—Any extraordinary act of nature—a deer or buffaloe having a white skin would excite their wonder and admiration—And they would throw around it a mystic influence, concieving such rarity to possess some power of charm—Our interpreter was informed that a war party had stricken their enemy—and here we saw the effects of that stroke—Here they had danced the scalp dance and here I saw sticks, stained with human blood and ornamented with human hair—and I was then perhaps standing upon a spot where but a short time before, blood and carnage clothed the ground in crimson, sounding with death groans. We ended our voyage and bloody thoughts about sunset."

"Medicine" we now describe as sympathetic magic, though in the *Handbook of American Indians* neither the article on "medicine" nor that on "magic" encompasses the present case. Anderson conveys the general idea of "medicine" in his second letter to the *American Turf Register*. Various notes on his homeward journey, reflecting the ideas of the hunter Emanuel Martin, show how the whites were influenced by Indian concepts of personal "medicine."

MAY 19, 1834.—*We have made but 17 miles to day. It has rained all day.*

All the buffaloes heads are placed with their noses down the river to draw the living fellows thither. This is the custom, and intention of the Pawnees and other Indians, who live below.

MAY 19—Owing to confused chronology in the various diaries, some perplexity attends Anderson's entry for this day. In the Narrative he calls this Sunday (it was Monday), and in the Diary says it rained all day. Wyeth writes, "19th. Rained hard all day." But Wyeth's entry seems to be a continuation of his entry for the 18th—which is the reason his diary got one day ahead of the true dates, a fact he noted on May 26. No rain is mentioned on the 19th by Townsend, Lee, or Shepard; and Wyeth on the "20th" (19th) says observations for latitude and longitude were taken, which could not be done under cloudy skies. It may be that Anderson did not write out his Diary entries until several days later and then wrote the rain into the wrong day. (Observe that Wyeth's entry for the "20th" correlates with Lee's for the 19th in mentioning a visit by two Pawnees.)

The word "caiac," used in the Narrative May 19 and in the Diary May 20, is explained by Sir William Drummond Stewart in *Edward Warren* (p. 364): "a name given to a bison bull by the mountain men." The term had long been used by the French *voyageurs*, who knew North or New Park as "Park Kyack," translated by the Americans as the Bull Pen.

once rejoiced in the beauties of nature; that, like me, he had seen, with admiration, the glorious uprising and down-going of the sun in this ocean of verdant prairie, and whilst beholding with satisfaction these plains, animated by immense herds of deer and buffalo, he had fallen the victim of an unseen foe.

In truth, the lonely sermon made the chill fear of death run through me, and I fancied that the grinning skull moaned in my ear, *Memento homo tu es pulvis, et in pulverem reverteris.* Adieu, kind friend; I have no more time to moralize. The sun is hot, and I must on and take my chances. From fancy, we have come to reality—a sad reality. We stand in the middle of a circle of blood-stained sticks, each bearing a lock of human hair. Near us are the peg marks of fifty or sixty lodges. At this spot there has lately been the scalp-dance. Here the *brave* and *noble* warrior minutely recited how he had crawled upon his enemy, in the dark, and killed him in his sleep; and here, tender woman, nature's sweet child, the squaw, screamed her song of triumph and revenge, as she plucked out the eyes, or hacked and tore the flesh of her quivering victims. This circle, the scene of savage joy, is what is called "a great medicine." This term I do not understand or appreciate. Is it not a French misnomer? The Indians do not, as far as I can learn, attribute medical qualities, physical or spiritual, to any wonder or extraordinary thing. Yet all rare and unusual occurrences, each and every variation from nature, they are made to call "a medicine." A white deer, or buffalo, Gen. Clark's red hair, was translated for them, a "big medicine." I have no doubt their idea was that of charm or amulet. Every warrior or hunter, when going forth to battle, or the chase, takes with him, in his charm-bag, a certain remarkable something, to protect or help him.

MAY 19, 1834.—Unless we have missed our count, this is Sunday. If it is so, then this is *the* rainy Sunday of our march. I noticed to-day another great big 'medicine.' I should rather term it, a huge Pawnee trick. They have pointed all the buffalo heads down stream, in order to draw the living browsers toward their villages. Might not this plan work against the hopes of the smart bipeds? Let us suppose some old shaggy fronted "Cai[a]c," after smelling at the nose of his dead brother, bellowing out to the "mobile vulgus," halt! hold on there! See big heap go down; mighty little heap come back.

91

MAY 20, 1834.—*This day one month ago I left St. Louis. I found another human skull on the prairie. This evening I beheld The first band of buffaloe I ever saw. I was disappointed in the appearence which they presented   They did not stud the plains like trees, as far as the eye could see. I do not know that I should be dissatisfied, as they were ten or twenty deep extending ten or twelve miles in length. This evening Mr Sublett proposed to me to take a chase after them. We accordingly girted our saddles, mounted Black hawk and companion, and put off. I wounded one, a Caiac badly, had a long and exciting race after him, but being so unfortunate as to drop my gun I was obliged to give him up.*

MAY 20—Although Anderson has miscalculated his dates, he was in fact one month out from St. Louis, having left there by April 20. Anderson again describes this day's buffalo hunt in his second letter to the *American Turf Register*. The "hunter stories of Beargrass" recalled in the Narrative hark back to the era before the buffalo was exterminated east of the Mississippi.

MAY 20, 1834.—We are now one month out from St. Louis. Found another skull on the plain to-day, but did not enter into conversation; did not ask its adventures. In fool-sympathy, with the rest smiled at the jest and ribaldry of some reckless packer, and passed on to finish another day-tramp in the march of time. This is, and I suppose will long remain a memorable day for me. The buffalo are in sight— herds or bands of buffalo. They do not, as I had expected, darken the plain far as the eye can see; they do not come with sullen sound and endless roar, realizing and fulfilling my boyish dreams—dreams excited by the hunter stories of Beargrass; but there are more than enough in sight to baffle all my figures. I will not indulge even in guess work. It is said to be a little band of a half mile front and ten miles deep. Mr. Sublette proposed a chase, and I assented. After examining guns and pistols, and tightening girths, we mounted our horses and started in pursuit. Heavens and earth, what excitement! The file-leaders flew to the sand-hills, and the whole sea of living things fled after them. Soon, very soon, everything was lost to sight. Below, around and above, clouds of dust, and we moved on, guided only by the snorts of the bulls as they scented their enemies, and the dull thudding of millions of feet. The hills are reached, and they divide off into lakes, islands, and rivers of black, moving masses. I skirted some smaller stream, tried to study its direction, and form some plan of action. Singling out an old and tired looking bull, I pulled towards him, but as soon as poor Blackhawk got a good sight and a full snuff of his horned majesty, he siezed the bit in his teeth, and was as unmanageable, for a while, as a rudderless steam boat. "After a long chase, and a strong chase," I succeeded in lodging an ounce of lead in his brown hide, but too far forward to bring him to a stand still. With true Kentucky ardor, and almost foolhardy, or Yankee perseverance, I followed on until I had given him the contents of my two pistols. After a few desperate plunges, he staggered, bench-legged, and fell. Was there then a prouder man on the face of the earth? It now became necessary for me to look for and regain my rifle, which I had let fall after my first shot. I found it by starlight, and it was then too late to go back and procure the evidence of my triumph, a buffalo's tongue.

MAY 21, 1834.—*To day the number increased much. Tens of thousands in view. I was once at a loss to know how so many animals can subsist, now tis no mistery. I am confident that providence has provided pasturage for them even were they ten fold increased. One may travel sixty, yea ninety days through grass covered bottoms of exceeding fertility. What wonder then, that one may see countless numbers of graminivorous animals, for three days continuous travel. We are a days march, or less from the crossing place of the Platte. The appearence of this river has not changed, from two to three miles in bredth, & up to the knee in depth.*

MAY 21, 1834.—The number of buffalo, or bison, properly speaking, have multiplied by thousands and ten of thousands. Formerly, when I heard of such immense numbers, I could scarcely believe it possible for them to obtain subsistance. But now all is comprehensible and within the scope of credibility. Where is the limit to their feeding range? Besides this rich, grass-covered bottom of the Platte, from two to three miles wide, and a thousand long, they rove over all of the streams of New Mexico; the Rio-del Norte and the Arkansas, and off and away to the streams of the North, East and West, on both sides of the mountains. Why then distrust the statement of the trappers who say they have made three days journey through dense herds of buffalo? My friend, Mr. Sublette, assures me he has seen such bands on the waters of the Arkansas. I know there are men of otherwise excellent information, and sound judgment, who discredit these prairie wonders merely because they have not seen them. I am aware that facts, monotonous facts, of these regions are cried down by certain city scribblers, as absurd and preposterous tales, utterly unworthy of belief. Well, all things get even after a while; when the old gambler, Time, shake[s] his dice-box, truth will win. The hardy trapper, who has not seen the face of a white woman for a dozen years, will have his say, he will assert, and swear it too, that such a fellow "was a fool, and couldn't dance, and his daddy had no barn." In other words, that he was not fit to inherit the brains of a dying idiot.

The Platte is still the platte, from two to three miles wide, and fully knee-deep.

DIARY

MAY 22, 1834—*We have made a long days march—at the least 30 miles. Now encamped at the crossing place, of the South branch of the Platte. Tis thought, from the almost total disappearance of the buffaloe, that there must be Indians in the vicinity. Few as they are to day I have had two unsuccessful shots at them. I have all along forgot to commemorate for myself the most beautiful, the most unusual & the deceptious spectacle I ever saw; tis the mirage or sahrab of the prairie—Large, clear and inviting lakes, rivulets and rivers as clearly seen, as the eye can distinguish any object. I would not for the world, have one of these mock streams, spread out before my longing senses when weary, worn & thirsty. After repeatedly beholding these strange ocular delusions, I had yesterday the great gratification of seeing it in contrast with the Platte—a lake of considerable magnitude, lay just before us, at a right angle with the river. To the keenest vision it appear^d as natural as the waters of the real stream. It was not reflection from the other, because there was a rise which intervened. Mr Sublette himself was almost imposed upon, tho he had passed repeatedly, & knew there could be none. I have also been gratified by being an eye witness of looming objects, Antelopes seeming as tall, as men on horseback. This not unfrequently causes some laughable alarms. "Indians, "Indians" &c—but, it is all a delusion.*

MAY 22—It is not possible from Anderson's record to say where he forded the South Platte, but Wyeth supplies the necessary information. The latter's note for May 23 (misdated the 24th) says he reached "the crossing of the South fork of the Platte about 8 miles above the forks." Shepard adds that they arrived "past noon." Hence Wyeth's company was only a few hours behind Sublette's. Wyeth encamped the remainder of the 23rd, so by nightfall was a full day's travel in the rear.

Anderson does not describe the actual fording of the South Platte on the 23rd. There was nothing to it in 1834. As Shepard writes on the 24th: "Crossed the South fork soon after breakfast, stream half a mile wide and very low water for the season—were soon all safe on the oposite shore—no injury excepting that one of Capt. W.'s men lost his gun by his horse steping into a deep hole in the river." Wyeth himself says on the 25th: "Crossed without difficulty and made up the N. side of the South Fork about 4 miles W. then struck N. W. about 1 mile to the North fork which is here the largest then made about W. by N. about 15 miles and near to some cut blufs which come close to the river." In all probability, this describes Anderson's travel of the 23rd.

The ford used in 1834 seems to have been standard during the fur trade era. It also served the Bartleson party in 1841, under the guidance of Thomas Fitzpatrick. Black Harris, in charge of the caravan of 1839, crossed farther up to avoid a Sioux concentration, and from 1842 emigrants regularly began to cross the South Platte at more westerly points. The uppermost of the early crossings, 4 miles west of present Brule, Nebraska, and some 87 miles above the Forks, was known by 1845, when Joel Palmer referred to it as a better way of reaching Ash Hollow than that which he and his fellow emigrants had taken. (Palmer's is one of the earliest references to Ash Hollow, a locality earlier called simply Ash Creek or the Upper Cedar Bluffs.) In 1846 the favored crossing was

MAY 22, 1834—We compute our march to-day at thirty miles. We shall probably cross the south fork of the Platte in the morning. Sublette thinks from the almost total disappearance of game, that Indians are near. Every man is now wide-awake and owl-like, his head and eyes turn in every direction. I am in luck. I have missed two buffalo to-day.

Oh, the mirage! the mirage! the waters of the plain! What a sight for a thirst-dying man. A terrible curse, and terribly expressed.

> "May he at last, with lips of flame,
> On the parched desert, thirsting die;
> While lakes that shone in mockery nigh,
> Are fading off, untouched, untasted."

This was looked upon by stay-at-home philosophers, as the fancy touch of that [a] child of genius, but "truth is strange, stranger than fiction," even on the plains of America. Here, in our unpoetic deserts, the traveler sees large, clear and inviting lakes—rivers and rivulets, flashing and sparkling in the sun—beautiful groves, fern-covered rocks, and mountain shadows making the land cool for many a mile. I would not, for the wealth of Potosi, have one of these mock, delusive streams, spread out before me, if burning with fever and longing for a cool draught of good, cool water. After frequently admiring, and sometimes almost fearing this "Sah-rab," as it is called in Persia, I had an opportunity yesterday of comparing it with the waters of the Platte. Just before us, and at right-angles with the river, ran a stream of almost equal magnitude, but much more clear and water-like than the muddy Platte. "Vive la bagatelle!" Before a thousand years roll by, I may feel no pride in these, my nightly scribblings. Perhaps, at some future time, I may turn up my wise, experienced nose, and say, what frothy nonsense! It may seem, and be, in fact, trifling; but whether trifling or not, it is pleasant trifling, so here goes "for some of that same."

---

at present Ogallala, 12 miles below the crossing just mentioned. The massive overland emigration of 1849 used all these fords.

The quotation in the Narrative is from Thomas Moore's "Lalla Rookh." The shimmering effect of a mirage was well depicted by Alfred Jacob Miller when journeying up the Platte in 1837. (See the reproduction in color in Bernard DeVoto, *Across the Wide Missouri*, Pl. IV.)

In his Journal Anderson continues: "A counterfeit resemblance of the real thing—in nothing, was there such a difference between the shadow & the substance. Looming, is another optical delu-

MAY 23, 1834—*I am now mentioning first impressions, which may seem hereafter, light & trivial. I have seen & been delighted with the little prairie fox, one of the most active & graceful creatures, I presume in the world. I must be again in the superlative, upon the subject of the hare—As much as the agility & grace of the Antelope is admired, I must decide that to my taste the hare is a more interesting 'cursor.' His leap is free [open?] straight upwards thrusting back then striking the ground with a "double coup" his bound is doubled with his hinder feet His head is born majestically up like the greyhound when his prey has dodged him. Of the prairie dogs I will not speak until I have seen more of them. I was decieved in their colour. Tis yellow, the colour of the lioness. We passed a large village of them to day.*

---

sion, that we almost every day behold. Many interesting and amusing incidents arise from this circumstance—The harmless little antelopes with their spindle legs and jet black horns, are at one time magnified into men in arms, dashing down upon us with spears and bows, when just as one opens his mouth to cry 'Indians, Indians', and another hears an arrow whistling over his head, the sun hides his face behind a cloud, and all proves to be but a dream at the best. 'Hale Mr Sublette, turn into the river, there is a good place to noon. We shall have a shade. I do wish to lay under a tree again.' S—— turned his unerring glance in the direction designated, and Spartan like said, 'No woods, but buffaloe.' Indeed I thought 'that Burnam's wood was coming to Dunsinane' for our trees were in motion.'

MAY 23—Anderson again describes the fauna of the plains in his letters to the *American Turf Register*.

MAY 23, 1834—As passing shadows of the mind, three little things, present themselves to be considered, and described, the prairie fox, the prairie dog, and the prairie hare. I have said shadows, and will stick to it, for who knows where or what they will be when the world ends? The first, or Reynard, [the] little, is nearly as round and about as long as a man's arm, the elbow terminating the body and beginning the tail. The color is a reddish gray, which renders it almost invisible, as it rapidly skims over the dry grass and sand of the plains. There is no labored, upward springing action of the body, no throwing out or switching from side to side of its well balanced tail. When at its highest flight we can scarcely realize the fact that our quadruped arrow is propelled by leg power at all.

The Prairie dog, is perhaps, the most remarkable of all super or subterranean animals, great or small. They are gregarious to an astonishing degree. They dwell in subterranean towns and cities, which spread over and through hundreds and thousands of acres. At a short distance they resemble the very young beaver, but in outward seeming the resemblance ends, as they have never been known to enter or touch the element in which the beaver delights to dwell. [I have seen a village on the top of the Black Hills—many thousand feet above the Platte's bed.] Their police regulations are as wise and as well understood as any ordained by the Lord Mayor and council of London. When enemies or strangers approach or pass through their corporate limits, here and there at long distances sentinels perched on hillocks, give the alarm. Some dozen clear, shrill barks are heard, when the whole wandering population rush home for safety. Though a hundred or a thousand may plunge into the same hole, it is never choked or filled, as streets and alleys lead off in every direction, thus connecting and relieving every thoroughfare from above. When the real or supposed danger has passed, first one head and then another pops up, and bark follows bark until the whole air is split and splintered with the ringing discord. These subterranean dry land teetotalers have been called, by some writers, Marmots. Clark and Lewis gave them the name of prairie squirrels, but the old trappers and traders have fixed upon them the honorable title of prairie dogs, and certainly if barking can make them so, these comical little sons of bitches will be dogs to all eternity. One word of apology to my tallow-candle. I really mean no disrespect, and unless I have entirely

99

MAY 24, 1834—*Yesterday we camped upon the north side of the south fork of the Platte. We are today on the north branch, where we shall continue, until we reach the mountains. I have killed to day my second rattle snake. Except occasional quarrels among the voyageurs, I find the tented life quite pleasant. Yesterday & to day clouds of buffaloe gnats have teased us beyond endurance. The pestiferous little devils! No bread, and no more till my return to civilization.*

MAY 25, 1834—*Travelled all day without seeing game. At night Mr Patten the clerk, killed an old poor Caiac. A few days ago I frequently saw wolves, elk, deer, antelopes, & buffaloe at one view. The first wild horses came in sight yesterday.*

MAY 26, 1834—*I have had the great gratification of seeing in their natural, free & independent state, the wild horse. Some may admire the Antelope, the deer, the fox or the wild hare, but tis my firm conviction that for majesty, beauty & grace there is not animal in existence which is the equal of the proud horse of the desert. I have nothing more this day worthy of remembrance.*

MAY 24—The miseries occasioned by the swarming gnats are also described by Townsend. Wyeth's party were finding the sandy aspect of the North Platte agreeable after the wearisome monotony of the "extensive and apparently interminable green plains," when they were suddenly assailed "by vast swarms of most ferocious little black gnats; the whole atmosphere seemed crowded with them, and they dashed into our faces, assaulted our eyes, ears, nostrils, and mouths. . . . These little creatures were so exceedingly minute that, singly, they were scarcely visible; and yet their sting caused such excessive pain, that for the rest of the day our men and horses were rendered almost frantic, the former bitterly imprecating, and the latter stamping, and kicking, and rolling in the sand, in tremendous, yet vain, efforts to rid themselves of their pertinacious little foes. It was rather amusing to see the whole company with their handkerchiefs, shirts, and coats, thrown over their heads, stemming the animated torrent, and to hear the greenhorns cursing their tormenters, the country, and themselves for their foolhardiness in venturing on the journey. When we encamped in the evening, we built fires at the mouths of the tents, the smoke from which kept our enemies at a distance. . . . The next morning I observed that the faces of all the men were more or less swollen, some of them very severely, and poor Captain W. was totally blind for two days afterwards."

MAY 26—In his third letter to the *American Turf Register* Anderson exceeds even his Narrative in rhapsodizing over the wild horses. They had spread northward from the Spanish frontier long before. In *Edward Warren* Stewart remarked that in 1833 the area between the forks of the Platte "was the especial haunt of the wild horse" (p. 133); here he "saw what at first startled, and then delighted me more than any thing I had yet seen, some half a dozen horses. . . . That they must be wild, was evident from the length of mane and tail of some two or three, who seemed the masters of the herd; they were . . . rearing up and striking out with their forefeet, one in particular of a dark brown, had the great neck, and a heavy mane falling to the ground" (p. 135). Compare the sketch of wild horses in *The West of Alfred Jacob Miller*, Pl. 176, and see Anderson's remarks in his homeward-bound journal, August 23 and 25.

mistaken the sex of their mothers, I do not think I have been guilty of any vulgarity. At all events I disclaim entirely any wish or intention of offending the prairie puppies, or such as may wear boots and breeches.

The hare is a bounder, and a beautiful bounder; with head borne proudly erect, he springs into action with a grace and loftiness which I have never seen surpassed by any other animal. There is a something very peculiar in his running, or rather in his succession of rapid leaps. After each elastic spring he seems to throw back and downwards his long hind legs, thus striking the earth with a double coup which propels him farther upward and onward. In the winter they are provided with a perfectly white robe, which makes it difficult for even the keen eyed hawk to perceive them as they sit by the sage bush, near a lump of snow.

MAY 24, 1834—We are now ascending the North fork of the Platte, up which we shall travel until we reach the Bed Ruutes [Red Buttes]. Save an occasional quarrel and a few loud "cusses" among the packers, all goes smooth and easy in our tented life. Yesterday and to-day we have met a new but not a very agreeable acquaintance, in the Buffalo gnat. Several of our men have become almost blind from their poisonous bites. The little devils seem to alight upon you with red-hot feet and billies. They bite, burn and blister you all over. Even my little thoroughbred Blackhawk has been almost run mad by their annoying, unceasing and invisible attacks. His head, neck and breast are swol[l]en to a wonderful degree, and his whole body hot with fever. [I begin to long for some bread.]

[MAY 25, 1834. *No entry.*]

MAY 26, 1834—I have just seen what of all wild, free things of earth I most desired to see—the wild, free horse—the masterless horse, fenced in by the horizon only, and with no rider but the wind. There he goes, the pure descendant of the Andalusian breed. Adieu for the present; I hope to make your better acquaintance at some future time.

A few days ago I beheld at one view, elk, antelope, deer, buffalo and wolves, all hitherto strangers to me. I had known them by hearsay, but now I have them before me, hide and hair, flesh and bones.

MAY 27, 1834.—*Of all the lan[d]scapes and scenery I ever saw, the view I had this morning was unsurpassed. It is a hill, in the range of those, which skirts the south side of the north fork of the Platte, the appearance of it is that of a castle situated upon a hill & commanding the country for 7 or 10 miles, down the river. The most delightful delusion was kept up until the base was within a very short distance. A most beautiful meadow-like plain was spread out before it. Flowers of every hue & odour bestarred the prairie. It would seem as if some wealthy scotch lord had fixed his aristocratic stronghold in the wilds of the new world. Antelopes and buffaloe were grazing in his extensive parks. To add to the charm and loveliness an active flowing stream broke out from its base and hastened to astonish the Platte with its clear waters. Would to God that I could design or describe well, tho I should then fail to do justice to this fascinating deception, I would nevertheless commemorate this scene for my own gratification! The chimney is a much more notorious point. It is singular truly, rising to an elevation of 150 feet, it is distinctly visible at the distance of thirty miles   Tis a pyramid or rather a funnel inverted—*

MAY 27—Anderson's commanding "castle" became known as Courthouse Rock, the name Jail Rock being applied to a nearby formation. Many of the landmarks along the overland trail had not received definitive names in 1834. Wyeth passed both Ash Hollow and Courthouse Rock without comment, though Jason Lee spoke of the "large rock which has the appearance at a distance of an old castle," and Cyrus Shepard mentioned the "singular bluff called the castle." Most travelers took note of the "romantic" scenery that distinguishes the valley of the North Platte west of Ash Hollow, but the name Courthouse Rock seems not to have been used until employed in Frémont's report of his 1842 expedition. Influenced by Frémont, emigrants began to use the name Courthouse familiarly in 1846.

What in the Diary Anderson describes as "the chimney," in the Narrative he discreetly calls "E. P.," a term he uses again in the Diary and Journal for August 24. Wyeth on June 9, 1832, mentions "the Chimney or Elk Brick the Indian name," which suggests that he was obtuse of ear or had a certain sense of humor. Zenas Leonard, as of 1831, remarks on the formation "known among the whites as 'Chimney cliff', and among the natives as 'Elk Peak.'" Warren A. Ferris, as of 1830, is unique in alluding to "The 'Nose Mountain', or as it is more commonly called, the 'Chimney.'" The phallic aspect of Chimney Rock, implicit in some of the above comments, is explicitly remarked by Stewart, whose *Edward Warren* in a footnote (p. 155) identifies "the chimney" as "Penus cervus of the Indians." Merrill J. Mattes, "Chimney Rock on the Oregon Trail," reproduces fifteen sketches of the rock made between 1841 and 1874.

MAY 27, 1834—This morning we have a most lovely view—a wild, picturesque landscape. There is a castle, situated on a range of hills which semicircles between its huge baronial walls and the river, a broad and meadow-like plain. The castle park is filled with the greatest variety of beautiful flowers, over which roam in native freedom horses, antelopes and buffalo. On each side of this oldtime defying stronghold are two well proportioned towers. To add to the charm of the scene, and keep up the delusion of a living lordly residence, an active, fine flowing stream breaks out from the base of the castle, and hastens to astonish the turbid Platte, with its bright, clear waters. [I wish to God I could paint or describe well, tho' I should then fail to do justice to this fascinating delusion. I would preserve a faint resemblance of this splendid scene.] But as I can neither paint or picture nature's grandeur, I will blow out my candle and sleep or scratch, until another day.

We are now in sight of E. P., or Chimney Rock, a solitary shaft, about one hundred and fifty feet high, and which can be seen at the distance of thirty miles. [Tis pyramidal, or rather a funnel inverted.] It is two miles from the river, on the left side ascending, and from its peculiar form and entire isolation, is one of the most notorious objects on our mountain march [but I think there is no comparison between the two].

DIARY

MAY 28, 1834—*We are encamped a little below Scotts hill. Violent winds all day. So much so that we have a very short days travel. We have but 3 days to the Black hills—Scott an old trapper, was left here in sickness and died upon the plains to glut the maws of the merciless wolves. His companions reported him dead, when they left him, but confessed afterwards that he was living, but to much reduced to be carried any longer, hunger, that cold hearted monster, compelled them to desert him.*

MAY 28—Anderson's report of violent winds this day better fits the narratives of the Wyeth party on May 27, though Wyeth said on the 28th that the wind was still high. On the 27th Wyeth spoke of "a severe gale from the N. N. W." that made "the sand cut like a knife." Jason Lee remarked, "The wind was so strong that it was with great difficulty that I could make headway when on foot, and it was of course very severe on the horses." Townsend commented that the whole camp was aroused that morning when a tremendous blast swept over the sandy plain, blowing down all the tents, and during the day "a most terrific gale was blowing directly in our faces, clouds of sand were driving and hurtling by us, often with such violence as nearly to stop our progress; and when we halted in the evening, we could scarcely recognise each other's faces beneath their odious mask of dust and dirt."

On reaching Scotts Bluff, Sublette's party camped at Robidoux Spring. In his comments on Scotts Bluff, Anderson makes major contributions to the record. His Journal reads: "We camp tonight a little below Scott's bluff. . . . The man after whom this bluff was called was an old mountaineer, who was taken very ill on his way to his home and friends. He died at the spot alone and unprotected—The cruel desertion of this unhappy individual, is an example of the most heartless & unchristian inhumanity—The human fiend who was the cause of such barbarity deserves the curses of mankind—This being, too called himself a disciple of the prince of peace—a presbyterian scoundrel—a monster of a human shape—The poor man's bones were found at the distance of two miles from where he was left—his unburied corpse became a feast for the raven and the wolf—Two of his companion[s] remained with him and bore him along for several days, but having no means of procuring food, they were compelled to leave him to famine and disease and pursue their barbarous leader."

Jason Lee writes: "A Mr Scott superintendent of General Ashley's Fur Company, was taken delirious in the Black Hills but at lucid intervals expressed a great desire to go home to die and the[y] thought it best to make a boat of skins and send him down the Platte some distance by water where the Com. if they arrived first were to await their arrival. Two men were sent with him but they were upset in rapids and narrowly escaped being drowned and lost their guns and everything but one knife and a horn of powder. The leader of the Com. did not stop for them and it was with the greatest difficulty that the men could find enough to subsist on until they overtook the Com. Their report was that he died and they buried him but his bones and blanket were found a 100 mi. from the place they said he had died and near the Bluff." Similar accounts are given by Ferris and Bonneville. Stewart (*Edward Warren*, p. 158) notes in the Black Hills the "cascade where Scott, who died at the bluffs below Larramé, was wrecked. . . ."

Hiram Scott, an Ashley man as early as 1823, was hired to pilot to Bear Lake the supply caravan sent out in 1827 by William H. Ashley and the American Fur Company. (See Dale L. Morgan, *The West of William H. Ashley*, index.) The business agent was James B. Bruffee of Washington County, Missouri. It appears that on the homeward journey Scott fell ill near the mouth of Labonte Creek, where the ill-advised voyage down the North Platte began. Matthew Field, who had the story presumably from William L. Sublette in 1843, pinned upon Bruffee the responsibility for not waiting for Scott below the Black Hills, and said, "The scattered remnants of his bones were sought after, found, gathered and buried the next summer [i.e., fall? spring?] by Wm. L. Sublette, and there lies poor Scott, with a mournful fate and a magnificent monument" (*Prairie and Mountain Sketches*, p. 65). The violent anathemas launched by Anderson upon the head of Scott's "betrayer" are to be understood as directed at Bruffee. For an examination of the Scott legend as it flowered in later years, see Merrill J. Mattes, "Hiram Scott, Fur Trader," pp. 127-162. A national monument now commemorates tragedy and scenic site.

MAY 28, 1834—We camp to-night a little below Scott's Bluff. The wind has been so violent all day that we have made but little headway. This place bears the name of an old mountaineer, who died here from sickness and starvation. The desertion and abandonment of this poor man, by his leader and employer, was an act of the most cruel and heartless inhumanity, uncalled for and unnecessary. His death has left here a traveller's land-mark, which will be known when the name of the canting hypocrite and scoundrel who deserted him, will be forgotten, or remembered only in hell. Two of his companions remained with him for several days, bearing him along as his weakness increased, and only left him when compelled by the want of food. The unburied corpse of poor Scott was found at this spot, having crawled more than two miles towards his father's cabin, and his mother's home. The only witness, the only watcher of his death-agony, was the dark raven and the ever hungry wolf. And keen, sharp and eager was the watch. I know the name of the soulless villain, and so does God and the devil. I leave him to the mercy of the One, and the justice of _____. Had such a being a father? I know not; for the sake of humanity, let us hope that he never had a mother, but "dropped from the tail of a dung-cart."

MAY 29, 1834.—*I saw to day, on horse creek for the first time, one manner of disposing of the dead, which was scaffolding—In the top of the tree fastened by chords of buffaloe hide, so firmly as to resist the wind for a long time, a frame upon which the deceased is placed with all of his movables—This body had fallen out, & the vacated place taken possession of by a hawk, who had deposited her eggs in the spot where the head of Sioux warrior lay. At the suggestion of Major Harris, Black H. one of my messmates I record for my future consideration, that on this evening, about 5 o'clock I bestrode a Caiac of my own slaughtering. We are within one days march of Laramy's fork.*

MAY 29—Horse Creek, alluded to in the Diary, has a considerable antiquity among the place names of the upper Platte, for on June 12, 1832, Wyeth mentioned "Wild Horse Creek." Robert Stuart observed wild horses in this locality as early as Dec. 24, 1812. The Sioux sepulture here shows that by the spring of 1834 Sioux penetration southwestward from the Missouri into the valley of the Platte was well advanced; thus they were not first drawn to the region by the founding of Fort William. On June 22, 1834, Sioux subagent J. L. Bean wrote Gen. Henry Atkinson from his Upper Missouri station as follows:

"The main band of the Yancton and Teton Siouxs left this place on the 2nd inst. for their Summer hunt—and about four hundred lodges of the Sowanné, Ogallallas, Minne Con-ojus and onkpaw-paw bands of Sioux separated with me at the little Missouri [Bad River] about sixty five miles above this place on the 12th inst—

"It was the intention of all the Siouxs that I have seen to pass the summer west of the Black Hills in the plains of the Platte river not only on account of the great Scarcity of Buffaloe on this side, but for the purpose of taking wild horses there, where they are alone to be found in abundance. . . ." He added that if the Sioux fell in with the Dragoons, they would be friendly. "But the Arickeraws whom you know to be the sworn enemies of any, and all the American people who visit this country, are now on the Platte river near the Base of the mountains where they passed the last winter—but the whole nation (say 500 men strong) would not dare to openly attack half their number of white men under any circumstances whatever . . ." (Records of U. S. Army Commands, Western Department, Letters Received, National Archives).

Placing the dead in trees or upon scaffolds was practiced by many tribes, including the Mandans, Gros Ventres, Arapahos, Siksikas, and Chippewas. In *Edward Warren* (pp. 156-157), Stewart intimates that as early as 1833 the cottonwoods along the Laramie River were thus employed; he speaks of "the mournful scaffoldings above, upon which the Sioux had built the nests of the dead; where waved the decaying blanket, escaped from the thongs which had tied it, with other household gods, to furnish out the last array of the departed brave. There were many such relics in this sacred grove. The living Indian left it for the dead, until it became the source whence fuel was procured for the forts afterwards built below. . . ." In 1843 Field observed: "At Laramee Fork, upon an eminence between the two forts there located [Fort John and Fort Platte], we found an Indian burying-ground, or rather a place of deposit for the dead—the bodies not being *buried* at all, but bound up in skins and elevated upon scaffolds in the air. Some of these scaffolds were so dilapidated by time that portions of the skeletons had fallen through, and the bones were scattered loosely around the vicinity" (*Prairie and Mountain Sketches*, p. 77). Charles Bodmer drew for Maximilian a striking representation of an Assiniboine sepulture on the upper Missouri.

When Anderson says in the Diary that he "bestrode" a bison bull of his own slaughtering, he means the term literally; Miller in 1837 sketched a hunter's "Yell of Triumph" from atop a carcass. The Journal varies slightly from the Narrative in saying, "This time I tied Black-hawk to his [the bison's] horns and took out his tongue as a trophy and bore it in triumph to the camp."

MAY 29, 1834—I found to-day, a hawk's nest, on a scaffold which had been the resting place of a Sioux brave. This bird of blood had deposited her eggs near the spot where a warrior's head once lay. This method of disposing of the dead is peculiar to, and common with that nation. A scaffold is securely fastened in the boughs of a tree so securely as to resist the action of the winds for years. The body, tightly wrapped in the honor-robe, his implements of battle and the chase within, is then bound to it, and the brave is left to the companionship of the birds of the air and his brothers of the Spirit land.

This evening, about 5 o'clock, I felled a mighty bison to the earth. I placed my foot upon his neck of strength and looked around, but in vain, for some witness of my first great "coup." I felt proud; I felt glorious; I thought myself larger than a dozen men. I tied little Blackhawk to his horns, danced upon his body, and made a fool of myself to my heart's content, then cut out his tongue and sat down to rest and moralize.

Nothing can be more revolting, more terrific, than a front view of an old bull buffalo. His huge hump, covered with long wool, rising eighteen or twenty inches above his spine; a dense mat of black hair, padding a bullet-proof head; a dirty dunkard[-like] beard, almost sweeping the ground, and his thick, dark horns and sparkling eyes, give him, altogether, the appearance and expression of some four-legged devil, fresh sooted from _____ Halifax [hell]. But nevertheless, and notwithstanding all this, his meat is good eating. Bosse, hump-ribs, side-ribs, tongue and marrow-bones. "Sufficient for the day," is the fatigue and rest thereof.

MAY 30, 1834.—*This evening we are encamped on the banks of the aforesaid fork. Tis here that* Mr S. *designs erecting a small fort. In a day or two he will recommence his march to the rocky mountains with such of his men as he does not leave for the erection of the fort. The Black hills are around us. They are spurs of the R. M.*

MAY 30—Little is known about the man who gave name to the Laramie River. In the autumn of 1831, when the U. S. government was gathering data on the fur and Santa Fe trade, John Dougherty at Cantonment Leavenworth included in his casualty list "J. Loremy," identified as "a free man" killed in 1821 "on the Platte" by "Arapahoes." Joshua Pilcher similarly listed "Loremy." This is the sum of the authoritative information about Laramie, though a considerable legend has evolved. The purported biography of "Jacques Laramie" by Grace Raymond Hebard seems speculative and imaginative in the light of what is now known of the fur trade around 1820, and the same may be said of the antecedent account by C. G. Coutant, *History of Wyoming*, pp. 296-299. See John D. McDermott's "The Search for Jacques Laramee: A Study in Frustration."

On June 13, 1832, Wyeth refers to "Larrimee fork of the Platte." Irving (or Bonneville) as of the same month employs the term "Laramie's Fork." Larpenteur, writing in 1834 respecting a journey of 1833, alludes to "fourche la Ramie or Rameis Fork." Ferris has the name "Laramie's Fork," and Leonard "Laramies river"; Stewart prefers "Larramé." Not until 1834 do diarists associate the name with a person. Jason Lee says of "Laramas Fork," "a man by that name was killed by the Indians on that Branch." Cyrus Shepard similarly comments that "Laramy's fork . . . is so called from the circumstance of a man by that name having some years ago been killed upon it by the indians."

On maps of the West the name Laramie is applied to the peak earlier than to the river. "Laramie Fork," as a legend on source maps, may have been misread by cartographers as "Laramie Peak." The first instance is Washington Hood's 1834 "Map of the Western Territory &c.," depicting "Larimers Peak" together with an unnamed Laramie River and a named Horse Creek. Two maps stemming from originals by Jedediah S. Smith are Albert Gallatin's (1836), showing "Lorimier's Peak," and David H. Burr's (1839), showing "Larimers Peak." Samuel Parker (1838) shows "Larama Fork" so as to suggest that all these peaks should have been forks instead. Frémont's first map (1843) named the stream Laramie River. After that the spelling became standardized.

Stewart refers in *Edward Warren* (pp. 157, 171) to "that finely shaped mountain, since [i.e., after 1834] called the Butte du Fort," or "the Fort Butte." *Les Côtes Noires*, or Black Hills, so called for their dark growth of conifers, persisted as the name for these hills south of the North Platte, though as early as July 22, 1842, Frémont made use of the expression "the Black or Laramie hills," while referring to "the lofty peak of Laramie mountain." The modern usage dates from 1870, when F. V. Hayden made a geological examination of the "Laramie Mountains, or Black Hills, as they are usually called." The change was helped along by a growing need to differentiate these Black Hills from those farther north, so known from very early times.

MAY 30, 1834.—This evening we arrived at the mouth of Laramee's Fork, where Capt. Sublette intends to erect a trader's fort. This is a bright, rapid stream of water, running out of the Black hills from the South. As soon as the fort is planned and commenced, we will resume our westward march. The Black hills are spurs of the great Rocky mountain range, and derive their name from the dark shadows which the cedar and pine growing upon their sides, forcibly suggest.

MAY 31, 1834.—This day we laid the foundation *log* of a fort, on Laramee's fork. A friendly dispute arose between our leader and myself, as to the name. He proposed to call it Fort Anderson, I insisted upon baptising it Fort Sublette, and holding the trump card in my hand, (a bottle of champagne) was about to claim the trick. Sublette stood by, cup reversed, still objecting, when Patton offered a compromise which was accepted, and the foam flew, in honor of Fort William, which contained the triad prenames of clerk, leader and friend.

MAY 31—See Introduction for a fuller discussion of the founding of Fort William. The Journal says: "This evening we arrived at Laramée's fork, where Mr Sublette designs erecting a trading fort—This is a very pretty, clear, rapid stream running out of the black hills from the south— As soon as the fort is planned & commenced, we shall resume our mountainward march—The Black hills are spurs of the Rocky Mountains, and are so called from the sparse growth of cedar & pine which give a dark appearance to their sides." The next entry reads: "Mr. Sublette left his clerk Mr Patton and 14 men to build the fort—reducing our number to twenty-three with which we recommence our still westward march." Later Anderson wrote between the lines that the fort "is to be called fort William, in honor Sublette & myself." Thus there is no suggestion that it reflected the name of Patton. Anderson is probably mistaken in saying in the Narrative that William was Patton's given name; see biographical sketches.

DIARY

JUNE 1, 1834.—*After calculating our days again, we found that our dates are in advance one day. We remained all the day yesterday [May 31] in our previous days encampment making arrangements for the fort builders. Mr Patton was left behind with 12 men, which reduces us to 23, to erect the works. I have at last reached the black hills. From the top of the highest eminence is distinctly visible the Rocky mountains. Some tracks of the grisly bear was seen this evening by some of the party. His majesty is yet to be seen by me. The fort on Laramy's fork is called J. William, in honour of its founder Mr S.*

JUNE 2, 1834.—*The mountains appeared to me to day in its most enchanting appearance. Nothing could more nearly resemble the glories of sun-set clouds than the metalic splendor of the mountains, substituting liquid silver for the accidental gold catching & retain-*

JUNE 1—Anderson this day lost a chance to straighten out his chronology. The Diary correctly observes that his dates up to this point were in advance one day; we have been able to establish that he reached the Laramie May 30, not May 31, and his dates have been corrected accordingly. It was on June 1 that Sublette left the Laramie, as is apparent from Anderson's comment that they remained "all the day yesterday" on the banks of the river, making arrangements for construction of the fort. We should note further that in the Diary, attempting to correct past mistakes, Anderson dated "May 31" both of the entries that we have redated May 30 and June 1. But he made a fresh error by overlooking the fact that the party had not moved on the true May 31. Thus from June 1 to June 18 his Diary entries are one day ahead of the true dates. We have corrected these further errors, supplying the correct dates for each entry.

The Diary says that Patton was left with 12 men while 23 went on, though on May 5 Anderson gave 37 as the total number of the party. Narrative and Journal do not help us in saying that Patton kept 14 men with him. On June 1 Wyeth "found 13 of Sublettes men camped for the purpose of building a fort." Three free trappers who had traveled out with Wyeth remained at the Laramie River to hunt beaver; Cyrus Shepard gives their names as Shanks, Sutton, and Oliver. Jason Lee adds that the three "left us here with the intention to catch Beaver in the Black Hills and thus they expose themselves their lives yea they run greater risks for a few Beaver skins than we do to save souls and yet some who call themselves Christians 'tell it not in Gath' would have persuaded us to abandon our enterprize because of the *danger* which attended it. . . ." See also the comment by Townsend.

Anderson describes rather vaguely his journey on to the crossing of the North Platte. The Wyeth party was only a half day behind (having nooned at the crossing of the Laramie on June 1). Wyeth camped, on the 1st, some 8 miles up the North Platte from its confluence with the Laramie. On June 2 he "Made along the river 5 miles then struck out into the hills about W. N. W. and made 12 miles to a little creek in the afternoon made 13 miles to pretty large creek and camped for the night the whole course this day about W. N. W." The first 5 miles would have been to the mouth of Warm Spring Canyon (up which the later [and earlier?] wagon road turned); the little creek beyond was probably Cottonwood Creek, and the "pretty large creek" doubtless Horseshoe Creek, the distances overestimated. If Sublette did not reach Horseshoe Creek on June 1, he must have traveled as far as Cottonwood Creek. Like Anderson, Jason Lee says on June 2, "Begun to see the snow-caped Mountains which to me are a most welcome sight."

JUNE 2—This day's travel can be followed only by reference to the diaries of the Wyeth party. On June 3 Wyeth made 15 miles northwest by north to noon on the river, crossing over the hills about half the way; then in the afternoon rode "6 miles cutting two very bad blufs but still fol-

JUNE 1-2, 1834—Leaving Patton and fourteen men to finish the job, we started upwards. From the top of the Black hills I got my first view of the Rocky Mountains—the snow covered mountains. My eyes have been fastened upon them all day, and at night I am not sobered, I must pen down my mind bubbles. My first thought, or feeling rather, was, Oh, ye toppling crags of ice, "summoned by the desperate Manfred," to crush him! Wherein are ye more terrific, more magnificently grand! See towering up to Heaven, the Kremlin of the winter God! Pillars and arches of gold and silver, with the rose dyed glories of the setting sun, flashing from tower to tower. There, palaces and pyramids of christal pierce the skies, and all around mansions of parian purity, spotless and white as virgin souls. Other portions of the range, not entirely wrapped in snow, were ever changing in form and color, whilst the summits were sporting with broad blades of light, the center was darkened by moving clouds, which like mighty billows surged onward and upward, or rolled back with resistless power, as if to tear the giant Oregon from its base. To me these mimic battles of clouds and mountains are supremely grand, and whether serious thoughts or wild imaginings, I write them down.

In six or seven hundred miles of weary travel, we have seen no trees, save here and there a cotton wood, near the banks, or on some island of the Platte. [To a forest-born Kentuckian, they are scarcely more entitled to the name of trees than a hemp stalk.]

Marvels, they say, will never cease, but the marvels of marvels is now before me. This muddy, slow and sleepy Platte—this water cheat, which, for so many days, we have seen floating downward, impelled only by its own weight—is here, one of the mightiest elements of the earth. It has come rushing with resistless power, over barriers of granite rock, and bursting and breaking through the Black hills, leaving perpendicular walls of eight [four] hundred feet on either side. I feel assured I shall never forget the grand spectacle, or cease to wonder at the change. I shall also mark this day with a white pebble, for another cause: I killed one of those fleetest of fast animals, the antelope. Moore calls it "the silver-footed Antelope." Those of our deserts are decidedly ebon-footed [& horned].

*ing the golden hues and dolphin dies of the changeable clouds &
making them her own. The mountain peaks are glittering with
snow, in the month of June, towering above the clouds, the middle
shadowed by these overhanging messengers of moisture, the lower
parts alone, showing the real composition of these enormous piles of
stone. All in all, tis a scene neither for the pencil, pen or chisel, but
far beyond the power of all to describe. Here and there were percieved deep black veins or chasms produced by the scraggy pines
which grow most sparsly on its sides. For the last thousand miles the
hills and eminences have been equally destitute of timber as the
plains. A few cotton-wood trees sprinkled ça et la on the waters edge,
is a most delightful sight. On the Platte again to night. To day I beheld the Platte, hitherto, a very shallow powerless stream, bursting through the black hills and leaving the perpendicular walls of
stone some four hundred & fifty feet above its channel. How it got
throug[h] I can no more tell than could Mr. Jefferson account for
the Potomac's release from its rocky prison. I think and hope I shall
never forget its appearance. Tis grand & beautiful—I killed an antelope, that most active and graceful of animals. The silvery footed
antelope, as Moore calls them. Mine was ebon footed.*

JUNE 3, 1834.—*We have marched since, we left the fort on Laramy,
N. N. W. crossed the Platte this morning—nothing strinkingly
strange, or at the least differing from what we see here every day.*

lowing the river." Jason Lee adds helpful details: "Started early this morning and came 15 m. before we could find grass and dined on the bank of the Platte. Started down [up] the bank of the
River under the Bluff but could not find a pass and were obliged [to] ascend the Hill and make
our way for some miles over hills and through ravines by far worse than any we have passed before." The morning travel brought Wyeth to the North Platte, east-southeast of present Orin, near
the site of the later "James Bridger Ferry." In the afternoon Wyeth rode west to a point a mile or
two east of the mouth of Labonte Creek, reached by the Sublette party the previous afternoon.
Here Sublette on June 3, and Wyeth on June 4, forded the North Platte. This trail must have been
used earlier, but we have no record. Possibly low water in 1834 encouraged Sublette to cross the
river farther down, instead of at the customary ford near the Red Buttes. To reach that ford, the
usual trail kept to the foothills of the Laramie Mountains, so as to avoid the bluffs and steep banks
of the creeks near their entrance into the North Platte. The trail left the river a few miles above
Fort William because of the deep canyons through which the North Fork of the Platte flows between present Glendo and Wendover, but when Anderson says he has seen the river flowing under
perpendicular walls of stone hundreds of feet high, he probably refers to the escarpment opposite
Labonte and Wagon Hound creeks, immediately west of the camp of June 2.

JUNE 3—Wyeth says on June 4: "Forded the river and made W. N. W. 17 miles along the river
and camped on it Sublette one day ahead." Jason Lee adds, "This morning forded the North Fork
of the Platte with safety scarcely wetting a bail which is seldom known to be fordable at this
season." Shepard's account is the most detailed: "After breakfast prepared to cross the main branch

JUNE 3, 1834.—We have crossed the Platte this morning. Our course is now about N. N. W. Rather deep fording; an inch or two more in this mixture of sand and water and we should have had a swimming match of up and down. We are having the variety of "always partridge," we decamp and camp again, precisely as we have done, for many and many a day. Had I to travel for weeks and months, over "these deserts idle," without hearing thunder, or seeing snakes, I might follow the example of that smart fellow who cut his throat, because disgusted with the everlasting dullness of putting on and pulling off his breeches.

---

of the Platte—The current is strong and rapid, the channel in some places deep and difficult—We were all however safe on the oposite side in about two hours with but little difficulty. . . . Had now to move forward over a tract of sandy and barren land, bounded on one side by the Platte and on the other by huge bluffs composed of a sort of hard clay sandstone sand and gravel—These rugged acclivities by the successive washing of the rains of heaven have assumed almost all shapes and appearances. . . . P. M. Crossed some high difficult bluffs covered with iron ore of the richest quality and also through deep ravines all which through good fortune we passed in safety and encamped early on the Platte. . . ." Sublette may have covered the same ground on the 3rd, making Wyeth's estimated 17 miles.

JUNE 4, 1834.—*Our course to day, is again nearly west. The prairies here are dry & sandy, grass very short and interspersed with wild sage which resembles very much the garden sage but is exceedingly bitter. We see every day, Indian forts, which are made of wood piled up in a circular form about as high as a man's head. Sometimes they are planted upright leaving crevices through which they send their missiles in defence of themselves and stolen property. Saw to day the tracks of two grisly bear—Our encampment to night is a little less than a days march from the red 'butes', the usual place of crossing to the N. side of the Platte; these are hills standing detached from their neighbours & compeers. I found upon a high piece of ground the most perfect piece of petrifaction I remember to have seen. It is a part of a tree, most probably cedar or ash, as the course grain is distinctly visible.*

JUNE 5, 1834.—*Direction to day a little N. of W. We have made about 25 miles. Not yet to the Butes. We leave the Platte this morning. We are moving on the N. bank of the river, where wild roses of a delicious fragrance is freighting the air with sweets while the tops of the mountains are glittering with snow. The indians are expected to pounce upon us every day & every minute. If they are to come I would that they come quickly. I dislike of all things, suspense.*

JUNE 4—Anderson does not estimate the day's travel. Wyeth on the 5th "Made along the river 24 miles."

JUNE 5—Anderson now gives us an estimate of the day's march, 25 miles, which compares with Wyeth's estimated 24 miles "W by N" on the 6th. Lee and Shepard note a weather change from warm to cool during the night. Shepard says, "wind very blustering on getting up found all the tents prostrated on the ground except ours and that threatening to fall every moment. . . ." The wind, Lee remarks, made the day's march disagreeable; and Shepard notes that the sand over which they traveled, "being agitated by the movement of the animals and wind, proved quite unpleasant to the organs of vision." Anderson's forecast in his Diary, "We leave the Platte this morning," was a mistake, corrected in the Narrative.

JUNE 4, 1834.—We are traveling [today] due west. The prairie change has been from sandy to clear sand, and the moist, green grass of the river shore has become a dry and yellow hay. The wild sage, or Artemisia, is now the common growth. It is a sapless, bitter shrub, and the leaves, though smaller, very much resemble our garden sage. [Tho very bitter, it is sometimes used for tea. Tis a very good diaphoretick.]

Since we reached the Black hills we are becoming acquainted with trees again. We occasionally pass Indian lodges, laid out in the quadrangular, or fort-form, made of saplings or large branches stuck in the ground and brought together at the top as a cone. Being of fresh ever-greens, they are pretty, and difficult to discover, when placed among, or in front of a thick grove. [They are cones, forward of the trunks of trees leaning against each other, and having shoot holes through which to tickle their visiters.]

I saw, to-day, the tracks of a grizzly bear, and the Irishman's remark about his game cock, (the duck) came to my mind: "Jasus, what a fut! but all hell couldn't up trup him!" I examined the most perfect petrifaction, I ever saw. It was almost a log, of either cedar or ash. The grain and bark was very wood-like.

JUNE 5, 1834.—Our direction is a little north of west, and we have, perhaps, made the distance of twenty-five miles. We are still a little short of the Red Buttes, the usual crossing-place, where the Platte is left for the Sweetwater, one of its tributaries. We have now a change, and that change the odd variety of roses, rattlesnakes and snow-covered mountains. With a wild flower in my lips, I have killed the diamond-coated tempter of mother Eve, and in sight of the Alps of America.

We are all keeping a very sharp look-out. [I have been afraid of loosing my hair for two days.] The signs indicate that "Yellow-jackets" are near, and we must take good care of our hair. Any hour, any minute, they may be here. This is no joke. These fellers wouldn't come to beg—they mean business. I wish it was all over, and we were all safe at the rendezvous. Sublette says I had better keep wide awake, as my white scalp would be prized as "big medicine." I confess I do not breathe freely yet. It would have been difficult to keep a better watch than I did last night. No wolf trotted in the moon-light; no elk whistled on the hill that I did not see and hear. But,

JUNE 6, 1834.—*10 o'clock in the morning. We have reached the Butes for breakfast. These are hills seperated from their fellows, as the term signifies—They are side-bound with red stones and earth. In their shape there is nothing singular or beautiful—On the divide, as it is called, of the Platte and its tributary the sweet-water, there is a most beautiful & extensive view. The mountains, on the yellow stone, snow capt are within reach of the unaided sight. I passed this evening an old encampment of Gordon's where he and Brown tarried 20 or 30 days. I have seen ten bands of buffaloe at a time—still they have not equalled my expectations. Our course to day is about S. W. We camp to night at a lovely little spring. The waters of the mountains are clear, cool & delightful. There is here so little dew that putrifaction or decomposition occurs very slowly. I have seen the skin, yet upon a buffaloe's head, which had been dead a year & more, perhaps. The mornings & evenings are quite cool. I regret very much my almost* total *inability to take home specimens of minerals. There are hereabouts very singular & beautiful ones.*

JUNE 6—From Anderson's Diary entry on the return journey, August 16, it appears that on arrival at the Red Buttes he carved his name on a tree, with the mistaken date June 5. This might account for Wyeth's entry of June 7: "Made 12 miles along the river to the red Butes so called and is the place at which the river turns S. W. and we leave to strike for Sweet Water Sublette 2 days ahead." Shepard says Wyeth's encampment, reached about noon, was "on a small island in the Platte oposite to the red bukes." Townsend comments: "In the afternoon, we arrived at the 'Red Butes', two or three brown-red cliffs, about two thousand feet in height. This is a remarkable point in the mountain route. One of these cliffs terminates a long, lofty, wooded ridge, which has bounded our southern view for the past two days. The summits of the cliffs are covered with patches of snow, and the contrast of the dazzling white and brick-red produces a very pretty effect."

The Red Buttes, 15 miles southwest of present Casper, Wyoming, denote the point where the North Platte rounds Casper Mountain after its long northward course from North Park. No "mountains of the Yellowstone" are visible from this locality. Possibly Anderson was viewing the Rattlesnake Mountains immediately to the west.

The reference to Gordon and Brown is not clear, but we have offered suggestions in the biographical sketches. The incident to which Anderson refers must have occurred no later than 1831. Sublette's camp must have been at the Willow Spring, the only watering place Anderson could have thought "lovely" or "beautiful." Gordon and Brown's encampment (again referred to on August 15) must have been on another of the sources of Willow Creek or on the creek itself, where they could have waited in greater security from passing Indians.

whatever I feel or fear, I keep to myself. [I bear as bold a front as the best of them—and I believe I shall fight as well too if it comes to it, but I don't wish for it I am not bloodthirsty.] Perhaps, if it comes to the worst, I shall do as the rest—fight or run. I know one thing, however, I don't wan't to be "tried and found" missing.

JUNE 6, 1834.—[10 o'clock A.M. at the red buttes and my scalp still on. I confess that I don't breathe loud yet.] We have breakfasted in front of the long-wished-for Buttes. They are two isolated hills, covered with a lake-colored earth or paint [as it seemed to me from the distance at which I saw them]. The stones hereabouts are impregnated with the same reddish matter. From the divide of the Platte and the Sweetwater, we have a distant, yet beautiful view of the snow-capped mountains of the Yellowstone. Far off, snow-covered mountains have very much the appearance of long banks of white clouds, from which they can only be distinguished by their brightness, for as the negroes say, "dey do shine like any glissen."

We have passed by the hiding place of [W.] Gordon and Brown, who stayed here [some] twenty days, watching for white men. There are immense numbers of buffalo in sight, and yet they do not come up to my expectations, as I can see the ground in many places. We are now living like fighting cocks. Here I am, at a beautiful spring, my skewer in the ground, at a hot fire of buffalo dung, a set of good, sweet hump-ribs roasting before me, legs crossed, knife drawn, and mouth watering, waiting for the attack. At just such a time I have forgotten home, Indians, everything but my ribs and my sweetheart, and but for hope and the association I think she, too, would have been put behind me. These clear mountain springs are charming places. They do so sweetly wash down a savory meal of buffalo meat. And is such meat really good? What a question to a hungry man! Ask a Catholic if he loves or believes in the Virgin Mary. At this elevation, where there is little or no dew, there is scarcely any animal putrefaction. I have seen the skin and flesh on the skull of a buffalo when the bone itself was nearly decayed [the animal had been dead for years]. These June mornings are so cold that I am compelled to ride, first upon one hand and then the other, to get them warm. The country around here is sparkling with bright and beautiful pebbles. I wish I knew what they are.

JUNE 7, 1834—*This morning there was a large frost. This is usual at all seasons. I saw to day, the earth covered for a half mile, with a white robe, resembling at a distance, lime, when closely viewed, is very similar to burnt alumn. This is on an average, three inches in depth. Its taste to me is compound of salt, some kind of alkali & salt petre of which last it seems to me to be principally composed. It is call[ed] by the mountaineers glober salts. It has a purgative effect of great suddenness. A little further on is a lake of the same basis of nearly three hundred yards by two hundred. Providence has made its wild animals, independent on man, in more ways than one. For several days I have seen, & travelled over the salt weed—a vegetable, which in some regions grows in great plenty and of which the buffaloe and other quadrapeds are very fond, particularly in the winter. Breakfasted at a very large rock on sweet-water river, called "The Rock Independence["] from the fact of eighty traders & trapers having kept the 4th of July in due style. I thought, when I looked upon its granite sides, that if our union & Indepen[den]ce coexisted*

JUNE 7—Anderson gives us the earliest description of the subsequently well-known "saleratus lakes," where emigrants shoveled up saleratus pure enough for use as baking powder. The lakes are situated 15½ miles from Willow Spring, 5 miles northeast of Independence Rock. There were other such deposits west of Devils Gate.

Anderson's remarks help to establish the year Independence Rock was named. Many travelers, like John Bidwell in 1841 and Matthew Field in 1843, noted that the name originated when William L. Sublette camped at the rock on July 4 with a mountain-bound caravan, but the exact year has not been determined. On July 23, 1843, while traveling in company with Sublette, Field commented, "The Rock was named by Col. Wm. L. Sublette, on the 4th of July 1831." (But Sublette on that day was arriving at Santa Fe with a caravan.) In his homeward-bound diary, Aug. 28, 1843, Field copied a number of inscriptions from the rock, including "Wm L. Sublette, with Moses Harris, on express, Jan. 1827, again on July 4th, 1841 [another mistake; Sublette was not in the Rockies that year] when the rock was christened—and again with us, July 22nd & Aug. 12 [sic] 1843." The year 1827 must be ruled out because the mountain-bound party of that year had reached Bear Lake by July 3. There was no caravan in the summer of 1828, which leaves only the years 1829 and 1830. In 1829 Sublette guided to the Rockies a party said to have numbered about 54 men; but in 1830, when he took his ten wagons to Wind River, he had 81 in company, a close match for Anderson's figure in the Diary. (Asahel Munger on June 25, 1839, commented, "This rock is called Independence from the fact that in 1830 the American Fur co. [sic] spent the 4th of July here and celebrated the day.")

Historians have been slow to accept an 1830 date because Ferris' narrative of his journey to the Rockies that year commented on June 13, "It bears the name of Rock Independence, from the circumstance of a party having several years ago passed a fourth of July, with appropriate festivities, under its ample shade." However, Ferris wrote up his experiences after leaving the mountains in 1835. Most early travelers, except Myra Eells on June 14, 1838, and John Bidwell on July 5, 1841, wrote "Rock Independence" rather than "Independence Rock"; so Anderson's usage has historical priority. F. V. Hayden measured the rock by odometer in 1870, finding it 1,552 yards in circumference.

Anderson does not say whether he left his own name on the rock. If not, he must have supplied the mistaken date of arrival afforded by his Diary, for Wyeth wrote on June 9, "Made S. W. 10 miles and made Rock Independence on which W. L. Sublette had noted that he had arrived on the

JUNE 7, 1834.—Jack Frost, how do you do? I am like "John Anderson, my Jo," with his frosty pow. My head is whiter than usual this morning. The ground is covered [for a half inch] with a white robe, all around a lake, which is about three hundred yards long by one hundred wide, and the exudation forms a fringe of one half mile, extending every way from the water's edge. The trappers call this "Glauber Salts Lake." [I have no means to test it. It has a sudden purgative effect.] It seems that luxuries, necessaries, and apothecary stuff are spread all over the earth, as well for the irrational as for the rational creature. And here comes in the salt weed. It is a short, withered looking plant, with small leaves, which are strongly saline, as if they had been steeped in brine. In the fall of the year, wild horses and buffalo are very fond of it, and it is said that in the winter the meat of all browsing animals is naturally and sufficiently seasoned by it.

We have breakfasted this morning at the base of Rock Independence [a very large and uncommon looking rock]. There are few places better known or more interesting to the mountaineer than

6th but I think he could not have done so before the 7th." As we now see, Wyeth was correct. Nevertheless, because he had made only a short march to the Red Buttes on June 7, Wyeth had lost another day. At Independence Rock Wyeth "noted my name then made S. W. along the creek 4½ miles to a place where the creek puts through cut rocks each side perpendicular and about 60 feet high [Devils Gate] the trail goes through another place on a level and about 100 feet South of the river the rock intervening then made 6 miles W. S. W. between mountains but on a level and along the creek." From Anderson's Diary for August 14 we learn that Sublette camped on June 7 a little above Devils Gate, not far from Wyeth's camp of June 9.

Despite his doubts that Sublette could be three days ahead, Wyeth was sufficiently troubled on June 9 to write "Mess Thomas Fitzpatric & Co": "Gent. I send this to inform you of my approach with your goods. I am now two days behind Wm Sublette, who I presume is with you by [the time you read] this. Milton informed me that you would rendesvous near the mouth of the Sandy. In case you do not I wish you would immediately inform me by express. I am now one days march above rock Independence and shall continue to come on at a good rate and for the present follow the same route which I came by two years since. I wish that you would defer making any contract for carrying home any surplus furs that you have or for a further supply of goods untill I come as I have sent a vessell to the mouth of the Columbia with such goods as you want and am ready to give you a supply for winter rendesvous if you wish, or for next year, and also to send home by her, at a low rate, such furs as you may have and can make you advances in St. Louis on them to pay men &c." Jason Lee tells us on June 10, "The Capt. sent an express to the Redevous this morning." On June 16, by which time the company had reached the Big Sandy, Lee notes, "The Capt. has heard nothing from his express nor from Rendesvous." Two days later, when nearly at Green River, Lee observes that the man sent on express had returned.

The origin of the name of the Sweetwater River (in the Diary) is veiled in obscurity. Two explanations became current, that the river was so called for the freshness of its waters; and that at some early date a mule lost a load of sugar in fording the stream. French versions of both names were early seen, *Eau Douce* and *Eau Sucrée*. The sugar explanation seems improbable, for William H. Ashley's diary uses Sweetwater as an established name in April 1825, up to which time Ashley himself had not seen the river, and no loads of sugar are likely to have then reached its banks. The earliest use of the name is David Thompson's on his maps of "The Oregon Territory," *with it, t'would have a brevet of immortality. The stone is about a mile in circumference; its shape is like an egg divided length wise—without an ounce of earth & consequently, destitute of all vegetation. Tis alone and independent on all the mountains around. We ascend this beautiful stream for four days—All the streams of this country, are as clear as cristal, and most excellent to taste.*

JUNE 8, 1834.—We are keeping a sharp look out for the 'Sauvages'. We have seen no sign but this is the region where they do their deeds of darkness. This morning I saw the distant snow clad summits of the Wind-river, or Sits-ca-dee mountains. This indeed was a lovely scene. I have heard of the ice castles of the north; I doubt not, in the least, that this equals or surpasses it. Tis like the purest and most fantastic white clouds of heaven, but more brilliant, not one dark spot to mar the charm and loveliness of the scene.

---

now in the British Museum. On these maps, drawn sometime between 1814 and 1824, and incorporating information obtained from the overland Astorians of 1811, Thompson named the Sweetwater and creditably depicted its general course, except for connecting it up with the Cheyenne rather than with the North Platte (see Carl I. Wheat, *Mapping the Transmississippi West*, II, 106-107, maps reproduced opposite pp. 98 and 99). The Astorians never laid eyes on the Sweetwater, so perhaps they got the name from the Crows—or perhaps the name became known after 1807 to Manuel Lisa's trappers, ranging south from Lisa's post at the mouth of the Big Horn.

JUNE 8—In the Narrative Anderson gives the translation of the Crow name for Green River, of which there were various spellings. Mountain men preferred the musical name Siskadee Agie to Green River or Rio Verde, a name applied at a fairly early date by Spanish traders coming up from New Mexico. The Wind River Mountains, as part of the Continental Divide, separate the waters of the Green from those of the Big Horn. Soon after white observers entered the region the mountains became known by their present name. Anderson's entry for August 13 shows that this night's camp was just below the locality later known to emigrants as the Three Crossings of the Sweetwater. On the cliffs of this narrow passage Anderson saw his mountain sheep (bighorns) on the morning of the 9th.

this huge boulder. Here they look for and often obtain information of intense interest to them. On the side of the rock names, dates and messages, written in buffalo-grease and powder, are read and re-read with as much eagerness as if they were letters in detail from long absent friends. Besides being a place of advertisement, or kind of trappers' post office, it possesses a reputation and a fame peculiar to itself. It is a large, egg-shaped mass of granite, entirely separate and apart from all other hills, or ranges of hills [upon a dead level plain]. One mile in circumference, and about six or seven hundred feet high, without a particle of vegetation, and with no change known but the varying sparkles of mica which are seen by the light of the sun by day and the moon by night. Some years ago, a party of buffalo killers and beaver skinners celebrated here our national jubilee on the great Fourth of July. What noise, what roar of powder and pomp of patriotism surrounded and echoed from this eternal monument my informant did not say, nor can I imagine. I shall suppose the immortal Declaration was talked over, Washington toasted, and Rock Independence baptised into the old confederacy. [In silence I laid upon my back gazing upon its grey granite sides—I breathed the prayer, that my country's *Union* & Independence might be co-existent with that Rock.]

JUNE 8, 1834.—[We are all on the qui vive for the red men—We have discovered no fresh signs, but this is the region of their dark doings, and we might as well, both watch and pray.] We are now in a very dangerous region, and our motto is, or should be, "watch and pray." There is a great deal of the first done, I know, and very little of the latter, I suspect.

Oh, lovely beyond all loveliness is the setting sun, gilding the snow-capped peaks of the Seets-ca-dee! But hold! scribbler! leave something in your inkstand! I must, indeed, for having exhausted all my superlatives, unless I resort to pure invention, I have nothing to add to the description of the Black Hill view. In apology for that night's overflow, I have this to say: I had never been more than fifty miles from home, was on very high ground, and had been reading Phillips' speeches for twenty days. Seets-ca-dee is called by some Mount of the Winds, but means, in the Crow language, Prairie Cock. They call Green River Seets-ca-dee Azh-ee, or Prairie Cock River.

DIARY

JUNE 9, 1834—*Nothing occurred to day worthy of notice, except that I saw five or six mountain sheep, high in air. There was one lamb pointed out to me, but five or six hundred perpendicular feet made them all seem lambs in size.*

JUNE 10, 1834—*This morning, a few seconds after discovering horses tracks we found a letter upon a stick from one L. Vasques who had been long unheard of & of whom alarming apprehensions were entertained. Yesterday & to day, the before mentioned mountains continued to appear as beautiful, and even more so than usual. Their congregated heighths so purely, spotlessly white, seemed like castles of Parian marble fit for angels mansions. Alas! like all sublunary beauties to which distance lends enchantment, these suburbs of heaven are now but barren rock with patches of snow. To morrow, with clean feet I shall tread upon the soil of Trans montane America. To day I drink of the waters of the Atlantic, to morrow I quench my thirst from those of the Peaceful ocean.*

JUNE 10—Sublette's camp on the 9th, as we learn from Anderson's entry for August 12, was in the locality of "Fitzpatrick's Cache," just below the mouth of Sweetwater Canyon, where the present Sand Creek (the Alkali Creek of Hayden's map) reaches the Sweetwater from the south. From the reminiscences of James Clyman, it is known that the party led by Jedediah S. Smith and Thomas Fitzpatrick sheltered at this point for several weeks in February 1824, caching many of their goods before making the spring hunt farther west, a trip that resulted in the effective discovery of South Pass. In June 1824 Smith and Fitzpatrick returned from their trapping grounds on the waters of the Green to rendezvous at this cache. The application of Fitzpatrick's name to the locality, however, may date from a later period. Fitzpatrick is known to have cached furs in the vicinity in 1832 and 1833, and it may be that the caches were all in the same locality, the site having proved favorable. (A clay bank was preferred, impervious to the water that might ruin the contents of a cache, as noted by Warren Ferris when Drips and Fontenelle cached goods in this area in 1830.)

The Journal says, in reference to Louis Vasquez: "a letter was found affixed to a twig, at the mouth of a 'cache' of Fitzpatrick's, which to Mr. Sublettes great delight was from one Lew. Vasquez—He had long been unheard of and it was feared that he had been killed." During the fall and winter Vasquez had been trading for Sublette & Campbell among the Crows, operating out of the fort at the mouth of the Yellowstone. There might have been some worry for his safety, in view of the fact that in September 1833 the Crows had robbed Fitzpatrick and Stewart. After a successful trade, Vasquez had come back to the fort on the Yellowstone and with ten men had set out again at the end of February. From Anderson's subsequent entry of August 31, we infer that Vasquez spent some time in the spring of 1834 with Long Hair's Crows; and from a letter Vasquez wrote his brother from Hams Fork on July 9, 1834, we learn that during the spring he was attacked by Blackfeet and lost two men.

JUNE 9, 1834.—I have seen the Big-horns, or Rocky mountain sheep. Passing through a narrow gorge [a very narrow defile where stupendous mountains of rock jut^d almost over the stream] they were pointed out, peeping at us from their unapproachable towers. I could not see the lamb which others saw, but to me they all seemed lambs, viewed through the gloom or dwarfed by their great elevation.

JUNE 10, 1834.—This morning, shortly after starting, fresh horse tracks were discovered. We followed them up and found a letter sticking in a twig near Fitzpatrick's "Cache." When Sublette read it and made known the contents there was a shout of joy from the whole company. It was from Lew. Vasquez, a great favorite of the mountaineers, who had almost been given up for lost. This letter was his resurrection. He was much talked of to-day, and always praised. One old trapper said "thank God he lives, and I shall hear his merry laugh again."

For two days the magnificent rivers [spectacle] of the Seets-cadee have rather increased than diminished. The congregated summits form themselves into cities, towns, and castles, bright and beautiful, as if built of spotless marble. Such they seemed but yesterday—to-day how changed! Their glories have faded away, and we see nothing now but immense masses of a dull dead stone; nature's rough ashlers, cracked and fissured into every size and form of angle, quadrangle and parallelogram.

To-day I drink of the waters which flow into the Atlantic; to-morrow I shall quench my thirst from fountains which send their tributes to the Ocean of Peace. We have had a restless, sleepless, and unhappy night. My anxiety is particularly great. Our hunter and young Walker, the grand-son of Major Christy, of St. Louis, have not returned, and serious fears are entertained. I have ascended all the highest hills, and eminences around, to look for them. Our guns have all been discharged, but no response, no sign.

DIARY

JUNE 11, 1834—*Last evening, our hunter & a youth belonging to our company, young Walker, became belated and lost. We fired several times for them, after we encamped for the night, but it did not produce the desired effect. I think I never passed a more anxious night. The Black-feet were present to all of our minds. To day about 11 o'clock we found them some twelve miles distant. In consequence of the aforesaid circumstance we did not pass from Oriental to Occidental America until late this evening. Tis strange what unbidden & chaotic masses of thought crouded upon my mind at the instant. I have not the regulating* fiat *to reduce all this confusion into order. I have now crossed to the eastern side of the snow crowned [valley of the] Seitskadee, from whence rises & flows to the rival oceans the Seitskadee, alias Sandy, alias Colorado of the west, the Columbia for the Pacific—the Platte & Yellow-Stone tributaries of the Mississippi flowing into the Atlantic. But of the first puddle hole of Pacific water, I saw two unpacific creatures, white wolves, start. The different names which the mountain & stream now in sight, are thus translated—Seitski or ka-dee is in the Crow tongue, prairie cock—upon which there are great numbers of that bird. Colorado or rayo—is spanish and means green river, Sandy, which requires no interpretation to those who have seen this river. These are all characteristic names whichever prevails.*

JUNE 11—Leonidas Walker's misadventure is recorded as follows in the Journal: "I spent last night in a state of mental anxiety not to be described, on account of the absence of two of our party, our hunter and a young man by the name of Walker, a grand son of my father's old friend Majr. Christy of St. Louis—I ascended all the hills around our camp to look out for them, we discharged all the guns in camp successively, and laid down at a late hour to dream of Black-feet and bloodshed—With heavy hearts we commenced our onward march, fearing their loss yet anxiously examining every quarter of the horison for the sight of them. At 11 o.clock, to our great gratification we discovered them, about twelve miles from our camp."

Anderson this day crossed South Pass. The name Colorado is indeed Spanish, as noted in the Diary, but means red, not green. The fitting name Sandy was applied to the well-known affluent of the Green by Ashley in 1825, but not to the Green itself. The "first puddle hole of Pacific water" was the boggy area later famous as Pacific Springs.

JUNE 11, 1834—We laid down, late at night, almost in despair, thinking of Blackfeet and bloodshed. Every quarter of the horizon had been scanned, when just as the most sanguine was about to surrender hope, they were discovered about twelve miles ahead, quietly waiting for us. This evening, with the sun, we passed from the Eastern to Western America. From the base of the Seets-ca-dee, or Mount of Winds, whose cold top is perennially clothed in snow, arises the many-named river of Seets-ca-dee, or Sandy, or Green, or Rio Colorado, whose waters flow into the Pacific; from neighboring fountains spring the Platte and the Yellow-stone tributaries of the mighty Atlantic. Yesterday, from a scarcely perceptible elevation, we could distinctly see waters flowing east and west, which enter far, far away into the two rival oceans of this continent.

JUNE 12, 1834—*This morning we were surprised by the fire of a gun. We sent out spies, caught up and picketed down our horses. The cry of "catch up, catch up,["] at such a time causes great bustle, excitement & confusion in a camp. The spies saw nothing and we recommenced our travels, but with great circumspection. Camped this night on another and a larger branch of Sandy. Never was a name more appropriately bestowed than "Rocky Mountains,["] to this chain of the N. American Andes. Masses of enormous nude stones. The colour & appearance of the stone, is that of demi-dryed mud, cracked by the sun, into immensely large slabs. It seems to me to be a composite, when broken it sparkles with various coloured pebbles & dyed with a chalybeate hue. I have seen large hills of iron-ore joined to & making a part of a chain of mountains. The whole face of the country from the red-butes on the Platte to sweet water, & from thence, to the main Seitskidee is sand, nothing but sand.*

JUNE 12—The day's journey took the company to the Big Sandy, near its confluence with the Little Sandy. Knowing the country, Sublette was heading straight for the Green River, near the mouth of the Sandy. Wyeth, coming along behind, lost Sublette's trail on the other side of South Pass and, as we see under date of June 18, wandered a good deal on the upper Sandy before reaching the Green.

The dark-colored vein remarked by Anderson attracted the attention of many early travelers, including Frémont in 1842 and Stansbury in 1849. When Anderson speaks of "Sweetwater Canon" in the Narrative, he refers to Devils Gate, a name not yet in use; see his entry for August 14. F. V. Hayden, examining the Devils Gate formation in 1870, commented, "These granite ranges are not unfrequently banded with old trap dikes, trending about northeast and southwest and varying in width from a few feet to two or three hundred feet" (*U. S. Geological Survey of Wyoming*, p. 31). Anderson's reference to iron ore is the more interesting in that in 1962 the United States Steel Corporation began large-scale iron-mining operations near Atlantic City, Wyoming.

JUNE 12, 1834—This morning about sunrise a gun was heard. It was but a moment's work to have all the horses driven in and picketed down. [Mr.] Sublette was soon upon the highest butte, spy-glass in hand; but discovering nothing we took up our line of march. If each man had not as many eyes as Argus he did not sleep with those he had. It was, perhaps, a false alarm, or some little volcanic puff, from the bowels of the mountains. These are emphatically Rocky mountains, accurately so named. Enormous piles of various colored granite, now dark and dull, now grey and sparkling. One time we see immense round boulders, then huge slabs, vertical, horizontal and slanting. Near the Sweetwater Canon, (pronounced as the last syllable of onion) there is a large vein of iron-ore which passes entirely through the spur of the mountain. The face of the country from the Red Buttes on the Platte to the Sweetwater, and from thence to the main Colorado, is barren in the extreme; it is sand and nothing but sand. In fact, except the bottoms, margining the streams up which we traveled from the Kaw west there is no soil visible. It is one immense desert; a true American "Sahara." If Providence has suffered civilized man to come here at all, it must have been *per gratia*, for surely such a waste and barren region could only have been intended for the gregarious prairie dog, or the migratory buffalo. [Camped tonight on a larger branch of the Sandy.]

JUNE 13, 1834—*Travelled to the main Seitskidee. Despatched two men over to Horse creek, to look for the companies. Since we reached the waters of the Pacific, we have journeyed a S. W. & S. S. W. direction sometimes directly South. Never was there a purer and more elastic atmosphere than we have been in for 16 or 20 days. I have not seen a piece of putrified flesh since I arrived upon the Platte. In truth our meats, spread out on our packs, are perfectly sweet and good five days after being butchered. The nights are beautiful and the moon & stars of clearer, brighter light than I ever saw elsewhere. I seriously believe in the country over which I have marched since I passed the Kansas there is not the average of a tree to a hundred miles. In 1200 miles I have not seen a hundred acres of timber in one place. The whole arborification consists of a few cotton wood and willows along the creeks. Even the hills and mountains are, most generally, destitute of everything of the kind, even scraggy cedars and pine. Black hawk is here, thin & jaded, tis to be confessed, but still able & I believe willing to bear me to the Pacific. Little Dick, my mother and sister often occupy my mind. God bless them, & improve me! Reached the point designed to be our haven of rest, when we left the settlements thirty seven days ago. I do not think the distance as great by two or three hundred miles to St Louis as is generally estimated. Six of Fontenelle & Dripps trapers came to us this evening They seemed really to be delighted to see the whites. No wonder, for they had been separated from their companions since last fall.*

JUNE 13—Sublette must have struck the Green about 6 or 8 miles above the mouth of the Big Sandy. Anderson says that for better grass on June 15 they moved a mile higher up, then on June 18 went "a few miles up the river." Here Wyeth found the camp located 12 miles above the mouth of the Sandy. As the vicinity of Horse Creek had been the scene of rendezvous in 1833, Sublette sent his express there to seek out the fur companies. For the operations of Drips and Fontenelle during the previous year, see the biographical sketches of these men.

Anderson wrote in the Narrative, but not in the Diary or Journal, of the "pair of pretty blue eyes" we suppose to have been Eliza McArthur's.

JUNE 13, 1834.—We are now in camp on the Seets-ca-dee, as it is generally called here, and I think should always be so called, for doubtless the Indians first found and named it. Never was there a purer, drier, or more elastic atmosphere than we have breathed and enjoyed for the last thirty [twenty] days. I have not seen, or smelt a piece of meat approaching to putrefaction, since I reached the Platte. Except the *heart* of man, I believe meat would petrify before it would putrify. I have frequently carried a piece of fresh buffalo, or venison, on my pack-saddle, without being cooked or salted and eat it at the end of five days, perfectly sweet and good. How lovely are the nights! The moon and stars shine with a purer and a brighter light than I ever saw them before. It is said "an undevout astronomer is mad." That may be so, but if I were an astronomer, I think I should go mad, or, like a child of Atlantis, curse the sun every day for depriving me of the sweet converse of the stars. How I long for a timbered country. In a thousand miles I have not seen a hundred acres of wood. All that comes near to arborification, is a fringe of cotton wood and willows along the banks of creeks and rivers. These everlasting hills have an everlasting curse of barrenness. Poor Blackhawk is thin, but game to his marrow bones. I believe he is willing, if not able, to bear me to the Pacific Ocean.

My mother, sisters, little Dick and a pair of pretty blue eyes, in Ohio, often occupy my thoughts. God bless them!

We are now at the place we started for when we left St. Louis. It is not so far, I think, by several hundred miles, as it has been generally estimated. I should not put it down at more than thirteen hundred.

This evening we were visited by six trappers from Dripps and Fontenelle's camp [Company]. They were exceedingly glad to see us. We gave them the news in broken doses; beginning with matters three years old. This was delightful, fresher by several years than any they had heard. Then we brought them up by degrees to the intelligence of the present day. To judge of the effect, we must consider that some of these men have been in the mountains for the last twelve years without a visit to the settlements.

JUNE 14, 1834—*Stayed all this day in one encampment on the main Colorado, sent our hunters for game & men—killed some buffaloe & our mono-tongued yankees saw three frenchmen to whom they could communicate, and from whom, they could learn nothing.*

JUNE 15, 1834—*Moved camp a mile higher up for better grass. I delighted myself to day in erecting the standard of my country, and liberty, upon the west of our Andes—the first I believed (and as Mr. S. supposed) that had ever been folded and unfolded by these mountain winds. It had scarcely smoothed its wrinkles, and began to dance its joyous measures with the breeze, than four men were seen, speeding across the prairie, upon their steeds—which were neighing, as if to salute the flag of the union, & hail its arrival in this region of danger and delight. A salute was fired and a huzza sent forth to the echoing hills, by the hardy, fearless mountaineers. The long lost Vasques, whom we he had sent in search for—was now ardently shake hands with his friend Mr S. and asking and being asked hundreds of unanswered questions. Mr Fitzpatrick one of the heads of the [Rocky] Mo. Fur company, and who seems to be a warm hearted, gentlemanly Hibernian was the second.—the third a Mr Grey who has long been with and is almost of the red skins—the 4th one of that hardy, revengeful race. Three or four of the companies are encamped within fifty or sixty miles of this place. In a few days I shall know what a mountain rendezvous means. Henceforth, as my travelling is done, I may not keep the date, but merely preserve here, en memorandum, such occurrances as will hereafter interest me.*

JUNE 15—Anderson may be correct about the priority of his flag-raising exploit, but it would be surprising if Captain Bonneville had not raised a flag over Fort Bonneville in 1832-1833. Flags would seem to have been carried into and across the Green River Valley by Ashley's men in 1824; Peter Skene Ogden mentions the flaunting of an American flag in Weber Canyon, near Great Salt Lake, on May 23, 1825. In November 1827, on the Snake River in present Idaho, Ogden encountered a Bannock chief, The Horse, carrying "an American flag." Note that Anderson afterward speaks of two flags in the camp of Sublette and Fitzpatrick.

For Thomas Fitzpatrick, John Gray, and the Flathead chief Insillah, see the biographical sketches. Gray was a half-breed Iroquois.

In saying that three companies are encamped within 50 or 60 miles, Anderson must have reference to Fitzpatrick's camp, a few miles higher up the Green; to Andrew Drips's American Fur Company party (which, according to Ferris, on June 2 was at the lake that "constitutes the source of the Western branch, of the New Fork," in the Wind River Mountains, and thereafter moved southward by slow marches toward a meeting with Lucien Fontenelle); and to Fontenelle's own party, known to have trapped during the spring in the Utah country. At the time Anderson made

JUNE 14, 1834—Capt. Sublette sent out some aspiring souls [*Greens*] to hunt buffalo and look for men. They found both, but *cui bono*, they could neither *kill* buffalo or *talk* French, so came home "with their fingers in their mouths."

JUNE 15, 1834—Have I, or have I not, immortalized myself to-day? I have raised with my own hands [this morning], our glorious flag, "the star-spangled banner," the badge of freedom and Union—on the brow of our great northern Andes. The first ever displayed on these unmeasurable heights. It had scarcely smoothed out its wrinkles and began to dance its joyous measures in the breeze, than four men were seen darting like Cossacks over the plains. Wild with amazement and delight, they screamed and shouted "hurrah, hurrah! well done for Bill," and "give us your hand old boy." Into the tent they rushed. Some how I learned their names. They were Vasquez, the long lost Vasquez, Fitzpatrick, Gray, and [a low well made, mild visaged Indian called] the Little Chief. Vasquez and Sublette are shaking hands with their right and smacking and pushing each other with the left. They both ask questions and neither answer. I set by a listener and a looker on. [The] Three Camps are now within fifty or sixty miles of each other. In a few days I shall know what a mountain rendezvous means.

---

this entry, Captain Bonneville was farther west investigating Bear Lake, while Joe Walker, whose detachment had gone to California the previous year, was encamped on Bear River, waiting for Bonneville to join him.

JUNE 16, 1834.—*Three of the Nezpercés came to us from the other camp. The elder of the Indians is called Kentuck. This is a nickname given to him in consequence of his continual endeavours to sing "the hunters of Kentucky.["]* He is called "the bulls-head" in his own language. This tribe like the flat-heads is remarkable for their more than Christian* [In margin: *I mean as practiced in what are called Christian countries]* *practice of honesty, veracity and every moral virtue which every philosopher & professor so much laud, and practice so little. There are now four missionaries on their route to the nation of flat-heads. If they can only succeed in making them such as the white-men are, & not such as they should be, it would be charity for the messengers of civilization, to desist. I believe these are the only people on the globe with whom the aforesaid virtues are generally practiced realities not admired Utopian dreams. They "bona fide" despise and discountenance lying, stealing and begging—I hear every day most interesting anecdotes of Indians &c, which I am very anxious to preserve for my future enjoyment, but the limits of my little* mem. *here, is so very contracted that I cannot possibly gratify myself in this respect.*

JUNE 17, 1834.—*Mr Sublette returned from a visit to our neighbours camps accompanied by a flat-head chief called by the whites the Little-chief. His indian name is Insillah—which means, in his tongue the 'war eagle's plume.' He is considered one of the best indians, of the best tribe in existence. He has an amiable, but not an intellectual face.*

JUNE 16—For Kentuck (Kentuc), see the biographical sketches. The Nez Percés, belonging to the Shahaptian linguistic family, ranged widely—from the Blue Mountains of Oregon to the Bitterroot Mountains of Idaho and Montana, and from the waters of the Snake to what is now southeastern Washington. Independent and brave, they were always held in high esteem by white men. That was also true of their neighbors, the Flatheads or Salish, members of the Salishan linguistic family, whose particular home was what is now western Montana, west of the Continental Divide. In his Journal Anderson wrote a further appreciation of these Indians: "The Nez percé and Flat Head tribes, are proverbial for their honesty & veracity—not as a people, admiring and teaching these virtues—but as invariably practicing them—The Flat-heads or 'Saalish' are especially distinguished for the strict observance of every moral excellence, that they can put in execution. There is not a vulgar trapper, however dissolute and abandoned he may be, but will declare that he has never known a Flat-head to lie or steal—From what I daily hear of these savage people, I believe they never have been surpassed, and have not now their parallel, in moral excellence. And these anomolous people are fast fading from the earth—They are daily being 'ground up into fine dust' by the execrable Black-feet—the Ishmaelites of the desert—I wish that these incorruptible people could be exchanged for some of our border tribes—There are four missionaries now on their way to them, if they design to make them, as the whites are, I pray for their failure—It

JUNE 16, 1834.—This morning we received a visit from three Nes Perces, who have come over from Fitzpatrick's camp to see how the land lies. The elder is called Kentuck, a name by which [he] is known even among his own people. [He is a good looking, good natured fellow, and acquired his appellation by trying to sing "the Hunters of Kentucky."] His Indian name is The Bull's Head. The Nes Perces, or Saap Tens and the Flat Heads, Saylish, are proverbial for their honesty and love of truth.

JUNE 17, 1834.—Mr. Sublette has just returned from Fitzpatrick's camp, bringing with him the Little Chief, Insillah, which signifies in English the War Eagle's plume. He is a short, well made, active man, and is, I understand, a splendid horseman. [He has, as I before remarked a very mild and amiable countenance, but I think not a very intelligent-looking one.] The amiable little fellow was looking intently at my white hair which Sublette observing, pronounced Gen. Clark's Flathead name, Red Head Chief, and putting the first fingers of his right hand on his tongue, intimated that we were relatives, (the white head and the red head) or had drawn sustenance from the same breast. He immediately pressed me to his side, and rapidly related his boyhood recollections of the Clark and Lewis expedition.

---

would be charity for the messengers of *civilization* to desist." (For Anderson's list of Nez Percé and Flathead chiefs in 1834, see Ethnological Notes, pp. 232, 235-236.)

The three (not four) missionaries mentioned in the Diary were Jason Lee, his nephew Daniel Lee, and Cyrus Shepard, besides two helpers, Philip L. Edwards and Courtney M. Walker. These Methodist missionaries went on to the Willamette Valley in preference to living among the Flatheads (whose name was a misnomer).

JUNE 17—"Red Head Chief," as in the Narrative, was a name very generally applied to William Clark by American Indians, who knew St. Louis as Red Head's Town. For an account from Flathead sources of Lewis and Clark's encounter with these Indians in 1805, see Olin D. Wheeler, *The Trail of Lewis and Clark*, pp. 65-68.

JUNE 18, 1834—*Moved camp to day a few miles up the river, where we were joined by Mr Fitzpatrick of the Rocky mountain company. There are with him divers & sundry indians. Nezpercés, Flat heads & snakes. Now every-thing is novel & interesting to me, but not as exciting as I had expected. While at dinner to day, the exclamation of "a bull is coming into camp", drew us all to the door of the tent— where we saw a large Caiac running with strength and velocity from the hill directly towards us, pursued by young Kentuck, bending forward with bow hard bent and arrow aimed Quick as fancy they passed on to the rivers bank, but before he had laved his ribs of strength in the cooling Colorado he had received nine balls in his brown carcass. He stopped not, died not until he reached the mid channel of the Seitskidee, and floated indignantly down its rapid current before our longing eyes.*

Capt Wyatt who left the settlements ten days before us joined us this afternoon. Capt Wyatt is on his way to the mouth of the Colum-bia, where he expects to meet with a vessel freighted at Boston, with articles of trade, and which he will refreight with salmon, furs, &c. I have neither accepted, or refused a very polite invitation to accom-pany him to the ocean. Mr. E. Christy returned to day from Fort Van. Couver, at the mouth of Columbia. He has been absent since early this spring—There has been but little else than policing in the

JUNE 18—We have combined under June 18 entries Anderson made in Diary, Journal, and Narra-tive for June 17 and 18. As we have observed, his chronology had been one day ahead of the true dates from June 1, but is correct for June 18, when his Diary can be checked against Wyeth's. It would seem that in writing up the Diary, Anderson described events of the 18th as those of two separate days, and by this inadvertence arrived at a correct chronology and was afterward able to keep the dates straight.

The arrival of both Wyeth and Edmund T. Christy, the latter with a contingent of Indians in-cluding the Nez Percé Rottenbelly, makes this a notable entry in Anderson's record. We last gave attention to Wyeth on June 9, the day he passed Devils Gate. On June 10 he advanced as far up the Sweetwater as the Three Crossings, but did not do so well on the 11th, traveling only 19 miles through following the river during the afternoon instead of cutting across a bend; Shepard says: "Travelled through a very wild, desert & broken region—very rough and covered with loose stones & wild sage of unusual growth are now off of the trail & have crossed the river eight or ten times." Thus Wyeth camped somewhat below Sublette's camp of June 9 near Fitzpatrick's Cache. Here there is some difficulty, for Wyeth's entry for June 12 is so similar to that for June 11 as to suggest that he repeated it. Jason Lee mentions no travel at all, merely describing a hunt. Cyrus Shepard indicates there was some travel on the 12th; he says: "Journey as usual—Plenty of buf-falo killed. encamped on the river an hour and a half before sunset."

Perhaps Wyeth simply moved up the Sweetwater a few miles to the vicinity of Sublette's camp of the 9th. (In any event it is impossible that Wyeth could have had two consecutive days of 19 miles' travel up the Sweetwater from the Three Crossings; there is not that much space.) On the 13th Wyeth got into trouble, which is not immediately apparent from his journal entry. He went 3 miles along the Sweetwater, up a ravine (Chimney Creek) about a mile, then west by south 9

JUNE 18, 1834—We have moved our camp a few miles up the river where we were joined by [Mr.] Fitzpatrick, of the Rocky mountain Fur Company. We are a motley set, Whites, French, Yankees, Nes Perces, Flatheads, and Snakes, or Shoshones.

Whilst dining in our tent to-day, I heard the simultaneous cry from English, French and Indian mouths, of *a bull, un caiac* [okâ-hé], *tsodlum* and oh, Spirit of Nimrod, what a spectacle! A huge buffalo bull, booming through the camp, like a steamboat, followed by an Indian yelling and shaking his robe. Loud shouts of "hurrah [for] Kentuck," "Oka-hey trodlum," "go ahead bull," and whiz, whiz, went a dozen arrows, bang, bang, as many guns, and poor John Baptist leaped from the bank and floated, broad side up, down the rapid current of Green river. This wonderful exhibition of skill, perseverance and daring, was performed by the Bull's Head in fulfillment of a promise, made the night before, to Capt. Sublette, that he would drive an old bull through the camp to please Hi-hi-seeks-tooah, his Little White Brother. And he did both.

Capt. Wyeth, of Boston, who left the settlements ten days before us, came into camp this evening. He is on his way to the mouth of the Columbia river, where he expects a vessel, freighted with merchandise, to be exchanged for furs, salmon, &c. I have declined an invitation to accompany him, although his return trip, by way of the Sandwich Islands, is a strong temptation. I think I am far enough from home for this time.

Mr. Edward Christy, of St. Louis, has just arrived [today] from Fort Vancouver, bringing with him a considerable number of Snakes and Nes Perces. Yells, songs and oaths are heard all day and

---

miles to a tributary of the Sweetwater (Strawberry Creek), and on west by south 7 miles to another tributary (Rock Creek). Jason Lee clarifies the picture: "Left the Sweet Water this morning to the left and soon after lost Sublet's trail." It would seem that after leaving Chimney Creek Wyeth got too far north, camping 4 or 5 miles above where Sublette crossed Rock Creek. (It is likely that Sublette on June 10 reached Willow Creek.) On the 14th Lee says he "Took the lead of Camp [Company?] while the Capt. went to see if he could ascertain where he passed when he went out before"—that is, in 1832. Wyeth says: "Made due West 5 mil[e]s and crossed a small creek of Sweet Water [Willow Creek] which comes from a point of granite rocks about 2 miles from which we passed then W. 7 mil[e]s to a spring of good cold water and good grass. ... Afternoon made W. 6 miles to Sweet Water creek main body going about S. E. and coming out of cut rocks [Wyeth's term for a canyon] then W. by S. 16 miles over broken ground to one fork of Sandy running S. by E." Thus Wyeth took his party on a course about midway between the later Lander Cutoff and the Anderson-Sublette trail (later the Old Oregon Trail past Fort Bridger), striking the Little Sandy some 5 miles northeast of Black Bluff (as depicted on the Hayden map).

On June 15 Wyeth journalized: "W. N. W. 9 miles to Big Sandy where we found Buffaloe plenty

two camps for the two past days. With Mr C. we have an addition to our red-brethren—more snakes or they [are] called per genera Panács. One is called by the whites—Rotten-belly—from a wound he recieved in his abdomen, in an engagement against the Black-feet. The Indian name of the flat heads, is Sālish. The Nez-percés in their own tongue are Sāãpten—I try to write them as they are pronounced. I have not seen as yet a pretty squaw.

My hunters not yet come in   been out 4 days   fearful they have been scalped." (These missing hunters, whose names Shepard gives as Stansbury [Nicholas U. Sansbury] and [Caleb] Wilkins, did not come into camp until June 17th.) Lee mentions that they "Passed some singular Mountains   one resembles a hay stack which we left on our left hand"—an evident allusion to Black Bluff. Camp was made on the Big Sandy near the point where it veers from south to southwest. The short march, Townsend explains, was to allow the animals to recruit. On the 16th the party followed the Big Sandy down, southwest by west 15 miles, then 4 miles southeast by east, the horses starving. Somewhat discouraged, Lee wrote: "Followed down Sandy and could find no grass until 2 O'Clock and then very poor. Sunday [the previous day] we traveled near W. and this P.M. S.E. and I judge we are not more than 10 m. from where we encamped on the night of the 14th. The Capt. has heard nothing from his express nor from Rendevous and hence he is wandering about not knowing whether he is going to or from it."

On the 17th Wyeth's party continued on down the Big Sandy, encamping without grass 6 miles below the mouth of the Little Sandy. Lee writes: "We are encamped on a dry sand plain where there is no grass except a few scattering spires but the opinion is that we are within 10 miles of Rendevous where we shall find plenty. The horses are nearly wore down but the mules stand it well and are in as good flesh as when we Started. The Capt. has just started in search of Rendevous." Lee also says that during the course of the 17th "Some of the Com. saw two men belonging to American Fur Com." Townsend writes: "we are now looking forward with no little pleasure to a rest of two or more weeks at the mountain rendezvous on the Colorado. Here we expect to meet all the mountain companies who left the States last spring, and also the trappers who come in from various parts, with furs collected by them during the previous year. All will be mirth and jollity, no doubt, but the grand desideratum with some of us, is to allow our horses to rest their tired limbs and exhausted strength on the rich and verdant plains of the Siskadee."

Wyeth set out with one man "on the night of the 17th . . . to hunt Fitzpatric and slept on the prairie   in morning struck Green river and went down to the forks and finding nothing went up again and found rendesvous about 12 miles up." Here, he says, "much to my astonishment the goods which I had contracted to bring up to the Rocky Mountain fur Co. were refused by those honorable gentlemen." See Introduction.

Meanwhile, on the 18th, Wyeth's company made some 19 miles down the Big Sandy to what Lee calls "a fine bottom of grass." He also says, "The man who went with the Capt. has returned also the one he sent out on express [from the Sweetwater on June 10]." On the 19th, as Wyeth tells it, his party traveled on about 8 miles and camped "1 mile above the mouth of Sandy on Green river or Seckkedee." Lee adds: "Met the Capt. about 12 O'C. near the Forks of Sandy and Green Rivers. Dined on the banks of Green R.   P.M. Crossed and encamped on the shore   grass pretty good. Here we met an Indian Free Trapper. . . ." Shepard says the Green was forded "with some difficulty" about a mile above where they had reached it at noon. This afternoon crossing, Townsend learned, was made because Wyeth had found good pasture on the west bank.

Thus Wyeth's own movements are brought into focus. To recapitulate: He reached the mouth of the Sandy on the early morning of June 18 to find nobody there. Going up the Green, after 12 miles he reached the camp of Fitzpatrick and Sublette. It was afternoon when he arrived, and by sundown Wyeth was assimilating the shattering news that Fitzpatrick would pay the $500 forfeit in preference to receiving the goods Wyeth had brought out. Next morning the combined parties of Fitzpatrick and Sublette began moving over to Hams Fork, as described by Anderson. Meantime Wyeth turned back down the Green, finding his party about noon near the mouth of the Sandy. On the 20th Wyeth led his company over to Hams Fork by a more southerly route all night long [since our camps have joined]. Like flies on a sugar-barrel, or niggers at a corn shucking, the red-skins are flocking to the trading tents. We have now perhaps not less than fifteen hundred around us. Mr. Sublette has met here an old acquaintance and friend in Rotten-belly, a tall, commanding-looking fellow, who was wounded in the same Blackfoot fight where the former received a ball in his arm and side. The bread-basket of the Nes Perce was so seriously damaged that he has ever since borne a name indicative of the fact. It was curious to see how those two iron men enjoyed their wounds. For a short time the scene was uproarious. Shouting, laughing, slapping and joking each other, then winding up by cursing the Blackfeet with a hearty and vicious eloquence.

---

than Fitzpatrick and Sublette had used: "Made W. S. W. 8 miles then S. by E. 15 miles to Hams Fork running here S. E. and a small stream." Shepard writes more fully: "Travelled across the prairie in a Southwesterly direction for Ham's fork, expected distance ten or twelve miles   it however proved to be at least twenty five—and both men and animals were nearly exhausted when we arrived at said fork. This fork is the place selected for rendezvous this season for the companies in the mountains—Made our encampment about two miles below the general rendezvous." Lee says the company got to Hams Fork about 4 P.M. "We call this Rendevous or the place where all the Companies in the Mountains or in this section of them have fixed upon to meet for the transaction of business. Some of the Companies have not come in yet most of them are a mile above us on the same creek."

Anderson's remark in the Diary identifying the Snakes as "Panācs" (Bannocks) he corrects in his entry for June 20.

JUNE 19, 1834—*We moved to day, to Ham's fork a very pretty tributary of the Seitskeidee. The cavalcade to day reminded me of bishops Heber's charming description of "the pilgrims on their winding way." Indians, male & female* [interlined: *all astride]—whites of every tongue—mules, horses & Jack asses—with here and there on the Sahara-like plains horsemen & dogs in full cry after the blowing buffaloe. The greatest and most striking peculiarity of taste, is constantly manifested. This morning I saw a squaw mounted astride, upon a handsome horse, with the most beautiful yet gaudy saddle, bridle and concomitant ornaments, I ever saw or heard described; pretty leggings &c—have her head covered with an old, stinking disgusting clout. They are perfect riders They mount and dismount with the ease and more than the grace of the men. There was killed a large grisley Bruin in the edge of the camp. He was started on a hill not far distant, and whilst I was preparing my horse and equipage he had been driven by two boys into the very camp. To fulfil my promise to 'mon petit neveu" Dick, I shall have it dressed for him.*

JUNE 20, 1834—*I was mistaken in supposing that the snakes were included under the designation of Panacks. The snakes are Shoshonees. The Crows are termed Absarokees. The Nez percés call the whites Alãim. By the snakes we are called Tãb ãboo. The flat-heads call the french Saimer—& the Americans Sooni â pi which means the long knives—*

JUNE 19—Hams Fork, a principal tributary of Blacks Fork of the Green, got its name in the spring of 1825 when it was trapped by Zacharias Ham, one of Ashley's lieutenants. Ham went to California from New Mexico in 1830-1831 and is said to have drowned while trapping on the lower Colorado River. (That would have been during or after 1836.) From Anderson's entries of June 28 and 29, it appears that this first camp on Hams Fork was some 5 miles above the confluence with Blacks Fork.

In mentioning Bishop Heber, Anderson has in mind the *Narrative of a Journey through the Upper Provinces of India, from Calcutta to Bombay, 1824-1825* ..., by Reginald Heber, Lord Bishop of Calcutta (3 vols., London, 1828): "The whimsical caravan filed off in state before me; my servants, all armed with spears, to which many of them had added, at their own cost, sabres of the longest growth, looked, on their little poneys, like something between cossacks and sheriff's javelinmen; my new Turkoman horse, still in the costume of his country, with his long, squirrel-like tail painted red, and his mane plaited in love-knots, looked as if he were going to eat fire, or perform some other part in a melodrama; while Mr. Lushington's horses, two very pretty Arabs, with their tails docked, and their saddles English ('Ungrigi') fashion, might have attracted notice in Hyde-park; the Archdeacon's buggy and horse had every appearance of issuing from the back gate of a college in Cambridge on a Sunday morning; and lastly came some mounted gens d'armes, and a sword and buckler-man on foot, looking exactly like the advanced guard of a Tartar army."

JUNE 19, 1834—Crossed the river, and moved our now large camp on to Harris' [Hams] Fork, a very pretty tributary of the Seets-ca-dee. Our cavalcade to-day very forcibly reminded me of Bishop Heber's charming description of "The pilgrims on their winding way." I rode to one side and watched it for a long time, with intense interest. Except in the language of the poet, it would be difficult to depict such a scene. It was an unbroken line of human beings, of several nationalities and varied costumes, constantly changing route and elevation. At one and the same time it was ascending and de-cending eminences; at one and the same time swaying both to the right and the left to avoid obstacles or overcome difficulties—the little front point, by some inscrutable power or resistless magnetism, seeming to drag the whole mass after it at will. There were whites of every caste and tongue, with their horses, mules and jackasses; Indians, with their dogs, squaws and lodge-poles, and away off (stragglers from another camp) were men in full chase after the blowing buffalo. In the dress of our aborigines there is frequently the most remarkable contrasts and contradictions. I saw to-day a squaw mounted astride [as they all ride, and elegantly, too], upon a handsome horse, most elegantly caparisoned, saddle, bridle and accoutrements shining with silver; she, herself, decked in corre-sponding attire, whilst her proud head was turbaned with a most filthy and disgusting clout.

These ladies are very fine riders, mounting and dismounting with the ease and grace of a cavalier.

A large grizzly bear, which had been frightened from the hills by two boys, ran through the camp, scattering women and children as a hawk scatters chickens, and took refuge in a dense growth of willows. In about twenty minutes, the discharge of a gun and the triumphant yell of Insillah announced its fate. [I was too tardy to be in at its death, but I hope I shall soon have an opportunity of meet-ing one of these monsters.] This evening the skin of the terrible ani-mal was presented to me by the brave Flathead chief, with the ears and claws still on. I do not know that I ever felt so much pride and surprise as I did upon that occasion. It was both a trophy of his dar-ing and proof of his high regard for the old "Red-head chief." Hi-hi-suks-tooah was as grateful and as gratified as if he had received a gift from royal hands and merited the compliment.

DIARY

JUNE 20—Anderson's ethnological remarks are correct as far as they go, though the translation of the Crow name Absaroka is more exactly Sparrowhawk People. The Snakes or Shoshoni are more fully discussed under date of August 31. Matthew Field says, "The Snakes call whites *Tab-i-bo*—Blackfeet call them *Napa-qua-na*—Flatheads *Su-yar-pe*—" (*Prairie and Mountain Sketches*, p. 137).

We could wish that Anderson on this and the next two days had given more attention to happenings at the rendezvous. On this day the Rocky Mountain Fur Company was dissolved. Also, about 4 P.M. Wyeth's party arrived, camping a mile or two below the camp of Fitzpatrick and Sublette. Shepard says that Wyeth's camp was visited "by several of the Flathead and Nez pierce indians, five of whom took supper with us—They are the most cleanly and respectable looking indians I have yet seen." Lee writes that some in the Fitzpatrick-Sublette camp "threatened that when we came they would give them Missionaries 'hell' and Capt. W. informed us and advised us to be on our guard and give them no offence and if molested to show no symptoms of fear and if difficulty did arise we might depend upon his aid for he never forsook any one who had put himself under his protection." Lee replied that he "*feared* no man and apprehended no danger from them when sober and when drunk we would endeavor to [keep] out of their way. I judged it best however to go immediately to their camp and get an introduction to them while sober and soon as possible went accompanied by the Capt. Found Wm. Sublette and was warmly received with all that gentlemanly politeness which has always characterized his conduct towards me [in St. Louis, before setting out]. Sup[p]ed with him. Was introduced to those who had threatened us and spent some time in conversation with them on the difficu[l]ties of the route changes of habit and various topics and made such a favourable impression on them and was tre[a]ted with such politeness by all that I came away fully satisfied that they would neither molest us themselves nor suffer their men to do so without cause. . . . Some of the men told the Pierced Nose and Flat Head Indians our object in coming into the country and they came and shook hands very cordially and seemed to welcome me to their country."

This same day, June 20, Wyeth wrote two letters, and next day five more, which are discussed in the Introduction. He wrote little in his journal until June 27, but the other diarists do better. Jason Lee noted on the 21st: "Felt more like laying down and resting than writing or work. Have had a visit from some 10 or 12 Pierced Nose and 1 or 2 Flat-Heads to-day and conversed a little with them through an indifferent interpreter. But being buisy arran[g]ing our things we requested them to come again when we were more at leisure. A man who had just come from Wallahwallah [Edmund Christy] gave us some encouraging information. Blessed be God I feel more and more to rejoice I was ever counted worthy to carry the glad news of salvation to the far western world."

On the 22nd, Sunday, Lee said further: "Was called this morning at 2 O'Clock it being my morning guard but having men enough to guard the horses and finding the atmosphere very cold I sat most of the time in the tent. Felt very stupid after breakfast. Tried to read my Bible but fell asleep and took a long nap. Soon after I awoke as many Indians as could [get] into our tent came to see us and we told them our object in coming showed them the Bible told them some of the Commandments and how they were given to all of which they listened with the utmost attention and then replied that it was all good. They enquired if we could build houses and said that the Indians at Wallahwallah gave horses to a white man to build them a house and when he got the horses he went off and did not build it. We of course expressed our strong disapprobation of his conduct. They said if we could build a house for them they would ca[t]ch plenty of Beaver for us which we take as a favourable indication showing their desire for improvement. One said he was going to St. Louis next year but he would leave his three children with his friend who was present and he would give them to us that we might teach them to read and write and be good. Some of them shook hands very heartily when the[y] left. One of the men went to purchase meat of the Indians but they would not bring it to him because it was Sunday. Thus while the whites who have been educated in a christian land pay no regard whatever to the Sabbath these poor savages who have at most only some vague idea of the Christian religion respect the Sabbath of the Lord our God. Though we might have a congregation of some hundreds of whites to preach to-day if they were disposed to hear yet we have no doubt if [we] were to propose such a thing that it would be rejected with disdain and perhaps with abuse, for all hands nearly are employed trading drinking or some such innocent amusement. My God my God is there nothing that will have any effect upon them?"

Cyrus Shepard writes to much the same effect. John K. Townsend, who had found the eight-hour ride of the 20th a racking agony, after which he was prostrated by fever for two days, manages to give us a better picture of the rendezvous on June 22, including the important intelligence that

JUNE 20, 1834.—I have, as yet, seen no Crows. In their tongue they call themselves Ab-sa-rokees, which means, as I understand, *the big bird*. I fancy that that tribe intended to call themselves "The Eagles," but the translator, supposing that their sign of flying resembled the flaps of our black corn-stealer, rendered it Crow. It is better so, perhaps, as I hear they are the most expert and incorrigible rogues on the face of the earth. I have made some inquiries as to the meaning of the names given by the mountain Indians to the Americans. So far as I can learn, they are all the synonyms of "long-knife," "big blade," or "sword." By the Crows we are called Mit-siats-ki—long knife; [they call the French Marshs*tishē* ri—grey-eyes;] the Black-feet, or Pug-ga-nes, term us Nisto-soo-ni-quen—long knife; the Nes Perces say we are Ala-im—big blade; the Flatheads [the French are called *Sai* mer—the Americans] Sooi-api—sword or long knife. Our name in Shoshone or Snake is Ta-ba-bo, but whether that has the same signification I did not ascertain.

Cerré's party, with Bonneville's goods, was now at hand: "We are now lying at the rendezvous. W. Sublette, Captain Serre, Fitzpatrick, and other leaders, with their companies, are encamped about a mile from us, on the same plain, and our own camp is crowded with a heterogeneous assemblage of visitors. The principal of these are Indians, of the Nez Percé, Bannock, and Shoshoné tribes, who come with the furs and peltries which they have been collecting at the risk of their lives during the past winter and spring, to trade for ammunition, trinkets, and 'fire water.' There is, in addition to these, a great variety of personages amongst us; most of them calling themselves white men, French-Canadians, half-breeds, &c., their color nearly as dark, and their manners wholly as wild, as the Indians with whom they constantly associate. These people, with their obstreperous mirth, their whooping and howling, and quarrelling, added to the mounted Indians, who are constantly dashing into and through our camp, yelling like fiends, the barking and baying of savage wolf-dogs, and the incessant cracking of rifles and carbines, render our camp a perfect bedlam. A more unpleasant situation for an invalid could scarcely be conceived. I am confined closely to the tent with illness, and am compelled all day to listen to the hiccoughing jargon of drunken traders, the *sacré* and *foutre* of Frenchmen run wild, and the swearing and screaming of our own men, who are scarcely less savage than the rest, being heated by the detestable liquor which circulates freely among them.

"It is very much to be regretted that at times like the present, there should be a positive necessity to allow the men as much rum as they can drink, but this course has been sanctioned and practised by all leaders of parties who have hitherto visited these regions, and reform cannot be thought of now. The principal liquor in use here is alcohol diluted with water. It is sold to the men at *three dollars* the pint! Tobacco, of very inferior quality, such as could be purchased in Philadelphia at about ten cents per pound, here brings two dollars! and everything else in proportion. There is no coin in circulation, and these articles are therefore paid for by the independent mountain-men, in beaver skins, buffalo robes, &c.; and those who are hired to the companies, have them charged against their wages.

"I was somewhat amused to-day by observing one of our newly hired men enter the tent, and order, with the air of a man who knew he would not be refused, *twenty dollars' worth of rum, and ten dollars worth of sugar*, to treat two of his companions who were about leaving the rendezvous!"

At the close of this day's entry in his Narrative, Anderson notes, "I have not written out for publication the balance of my notes—It is perhaps as well to chop off here—" Consequently the Journal text supplies the place of the Narrative from June 21 to the end of this book.

DIARY

JUNE 21, 1834.—*I have nothing to do to day but keep the time.*

JUNE 22, 1834.—*Do—*

JUNE 23, 1834.—*Unwell to day. Last night is the second time only, that I have pleaded indisposition to be excused from standing guard —I went to a lodge where worship was held this evening. Not wishing to disturb them in their devotions I remained on the out-side—& per consequence saw none of their expressions or gesticulation. Their music or hymn, which was accompanied by the solemn death [?] drum tapping on some rude representative of that instrument, was not uninteresting. I should fancy that there is some similarity betwixt it & the Welsh-howl—rude—wild & affecting   A Mock war dance was held also in Mr Fitzpatrick's camp in compliment, I believe, to me. Baptiste Charboneau, a half breed, & born of the squaw mentioned by Clark & Lewis, on their journey, was the principal actor in this scene. Of him there is something whispered which makes him an object of much interest to me. At all events he is an intelligent and interesting young man. He converses fluently & well in English, reading & writing & speaking with ease French and German—understan[din]g several of the Indian dialects—*

JUNE 23—Jason Lee writes: "Went to Mr. Sublett's Camp to see about purchasing a mule of Mr. Trapp [Fraeb]. Heard the Indians in one lodge praying and singing   went to listen to them but they were just closing as we approached. How encouraging to see these red men thus religiously inclined. Soon after dark a fire was built in the prairie for the purpose of a war dance. One with a thing that answered for a drum stood near the fire and sung with others. While the three half-breeds who were all that joined in the war dance were making preparations the whites made themselves perfectly ridiculous by jumping about the fire trying to imitate the Indian dance while none but the little boys would join them. At length they came and went through their dance which was rather interesting especially that part where they killed and scalped one and went off with the gun in triumph—Slept with Mr. Sublette and returned in the morning."

The Diary's "something whispered" about Jean Baptiste Charbonneau was doubtless the tale that William Clark, not Toussaint Charbonneau, was his father. However, Lewis and Clark did not reach the Mandan villages until November 1804, and Sacagaweah's child was born the following February. This is not to say that Clark and Lewis did not share the pleasures of their men, though their journals describe the amatory activities only of the rank and file. L. V. McWhorter records the 1926 statement of a Nez Percé informant, Wottolen, that Clark took a Nez Percé woman at the time Lewis and Clark returned from the Pacific in 1806, and had a son by her named Halahtookit (Daytime Smoke). This Nez Percé was one of those captured with Chief Joseph in 1877, along with his daughter and her baby. (*Hear Me, My Chiefs!*, p. 498.)

Journal

JUNE 21, 1834—Nothing done to day—Yet to day's a day for a, that.

JUNE 22, 1834—I have nothing more to say of this day than yesterday.

JUNE 23, 1834—I am very unwell to-day, as I was last night—twas the second time that I have excused my [self] from guard duty since I have been out—Tis night, and I have just returned from a lodge in which they were holding a family worship—wishing not to disturb them I remained on the outside and heard only their humdrum hymn—This song to the great spirit is of the simplest sort—it has a monotonous drowsy sound, tho not devoid of a kind of solemnity, tis accompanied by the tapping of an instrument like the tanbourin— They keep time with their hollow guttural cadences—Occasionally there broke out from their *sourd* [?] tones, some sharp, quick yelps, which made me think, I know not why, that there was a similarity to the Welch howl—rude, wild and affecting—A mock war dance by two or three half breeds and several young Indians was performed in our camp, for my satisfaction—Baptiste Charboneau, the son of Lewis and Clarke's intrepreter, who was born on their expedition, was the principal actor in this scenic representation—To me it was a very agreeable spectacle—

JUNE 24, 1834—*My 27th birthday finds me far away from the busy haunts of man, from my home, my mother & friends. I have had this day none but lonely & restless reflections—Regretting the little good which I have done for myself, my God or my country. Hope still pointing forward, & promising me better health, better prospects & better mind, as each revolving year rolls o'er the track made by those that passed before. How vain have been my wishes & my hopes! Mr Stewart an Englishman & I am told a gentleman and a scholar, has just arrived from Mr Bridgers party. He reports him to be within a few hours march—The black-feet who are the terror of the white & red man, whose hands are raised against every man & against whom every man's hands are raised, are called in their own tongue—Pāgănis—There is a band among them, who by superlative distinction are called "Blood Indians" being a little deeper dyed than the rest.*

JUNE 24—For William Drummond Stewart and James Bridger, and their adventures after the 1833 rendezvous, see the biographical sketches. They came to the rendezvous from the Colorado Rockies. Stewart was a captain in the British Army, not the Navy as Anderson says in the Journal.

Three subtribes of the Blackfeet frequented the American West—the Piegans, the Bloods (or Kainahs), and the Blackfeet proper (Siksika). Among them lived a detached branch of the Arapahos, the Atsina, known to the trappers as the Gros Ventres of the Prairie (often confused with those cousins of the Crows, the Hidatsa or Minnetarees, who dwelt near the Mandan villages and were known as the Gros Ventres of the Missouri). Every few years the Atsina journeyed to the Southern Plains to visit the Arapahos. Coming and going, they left a trail of blood; many of the killings attributed to Blackfeet were actually done by the Atsina.

In Wyeth's camp this day the routine, Shepard says, was "washing, mending and preparing for our future journey." Lee "Purchased some things of the Indians and a mule of Mr. Frapp. Paid in red cloth at 100 per cent $55.00 Found that our red cloth was minus 12 yds."

JUNE 24, 1834—This day twenty seven years ago I came into this world at 'Soldiers Retreat' near the fountain of Bear-grass, which waters one of the most fertile and beautiful countries in the world. Then I was watched over, by my loving parents, and from my infancy upwards, on that spot, I was surrounded by every person and thing that could bind me to life—How unlike the first, and all intervening, is this last anniversary of my birth—Far, far away from the grave of my father, the dear home of my mother, and the land of my countrymen, I am in a social waste, as soil-less and as desolate as the Desert which I dwell in. Here is no heart that ever beat in unison with mine, at the joyous incidents that gilded the wings of Time when boyhoods blood shot sparkling through my veins, or sympathized at tales of woe which cast a fleeting cloud oer the smooth bosom of youths peaceful lake—This day which often has been a day of happiness and pleasure, has proven itself a day of penance and of sorrow. Apart, in this 'vast wilderness' I have regretted the little good that I have done the great good that I have left undone—I've reflected with bitterness on the false promises that hope had made me, always pointing forward to a bright sunny path, which was too surely overshadowed by the darks clouds of disappointment—Deceitfully promising me health, fortune and knowledge—as years revolve, the last billows of time efface the wavelets of the first, and where is my knowledge, my health or my fortune—Why should I repine? even the shrubs of the earth are bitter and salt._____An Englishman by the name of Stuart and as I hear, a Capt in the Royal na[v]y of G. B. arrived from Bridgers company. He says B. will join us to morrow. We shall then be free from the symptoms of the Blackfoot fever which now and then manifests itself. [*Author's footnote*: Sir Wm Drummond Stuart, of the old royal stock of Scotland, England & Ireland]—These red devils, whose hands are raised against all men, are called in their own language Peugàni—(the first syllable sounded as the '*eu*' in the french "*peur*," or like the *u* in tub.) There is a band among them who "par excellence" are called blood Indians —What *tigers* they must be!

JUNE 25, 1834.—*Bridger of the R. M. F. C arrived in camp this morning. A most interesting meeting took place between two parties of Indians. A band of about 20 galloped in sight, hooping, singing, & beating an instrument resembling a tamboreen. On nearing the camp an Indian belonging to it [the camp—WMA] (a soldier of a village) mounted on horseback & gaudily dressed, dashed out to meet them—when he reached all stopped—the leader advanced, and after a seeming [?] parley they shook hands with their left hands—The soldier then returned and by the time they had almost reached the tents—he had placed himself at the head of an equal number and marched out to meet the visitors—when within thirty or forty yards, both parties halted. the horsemen dismounted—disarmed themselves and placed their weapons on the ground in a pile. then both sides slowly advanced in single file until the foremost individuals were within arms reach—then reaching out their hands they held each other thus, for perhaps, 4 minutes and passed each to the left taking hands in succession of every one. I heard nothing spoken, until every one had held with stiffened arm, the hand of a guest or a visitor.*

JUNE 26, 1834.—*Nothing in the camps, now but drunken songs & brawls day or night—*

JUNE 27, 1834.—*Write not, & spare the ink, may be put after this day's date.*

JUNE 28, 1834.—*We left our first lodgment on Ham's fork and pitched our tents a few miles above on same stream. Not a drop of rain has fallen from the clouds, for weeks, yea, almost months. My pet, the young eagle grows finely. The young gentleman is possessed of an admirable appetite.*

JUNE 25—Wyeth writes on the 27th (a mistaken entry for the 25th): "Moved up the river N.W. 10 miles grass here pretty good but little timber and none but willows for the last six miles." Shepard says the move was "for the better accommodation of pasture for our horses." Lee, who concurs in Wyeth's estimate of the distance: "Removed 10 mi. up the creek," adds that he began "writing letters in good earnest, but found it very hard to bring my mind to the work."

JUNE 26—It was not only Anderson who found life dull this day and the next. "Made some repairs of saddles &c, and wrote some letters," says Lee on the 26th; and on the 27th, "Copied a long communication for the Advocate. Found peace in believing."

JUNE 25, 1834—Bridger arrived this morning—I was very much interested in witnessing the meeting of two friendly parties of Indians to day—A small party of 20 or 30 galloped in sight, whooping, singing and beating their rude drum. At the distance of about a half mile they were met by a gaudily dressed savage handsomely mounted, who was the soldier of the encamped village—they were all halted when he arrived, the leader advanced and after a seeming parley, the soldier returned, and placing himself at the head of a nearly equal number, of the best dressed fellows in the village, advanced on foot to meet the others—When within forty or fifty yards of each other they mutually halted—the horsemen dismounted and disarming themselves placed their weapons on the ground—both sides now slowly advanced in single file, till their leaders met, who took each other by the left hand, their right placed over their hearts—stood at arms length looking one another in the eyes and uttering not a word for about 2 minutes—then passed to the left—till the same silent ceremony was performed successively by all. After the first had become last and the last first, they entered togethered into the lodges, visiters and friends—

JUNE 26, 1834—There is nothing now in the camps but drunken brawls and songs, night and day—

JUNE 27, 1834—When I had written the figures, which indicate this day, I might have stopped, for it has given me no incident to record—

JUNE 28, 1834—We moved a few miles up the creek for fresh grass— I believe we have not had even a gentle shower for months—say two —I have a young eagle which I bear about from camp to camp—He rides very majestically on my pack-horse, looking farther into the surrounding prairies than any one else in the company, but whatever he sees or thinks, he sagely keeps to himself—The young gentleman has an excellent appetite and relishes buffaloe meat very much —I commend his taste. It gives me much pleasure to divide my meals with him.

JUNE 29, 1834.—*Paid a visit to the American Fur Comp. about eight miles below at the junction of Hams fork & Black's do. This company is conducted by Dripps & Fontenelle. Rice pudding & plumb pudding &c in the mountains were not unwelcome, but most unexpected rarities. A larger & more interesting collection of "Sauvages", than I have seen elsewhere—were around their trading pen or store—*

JUNE 30, 1834.—*The sun arose and set to day as usual.*

JULY 1, 1834.—*My grisley bear skin which was given me by Insillah a Saalish chief, is stolen by some red face—C'est egal!*

JUNE 29—Blacks Fork, we gather from Ferris, was so known by 1830. The name may date from the spring of 1824, when Arthur Black perhaps trapped there as one of Jedediah S. Smith's party. This view contradicts what Heinrich Lienhard was told in 1846 by an informant (obviously Miles Goodyear, who came to the mountains in 1836 with Whitman): ". . . fourteen years ago at this spot [Fort Bridger] over there in the willow thicket, a man named Black had been killed by a band of fifty Blackfoot Indians. For some time he had courageously defended himself and killed or wounded several of them before they succeeded in doing away with him." See Erwin G. and Elisabeth K. Gudde, eds., *From St. Louis to Sutter's Fort*, p. 95. Field relates an adventure that occurred in 1828 when Joseph Pourier "was in the employ of a trader named Black, after whom the mountain stream now known as 'Black's Fork' was christened." (See *Prairie and Mountain Sketches*, pp. 102-104.) In 1828, however, Black was on the Oregon coast with Jedediah Smith. He was still living as late as Nov. 24, 1832, when he signed a deposition in St. Louis (Floyd E. Risvold Collection).

Drips and Fontenelle were encamped at present Granger, Wyoming. The mention of their "trading pen or store" is of interest. Etienne Provost must have reached Hams Fork a week earlier, bringing the wherewithal for the rice and plum puddings. Warren A. Ferris, who recorded his experiences with Drips and Fontenelle during his first four mountain years, has only an elliptical narrative after early June 1834 and affords no more information until August.

JUNE 30—Townsend, silent since the 22nd, writes on this day: "Our camp here is a most lovely one in every respect, and as several days have elapsed since we came, and I am convalescent, I can roam about the country a little and enjoy it. The pasture is rich and very abundant, and it does our hearts good to witness the satisfaction and comfort of our poor jaded horses. Our tents are pitched in a pretty little valley or indentation in the plain, surrounded on all sides by low bluffs of yellow clay. Near us flows the clear deep water of the Siskadee [Hams Fork], and beyond, on every side, is a wide and level prairie, interrupted only by some gigantic peaks of mountains and conical *butes* in the distance. The river, here, contains a great number of large trout, some grayling, and a small narrow-mouthed white fish, resembling a herring. They are all frequently taken with the hook, and, the trout particularly, afford excellent sport to the lovers of angling. Old Izaac Walton would be in his glory here, and the precautionary measures which he so strongly recommends in approaching a trout stream, he would not need to practise, as the fish is not shy, and bites quickly and eagerly at a grasshopper or minnow.

"Buffalo, antelopes, and elk are abundant in the vicinity, and we are therefore living well. We have seen also another kind of game, a beautiful bird [the sage hen], the size of a half grown turkey, called the cock of the plains, (*Tetrao urophasianus*.) We first met with this noble bird on the plains, about two days' journey east of Green river, in flocks, or *packs*, of fifteen or twenty, and so exceedingly tame as to allow an approach to within a few feet, running before our horses like do-

JUNE 29, 1834—We paid a visit to the American Fur Company's camp, which is at the junction of Blacks and Hams forks, about 8 miles below. This company is conducted by Messr⁵ Fontenelle and Dripps—they recieved us very politely and treated us very kindly Rarities I little expected to meet with here were given us for dinner —rice and plumb puddings—There was a larger and more interesting collection of savages around their trading pen, than I have before met with—

JUNE 30, 1834—30ᵗʰ and last day of June—The sun rose and set to day as it has done on thousands before—

JULY 1, 1834—My bear skin, given to me by Insillah the Saalish chief, was stolen by some red rascal—C'est égal—T'will be all the same thing a century hence—

---

mestic fowls, and not unfrequently hopping under their bellies, while the men amused themselves by striking out their feathers with their riding whips. . ."

JULY 1—Cyrus Shepard writes: "Quite recovered from the fatigue of our past journey—Rode with J. Lee to Messers Sublette's & Fits-Patrick's camp a few miles down the Creek, were politely received &c took tea with Mr S. and returned to camp soon after Sunset." Jason Lee says that after sealing up various letters he "carried them down to Wm. Sublette's Camp and he kindly took charge of them. May they safely reach those for whom they are designed. Took my leave of Mr. Sublette and Mr. Fitzpatrick & Christie and they all wished me success expressing a hope that we might [meet] again in this country. But in what they wished me success I know not as some of [them] at least are opposed to our enterprise." These entries help to locate the various camps on Hams Fork. Wyeth's was the highest up after June 25.

JULY 2, 1834.—*The sun rose & set this as on any other day, tho the night passed not away as every night passeth. Prayer & song was heard the live long night—This was occasioned by the coming departure of a part of the Flat head & pierced-nosed tribes—There is something wild & consistent in their war songs even when sung as valedictories. There life is one scene of continious struggle for blood and rapine. Who of them knows then, when he bids adieu to a friend or a brother but that that brother will soon be weltering in his blood that blood soon to be lapped up by the hungry wolves or baked into black goutes on the burning sands of the prairie.*

JULY 3, 1834.—*I can not now say I have seen no pretty squaw. I have seen one, & but one—she is the companion of Dr. Newell of ⸺ [Ohio]. Tis strange there are so many finely formed men & so very few well shaped women amongst them.*

JULY 2—Anderson records the departure only of the Indians, not of Wyeth and his varied companions. Jason Lee writes on the 2nd that he sent various letters "by Mr. Greenow"; then: "Left Rendvous rather late being detained on account of some horses that had run away. Had been quite long enough in Camp and glad to pursue our journey. A band of Indians No. Pierce and Flat Heads came with and camped with us on Ham's Fork. They are on their way to the Flat Head camp."

Townsend writes more fully: "We bade adieu to the rendezvous this morning; packed up our moveables, and journied along the bank of the river. Our horses are very much recruited by the long rest and good pasture which they have enjoyed, and, like their masters, are in excellent spirits.

"During our stay at the rendezvous, many of us looked anxiously for letters from our families, which we expected by the later caravans, but we were all disappointed. For myself, I have received but one since I left my home, but this has been my solace through many a long and dreary journey. Many a time, while pacing my solitary round as night-guard in the wilderness, have I sat myself down, and stirring up the dying embers of the camp fire, taken the precious little memento from my bosom, undrawn the string of the leathern sack which contained it, and poured over the dear characters,till my eyes would swim with sweet, but sad recollections, then kissing the inanimate paper, return it to its sanctuary, tighten up my pistol belt, shoulder my gun, and with a quivering voice, swelling the *'all's well'* upon the night breeze, resume my slow and noiseless tramp among my sleeping companions.

"Many of our men have left us, and joined the returning companies, but we have had an accession to our party of about thirty Indians; Flat-heads, Nez Percés, &c., with their wives, children, and dogs. Without these our camp would be small; they will probably travel with us until we arrive on Snake river, and pass over the country where the most danger is to be apprehended from their enemies, the Black-feet.

"Some of the women in this party, particularly those of the Nez Percé nation, are rather handsome, and their persons are decked off in truly savage taste. Their dresses of deer skin are profusely ornamented with beads and porcupine quills; huge strings of beads are hung around their necks, and their saddles are garnished with dozens of little hawk's bells, which jingle and make music for them as they travel along. Several of these women have little children tied to their backs, sewed up papoose fashion, only the head being seen; as they jolt along the road, we not unfrequently hear their voices ringing loud and shrill above the music of the bells. Other little fellows who have ceased to require the maternal contributions, are tied securely on other horses, and all their care seems to be to sleep, which they do most pertinaceously in spite of jolting, noise, and clamor. There is among this party, a Blackfoot chief [Kosato?], a renegado from his tribe, who sometime since

JULY 2, 1834—Nothing more—Yet last night passed not as every night passes—Prayer and song the live long night—The long & short "Hō-hŏ-hō-hŏ! with an occasional wild High-hi-o-huh—rose upon the air and shewed that all were not calmly resting from the labours of the departed day—This was occasioned by the seperation of Indian brothers and friends—A portion of the Flat-head and Nez percé tribes were going to return to their homes on the Columbia—There is something solemn and affecting in these valedictory songs of natures children—Their life is one continued struggle for blood and rapine—Which of them knows, when he bids adieu to his father, his brother or his friend, but that the blood of his father is soon to be lapped up by the thirsty tongue of the gaunt and coward wolf. Does he know that his brother will not soon be writhing in his own frothy gore? How can he tell that his friend will not be struck down by the unseen hand of a foe, and his scalp torn off by some heartless demon amidst scoffs and cuffs—His brothers blood may mingle with the pure fountain from whence he is quenching his thirst—The life stream from his father's heart, may be dried into black gouts on the sands of the desert. And the flesh of his friend be hacked from his living body by squaws and children as he is tied to the stake of sacrifice—

JULY 3, 1834—I have seen only one squaw that I can consider at all handsome. She [is] a Pierced-nose woman, belonging to Newell a trapper—Tis strange, where the men are such well made, fine-looking, handsome fellows, that the females should be the reverse in every particular.

---

killed the principal chief of his nation, and was in consequence under the necessity of absconding. He has now joined the party of his hereditary foes, and is prepared to fight against his own people and kindred. He is a fine, warlike looking fellow, and although he takes part in all the war-songs, and sham-battles of his adopted brothers, and whoops, and howls as loud as the best of them, yet it is plain to perceive that he is distrusted and disliked. All men, whether, civilized or savage, honorable, or otherwise, detest and scorn a traitor!

"We were joined at the rendezvous by a Captain Stewart, an English gentleman of noble family, who is travelling for amusement, and in search of adventure. He has already been a year in the mountains, and is now desirous of visiting the lower country, from which he may probably take passage to England by sea. Another Englishman, a young man, named [Charles Howard] Ashworth, also attached himself to our party, for the same purpose.

"Our course lay along the bank of Ham's fork, through a hilly and stony, but not a rocky country; the willow flourished on the margin of the stream, and occasionally the eye was relieved, on scanning the plain, by a pretty clump of cottonwood or poplar trees..."

JULY 3—For "Doctor" Robert Newell and his wife Kittie, daughter of the Nez Percé chief Kowsoter (or Cow-sotum), see the biographical sketches.

JULY 4, 1834.—*Startled this morning by the loud, & quick rattle of fire arms, & the rapid & irregular hooping, each man sprang to his gun and prepared for action. For a moment there was a most singular scene of hurry & confusion, & alarm, but lo! the magic words "4th of July["] charmed all into order & security. Laughter & jesting succeeded to preparation or trepidation. This evening both camps are nearly deserted from vanity—Mr Fitzpatrick & Mr Sublette have gone, attended by the greater part of both parties, bearing two flags, to return a visit, made us yesterday by the Ameri. Fur. Comp; & to outbrag them, if practicable. Two race horses are taken down to sweat for their folly or convince where their arguments avail naught—Black-hawk was applied for but, I pleaded indisposition for him.*

JULY 5, 1834.—*This is another day like those beyond the flood (or soon will be) gone, unreturnable. Yesterday the horse from this camp outran the horse from the lower camp; and and a man from this camp beat a bully from their camp, ergo in our opinion, we are the best men, individually. I think it is a proof that we are or have, only the best animals.*

JULY 4, 1834—About day-break, startled by the loud discharge of fire arms and the quick sharp yells from a thousand tongues, each man sprang to his gun and awaited in breathless expectations the charge of a fearful foe For a time all was confusion and alarm, some stole from their tents and plunged into the willows, some laid close upon the ground their hands upon the lock—once more—all was death-like stillness—awful pause!—4th of July—4th of July—& the cold drops that had gathered on many a brow were soon wiped off, and they looked up to the flag which floated over Fitzpatricks tent & were cured—Cachinnation succeeded trepidation—You were alarmed—and you were scared—were bandied to and fro—This evening I am left nearly alone. Messrs. Sublette and Fitzpatrick have gone with most of the men, to the other camp to dazzle them with our two flags—They have gone prepared to out brag or to bet their friends, that we have two horses in our camp, faster & better than theirs—As the last, they have two horses upon which they are to rely —They propose to make a horse to sweat in their places and to convince by his heels, for their lack of argument—

JULY 5, 1834—They have returned with songs of triumph—The horse from this camp beat the horse from their camp—And our bully beat their bully—Ergo, say we, our's are the best horses and best men —Querie? Wouldnt it be better, to say *generally* that we have the best *animals*—

JULY 6, 1834.— *I have been busy all this day writing a letter to my mother, which I am not yet convinced will ever be necessary, as I cannot determine until the very moment of Mr Sub's departure, whether I shall go or stay. When on guard this night I combed my hair with a wooden comb & I percieved it crackled like burning grass —At this elevation I suspect that every nonconductor will do the same by friction, having been told a day or two before that a silk handkerchief and an opishomo would produce fat [?] sparks at night —A false alarm yesterday & to day, about Crows or black feet being seen in the vicinity of the two camps has stirred our blood—200 red skins were reported to be in a short distance of the lower camp, by a frightened, root digging squaw—twelve antelope were aggrandized into as many men by an unarmed fisherman from our own—Speaking of digging, the Snake Indians call diggers, Shokonee's. There are savages, I have been frequently & I believe credibly informed, living upon the waters of the Calafornia who in all things subsist like quadrapeds eating grass & roots & have no covering but that which nature has given them. For three days & nights there has been nothing heard but drumming & singing the invariable accompanament of gambling—Tis truly astonishing what excessive love these red beings have for sport almost equal to that of their white bipeds—This day I know that a superannuated old squaw has broken eight or ten of the youths of the camp. A young gentleman white man lost every shirt he possessed, but the one he wore, on the game of hands, at which Madam Flathead is invincible.*

JULY 6—Anderson's letter to his mother has not been found. His remarks about the "Shokonee's" or "*Shoshokoes*" (as variantly rendered in Diary and Journal) are interesting in that ethnologists deny that the name has any meaning. The distinction is so consistently made between Shoshonis (Snakes) and Shoshokoes in the annals of the fur trade that the latter term should be studied further. The term "Digger" was very elastic, applicable to nearly all the mountain-desert tribes, particularly those of Shoshonean stock, who dug for camass and other roots to supplement their diet of animal food.

The gambling game "Hand" is also described by Stewart: ". . . a group of gamblers . . . were seated in a circle, and chaunting the air which accompanies their game. A small piece of carved bone, often taken from the body of the fox, was held by the gambler, who joining his closed fists together, one above the other, could thus pass it into either, he then separated them and threw his arms wide apart, singing and jerking his body up and down, and again bringing his hands together, and changing or pretending to change the bone, the gamblers choosing only when the hands were held wide apart; if the guess is right, the guesser pulls away his pile with that of the bone holder, previously arranged beside it; and if inclined, a new bet is made, when the juggler or the bank, as he might be called, has nothing more to bet, he gives up the bone, or if the successful guesser chooses, he may, as is generally the case, take his place. [In a footnote Stewart says, "There is also the bye-play of those who back the caster, especially if he is an adept, and this sometimes supersedes the necessity of his backing himself."] The scene is particularly animating from

JULY 6, 1834—It is very strange, how irresolute the mind will sometimes become—I can not detirmine whether to return with Mr Sublette or to remain until next spring—I have been employed all day writing a letter to my mother, yet I fear I shall yield to my wishes, and homeward go—When on guard last night I heard my hair crackle, like burning grass, as I combed it with a wooden comb. One of the men, a few nights before, told me that a buffaloe-robe and his silk hankerchief had given out sparks—Yesterday & to day we have had alarms in both upper and lower camp—At the A. F. C. a root digging squaw reported that she saw two hundred Crows, near that camp—One of our silly fellows who had wandered off a fishing without his gun, was taken with the Black foot fever and aggrandized a dozen harmless antelopes into as many Indians—All this is exciting, but not very funny—The *diggers* are a small poor band of the Snake Indians who are unable to follow the buffaloe, having no horses— hence they are compelled to live on fruits, roots and what small game they can kill on foot—The wealthier and more cavalier part of that nation, who can afford horses are called buffaloe Indians—the sans culottes portion, Diggers or *Sho*shokoes—I have frequently been told, that there is a nation living on the waters of the Calafornia, who are

the exciting song and action, being joined to the deep and desolating passion of play" (*Edward Warren*, p. 271).

A different description is that by Warren A. Ferris: "Gambling seems not to be disallowed by the religion of the Flatheads, or rather perhaps is not included among the number of deadly offences, for they remain incurably addicted to the vice, and often play during the whole night. Instances of individuals losing everything they possess are by no means infrequent. Their favourite game is called 'Hand', by the hunters, and is played by four persons or more.—Betters, provided with small sticks, beat time to a song in which they all join. The players and betters seat themselves opposite to their antagonists, and the game is opened by two players, one of each side, who are provided each with two small bones, one called the true, and the other false. These bones they shift from hand to hand, for a few moments with great dexterity, and then hold their closed hands, stretched apart, for their respective opponents to guess in which the true bone is concealed. This they signify by pointing with the finger. Should one of them chance to guess aright and the other wrong, the first is entitled to both true bones, and to one point in the game. Points are marked by twenty small sharp sticks, which are stuck into the ground and paid back and forth until one side wins them all, which concludes the game. The lucky player, who has obtained both the true bones, immediately gives one to a comrade, and all the players on his side join in a song, while the bones are concealing. Should the guesser on the opposite side miss both the true bones, he pays two points, and tries again; should he miss only one, he pays one point. When he guesses them both, he commences singing and hiding the bones, and so the game continues until one, or other of the parties wins." Ferris adds, "The women are as much addicted to gaming as the men. They play at Hand, and have also a game which is never played by the other sex."

The addiction of Indians and whites to Hand is well attested by the literature. See, for example, Wyeth, April 30, 1833; Victor, *River of the West*, pp. 227, 261; Field, *Prairie and Mountain Sketches*, p. 138; Wislizenus, *Journey to the Rocky Mountains*, p. 89; Irving, *The Rocky Mountains*, II, 185-186; and Marsh, *Four Years in the Rockies*, pp. 191-193.

DIARY

JULY 7, 1834.—*God has made this for another day therefore let it pass.*

JULY 8, 1834.—*Vacillating all day between tarrying or returning. Rode down to Dripps camp to defend a murderer but conscience made a coward of him & he fled.*

JULY 9, 1834.—*We expect to commence a homeward march today. Great God, how wearisome & monotonous will be the way—*

To resume, as I wish, my task of journalising, I shall have to go back to the day of Mr Sublettes return & set down events and time subsequent to it, upon the faith of a shadow of a sketch.

JULY 8—Anderson's Diary shows how difficult was the decision whether to return with Sublette or remain in the mountains with Fitzpatrick. Both Diary and Journal mention a murder trial that did not come off. This may have been the affair underlying the episode in Stewart's novel *Edward Warren* in which a character is tried for murder and found guilty (though Stewart had departed with Wyeth six days earlier). In one of his factual footnotes (p. 321), Stewart says: "The death of Reece really took place by the hand of a man he had threatened, in the way described. The object of Reece's mad love was this man's wife; thinking, if it was reported to him that he had sworn on the Bible to destroy him the first opportunity, he would believe him in earnest and let her go. He met with his death from the husband on one of the small streams which run into Snake River, near [the site of?] Fort Hall, waylaying him on one of his visits. There was a court of inquiry, or something of the sort, but the threats had been so notorious, that the act was universally considered justifiable; and Reece himself, in dying, declared that he had nothing to say against the hand by which he fell." The name of the husband does not appear. The murdered man was perhaps T. S. Reese, whose name recurs in mountain annals from 1829 to 1833, then disappears, except for an ambiguous entry in the Fort Hall Account Books, which may or may not indicate that Reese was still alive in 1835.

in the most complete state of nature, the truest disciples of Pythagoras, refraining from flesh (because they cannot get it) and subsisting on grass, herbs & roots like the beast of the field—The only covering, a small plaited mat of grass, after the fashion of good mother Eve's fig-leaf dress—For three nights in succession I have heard the songs of the gamblers all night long—Their excessive fondness for this practice, cannot be surpassed by our own most accomplished faro-dealer—If they have no *dandy bird-lime*, to entice the young and thoughtless into their hells of corruption, they have other enticements, a rich bank of "fanfaron" articles, drums and songs, and woe to the victim, who is found betting on the game "of hands" against the Flat-head *Sin si pee*. I know that she has to day relieved a young man of my acquaintance of all that he possessed except the shirt he wears—It merely consists in passing a bone, from one hand to the other, while you are looking at her. And in such a manner as to defy your senses—

JULY 7, 1834.—This is another day gone—

JULY 8, 1834.—Uncertain yet whether to hie me home, or not—I was offered a fee of $150 to defend a man accused of murder before a self constituted court—I rode down to the other camp to appear for him, but conscience made a coward of my client and he fled—

JULY 9, 1834.—Mr Sublettes starts to St. Louis to morrow—I shall not go with him—I know I shall feel his absence very sensibly, never have I seen a man, in whose skill, prudence and courage I have more confidence—Every way, I think he is an estimable man, and I think I know him—I have slept with him, I have eat with him and if I have not fought with him, at least I have been with him, where we thought it would have to be done—There is no man in whose company I would rather do it—To morrow I shall bid adieu to him, a good and brave man—

JULY 10, 1834—*Then I find that he struck his tent & marched away. Capt Çéri joined him. Same evening Mr Vasquez, with 10 men started on his hunt.*

JULY 11, 1834—*We moved not camp.*

JULY 12, 1834—*Moved up stream.*

JULY 13, 1834—*One of Frapps men—old Vollier getting lost came to us.*

JULY 14, 1834—*A large party of Snakes came to us under Brâcelette de Fer—a talkative, humourous, graceful, tall & rascally savage. Tis said that he begins to find that "the sceptre is passing from Judah."*

JULY 10—The second volume of Anderson's Diary begins on this date. Sublette must have given Anderson a partially blank notebook to continue his diary. Obviously Anderson allowed the Diary to lapse for several days, then at an undetermined time brought it up to date.

What little is known concerning Sublette's inbound journey comes principally from an item in the St. Louis *Missouri Republican*, Aug. 26, 1834, which obviously owes to Edmund T. Christy: "A gentleman who reached this city yesterday from the Mountains has sent us a note, in which it is stated, for the information of the friends of those who accompanied Mr. Provost (of the American Fur Company), 'that his party had not been attacked by, nor had they a fight with the Pawnee Indians last spring', as was reported. Mr. W. L. Sublette and Capt. Cerre have perhaps arrived at Independence [i.e., Lexington?] by this time—the former with 60 or 70 packs, and the latter with about 20 packs of Beaver. Mr. Provost intended leaving the rendezvous on Ham's fork of the Rio Colorado, six or seven days after the writer of the note, who left about the 10th of July. Last spring the writer visited Fort Vancouver, an establishment of the Hudson's Bay Co., situated 90 miles above the mouth of the Columbia; he left there on the 31st May [March?], and lying by 37 days reached Independence on the 16th of August."

A letter to Sublette from James Aull, dated Lexington, Missouri, Aug. 30, 1834, says: "On Wednesday the 27th inst. I loaded John L. White & A. Marshals waggon with your fur. Took a receipt from each which I forwarded to A. & G. W. Kerr & Co. by the waggons and retained the duplicate. I advance each waggoner $20. and am to pay them the remainder on their return to this place. If the fur is delivered according to contract, you will please pay over the amount to E & A Tracy on a/c J & R Aull. . . . Your waggons left Thursday morning and expected to reach St Louis in 11 or 12 days. They carry this loading low and I hope you will try and get them a back load" ("Letters of James and Robert Aull," V, 282).

Michel Cerré and Joseph R. Walker were encountered by Wyeth in the highlands between the Green and Bear rivers on the afternoon of July 4, en route east with Bonneville's furs. They must have reached the rendezvous on Hams Fork July 5 or 6.

Anderson's separate mention of Vasquez in the Diary may indicate that the latter did not accompany Sublette on leaving Hams Fork. With his ten men he began to operate out of Fort William on the Laramie. During the fall Vasquez apparently made his way to the South Platte. He wrote his brother on December 30 from a locality he designated as "Fort Convenience," giving his mail address as Fort William.

JULY 12—Fifteen or twenty miles' travel, noted in the Journal, might have brought the camp to the great bend of Hams Fork below present Kemmerer, Wyoming.

JULY 10, 1834.—Mr Sublette accompanied by Capt Céri and Mr Christy, took his departure for the whiteman's country.

JULY 11, 1834.—0—

JULY 12, 1834.—Moved up stream, fifteen or twenty miles—

JULY 13, 1834.—Continued our march up the fork and camped in a fine bottom of grass, not far from where the St. Louis trail crosses it— One of Mr Sublettes old hands who had remained with Frapp, being lost from his party came back to us—

JULY 14, 1834.—A large party of Indians, Snakes, under Bracelette-de-fer, joined us this evening—This chief is a very fine specimen of an Indian leader—He is a tall and well made man—he has an intelligent, but cunning face—Tho he can wear a very strikingly grave and commanding countenance, it is most frequently brightened with smiles—He is very fond of laughing and talking, and I was told by those who understand his tongue, that he is very humourous—In postures and gesticulation he is extremely graceful and expressive— These are things however by no means confined to him—Every savage of these deserts, is as graceful and dignified, as a Roman Senator —The dirtiest hunter in his lousy robe, will display finer and nobler attitudes than the most accomplished actor—The slightest observation, will prove this fact, to any one, who has seen them, and the least reflection will suffice to shew the reason—Each child, male or female, has its little blanket or rabbit-robe, in which it sits, stands or walks— Nature and example soon teach it to envelope its little limbs in such

---

JULY 13—The "St. Louis trail," referred to in the Journal, would have been used primarily between 1826 and 1831 in traveling to the rendezvous in Cache Valley and at Bear Lake. From the Green River westward, the trail was evidently what became known after 1844 as the Greenwood Cutoff and after 1849 as the Sublette Cutoff. It crossed the Green below the mouth of Labarge Creek, turned southwest to Fontenelle Creek, followed this stream up a few miles, again veered southwest to the head of Slate Creek, crossed the divide to Crow Creek, and descended this stream to Hams Fork. From Hams Fork west to Bear River Wyeth's party traveled the "St. Louis trail" in 1834; and it was described in its entirety by William H. Gray's letter of Sept. 9, 1836, to David H. Ambler (Whitman's wagon having been taken to Fort Hall from the 1836 rendezvous by this route).

To judge from Anderson's comment, Henry Fraeb was evidently not far off, though he had sold out his interest in the Rocky Mountain Fur Company on June 20. No information has appeared about his man "old Vollier."

JULY 14—For "Bracelette de Fer" or "Iron Wristbands," see the biographical sketches.

JULY 15, 1834.—*A blank.*

JULY 16, 1834.—*Do.*

JULY 17, 1834.—*To day Messrs Shoshonees took their leave of departure.*

JULY 18, 1834.—*A day of sleepy indolence.*

JULY 19, 1834.—*Mr. Fitzpatrick & B. visited the A. F C.s camp, which has moved up within 8 or 10 miles, to transact some business which is as yet sub rosa. The arrival of a war party of Snakes, about 150, with some female prisoners dissipated all thoughts of business. A gentleman of the lower camp, very generously ransomed three of these unhappy captives who would otherwise have been doomed to inevitable death. The eldest, a mother with one infant child, was the wife of their antagonist chief, a Eutaw, & one of the most dreaded of the savages of this western world. His name as pronounced by the Whites is Gomorrow-wop. I think this woman is the best specimen of a squaw which I have yet seen. She has a reflective matronly countenance. Her captor alone, displayed some humanity and magnanimity—he sought a purchaser for his prize, saying that he liked her & did not wish to see his women kill her, as they would do, with all the barbarity of hells angels, dancing, singing & laughing at her mortal pangs. He wished to reserve her boy but she said, "no, no. "I will endure all rather than leave Gomorrow wops son" he surrendered the handsome infant to its mother, recieved his trifling recompense and departed. Sad is the fate of us poor mortals but far more so is that of captive females of a savage tribe.*

JULY 19—The "sub rosa" business with which Anderson tantalizes us was the merger of Fitzpatrick, Sublette & Bridger with Fontenelle, Drips & Co. in consequence of the division of the fur country between the American Fur Company and Sublette & Campbell; see Introduction. For the Ute Chief "Gomorowop," see Conmarrowap in the biographical sketches; and for the ransom of the Ute women, the sketch of William O. Fallon.

manner, as to allow the most free, easy, and consequently graceful motion. As the right hand and arm, are frequently in use, in gesture, the robe is thrown around the body passing over the left shoulder and retained by a slight pressure of the left arm upon the breast, leaving the other, its free and unrestrained action—The language of signs which is understood by all savages, gives grace, flexibility and impressiveness to every possible motion of the head, hands, arms and body—I am certain that I have several times seen in a small camp, a motion of the hand and arm, an inclination of the head, with an erection of the form, as dignified and statue-like, as I ever saw made by Booth, Cooper or Forrest—Their—pause—is peculiarly forcible— I had rather hear and see after an animated harangue the "Cara-*ho-mick*" I have *done!*—of ["]Bracelette-de fer," than to listen to the majority of the best speakers of our country throughout—Old "Bracelette" percieves that his authority is on the wane—The sceptre is passing from Judah—His brother, the Soldier, it is supposed will soon supplant him.

JULY 15, 1834—O.

JULY 16, 1834—do.

JULY 17, 1834—The Shoshonees took leave of us—

JULY 18, 1834—These days in camp are fit only to be slept away and counted—

JULY 19, 1834—M. m. Fitzpatrick and Bridger visited the A F camp which is now only a few miles off, to negociate an affair of business which is yet "sub rosa["]—The arrival of a war party of Snakes with some Eutaw prisoners put an end to all business—The little Soldier, already mentioned, who is a restless, busy warrior had met with a party of Gomorowop's band defeated them and brought off five women and several children—Among them the wife and child of the brave Eutaw chief—Her captor, the Soldier, shows a noble and a generous heart. He seeks to dispose of her—declaring that he likes her too well to take her to his camp, where his women would like hells dark angels, tear her flesh & yell and dance and sing, while she

JULY 20, 1834.—*Our camps are joined for several days march, when there will probably be a general breaking up till winters cold shall drive them to their folds.*

JULY 21, 1834.—*We crossed a very precipitous mountain on to a small branch which runs into Clyman's fork or New fork which ever shall prevail.*

JULY 22, 1834.—*Passed through Fontanelle's hole on Clymans fork—and camped after passing it on Le Barge's fork.*

JULY 23, 1834.—*On a small creek about which there is a disputed name—Harris terming it marsh-fork—F & others denying that this, or any other bears the name.*

JULY 24, 1834.—*In same camp, where we expect to stay on 3 days—*

JULY 20—By inference from the geography, supported by the phraseology of the Diary, the combined camps this day moved another 20 miles up Hams Fork to present Dempsey Basin.

JULY 21—Anderson had followed the old Indian trail northeasterly up Beaver Creek from Hams Fork, as shown on the U. S. Geological Survey's *Cokeville* quadrangle. The trail climbed over the Absaroka Ridge to strike the bend of the South Fork of Fontenelle Creek where this stream emerges from its deep, southward-trending canyon, continuing east a few miles to the open expanse now called Fontenelle Basin. Fontenelle Creek itself was then known as Clyman Creek, James Clyman having trapped there as one of Ashley's men in the spring of 1825, and perhaps in 1824 as well. By a misreading of Jedediah Smith's manuscript map, the creek is termed Ryman Creek on the Gibbs copy of this map, reproduced in Morgan and Wheat, *Jedediah Smith and His Maps of the American West*. Anderson is the next to use the name. The last known reference to Clyman Creek as such, "Clamons fork," is by W. H. Gray in his letter of Sept. 9, 1836. When Fontenelle's name displaced Clyman's is not known, but it must have come as an extension of the term "Fontenelle's Hole," mentioned by Anderson on July 22. Neither is it known why the name Fontenelle's Hole was applied. Lucien Fontenelle, after coming to the mountains with Joshua Pilcher in the autumn of 1827, may have trapped this area in the spring of 1828. The maps of Bonneville and Warren A. Ferris showed no awareness that such a stream as Clyman or Fontenelle Creek existed.

JULY 22—This day the combined parties turned north up the Fontenelle Basin, following Fontenelle Creek some 10 miles to Pomeroy Basin, then on a north-northeast course went about 5 miles across the ridge to Labarge Creek. The name of this stream dates from 1825, when one of Clyman's men was killed by Gros Ventres on the stream's lower course. (He was perhaps the Charles Labarge recorded as living in St. Louis in 1819.) Bonneville's map represents the creek as "Libergos Fork." In the literature of the fur trade, Anderson's is the only connected record of travel on this route, though Joseph Williams may have traveled it southbound in 1842.

JULY 23—Travel this day was perhaps up Labarge Creek about 10 miles, to the Lander Cutoff of later years, then east across Thompson Pass to South Piney Creek in the Snider Basin. It is possible a shorter trail was followed, leaving Labarge Creek 5 miles lower to ascend Packsaddle Creek, climb Packsaddle Ridge, and descend Trail Creek to the South Piney and Snider Basin. Again see the *Cokeville* quadrangle. Piney Creek is represented on Bonneville's map as Grand Encampment Creek.

writhed in the agonies of death—Her son he wished to keep, but she said—no! no! no! I will go to your women, I will not leave Gomorowop's son. He yielded both for a pittance and departed—Two other young squaws were rescued from a miserable end—The inhuman and shocking indignities offered to the dead bodies of their victims are the effects of female rage—They follow after their warriors and commit the most unheard of atrocities on the bodies of those, who may possibly have slain their friends or relatives—

JULY 20, 1834—We are now all together, and will perhaps remain so until each trapping party shall start for the scene of its labours. They will not reassemble until winter shall again drive them to their folds—

JULY 21, 1834—In our westward [i.e., eastward] march, leaving Hams fork, we descended one of the most frightful points of the mountains, that ever man or beasts slided down—I dont know how I did it—but here I am safe, in a sweet little valley, surrounded by thousands of balm o[f] Gileads and Aspen, with a clear, noisy little brook of liquid crystal, running through it. We are on the waters of Clymans-fork—

JULY 22, 1834—Passed through Fontenelle's hole on Clymans fork, and shall roost for this night, on the banks of Le Barge's fork—.

JULY 23, 1834—We camp on a little tributary of the Seitscadee, which seems to have no fixed name—some call it Piny-fork, others Marsh fork—I should be inclined to baptise the little stream Council creek, as we are to be detained on it several days for that purpose—

JULY 24, 1834—nothing to write, except that we are stationary.

JULY 25, 1834.—*The songs of the gamblers sounded in my ears the livelong night. The old Flat Head Sybele Sinsipee invariably presides at those concerts—This is a scene for the memory, not for the tongue. Perhaps all people, civil & savage deem it necessary to dress up this demoralising vice with meretricious ornaments to seduce the fascinated victims to their ruin.*

JULY 26, 1834.—*A desire to find a pair of ram's horns lead me to attempt the ascent not of the hill of "Fame's proud temple", but of one equally difficult. So much so that I could not effect it. I found some old acquaintances on the mountain's rough side—the little snow birds. They are now in the season of incubation. The feathers of the belly are of a brownish red. The tail feathers when spread showed the two bordering whites. I find a bird of the jay species here, resembling strongly the citizen of the states, but of a paler blue—no bands —no top knot—having the head[,] in front of the eyes & including them above and below[,] white. Pine squirrels are very much like the common or grey squirrel in shape & dress—a little more reddish on the back—about as large as the blue rats which were the predecessors of the Norwegian strain. A few pieces, of, distinctly marked, petrified pine likewise rewarded my labours.*

JULY 27, 1834.—*Moved camp about fifteen miles on to another fork of the Seitskeidee—We are moving now East. Eastward let us go! In three or four days a party of sixty or more will leave for St. Louis, I may go too It remains to be seen—Ah capricious youth!! I fear that my dear little friend Blackhawk is lost. He is missing all this day. A second Black-foot fort upon the trail was seen to day. These gentlemen seem to have been waylaying the trappers last fall.*

JULY 26—Anderson's climb may have been up the slopes of the Thompson Plateau immediately east of Snider Basin, or more probably in the Wyoming Range to the west, where Mt. Thompson, 9,728 feet, is the commanding peak.

JULY 27—This day's travel probably was northeast to present North Piney Creek. Anderson's comment in the Journal makes us reflect that in the eighteenth century it was thought that mastodons and mammoths might still roam the western wilderness. Jefferson's instructions to André Michaux in 1793, in connection with a proposed transcontinental journey, envisioned this possibility.

JULY 25, 1834—The songs, or the see-saw whines, of the gamblers were sounding in my ears all night—The old Flat head female, who in person and form is a Sibyl and a Circe, in her seductive allurements, is always presidente at these meetings—No people civil or savage but are resistlessly attracted by the smiles of the divinity of Chance, and yet all deem it necessary to adorn this lascivious queen with guady trappings to seduce the victims to her stye of infamy—

JULY 26, 1834—A desire to find a pair of rams horns induced me to attempt a steep, (not of Fame's proud temple,) but of one equally difficult upon which I had hoped to have planted my solitary feet and where I expected to obtain the objects of my search—I struggled upwards with praiseworthy assiduity and perseverance, but to no avail, my exhausted breath and overexerted muscles made me turn my unwilling steps and sight downward again—On the side of this unscaleable mountain I met with some little friends, the snow birds, in the time of their incubation—At this season they are paler on the backs, and the pure white of the breast and belly are of a reddish cast now—The jay of the mountains resembles the citizen jay very much, in shape—but his colour is a paler blue—no bands of white & no top knot—about one half of the head, including the eyes, is white —The little pine squirrels which I here saw distinctly, for the first time, in shape and colour are very much like the common grey— Their size is near that of the old fashion blue-rat, or perhaps between his and that of his Norwegian successor—A few specimens of undoubted petrifaction, the wood and bark of the pine likewise rewarded my labours—

JULY 27, 1834—Moved camp to a small creek, fifteen miles east—A party will start for St. Louis, in a few days, with the furs belonging to the American Fur company. If my only acquaintances Fitzpatrick and Fontenelle, (I mean associates) return with them, I think I shall look towards sunrise and turn not back till I see Kentucky, that land of the east and of chivalry—My own state is the only one, according to the traditions of the first Americans, according to the fathers of Philip and Tecumseh, from which they have not been forcibly driven. Our fathers have taken possession of the neutral ground, to which none laid claim—they have done no one injustice—twas the

JULY 28, 1834—*I went out to look for my wandering Diomed, but looked in vain. I fear much that he is to enrich some villain pied-noir. It would be less felt (his loss) if I thought he would enjoy unbridled liberty on these mountains—In a short time he would become a beautiful wild rover of the prairies—Adieu my faithful charger! No more shall you bear me fleetly to the frightened herds of buffaloe. I hope no savage shall profit by your speed.*

JULY 29, 1834—*Four hunters were sent out to look for the two lost horses—one of the company's—they returned unsuccessful.*

JULY 30, 1834—*Rien pour écrire.*

JULY 31, 1834—*Presque la même.*

battle ground of the savage, the unpossessed pastures of the Mastodon and the buffaloe—My little charger Blackhawk is gone, I fear forever. He strayed this morning and no one has seen anything of him. We passed to day a large Black-foot camp—It consisted of numerous cedar-log forts—Whenever they can, they make their encampment in the woods, and fortify themselves by cutting down the trees and fastening them together at the top, leaving an entrance near the churn-like base quite ingenious and singular—The trees are made to lap over so as to resemble somewhat the winding opening of a conch shell—One may concieve the singularity and beauty of such a road-side village when the limbs and leaves are all fresh and green, which are allways suffered to remain. Some of these verdant pyramids had not yet gone into the seer and yellow leaf, this betokens that we have had neighbours, and such as would have visited us, if they had dared.

JULY 28, 1834—I have been hunting for my horse all day. No signs of him—He is gone—I believe I should be less grieved at his loss if I did not fear that some villain black-foot would catch him and ride him to death in chase of some ignoble beast or savage—In a short time he may become a beautiful, free rover of these desert mountains—He will gaze in wild liberty, from some lofty eminence, upon the immense herds of buffaloe feeding beneath him   His bright eyes flash, when the morning sun awakes the eagle in his cloud encircled eyrie, and summons the graceful antelope to outstrip the winds in speed—

JULY 29, 1834—Four men were sent upon a fruitless search for the two lost horses—One of the company's is gone too—

JULY 30, 1834—A blank—

JULY 31, 1834—"Toute la même chose—"

AUGUST 1, 1834.—*This morning of three Eutaw women ransomed by Mr. Fallon, two have run off. Poor creatures if they have done thus merely to exchange Masters they are sadly deluded—if they are endeavoring to return to their own homes & friends they are attempting a hazardous but praiseworthy action—We have moved on to a little creek about six miles from Horse creek, in about twice the distance from the wind-river mountain whose sides are blanched with snow. I believe two suns more will lighten us on our route homeward. Okahaī! Okahaī! which is equivalent to 'hurrah—go ahead.['] I have been searching unsuccessfully for several days, a pair of rams horns to stock my pistols with. This suggestion of mine has been highly applauded by the ingenious. They think it would answer in respect, of both beauty & strength—Sorry I am that I can not put it to the tests!*

AUGUST 1—For the Ute women who ran off, see Anderson's entry for July 19. The day's travel was probably again northeasterly to a camp on present Cottonwood Creek, shown as Marsh Creek on the Hayden map. According to Irving, Horse Creek was so named because on its banks "Smith and Fitzpatrick" were robbed of their horses. (*The Rocky Mountains*, I, 216.) This event occurred in the spring of 1824 when Smith and Fitzpatrick were trapping entirely different parts of the Green River Valley; Clyman, who was with Fitzpatrick, has a fuller account. Beckwourth's story that the stream was named in the spring of 1825 for a wild horse that Ashley's party found on its banks cannot be correct; Ashley did not travel so far up the Green River. Anderson's mountain-climbing exploit, described in the Journal, may have involved the comparatively low Aspen Ridge, between Cottonwood and Horse creeks. See the U. S. Geological Survey's *Big Piney* quadrangle.

AUGUST 1, 1834.—This morning two of the Eutaw squaws, ransomed by Mr Fallon of the Snakes, ran off—If they have gone with no other motive than to exchange one master for another I apprehend they have not sufficiently weighed the dangers to be incurred against the advantage to be gained—I hope that the wife of Gomorrowop and the mother of Gomorrowop's son, will return safe to the fealty of her lord and restore the beautiful boy of the chief to his father's arms—We are camped on a little brook about six miles from Horse creek, and twelve from the Wind-river mountain—It is still silvered o er with snow—Last night when visiting my guard, I had an opportunity of witnessing the intense enthusiasm or Swiss love of country—I found one of the guards an Alpine mountaineer stretched upon the ground leaning on his arm and gazing by the moon's silver light upon the Alabaster Andes—I approached him softly and found him melted into tears—I spoke to him but he could not answer until relieved by the overflowing of his heart—He exclaimed, Oh! Switzerland! Oh mine country! He then, as if unable to restrain himself, sang "heim ava' in a touching an[d] affecting style—So much so that I could not refrain from giving a few drops of dew in sympathy with his longing soul—I this day also felt a fellow-feeling with Goldsmith, or at least claimed the priviledge of echoing his noble and manly sentiment which his proud heart cherished, when looking down from a mountain's height on a lovely mass of green—"The world, the world is mine." When about leaving our encampment, our little foundling was not returned from a buffaloe chase—This morning, on my Spanish horse Blanco, a good climber, I ascended a very lofty and steep Mountain to look for a straggler from our camp—Twas the highest of the high—How bright and balmy was the air! how distant and how rugged the view! On one side bands of buffaloe feeding peacefully in their undisturbed pastures, on the other, tens of thousands rushing wildly from the terrifying sight, and still more alarming scent of man! Here, a solitary eagle, circles in the air. There shines, with modest light, a huge rock of unstained Chalcedony—Far far down chrystal streams glisten in the distance—And here and there I catch a faint view of a long line of pigmies, winding through a narrow pass —I stood alone up, high up. No living thing, that touched the earth above me, & Nothing that breathed, between me and the heavens, save the lone eagle, which sprang from the spot on which I stood—

AUGUST 2, 1834.—*I have had a conversation to day with several of the mountaineers by which I have learned some particulars concerning the Big & little lakes and Bear river—This latter is a river quite as large as the Seitskeidee and affording nearly as much water as the Platte—it first runs nearly a due north course, then capriciously, & as some one said, foolishly, leaves a plain of easy passage, & turns south to bully & break up immense granite bound mountains in its way. The last mentioned lake is the 1st on the borders of the river— it is a most exquisitely beautiful "tableau d'eau" its length is about twenty five miles, its breadth seven or eight, by a small stream of a few miles it communicates with Bear river. Surrounded by mountains & interspersed with a few mountainic oasis as islands. The Big lake is at the termination of the river—it is about one hundred and fifty in length forty or fifty wide   This too has its islands of mountains but at so great a distance as to seem but mole hills. The waters of this lake has this remarkable difference from the river & lake beforementioned, that whilst they are* very *sweet & pure they—the waters—are so very saline as to encrust every thing with salt so soon as it is withdrawn from them—even hands bathed in it will whiten as soon as dried. Between the two lakes, on bear river, there are every variety of mineral springs—one of soda or so like it as to be so termed by every one who has tasted it.*

The longest branch of the Arkansas heads within a few miles of Grand river—The South branch of the Platte rises in the black hills, near to the heads of the Arkansas. The waters of the green river which loses its name in the Spanish country & becomes Grand river rises between the big lake & the Rio del Norte—

AUGUST 2—Anderson's is a good hearsay description of Bear River and Great Salt Lake; the elaboration in the Journal is not an improvement on the Diary. Bear River, scarcely the size of the Platte, rises in the Uinta Mountains, flows north and west to Soda Springs, then capriciously turns in the open plain where it almost joins the Portneuf, to cut its way southward through lava canyons to Cache Valley and wind on down to Great Salt Lake. The first known white men to see the Bear were detached Astorians with Joseph Miller in the fall of 1811; thus the returning Astorians under Robert Stuart who traversed it from Soda Springs to Thomas Fork next summer called it Miller's River. The name Bear River was applied in 1819 when a detachment of North West Company trappers under Michel Bourdon reached its banks from the north, finding it frequented by black bears. The river was familiarly known to the American mountain men from the autumn of 1824, when John H. Weber's party from the Big Horn reached it after crossing South Pass and the upper Green River basin. The southern shore of Bear Lake (also known in the era of the fur trade as Black Bear's Lake, Sweet Lake, Sweet Water Lake, Weber's Lake, Little Lake, Little Snake Lake, and Trout Lake) was the scene of the rendezvous in 1827 and 1828. Anderson's description of the lake is excellent, except that it has no islands worth mentioning. He overestimates the length of Great Salt Lake, which is about 75 miles, and understates the size of its islands, most of which are large. The

The little moving things, I scarce could see, were men. To any up-turned eye I must have seemed a horseman in the clouds—But! What a little thing is man! One moment filled with the pride, the ambition of Lucifer, & before a second heart throb, humbled into dust with self abasement & terror—I found myself on the edge of [a] precipice, in an instant—all sense of sublimity gone   The stiffness, the coldness of absolute fear seized upon me—There was no self-help in me, but thank God my dear old Blanco, with less sensibility, & I think more sense, saved his almost mind-less master—I descended, but did not boast of my adventure—

AUGUST 2, 1834.—Some inquiries of mine, elicited a conversation and a description of the great salt lake from two or three of the oldest and most intelligent trapers, the particulars of which were of uncommon interest and curiosity to me—It is an inland body of water without any visible or known outlet—one hundred and fifty miles in length, and from forty to fifty in breadth—of the deepest and most beautiful green—The shores are encrusted with salt, formed by the exhalation of the *spray*—the same indeed running some distance in to the lake, like a pure and shining pavement of alabaster—A far in are mountain islands, sunk by distance, almost to the waters edge—Such is the extreme saltness of its waters, that a hand will be whitened by the saline particles which evaporation leaves upon it, *if washed in this*

---

mineral springs on Bear River are now mostly lost in the waters of the Soda Point Reservoir, though a spring above the town of Soda Springs is maintained in a municipal park. The Journal mentions the Steamboat Spring, described by Wyeth, Bonneville, Frémont, and innumerable others. Anderson is to be understood as saying in the Journal that Bear Lake is about 10 miles from Bear River, not that distance from Great Salt Lake.

The scientist Anderson alludes to in the Journal is George Louis Leclerc, Comte de Buffon (1707-1788), whose *Histoire Naturelle, Générale et Particulière* was published at Paris in forty-four volumes between 1749 and 1804. On this page of the Journal, Anderson wrote, at a later date, "In a late number of the F. library, Fraser, Persia, is a beautiful description of just such a lake—the Uremiah." The allusion is to James Baillie Fraser (1783-1856) and his *Historical and Descriptive Account of Persia*, first published at Edinburgh in 1834, republished by Harper and Brother at New York in 1836 as No. 70 in their Family Library. (Another edition appeared in 1842 as No. 74 in the Family Library.) Fraser refers to "the great salt lake of Urumeah or Shahee" in the province of Azerbaijan (pp. 50-51).

Anderson wrote the paragraph on the river systems of the West in the end pages of his Diary; for convenience we have placed it in his text here. He does not fully distinguish between the two principal heads of Grand River—the Colorado itself, known to mountain men as Blue Fork, and the Grand River proper, later called the Gunnison. In his remarks on the South Platte, as in his third letter to the *American Turf Register*, Anderson seems to regard the Black Hills as identical with the Rocky Mountains; he conceives of the Rio del Norte (Rio Grande) as extending much farther north than is the case—a common failing of maps in the 1830's.

AUGUST 3, 1834.—*The arrangement some time contemplated between the two neighbouring camps, has been this day effected. They are now una anima, uno corpore—I have been thinking, perhaps presumptuously, of giving some information to the heads of department of the state of the best people in the world—the Flat-Heads & Nez-percés—It would be national charity & policy to assign them a country, exempt from the annihilating visits of the Black feet—to give them protection & encouragement—tho virtuous & warlike they are too few to contend with their numerous foes. Such a people upon our borders would be the best terminal defenders possibly to be had.*

AUGUST 4, 1834.—*Another day of indolence gone.*

AUGUST 3—Anderson makes an important contribution to the fur trade record, in that on this day he notes the birth of the new concern, Fontenelle, Fitzpatrick & Co., which two years later was swallowed up by Pratte, Chouteau & Co.

The Flatheads and Nez Percés afterward needed protection less from their enemies the Blackfeet, who were much subdued by the devastating smallpox epidemic of 1837-1838, than from their friends the Americans, who wrested their lands from them. There is no evidence in the government archives that Anderson fulfilled his promise to plead the cause of the Flatheads and the Nez Percés.

briny sea—This lake is supplied with an abundance of water from two sources, the little lake, and bear river The smaller lake is a very lovely "tableau d'eau" about ten miles from the first, and contributes to it by a canal, a natural feeder of Bear river—This and the river are neither saline, but perfectly sweet and clear—The river is said to be a large one, and runs with considerable boldness. It rises not far from the head of the Seits ka dee—runs north, along the western base of Rocky mountains, leaves the plain by a southward turn and goes to bully and break up a huge arm of the rock bound Oregon, thence smoothly flows on until it recieves the addition of the smaller lake and pours itself into the strange and anomalous gulph—Buffon says there are many running waters which hold salts in solution, that are not perceptable except 'en reservoir' There are various mineral springs in the vicinity of the lake and river—among them a soda fountain, one of natures. A hot spring, which in discharging its heated air through a hole in rock which covers it, produces a sound like a miniature steam-boat and has caused it to be christened the puffing spring—This rises not far from, and flows into the Bear river, near its débouchement into the lake—

AUGUST 3, 1834.—The members of the two rival companies have associated themselves—They hunt and exist now "una anima, uno corpore"—As our government has, perhaps arrogantly, constituted itself the protector of the Indian tribes, within her claimed territory—I could wish that she would extend her helping power to the best Indians and incomparably the best people in the world, the Flatheads and Nez-percés tribes—Indeed I promised *Takin sherae tish*—or Rotten-belly that I would tell the Big Capitan of All the Whites,—that his heart was good. That he loved the Great Brave—That he had heard how he had struck the red man, where the sun was near (in the south, how he had ground up the White men that came over the broad water—I promised to tell our 'Chief" that he and his people had fought many fights with the Pugānies—That tho they had strong hearts, they were getting very weak—Tell the big capitan to grind up the Pugānees—I wish I could eloquently plead their cause before those who term themselves, 'fathers' of the Red-men—

AUGUST 4, 1834—No unusual occurrence to day—I have neither seen or thought anything, to make me wiser or better—

AUGUST 5, 1834.—*To vary the scene and banish the accursed monotony, we had a stabing match in the lower camp. Young Charbonneau stuck his butcher knife into a fellow for wishing to flog him, for merely telling him that he was a rogue.*

AUGUST 6, 1834.—*Bridger has started & I have bid adieu to my new acquaintances of the mountains. I have moved down to Fontenelle's camp—to await the departure of the St. Louis party, which I trust in God will be to morrow.*

AUGUST 7, 1834.—*This is the day & sacred & prosperous be it, of our return. There is a most general joy on the occasion. Our lodge this night will be the golden eyed heaven.*
    Day of departure descended the creek about—7 miles.

AUGUST 5—Anderson uses the term "lower camp" in the Diary in reference to that of Drips and Fontenelle. His mention of the stabbing match is the last reference to Jean Baptiste Charbonneau for five years.

AUGUST 6—With Bridger went Kit Carson, the best chronicler of the fall hunt. Carson says that about 50 men made up the party. "We set out, for the country of the Blackfeet Indians, on the head waters of the Missouri. . . . Five of our men were killed. A trapper could hardly go a mile without being fired upon. As we found that we could do but little in their country, so we started for winter quarters. In November we got to Big Snake River, where we camped. We remained here till February. . . ."

AUGUST 7—The details of travel which we have placed at the end of each day's entry in the Diary, from August 7 to September 11, are recorded in a separate memorandum Anderson kept in the end pages of the Diary.

AUGUST 5, 1834—A stabbing match took place, which had like to have produced serious disturbances in both camps. Last night—horses were cut loose and halters were stolen, which led this morning to the charges and recriminations that produced the difficulty—Charbonneau accused a young white fellow whom he had discovered prowling about in the night with having committed the theft—for which compliment he was kind enough to offer Baptiste a flogging—not choosing it, and being somewhat liberally inclined he lent the accused his butcher-knife up to the hilt in the muscles of his shoulder—This is, per variety—

AUGUST 6, 1834—The trappers under Bridger left us for their "*springs of action*["] this morning—There are many brave, rough fellows among them, whom I do most heartily wish well—They have been kind and accomodating to me, a stranger—I have been hungry in the desert and they have given me elk and buffaloe meat—I doubt not, that they would also have given me drink and raiment, if I had needed them—Soon I shall turn homeward—Forty days I shall travel towards the Sun, yet I shall not touch his home—I shall only be in the far West—Where is the West? Where is the East? I know no East—no West—

AUGUST 7, 1834—To day is fixed upon for our homeward march—Where shall I be on this day's anniversary? What changes will have taken place in my life and fortune in one short year? May not kingdom's perish, sovereigns die in the same space of time? To day I shall measure my stirrups—tighten my girths—Examine my rifle and prime my pistols all preparatory to a secure safe and easy voyage home—All bear faces brightened with joyous hope—To night we shall lodge in a vast lodge—the earth its floor—the heaven its roof, the golden eyes of heaven will keep watch over us. Sweet be our sleep, safe our waking!

AUGUST 8, 1834.—*We had a lodge in "a vast wilderness—a boundless space of contiguity, and never have I slept more profoundly—never was my rest more unbroken. My head this morning was silvered o'er with frost—still I am stout & well. Thousands & thousands of wolves on the perpendicular hills, over our heads, serenaded us the live long night. One most singular change in the temperature of the water, I have percieved as we have reached nearly the base of the continents great back bone, from an icy coldness it has become milk warm to the taste.*

We nooned on the Seitskeidee—camped at night on New-fork. [22 miles]

AUGUST 9, 1834.—*We made about 22 miles yesterday going about N.N.E.—. We are fifty seven strong. A guard every second night for each man. There has once been witnessd a most singular atmospheric phenomenon. On the 20th of June 1829, my informant Mr. Fitzpatrick was encamped at the forks of Wind river—a fork of the Big-horn, which is the main branch of the Yellow stone—when all of a sudden the air became of a dull smoky appearance so excessively heated that the skin seemd to be blistered at its touch. He states that he believed that his eyes would melt from his head. Tracks of Indians on foot, very fresh, were discovered yesterday. I will mark this day with a white-stone. I have been fortunate Black hawk & the grey is found—Mr. Fitzpatrick toted them into camp after following them four or five miles. They have been lonely wanderers 13 days. This evening we are encamped on a fork of Sandy, having made a long day's march—say thirty miles.*

Nooned on another fork of the new fork—three or four miles above a noted bute & a little above where the horses were found—15 miles since morning. [30 miles]

AUGUST 8—The previous day Anderson seems to have traveled down Cottonwood Creek some 7 miles. On the 8th he struck nearly east to the Green River, on which he nooned after traveling perhaps 6 miles. He continued on, another 16 miles by his estimate, to New Fork. The distances seem overestimated, and identification of the route is complicated by the Diary for the 9th, which gives the direction of travel on the 8th as north-northeast. Possibly the course should be east-northeast, and the night camp on New Fork, about 5 miles below present Pinedale, Wyoming. The day's journey would more nearly have approximated 12 miles than 22. Anderson's travel over the next few days may be compared with Wyeth's journal for July 24-28, 1833, eastbound from Horse Creek to the Big Horn.

AUGUST 9—Anderson did evade guard duty by the plutocratic method, as the Journal indicates he would, for in the end pages of his Diary a note says: "Charles Matt to stand my guard—50.00." No further information appears about the man (Matthews?) with whom this engagement was

AUGUST 8, 1834—Last night the wolves long howl, (and big wolves and little wolves, old wolves and young wolves, all joined in that howl), made the shores of Seitskadee reverberate with their hellish songs—My white locks were still more blanched by the hoar *rime* which glittered on my *un*covered head. The temperature of the water which has been hitherto insupportably cold, has changed here under the brow of the mountain, to milk warm. 22ms—

AUGUST 9, 1834—We are in number 57, which reduces us to the necessity of standing guard every second night—I shall buy off. There is sometimes felt in these plains, heat, as oppressive as on Petra's scorching steppes—When Mr. Fitzpatrick was encamped at the forks of Wind river he experienced a simoom or something similar—On 20th June the sun became red, the atmosphere was substantialised and bore a dull, hazy appearance, and the heat was so intense that his eyes felt as if they would have melted out of their sockets—Where the gusty wind touched the unprotected skin it crisped or blistered— His lungs notwithstanding the hot air circulated, laboured as tho he were gasping in an empty reciever.—our sentinels would have challenged a mole for stirring last night—The bare tracks, very fresh of some ten or a dozen Diggers, put them upon the "who comes there"? *Bang!* A little fright now and then, is your best soldier maker. I found my horse to day, which left camp 13 days ago—Poor Black hawk, he has run and starved himself nearly to death—His eyes and nostrils seem to be enlarged one third, such has been the effect of constant terror—Tho there is nothing which more terrifies a horse, than the sight and scent of buffaloe, yet by some insuperable and unaccountable power they rush into the midst of them and surrounded by that terror of terrors fly as long as their legs will bear them onward—At first sight of these fearful looking creatures—the perspiration will sometimes break out from their loins—their ears become stiff and forked, and their neck ridged with fear—I have heard my horse sigh as piteously as any truant school boy condemned to his score—An untried horse will tremble as in ague fit, and complain audibly—In truth no Devil, fresh sooted from hell, can look more horribly, than these black bearded monsters—

---

made. Anderson's anecdote concerning Fitzpatrick helps to fill in the latter's scanty biography during the previous decade. The day's march would have been to Willow Creek, a southern tributary of New Fork, past Fremont Butte, and on to a night camp on the Little Sandy. As on the 8th, the estimate of distance traveled seems excessive.

AUGUST 10, 1834—*Another long march—say thirty one or two miles & short grass without the prospect of having better for several days. Poor horses! I am almost desirous of swaping fare with them. We bid adieu to the waters of the Pacific this morning and nooned upon those of the Atlantic. The little stream upon which we stopped was so very stingy with its contribution that we were compelled to cut holes through the sod & gravel to get water to drink, tis not wonderful tho that it doles out so little, for it calls itself sweet water. To night we shall sleep on the main sweet water. This is quite a bold pretty stream. I have picked up some specimens of isinglass near this spot.*

31 miles & camped on sweet water.

AUGUST 11, 1834—*We have been compelled to make a short march in consequence of the great scarcity of grass. Poor animals in a country where there is no grain tis distressing to see them suffer for the only substitute. Fifteen or sixteen hundred miles with little grass & less water is too hard. This evening a conversation was had upon the subject of the diminution of the buffaloe, which several of the oldest mountaineers pronounced to be very considerable. This lead to an enquirey as to the number of robes traded of the Indian Tribes by the American Fur Company, which seems to be enormous. Mr. Fontanelle lately of said company told me that three years ago there was traded from the Sioux fifty thousand robes. From this an idea, of the immense numbers of these animals which are yearly destroyed, may be formed. The uninformed too are to be taught, that for the purposes of trade, & for no other purpose, save the making of parfléches, are the bulls stripped of their hides. The season too of killing them is confined to about 2 months of winter; I mean for the making robes—for clothing, lodge making & eating they are destroyed throughout the year. In four days our hunter alone has butchered fourteen cows.*

On sweet water again—a short march, not more than 17 or 18 miles.

AUGUST 10—The party seems to have nooned on the Sweetwater where it emerges from the Wind River Mountains. The night camp was probably near what became known as the Last Crossing of the Sweetwater.

AUGUST 11—Anderson has now reached the trail traveled with Sublette when outbound in June, but the campsites vary. This night's camp appears to have been on the Sweetwater, near the mouth

AUGUST 10, 1834.—in the evening—A long and tiresome march—30 miles or more—short, dry grass and little prospect of better for several days to come—Poor horses! I wish I could divide my fare with you—We are enjoying rich, delicious food, whilst you are faint for want of sustenance—Farewell to the waters of the Pacific.—Pacifick, why pacifick? Upon the principle May be—of "lucus à non lucendo." To day we nooned upon the Sweet water—Twas sweet enough when we got it—Every man had to dig a partnership well, for himself and horse, with no other spades than his butcher-knife and fingers—This is the same long, clear and active stream which we struck at Rock Independence on our outward march—I found some beautiful specimens of isinglass—

AUGUST 11, 1834.—Stopped early this evening in consequence of the great scarcity of grass ahead—It is too distressing to see our poor horses suffering for a few blades of grass—after bearing us patiently all day through the hot sand—Tis a cruel necessity which compels each rider to shorten his rope, when he pickets his animal for the night—The old hunters in the camp conversed about the diminution of the buffaloe—There is a contrariety of opinion—Some assert that the number is fearfully less; others merely, that they have changed their regions of pasturage—Tho I have seen million and tens of millions at a view, I believe they are fast diminishing—And why should they not?—Mr. Fontenelle asserted this evening, to knowing ones, that the American Fur company at their posts on the Miss & Missouri rivers, traded with the Sioux alone, in one winter, for fifty thousand robes—For this trade, it is to be remembered the cows only are killed —The robes of the bulls are not saleable—Bulls are killed sometimes, for meat, when the cows are gestating, and sometimes to make lodges

---

of Willow Creek. The year before, Wyeth used a somewhat more northerly route, approximately that of the Lander Cutoff.

The record of Emanuel's hunt (see p. 181) should be compared with the Diary for the corresponding days. It is so abbreviated in form as to be easier to follow when quoted in its entirety: "August-8-9-10 & 11th Emanuel—has killed 15 buffaloes—12--but 5—13th-5—14th-1. c[ow]-15th 3. 16th. 4. 17th 5.—18th 4. killed & three wounded. 19th 7. Emanuel killed & butchered these buffaloes in a bout 2½ hours—This I know for a verity. Among them was a steer the ribs of which we shall eat this night. 20th & 21st While gone Emanuel has killed but 2 cows—a ram and an eagle— The skin of the ram, if I have good fortune, I shall take home—hoofs, horns and all—22nd 1-b[ull] —23d-1. c[ow] & 2 wild steeds a bay & a black. 24th 2 cows—25th 6 cows—26th-8—In addition to these there were killed by others 18 cows—27th 3—28th 6. 29th 1. 30th 3 2 bulls & 1 cow. 31st 3 1 c. & 2/b Sept 1st & 2nd-0." For Emanuel Martin, "One-eyed Manuel," see the biographical sketches.

AUGUST 12, 1834—*Nooned about eleven, upon a small tributary of sweet water, where I found a piece of mineral with which I am unacquainted. It looks as if it might have been in a liquid state, as lava &c, & hardened in cooling. There must be much mineral substance upon the head waters of this stream. I have found various beautiful specimens of isinglass, pure & mixed. We are camped this evening on the main sweet water, a mile or two below Sublette's camp where he found Vasquez letter at Fitzpatrick cache.*

We are this night on the sweet water near Mr. Fitzpatrick's cache —the water is low & grass very indifferent. [25 miles]

AUGUST 13, 1834—*We have encamped on sweet water below a very narrow pass between very high hills of stone, near where Sublette's camp, (one below the cache) was, ascending. Here within a few hundred yards of the spot where I saw the only sheep I have yet seen, I saw and gave chace to a fine large bear—he escaped into the brush & thereby avoided inflicting or recieving a wound of mortality.*

We have again made about 25 miles. We camp on sweet just below the narrow pass where Sublette took much precaution in passing.

AUGUST 12—The noon camp very likely was on Strawberry Creek. Concerning the geology of the area, Dr. Paul O. McGrew, Professor of Geology at the University of Wyoming, informs us: "About one mile up the Sweetwater from the mouth of Strawberry Creek the old trail enters an area of metasediments with 'graphite bearing layers and graphite schists' (see Spencer, *U. S. G. S. Bulletin 626*). The same zone is found beginning about three-fourths of a mile up Strawberry Creek from its mouth. Graphite schists would certainly fit Anderson's description. They would be wave-like, resemble both (or neither) stone or metal, resemble lead in *color*, have a soapy feeling and would be light for their bulk. The area also produces abundant mica or 'isinglass.'" Anderson was right in stating in the Diary that there must be "much mineral substance" on the headwaters of the Sweetwater. There the "Sweetwater Mines" boomed, beginning in 1867, and in 1962 a great iron mine was opened. For Fitzpatrick's cache, the Vasquez letter, and Sublette's camp, see the entry for June 10 and accompanying note. The Journal scales down the Diary's estimate of the day's travel from 25 to 11 or 12 miles.

AUGUST 13—Anderson here describes the Three Crossings of the Sweetwater much better than he had in June. The later wagon road had to cross the Sweetwater three times in 2 miles; hence the name.

of their thick hides. It would sound a little strange to persons in the settlements to be told that of our whole company, in which there [are] many good hunters, not more than one or two can enjoy the pleasure or the privilege of the chase—that only one or two can go into a grove of moving quadrupeds & kill & take meat at their will— Yet this is almost strictly true—and for good reason—It is the customary police [policy] of every moving camp, to employ a hunter who is acquainted with the route to be travelled, and who is skilful enough to feed a certain number of men—This will provide against unnecessary firing whilst we are in an Indian country; and also prevent rawhands, from giving the wind to the herds and thus the balance to the pangs of hunger—I shall perhaps keep a record of the cattle killed by Emanuel on our homeward march.

AUGUST 12, 1834—Moved to day only eleven or twelve miles—Still upon Sweet water—Near this place I saw a certain something—neither stone nor metal—In colour it resembles lead, it has a soapy feeling, and for its bulk, very light—It seems to me to be volcanic—There is a wave like mass upon a brow of a hill—which looks as if suddenly cooled in "rudis indigestaque moles"—In the same vicinity, I saw specimens of isinglass, and pebbles of every hue—We camp to night near Fitzpatrick cache where Sublette found Vasquez' letter—Not far from this spot I staid last June—Shall I ever sleep again near the same place, or on this river? God is great! I am in his hands—& *may* sleep the sleep of death here—"*Amen*"

AUGUST 13, 1834—We wallow to night near the sweet water pass— where Sublette halted last spring, going out—This is a place where the high hills of rock jut in on both sides to the very waters edge, and is always considered a very dangerous place; for an enemy could hover like a raven perpendicularly over our heads and send unavoidable death upon some of us—Here, in the spring, I saw the notorious big-horns for the first time—They were standing at an immense height above me—They were truly dwarfed by distance. The old buck and ewes seemed no larger than lambs—Near this place last night, I had the gratification of making a grisley bear, leave his dinner, and take to his heels—Tis well for my reputation he did, for had he made show of fight, I think I should have taken to my heels with a

AUGUST 14 1834—*A few hundred yards below an old camp of Sublette's ascending, & immediately above the very remarkable Kenyion of the sweet water through the mountains. This small, peaceful & now almost waterless stream after a running a long and noiseless course towards the east turns suddenly, without obstruction, to the north to attack a rocky earthless mountain which frowns indignantly upon its Liliputian foe from a 200 feet. Through this which may be three hundred yards in the distance is seen [i.e., the view extends] to blue mountains dwarfed into mole hills. The perspective is beautiful—I shall once more & perhaps for the last time, see the rock of Independence, in the morning.*

At the Kenyon, near rock Independence—I think we are this night 27 miles from last nights lodge.

AUGUST 15, 1834—*We are camped at a spring about midway between the Rock Independence and the red butes. This spring as, I believe, I before noticed is about three miles from one, where Gordon & Brown stayed a long time. We see a trail and a fresh encampment near where Sublette passed and camped ascending.*

Where we camped the 5th [6th] of June. [25 miles]

AUGUST 14—Anderson's is one of the best early descriptions of what became known as Devils Gate. Nathaniel Wyeth and Captain Bonneville passed without comment in 1832, though in returning to the mountains in June 1834 Wyeth observed the geological oddity, as did Cyrus Shepard. Father De Smet first seems to have recorded the name—may even have originated it. He went to the mountains in 1840 without mentioning Devils Gate, but on his second journey, in a letter dated Fort Hall, Aug. 16, 1841, he said that "travellers have named this spot the Devil's Entrance" (*Letters and Sketches*, p. 99). Frémont's *Report* of his first expedition to the Rockies (published, like De Smet's letters, in 1843) uses as of Aug. 2, 1842, the name "Devil's Gate," though Charles Preuss, one of his party, records in his diary neither name nor geological formation. The name came into common use after the appearance of Frémont's *Report*. Most travelers afterward took note of the curiosity. Literary force aside, the name was not particularly appropriate. It probably migrated from Hell Gate in Montana, the canyon east of present Missoula. Hell Gate, the Porte d'Enfer of the French trappers in North West Company service, was so named because it spewed predatory Blackfeet into the country of the Flatheads.

AUGUST 15—The camp was at Willow Spring. See the entry for June 6.

will—I should have run away, ["]to live to *run* another day"—By some, in camp, I was applauded as if I had taken a scalp—

AUGUST 14, 1834—This evening we are again in sight of the sweet-water cañon—which I mentioned before—This small, peaceful, and now almost waterless stream, after running a long and noiseless course, from East to West, turns a right angle to the north, and rushes, with its pigmy power, against an earthless, shrubless mountain of rock, two hundred feet in height and "mirabile dictu," by some aid—the aid of God, tears asunder the mighty opponent and passes on to its mother Platte—The perspective seen through this mighty cleft, is very beautiful. Looking through this casm, we see, rising out of the distant plain a hint of mountains, the Wind river mountains--blue, blue, pale blue and still more pale, until all form and colour melt into the far-away   To morrow I shall salute again perhaps for the last time Rock Independence. Will it be the last time? Who knows?

AUGUST 15, 1834—We ground arms again at an old camp—Here I feel as if I am with old friends—Here I have knelt and drank before—These trees I have seen—here was my fire—here I stood guard, and there fed my horse—This is a spring in the prairie, midway between Rock-Independence, and the red-butes on the Platte—About three miles from this place, Gordon and Brown, spent several summer months, waiting for traders—

AUGUST 16, 1834.—*We have again reached the Platte. Nooned at the red butes the second time. A. W. Sublette left his name on a tree, where I carved mine 5th June, indicating that he had reached that place from the Yellow Stone—he was at the butes 30th of July— 1834. I every day hear very interesting anecdotes of the Diggers. They are certainly the most singular and simple people in the world. Living, in consequence of their poverty, principally upon rootes, berries & such small animals as they can kill conveniently on foot with bows & arrows. Women & children are almost destitute of clothing at all seasons, in winter, covered, solely, with rabbit skins. An anecdote told me to day of the "black bird,["] chief of the Mohaws—sometime dead, evinces the despotic assuming tyrant as completely as any that history can shew. This chief when asleep, ordered that none should dare awake him save by tickling his nose with a feather. And upon no occasion could his subjects be induced to break this order—even tho an enemy approached. The dread of this man continued after death, he was buried on horseback upon the top of the highest hill on the shores of the Missouri— to observe as he said, the approach of the Whites.*

Camped on the Platte once more; thank God, about 8 miles below the red butes. Distance to day—28 miles.

AUGUST 16—For Andrew Whitley Sublette, younger brother of William, see the biographical sketches. For the Diary's mistaken date "June 5," see our note for June 6. An account of the Omaha chief Blackbird (Wash-ing-guh-sah-ba) is supplied in the biographical sketches.

AUGUST 16, 1834.—We noon on the Platte at the identical spot where we dined before—On a cotton tree hardby, is a woodman's letter, A.W. Sublette's name,—written with grease and charcoal, on a pealed place—stating that he had arrived there July 30ᵗʰ 1834, from the mouth of the Yellowstone, and was bound for Laramy's fork—Every evening, stre[t]ched out upon the grass around our welcome suppers, we while away the time, by telling stories of the past, reflecting upon things of the present, or anticipating those of the future—Accounts of those most strange and unparralleled people the Diggers—serve to give wing to many, an else weary moment—They, certainly are the most natural of all the children of Nature. They are called Shoshocoes in their own tongue, They are of the great family of Shoshonee's or Snakes—Their poverty prevents them from following the buffaloe, like the riding, or buffaloe Indians, (as they are called, that have horses) and are consequently obliged to content and support themselves by killing such small game as they can approach on foot—In default of this sustenance, they betake themselves to berries, roots &c—Sometimes even eating grass like a King, or a quadruped—Men, women and children, substitute for our progenitors figleaf, a covering of the skins of rabbits &c—Mr. Fontenelle related an anecdote of the Black-bird, a chief of the Mohaws which evinces as much of the haughty, supercilious tyrant as anything can do—One of his mandates, was that no one, on any occasion, should presume to awaken him, except with a feather. During his slumbers, should an enemy attack his camp, none would dare to arouse the sleeping lord, save by tickling his nose with the downy pinion of a bird—They obeyed his decrees with trembling, when living—and reverenced his order given when dying—He was interred according to his directions, astride his favorite steed on the highest hill on the shores of the Missouri—"Place me here, he said, on my war-horse, that I may see my friend the white-man when he shall come to the Mohaw's land."—The Black bird and his steed have crumbled into dust, yet the old man shudders at the terror of his youth. At his word an opponent would pine, and pining, die—Hundreds at the appointed time, would sicken, & die the death of agony—His prophecy was considered as fatal as the scythe of Time. Even the white man wondered at the unerring accuracy of his sinister predictions—To incur the displeasure of the Black-bird, was mortal—All felt and dreaded his blighting power.

AUGUST 17, 1834.—*All I can say of this day, is that it [is] worthy of praise in as much as it has help[ed] us on our way homeward some twenty seven or eight miles.*

This evening on a small creek on the right bank descending, made to day about 27 miles.

AUGUST 18, 1834.—*We have travelled about thirty miles down the Platte. I am now doing, what I had not an opportunity, & but very little inclination to do, when I came up—i e with a single companion I go ahead of the camp three five & sometimes ten miles. I believe I am becoming, what almost all who remain in the mountains are, callous & foolhardy. They have sometimes, & I may yet, regret the want of caution.*

On the north bank—to day we count thirty miles.

AUGUST 19, 1834.—*We have made a short trip to day. We laid by this evening at La Bonte's camp for the purpose of having some mules shod to send ahead on express. Mr. Fitzpatrick & myself will start ahead in the morning to Laramy's fork. It is about 50 miles. We shall possibly get there to morrow night by moonlight. A steer buffaloe was killed to day—A no uncommon thing I am told.*

At la Bonte's cabins—say 15 miles to day.

AUGUST 17—From the Diary it is evident that Fontenelle and Fitzpatrick crossed the North Platte near the Red Buttes instead of continuing down the left bank to the ford used in June. Frémont mentions this upper ford in 1842; it was well above the ferry site employed in later years, near present Casper, Wyoming. The party perhaps camped on Deer Creek.

AUGUST 18—Fitzpatrick and Fontenelle apparently recrossed the North Platte in the vicinity of Deer Creek to descend the left bank in preference to taking the trail through the Black Hills. The evening camp was near present Orpha. Anderson had camped here on June 3.

AUGUST 19—As seen in the note for August 11, on this day Emanuel "killed & butchered" seven buffalo in about 2½ hours, including "a steer the ribs of which we shall eat this night." Apparently the company again crossed the North Platte where Sublette and Wyeth forded the river in June, just below the mouth of Labonte Creek. Anderson's use of the expressions "La Bonte's camp" and "la Bonte's cabins" is tantalizing, for the name reflects some incident of the fur trade era, undated and unexplained, from which Labonte Creek derived its name. Rufus Sage, passing by with a company of trappers toward the end of February 1842, "encamped at the forks of a small stream called La Bonte's creek. Near the confluence of its waters with the Platte are the remains of a log cabin, occupied by a trading party several years since" (*Scenes in the Rocky Mountains*, p. 114). Field's account of the Hiram Scott tragedy, written in 1843, mentioned Scott's having become too ill to ride a horse at "a point known as 'Lebonte's Cabin,' on the Sweetwater" [i.e., the North Platte] (*Prairie and Mountain Sketches*, p. 64). Theodore Talbot on Aug. 7, 1843, alluded to "the

The secret was explained, however a short time before his death—A mercenary wretch, some hell doomed whiteman sold him a quantity of arsenic, with which, in secret he wrought his devilish will.

AUGUST 17, 1834—The day has passed as other days, the earth revolved and gave us a rising and a setting sun, darkness succeeded light—& fatigue has followed travel—

AUGUST 18, 1834—I find myself doing every day what I had no opportunity and very little inclination, in my Eastward march, with a single companion I leave the morning camp, and precede the company to our dining place—thus being seperated from them by 10 or 12 miles. I believe I should in short time become as callous, or more properly, fool-hardy as the rest—They have sometimes & I may, yet, pay the forfeit of my imprudence—

AUGUST 19, 1834—We have made but an indifferent march to day. We stopped early at La Bontee's cabins, to shoe the horses and mules of three men, to be sent express to the Bluffs. Mr Fitzpatrick and I will accompany them, to Fort William on Larameé's fork, where we will remain until the company shall overtake us. This will be the longest days ride I shall have made say fifty miles—Emanuel killed a very large and exceedingly fat steer buffaloe. This is no very remarkable circumstance, the Crow Indians alter a great many calves—and some suppose that accidents arising from the attacks of the wolves reduce others to this condition—

---

valley of 'La Bonte's cabins'" (*Journals*, p. 35); and Francis Parkman, between June 21 and July 10, 1846, referred to "La Bonte's Camp" (*Journals*, II, 445-454).

The identity of Labonte, the year he was in the area, and the special circumstances are unsolved questions. The name may date from the winter of 1831-1832, when a party under Drips is reported by Ferris to have wintered "at the foot of the Black Hills." The same year various detachments of the Gantt & Blackwell party wintered in the Black Hills. Zenas Leonard, with the group led by A. K. Stephens, told of building "houses, stables &c. necessary for ourselves and horses"—but that was on the Laramie itself, above its canyon, and no one named Labonte appears on the license issued to John Gantt and Jefferson Blackwell (Ritch Collection, Huntington Library). In the Chouteau Collection "Labonte" appears as an *engagé* at Fort Jackson on the South Platte in 1837-1838. David (or Davis) Labonte's name recurs in the records of the fur trade on the South Platte after Anderson left the mountains. A letter from Abel Baker to Sarpy & Fraeb, Fort Lookout, April 1, 1839, says: "Davis Labonte who left Guerrin in Taos, winter before last, is now in this country; but has no available property, and is out of employ." It is possible he was the Labonte involved.

AUGUST 20, 1834.—*As contemplated Mr. Fitzpatrick, & myself, accompanied by the express, left the company at La Bonté camp for the Fort, which we reached late in the evening. We travelled about 50 miles—without accident or adventure. The great gratification at length was afforded me of seeing the far famed Big horns. They are fine stately looking animals. This is Fort William where we drank the champaigne a few weeks ago—now there is enclosed one hundred feet, which gives protection to men and animals.*

From La Bonté's cabins to Fort-Wm, 50 miles.

AUGUST 21, 1834.—*The company reached Laramy's fork about 4 o'clock. All well & no accident. I have just found a long lost acquaintance, the day of the week. This day is Thursday.*

Laid by at the Fort for the arrival of the company.

AUGUST 22, 1834.—*We moved our bones from the fort this morning all in good health & spirits. Patton treated us very kindly, hospitably. I have sung and bid 'adieu, adieu to the mountain's brow" &c. I think I am taking a long farewell to them.*

Left Laramy & descended about 25 miles.

AUGUST 20—The distance from Labonte Creek to Fort William by Wyeth's reckoning was 59 miles. Both Diary and Journal now allude to the champagne episode of May 31, described in detail in the Narrative for that date. The Diary also gives the first stated dimensions for the fort.

AUGUST 21—Thursday was the correct day of the week; evidently Patton had been keeping a journal at Fort William. Anderson's mention of Patton on August 22 is the last contemporary reference we have. Very little is known about developments at the fort during the next nine months, until its sale by Sublette & Campbell to Fontenelle, Fitzpatrick & Co. in April 1835. Writing from St. Louis on Feb. 10, 1835, Robert Campbell commented, "We have now about 35 men engaged in hunting and trapping in that country." Even if Louis Vasquez and his ten men are included and allowance made for those brought by Andrew Sublette from the Yellowstone, Sublette must have hired a number of men at the rendezvous to join the dozen or so detailed in June to build the fort. His party had originally numbered only "about 37 men," and most of those who had accompanied him from the Laramie to the rendezvous were probably needed to bring down the returns of the R. M. F. Co. and furs bought on his own account. As seen in the note for August 11, when the company arrived at Fort William, Anderson remarked the fortunes of the hunter Emanuel in the two days they had been separated: "While gone Emanuel has killed but two cows—a ram and an eagle —The skin of the ram, if I have good fortune, I shall take home—hoofs, horns and all."

AUGUST 22—It is apparent that on leaving Fort William, Anderson forded the North Platte for the fourth time, presumably using the ford half a mile above the mouth of the Laramie.

AUGUST 20, 1834—As determined, Mr F. and my scribblership, left La Bontee's camp this morning with the light and reached Fort W^m with the night. On our ride—we saw a half dozen mountain sheep. Two were rams—noble looking fellows—they bore most admirable burdens on their heads. I did not get a shot at them—Well—here I am, at, and in Fort William—here a month or two ago, I aided in emptying a bottle of good, genuine, New York imported champaigne, to the "to be built["] fort, now, here she stands defying wind, rain & Indians.

AUGUST 21, 1834—Our companions of the Plains arrived at 4 o'clock —all are well—I have found at this place a long lost (it seems long) friend—the day of the week—This is thursday—Eh bien—Ill hold on to you, henceforth—

AUGUST 22, 1834—Friday—We moved all of our bones from the fort this morning, in good health and spirits—I took as warm a parting from Patten as if he had been an old friend—He has on all occasions treated me in a friendly manner—And here such treatment is particularly agreeable—I hope he may keep his hair on his head a hundred years—Farewell to him, the remembrance of his kind hospitality I will bear with me—I think I have taken a long "adieu to the mountain's brow—"

AUGUST 23, 1834—*Saturday. This night we are camped a short distance below Scotts Bluff on the opposite side. There is an island immediately by us, upon which a few years ago a frenchman was interred. The night previous he had a singular dream which was more singularly verified. He said, "I dreamed that I was descending the river Platte & stuck upon this island from which I could not be taken by the united efforts of my companions. I remained & died here.["] In a few hours he died & was buried there. Rest islander, Rest. This is a memorable day. I attacked, defeated but not killed a brown monarch of the Plains. I shot him in the shoulder and made him "traverse la riviere" cursing me from his hearts core every 10 minutes. Bands of wild horses are now sweeping over these wilds. Our hunter killed two stallions this evening.*

A short distance below the spot on which poor Scotts wolf-eaten carcass has long since mouldered. Nearly thirty five miles to day.

AUGUST 24, 1834—*Sunday. A few miles below the chimney. We consider ourselves about halfway to the Bluffs, we are 17 days en route and including 2 meat making days we think we shall be the same to the C. B. This evening I killed a wolf & robbed him of his brush—tis "une bonne medicine", says Emanuel. Saw C. Lajeunesse who had been sent from the fort in search of the Sioux & Chians. They saw none. Supposed from the trails that they have gone into the Black hills. Perhaps in search of the Crows. God grant it. They want a good flogging.*

E. P—about 30 miles to day.

AUGUST 23—We have found no other account of the unfortunate Frenchman buried near Scotts Bluff unless this was the man Brada or Brady, diversely reported to have been killed in 1827 or 1833, who gave name to Brady's Island.

As Anderson says in the note for August 11, the hunter killed "2 wild steeds a bay & a black." Men sometimes sought to capture wild horses by "creasing" them—stunning them by a shot that grazed their necks. Wild horses were occasionally shot for food, and sometimes just for sport.

AUGUST 24—Charles Lajeunesse was probably left at Fort William with Patton in June. As suggested by the Diary and Journal, the trappers were much dissatisfied with the Crows this summer in consequence of their having robbed Fitzpatrick, Stewart, and others the previous year. For "E. P.," or Chimney Rock, see the note for May 27.

AUGUST 23, 1834.—Saturday. Camp to night a short distance below Scotts bluff, on the opposite side—Just by us is an islet where, a few years ago, a frenchman was interred—The night previous he had a strange dream, which was more strangely verified—He thus related it—"I dreamed last night that I was descending this river in a small boat, which struck and fastened on that island, pointing at it, In vain did I labour to remove it—I called in vain for help, my own call was echoed back to my list[e]ning ears—I heard the mournful cry of —Oh help! The sound died on the waters—my knees bent beneath me—cold drops of sweat broke out upon my brow—I fell there & rose no more—Sinister foreboding! a few hours, and he was indeed a lonely tenant of that island—Poor solitary dreamer, peaceful and sweet be your slumbers—Tho far away from the home of your childhood, thy spirit shall reach the "bright hall of judgement" ere the sounds of the trumpet have ceased in the air____I had a memorable engagement with a grisley bear   I found his *majesty* mid sides in water, affectionately dandling an old buffaloe bull, as a mother would dandle her child—He evinced no disposition to leave me his prize—but on the contrary showed a most bear like indifference for me and my bearlike preperations—I shot him (as Johnny Gladen did the devil, with a leaden bullitt—I shot him with two, and after that, with my two ounces of lead in his huge carcass, he cursed me and quit, dragging his huge bulk along, he crossed the Platte and gave up the ghost with his scalp on his head—

AUGUST 24, 1834—Sunday. We have put the chimney or E. P. a few miles behind us. We consider ourselves about half way to the Bluffs from the mountains. We have been seventeen days "chemin faisant" & and including the meat making days, we expect to be as many reaching the above mentioned place—This evening I killed a wolf and robbed him of his brush—I bear this on my gun cover for "une bonne medicine" as Emanuel recommends—He almost every day adds some thing to his charm bag—I met Charles Lajeunesse who had been despatched from fort William in search of the Sioux and Chians—He did not find them—Supposes from the trails, they have gone into the black-hills in search of the Crows—The trappers think, and wish thus—They, the Crows, are becoming suspiciously audacious—

AUGUST 25, 1834—*Monday evening. More buffaloe to day than we have seen since we reached the river. Ten or fifteen wild horses peaceably feeding with them. The horse is an animal which did not originally belong to this continent. Even at the present day there are many indians who have but a common name for the horse & that animal which was its predecessor in domestic drudgery, viz the dog. This is a singular circumstance to us, yet I am most credibly informed that it is only the minority of savages who called them differently.*

30 miles to day.

AUGUST 26, 1834—*Teusday. Nothing unusual to day—the same old business of packing up & marching on till noon, from noon till night again, the same thing to be repeated to morrow and to morrow and to morrow for perhaps 18 or 20 to morrows before I shall be able to say this is my own, my native land. 'La Platte! La Platte! La Platte, is as wearisome, as "tourjours perdrix." We shall stop to morrow & maybe the next day to kill and make meat for the remainder of the journey. This is usual & necessary, for the buffaloe may give out, and in that case we should be meatless 15 days, to the settlements, or else eat our poor horses. Black hawk is dog poor & shoeless. Blanco has sores on his back, what I shall do when the hawk gets lame and the Espagnol refuses longer to bear the saddle —"sais pas" as the v. french say.*

32 miles, camped on a cotton wood grove about 12 miles above the cedar island.

AUGUST 25—Anderson's remarks on the wild horse are well taken. Paleontologists later discovered that the horse had flourished in the New World prior to the ice ages. It died out along with the mammoth and other Pleistocene fauna some 6,000 years ago, during a warm climatic period.

AUGUST 26—The night camp may have been near present Lost Creek, Nebraska. We have not identified the "cedar island" noted in the Diary. Before traveling 12 miles next day, Anderson comes to a noteworthy landmark, "the cedar bluffs." Possibly he wrote "cedar island" by mistake.

AUGUST 25, 1834—Monday. Immensely large bands of buffaloes to day, greater than any we have seen, since we reached the river. On the skirts of some of the herds were ten or fifteen wild horses peacefully feeding—Previous to the invasion by De Soto, of Florida the horse had perhaps been never seen on this continent—Tis asserted that the savages had long, a greater dread of this remarkable animal than of the steel clad Spaniard who directed him—That they have not been long acquainted with this invaluable friend and servant of ungrateful man, may be sufficiently proven by this fact,—that there is scarcely a single tribe that has given it a name—Most of the Indians that now make use of them—have but one name for the dog and the horse—The latter in fact has, in most things, been but the successor to the former—where he now is made to pack the lodges & provisions of the village, the dog formerly did it, the dog was once used to drag the sleigh in pursuit of the elk and the deer, the horse has now learned to bear the harness—Those Indians that have a different name for these two useful brutes are a small minority of those that now make use of the larger and more serviceable—He is called, the big Dog—

AUGUST 26, 1834—Nothing unusual to day, the same old business—some of it I can do with my eyes shut, *sleeping*, eating, packing, marching, unpacking and resting—Oh me! I wish I was done! the same thing to-morrow, and to-morrow, and perha[p]s twenty to-morrows, before I shall say this is my own, my native land—We shall ease-oars to morrow and the next day to make meat for the balance of the trip—This is a highly necessary precaution, for the buffaloe may give out, in that case we should be meatless 15 days to the settlements, or else eat our poor cavalry—My share would be hard-fare—for Black-hawk is dog poor and Blanco is covered with sores—What I shall do, when B. h. gets too lame and the old white no longer saddle*able*, "scais pas"—as the vulgar french would say—

DIARY

AUGUST 27, 1834.—*Wednesday. We have camped to day very early at a spring immediately above the cedar bluffs. This is a very charming place, a spring surrounded by an ash grove. A convenient and sometimes used, wintering place for the Indians. The Pawnee village was here 4 winters ago. To morrow we shall remain here meat making. Thence we shall home sweet homeward go.*

Not above ten miles to day.

AUGUST 28, 1834.—*Thursday. This day like its predecessor devoted to making provision for the remaining march. In the three days which we have been killing cows for the aforesaid purposes, there have been fifty slain. An anecdote has been confirmed to day, which was related sometime since—tis this, when a part of the R. M. company was encamped on black-foot river they were driven from there camp by an unequal yet resistless foe, yes thirty five or forty well armed men were defeated without the loss of a drop of blood by fourteen polecats. They marched all abreast, hair bristled & tails erect into the midst of the tents, ere they were discovered, by the surprised mountaineers. These comely gentlemen surveyed the premises & retired at their leisure unharming & unharmed. This singular story is asserted by the most intelligent & veracious persons belonging to these countries. The great salt lake at the termination of Bear river, which has been claimed to be discovered by Genl Ashley & which in the U. S. bears his name, I am informed by good authority has never been seen by him. False ambition often doubtless prompts to false assertion! Tis believed the credit, if there is any in the accidental discovery of a place, is due to Weaver or Provost. C'est egal.*

AUGUST 27—Anderson describes the locality later famous as Ash Hollow, as the Journal makes clear; so he had again forded the North Platte. He must have recrossed to the north bank the next morning. The rugged terrain below, which made travel difficult for many miles, was known during this period as the Upper Cedar Bluffs. Anderson's reference to the Pawnees at Ash Hollow must reflect the winter journey of William Sublette and Black Harris to St. Louis from Wind River. They would have passed by in January 1830.

AUGUST 28—Anderson's remarks on Ashley, Provost, Weaver (Weber), and the discovery of Great Salt Lake are an important contribution and should be read in conjunction with his third letter of 1837 to the *American Turf Register*, his letter of 1860 to the *National Intelligencer*, and our discussion on pp. 244-248.

194

AUGUST 27, 1834—and Wednesday—We are encamped quite early in the day, at a beautiful grove of mountain ash—I shall call it the ash-grove spring—This spot is on the south Side of the Platte in a deep cove, & bounded to the East & West by high perpendicular hills and immediately above the cedar bluff—The Pawnees have now & then, used this as a wintering place—To morrow we shall give general license to all disposed, to hunt the sullen buffalo—then we shall wend our way to sweet home—

AUGUST 28, 1834—Thursday. Counting this and its two predecessors fifty odd fat cows have fallen to silence the calls of our famelic stomachs—I have more than once heard the strange story which I am about to relate—I consider it corroberated sufficiently to bear the stamp of truth—A party of the Rocky mountain fur company, encamped on a branch of Black-foot river, was defeated and driven out of their tents by a small yet powerful foe, yes fifty well armed men, without a drop of blood, were compelled to take to an inglorious flight by fourteen pole cats   Without sound of horn or beat of drum they marched over the field of action their tails aloft and waving like banners of victory—These comely, sweet scented gentlemen, unharming & unharmed, surveyed the premises and retired—I suppose the worthy trappers, if challenged by the petty warriors, would have excused themselves in the same manner as a lion was reported to have done when a skunk threw down his gauntlet & dared him to the field—I will not fight, said the monarch of the woods, Why not? are you afraid? demanded the little brave—No—was the reply—but if we should contend, you alone would gain glory, if victorious, whereas, it would be known to my discredit for a month that I had been in the company of skun[k]s—It has been asserted by, or for Gen¹ Ashley, that he was the first white discoverer of the great salt lake; in either case, he is to blame, as it is not the fact—The credit, if the accidental seeing of a spot is entitled to any credit, is due to Mʳ Provost of St. Louis—At all events it seems to be generally believed that Genl A. not only did not first find that remarkable inland sea, but, that he has not ever yet seen it—From the accounts of others, he gave a description of it—on which account it is sometimes called by his name—prompted by false glory he acquiesces in the reception of false honours—

AUGUST 29, 1834—*Friday. After our two days rest we have again made on our homeward march about 25 miles. Camped to night at the foot of the cedar bluffs. In my thirst for blood, I sacrificed at noon a large Caiac & on this evenings march the largest & oldest rattle snake I ever saw. "Prenez garde, voila un gros serpent!" turns every horse from the trail & every french tongue to rattling in concord.*

AUGUST 30, 1834—*Saturday. Last night or rather evening we were terribly bedevilled by the musquitoes. I fear the same this evening & every succeeding one on the Platte. I find a very great difference between lying out here & in the mountains—there we arose fresh and dry from our blankets, here we are bathed in the dew of these bottoms & have our limbs to feel stiff & old—this latter will be all the better to think, laugh & talk about, in futuro. I think we shall noon at or about the forks tomorrow. In that case we shall be three hundred miles from its mouth, which is 12 days march for us. Eh bien, okahée, okahé.*

   28 [miles]—or about.

AUGUST 29—The night camp was doubtless on present Whitetail Creek, Nebraska. The "cedar bluffs" immediately below are located by the Mormon journals of 1847 and are mentioned by Samuel Parker on July 17, 1835.

AUGUST 30—Camp was probably on present Birdwood Creek, Nebraska. The reference in the Journal is to Stephen H. Long, and more particularly to Edwin James, *Account of an Expedition from Pittsburgh to the Rocky Mountains, Performed in the Years 1819 and '20 . . . under the Command of Major Stephen H. Long.* In the spring of 1820, by much the same route Anderson was now traveling in reverse, Long's party made its way to the Forks of the Platte, then up the South Fork into present Colorado. William H. Ashley followed approximately the same route to the Rockies in the winter of 1824-1825.

AUGUST 29, 1834—Friday. After our two days rest we have again made 25 miles on our homeward march—Camp to night at the base of the cedar bluffs   In my blood thirsty mood I killed an unusually large Caïàc, and the oldest rattle snake I have yet seen. The quick, clear cry of, "Prenez garde, prenez garde, voila un gros serpent à sonnettes" turns every horse from the trail, and every french tongue to rattling discord—I may say that I (having nothing to do) have been snake pelter general to the expedition—I have taken, as I have before said, most ample vengeance on the whole serpent race, for the seduction of old Father Adam's helpmate "the *rib*, and crooked part of him'—

AUGUST 30, 1834—Saturday. Last night or rather evening we were *bedevil*ed by myriads of kin claiming musquitoes. I fear the repetition, this and every succeeding night, whilst on the Platte—The Lord of comfort forbid! There is a very wide difference, between sleeping in the open air, here in the plains, and in the mountains. Here we arise with difficulty, wet & stiff, from the cold dews; there, we sprung up dry and gay, from our unmoistened robes—To morrow I think we shall noon at, or near the forks—in that case we shall be three hundred miles from the mouth, according to Mr. Long, which will occupy us twelve days more—Oka-hai—oka-hai—

AUGUST 31, 1834.—*Sunday, or as near to it as may be. We have seen much greater numbers of buffaloe than we had anticipated. We passed this evening a large Indian encampment, supposed to be of the Pawnees. They have been here, since I passed last spring, to make meat. From information to be relied on, I believe they have been a powerful tribe. Mr. Fontenelle has seen at one time 1500 lodges. Some notion of their strength may be formed, by allowing the general average of 10 souls to a lodge. We have not passed the forks yet. Since he saw their large encampment, they have been much weakened by war & small pox. The Crow nation claims to have 300 lodges. This tribe, as well as almost all of the mountain nations, except the poor Flat-heads & Nez percés, have very much increased of late years. Burns alias The long hair is now an old cheif, he still however wears his power as well as his hair. His*

AUGUST 31—The Crow chief Long Hair was one of the most interesting personalities of this era; see the biographical sketches. The Rain was pistol-whipped by Benjamin O'Fallon in 1825, when the Atkinson-O'Fallon expedition ascended the Missouri to treat with the various tribes, O'Fallon being Indian Agent for the Upper Missouri. The Crows (except for six lodges and forty warriors that were with Rotten Belly near the mountains) came in to the Mandan villages at Knife River on Aug. 4, 1825. Gen. Henry Atkinson's official journal relates: "at 11 went into council with the Crows & concluded a Treaty with them. Two Iriquois prisoners were demanded of the Crows; from this or some other cause unknown to me the Crows became very very hostile in their conduct, and from their attempting to take the presents before they were told to do so Maj. O'Fallon struck three or four of the chiefs over the head with his pistol. About this time Gen. A. [himself] who had been a few minutes absent from the council, to get his dinner, in returning to the council saw the commotion & ordered the troops under arms—this probably saved blood-shed" (Reid and Gannon, "Journal of the Atkinson-O'Fallon Expedition," IV, 36). Also see Irving's *The Rocky Mountains*, I, 216-217, which gives chief prominence to the interpreter Edward Rose; and T. D. Bonner, *The Life and Adventures of James P. Beckwourth*, pp. 83-85. Beckwourth says O'Fallon struck the Crow chief "a violent blow on the head with the weapon, inflicting a severe gash."

The Indians whom Fitzpatrick describes as the "buffaloe Snakes" first appear in the literature of the fur trade as "Plain Snakes." Alexander Ross says that when encountered by Donald Mackenzie in the Snake Country in the fall of 1819, their principal chiefs were two brothers, "Pee-eye-em" and "Ama-qui-em." Ross himself met Pee-eye-em in the Snake Country in the summer of 1824, and in the spring of 1825 Peter Skene Ogden heard of him while in Cache Valley: "Pe-i-em with all the Snakes are now absent on a trading excursion for Shells with another nation Some distance from this & are expected back this month."

William H. Ashley in his diary and narrative of 1825 leads us to think that the "Southern Snake Indians" had wintered in Browns Hole on Green River. Peter Skene Ogden in a "Snake Country Report 1825/26" commented that "Indians resident in the Snake Country are known by the name of Baniques [Bannocks] or Lower Snakes in number about 1500 men headed by 4 Chiefs and the plain Snakes, headed by 6 Chiefs, about 2000 in number. They in the Fall resort to Buffaloe, and in the Spring descend the South Branch [Snake River] and support themselves on Roots and Salmon. . . . The plain Snakes in their conduct towards us have so far comported themselves with propriety. They reside entirely in the Buffaloe Country—both tribes however annually resort to the Spanish Settlement called *Toas* more with a view of stealing Horses than trade, Leather and Buffaloe Hides are occasionally bartered with the Spaniards." Wyeth commented in a letter of May 20, 1848, to Henry R. Schoolcraft: "I am uncertain if any Indians inhabit any portion of this [Green River] valley, as being particularly their own, above Brown's Hole. If so, it is the Green

AUGUST 31, 1834—Sunday, may be. Having no divine one, we set off sermonless on our route to the great giant of waters—More numerous herds of buffaloe than we expected to see so low down—We passed this evening, an encampment recently deserted, supposed to be the Pawnee's—It seems they had been up buffaloing since I passed here in the spring—Their old camps point out their whereabouts—From authentick information the Pawnees have been a more powerful tribe than they are commonly supposed to be—Mr. Fontenelle was once in a village, in which he computed 15,000 souls. Allowing the usual number of 10 to a lodge, this would make a town of fifteen hundred moveable houses—Since that time, the double desolations of war and small pox, have waved their besoms, over their country, and swept off many a gallant brave, and very many expert horse stealers—The Crows—Absarokees claim to have 300 lodges, which would make them tell 3000 souls—These are a brave, boastful, stealing & lying nation—Their language is very expressive and is more susceptible of being reduced to written order than most other tongues—They have fine, poetic imaginations, & possess many eloquent men—This tribe, as well as most of the mountain nations, have encreased very much of late years—The Flat-heads and Nez perceés excepted. Old Burns, alias Long-hair, is, and has long been a principal chief—Like Sampson, his strength lies in his hair—Some of our belles, might envy his luxuriant head ornament—When Mr Campbell measured it (tis a great favor to touch it) two years ago,—twas eleven feet & four inches—This spring my friend Mr Vasques took its dimensions and found it to be 11.ft. 8 in^s This sacred

River Snakes, whose village of 152 lodges, I met on the main fork of Grand River, on the 18th July 1836. These Snakes appear to me to be of the same stock as those of Lewis River."

The first chief mentioned by the American trappers in connection with these Snakes appears under the sobriquet Petticoat (Le Cotillon). Whether he is to be identified with Pee-eye-em or Ama-qui-em has not been established. For his sons Iron Wristbands and Little Chief, see the sketch of Bracelette de Fer. In later years Washakie emerged as the leader of the Snakes who ranged into the Green River Valley and who were settled on the Wind River Reservation in 1868. Widespread though the Shoshonean linguistic family was, embracing the Northern and Southern Paiutes, the Chemehuevis, the Bannocks, the Utes, the Hopis, and the Comanches, as well as the Western and Northern Shoshoni, they extended to the Pacific only in the southerly parts of California.

These notes on the Indians are interesting and valuable, and we could wish that on his journey to and from the Rockies Anderson had been at all times so conscientious in making inquiries. His reference in the Journal to Hunter must be to that work, curious and of doubtful authenticity, John Dunn Hunter, *Manners and Customs of Several Indian Tribes Located West of the Mississippi* . . . (Philadelphia, 1823), reprinted in London the same year as *Memoirs of a Captivity among the Indians of North America.* . . . However, we do not find in this book any statistics regarding the Sioux.

strength like Samsons is located in his hair. When Mr Cambell measured it a year or two past, it was eleven feet & four inches long. Now it measures 11 feet, 8 inches according to Mr Vasques rule. The rain is likewise an old chief. This is the same distinguished individual who suffered the degredation of being knocked down in the presence of his whole nation by Maj. O'Fallon. The most warlike & dangerous savages of the R. mountains, stand next to the Sioux in number. They are said to have 1200 lodges. The Black-feet. The number of the Sioux can not accurately be ascertained, including the Asiniboines they are supposed to rise above 40,000. The Chians who accompany them & try to be assimilated to them, have about 150 lodges. The buffaloe Snakes or such as are rich enough to have horses & live on meat are thought by Mr. Fitzpatrick to have about 350 lodges—taking in however all the petty tribes who speak their language in his words they are innumerable, not innumerable if the computation by guessing were allowed. They extend to the Pacific.

I think we have travelled to day the same distance as yesterday 28 miles.

SEPTEMBER 1, 1834.—*I am about thirty miles below the forks of the Platte. This time will pass and give place to successive hours days & months, but I can not concieve a thing that will ever bring me to the same place at any given hour day or month. I think I am still between 900 & 1000 miles from home. Tis a long distance for very poor and diseased horses to carry me. This thing is unpleasant enough at present to make it very agreeable in future. I hope it may be so—it is anything but interesting now.*

30 miles.

SEPTEMBER 1—From Anderson's reference to the Forks of the Platte, we infer that the previous night's encampment was in that vicinity, a locality difficult to distinguish precisely, owing to the sloughs and islands. Anderson's mileages the rest of the way are frequently overestimated, sometimes by as much as 20 percent. Camp this night was probably near the present Union Pacific station, Vroman; on the next night, near present Coyote station, both in Nebraska.

growth, is revered as a great medecine—After winding twice around his body, it is secured over his stomach, in a ball, as large as a man's head—When it is let out, to be examined or combed, no one is to be present, but some bosom friend and a favoured stranger. Then, no one must spit in the presence of the chief—His hair at present is decidedly the pride of the band—The Rain, is another very old and distinguished chief. He is the same individual who suffered the degradation of being knocked down in full council, by Majr. O, Fallon— The Black-feet, Puhganees, are the most dangerous bloody thirsty, & next to the Sioux, most numerous of the N. American savages— They are the irreconcilable enemies of all mankind—With them, a coup is a coup—and a scalp is a scalp, be it of white, black or red—and they will make and take them, wherever, & whenever they can— They are believed to be 12,000 in number.—The numbers of the Sioux, are variously estimated. My informants, Mssrs. Fontenelle, Fitzpatrick & Provost, compute them at 25,000 including the Assiniboines. Hunter, exclusive of the latter, declares the nation to contain 40,000—The Chaians are very desirous of being incorporated into this powerful family—They keep as near to them as possible— They have about 150 tents—The buffaloe Snakes, (or such as are wealthy enough to own horses & live on meat,) are thought by Fitzpatrick to have 350 lodges, containing nearly thirty five thousand [more properly 3,500] souls—Including all that speak nearly the same dialect and belong to the Shoshonee *genus* they are incomputable—They wander, from the waters of the Calafornia to those of the Colombia, and from the R. Mountains to the Pacifick ocean—

SEPTEMBER 1, 1834—I am now about thirty miles below the forks of the Platte. This time will pass, and gave place to coming time— hours, days & months shall glide on and other hours, days & months shall succeed to them, but I cannot concieve a circumstance that will ever again bring me to the same place I am now on, at any hour, or day, or month. I think I am still 900 or 1000 miles from home. A long way, for poor wayworn horses, to carry me. This is very unpleasant at present, but I hope it will at least be like the negro's sore shins—"feel so good when he gettin well! ["] The troubles of the present, prove frequently the pleasures of the future!

SEPTEMBER 2, 1834—*Teusday. I have been astonished this evening at the immense numbers of buffaloe which are visible on the right bank, descending. This is low down for such large herds. The coarse and most unmusical guttural rumbling of several hundred bulls, are now rolling over the waters and prairie. It can be likened to nothing, that I know, except that hoarse ugly sound which is uttered by the lion, when enraged. These sounds which are always given during the running season commence in June & end in the latter part of August or 1ˢᵗ part of Sept. Frequently they seem almost present when they are several miles distant.*

30 miles.

SEPTEMBER 3, 1834—*Wednesday. We have made a good days journey, yet have fallen short of our haven contemplated at our mornings start, the mouth of the sheep's eye, a little wooded tributary of the Platte. To day and yesterday we have passed some eight or ten Pawnee encampments. To day some tracks much fresher then their camps seem. Seven days are allowed to reach the Bluffs. I hope it will require no more.*

At the least, 30 miles.

SEPTEMBER 4, 1834—*Thursday. Still travelling on the left bank of the river—Amidst fields of sun flowers & wild rye—The rye has a very long head with small grains. At several places in the mountains I saw a wild flax, resembling in every particular the cultivated plant, being only in bloom I could get no seed.*

35 miles this day.

SEPTEMBER 3—The night camp was perhaps near present Overton, Nebraska. The stream Anderson calls the Sheep's Eye may be Elm Creek, named by the Mormons in 1847.

SEPTEMBER 4—Interesting is the mention of sunflowers in Nebraska at this date. The night camp seems to have been near present Kearney.

SEPTEMBER 2, 1834.—I am amazed, this evening, at the immense herds of buffaloe that are in sight on the right bank descending— The coarse and most unharmonious guttural rumbling of several thousand bulls, is now rolling over the prairies—I can compare it with no other sound, that I am acquainted with, except the low, deep growl of the lion.—These rumblings, which are only heard in the running season, commence in June and end about the last of August or 1st September—Frequently they seem to indicate the animal very near, when he is several miles distant.

SEPTEMBER 3, 1834.—Wednesday. We have made a good days journey, tho we have not reached our contemplated haven, the mouth of the Sheep's eye, a little wooded tributary of the Platte. To day and yesterday we have seen several Pawnee encampments—We discovered some fresh mocasin tracks in the sand to day—Seven days to the Bluffs—I hope no more—I am so tired—

SEPTEMBER 4, 1834.—Thursday, descending the left bank of the Platte, through fields of sun-flowers and wild rye—The rye is exactly similar to that cultivated—At several places in the mountains I saw the wild flax in bloom—It grows in the most rocky and sterile spots—Being the wrong season, I could procure no seed—

SEPTEMBER 5, 1834—*Friday. We have nooned, and camped for the night on creek, which runs in to the Platte on the north side, called Gros-bois. Tis a small, wooded, clear stream with steep banks. We have all, to a babe, eaten to repletion of plumbs. We have travelled nearly ever since we reached the forks, on the Pawnee trails. This is very beneficial, otherwise the high rough grass would lame our horses feet. Tis rather discouraging to think that after so many days hard riding, I am still more than a thousand miles from home, but as Larz once said "B. A. S" & go ahead! This panacea I will try at all events.*

32 [miles]—On Gros-bois.

SEPTEMBER 6, 1834—*Saturday. We sleep again on the Platte to night, and as I hope & believe the last—at least so far as concerns myself "nunc aut in futuro." Nothing but great pecuniary interest could induce me to launch out again into these endless, everlasting prairies, where I hear every day the cry of "no bottom, no bottom!" & land, land, land, whenever timber is in sight—curiosity can no more prompt me. We have this evening passed the Grand Island, the longest* fresh water *river island, perhaps in America—it is at the least ninety & the Indians say 120 miles in length. It commences indeed, God knows where, & ends God knows where. This river like all other natural wonders, is an inscrutable mystery. I have a fine chance of being horseless by the time I reach the Missouri river, if not before. "Comme le Bon Dieu veux."*

On to the Platte again & 35 miles further on.

SEPTEMBER 5—Wood River, first depicted on Long's map of 1820, was called Great Wood River in the James narrative. The map accompanying the French edition of Father De Smet's *Letters and Sketches* (1844) uses the name Gros-bois. Anderson may have nooned near present Gibbon and made a night camp at present Wood River. Mention of a babe shows also the presence of Indian wives in Fontenelle's company.

SEPTEMBER 6—The camp was probably near present Chapman.

SEPTEMBER 5, 1834—Friday. We have nooned and are encamped for the night, on "Gros bois," which runs into the Platte from the North This is a very clear-watered, well wooded and steep banked creek—This evening we have all, even the babe, eaten to repletion of wild plumbs—And excellent ones too—Weve been travelling ever since we left the forks on the Pawnee trails—This is a great advantage—the tall, rough prairie grass would otherwise have rasped our horses hoofs to the quick—Tis rather discouraging, to know that after so many days good hard riding, I am more than a thousand miles from "heime ava"—yet—but as Larz once said to me B. A. S. & go ahead. I will *now* try the virtue of his panacea—

SEPTEMBER 6, 1834—We sleep on the Platte again, and as I hope and believe, (at least so far as concerns myself [ ]], for the last time. Nothing but a great pecuniary acquisition could tempt me again to launch out into these endless, everlasting prairies—where every day, I hear the comic and yet not unmournful cry of "no bottom, no bottom"—and whenever a timber lined stream is come in sight of, the reviving and pleasing ex[c]lamation of "land land, land"—Curiosity can no more prompt me, and health I hope I never more shall require to take the trip again. We have the long island in our rear at last—Grand Island is perhaps the most extended river isle, in the world—If not one, there are many chained together and bearing that name, which extend as many as 120 miles—I have mentioned this before —I may every day see and describe something which I saw and described before, but with additional knowledge and information—Of this island however, I believe that neither the ending or beginning is well known—it is so cutoffed & bayoued—I have a fair prospect of being horseless soon, as they are getting poorer and lamer. As the Good God wills—I will then take to my ten, in the best style I shall be able—

SEPTEMBER 7, 1834—*Sunday. We left the main Platte, and our usual east course, this morning, and started a northerly direction. About eleven, we descried Indians, the first we have seen. We camp to night on the Loup fork. The little chief, as he is termed by the whites are with us, & three other of the Tapage tribe of Pawnee's. I fear the musquitoes to night more a great deal, than I do the savages. This has been the most crooked days march I ever saw made.*

34 [miles].

SEPTEMBER 8, 1834—*(Loup fork) Monday. Last night the aforesaid gentlemen red-skins stayed with us. One is the chief of the Tapage band—the other chief of the Republican—Another—a son of a very noted chief & brave, named Long-hair. He is not yet a chief, is in a state of expectancy. They are all three very looking intelligent Indians. They speak a very manly fluent language & are very expert at signs, more signs than others I have seen.*

30 miles.

SEPTEMBER 9, 1834—*Coquille creek. Teusday. We have started & stopped—Nothing else!*
On Coquille creek—about 25 miles from our starting place.

SEPTEMBER 7—Fontenelle's company left the Platte between present Central City and Clarks, traveling north to strike the Loup Fork about 3 miles east of present Fullerton, Nebraska. Fontenelle had perhaps gone this way from Wood River to avoid the Pawnee villages farther up the Loup Fork. "The little chief" had been one of the signers of the Pawnee treaty of 1833; George Hyde notes that he was a Pitahauerat, and that his Pawnee name Tarawicadia does not mean Little Chief (*Pawnee Indians*, p. 136). Charles Augustus Murray, who spent the summer of 1835 among the Pawnees, termed "Tarawicadi-à (or the Little Chief)" "the head chief of the Tapage tribe, and a man of considerable influence and ability" (*Travels in North America*, I, 211). The Presbyterians maintained a mission among the Pawnees from 1834 to 1846. Letters of these missionaries, printed in Kansas State Historical Society, *Collections*, 1915-1918, XIV, 570-784, are informative but say little about individuals; however, John Dunbar perhaps refers to Tarawicadia when he says that on April 6, 1836, he "took lodgings with the first chief of the Tapage band, who has always treated me kindly" (ibid., p. 617).

SEPTEMBER 8—Anderson possibly camped this night about 5 miles west of present Columbus, Nebraska. His remarks about the Pawnees vary from those of the day before. The Republican (Kitkehahkis) chief might have been Capot Bleu or Blue Coat, whose Pawnee name has not been recorded. Long Hair was a chief of the Grand Pawnees (Chauis), "the second warrior of the village," described by John Treat Irving in 1833 as "a stern, gloomy looking man, with an anxious, wrinkled brow, a mouth like iron, and an eye like fire," even his smile more resembling "the angry snarl of a wildcat, than the evidence of any pleasurable emotion" (*Indian Sketches*, pp. 132-133).

SEPTEMBER 9—Coquille or Shell Creek was probably reached about 2 miles east of present Schuyler, Nebraska.

SEPTEMBER 7, 1834.—Sunday. Sans prayer, sans preach, we shook off the fleas and pushed on, in good style—This morning, we left, both our usual east direction, and the Platte, and steered north. About 11 o'clock we descried Indians in the prairie—the first we have seen—To night we roost on the Loup-fork of the Platte—The little chief and three other of the Tapage Pawnee's joined us this evening and accompanied us to camp. I am more afraid of the musquitoes, than I am of the yellow jackets, to night—A very crooked march.—

SEPTEMBER 8, 1834.—Monday. Loup-fork—Last night the above mentioned gentlemen redskins stayed with us—One gives himself out as chief of the Tapage Pawnees. The other is of the Republican band. A third is an uncommonly low, fat young man; the son of a very distinguished brave, named long hair—He is not a chief, but is looked upon as a young aspirant, in the line of promotion—All three of these had medals, with the impressions of Presidents upon them—The two first seemed to have been honoured in the time of Adams 2nd the junior bore the brave of New Orleans [Jackson] over his breast—They enquired into the respective merits of our "big captains," we placed our first fingers even together, and said, "tour-aha," which is, that they were just equal, and very great. A fourth indian accompanied them, I suppose, in the capacity of 'toad-eater' as he was subserviently attentive to all they said and did, grunting & shrugging approbation to every word or action. These, are fine, intelligent-looking Indians. They speak a very fluent, manly language; and are more quick and expert at signs than any that I have hitherto seen—

SEPTEMBER 9, 1834.—Teusday. Coquille creek, I have the satisfaction to know that:

> "I daily pitch my moving tent,
> A day's march nearer home."

The record of such a conviction is sufficient for the day.

SEPTEMBER 10, 1834.—*Wednesday. We camp to night at a small pond of water in the prairie between the coquille & the Horn. There are now four Ottos. They differ somewhat from the Pawnees and a great deal from the Mountains indians—the cheek bones of the latter are less prominent than those of the tribes more eastern. Say 30 [miles].*

SEPTEMBER 11, 1834.—*Thursday. We have at last reached the banks of the Missouri river, & I have seen the ruins of the "council Bluffs." To see men with boots & shoes on, & to dine at a table with knives & forks is a right pleasant thing. Another unwished for, yet amusing occurence, is the absence of all ardents, which has given exceeding*

SEPTEMBER 10—Even before Lewis and Clark ascended the Missouri in 1804, the Elkhorn, or Horn River, a principal tributary of the Platte, was well known to the French traders as the Corne des cerfes. The camp this night was probably near present Fremont.
For the Otos, see the note for May 13.

SEPTEMBER 11—By "ruins of the 'council Bluffs'" Anderson refers to Fort Atkinson. The Council Bluffs, west of the Missouri in Nebraska, about 25 miles above the present Iowa city of that name, were so called by Lewis and Clark in 1804. In 1819 the "Yellowstone Expedition," intended to establish a U. S. military outpost on the upper Missouri, came to a halt here. At first called Camp Missouri, but soon renamed Fort Atkinson, this post was maintained until 1827, when it was abandoned in favor of Cantonment Leavenworth. When Prince Maximilian passed the site in May 1833, he could see "only the stone chimneys, and, in the centre, a brick storehouse under roof. Everything of value had been carried away by the Indians."
Anderson's amused references to William O. Fallon show that he had traveled down from Green River with him. For John P. Cabanné and Joshua Pilcher, see the biographical sketches, which also explain Cabanné's surprising presence here at this time. What had been known since 1823 as Cabanné's House, the Establishment at the Bluffs, or the Oto Post, had been founded the year before by Joseph Robidoux. It was located several miles below Fort Atkinson and the same distance above the Missouri Fur Company's Fort Lisa. En route up the Missouri in 1833, Maximilian commented: "This trading post consists of a row of buildings of various sizes, stores, and the houses of the *engagés*, married to Indian women, among which was that of Mr. Cabanné, which is two stories high. He is a proprietor of the American Fur Company, and director of this station. He received us very kindly, and conducted us over his premises. From the balcony of his house was a fine view over the river, but the prospect is still more interesting from the hills which rise at the back of the settlement. Between the buildings runs a small stream, with high banks, which rises from a pleasant valley, in which there are plantations of maize for the support of the inhabitants. Mr. Cabanné had planted fifteen acres of land with this invaluable grain, which yield, annually, 2,000 bushels of that corn, the land here being extremely fertile. The banks of the stream are covered with fine high trees. . . ."
We have no additional information about the embroilment of Anderson's brother Charles. Johnson may have been Col. Richard Mentor Johnson, Vice-President of the United States from 1837 to 1841. News might have arrived by the steamboat *Diana*, which had just completed her second trip of the year to Council Bluffs. The missionary Samuel Allis, about to begin his work among the Pawnees, relates that the *Diana* started from Fort Leavenworth September 1 loaded with "a large quantity of goods for the traders above, & the annuities for the Otoes, Omohas & Pawnees" (Kansas State Historical Society, *Collections*, 1915-1918, XIV, 695). The *Diana* reached Bellevue September 7, and to judge by Anderson's comment, within twenty-four hours completed her voyage to Cabanné's post and started back down the river.

SEPTEMBER 10, 1834.—Wednesday. We are encamped to night at a small pond of water in the Prairie, midway between the Coquille and Horn creeks—Soon after unsaddling, four Ottoes came to our fires—In appearance they differ a little, from the Pawnees, and considerably from the mountain tribes—The cheek bones of the first are more prominent than the latter—They are more aquiline in the nose too, than those of the far-west—(not the farthest west—so very far, my knowledge does not extend).

SEPTEMBER 11, 1834.—Thursday. Why is it that I am not satisfied? I have always had some place in advance, to reach which, I intended to be contented—I expected, when I arrived at the fort on Laramee's fork, I should feel entirely free from personal alarm—perhaps I did, yet another engrossing desire took possession of me, I reckoned, & found myself a great way from the big river in hope, a place of rest. I next was all anxiety to be at the forks of the Platte, where I knew I should be only three hundred miles from the mouth—There—I wished myself at the Bluffs. Now here, my calculated figures tell me I am 900 miles from Louisville, my home—Restless being! I fear I shall never be settled & happy—Now for St Louis, then for Kentucky & again, for,—God Knows—where! for a man that cant be satisfied there—ought to roam 'toujours'.—We passed by the ruins of the old Council bluffs. Emblem of human fortunes—! One day—all a wilderness—another day—the strong-place of strong men—the next, a heap of rubbish—So with man—One minute, a child a helpless, puking child, In a little while, a proud strong man —lord of creation! and, yet, a little while a carcass, a rattling skeleton of dry bones—Where those chimnies stand—once was *Fort* Atkinson—This hollow bone, was once the beautiful head of a brave chief! Earth to Earth, dust to dust—ashes to ashes!—and all is done! _____To see men with boots & shoes on, to dine at a table, and to eat with forks again is a right pleasant thing—Who would have thought, 8 months ago, that such would be my thoughts at this time? Another unwished for fact, (the absence of ardents) has given me an occasion to feel secretly pleased at the disappointment of poor Fallon—He had set his affections upon a Miss-Jolie he expected to have had great fun in the wooing, and exceeding happi-

uneasiness and distress to one of my "companions du voyage" who had fixed his affections upon a "Miss frolic" at this place. The gentlemen in authority here (Mssrs Cabanis & Pilcher) have recieved us with all marks of open sincere hospitality & seem disposed to make us as comfortable & as easy as possible. The gentlemanly urbanity & ease of the first, which would distinguish him even in our western soireés, was as unexpected and agreeable in these wilds, as would the songs of the nightingale among Jack-asses—Not intimating that there are not gentlemen and men of genteel deportment wherever I have been, far from it, but that I have not seen & little expected to see, hereabouts, one who so entirely possessed the "tournure du beau monde." Mr. Pilcher is an acquaintance of Robert's & recieved me with politeness. He gave me some intelligence of a difficulty which has arisen between Charles & a certain gentleman *that has excited more apprehension & uneasiness in me, than all the trails & signs of Black-feet or Crows. I know nothing now except that there has been some publications upon the subject of Charles refusal to recieve an introduction to the said biped, who has accidentally been given the shape of a man. I hear that Noland stepped forward as C's representative in his absence & offered himself to that creature for any kind of satisfaction. I hope that N. will not be suffered to put himself into the least jeopardy on our account. I shall be uneasy until I hear & know more about it. It is no doubt, now, all passed, but all is to be learned by me. We most unfortunately reached here too late, a steam-boat left this place three days ago. Good patience! six or seven hundred miles more by land, on poor worn down horses! Alas poor Yoricks!*

25 [miles].

ness in the winning of her—His gala, spanish dress, he had whitened over—his milk white steed, he long had rubbed and dusted—and lo! there is no steam—his joy is dead—such a wo-begone phiz I have not seen these many days, & yet I cannot sympathise with him. Never mind, he tells himself—there will be a carnival among the still houses, when he reaches the settlements—I am very agreeably disappointed here, I have met with no acquaintance, & did not expect it,—but my brother Roberts name, is as good as a warrant of hospitality for me—The gentlemen in authority, at this place, Messrs Pilcher and Cabanis, have recieved me and my companions with marks of sincere friendship—Their generous offers and kind attentions, have made my heart glow with the warmth of unspoken gratitude—Pilcher, *almost*, made me cry, praising Bob! He has a friend in the desert—He ought to rem[em]ber that—if he, R does not, I will—May God bless Pilcher! But the polished ease and gentlemanly urbanity of M. Cabanis is what most surprised me—I might have looked for his accomplis[h]ed manners in the refined soireés of St. Louis, but I certainly did not, up here among these aboriginals—It was as unexpected and as agreeable, as the song of the nightingale, would be, among the dutch nightingales (croaking *bull frogs*).— He has, in eminent degree—what the French term "tournure du beau monde." I have just been informed of a difficulty which has occurred, between Charles and a certain being, misnomered! gentleman—This circumstance has excited in me much uneasiness— more I confess, than the tracks of the Blackfeet and Crows, altho I have a conviction that he is too mean to have courage—Yet he is to be feared, and for that reason—One may sometimes be stung by the flying adder—I know nothing, except that C. has been challenged and published, for not recieving an acquaintance that this biped wished to cram on to him. I also hear, that C. Noland, in Charles absence, from St. Louis, offered his services to [Col. Richard?] Johnson —I hope that Noland will not be permitted to soil his fingers with the creature If he must have a flogging, let it come from the right place—Besides I know, that no one can handle a skun[k], that will not be perfumed by it—And as C. has been near its hole, he should bear the sin of it.—"Hen me miserum!" three days ago, a steamboat left this place, for St. Louis—Bad luck to us, six or seven hundred miles by land on worn out horses—'Alas Poor Yoricks!

DIARY

SEPTEMBER 12, 1834.—*Friday. This day we have remained all day at Mr. Cabanis' establishment. I have not yet determined whether I shall go to the St. Louis by water or land—in either way, I expect to be blood sucked at all events.*

SEPTEMBER 13, 1834.—*Saturday. We bade adieu to Mr. Cabanis establishment & its inmates this morning, and are now resting for a time at Mr. Fontenelles about sixteen miles below. This is a very pretty situation well deserving the name it bears—"belle vue." Old human nature is again at work! and I am, by way of change anxious to put of[f] by water—This if the winds continue fresh up the river will be a long and tedious manner but my horses are too poor to start upon.*

SEPTEMBER 14, 1834—*Sunday. This is the first sabbath that has been observed by all for sometime I mean by our travelling party & I mean also observed only as to the article of rest. In honour of this remarkable fact I suppose, there was the greatest thunder & hail storm I ever witnessed. In the after noon was heard the most uninterrupted prolongued grumbling of thunder, which we all agreed in the supposition, betokened something unusual—I consciensciously believe I could have ridden eight or ten miles during the continuance of it. A large flock of pelicans rose from the river near us, & commenced their spiral ascent, mounting higher & higher as the clouds darked and the noise increased, until they supposed that their elevation would secure them a passage from the shower of frozen grapeshot—Scarcely had they disappeared from the N. E. horizon when heavens musketry & cannister was fired upon the earth—then*

SEPTEMBER 13—Bellevue was founded by Joshua Pilcher in 1823 to replace old Fort Lisa as a base of operations for the Missouri Fur Company. Maximilian notes that when the Missouri Fur Company was dissolved, the post was bought by Fontenelle, one of its partners. He in turn disposed of it to the government as headquarters for the Council Bluffs Indian Agency and established himself about a half mile below. Maximilian adds that Fontenelle's dwelling consisted "of some buildings, with fine plantations of maize, and verdant wooded hills behind it."

Bellevue, Nebraska, has grown out of the trading post and Indian agency. A voyage from Bellevue to St. Louis is contemplated when Anderson speaks in the Journal of "Pain-court" (short of bread), a derisive nickname applied to St. Louis by the early French inhabitants. Samuel Allis, who had reached Bellevue on the *Diana*, says that on September 13 he "saw a gentleman that had returned from the Mountains, that went out last spring in Com with Messrs Lees & Shepherd, (Missionaries to the Flatheads) who says, thes Brethren were in good heal[t]h & spirrets. had a good time in getting to the mountains; He thinks the prospect good to establish a mission, among the Napecies, were they not at war with the Blackfeet & some of the Snakes. I am told the fullblood Flatheads are most of them killed off, but the Napercies, are nearly the same people" (Kansas State Historical Society, *Collections*, 1915-1918, XIV, 696).

SEPTEMBER 12, 1834.—Friday. To day we shall remain with M. Cabanis, at the A. M. F company's post—He advises me to leave my horses and descend the river with him—In either route I shall be bloodsucked—Curse all musquitoes, I say—Amen, they all say—

SEPTEMBER 13, 1834.—Saturday. We bade a dieu to our friends of the trading post and descended the river to Mr Fontenelle's bellevue sixteen miles lower down—This is well worthy of its name—The prospect is extensive and interesting, above & below, his commanding situation—Old human nature is again at work, and by way of change, induces me to wish for a canoe trip from this to "Paincourt—' If the wind should continue, as now, to blow up the river, this would be a long and tedious voyage—My cavalry is so poor that I think I shall determine in favour of the water route.

SEPTEMBER 14, 1834.—Sunday. This is the first sabbath that we have all coincided in keeping, even in one particular, and that particular we did most gladly observe, rest—Yes—horse, man & mule—rested. Tis a sabbath of rest—This day too, is farther signalised by the most terrifying hail and thunder storm I ever witnessed—In the evening—about 4 °clock the heavens were darkened, & the distant thunder rumbled, in low & prolongued sound, over the whole arch of ether—The continued, and continuing sound, was the most remarkable that any of us had ever listened to—Some believed that they could have galloped eight or ten miles during the sound—A large flock of pelicans with their snow white bodies and black wings, rose from the river, just below us, and commenced their spiral ascent, winding higher & higher as the clouds grew darker, and the thunders louder, until they could steere a course above the thickening elements, that were soon to wage war upon the earth and all the unprotected tenants thereof. No sooner had they disappeared from the N. East horizon, than heavens artillery, grape-shot and cannister was fired upon all below—How grateful did I feel for the shelter of the cabins roof, that I was not an uncovered wanderer upon the prairie—Few unprotected animals, human or bestial, could have escaped unmaimed, from that pounding storm—The wisdom of Providence, has circumscribed their extent—How great a blessing! One of the most remarkable natural curiosities I ever

I felt indeed grateful that I was not shelterless upon the desert plains of the Platte—few unprotected beings, human or bestial, could have escaped unharmed, unmaimed from the pounding storm. I forgot to mention, that while at Mr. Cabanis establishment I was shewn one of the most curious & beautiful things I ever have seen—a perfectly white & spotless deer skin. This animal was a doe, differing as much in the smoothness & fineness of her hair as in the colour. The white too is of the clearest kind. Such things among the Indians are looked upon as very great Medicine. In one sense I consider it so too—as a curious unique excentricity of the Big Spirit. White beaver have various times been caught.

SEPTEMBER 15, 1834—*Monday. The storm has passed, & our flock of pelicans have returned in increased numbers. Much more numerous than the la[r]gest flocks of buzzards in the West. Fleas by the handful are my nightly companions—the devil kill'm—*

SEPTEMBER 16, 1834—*Teusday. Belle vue encore—To morrow, there are some prospects, we may depart "en canot. ["] Then I shall be in favour of "rowing swiftly there, my gondoliers ["] &c &c. I can tell my settlement friends that musquitoes fleas & big lice make a strong hotch-potch*

SEPTEMBER 17, 1834—*Wednesday. I have been all prepared for several hours to start, but it would have been to[o] little in accordance with my general fortune, to have thus departed, without suspense. The big canoe, our "compagne de voyage" can not be ready until to morrow—"C'est egal, ["] or will be a hundred years hence. Perhaps we shall take leave of Belle vue & its too hospitable master to morrow. Nous verrons. I am certain of one thing—ie my perfect willingness to do so—*

SEPTEMBER 17—On this day Lucien Fontenelle wrote Pierre Chouteau: "I arrived here three days ago with my expedition and returns from the mountains for the last year. I shall be able in a few days more to ship the beaver down. I am waiting for the boat which is now building at the Oto post [Cabanné's establishment]. It is probable that you may wish to have the beaver insured and I am extremely sorry that I can not give you the correct weight. However, the number of skins I have amount to 5,309 beaver, 90 of otter, 18 of bear, 130 of muskrats, and about 150 pounds of castorum. I hardly think it necessary to have them insured, although the river is very low, but the boat will be very strong, and will have a double crew formed of the very best kind of voyageurs under the eyes of Mr. Cabanne, and the superintendence of Etienne Provost.

"I am sorry to say that I would have sent down more beaver had it not been for the misfortune of losing a cache in which there were eight or ten packs lost, destroyed by wolves and bears, and saw, was shewn me by Mr Pilcher the other day—It was the skin of a deer purely spotlessly white—It was as uncommon in the softness and smoothness of the hair as in its colour—Such things among the Indians are held in religious admiration, to them they are great medecine—In one sense I consider such a "luxus Creatoris" a great medecine—as a very interesting eccentricity of the BIG Spirit—Beavers with nearly white skins have frequently been caught.

SEPTEMBER 15, 1834.—The pelicans have returned in increased numbers, with the bright sun that enlightens this monday—The flocks of these birds are much more numerous than I expected, altho told they were very large—Of fleas we have any quantities—The frenchman's ["]queer bugs"—now here, now, he no here—

SEPTEMBER 16, 1834.—Teusday. Belle vue still—To morrow I hope we shall leave it—Then I shall wish to be rowed gently there—My gondolier & c—If Job had been tried by gallanipers, fleas & fat lice, at one time—as I have been I think he would have complained as much as he did any how—

SEPTEMBER 17, 1834.—Wednesday. I have been ready these several hours "pour descendre la riviére," but it would not have been in accordance with my usual ill luck, to have departed without suspense—We have to wait, until the *big canoe* is finished—Thus—oh stars of misfortunes, this cursed dugout, is made of as much consequence as a steamboat—The *Big Canoe* is not *ready* to be *launched*! Well, I suppose it will be all the same a hundred years hence—

---

eight or ten packs more which we have lost by the rascality of a few men, who were largely indebted to us and who traded their fall's hunt with other companies during the winter as it happened they did not winter near any of our parties. I am in hopes that it will not so happen in the future as I have so arranged that it will be hard for any of them to defraud us hereafter.

"You must have heard before this of the returns that were made by Mr. Sublette and the company of Bonneville and Company. The latter I think by next year will be at an end with the mountains. They have sent down from twelve to fourteen packs of beaver and admitting that it should sell at a high price it is not enough to pay their retiring hands. Wm. Sublette takes down about forty packs. The heretofore arrangements between him and Messrs. Fitzpatrick, Milton Sublette and others having expired last spring, they concluded not to have anything more to do with William Sublette and it will surprise me very much if he takes more than ten packs down next year. I have entered into a partnership with the others and the whole of the beaver caught by them is to be turned over to us by agreement made in concluding the arrangement. William Sublette has built such a fort as Fort Clark (Mandans) on Laramie's Fork of the River Platte and can make it a central place for the *Sioux* and *Cheyenne* trade. He has now men running after these Indians to bring them to the River Platte. Buffalo is in abundance on that river during all seasons of the year, and the situation may turn out to be an advantageous one for the trade . . .—Fontenelle" (H. M. Chittenden, *The American Fur Trade of the Far West*, I, 304-305).

SEPTEMBER 18, 1834.—*Thursday. We left to day at 12 o'clock our urbane companion & host Mr. Fontenelle. We are descending the Big Water in two canoes joined, propelled by six rowers—with a relief every two hours. We are seventeen in number—The appearance of the hills which smile, frown, or cast a beautiful shade upon one side or other of the river according to situation or circumstance, is peculiarly interesting. This evening, & especially at this time of it —sunset, they are beautiful—All of the hills are covered with a meadow-like verdure & which, when seen beneath & between the scattered trees which are just placed far enough apart to shew the rich green, present a charming appearance—I can not undertake to describe any particular landscape. I would then be monotonously saying that here was a hill, here a delightful, here a pearly brook —here shade & here sunshine—No—I will only say that 'lac de fer' & some others just below are very pretty—*

SEPTEMBER 19, 1834.—*Friday. We have travelled unceasingly all this day, yet I think we cannot flatter ourselves with having gone very far from the roosting place of last night, on account of the crooked course of the river to day. Our six "rameurs," by hourly relieves make us descend about 5 miles an hour. In two days I hope to get something new of home. My hopes are founded upon seeing some acquaintance at the little Bluffs or cant. Levingworth.*

SEPTEMBER 20, 1834.—*Saturday. All day in a cold rain upon the Missouri river, without a stop from morning's dawn till night begins is no delightful thing—add to this the most tortuous course that ever river ran—& through 10000 chicots—such are the things of this day.*

SEPTEMBER 18, 1834—Thursday. We set sail, with no sails, to day at M. biding a dieu to our kind host Fontenelle We have begun the descent of the strong water, in two canoes lashed together—propelled by six oars—with a relief every two hours—The hills, that alternate with sunshine and shade, are beautiful on both sides—by turns—This evening, and particularly at this time, sunset, they are lovely—The hills are all covered with a meadow-like green, which, when seen through the trees, which by the hand of nature have been just sparsely enough placed, to show the rich verdure, are exceedingly beautiful—I will not undertake to describe a scene, that is lovely *beyond description*. I can only say of "lac de fer" that to have a tolerable idea of its beauty, one should recall the image of the most charming landscape they had ever seen & then redouble the charm, to approach that spot.

SEPTEMBER 19, 1834—Friday. We have rowed unceasingly all day, yet I think we cannot flatter ourselves on having made very great progress, on account of the extremely crooked course of the river. Our six rowers, with frequent changes make us descend about 5 miles per hour. I hope in two days to hear some thing from home, this is founded upon the expectation of seeing some acquaintance among the officers at the little Bluffs, cant. Leavinsworth.

SEPTEMBER 20, 1834—Saturday. All day uncovered, we have kept the channel exposed to a cold rain, No stop, no stay, from mornings dawn till night—hungry, damp & cross—We all look this evening as sour as unfed tigers—The river has been twisting and turning, as tho it would wind itself into a ball, Add to this, its dashing the foam out of itself against ten thousand, ['] chicots'—and threatning to dash our bodies, not into foam, but into jelly—There are in the river 10,000 "chicots," as the french steersman calls them—Every few minutes we hear his hoarse ungramatic voice "saying "rame rame" —"attrape les chicots—" I observe that almost all the Canadians, like the friends make use of the imperative singular—using thee and thou— —Our old camp-leader, every night, cried "omphage, omphage les chevaux;' when commanding the whole company to hobble the horses—

SEPTEMBER 21, 1834.—*Sunday. We arrived about 9 o'clock at the Black-snake hills where there is a trading post for the Ioways. These indians like the Pawnees either shave their heads or wear the hair short. The features were prominent, nose more of the Roman than the 'savages' of the mountains. I think in general, the indians of the plains are taller, but not so well made as those of the mountains. We could not, with uncommon exertion reach the garrison. we camped a few miles above it.*

SEPTEMBER 22, 1834.—*Monday. We have descended below the mouth of the Kansas river. In our passage down this mighty stream we passed the little Bluffs or Cant. Levinsworth. I was very unexpectedly & cordially recieved by Mssrs. Morgan, Wickliffe, Hughes*

SEPTEMBER 21—The trading post at the Blacksnake Hills was established in 1831 by Joseph Robidoux, returning to the Indian country after two years, during which the Chouteaus had paid him $1,000 a year to stay out of it. By 1833 Maximilian noted that Robidoux' "white house, surrounded by the bright green prairies, had a very neat appearance." Samuel Allis observed when the *Diana* stopped to unload freight on Sept. 2, 1834: "There is a trader stationed there, who trades with the Ioways, the Ioways with a small band of the Sac & foxes, live about 7 m. east, the Country is beautiful, the soil productive." In the spring of 1835 Samuel Parker mentioned the nearby agency for the "Iowa, Sioux [Sauk], and Fox tribes," and said the Sauks were "only a small band, who would not join Black Hawk in his war against the United States, and who are now afraid to return to their own country." Parker went on to the Blacksnake Hills, where "Mr. Rubedoux has a trading post, and an uncommonly fine farming establishment on the Missouri river. His buildings are on a small elevation of land, having a delightful prospect in front of more than a thousand acres of open bottom land, lying along down the river; and hills on the north and east partially covered with woods." Out of this "Ioway" trading post evolved present St. Joseph, Missouri. The Indians who gave name to the State of Iowa were of Siouan stock, closely related to the Otos and Missouris. In 1836 they were placed on a reservation in northeastern Kansas. Part of the tribe later moved to central Oklahoma.

SEPTEMBER 22—Cantonment Leavenworth was founded in 1827 and as a permanent post was renamed Fort Leavenworth in 1832. By coincidence Anderson reached the fort on the morning of the day three companies of the Dragoons arrived from Fort Gibson after the summer campaign to the Pawnee-Pic country. John Dunbar, in late June 1834, described Fort Leavenworth as "beautifully situated on a rising ground near the southern shore of the Missouri. The bank of the river at this place is composed of lime rock, rising several feet above the surface of the water, and is covered with verdure to the very edge. . . . the neat white buildings of the establishment, including the residences of the officers, the quarters of the soldiers, the hospital, etc., the fine scenery of the back ground, the wide spreading prairie, the deep green forest, and the distant highlands, are all presented to the view of the enchanted beholder at the same time, and he finds himself at a loss which most to admire . . ." (Kansas State Historical Society, *Collections*, 1915-1918, XIV, 584-585).

The Kentuckians Anderson met at Fort Leavenworth were Alexander G. Morgan, sutler and postmaster, whose wife (Samuel Allis says) was a Presbyterian from Lexington, Kentucky; William N. Wickliffe, then a captain of the Sixth Infantry, who resigned from the Army three years later; Andrew L. Hughes, in charge of the Iowa subagency from 1830 to 1836, and of the Great Nemahaw subagency in 1837-1838; and John Dougherty, one of the best-known personalities along the Missouri. Dougherty was born near Bardstown, Kentucky, on April 12, 1791. He was associated with Manuel Lisa and the original Missouri Fur Company for many years, beginning in 1808, and from 1819 to 1826 was interpreter and subagent under Benjamin O'Fallon at Council Bluffs. After O'Fallon's resignation, from 1827 to 1839 he was U. S. Indian Agent at Fort Leavenworth and Council Bluffs. He then settled in Clay County, Missouri, served in the legislature as a

SEPTEMBER 21, 1834.—Sunday. About 9 o'clock we reached the trading house of the Ioways, at the Black snake hills.—These Indians, like the Pawnees either shave their heads or wear the hair short. The features, of these, are more prominent, than those of the mountain savages—I saw very few Roman noses among the red men of the mountains—among those of the Plains they are very common—I am of opinion that the Indians of the Missouri regions are taller—, but not so neatly built as those of the mountains. This is the reverse of what I expected—The Flat heads are of a lower stature than the Ioways or Ottoes, but are broader shouldered and more tapering, thence down—To day we could not reach the garrison, tho we made a manly pull for it—We slept within gun sound of it—

SEPTEMBER 22, 1834.—Monday. We have landed and camped below the mouth of the Kaw; after merely pausing a few minutes at Fort Leavensworth or the little bluffs—The site is beautiful—On the south bank of the Missouri river, commanding a wide prospect of land and water—Immediately above, is a noble and majestic bend of the father of rivers, which morning and evening recieve and retain the salutations and a-dieux of the God of Light—Nothing is more lovely than the sunshine and shade—, which this mighty stream and the lofty forests here afford—I was most agreeably surprised, at the reception I here experienced—I landed, a dirty, almost shirtless stranger, in a few minutes, my little heart with grateful warmth was bounding at the Kentucky welcome, given me in the far western wilds, by my fellow statemen Morgan, Wickliffe, Hughes and Doherty—Gen¹ Hughes enquired after my father and

---

Whig, developed extensive sutlering and freighting interests, and died at Liberty, Missouri, Dec. 28, 1860. For fuller accounts of him, see the Walter B. Douglas edition of Thomas James, *Three Years among the Indians and Mexicans,* passim; John C. Luttig, *Journal of a Fur-Trading Expedition on the Upper Missouri, 1812-1813,* pp. 151-153; and William E. Eldridge, "Major John Dougherty, Pioneer."

The Kickapoos, like their relatives the Sauks and Foxes, were of Algonquian stock. At one time they lived in Wisconsin but drifted south into Illinois and Indiana. By 1819 they had ceded their lands in these states and moved to extreme western Missouri, later going to Kansas. The Sauks (or Sacs, as their name was usually spelled at this period) lived in Michigan when first known, later in Wisconsin, Illinois, and Missouri. They were very closely associated with the Foxes, but about 1804 one Sauk band near St. Louis ceded all rights to territory in the above states, outraging the other bands and estranging the Foxes. The Sauks and Foxes were British allies during the War of 1812, and continued disaffected until crushed in the Black Hawk War of 1832, a conflict named for a subordinate Sauk chief who was the principal figure of the resistance and who after a period of captivity died in Iowa in October 1838. In 1834 the Sauks and Foxes had their principal homeland in Iowa, from which they had driven the Sioux, but by 1837 had ceded the last of their lands. They were placed on a reservation in Kansas, from which some moved in the 1860's to present Oklahoma.

& Doherty. The liberal & generous kindness of Majr. Morgan was cheering to a fellow Kentuckians heart. The Kickapoos & a small part of the Sacs are at the garrison. The latter are taller & finer looking fellows than the former.—I observed that several of the Sac's wore the medal of his B. Majesty—

SEPTEMBER 23, 1834—*Teusday. This evening at sunset we arrived at Lexington from whence I took my departure last April. I have again supped at a tavern amidst village philosophers, pedantic doctors & sage looking lawyers—Our dirty coats & greasy breeches seemed to offend their nice eyes & delicate noses—God help them! A few white squaws were quite a treat. Happily too the first I have seen is worth seeing—a fat, healthy looking amiable countenanced lady—the wife of Majr. Ryland.*

SEPTEMBER 24, 1834—*Wednesday. I had forgotten to make my dayly record until this time, about "minuit" when being disturbed by several thousand fleas, I lighted my fire rubbed up my memory & wrote down in pencil marks as follows—Tis pleasant at the dead hour of night, in the dense forests of the western world, to be alone in mental life & activity & think of our own firesides, our parents & our country—Tis very pleasant to hear, at this time, the deep mouthed owl in lonely independence hooting to the midnight echoes of these shores, to hear the wolves in rapid discord howling on Missouris avalanching shores. I love to watch the moon at noon of night, when mildly gilding the quiet features of a sleeping friend, she walks in beauty through the fields of air, then hides her modest face behind the "mt. of winds"—& now I ll dry my shirt, burn the lice & try to dream of home & Dick—*

SEPTEMBER 23—In the Diary Anderson refers only to the wife of Major Ryland, but in the Journal he speaks of "Majr Riley and his wife" and "Ryland the receiver" and wife. E. M. Ryland was a receiver of public monies for the General Land Office at this period, with headquarters in Lexington. Bennet Riley made more of a mark in Western history. Born in 1787, he entered the U. S. service as an ensign of riflemen in 1813; saw active service in the War of 1812 and on the Mississippi frontier, rising to the rank of captain; was transferred to the infantry on the disbanding of the rifle regiment in 1821; participated in the Arikara Campaign of 1823; commanded the first military escort on the Santa Fe Trail, 1829; and served in the Black Hawk War, 1832, the Seminole wars, 1839-1842, and in the war with Mexico, 1846-1848. He was promoted to major in 1837, lieutenant colonel in 1839, and colonel in 1850. For his services in the Mexican War he was breveted brigadier general, then major general. In 1849-1850 he was commanding officer and military governor in California. Riley died at Buffalo in 1853, leaving a widow, Arbella, and five children.

brother—I blessed him for knowing them. I thought he had intrinsic merit because he had seen them—Oh! what a pleasure! when nearing friends and home, to meet *those* who have known & esteemed those that we have loved! All met me as stranger and parted with me a friend—The Kickapoos and a small dejected looking squad of Socs were at the garrison—The latter in truth to speak, are a taller better looking race, than the first mentioned—I remarked his Brit. Majesty's profile, pendant from several Soc necks. It was this doubtless, or the spirit incident to their bearing his favours that caused their late disasters—

SEPTEMBER 23, 1834—Teusday. Sunset, this evening, we landed opposite to Lexington—From this place last April I started westward— A short time ago, I consider^d this town far West—now after travelling *east* some thirty days I have just reached my quondam western 'Thule[']—I supped this minute at a tavern table, amidst village politicians, pedantic doctors, and wise *looking* lawyers—My dirty hunting shirt and greesy leather breeches seemed to offend their hypercritical eyes and too curious olfactories—God help them! Majr Riley and his wife—I hope to see them again, if not, I hope to hear that they are prosperous and happy—They have acquired my good wishes cheap—but the same bargain under similar circumstances can be had by anyone else—by being polite and kind to a dirty pilgrim—Ryland the reciever, has a gentleman's heart, moreover, he has a handsome and ladylike wife—Her good natured, fat face looks like his own—

SEPTEMBER 24, 1834—Wednesday. I forgot to scratch down my daily task, until this, the night's noon—, when being roused by several regiments of fleas, I lighted up the fire, rubbed up my memory and with pencil blue, wrote as follows—"Tis pleasant at the dead hour of night, to be alone in thought and wakefulness, and look upon the temporary dead, and know that none watches with you, save the unsleeping One—Tis very pleasant at such an hour in the dark and mighty forest of the unknown wilderness, where all is hushed, but the deep mouthed owl, hooting in lonely Independence, and think of home—I love to hear the wolf's long cry, to watch the moon climbing the mountain clouds, now gilding the features of a sleeping friend, now casting the shadow of a giant tree upon the scenes

SEPTEMBER 25, 1834—*We have passed to day the Grand riviere, which empties into the side towards the Mississippi—also Chariton on the same side—This morning I remarked that we followed the river to the four points of the compass. The north, east, south & west. Mr. Fitzpatrick's little foundling, Friday is becoming, every day, an object of greater & greater interest to me, his astonishing memory, his minute observation & amusing inquiries, interest me exceedingly. He has been from his band & kindred, 3 or 4 years, yet some scenes & incidents he describes with wonderful accuracy. He still remembers that he was called Warshinun which he tells me means 'black spot.['] "His tribe are called by the Snakes, Chariticks, dog-eaters"*

SEPTEMBER 26, 1834—*Friday. We have had a very pleasant little rebellion on board of our vessel, on account of Mr. Fs not getting food last night & this morning—tho he made every exertion, they refused to go any farther and landed & unloaded accordingly—We did not stay to court them back to labour, but made up a sub-crew of seven, parted the canoes and set on our way lamenting. The appearance of the banks have changed to what I had desired them— i e meadows & corn bottoms on one side, and high Gibraltar walls*

SEPTEMBER 25—In April 1833 Maximilian found the mouth of Grand River, then very shallow, almost as broad as the Wabash. Samuel Allis in June 1834 thought the entrance of the Grand "truly Grand and the country around." Maximilian said that at the mouth of the Chariton there were "several islands, covered with willows, poplar, and hard timber. The river here makes a considerable bend. . . ."

For the waif Friday, see the biographical sketches. The Arapahos belonged to the Algonquin family and were closely associated with the Cheyennes during most of this century. Their name for themselves is Inuñaina. They early separated into two groups, of which the Atsina, or Gros Ventres of the Prairie, took up residence among the Blackfeet, while the Arapahos drifted farther south. A deadly enmity persisted between the Arapahos and the Shoshoni, Utes, and Pawnees. During the latter half of the eighteenth century the Arapahos were divided by various exigencies into two groups, one being placed with their old enemies, the Shoshoni, on the Wind River Reservation in Wyoming, while the other settled in present Oklahoma.

SEPTEMBER 26—Concerning the three river towns passed this day, Maximilian wrote in April 1833: "the village of Boonville [stands] on the left bank, opposite of which is Old Franklin. As this place was threatened by the river, and is besides in an unhealthy situation, the people founded New Franklin, rather further inland, now a thriving village, near which salt springs have been discovered." Rocheport ("Rockport") was "a village founded two years ago, on the Manito River, six miles up which river Columbia is situated." Samuel Allis called Boonville "a small village situated on a high bluff on the south bank of the River, the most delitefull I have seen on the banks of the Mo—."

Alphonso Wetmore in his 1837 *Gazetteer* said of Boonville, the principal town of Cooper County: "The site of this flourishing and rapidly-growing place is beautiful in the estimation of and burying them in darkness—And grandest of all, I'll dry my only shirt, smoke off the lice, and dream of home and Dick—

SEPTEMBER 25, 1834—To day we passed the mouth of Grand River, which flows from the north—or from the direction of the Mississippi, the bride of the Missouri—Also the Chariton entering on the same side—This forenoon we were carried by this river to the four points of the compass—just as soon as it could change from one course to another—North, East, south and west—We have a little Indian foundling, belonging to Mr Fitzpatrick, named from the day of his discovery, Friday,—he is a very interesting object to me, growing more so each day that passes—His astonishing memory, his minute observation, and his amusing inquiries—make an extremely entertaining companion—He still remembers his name, his sisters and many of his tribes fireside anecdotes, tho he has been absent 4 or 5 years, and was not over six years old when found almost starved in the prairie—He is of the Arapahoe tribe—his Indian name was "Warshinun" or Black-spot—The Snakes call that nation Chariticks or dog eaters—The Snakes by the by are almost the only savages who do not feast on that animal—Of the Sio[u]x it is the *Epicurean* dish.

SEPTEMBER 26, 1834—Friday. We had a tempest in a teapot—Our canoe crews raised a rebellion on account of the scarcity of food—It was unpardonable in Fitzpatrick not to have gotten it for them, particularly, as their was none to be had—But with them, the impossibility, was nothing—without, "they couldnt & wouldnt work.["]

the strangers who visit it, as well as the inhabitant. . . . The courts are held here; and the courthouse and clerk's office are creditable public buildings. The Methodist church is likewise a respectable house." The town was named for Daniel Boone (pp. 67-68). Concerning Franklin: "The old town bearing this name was situated on a high alluvial bottom on the left bank of the Missouri, opposite Booneville. This town was very populous and increasing in consequence up to the year 1818. But the mad whirlpools and the insidious eddies of the Missouri river tore asunder its foundations, and the inhabitants, bearing away the wreck of their domiciles, fled to the neighboring hills, where they rebuilt New Franklin. Here health and rural enjoyment are in store for the diligent and frugal denizens of an unobtrusive corporate town situate two miles from the river, on high ground, to which a railway will be constructed" (pp. 79-80). And as to Rocheport: "situate on the Missouri, at the mouth of Manitou, and in the southwest corner of Boone county, [it] is attracting the attention of business men by its local advantages, and the activity of business operations at present carried on in this new town." Wetmore enumerated thriving commercial enterprises, mentioned the "good horseboat" employed at the ferry, then said: "The Manitou spring is a curious, and probably a valuable production of nature. It breaks out of an abrupt cliff on the bank of the Missouri, four miles below Rocheport, and falls twenty-five feet perpendicularly. . . . Near to this, in a cave, is a good site for a mill or a distillery" (pp. 44-45).

of stone on the other. Opposite to Franklin is beautifully situated the little town of Boonsboro—on such an eminence—on the same side with Franklin, to & below Rushport, the hills are very bold & perpendicular. The everlasting monotony of the Platte is changed into Time-built & Time-enduring towers of strength—not bleak & bare as if God's withering curse of everlasting barrenness had fallen on their miserable brows, but crowned with oak & gladdened with the perennial green of the cedar & the pine. In the midst of some of these towers, not built by hands and sometimes midway up, are seen the mouths of caves which seem large and dark enough to admit a thousand pious sons to the depths of classic hell to seek their sires. If any dear lover of Virgil and Romance should wish to follow the excellent praiseworthy example of his hero, I recommend him to search his entrance into the Stygian realms a few miles below Rushport, in the stony pillars which protect Missouris shores from the threat[e]ning clouds—&c &c &c.

SEPTEMBER 27, 1834.—*Saturday. To act out my usual fortune—there was another defection this morning, the seat of one of the three rowers was vacated, "par consequence", behold a little man of my complexion & stature tugging at the oar like a good fellow. This lasted till nearly mid-evening, when by a turn of the meadows wheel, a quarrel & fight on board the rebellious vessel sent me relief in the shape of a deserter from it—Passed about 10 o'clock Jefferson city—["]ville capitale" of Mo. They are erecting a fine looking penitentiary of fine white marble—It seems to me to be superior to any that*

SEPTEMBER 27—Jefferson City was selected as the Missouri state capital in 1821, two years after the first house was built. The original capitol building, completed in February 1825, was destroyed by fire in November 1837. The penitentiary mentioned by Anderson was provided for by law in 1827. See *History of Cole ... Counties, Missouri*, pp. 276-282. In 1833 Maximilian saw Jefferson City as "only a village, with a couple of short streets, and some detached buildings on the bank of the river. The governor's house is in front, on the top of the bank, and is a plain brick building of moderate size. The gentle eminences, on which the place was built about ten years ago, are now traversed by fences, and the stumps of the felled trees are everywhere seen." John Dunbar in 1834 observed that the Missouri capital was "situated on a high bluff. The site is quite uneven and not remarkably pleasant. It is built on no less little hills than old Rome." Alphonso Wetmore said in his *Gazetteer* (p. 62): "The place is now improving, and promises to be that which it is named, although Nature left the entire task for art to perform. In justice, however, to the much-abused and suffering city, there are some local advantages at Jefferson. It is a central position; the 'mad waters' flow at the base of the Rome-like hills on which it is being built. The place is based on very valuable quarries of gray building-stone, resembling marble [limestone]. ... The governor is furnished with a house, built for his residence, which is creditable to the state, on the score of munificence and taste. The penitentiary is on a substantial scale, and much more spacious than the state of morals in Missouri requires."

To delay as little as possible—We landed cut loose, and each went floating on, growling—The appearance of the shores is now what I could have wished—that is to say—we may see corn bottoms on one side and huge Gibraltar walls of stone on the other—Franklin and Boonsboro are situated on opposite sides,—in just such sites, the latter towering above her humble neighbour, and peering into all her domestic concerns—The hills change sides a short distance below, and continue to, and below Rushport—They are bold and beatling ramparts—worthy associates of such a stream—I rejoice, that the everlasting monotony of the Platte, is exchanged for these Time built & Time enduring monuments of nature—Nor are they bleak and desolate, as if God's withering curse of barrenness, had fallen on their brows,—but oak-crowned, and ever-verdant with the lively fir and pride of Lebanon—In the midst of some of these ramparts, "not built by hands, perennial on the Earth' are Caves large and dark, whose mouths are wide enough to admit any number of pious sons to descend to the depths of classic hell, to seek their irredeemable sires—If any lover of Romance, and Virgil should wish to follow his pious, praiseworthy example, let him seek an entrance a few miles below Rushport on the north side of the roaring Missouri—

SEPTEMBER 27, 1834—Saturday. To exercise me in patience and fatigue a rower deserted from our single pirogue "par consequence" a little man of my size had to take to the tugg, like a good fellow—This looked squawly, but lasted only till near sunset—A quarrel among the friends of the rival vessel, sent me relief in the person of a runaway from their side—About 10 °'clock we passed by Jefferson city—"ville capitale' of Missouri—Here is being built a penitentiary of very handsome marble—Much whiter and firmer, I think, than that of the Kentucky river hills—Save this unfinished edifice, this little capital contains no buildings worthy of a seat of Government—If the state of Missouri and its *chief* city, shall coexist with the hills upon which the latter is founded, its duration will exceed all sublunary things—but this cannot be—these God-created ashlers will endure, when the marble monuments, of man's transient glory, shall have mouldered into dust—All is vanity! Of the frowning grandeur of these hills, man will never say 'sic transit gloria mundi"—

*I have seen in the hills of the Kentucky—This town is very small &
contains no buildings worthy of mention—The state prison is not far
enough advanced to be described.*

*If the state of Missouri & its capital shall coexist with the hills upon
which it is built, it would have a term less than no sublunary thing,
but, the God-created ashlers of eternity shall endure, when the
marbled monuments of man have crumbled into dust. Never shall
man say of the frowning grandeur of these hills, "sic transit gloria
mundi".*

SEPTEMBER 28, 1834—*Sunday. Passed yesterday the mouth of Osage
river—slept immediately below the town of Portland. Passed the
mouth of Gasconnade—*

SEPTEMBER 29, 1834—*Monday. A long days march partly by water
& partly by land   Reached St. Charles this day about 1 o'clock & here
ends, I think for a time my canoe travailing. No more perhaps shall I
hear the facetious order of "fumez la pipe", from our old Canadian
Charon, whenever he wished to rest from his labours—"Garde aux
rames"—["]attrape les chicots" & a thousand other such expressions
will sound in the ears of my imagination for many a day to come—
This night after supper I returned to St. Louis which I left, it is now
six months—I learn with regret that I am left with no other wardrobe
than I have worn night & day this half year. I smile & shudder at the
figure I shall cut tomorrow calling on my kin & acquaintance—*

SEPTEMBER 28—The Osage and Gasconade rivers are principal tributaries of the Missouri. Maximilian noted only the latter: "an inconsiderable river . . . [which] expands behind a high, bold eminence, the summit of which is covered with rocks and red cedars. The hills near it are frequently covered with the white and the yellow pine, which supply St. Louis with boards and timber for building. Its mouth, which is reckoned to be 100 miles from that of the Missouri, is picturesquely situated in a lofty forest." In June 1834 John Dunbar described Portland as "a comparatively new settlement on the right bank of the river." His companion Samuel Allis thought it a "pleasant village houses built principally of logs." Alphonso Wetmore commented: "the landing being good at all seasons of the year, [Portland] is a considerable place of business. Although it is only about three years old, it contains four stores and three groceries. The steam saw and flour mill of Messrs. Benson and Childs, gives Portland an advantage which will tend greatly to accelerate its growth" (p. 47). The town no longer exists.

SEPTEMBER 29—As was customary for travelers who did not have to stay with their boat for the 40-mile trip by water from St. Charles to St. Louis, Anderson left the river at St. Charles and made the rapid 19-mile passage overland. He did not pause to describe St. Charles. Samuel Allis was content to picture "a small village, one Catholic, one Presbyterian church," but the previous year Maximilian called St. Charles "one of the oldest French settlements on the Missouri, consisting of

SEPTEMBER 28, 1834—Yesterday we passed the mouth of the Osage—
Slept immediately below the town of Portland—To day passed the
Gasconnade—

SEPTEMBER 29, 1834—A long, a strong pull and a pull altogether,
brought us to St. Charles, about 1 °'clock—Here ends for a *time* my
canoeing—I shall not be in a hurry to blister my palms, to the tune
of "les bonnets blanches"—&c—Never again, perhaps, shall I hear
the facetious and characteristic command of "fumez la pipe" from
our weatherbeaten, bronzefaced Canadian Charon, when he willed
that his galley boys should rest—His other dits' 'Garde aux rames"
attrape les chicots, & a hundred & one such sayings will sound in
the ears of my memory for many an hour unborn—Adieu old friend
—adieu! you have piloted me through many a straight—you have
safely brought me over many a hinden [hidden] danger—I hope
that I may succeed as well in steering my bark past all the visible
and invisible *Scyllas* which shall lie in life's voyage—This night I
end where I began six months ago—in *St Louis*—I shall not stay to
display my greasy carcass here—As soon as possible, unwashed, un-
combed I start for home———Okahée____Here ends my travelling
notes—

---

about 300 houses, where the massive church, with its low tower, has a very good appearance. The
environs of this scattered village are rather bare, but there were many European fruit trees in
blossom. Most of the houses are built of wood, but a modern part of the place is of brick. On an
eminence, rising behind it, stands an old stone tower, which formerly served as a defence against
the Indians."

Anderson Miscellanea

Ethnological Notes

Notes at End of the Journal

I will now add, from memoranda taken when amongst them, a few Indian words —Such as I believed would be most useful to me in my intercourse with them—In my limited vocabulary I find the Flat-head numerals—as follows—Inco—1, Asale 2, *T*chat *les* 3, *mose* 4, *T*sule 5, Tacan 6, Seispel 7, Haine 8, Hâ *n*oot 9, Open 10. These Indians by using the preceding numbers, with the last of the above, formed our compounds—e. g. Asale-open is twice ten, or twenty—and so on to open open —or 100—Figures they have none—When the words were not used, they counted by the exhibition of their fingers—open-open, is called In-kaw [?] kīne—*I si a h* all,—I have seen black feet—they would render into *Squoishen* weitah *t*chum—a great many black feet, *Who* it *squoi*shen— —Other Flat head words—as near as I could write them—skoin*t*ch a bow, Tâ po min an arrow, So ma*i*ntoo tobacco, So mai noots a pipe, Ta pai *p*ah too pipe stem, So *p*ō lee grass, Skī u mi lodge poles, Sei too a lodge, Sow-oo*l k* water, s*p*âpe smoke, *so*lseits fire, Āts min a trap, Seâ *lou* a beaver, Tiltico an otter, Kī shine moccasins, *Sei*-tklish breeches or leggings, S*nasle* —kīte a coat, star koi a blanket, ēkoine star koi, a green blanket, Ekoinih [?] star koi a red do, Y*ar* koi star koi a black do, kouil-kouil scarlet cloth—Koi koite black cloth, Hâ yux a shell, S*p*uck-u*n nĭ* the Sun, *Nin tch*ou min a knife, Kou k, kou u mi nin tchou min a little knife, Kou tou ni-min tchou min a large knife, Sodle-lodle-mints a gun—Mpuck omin powder, *T*so-dle-um a buffalo bull. *T*so-matt a do cow, *S*ei-*tsum* buffaloe robe.—Kou d le chip a kettle, *T*chin-pucki a ring, Kaw-muck er hair, Sin-ko-sow a brother, Sou.i.â pi—Americans—S*n*o the Snakes, *S*to mist to trade, *S*mai-cout snow on the ground, Smohope the falling snow, Tuh pai-ish [*interlined*: Tuh Tuh.pai.ish] rain, Quil-kouil to talk, Is-in sooh to hear or understand. An Indian when he does not comprehend, will say that he does not hear—or understand—Tā is in sooh—I dont hear or understand—

Words of the Snake tongue—Hāckgunni? how do ye do—a general salutation, and enquiry—what do want &c—what is it & &c. Ka *cu*nni hanche how-dy friend, Kai-no, or none, Kai-wiet have none, *T*ch*a*nt good—kai tchant not good or its bad, Mi-*yah* give me some, Pâ mi yah, give me some water,—Shin-bun-nah—I know it, Mâ-bō*n*ì I see it, Bung-go a horse, Mish, what is it? Weet a knife, *Wi*pe a woman, E-weet—this way, Pâ mo tobacco, Bishey buffalo, *Tai* quan to talk, Tai-kup something to eat, *bou* -na fire, *Ca*-tone smoke, Kâ *ne*e a lodge—Wan-ton lodge poles, S*ho* nip grass, *Share* a dog—Peup—large [*crossed out*: peup share a horse, or *big dog*] Na ry ant powerful, Kai-peup little, Namp moccasins—Na ro to trade And 1ˢᵗ of [?]

Names of Indian Chiefs & Braves—

Saylish or F Heads— —1ˢᵗ Insil lah, called by the Whites the Little Chief—his name is descriptive of his battle cap, ornamented with the War Eagle's plume.

2nd Tsom shoum ki—3rd *Kow* kots-up-ski or Big face, 4th Quoil. quoil. ski onis, or red pole—

Of the Sâ a pe ten or Nez-Percée Tribe—

1st Nose—nési-ow—Cut nose. 2nd Cow-so-tum—3rd Ot-lot-coat-sum The talker—The whites know him by the name of the lawyer. 4th Ko-ko-kel-pip, the red crow, 5th. Push-*wa*-hi-kite, 6th Mel-wel-tshin-tin-tini—7th Koul-koul-ta min or the red beard, Tiel-licki-nichiti, 8th Ta kin-shwai tish—Known to the whites as rotten Belly—Wounded by the Black-feet at the same time that Sublette was shot.[1]

Of the Absarokee's or Crows— ——

1st Old Burns or *Long-hair* [*footnote: 11 feet 18 inches*], 2nd Rotten-belly 3rd High-bull, 4th Mad-bull, 5 'Gros ventre' horses 6. Two Face, a good fellow, 7. Three Crows, 8, Pa pâ ge, 9th. Wooden-bowl, 10th The bear's tooth, 11th The Lawyer, 12th The Rain. Knocked down in full council by Ben O'Fallon, 13th Om o tashi. 14th Spotted water, A-ca-co-wa-ca-shei, or War Eagle, 15th The Wolf, 16th The breast that gives no milk, 17th Rotten Tail, 17 [sic] Yellow-bull, 18th Yellow-belly. 19th Mi niki [?] a chi, or Hot water, 20th Na-ki-o shish, or the burnt Child———Bar.chi.tucki—White-flower or the Cherry blossom—a Gros-Ventre squaw.

[1]In *The Nez Perce Indians and the Opening of the Northwest*, pp. 122-123, Alvin M. Josephy, Jr., comments on these Nez Percé chiefs (whose names Anderson spells variantly in Journal and Diary): " 'Nose nicion' (The Cut Nose) bore the same name as Neesh ne park kee ook, The Cut Nose from the vicinity of Colter's Creek on the Clearwater, who had welcomed Lewis and Clark in 1806. 'Cowsotum', whom Bonneville had met near the forks of the Salmon River in 1832 and had called Kowsoter, was perhaps a Nez Perce; but because his name was Salish, he may have had a Flathead father or been called after a Flathead leader. 'Otlotcoutson' was Hallalhotsoot (The Lawyer) from Kamiah, who had been wounded at the Battle of Pierre's Hole in 1832. He was the man who had heard Spokan Garry preach during the winter of 1829-30 and who would later tell the missionary A. B. Smith that his people had sent the messengers to St. Louis. 'Ko ho kelpip' was Qoh Qoh Ilppilp (Red Crow, or Red Raven) from the area of present-day Stites, Idaho, on the Clearwater River above Kamiah. 'Pushwahikite' was Bonneville's friend, Apash Wyakaikt (Flint Necklace, later known as the senior Looking Glass) from Asotin on the Snake River. 'Melmelstin tinton' was a Cayuse. 'Koulkoultamin' was Koolkooltami, a noted warrior from the Stites area. 'Tieltickinickiti' may have been Tilaukait, a Cayuse leader from the Walla Walla Valley; and 'Takinswhaitish' was the Nez Perce whose stomach wound at the Battle of Pierre's Hole had gained him the name Rotten Belly." Josephy reproduces portraits of Hallalhotsoot (Lawyer) and Apash Wyakaikt (Flint Necklace), drawn by Gustavus Sohon in 1855.

Notes in End Pages of the Diary

{ nez-percés } e tomi as clape cut. I want to trade for moccasins—
{ Sããpten   }   Tsumtoohs. the sun.—

Snake or Shoshoney naro Namp I wish to trade for moccasins—gun piéãti—
nãotoks—powder horn—
râantshomi—buffaloe robe) (Saaptens—Timooks—gun

---

high-high Téicuhbi [?]—white blanket—
ilp hilp suskuh—simoosick
moo mothe[?] modle—buffaloe powder horn or soot-ki
    buffaloe robe—ipsoos hand—
Teiks toah brother or friend—

Wals butcher knife—
"Hai-hai, seikstooah," or Little white brother." My Nez-perce name
Hã cunni hãnch—What do you want friend? What are you looking for? &c &c.

Kai wut. I have none—
    The Crows [*interlined*: Absarokis] call the Americans mitsiãtski"—long knife—
The French Mans koti [?] shãri grey eyes"—The black feet term the Americans
Nistosuniquen long knives Nistosuniquen—

W. Marshall Anderson

The gray eagle is called in the Nez perce "Wãipitish—The bald eagle is Suc-
cuntish—

Flat-Head—numbers—

Inco-	one		
Asali	2	-open	20
In kar-koine	100		
Tchatlan	3	-open	30
Mase	4	do	40
Tsule	5	do	50
Tâ can	6	do	60
Seispel	7	do	70
Haine [Hame?]	8	do	80
Hâ nool	9	do	90
Open	10	a sali open 2-10 or twenty	
Isi-ah—all			

Squoishten—weitsthum—F Head I have seen black-feet—
Whent squoishten—plenty of B. Feet
Inco—one

Squoishen weitsthum—I have seen Black feet. Whoit squoishen—a great many Black-Feet.

[Horace] Everetts Report on the Indians department—May 20th 1834 [23rd Cong., 1st Sess., H.R. Report 474, Serial 263].

Snake words

Ha gunnin? seems to be a general method of enquiry, as how do you do? What do [you] want? What is it? &c. *"Ha gunni hanch"* how do you do friend or what do wish friend? *"Kai"*—no or none—*Kai weet*—I have none. *"Tchant* or *Tsant"* good— *Kai tchant* it is not good. *Mi yah* give me. *pâ mi yah,* give me some water *Shambunna* to know any thing. *Mabonie* to see any thing—*"Pun* or *Bungo"* a horse *Mish?* what is it? *weet* [*meet*?] a knife. *wipe* a woman—*e-weet* this way, in this manner—*pâ mo* tobacco. *bishey*—buffaloe *Tai-quan* to talk—*tai keep* something to eat—*conna* fire *cotone* smoke. *Kanee* a lodge—*wanton* lodge poles—*shonip*—grass *Sharee* a dog—*peup* large *nary ant* powerful *kai pe* or *beup*—little *namp.* moccasin—*naro* to trade.

---

words of the Flat head tongue—

Inco—one
Skointch—a bow
Tā-pomin—an arrow.
Somaitoo—tobacco—
So mainoot. a pipe
Tapaipotoo—pipe stem
Sopolee grass
Skiume—lodge poles
Seitoo a lodge
Sowoolks water
Spâpe smoke
†*quoil-quoil*—scarlet cloth

Solseits fire
Ats-min—a trap
Sealow—a beaver
Toltico—an otter
Kīshin—a moccasin—
Sithlish—breeches or leggings
Snasle-kite—a coat
Starkoi. a blanket
Ékoine starkoi—a green blanket
Ekouil do a red do
Yakoie starki a black do

---

†quoil-quiol. tschá—Scarlet breeches—a name given to the little son of the Little Chief of the Flatheads called "*Insillah* or "War Eagles plumes—Insillah was the first convert to Christianity, by Father De Smet and called "Michael"—I knew him several years before Father De Smet went to the Rocky Mountains—[*This note written in pencil, at a later date.*]

234

Koi-koite—black cloth—
Hâ yun   a shell   spuckuni   sun
Neint.chou min   a knife
Kou kou-ami neint—a small do
Kou ton ni   do—large do
Sodle lodle mints—a gun—
M puckamin   powder
Tsodle-um—a bull-buffaloe
Tsomalt   a cow
Koudle chip a [*crossed out; elsewhere*: kettle]
Seitsum—a buffaloe robe
Tchinpuckiē a ring
Kaw mucker—hair—
Sinkosoo—a brother—
Kalispelum Spokan tribe of the F. Heads
Soui a pé the Americans
Sno the Snake—F H
Stomiste to trade
Smohope the falling of snow
Smaicout   snow on the ground
tepaish   rain
Stolehoe   ground
Hootshole   mountain

Noah [?] koil   to talk—isinsooh to hear or understand. Ta isinsoohoo, I don't understand. Tapskillsto [?] the act of shooting. Ta pen   to shoot.   quellah [?] kai en tapin—stop I'll shoot them or it   Ta sen ché sodle lodle incals [?]—My gun is not loaded—aihote to be tired—koin kointe to be exposed [?] is hard [? bad?]— repanaunts [?] great count [?] or treaty [?]—Sou en name [?] a squaw   trape it [*word illegible*] Kapelth [?] a pan—sidle min   an ax—espoode a heart) asale, I have two hearts or to be uncertain—Scaminch bring some wood. idlemodle bring some water—tichsooslk [?] for me to drink   snou dot   wind

---

Chieftains & Braves of the Crows—
Burns. Rotten Belly—High Bull   Mad Bull—Gros ventre Horse Two Face good-fellow,—Three Crows—Popa-age—Wooden Bowl—Long Hair. The Bears tooth—Lawyer. The Rain—Wami [?] tushi [?]   Spotted Warter—War Eagle Acoweon-wacashei [?] High Tail   Wolfe—The breast that gives no milk—Rotten Tail—Yellow Bull—yellow Belly—Minksache [?] or Hot water Nakioshish [?] or burnt child-

---

As near as I can write them, names of chiefs of the Nez-percé tribes—Cut nose—is nose nicion—Cow so tum—Ot lot cou ts sum ote [?] or the Lawyer—red crow—&

three others Pusherahikiti-Melmelsthin tintini—Kokokelpip [*in margin*: Grand visage]—Koul koultamin or red lead [i.e., beard?]—Tiellickinickiti Takinswhaitish —or rotten belly—Insillah—Stomshoumki—Quao kots lapski—Quoil—quoilskve*mi*. red pole—Flat heads & pond-de-rey's—Spokane—or Coeur de lions—Kalispelum—

Bar-chi tucky—White cherry. Gros ventre squaw—

Chiefs of the Sāpeten or Nez percé tribe
Nouse nacēon—or Cut nose—Cowsotum. Otlotcoutson—or the Lawyer—Ko ho kelpip the red crow. Pushwahikite—Mel. meltohintintini—Koulkoultamin or the red beard—Tiellickinickite—Takinswhaitish or rotten belly— —

Saalish or Flat heads.—
Insillah, called by the whites Little chief his name is descriptive of the war cap, with the war eagle's feathers in it— —Tsom shoumki. Konou-kots upski grand visage. Quoil quoilskiemi—red-pole—
Chiefs & braves of the Absarokies or Crows—Burns. Rotten Belly—High Bull, Mad Bull—Gros-ventre horse—Two face, a good fellow—Three Crows—Popāge—Wooden bowl—*Long hair—The bear's tooth. The Lawyer—The Rain—Omotashi, spotted water. Acacowackshei the war eagle Wolf—The breast that gives no milk. Rotten Tail—Yellow bull, yellow belly, Minisachi or Hot water. Nakioshishi or Burnt child [*Marginal note*: *vid 31ˢᵗ August.]

Articles in the *American Turf Register*, 1837

ADVENTURES IN THE ROCKY MOUNTAINS

DEAR SIR:

I accept the invitation to occupy a few pages of your Register with a description of my horseback adventures to and beyond the Rocky mountains, the fear of the *devil*,* notwithstanding. I hope it may prove instructive or interesting to your readers; if not, my *labours* are in vain, and my first bantling dies for want of nursing. Preparations were soon made for the trip—consisting of a light Tryon rifle, fifty to the pound, a compact little horse below fourteen hands, two blankets, a butcher knife, and of powder and ball quantum suff [sic]. I left Louisville, Ky. in April [March], 1834, low in flesh, lower in spirits, and as sensitive as the plant. In the course of an hour I encountered a teamster, who reminded me that I was at least enjoying the inestimable blessings of liberty and democracy—when in the act of passing, he bawled out, 'see here Bet, did you ever see a tighter fit, horse, man and gun? *Hell-low* mister!' 'Well, sir.' 'You've forgot one thing.' 'What is that?' inquired I. 'A coffee-pot to put the whole works in when it rains.' Zounds and death, thought I, shall I ever get to the mountains. I replied not a word, and smothered rage soon sweated itself off. Now, sir, I never bear malice, for I like such fellows, though they do hurt sometimes confoundedly. On we trotted, horse, gun and little *i*, without further bruise or blow, to St. Louis. Let us now, 'all on horses, gee up and gee oh,' set off for the mountains.' I hope you will not anticipate my dullness and fear that I am about to put a journal on to you. No, I shall not, I will delay you only long enough in the states, to say that the counties of Jackson and Fayette, on the south bank of the Missouri, are as beautiful and rich as 'bella Italia,' which Byron declared was 'the world's granary, ploughed by the sun-beams only.' Such ploughing would give but a light crop any where I opine. Our company consisted of but thirty-seven men, headed by a good trapper and a brave man —all in all, just such a one as you would like to know—gods what a country this would be, if every man was such as he. This tall Jackson-faced, raw-boned brave, is W. L. Sublette, with as quick an eye and steady a hand as ever lead company or shot a Blackfoot. When in camp, he resembled an old bruin in one respect, and that was, that you could touch in no place, that he was not ready to fend off. But, to the trip, at a dinner's halt on the Blue [May 16], the day we expected to reach the Platte, there sneaked upon us, three sly-looking naked Indians, who proved to be Pawnee republicans. They informed us that a large party were encamped on the river some miles above us, on their way to the Arkansas to make a buffalo hunt, taking with them, as our informants said, none but good hunters and great warriors. As we were obeying the order of 'catch up,' one of the yellow-jackets threw his Opishomo (a piece of buffalo robe to ride on) on to his shabby steed and

---

*The writer had expressed to the editor a dread of appearing in *type*; it is the *printer's devil*, therefore, that our respected correspondent alludes to [Ed.—*American Turf Register*].

flew up the river. The other two remained with us for two or three miles, or until we directed our course from the Blue towards the Platte, when another dashed off with savage speed in the direction of the first. Mr. Sublette directed my attention to a blue line of hills, beyond the river we had just left, my unpractised eyes discovered a scarcely perceptible something which seemed to move along their brow. 'There they are,' says he, 'that is the dust kicked up by the red rascals. Let us move on quickly, we must reach that hollow before they overtake us.' In a short time we were snugly unpacked and picketted in one of those ravines which run from the prairies into some near stream. From the bottom of this, when standing erect, we commanded an eminence or rather elevation in the ground riverward, about a hundred yards distant. When all was done, each horse and mule fast to his own picket, and each man's lungs relieved of the long breath, Sublette standing on our right, leaning on his gun, his eyes fixed on the little rise, said in a low but distinct voice, 'I suppose there is no man here who would rather *walk than ride.*' That was understood. Now, sir, I may be a brave man for aught that I do know, but indeed, I did not feel very pugnacious about that time, and if I ever am impertinently asked if I was scared, I will say yes—laugh who will. In one minute after our captain's comprehensive speech, one hundred and thirty fellows in paint were drawn up in battle array before us. Then, sir, oh where was my coffee-pot, where. I had neglected the caution, and was therefore compelled to stand and take it like a man. An awful pause! gad, though I did'nt feel funny, I could observe that the red bellies were right, and that there were indeed pale faces among us. I mean not to insinuate that any were cowards in that little band —far from it, for though their cheeks did blanch, their lips quivered not, neither did their knees shake; and I am bold to declare, from after knowledge, that there was as good game in some of them as ever pulled a trigger. But I'll spin my thread faster—our head sent up a young man who spoke a little Pawnee to desire the tall* men or captains to come down, but by no means were any others to leave the place where they had halted on. Immediately one rode from the ranks and after addressing a few words to the hunters and braves, descended accompanied by three others to our burrow. A talk ensued, which forthwith banished all my apprehensions, for after diplomatically inquiring into our whereabouts, whereto and whatfor, they graciously signified their willingness to let us depart, *provided,* we made something like an equal divide of all our goods and *cattles.* To this we demurred. They fell a few snakes, they would condescend then to accept a third, being as we were friends—another demurrer—then they would put up with a bundle of guns, a few sacks of powder and one or two etc. Still too deep—huh, huh, went from one mouth to another. Well, what will you give us? Five pounds of tobacco, ten bunches of blue beads, and six papers of paint—another 'huh,' a few words, many more grunts, and the bargain was closed. Mark the shrewdness of these men; when the articles agreed on were placed before our ministers plenipo, a light smile

*Signs, among Indians, constitute a universal language, those made by one tribe being used or understood by all others—the sign for chief or captain being one finger placed by the side of another so as to be longest—when two are equal they are placed evenly together [WMA].

rippled around the mouth of their Talleyrand, and at a sign from his hand, the four who had hitherto stood together, paired off, and touching his companion and pointing to the others, said, 'we are one village, and there stands another. This was enough, we paid duty to two ports. Before I close this letter, I will merely say that the Pawnees of the Platte, reside in four villages and have their separate, independent chiefs, though they are all one people originally, viz: the Grand Pawnees—the Pawnee Loups—the Pawnee Topagies and the Pawnee Republicans. That day [rather, on May 17] we tented on the Platte. Adieu, yours, &c.

MARSHALL.

SCENES IN THE WEST—THE PLATTE, &c.

DEAR SIR: May 27th, 1837

I believe it is true that 'use can almost change the stamp of nature, and either curb the devil or throw him out with wondrous potency;' for having once ventured into the presence of your *little demon*, I feel much less fear of him than I formerly entertained. Nevertheless, I hold it both wise and christian to love God and fear the devil. Of this enough! We tented on the Platte, and happy shall I be if I make your readers con tented with my account of the same. This river, as its name signifies both in French and Indian, is flat, i. e. it runs without fall or rapid, from its source in the Black Hills to its 'embouchement' into the Missouri: course almost due east.[1] We struck it about midway Grand Island. This, if the white or red man's account be true, is verily a grand island, being according to the first eighty, and from the description of the latter, about one hundred and twenty miles long. Spreading around said island, the river is generally two or two and a half miles wide. In appearance that broad and muddy stream resembles the Mississippi; but only in appearance. I imagined it as bold, impetuous, and deep. Standing on its banks and seeing its waters whirling and boiling about, I supposed that a seventy-four, with her full compliment of men and guns, could float upon her bosom; what then was my surprise to see a man jump in and wade a considerable distance, without wetting his breeches' flap. I found on examination that the deceptive appearance was occasioned by the motion of the quicksands, which constantly giving way, the water would sink into the holes, then burst upward and thus keep a perpetual agitation on the surface. Near our camp on that day, the earth was covered with a robe almost as white as snow. It was a salts, a feathery, frost-like exhudation; and as well as I remember was glauber tasted. The next day on our march, I saw for the first time the shy elk and ebon-footed antelope; but saw them only in their wild liberty; for although my gun was poised and mimic thunder and lightning was heard and seen, they passed unharmed from my vicinity, (indebted no doubt to the young hunter's ague for their safety.) The antelopes of the American desert are shorter and lower, but not much lighter than our common deer. The bucks have short black horns, from eight to ten inches in length, turning in towards the ends. They have no distinct prong from them but the bud

[1]Anderson is ill-informed in saying that the Platte has its source in the Black Hills, not the ultimate source even of the Laramie.

or semblance of one about three inches from the tip. Their general colour is that of our deer in the red, having two large white spots, the one extending from a hand's breadth of the shoulder to the same distance of the hip, the other covering the haunches so as to make them look like white animals when moving from you. The hair is soft, spungy, and swollen at the ends. The French 'voyageurs' call this animal 'cabri;' but there is no similarity between it and the goat, save that the tail is short. I have seen nothing so fleet; far more so I think than the greyhound or deer. The next day I saw a human skull laying on the plain, and as our motley crew passed by with jest and gibe, I could not help feeling saddened at the sight. My busy brain soon gifted it with all the attributes of living man, a body, flesh, and mind. He told me, that impelled by the spirit of adventure, he had years gone by bade adieu to his kin and country and sought to behold the wonders of the far-off west—that he had once rejoiced at the beauties of nature—that, like me, he had with admiration beheld the glorious sun rising and setting in the prairies' verdant sea—that he had seen with satisfaction these plains animated with immense herds of buffaloe, and whilst rejoicing in the pleasures of the day and thanking kind Providence for the favours he had bestowed, he fell the victim of an unseen foe. Indeed despair almost took possession of my soul, and I fancied the grinning head an eloquent 'memento mori', warning me with solemn voice, that 'in the midst of life, I was in death'. Sad, sad is it to behold that citadel of intellect tenanted by the slimy wanderer or the loathsome toad. But such is the fate of man! Such is death. On the same day we passed a spot where signs of destruction were still fresh all around. The demi-devils had lately been successful in some warlike fray. There stood their charmed circle of blood-stained sticks, on each of which was a small lock of their victim's hair, around which they had whooped, and danced, and sung with savage joy—stopping the while to tell how they had crawled upon their enemy and killed him when asleep, describing by voice and gesture this most manly act—how stealthily they had sneaked upon the foe and struck him when unseen, this too is an Indian's boast—and finally, how they had driven the tomahawk into his brains and torn off the precious scalp with their teeth. These scalp dances are what the French call 'grandes medecines'. I have heard an old trapper remark, and I think with justice, that the term 'medicine' was inappropriately used; for their medicine bag certainly is not supposed to contain any thing of medical virtue, either physical or spiritual, but is similar to the Jewish phylactery or Arab amulet, a charm for good or evil purposes. All along we found the nose of every buffaloe head turned down stream, towards the Pawnee villages. This is another French medicine; but I should rather call it a Pawnee trick, practised by them to entice the living browsers in the same direction. Quere —if those brutes could reason at all, would not some broad-headed old bull sagely say, 'that it was strange so many had gone down and none seemed to have returned?' Therefore he would conclude with Mr. Crapaud 'that it was no good medicine to go farther that way'.

Never shall I forget the evening when I first saw the 'sullen buffaloe'—when, in their state of nature, I first beheld the black bands of those terrific looking creatures, which once slaked their thirst even in the stream on which I was born —the sweet rolling Beargrass. Their number did not equal my expectations, for I had heard of their covering the ground like trees, as far the eye could see; but why be discontented, for there were thousands in view? My friend and leader S. proposed to me to take a chace. I cheerfully assented, and in preparation, we examined our guns and pistols, tightened our saddles, remounted our horses and off we put. Never before had I been so much and so agreeably excited. I had followed the close-pressed fox and panting deer when pursued by the joy-maddened pack, but what was that to the chase of a snorting band of shaggy shouldered buffaloe, in which each man had to depend on his own firm seat, steady arm, and fleet steed? Away we bounded. My little Black Hawk soon brought me up with a sergeant's guard on the outskirts. The first view of one of those dunkard quadrupeds, alarmed him as much as if he had seen a four-footed devil fresh sooted from ———; but, sir, when he caught the sweet odour of his horned majesty in his *green* nostrils he set off at a right-angled tangent, and was for a while as unmanageable as a rudderless steamboat. After a long chase and a strong chase, I lodged a pill of lead into the brown robe of one of the big ones, but too far forward to bring him to the earth. What threatening fire then flashed from his eyes—what desperate plunges did he make towards his pursuer—and the way Black Hawk made the sand fly was pleasing to his rider. I made a circle, got again into his wake, and with Kentucky ardour dashed up alongside my first friend and discharged both pistols into his carcass. This time his eyes dimmed, his nostrils ran blood, he staggered, bench legged, and fell down. What a fall was there! It is not always a final fall, for unlucifer-like, he may rise again; and if he should, wo betide the man or horse that comes within the reach of him—'habet fœnum in cornu.' To any but a victor in such a contest, the mighty and struggling throes of a dying bull is a painful spectacle; his efforts to rise, his tossing from side to side, his sitting on his narrow haunches reeling to and fro, his beating the earth with his cloven feet, and lastly the deep and mournful groan, which sounds his death when he sinks into his own blood, is indeed a painful sight. My hurry and anxiety had like to have cost me my gun, which would have been an awkward predicament. In tugging at my holsters, after the first fire, my rifle slipped from my grasp and fell to the ground; I passed on to finish the deed, after which it required nearly two hours search to find it. Sunset was approaching, and camp was distant about five miles. I hastened thither to receive the congratulations, which I thought were justly due. What was mortification and surprise to find all honour denied me, and for why? Simply because I had not brought in the tongue. This with the hunter is as invariable a trophy as is the scalp of the warrior. In neither case can the 'coup' be counted without the proof. I was a raw—not so our captain, who shortly returned with tongue, bosses, and hump ribs. Adieu until my next, in which I shall start a few wild horses, prairie-dogs, prairie-wolves, prairie-cocks, prairie-foxes, and some other prairie wonders. Wishing you both domestic and editorial prosperity, I remain yours respectfully,

W. MARSHALL.

SCENES AND THINGS IN THE WEST

MR. EDITOR: September 29, 1837

Before I start the 'wild things of the west', promised in my last, I will endeavour to describe two of the most beautiful and remarkable creations of nature—the mirage and looming. When I first read [in Thomas Moore's *Lalla Rookh*] the curse of the traitor—

> 'May he at last, with lips of flame,
> On the parched desert thirsting die,
> While lakes that shone in mockery nigh,
> Are fading off untouched, untasted.'

I looked upon it as the wrathful imprecation of a pagan heart, or a poetic variation on the punishment of Tantalus. Now, sir, I am convinced that 'no fiction is stranger than truth', for I know that every day on the American sand plains are to be seen the 'lakes that shine in mockery nigh', which 'fade away untouched, untasted.' What a terrible curse that would be! Such a judgment should be reserved for the traitor—and Arnold or Iscariot—a traitor to his country or a traitor to his God. Wonderful phenomenon! Who can look upon thy broad lakes, bold rivers, and sweet little brooks, which rise into billows, flow on with the might and majesty of the Father of waters, or leap and sparkle like a meadow stream, 'kissing the clover which hangs over its banks', without admiration and delight. But, 'on the parched desert thirsting die'—oh! I would not, for the wealth of a thousand mines, have one of them spread out before my longing eyes, if, like the rich man in the parable, I was praying for a drop of water to cool my burning lips.

On one occasion I had an opportunity of comparing this Persian *Sahrab* with the broad and muddy Platte. Just before us we saw a clear and rapid stream, hastening to mingle its bright and flashing particles with the river at our side. Even S[ublette]. paused to gaze upon the perfect delusion—'we looked on this and then on that', the eye of man could not perceive a difference, save that the 'counterfeit resemblance was far more inviting than the real thing.'

Looming is another spectacle which nature shows to the adventurer of the wilds that she denies to the woodsman. Many interesting and amusing incidents arise from this cause. 'See! look there!' whispers a voyager to his neighbour—and behold a band of mounted warriors, with bows and battle axes, are descending like a whirlwind upon them. One dodges from an arrow, another draws in his breath to bawl out 'Indians! Indians!' when the sun is suddenly obscured by a cloud, and lo! the harmless little antelopes, with their jet-black horns and spindle legs appear. I once requested my friend Arra-raish, (a name given to Mr. Sublette by the Crow Indians, and which means the straight walking cane,)[2] to go to a certain grove which I pointed out toward noon; he turned his unerring glance in the direction designated, and observed 'they are not trees but buffaloe', and truly, it

[2]The word "cane" was probably a misprint for "rain." See note for May 16.

seeemed as if my 'Burnin's wood was going to Dunsinane,'[3] for the forest was in motion. Every day in fact, when the sun was bright, the accuracy of our vision was tested by some unusual appearance in the prairies. I have actually known a man to dash off in pursuit of a grizzly bear, and return to be jeered at for making war on a prairie wolf.

Now, at length, for my promise. And first in order, as in rank, the horse. I cannot describe the sensation of more than pleasure which I felt when I first saw that paragon of animals in the full enjoyment of liberty—and no bird of the air could be more proudly exultant in that great privilege. One brown stallion, the leader of his band, defying all danger, came boldly up, walking with a firm and elastic step, reconnoitered us with an air of authority, paused to gaze more deliberately at us, his little sharp ears pointing directly in our faces. While standing in this position, from time to time tossing up his head, as if to display the red chambers of his nostrils, a young Alabamian who was with me, discharged his rifle into the ground just beside him, with a leap and a snort that would have done honour to a buck, he dashed off to his company, every hair in his long tail in a straight line with his back, and was soon lost to our sight forever. It may not be improper to mention a fact, which I think goes far to prove that this noble creature did not originally belong to this continent, but came over perhaps with the conquerors of Florida; it is that no word in any of the dialects of the mountain Indians, from south to north, is solely appropriated to the horse. In most of them, he is called the 'big-dog' from the circumstance of his succeeding that faithful servant and companion of man in the duties allotted him by the savages—packing lodges, drawing tent-poles, and in winter of being harnessed to their sleighs, laden with the rich treasures of the chase, or the more glorious 'spolia opima' of war.

The prairie dogs, from their social or gregarious habits, are the most interesting of quadrupeds. They live in villages, or more properly cities under ground. Their residences are formed by boring holes into the earth to a very great depth. Near each hole is a tumulus which was thrown up at the time of the excavation. On these each citizen perches himself like a kangaroo, and chatters to the air: for here, as in a frog-pond, every musician sings to his own delighted ears. If any thing passes near them a signal is given, and down sinks music and musicians, *sub terra*,—and on the area of six hundred acres are only to be seen one or two sentinels, perched on their watch towers, keeping up a fierce and incessant bark as long as the offensive intruder continues in their vicinity. The most remarkable fact in the history of these petty burghers is that they have never been seen to make use of water. Their villages are sometimes found at a great distance from any stream—sometimes on the tops of the highest mountains. I myself passed through one on the Black hills, several hundred feet above the bed of the Platte. The Indians say they never drink. They are yellow or lion-coloured, shaped not unlike the kangaroo, with broad quarters, tapering thence to the head; their fore-

[3]The quotation from Shakespeare's *Macbeth* is pleasant in that at the rendezvous Anderson met William Drummond Stewart, who succeeded in 1838 to the estate in Scotland that included Birnam Wood.

legs are much shorter than the hinder, and when sitting erect they look like little arms folded on their breast: and to finish the description, their ears, like those of the beaver, look as if they had been cropped with the knife.

The prairie fox is another wonder of the wilderness. This beautiful little animal is one of the swiftest things of its size in the world. So smoothly and evenly does it go that it seems to be propelled by some arrow-like power, rather than the action of its legs, as it skims along the earth. Its pretty long bushy tail seems to add just another length to the body, so alike is the proportion of the two. They are rarely seen together, and are very wild.

The hare is a *bounder*. There is a grace and loftiness in its motions which are unsurpassed. His stroke is peculiar, after leaving the ground his long and muscular legs are thrown downwards and back, so as to form a 'double coup' on the earth, which propels him a half-length farther than he would otherwise have gone. His head is borne proudly up, and every leap is similar to those beautiful springs which the greyhound takes when he is dodged by his prey. In the fall his coat becomes somewhat tawney, approximating the seared and yellow vegetation of that season—in winter he is as white as the snow which covers the earth—being thus aided by a favouring Providence in concealing himself from his enemies of the air and the land.

Here for a time I will end my description of the animals of the boundless prairies, and here too I will end this hasty letter, after protesting, solemnly protesting, against an act of injustice done against a numerous, brave, and adventurous class of our western citizens by our much admired Irving, or rather by Captain Bonneville through him. In the name of Sublette, Fitzpatrick, Fontenelle, Dripps, Bridger, and Campbell, I protest against the name 'lake Bonneville', given by the author of 'Astoria and the rocky mountains' to that great inland sea, the Urimiah of our continent. In the name of Ashley, who had described this lake eighteen or twenty years before Captain Bonneville ever crossed the mountains, I protest against that name. What justice, what honour can there be in claiming the right of naming that 'wonder of western wonders' after Bonneville, when it had been found, circumambulated, and trapped on as early as 1820 by Provost? All these men are his predecessors, and he knows it. They have all seen and been intimately acquainted with it, and he knew it. This lake was once called lake Ashley, and with how much more propriety. High and respected as is the authority of Irving— 'fiat justitia'.[4]

Yours, &c.

W.M.A.

[4]Washington Irving's account of the adventures of Capt. B. L. E. Bonneville, originally titled *The Rocky Mountains*, had been published earlier in 1837. The maps in *The Rocky Mountains*, based on originals by Bonneville, apply the name Lake Bonneville to Great Salt Lake, and in Vol. I, Chap. xxi, Irving gives a considerable account of the lake as supplied by Bonneville from hearsay. In a letter to Lieut. G. K. Warren, dated Gila River, New Mexico, Aug. 24, 1857, Bonne-

ville said: "On all the maps of those days the Great Salt lake had two great outlets to the Pacific ocean: one of these was the Buenaventura river, which was supposed to head there; the name of the other I do not recollect. It was from my explorations and those of my party alone that it was ascertained that this lake had no outlet; that the California range *basined* all the waters of its eastern slope without further outlet; that the Buenaventura and all other California streams drained only the western slope. It was for this reason that Mr. W. Irving named the salt lake after me, and he believed I was fairly entitled to it. . . ." See Gouverneur K. Warren, *Memoir To Accompany the Map of the Territory of the United States*, p. 33, which also appears in Vol. XI of the *Reports of Explorations for Pacific Railroads*.

Anderson's protest is echoed by Warren Ferris (*Life in the Rocky Mountains*, p. 69): "An attempt has been recently made to change the name of this lake to Lake Bonnyville, from no other reason that I can learn, but to gratify the silly conceit of a Captain Bonnyville, whose adventures in this region at the head of a party, form the ground work of 'Irving's Rocky Mountains.' There is no more justice or propriety in calling the lake after that gentleman, than after any other one of the many persons who in the course of their fur hunting expeditions have passed in its vicinity [as Ferris himself did, two years before Bonneville went to the mountains]. He neither discovered, or explored it, nor has he done any thing else to entitle him to the honour of giving it his name, and the foolish vanity that has been his only inducement for seeking to change the appellation by which it has been known for fifty years, to his own patronymic, can reflect no credit upon him, or the talented author who has lent himself to the service of an ambition so childish and contemptible."

Both Ferris and Anderson exaggerate somewhat. Ashley brought back reports of Great Salt Lake in 1825 and 1826, not eighteen or twenty years before Bonneville crossed the mountains in 1832; and there is no reason to suppose that Étienne Provost penetrated to the Great Salt Lake region before 1824; his trapping operations out of New Mexico came after the opening of Santa Fe to trade in 1822. It is amusing that Anderson, critical in his Diary of Ashley's claims to distinction, now appears as Ashley's defender.

Letter to the *National Intelligencer*, 1860

WHO DISCOVERED SALT LAKE?

Among the "thousand and one" articles of freight and baggage which went down to the Bay by the steamer Queen City yesterday were two old flint-lock, smooth-bore rifles of the real old "Kaintuck" stripe. They were brought on board by a man who looked as weather-beaten, flinty-locked, and hard-stocked as themselves. Being curious to learn their history and who it was that possessed them, we made a few inquiries, and the owner, being mellowed by the genial influences of the corn vintage, communicated the following facts: His name was Seth Grant, a Scotchman by birth, who come to America at an early age, in the year 1819, and joined the American Fur Company. In 1826 he accompanied Bridger—the founder of Fort Bridger—and his partner, Col. Vasquez, to the then unknown wilds of the West, far beyond the head waters of the Platte or Yellowstone. It was on one of those fur-seeking, marauding expeditions that the Frenchman, Col. Vasquez, while out on an excursion, discovered the Great Salt Lake of Utah. The immense extent of the lake, with its mountains and islands, so deceived Vasquez and his party that they reported to their fellows that they had discovered an arm of the Pacific ocean; and so, indeed, it seemed, for it was years before the error was corrected. The two rifles in possession of Mr. Grant were a portion of the arms of the original party, and bore the marks of having seen long and honorable service. Mr. Grant values them highly, and, being on his way back to his own native land, intends taking them as trophies, to be hung up with the tartans and claymores of his countrymen.[1]

[*Sacramento Standard.*]

SEVEN OAKS, FEBRUARY 16, 1860.

Messrs. Editors of the National Intelligencer:

Allow me to call your attention to the above paragraph, credited to the "Sacramento Standard." The writer, on the authority of a Mr. Seth Grant, says that my old friend Vasquez, of the Rocky Mountains, was the discoverer of the "Great

[1]Everything known of Grant comes from this paragraph in a Sacramento newspaper. He was possibly one of John H. Weber's party, including Bridger, which left the Big Horn in the summer of 1824 and crossed South Pass to reach the Great Basin. If Grant journeyed to the mountains as late as 1826, he may have come with Vasquez, but not with Bridger.

Salt Lake" of Utah.[2] The honor could not possibly have been bestowed upon a worthier man. Can this geographical fact be now ascertained and settled beyond dispute? Was Col. Vasquez the discoverer of that remarkable body of water? My answer is, no. I not only doubt, but I emphatically deny that statement. A little more than a quarter of a century ago I heard the very subject of the priority of its discovery debated by old mountaineers almost in the vicinity of the Lake itself.[3] To furnish better proof than unassisted memory I send you the following extract from a letter written by me in 1837, at the request of the venerable [John Stuart] Skinner, and published in the 8th volume of the American Turf Register:

"Here for a time I will end my description of the animals of the boundless prairies; and here, too, I will end this hasty letter, after protesting, solemnly protesting, against an act of injustice done to a numerous, brave, and adventurous class of our Western citizens by our much-admired Irving, or rather by Capt. Bonneville through him. In the name of Sublette, Fitzpatrick, Fontenelle, Dripps, Bridger, and Campbell, I protest against the name 'Lake Bonneville,' given by the author of 'Astoria' and 'The Rocky Mountains' to that great inland sea, the 'Urimiah' of our continent. In the name of Ashley, who had described this lake eighteen or twenty years before Capt. Bonneville ever crossed the mountains, I protest against that name. What justice, what honor can there be in claiming the right of naming that 'wonder of the Western waters' after Bonneville when it had been found circumambulated and trapped on as early as 1820 by Provost? This lake was once called 'Ashley,' and with much more propriety, high and respected as is the authority of Irving. *'Fiat justitia.'*"[4]

---

[2]The particular celebrity of Vasquez at this time rested on a story in the San Francisco *Daily Evening Bulletin,* Oct. 29, 1858, a correspondent having written from Great Salt Lake City on Oct. 11: "I have had the pleasure of meeting, during the past week, Major Vasquez, the oldest mountaineer in this country, and the discoverer of Great Salt Lake. He first entered this valley 36 years ago. In the fall of 1822, he, with a company of trappers, arrived in Cache Valley, where they determined to spend the winter, and trap in the numerous streams with which it abounds. The winter, however, became so severe—the snow falling to the depth of 8 feet—that they found it necessary to hunt out a better valley, in order to save their animals. Accordingly, Major Vasquez, with one or two of his party, started out, and crossing the divide, entered this valley, and discovered Great Salt Lake. This they at first took to be an arm of the Pacific Ocean. They found the valley free from snow, and well filled with herds of buffalo. Returning to their party, they guided them over into this valley, when they divided—one party, under Weber, wintering on the river which now bears his name; the other party wintering on Bear river, near its mouth. The following spring, Vasquez built a boat, and circumnavigated this sheet of brine, for the purpose of finding out definitely whether it was an arm of the sea or not, and thus discovered that it was in reality merely a large inland lake, without an outlet. Since that time, the lake has been gradually receding."

This tale appears to be a composite of mountain experience. Vasquez may have reached the Yellowstone in 1822, but he must have first come to the Rockies in the Ashley party that reached Cache Valley in June 1826. The circumnavigation of Great Salt Lake had been accomplished that spring by others. The severe winter clearly was that of 1827-1828, though John H. Weber left the Rockies for home in 1825 or 1826. We judge that Vasquez is describing events of the winter of 1824-1825, and that the discovery for which he takes credit was made by James Bridger.

[3]Anderson exaggerates the nearness to the Great Salt Lake of this "debate by old mountaineers," but compare his Diary for August 2 and 28.

[4]See Anderson's third letter to the *American Turf Register* and the concluding note.

The above was written, at the time indicated, from my journal notes, taken down in the presence of the interlocutors in 1834. Provost was then "no more." Neither praise nor censure could reach him. His survivors and brothers in the hardships and hazards of mountain life gave to him alone the credit of having discovered and made known the existence and whereabouts of that inland sea. Notwithstanding the positive assertion of Seth Grant, "made under the genial influence of the corn-vintage," I deny its truth. I will not pursue the subject further than to add that only eight years had elapsed since Vasquez and his companions had come upon "that arm of the Pacific ocean," and yet he, then present, made no claim, and his associates and equals, of both the American and Rocky Mountain Fur Companies, with whom he was the general favorite, did not assign him even a secondary honor.[5]

Confidently appealing to my surviving friends and acquaintances of the mountains for correction or confirmation, I assure you, gentlemen, of the reverential esteem of

W. MARSHALL ANDERSON.

[5] In 1834 Etienne Provost was by no means "no more," unreachable by praise or censure; he was in camp and could have participated in any discussions. Vasquez was not on hand, having left the rendezvous on July 10. But Anderson's denial that Vasquez was the discoverer of Great Salt Lake has been vindicated by the march of knowledge.

A Galaxy of Mountain Men

BIOGRAPHICAL SKETCHES

WILLIAM HENRY ASHLEY

Ashley was born probably in 1778 at Manchester, Chesterfield County, Virginia. He moved to Powhatan County at an early age, and made his way to Ste. Genevieve, Missouri, in 1802. After a varied career, described in Dale L. Morgan, *The West of William H. Ashley, 1822-1838,* he emerged in 1820 as the first lieutenant governor of Missouri and thereafter as a brigadier general of militia. In the summer of 1821 he and Andrew Henry organized a fur trade partnership.

Henry led their first expedition up the Missouri in April 1822, reaching the Yellowstone by October to begin the construction of a fort at its mouth. A second boat, started upriver in May, sank with most of its cargo in the Missouri below Fort Osage. Ashley obtained another keelboat and a new outfit, set out from St. Louis in June, and joined Henry at the Yellowstone in October. Soon after, he returned home in a pirogue.

In March 1823 Ashley led a second expedition up the Missouri. At the Arikara villages on June 2 he was attacked and defeated, losing fifteen men and a considerable amount of property. A military campaign against the Arikaras was so ineffective that the Missouri remained closed to the fur traders. Ashley and Henry had already given thought to sending parties overland from the Missouri, and accordingly, in late September 1823, Ashley launched Jedediah Smith, William L. Sublette, Thomas Fitzpatrick, and others from Fort Kiowa (Lookout) toward the Black Hills and the Crow country beyond. He then returned to St. Louis. Next summer he made an unsuccessful campaign for the governorship of Missouri. Shortly thereafter Andrew Henry returned, discouraged.

Having received word from Fitzpatrick that he and Smith had been successful trapping beaver beyond South Pass (the effective discovery of which they had made in March 1824), Ashley mounted a new expedition and left St. Louis the last week of September to seek out his men in the mountains. He and Henry had introduced a change in fur trade practice by which men taken to the fur country received no wages but agreed to sell their beaver at three dollars a pound. This free trapping reduced Ashley's overhead, but nullified his claim on the beaver caught unless he could supply the trappers with goods.

On Nov. 4, 1824, Ashley therefore left Fort Atkinson, which he had reached October 21. He started out with a wagon, but soon had to abandon it in heavy snow. After wintering on the Platte and the South Platte, in February 1825, from the vicinity of the Cache la Poudre in present Colorado, he started into the Rockies. By way of the Laramie Plains, and the north end of the Medicine Bow Mountains, he reached the North Platte in late March, and went on to Green River through the Great Divide Basin, south of South Pass. On April 22, 1825, Ashley started down the Green on a voyage of discovery. Descending the river through its canyons, he reached the Uinta Basin, where he encountered trappers brought from Taos by Etienne Provost and his partner (François?) Leclerc. Ashley headed west up the Duchesne and the Strawberry and soon fell in with Provost, returning from a spring trapping tour to the basin of the Great Salt Lake. He hired Provost to transport his cached goods, then completed his circuit of the Uinta Mountains, arriving at his appointed rendezvous on Henrys Fork of the Green about July 1, 1825. On this expedition Ashley did not get much closer to Great Salt Lake than present Coalville in the valley of the Weber River.

The Henrys Fork rendezvous was the first of the famous gatherings that have come down in history as the distinguishing institution of the mountain fur trade. After trading with the trappers and forming a partnership with Jedediah Smith, Ashley set out for the Big Horn River. Reaching a navigable point below the Big Horn Mountains, he constructed bullboats and floated his furs down to the mouth of the Yellowstone, where he encountered the Atkinson-O'Fallon expedition. Atkinson agreed to transport Ashley's furs to Fort Atkinson, and Ashley went on from there to St. Louis, arriving the first week of October 1825.

By the end of that month, Ashley had assembled a new outfit with which Jedediah Smith set off to the mountains. Smith lost pack animals, was forced to send back to Ashley for more, and wintered at the Pawnee villages on the Republican River. In the spring Ashley joined him in the valley of the Platte and went on to Cache Valley, where he arrived in June. This is probably as close as Ashley ever came to Great Salt Lake; Anderson no doubt heard rightly in 1834 that the General had never laid eyes on that famous body of water. According to Robert Campbell, after the rendezvous was over, Jackson and Sublette were encountered on Bear River, and negotiations then undertaken by which a new partnership, Smith, Jackson & Sublette, bought out Ashley. They purchased the goods on hand and gave him a provisional contract to buy more. Ashley continued to St. Louis and arrived safely with his furs in September, thus having retrieved his fortunes.

Ashley never returned to the mountains. For a few years he acted as supplier, banker, and sales agent, first for Smith, Jackson & Sublette, later for Jackson & Sublette, finally for William L. Sublette. He won a special election in 1831 to become representative from Missouri, and thus reestablished himself in politics. Originally a Jackson man, he differed with President Jackson on the U. S. Bank issue, which led to a difficult situation for Ashley politically. Nevertheless, Ashley was reelected twice, serving in the House of Representatives until March 1837. In the summer of 1836 he ran for governor against Lilburn W. Boggs, but was decisively beaten. He was again preparing to run for the House when he died of pneumonia on March 26, 1838. Ashley had been twice a widower, and he left a widow. He had no children.

Frederic Billon describes him as: "A man of medium height, say about five feet nine inches, of light frame, his weight might have been from hundred and thirty-five to one hundred and forty pounds; thin face, prominent nose, not Roman, but aquiline or Grecian, so that a profile view of his face presented a projecting nose and chin with the mouth drawn in."

HENRY ATKINSON

Atkinson was born in North Carolina in 1782, entered the Army in 1808, and rose to the rank of colonel in the infantry. He commanded the Yellowstone Expedition of 1819, out of which came the founding of Fort Atkinson and Long's expedition to the Rocky Mountains; and in 1825 he was co-commissioner with Benjamin O'Fallon, Indian Agent for the Upper Missouri, in negotiating treaties with various Missouri River tribes. Before returning, he ascended the Missouri to Two Thousand Mile Creek above the mouth of the Yellowstone. Made brigadier general in 1820, he was in general command of the troops in the Black Hawk War of 1832 and was in immediate command when the Sauk chief's forces were crushed at Bad Axe. In 1840 Atkinson supervised the removal of Indians from Wisconsin to Iowa, and two years later, on June 14, 1842, he died at Jefferson Barracks (the site of which, ten miles south of St. Louis, he had selected). Atkinson married Mary Ann Bullitt at Louisville, Kentucky, on Jan. 16, 1826, and one son was born to them. W. J. Ghent, from whose account in the *Dictionary of American Biography* the foregoing is principally taken, says: "His name is inseparably connected with the earlier period of the conquest of the frontier, and the part he bore is equaled in importance by that of no contemporary with the possible exception of William Clark." For a fuller biography, see Roger L. Nichols, *General Henry Atkinson: A Western Military Career.*

BLACKBIRD (Omaha Chief)

Blackbird, or Wash-ing-guh-sah-ba, gave the Omahas, a Siouan people, their only hour of greatness. According to Philip St. George Cooke, *Scenes and Adventures in the Army*, pp. 130-135, Blackbird was born about 1750. He was a "great chief" by 1794, when Jean Baptiste Truteau summed him up as "the most shrewd, the most deceitful, and the greatest rascal of all the nations who inhabit the Missouri." Truteau thus early recorded the tales Anderson heard from Lucien Fontenelle forty years later, that he was an accomplished poisoner and that he was to be awakened only by passing a feather lightly over his face, or tickling certain parts of his body. James Mackay added to Blackbird's tough chronicle in 1795-1796; see A. P. Nasatir, *Before Lewis and Clark*, I, 282-290, 357-363. Although Alphonso Wetmore's "Biography of Blackbird" in his *Gazetteer of the State of Missouri*, pp. 299-305, says that the chief died in 1802, Lewis and Clark noted on Aug. 12, 1804, that Blackbird had died of smallpox four years before with some four hundred of his tribesmen. "Blackbird's Hill," where he was buried astride a favorite riding animal, was thereafter a famous landmark along the Missouri. Tales about Blackbird were recorded by many later travelers up the river, including John Bradbury and H. M. Brackenridge in 1811, Stephen H. Long in 1819, George Catlin in 1832, and Maximilian in 1833. Catlin carried off his skull, and in the Smithsonian *Annual Report* for 1885, Vol. II, p. 263, it is reported among the collections of the National Museum. However, we are informed by the Smithsonian Institution that the museum contains only "one skull identified as Omaha, and this particular skull does not belong to Chief Blackbird."

BENJAMIN LOUIS EULALIE DE BONNEVILLE

Bonneville was born in or near Paris on April 14, 1796, and migrated with his family to New York in 1803. He entered the Military Academy on his seventeenth birthday and graduated Dec. 11, 1815. After serving in New England and the recruiting service, on military road construction in Mississippi, and at the frontier posts of Fort Smith and Fort Gibson, as also in San Antonio, Texas, and St. Louis, he was detached to serve as aide to Lafayette during the famous visit to the United States in 1825, afterward accompanying the Marquis back to France. By November 1826 he was back at Fort Gibson, and there he spent most of the next four years. (On Oct. 4, 1825, he had been made captain in the Seventh Infantry.)

Perhaps influenced by the Bean-Sinclair trapping party, which with considerable publicity was organized on the Arkansas frontier in 1829-1830, Bonneville became interested in the fur trade. (See the sketch of Joseph Reddeford Walker.) He went to New York, won backing from the onetime Astorian, Alfred Seton, and in the summer of 1831 obtained from the War Department a two-year leave of absence, professedly to gather information about the Far West. A certain ambiguity has always attended this furlough, leaving it doubtful whether it was a money-making venture cloaked in military propriety, or a military undertaking the government was pleased to have carried out at no expense to itself.

Bonneville's two-year license to trade, dated Feb. 28, 1832, gave the value of his goods as $17,254.77. On May 1, 1832, with 110 men, Joseph Reddeford Walker, q.v., and Michel Sylvestre Cerré, q.v., recruited as his principal lieutenants, he set out from Fort Osage, Missouri. The twenty wagons in which he transported his goods as far as Green River were the first to cross South Pass, though Ashley had sent a cannon on a carriage to Bear Lake in 1827, and William L. Sublette had taken ten wagons and two dearborns to Wind River in 1830. Bonneville made a leisurely passage westward, reaching the Platte June 2, the Laramie June 26, South Pass July 24, and the Green River near the mouth of Horse Creek July 26. While his horses and mules recruited, Bonneville built a "breastworks of logs and pickets" thereafter known as Fort Bonneville, "Fort Nonsense" to the trappers. This rude fortification had no military utility; only troops maintained in the country could have had any meaning, and to their presence "Fort Bonneville" would have had no power to add or detract.

Advised that Horse Creek was not suitable for a winter camp, Bonneville moved over to the Salmon River, first detaching a party under David Adams to trap the Crow country and circle around to the Salmon via the Three Forks of the Missouri, and another party under (A.?) Matthieu to trade with the Snake village on Bear River, then join Bonneville on the Salmon. The main body he himself conducted to the Salmon. While he occupied himself building another establishment (also called Fort Bonneville), he sent Joe Walker to trap in the Flathead country.

Adams' party was broken up completely; Matthieu's party had to winter in Cache Valley, and four of his men were killed; Walker alone accomplished very much. Bonneville, who had reached the Salmon September 26, was rejoined by Walker the first week of November. About two weeks later "the bald chief," as the Indians had begun to call Bonneville, dispatched Walker off to the south with forty or fifty men to set up a winter camp on the Snake. He himself remained on the Salmon until December 26, when with thirteen trappers he headed for the Snake. He found some of Matthieu's men there January 12, and according to Irving, Matthieu and the rest arrived from Bear River three weeks later. Walker is not mentioned, but his camp must have been the scene of the reunion. On Feb. 19, 1833, Bonneville set out on his return to the Salmon, which he reached about March 12. He detailed W. D. Hodgkiss to accompany a group of free trappers up the Salmon and himself organized a party to hunt westerly into the Snake country. The Rocky Mountain Fur Co. had detailed Milton Sublette and Gervais to trap the same country, and Bonneville did not do well. In his letter from Wind River, July 29, 1833, he says he trapped the "Malade [Big Wood], Camanche [Camas], Boisey and La Payette rivers—at last found that living upon fish, horses and roots would not do—I then tried to cross the mountain to the North, (1st July [June])—the great debth of snow forced me to seek another pass, at last reached the forks of Salmon river on the 15th of July [June], here I waited 4 days for my parties, having found their path, I took it, and on the 29th found them, much to my surprise with the Pends, Orrielles & the Cottonains, the Flat heads & Nez Percey, having been driven from the country by the Black foots, who that Spring consolidated for that purpose." Amid many hazards, he made his way over to Horse Creek (accompanied part way by Nathaniel Wyeth; briefly they considered a joint trapping venture to California to be headed by Wyeth). Bonneville got back to his fort on Green River July 13, 1833, as Irving says; Wyeth makes the date July 15.

Again Walker had produced the only returns of consequence. He was placed in charge of an expedition which, Irving maintained later, was to have explored Great Salt Lake, but which at the time was understood to be bound for California. To Cerré was entrusted the year's returns, said by Wyeth to have totaled only thirty packs. Bonneville accompanied Cerré to the place of embarkation on the Big Horn River. They set out July 25, the day after Walker left the rendezvous for California, and reached the Big Horn via South Pass on August 12, having journeyed much of the way in close proximity to Wyeth, Fitzpatrick, and Campbell.

Having seen Cerré off, Bonneville turned back through the Crow country, but his parties had no success trapping the western tributaries of the Big Horn, his fall hunt according to Thomas Fitzpatrick netting only 112 skins. After revisiting his fort at Horse Creek, Bonneville moved southwesterly to the Bear, where he arrived November 6. Finally, in December, he set up a winter camp near the mouth of the Portneuf.

Taking three men with him, on Christmas Day, 1833, the Captain set out on a tour of investigation toward the Columbia, starting down the left bank of the

Snake, and after many vicissitudes reaching Fort Walla Walla on March 4. Not until May 12 did he get back to the Portneuf, the trip having taken two months longer than anticipated. He found his men encamped on the Blackfoot River; apparently they had realized little from their spring hunt. With his party Bonneville moved over to Bear River, and on its banks (about June 20) he found Walker, who had returned from his California venture twenty days earlier.

Cerré put in his appearance with the next year's outfit on June 28. He had obtained in St. Louis, on April 16, a new two-year trading license, curiously issued to "Astor, Bonneville, & Co.," the capital stated as a modest $2,957.12 (though this would have covered only goods to be traded to the Indians). The arrangements Bonneville made on Bear River are somewhat murky, but it appears that Cerré was asked to take down the returns, accompanied at least part of the way by Walker; that a company was sent to trap the Crow country under Antonio Montero (or the company may initially have had two leaders, Walker being the other); and, finally, that Bonneville himself took a twenty-three-man party toward the Columbia. The several detachments separated July 3. Bonneville went slowly at first, to give his horses an opportunity to recruit, and thus he was overtaken by Wyeth, en route to found Fort Hall. Bonneville continued down the Snake by his route of the previous winter, but no dates are given by Irving until August 26, when Bonneville reached the Grande Ronde. He moved on to within thirty miles of Fort Walla Walla, but the Hudson's Bay Company would furnish him no supplies, and he could not get the Indians to trade him fish or other provisions. Turning his back on the Columbia to ascend John Day River, Bonneville reached the Snake again on October 20, and was happy to get back to buffalo country at "the head waters of the Portneuf" about Nov. 15, 1834.

Soon after, Bonneville received word that Montero's company was still in the Crow country, and that a June rendezvous on the Arkansas, which Irving says had been contemplated, was not feasible. A Wind River rendezvous was agreed upon instead, and Bonneville set up a winter camp on Bear River. His spring hunt, launched April 1, 1835, was made in the Green River Valley. Late in June he joined Montero (and Walker?) on Wind River, after which he started home via "the head of Powder River and its mountains," reaching Independence Aug. 22, 1835.

Bonneville learned on arrival that he had been dropped from the Army for having overstayed his leave. The details of his fight for reinstatement need not be discussed here, having been touched upon by Edgeley W. Todd in a new edition of *The Adventures of Captain Bonneville*. Bonneville fell to work on the manuscript account of his adventures, which in March 1836 he sold to Washington Irving for a thousand dollars and which Irving made the basis of his book originally titled *The Rocky Mountains*.

The Captain was ordered reinstated in the Army on April 22, 1836, but before the news reached him he had set off for the mountains again. He got a license in St. Louis, April 19, 1836, for fifteen men, with a stated capital of $1,122, Daniel Lamont being his surety. This venture of 1836 is the least-known episode of

Bonneville's involvement with the fur trade, having been passed over by Irving; his purpose was to provide an outfit for Montero, who had remained in the Crow country. Leaving Independence May 8, Bonneville reached Fort William June 6, eight days ahead of Fitzpatrick. A letter from Fort William written by L. Crawford on June 29 says: "Capt Bonaville has settled his affairs in this country and is on his way down with part of his equipment which he expects to sell here, but I'm afraid he's coming to a poor market. I'm told he has eight Kegs of liquor to dispose of, that we never have too much of, if he will take a reasonable price for it I may bargain with him, the Sioux are all along Riviere Platte and if he should attempt to take it down he's sure to be robbed."

Bonneville got back to Fort Leavenworth Aug. 6, 1836. Next day he wrote the Adjutant General that he would go at once to Fort Gibson, and by October 20, via St. Louis, he had done so. To Brev. Brig. Gen. Mathew Arbuckle, commander of the South Western Frontier, Bonneville then reported that in view of "the liberty granted me by the Honorable Senator T. H. Benton, who as chairman of the military comm. assured me my presence was entirely unnecessary," he had been impelled "to prevent wasting the small means yet within my reach," to turn his personal efforts to sustain himself in case of failure. This was a way of describing his final fling in the fur trade, in the face of the hostility of his brother officers of the Seventh Infantry, who had opposed Bonneville's reinstatement.

Many years later, in 1876, Bonneville wrote the Historical Society of Montana concerning his Western operations: "One of my parties was sent through the Crow country and came round by the north, and wintered with me on Salmon river [Adams' party was to have done this but did not]; another party was sent south and wintered on the shores of Salt Lake [Matthieu's party got no farther than Cache Valley]; another journeyed into the Utes country, farther south, until it met the traders and trappers from New Mexico [unidentified, unless some arrangement was reached with Fallon & Vanderburgh in 1833-1834, or unless this describes where Walker actually went in the fall of 1834]; another [led by Bonneville] went down Salmon [Snake] river, to Walla Walla, on the Columbia; another [Walker in 1833-1834] to coast around the Salt Lake; being out of provisions, it turned north, upon Marias [Mary's] river, followed this river down west to the eastern base of the California mountains, where it empties itself into large flat lakes, thence westward, clambering for twenty-three days among the difficult passes of this elevated range, before it reached its Western or Pacific slope; thence to Monterey on the coast, where it wintered...."

Bonneville must never have had the opportunity to review Irving's manuscript, for obvious misinterpretations were not corrected. Irving worked at one remove from Bonneville's journal, utilizing a narrative Bonneville wrote in Washington during the fall and winter of 1835-1836, a situation which enlarged the realm for error. Bonneville's fight for reinstatement also colored the materials that came into Irving's hands. The last word on Bonneville remains to be written.

A summary of Bonneville's military career prepared by the Adjutant General's Office for J. Neilson Barry may be found in *Annals of Wyoming*, VIII (April

1932), 632-633. Here it is enough to say that he was promoted to major, Sixth Infantry, on July 15, 1845; lieutenant colonel, Fourth Infantry, on May 7, 1849; colonel, Third Infantry, on Feb. 3, 1855; and retired on Sept. 9, 1861. He was breveted lieutenant colonel on Aug. 20, 1847, for gallantry and meritorious conduct in the battles of Contreras and Churubusco; and brigadier general, March 13, 1865, for long and faithful service in the Army. When he died at Fort Smith, Arkansas, on June 12, 1878, Bonneville was the oldest officer on the retired list.

On Dec. 12, 1842, he married at Carlisle, Pennsylvania, Anne Callender, daughter of Dr. Charles W. Lewis of Monroe County, Virginia. She and their young daughter died at St. Louis. After his retirement, at Fort Smith in 1870, he married Susan Neis, who survived him.

BRACELETTE DE FER (Shoshoni Chief)

The Snake chief who was known to the whites as Bracelette de Fer or Iron Wristbands, according to Osborne Russell was known to his people as "Pah-da-her-wak-un-dah," or "The Hiding Bear." His father, termed by the French trappers Cotillon (Petticoat), is referred to by William Drummond Stewart in *Edward Warren*, p. 222; and in a letter to his brother from Green River, July 20, 1833, Robert Campbell mentions the "Iron Wristband," who "had lately succeeded his father, 'Petticoat', as chief of the nation." Warren Ferris did not have an elevated view of this eldest son of Cotillon: "The principal chief of the Snakes is called the '*Iron Wristband*', a deceitful fellow, who pretends to be a great friend of the whites, and promises to punish his followers for killing them or stealing their horses. . . . The 'Little Chief', a brave young warrior, is the most noble and honorable character among them."

Stewart terms Iron Wristbands "a good-natured cunning-looking Indian, who did not much meddle with the more important affairs of the tribe, and contented himself with interfering in the intrigues of the women [as marriage broker, etc.], and the profits of trade" (p. 273). He elaborates on "the Soldier," or Little Chief, Bracelette de Fer's younger brother, by saying (pp. 244-245) that he "was a man of about six feet, not thirty years of age, with a countenance whose simple and grand expression was not in any way weakened by the mildness and gentleness so clearly stamped upon it. He wore one middle lock, cut square, in the centre of his forehead, ornamented by a knot of small turquoise beads; the division of his fine hair along the ridge of the head was filled with vermillion, with which his face was highly rouged, and certain figures marked on it with great care and accurate drawing in bright yellow ochre; his arms were loaded with bracelets, all but one of shining brass, that one was of iron, it was the distinctive badge adopted by his house; and his elder brother, the principal chief, took his name from it, Bracelet de Fer. But in all matters of importance in war, in the sustaining of authority, and the repression of theft, the voice of the younger brother, the Little Chief, was alone that which insured obedience in the Shoshone camp."

The Little Chief, more properly Ma-wo-ma, was painted by Alfred Jacob Miller in 1837, together with his son Si-roc-u-an-tum, then said to be about twenty-two years old. (Of this son no more is heard; he may have died early.) Both Stewart (p. 381) and Miller remark on Ma-wo-ma's opinion of his own portrait, which virtually expressed the attitude of a modern school of art—"it was too like, which he considered a vulgar and familiar species of art, such as he said, could be made by his looking glass."

Anderson's Biblical allusion to a time not far off when Bracelette de Fer would be replaced by his brother as head chief expressed the view of many, but the event was continually deferred. Osborne Russell, reporting gossip among the Snakes in December 1840, said that "the Snake *Chief Pah da-hewak um da* was becoming very unpopular and it was the opinion of the Snakes in general that *Moh woom hah* his brother would be at the head of affairs before 12 mos as his village already amounted to more than 300 lodges and moreover he was supported by the bravest men in the Nation. . . ." In some remarks on the Snakes penned later in the 1840's, Russell commented: "In the winter of 1842 the principal Chief of the Snakes died in an appoplectic fit and on the following year his brother died but from what disease I could not learn. These being the two principal pillars that upheld the nation the loss of them was and is to this day deeply deplored—immediately after the death of the latter the tribe scattered in smaller villages over the country in consequence of having no chief who could control and keep them together—their ancient warlike spirit seemed to be buried with their leaders and they are fast falling into degradation, without a head the body is of little use." (This was before the emergence of Washakie as principal Snake chief, though in 1840 Russell mentioned him as a man of note.) Stewart has another reference to Little Chief, doubtless picked up at the time of his final visit to the Rockies in 1843: "this last brave of the once great tribe . . . was . . . fated to die of chagrin at the decadence of his people, and of unavailing wounds in their defence" (p. 245).

In his 1871 letter to Robert Campbell (see the Introduction), Anderson refers to another Shoshoni notable, "the Coughing Snake." Concerning him, we have no information.

JAMES BRIDGER

Bridger is said to have been born at Richmond, Virginia, on March 17, 1804, and to have come west with his parents in 1812, settling opposite St. Louis on Six Mile Prairie, Illinois, a locality also known as the American Bottoms. His mother died in 1816, his father the next year. It is written that Bridger supported himself and his only sister for a time by running a flatboat ferry between St. Louis and Six Mile Prairie. He was then apprenticed to a St. Louis blacksmith, but tiring of this work, left for the Rockies in 1822 with the first Ashley-Henry expedition. He is thought to have been one of the party under Andrew Henry who descended the Missouri to reinforce Ashley after the Arikara Defeat of June 1823 and to have participated in the Arikara Campaign the following August.

His first-known adventure occurs when Henry's party was crossing present South Dakota, en route back to the Yellowstone after the Arikara Campaign. One of the company, Hugh Glass, was torn to pieces by a grizzly, and Henry had to leave him in the care of two men till he should die. John S. Fitzgerald was one of these, the youthful Bridger the other. They abandoned Glass as a dead man, but miraculously Glass survived to rejoin his comrades at the mouth of the Big Horn in the winter of 1823-1824. Fitzgerald had left the fort, and Bridger was forgiven.

In the summer of 1824 Bridger was one of the party under John H. Weber that crossed South Pass in the track of Jedediah Smith, eventually making a winter camp on Cub River in Cache Valley. From this camp, to settle a bet as to the course of Bear River, Bridger made the reconnaissance down the Bear that resulted in his discovery of Great Salt Lake. Bridger recalled the circumstance on a visit to Denver many years later; the *Weekly Rocky Mountain News*, May 15, 1861, reported from its interview with Bridger: "This well known pioneer came to this country forty years ago, (1822) with Henry's expedition, and afterwards with Sublette, and was of Weaver's party when they came on to Salt Lake in that winter, supposing it certainly to be the Gulf of California or the Pacific Ocean." The circumstances were described by Robert Campbell in a letter of April 4, 1857, after a discussion with Bridger and Samuel Tulloch: "A party of beaver trappers who had ascended the Missouri with Henry and Ashley, found themselves in pursuit of their occupation on Bear river, in *Cache* (or Willow) valley, where they wintered in the winter of 1824 and 1825; and in descending [discussing] the course which Bear river ran, a bet was made between two of the party, and James Bridger was selected to follow the course of the river and determine the bet. This took him to where the river passes through the mountains, and there he discovered the Great Salt lake. He went to its margin and tasted the water, and on his return reported his discovery." Historians have said that Bridger made this tour of discovery in a bullboat, but the reconnaissance must have been made on horseback, for Bridger told Capt. E. L. Berthoud in 1861 of having discovered the water to be salt "when he, with some other trappers, dismounted to get a drink" (Frederick S. Dellenbaugh, *Frémont and '49*, p. 135). Etienne Provost, coming independently from the direction of Taos, may have seen the lake some weeks or months earlier. This is the basis of the argument, recorded by Anderson in 1834, whether Provost or Weber should be considered the discoverer of Great Salt Lake.

Presumably Bridger was present at the initial rendezvous of July 1, 1825, on Henrys Fork of the Green, as he was at every succeeding rendezvous except that of 1833. He may have been one of the party that escorted Ashley to his place of embarkation on the Big Horn in July 1825. George Gibbs's copy of Jedediah Smith's lost map of the American West includes a notation at Bad Pass of the Big Horn: "Here the river runs for 40 miles through the mountain, the Gap but just wide enough for the river—with few exceptions on both sides precipices 1000 feet high. In 1826 J. T. Bridger passed through on a raft." As Bridger told Capt. W. F. Raynolds in September 1859 that he had "descended the lower cañon of the Big Horn some years since upon a raft," the fact seems established; the question is whether Smith had the date correct. If 1826, the time would necessarily have been in the spring, but no trapping is known to have been attempted in the Crow country that year. Perhaps the date should be August 1825. Also interesting in Smith's comment is the middle initial given Bridger. (In a popular biography published in 1961, *King of the Mountain Men*, Gene Caesar notes a prevailing story in the Bridger clan that his middle name was Felix, the name borne by his eldest son; an "F" might have been misread by Gibbs as a "T.")

Robert Campbell, who came to the mountains in 1826, places Bridger among the party under William L. Sublette and David E. Jackson which the next fall made the first known penetration of the Yellowstone Park area; and he may have accompanied Jackson on the latter's hunt in the Green River Valley in the spring of 1827. No definite information exists on the fall hunt of 1827, unless Bridger was one of those who ranged the lower Snake country. He would seem to have returned to Cache Valley for the winter and to have moved on down into the valley of the Great Salt Lake, where he is mentioned by Beckwourth. Perhaps he accompanied Fitzpatrick in the spring hunt on the Portneuf and the Bear, also described by Beckwourth. After the Bear Lake rendezvous of July 1828, he went with Robert Campbell to trap the Crow country, a hunt continued in the spring of 1829. Unless he was with the main party headed by Jedediah Smith, where he trapped in the fall of 1829 and the spring of 1830 is not known. But at the rendezvous on Wind River in July and August 1830 he joined with Fitzpatrick, Fraeb, Gervais, and Milton Sublette in founding the Rocky Mountain Fur Company.

Bridger's movements from the fall of 1830 to the spring of 1832 are mirrored in the sketches of Fitzpatrick and Milton Sublette. Warren Ferris encountered him and his party on Grays Creek about May 15, 1832, which fits in generally with Newell's account of that spring hunt. The sketches of Fitzpatrick and Fraeb again keep track of Bridger from the Pierres Hole rendezvous of 1832 up to the time he and Fraeb joined Fitzpatrick on Hams Fork in late October or early November 1833. He seems to have wintered with Fitzpatrick in 1833-1834, first in the Green River Valley, later on the Snake. In late March 1834 he headed a party to the three Parks of the Rockies, as described in the sketch of Stewart. Anderson reports his return from the south on June 25, 1834.

Anderson again notes Bridger's separation from Fitzpatrick and Fontenelle on August 6, en route to his fall hunt after the organization of Fontenelle, Fitzpatrick & Co. Kit Carson, one of Bridger's party, says they "set out for the country of the Blackfeet Indians, on the head waters of the Missouri. We made a very poor hunt as the Indians were very bad. Five of our men were killed. A trapper could hardly go a mile without being fired upon. As we found that we could do but little in their country, so we started for winter quarters." Newell, who had taken goods to the Flatheads after the rendezvous, says: "Bridger came to us on piers fork near horse prairie from thare to Snake River and wintered." Carson adds: "In November we got to Big Snake River, where we camped. We remained till February." On November 20 Osborne Russell heard at Fort Hall that Bridger's party was at the Forks of the Snake and proposed to winter there. In February 1835, as Carson relates, Blackfeet ran off a number of their horses. Soon after, they launched their spring hunt. "We trapped the waters of the Snake and the Green rivers, made a very good hunt. . . ." Russell met Bridger's company on an affluent of Salt River May 11 and heard "that the country around and below was much infested with Blackfeet. They had had several skirmishes with them in which they had lost a number of horses and traps and one young man had been wounded in the shoulder by a ball from a fusee."

Bridger was at the rendezvous on Green River when Samuel Parker and Marcus Whitman arrived with the annual caravan on Aug. 12, 1835. Next day, Parker writes, Dr. Whitman "extracted an iron arrow, three inches long, from the back of Capt. Bridger, which was received in a skirmish three years before, with the Blackfeet Indians [on the Gallatin in November 1832]. The doctor pursued the operation with great self-possession and perseverance; and his patient manifested equal firmness."

When the rendezvous broke up on August 22, Bridger left for the Tetons with some fifty men. Parker traveled with him through Jackson Hole and over to Pierres Hole, whence, about August 30, Bridger went northwest into the mountains to the Flathead hunting grounds. "The first chief of the Flatheads and his family, with a few others of his people, went with Captain Bridger, that they might continue within the range of buffalo through the coming winter." On September 8 Russell met fourteen whites "of Mr. Bridgers party who was encamped at Henry's Lake about 20 mls in a South direction and expected to arrive at the Madison the next day his party consisted of 60 white men and about 20 flathead Indians." Russell's group joined Bridger on the Madison and stayed with him until September 28, when they reached Camas Creek, "at the NW extremity of the great plain of Snake River." In February 1836, as a free man, he "joined Mr. Bridgers Company who were passing the winter on Blackfoot Creek [River] about 15 Mls. from the Fort [Hall] where we staid until the latter part of March." On March 28 Bridger commenced his spring hunt; he moved north to the Snake "and ascended it S E to the mouth of Muddy Creek where we arrived on the 7th of April." Russell left the main party here and rejoined it at the mouth of Thomas Fork on Bear River May 8, Drips's party also being on hand by then. Bridger's "whole company of Indians and whites" moved over to Hams Fork, and after separating from the Indians, "laid about on the branches of Green river until the 28th of June," when they arrived at the Horse Creek rendezvous.

When the rendezvous broke up about July 16, 1836, Russell says: "Mr. Bridgers party were destined as usual for the Blackfoot country." It consisted of sixty men, including most of the American trappers. Russell traveled with a separate party that met Bridger August 16 at "the inlet or southern extremity" of Yellowstone Lake. The combined party was in Gardner's Hole on August 27, and next day on the Yellowstone. On reaching the plain, the trappers scattered in small parties, while Bridger with twenty-five camp keepers moved slowly down the river. On September 1 the camp was at the mouth of Twenty Five Yard (Shields) River, and on the ninth had a fray with Blackfeet below the mouth of Clarks Fork, one trapper being killed. After trapping on Pryors Fork, Clarks Fork, and the Rosebud, on October 10 Bridger set up his winter camp on Clarks Fork, four miles above its mouth. At Christmas he moved down to the Yellowstone. In February his party had another fight with the Blackfeet, a Delaware named Manhead being slain, and at the end of the month Bridger moved over to the Big Horn. The party remained at the mouth of Bovys Fork until April 10, then began its spring hunt, reuniting on Rocky Fork at the beginning of May. The camp crossed the Big Horns to Stinking (Shoshone) River, went on south to Wind River, and by May 26 had reached the Oil Spring on the Popo Agie. After an eight-day halt, the trappers rode to South Pass and the Green, where they arrived June 10. "Here," says Russell, who has enabled us to follow Bridger in unusual detail, "we found the hunting parties all assembled waiting for the arrival of Supplies from the States." While they waited, they engaged in the battle with the Bannocks in which Meek's Snake squaw Umentucken was killed (see the sketch of Milton Sublette).

The rendezvous of 1837 is memorable with respect to Bridger because as a pleasantry, Stewart brought him a present—sometimes referred to as "a suit of armor," but described by Bernard DeVoto as cuirass and greaves; he is shown wearing it in two of Alfred Jacob Miller's sketches. David L. Brown, who had come up to join Bridger's brigade, later wrote a striking description of him: "Tall—six feet at least—muscular, without an ounce of superfluous flesh . . . he might have served as a model for a sculptor or painter, by which to express the perfection of graceful strength and easy activity. One remarkable feature . . . was his neck, which rivalled his head in size and thickness, and which gave to the upper portion of his otherwise well-formed person a somewhat *outré* and unpleasant appearance. His cheek bones were high, his nose hooked or aqueline, the expression of his eye mild and thoughtful, and that of his face grave almost to solemnity. To complete the picture, he was perfectly ignorant of all knowledge contained in books, not even knowing the letters of the alphabet; put perfect faith in dreams and omens, and was unutterably scandalized if even the most childish of the superstitions of the Indians were treated with anything like contempt or disrespect; for in all these things he was a firm and devout believer."

After the 1837 rendezvous, Lucien Fontenelle took the main brigade back to the Yellowstone, with Bridger as "pilot." Carson, one of the party, relates: "We had met with so much opposition from the Blackfeet that this time, as we were in force, we determined to trap wherever we pleased, even if we had to fight for the right. We trapped the Yellowstone, Otter, and Musselshell rivers and then went up the Big Horn and on to Powder River, where we wintered." Russell says they started out via the Hoback River and Jackson Hole and adds that the winter camp was set up by early December. Robert Newell, who reached the camp January 4, says: "We left Powder river on the 29th of March in search of bevver by the way of tongue river to the little horn met the crows onto the big horn to the yellow Stone. . . . We are at this time Lying at the mouth of 25 Yd River and our hunters out in Search of Beever May 15th 1838 Up 25 Yd River onto the Missourie the Galiton fork from thare to the Madison fork found the blackfoot trail about 5 or 6 hundred Lodges they Seperated and the largest part of them went over to the

Jefferson fork of Missourie the ballance went up the Madison that being our route we overtook them in a fiew days a battle ensued the first Scrimage we Killed 7 wounded 15 as we was informed afterwards the following morning in attempting to pass up the river they made a second charge but had to give way for us to pass we past in sight of thir village Keeping up constant fire untill we had past." Bridger went on to Henrys Lake, thence to the Snake, over to Jackson Hole, and after learning that the rendezvous had been changed to Wind River, "went on to the head of wind river from thare down to the fork of po po isha [Popo Agie] whare we found Mr Drips with our Supplies." Myra Eells and other Oregon missionaries record their arrival on July 5, 1838. "They had the scalp of a Blackfoot Indian, which they carried for a color, all rejoicing in the fate of the Blackfoots in consequence of the small-pox." (The Blackfeet by now had been badly hurt by the epidemic of 1837-1838.)

According to Sarah Smith, Bridger's party consisted "of about 100 men & perhaps 60 Indian females & a great number of guns & noisy shouts. Thought perhaps that we would be interested, therefore came & saluted us with firing, drumming, singing & dancing. Their appearance was rude & savage, were painted in a most hideous manner. One carried a scalp of the Black Foot in his hand. . . . Bridger's party have just been among the Black Foot tribe. This tribe have long been a terror to neighboring tribes & to the whites, but now their number is most reduced by the smallpox & it is still raging. The Indians made no attack on B's party but this party attacked them & shot 15 of them dead without excuse but to please their wicked passions. . . ."

Bridger had been in sole charge of the spring hunt, Fontenelle having left the party at its winter camp and come in to Fort William. At the rendezvous Drips, as agent for Pratte, Chouteau & Co., gave Bridger an order on the company, "due James Bridger on his arrival at St. Louis three thousand and three hundred and seventeen dollars and thirteen cents for services rendered the R. M. outfit for the two last years services." Bridger on this date, July 12, may have contemplated returning to the states. Instead, next day, he arranged to send the due bill down with the returning caravan, with a power of attorney that would enable William L. Sublette to collect the sum for him; in this document Bridger describes himself as "late of Illinois and now in the Rocky Mountains."

In 1838-1839 Bridger accompanied Drips as he had Fontenelle the previous year. The brigade went up Wind River, over Togwotee Pass to the Grosventre, and down to Jackson Hole, thence to Pierres Hole and to Falls River, the middle branch of Henrys Fork. Newell says that later in the autumn he joined Drips at Pierres Hole and "went from thare [to] the head of Green River commen[ced] winter quarters with 8 men and verry Cold Nov 20 1838." This sounds as though Newell had separated from the main party, but he goes on to say: "Capt. Drips left in Dec for wind river with his camp Capt Walker remained on Green river with a Small party whare we are now. . . . Jan 26 1839." It would seem that Drips and Bridger made their winter camp and spring hunt in the Crow country. Carson tells of joining Bridger in "the spring of 1838 [1839]," but only to get an outfit, apparently, for he and four others hunted in the Black Hills (Laramie Mountains) for three months, then "started to find the main camp, which was on a tributary of Green River."

The scant narratives of the 1839 rendezvous do not mention Bridger. After the rendezvous (no brigade was put in the field for 1839-1840), he set out for the states with the returning caravan, his first visit home in seventeen years. (During all this time, as he later commented, he had not once tasted bread.) Bridger's visit to St. Louis is reflected in the Chouteau account books, which record transactions with him in St. Louis between Sept. 17, 1839, and March 13, 1840. The small sum of $408 credited to him on the former date exemplifies what had happened to the fur trade. Most of the money was gone by November 19. Some recollections of Bridger in St. Louis at this time by H. J. Clayton are printed in the San Francisco *Alta California*, April 21, 1872: "Bridger was tall—fully six feet high—erect, thin, wiry, and sunburnt almost to the complexion of an Indian—a light olive—with a face noble and expressive of generosity, dark brown hair and liquid hazel eyes, bright almost to blackness. . . . In form he was straight as an arrow, wore moccasins, and, as an Indian, turned his toes as he walked slightly inward, so strikingly did his manners conform to those of the wild denizens of the forests. So also when walking in the streets of St. Louis with Mr. Dripps he followed him in single file— never at his side, never leading."

Clayton recalled further that, having visited his old home in "the American Bottom" and having within a few days "fully gratified his curiosity in St. Louis," Bridger became despondent, like a homesick boy, and [said] he wished to go back to his free life in the mountains. At St. Louis, he had an attack of chills and fever, which made him still more impatient to leave. . . ." Fortunately, Henry Fraeb was at loose ends after the dissolution of his partnership with Peter A. Sarpy. The two formed a new concern, "Fraeb & Bridger," began buying goods on March 13, 1840, and soon were off to the mountains. There was, after all, something of a final rendezvous in 1840, for Drips traveled up to Green River with the partners, as did Father De Smet, seizing the opportunity to make his first visit to the Flatheads. A few Protestant missionaries to Oregon, and Joel Walker, elder brother of Joe, rounded out the party. According to De Smet, they left Westport April 30, reached Fort Laramie June 4, and arrived on Green River June 30. Newell recorded the coming of "Mr Drips Feab & Bridger from St Louis with goods," but lamented, "times was certainly hard   no beaver and everything dull."

William L. Sublette, in a letter of September 1842, recalled that Fraeb and Bridger "left here 2 years since with about 30 men trading and traping on the watters of the Columbia River." There is no clear record of Bridger for most of the first year, but it seems likely he went to southern California with Fraeb and Joe Walker, reaching Los Angeles Feb. 10, 1841, as recorded in the sketches of his associates. It may have been at this time that Bridger first had a look at the Hopi villages, as reflected in a story in the San Francisco *Daily Herald*, Oct. 9, 1853, though the experiences referred to may have attended his California venture of 1844-1845. Narcissa Whitman, in a letter completed Nov. 19, 1841, speaks of having had Bridger's (six-year-old) daughter, Mary Ann, at Waiilatpu for three months, but it does not seem possible that Bridger himself can have taken his child to the Whitmans in August 1841, for he was then occupied in building the first Fort Bridger, on the west bank of the Green a few miles below the mouth of the Big Sandy. Fraeb, sent out to "make meat," was killed in a famous battle with the Indians.

Bridger is next referred to by Joseph Williams. On June 1, 1842, at Fort Boise, Williams "heard some dreadful oaths from Mr. [Richard] Grant, about some threats which he had heard from Mr. Bridger, one of the American Fur Company, against Fort Hall; and respecting some goods which had been stolen by Mr. Bridger's company from the Hudson Bay Company." Williams went on to Bridger's fort, arriving early in July. Bridger's company "had left for the United States about thirty days before, and we saw nothing there but three little, starved dogs. We saw the grave of an Indian woman, who had been killed by the Shiennes." Bridger had indeed started down to the states, accompanied by Fitzpatrick and probably by Walker. He reached Fort Laramie July 2, taking an unusual route through the Black Hills to avoid the Sioux and Cheyennes, then continued down the North Platte. On July 8, below Chimney Rock, he fell in with the detachment of Frémont's party with which Charles Preuss was traveling. "He informed us," says Preuss, "that the condition of the country had become exceedingly dangerous. The Sioux, who had been badly disposed, had broken out into open hostility, and in the preceding autumn his party had encountered them in a severe engagement, in which a number of lives had been lost on both sides. United with the Cheyenne and Gros Ventre [Arapaho] Indians, they were scouring the upper country in war parties of great force. . . . This gentleman offered his services to accompany us so far as the head of the Sweet Water; but the absence of our leader, which was deeply regretted by us all, rendered it impossible for us to enter upon such arrangement."

William L. Sublette, in his letter of September 1842, observed that "Bridger has come in with about 20 men and 30 packs of Beaver and also Lewis Vasques who remained behind to setle up the Business of Vasques & Sublette. . . . Brother A. W. Sublette is now on the farm and Vasquez and Bridger has left here lately [approximately August 20] with about 30 or 40 men fitted out by the American Fur Co. to trap on the watters of Missouri, Say near the 3 forks."

Thus Bridger entered on his partnership with Louis Vasquez. In a letter dictated at Fort Union on Dec. 10, 1843, he says that Vasquez was "strongly recommended by the Company in St. Louis, as a very capable man. . . . It was an understanding between him and me, that as he had been so strongly recommended as a capable man by the Gentleman of the Company in St. Louis, that I would give him all the goods and means of carrying on [trade with Indians], and start myself, with a few *green horns*, and try to trap as many Beaver as possible; the calculation is that if he succeeds, as I have no doubt he will, his return will pay the whole of our equipment, and whatever I have, or will make next spring, will be a clear profit for he and I."

Nothing is certainly known of the partners for almost a year after they re turned to the mountains, except that an express sent to Fort Laramie in the winter of 1843 spoke of an unsatisfactory hunt, traders supplied by the Hudson's Bay Company having strongly opposed them. Bridger was at his fort, reestablished on Blacks Fork west of the original location, when Cheyenne and Arapaho raiders ran off a horse herd toward the end of July 1843. He was still there as late as August 2, but in the absence of his partner was unable to join Sir William Drummond Stewart's excursion party in the upper Green River Valley. He must have left the fort soon after Vasquez arrived on August 13. When Theodore Talbot, traveling with Fitzpatrick's detachment of Frémont's Second Expedition, reached Fort Bridger on August 30, he noted that Bridger, "the most celebrated trapper of the Rocky mts. has started with a party of forty men to trap on Wind River."

This fall hunt brought Bridger to Fort Union; Larpenteur tells of a visit by him (misdated 1844), and indicates that he made some effort to trap on Milk River. In his previously quoted letter of Dec. 10, 1843, Bridger said: "I arrived here [Fort Union] some days ago from my beaver hunt having been particularly unsuccessful owing to the lateness of the season, and caught only about three packs, but I believe that a good hunt could be made in the same country, and will therefore try it next spring." He spoke of leaving Vasquez at the Platte, where he "gave him all the goods designed for the trade with the Indians, in the mountains," and hoped that with no opposition Vasquez would do well. With "fair prospects of a hunt next spring, and a perfect reliance on Mr. Vasquez for his success in the trade," Bridger sent in an order for the next year's outfit: "only things that are absolutely necessary for the carrying on of our business"; and explained, "I have established a small store with a Black Smith Shop, and a supply of iron in the road of the Emigrants, on Black's Fork, Green River, which promises fairly. They, in coming out are generally well supplied with money, but by the time they get there, are in want of all kinds of supplies. Horses, Provisions, Smith work, &c, brings ready cash from them; and should I receive the goods hereby ordered, will do a considerable business in that way with them! The same establishment trading with the Indians in the neighborhood, who have mostly a good number of Beaver among them." Bridger remarked that the conduct "of Mr. Vasquez at the Platte was not such as it should have been considering the recommendation he had in St. Louis, and I was sorry for it." He intended "to make a spring hunt and deliver up my returns, and after receiving the inclosed equipment, to make an expedition into the California, which country is now the only one remaining unexplored, and is rich with Beaver. I shall take from 30 to 40 men for that purpose to trap it thoroughly and make also a large return of Horses, Valuable Shells &c, which, together with the returns that Mr. Vasquez will make, ought to realize a good profit for all concerned. . . . Should it be necessary for us to have our license renewed, you will be so good as to have it done, and forwarded by the equipment, as also a passport to travel in the California and return therefrom, which you can forward at the same time."

William Laidlaw, who forwarded Bridger's letter to St. Louis, commented sourly: "Bridger has come in with a mountain party of thirty or forty men. He is not a man calculated to manage men, and in my opinion will never succeed in making profitable returns. Mr. Vasquez, his partner, is represented to be, if possible, more unable than he, as by drinking and frolicking at the Platte, he neglected his business."

Bridger went to California next year. James Clyman, arriving at Fort Bridger on Aug. 31, 1844, noted that "thirty men . . . started out under the command of Mr. Bridger yesterday on an excursion through the mountains of northern and Central Mexico." Bridger seems to have taken a northern route to California, past Fort Hall, and to have returned in the spring of 1845 by way of the lower Colorado. Some of the stories about him intimate that his travels had extended as far south as the Gila, and unless he trapped there in 1840-1841 he had no other opportunity to look at that country.

In any event, he came back to his fort by the route up through Utah, not reaching Fort Bridger until after the 1845 emigration had passed. According to a letter by A. R. Bouis to Pierre Chouteau, Jr., from Fort Pierre, Sept. 17, 1845: "Mr. James Bridger arrived at Fort John [Laramie] on the 2nd inst and delivered Mr. Jos Picotte 840 beaver skins and castoram 675 dressed deer skins 28 mules 24 horses 1400 California sea shells H. C. the whole amounting to about $5000 exclusive of the California shells, as I do not know what Mr. Picotte will allow for them. . . . Mr. Bridger was in California, and plenty of beaver there, but he wouldn't trap as the Indians stole the traps as soon as the hunters had set them. . . ."

Bridger had not yet left Fort John when the California-bound pack party led by Lansford W. Hastings arrived. Napoleon B. Smith, one of the nine men who accompanied Hastings, recalled later that there was considerable anxiety over the hostile mood of the Sioux and Cheyennes. Bridger "with 2 Frenchmen, trappers in his employ," had in consequence been detained for some days, and proposed to the Hastings party "that if they would accompany him, he would take them by a trail through the Wind River Mountains to Fort Bridger, by which the Country of the hostile Indians would be avoided." Via a rugged mountain route, he brought the party in twenty days to his fort. That would have been about mid-October. He then disappears until the spring of 1846.

James Clyman, returning from Oregon and California, reached Fort Bridger on June 7, 1846, to find the post deserted. He gathered that "Bridger and his whole company had taken the road N. W. Toward the Lower part of Bear River," at least a month before. Bridger and Vasquez had gone to Fort Laramie, where their presence is recorded by May 29. The partners were back at their fort when the Oregon and California emigration passed; James Frazier Reed mentions Bridger favorably in a letter written from Fort Bridger July 31.

Reed said that Bridger and Vasquez intended to visit the states in the fall of 1846, but Bridger remained in the mountains. On June 28, 1847, when the westbound Mormon pioneers met him at the Little Sandy, Bridger was en route to Fort Laramie. He paused overnight to confer with them about likely places for a settlement in the Great Basin. When he resumed his journey, Brigham Young gave him a note to Thomas Grover at the newly established Mormon ferry on the North Platte, asking that Bridger and his two men be crossed "on account of B. Y." Bridger presented this note at the ferry on July 3, at which time Appleton Harmon wrote in his diary that "he was agoing to Laramie & expected to return to his fort in time to Pilot the Pioneers through to Salt Lake he said that he could take us to a place that would Suit us." Bridger returned too late to be of further service to the Mormon pioneers, though he was back at his fort by July 31.

The settlement of the Saints in the Great Basin marks a period of change in the West, the effective conclusion of Bridger's personal fur trade era, and no further effort will be made to document his life in detail. He is known to have been at his fort in July 1848, and again in June 1849, when he and Vasquez had traders doing business with the forty-niners on the Sweetwater. On July 1, 1849, he was re-marked among these traders by Henry R. Mann, but next day he set out on his return to Fort Bridger, and was back at his post by July 11, when John F. Lewis talked with him. On July 31 William B. Lorton, en route to California, recorded a conversation with Bridger in the course of which the latter said that he "used to own Fort Larimie sold with every thing around for $7,000 to Am. fur comp"— an interesting allusion to the transaction by which Fontenelle, Fitzpatrick & Co. sold out to Chouteau at the 1836 rendezvous. In August Bridger hospitably received Capt. Howard Stansbury, who employed him to reconnoiter a possible emi-grant road to Cache Valley. They left Fort Bridger August 20 and reached Great Salt Lake City eight days later.

In the late summer of 1850 the homeward-bound Stansbury hired Bridger to guide him via Bitter Creek and Bridgers Pass; they left Fort Bridger September 10 and reached Fort Laramie October 12. Next year, in the late summer, Bridger accompanied a Shoshoni delegation to the great council with the Plains Indians east of Fort Laramie. In the summer of 1853, after a long period of friction, the Mormon authorities in Great Salt Lake City sent a posse to arrest the veteran mountain man, forcing him to abandon his fort. The Mormons purchased the property from Vasquez two years later. Afterward Bridger had a distinguished career as guide for Army detachments and emigrant trains until his withdrawal from the mountains in the winter of 1868-1869. The rest of his life, in gathering blindness, was spent on a farm south of Westport, where he died July 17, 1881. These latter years may be followed in J. Cecil Alter, *James Bridger, Trapper, Frontiersman, Scout and Guide* (Salt Lake City, 1925; expanded edition, Colum-bus, Ohio, 1951; recast and updated as *Jim Bridger*, Norman, Okla., 1962).

Bridger was known to the mountain men as Old Gabe. To the Crows he was Casapy, the Blanket Chief. His first wife, taken about 1834, seems to have been a Flathead. His first daughter, Mary Ann, then about six years old, was carried in the summer of 1841 to Waiilatpu. She was captured by the Cayuses at the time of the Whitman massacre; though released, she died at Oregon City soon after, as recorded in the *Oregon Spectator*, March 23, 1848. Two more children by Bridg-er's Flathead wife, prior to her death in 1846, were Felix Francis, born in December 1841, and Mary Josephine, born about 1846. Bridger's next wife is reported to have been a Ute. He had married her by July 31, 1847. She is said to have died July 4, 1849, in giving birth to a daughter, Virginia. An entry of May 10, 1854, by Father De Smet in the Register at St. Charles, Missouri, records the baptism of "John Bridger, about four years old, and Virginia Bridger, about six years old, children of Maj. James Bridger and of his Indian wife of the Shoshone or Snake nation in the Rocky Mountains." His last wife, who bore Bridger a daughter, Mary Elizabeth, in 1853 and a son, William, on Oct. 10, 1857, lived with him on his Missouri farm. Tales that Bridger once had a Mormon wife can hardly be true.

(WILLIAM F.?) BROWN

Identification of the Brown coupled with (William?) Gordon by Anderson is complicated by the floating date of the association. It is unlikely the man could have been Henry ("Boatswain") Brown, who died in the Mohave massacre of August 1827 as one of Jedediah Smith's party. A possibility is Joseph Browne, who had dealings with Smith, Jackson & Sublette prior to 1830. Less likely possibilities are David Brown, who went up the Missouri on the steamboat *Yellow Stone* in April 1831 and Thomas G. Brown, who left St. Louis for the Rockies in May 1831 in the party of Gantt and Blackwell. Perhaps the most reasonable hypothesis is that the man was William F. Brown.

In the Sublette papers of the Missouri Historical Society is a receipt signed by Thomas Fitzpatrick at St. Louis Dec. 17, 1834, which refers to "our note on Wᵐ F. Brown for $237.62½, and on William Thompson for $145, placed in William L. Sublette's hands for collection in 1830." This document would seem to place William F. Brown in the Rockies prior to the Wind River rendezvous of 1830. He is next listed in the American Fur Company's license of March 26, 1832.

From July 8, 1832, we have a terminal record of this man's life. The Fort Pierre Journal on that date records that "Messrs. Brown, Durand and 2 Americans (all beaver trap[p]ers) arrived." On July 30 "Mr. Brown left us with 26 Pork Eaters to cut fort Timber about 12 miles above this." On August 23 Brown arrived with two men who had deserted two days before: "He caught [them] in the middle of the Big Bend." On September 11 "Mr. Brown left us for the Navy Yard, otherwise called the lumber yard." On December 31 "Mr. Brown left us for the Island (Roy. Is.) with eight or ten men to clear a plot for a garden." And finally on Jan. 10, 1833, "Mr. Brown left us in the afternoon on his return to Bloomfield farm, which place, however, the unfortunate gentleman never reached alive. The ice was so weak that he broke through and was drowned not more than 20 paces from the shore of the Island. He had men with him but they were too far from him to render him any assistance."

JEAN PIERRE CABANNÉ

Cabanné, whose first name became anglicized as John, was born at Pau, Béarn, France, on Oct. 18, 1773. It is said he was educated and trained to mercantile pursuits and came to the United States with considerable capital. He engaged in the sugar trade at Charleston, South Carolina, but lost two vessels and went to New Orleans. According to one story, he became involved in a duel, which in 1798 made it expedient for him to move along to St. Louis. There, on April 8, 1799, he married Julia, daughter of Charles Gratiot, one of the leading citizens of the town. To them were born six sons and five daughters.

Like his father-in-law, Cabanné early engaged in the Indian trade. From 1798 to 1800, and perhaps for some years thereafter, he and Gregoire Sarpy were licensed traders among the Kansas Indians. In September 1816 he was given a license to trade with the "Ayouas, Sacs, Foxes & Sioux" on the Mississippi, and eleven months later "Cabanne & Com^y" was licensed to trade with "the Indians of upper Missouri." His partners in 1817 were Bartholomew Berthold, Bernard Pratte, Sr., Manuel Lisa, Pierre Chouteau, Jr., and Theodore Hunt. The firm was dissolved by mutual consent on June 1, 1819.

In May 1823 Cabanné entered into a new association with Berthold, Chouteau & Pratte, the firm name being B. Pratte & Co. until its transformation as the Western Department of the American Fur Company in 1827. In the fall of 1823 Cabanné took over at Council Bluffs the Oto post that had been founded for the company by Joseph Robidoux; thereafter it was commonly called Cabanné's Post, or "the Establishment near the Bluffs." Cabanné continued in charge, with occasional visits to St. Louis, until he and Peter A. Sarpy stirred up a political storm by seizing a liquor cargo being taken up the Missouri by a rival firm, Valois & Leclerc. This seizure, on Sept. 17, 1832, all but cost the American Fur Company its license. The Company had to repudiate Cabanné and Sarpy and withdraw them from the Indian country. In consequence, Cabanné was replaced at the Council Bluffs post by Joshua Pilcher in May 1833.

On Aug. 11, 1834, William Clark asked that Cabanné and Sarpy be allowed to return to the Indian country, and approval of this was given by the Secretary of War on September 8. Cabanné did not wait for approval from Washington, and Anderson found him at the Bluffs on September 11; he had probably just arrived on the steamboat *Diana*. Cabanné continued at the Oto post at least until the fall of 1835. Marcus Whitman met him there on arriving from the mountains, Oct. 10, 1835, and ten days later set out from Bellevue with him in "a fur boat," laden with Fontenelle's returns. They reached St. Louis November 4. In a letter of Dec. 17, 1835, Whitman indicated that it was Cabanné's intention to return upriver: "He kindly invited me to go up in the *Diana*, the Company's boat, and remain at his post until Mr. Fontanelle goes in the spring." If Cabanné returned to the Oto post, he did not reside there any length of time. He died at his home in St. Louis on June 27, 1841, and is remembered as a man who had done much to build the city from his interest in its churches and schools and its political and economic institutions.

ROBERT CAMPBELL

Of Scotch-Irish parentage, Robert Campbell was born at Aughalane, County Tyrone, Ireland, on Feb. 12, 1804. In August 1822 he came to Milton, North

Carolina, whither his brother Hugh had preceded him in 1818. Campbell moved on to St. Louis early in 1824 and entered into the employ of John O'Fallon and James Keyte. Afflicted with hemorrhages of the lungs, he was advised by Dr. Bernard G. Farrar to go to the Rocky Mountains. Accordingly he left St. Louis at the end of October 1825, in the company headed by Jedediah Smith. The enduring friendship of the two men dates from their shared experiences of the next nine months; they wintered together at the Pawnee villages on the Republican River. In the spring of 1826, after being joined by Ashley in the Platte Valley, Campbell went on to the rendezvous in Cache Valley. He accompanied Sublette and Jackson on their fall trapping tour to Yellowstone Lake and back, and in the spring of 1827 hunted with Jackson in the Green River Valley.

Following the 1827 rendezvous at Bear Lake, Campbell took a party to the Flathead country. In the course of this hunt, the Iroquois "Old Pierre" was killed by Blackfeet; so the other members of the company declined to return to the winter camp in Cache Valley. With an old French Canadian, Jacques Fournais, and one Flathead Indian, Campbell nevertheless made it back to Cache Valley. In the course of the winter, an exceptionally severe one, Campbell set out to rejoin his party, accompanied only by two half-breeds. They traveled on snowshoes with dogs and sleds. Peter Skene Ogden recorded Campbell's arrival from Bear River at the Snake on Feb. 17, 1828, and his departure northward six days later. Campbell found his men beyond Clarks Fork after forty-four days on snowshoes. The party trapped its way back to Bear Lake, but on arrival in June 1828 was attacked by Blackfeet, one man being killed. Campbell saved his party by breaking through the besiegers, accompanied by "a little Spaniard," to summon help from the rendezvous.

He had intended returning to St. Louis but was persuaded to make a hunt in the Crow country with Jim Bridger as pilot. The twelve-man party trapped during the fall on the Powder, the Tongue, and the Big Horn, then wintered with Long Hair's Crows on Wind River. In the spring of 1829 he hunted back over the same country and as far east as the Red Buttes, "in order," Campbell says, "to meet Sublette coming up. Not meeting him, I went to Sweet Water and over to Wind River . . . and waited there till he came up." After this rendezvous with Sublette in July, he set out for the states, reaching Lexington, Missouri, on August 20. The value of his returns, which may have included furs traded from free trappers, was $22,476. For his services Sublette gave him a draft on Ashley for $3,016, which probably covered his whole four years in the mountains. During those years he had recovered his health.

Campbell had various projects under consideration: a partnership Jedediah Smith had broached at the 1827 rendezvous and a more concrete offer Fontenelle and Drips made when he left the mountains. Instead, he revisited Ireland, sailing from New York in February 1830 and returning in June 1831 by way of Richmond, Virginia. Campbell got back to St. Louis late in July 1831. During the fall, on a visit to Lexington, he met Thomas Fitzpatrick, just arrived from the mountains, and William L. Sublette, coming in from Santa Fe. Sublette undertook to provide the outfit Fitzpatrick sought for the Rocky Mountain Fur Company, and Campbell assisted him. He also did clerical work for William H. Ashley.

When Sublette set out for the Rockies in May 1832, Campbell went along, having mounted an outfit of his own, consisting of "goods, blankets, clothes and only five men and fifteen horses. Ten of the horses were loaded with merchandise." Campbell fought shoulder to shoulder with Sublette in the battle of Pierres Hole after they reached the rendezvous; and when Sublette was wounded, Campbell carried him to safety. Afterward he sold his merchandise to William Fallon and James Vanderburgh and conducted the Sublette party back to the states, reaching Lexington on September 21.

On Dec. 20, 1832, Sublette and Campbell entered into articles of copartnership and agreement, to continue three years from Jan. 1, 1833. (The agreement was twice renewed and finally allowed to expire in 1842.) In the spring of 1833 Sublette voyaged up the Missouri, establishing trading posts as he went, so as to open a full-scale competition with the American Fur Company, while Campbell made for the Yellowstone via the mountains with a pack party of forty-five men. Supernumeraries included Capt. William Drummond Stewart on his first visit to the Rockies, Edmund Christy, Dr. Benjamin Harrison, and Fitzpatrick's Arapaho boy Friday. Campbell's operation was speculative, no advance order having been given by the R.M.F. Co.; but, as seen in the sketches of Fraeb and Fitzpatrick, he was able to sell his outfit on reaching the Laramie River. With Fitzpatrick, Campbell went on to the Green River rendezvous, arriving July 5. After a side trip to Pierres Hole to retrieve some cached furs, he set out for the Yellowstone July 24 with Fitzpatrick and Wyeth. He arrived on the Big Horn below Bad Pass August 12 and two days later embarked. In his diary Campbell writes retrospectively: "In the Big Horn the Skin Boat in which I was sunk and I had like to have perished— thrice I went under water and but for an allwise and all merciful God I whould never have seen the termination of this Year I got safe to shore and succeed in recovering all but about 4 packs of Beaver and our arms besides I lost my saddle bags &c I recovered again my boat and next day was joined by all the Crow Indians—and here again I must acknowledge my dependence on God who inclined these Indians to treat me kindly and return most of my beaver when they had us completely in their power and I may here observe that these same Indians 17 days after this [on September 5] at the instigation of the American fur Cᵒ robbed Mʳ Fitzpatrick of all he had with him but of themselves afterwards returned animals for nearly all they had taken I proceeded on down to this place [mouth of Yellowstone] where I arrived on the 30th of August and found Mʳ Sublette who had got here the day previous. . . ."

To Campbell fell the responsibility of constructing Sublette & Campbell's principal base, Fort William, situated near the mouth of the Yellowstone, several miles below the opposition post, Fort Union. Here Campbell conducted the trade until he received word about the last week of June 1834 that Sublette had effected a division of the fur country with the American Fur Company. Closing up the business, he set out down the Missouri, passed Fort Clark at the Mandan villages July 11, and reached St. Louis early in August.

Meanwhile, as recorded in Anderson's journal, Sublette had gone out to the mountains and founded a new Fort William on the Laramie. In consequence of developments after the 1834 rendezvous, the partners sold out to the new firm, Fontenelle, Fitzpatrick & Co. Campbell went out to Fort William to transfer the property, leaving St. Louis with two companions April 9, 1835. He returned July 15, bringing down his buffalo robes by water—a notable feat. He and Andrew Sublette with a small party packed out the beaver on horses via Council Bluffs. Afflicted with an "intermittent fever" after his return, Campbell had a long convalescence in Philadelphia.

Robert Campbell never returned to the mountains as a fur trader, though in 1851 he attended the great council with the Plains Indians at Horse Creek and in 1870 revisited Fort Laramie to treat with Red Cloud as a member of the Board of Indian Commissioners. He and Sublette became St. Louis merchants. Campbell prospered in mercantile ventures and in real estate speculations. By the time of his death, Oct. 16, 1879, he was one of the wealthiest men in Missouri. Campbell married Virginia Kyle on Feb. 25, 1841, and had thirteen children, most of whom died in childhood.

CHRISTOPHER (KIT) CARSON

Born in Madison County, Kentucky, Dec. 24, 1809, Carson early moved with his family to Howard County, Missouri. As a youth he was apprenticed to David Workman, to learn the saddler's trade, but after two years ran away, joining a caravan bound for Santa Fe. Workman took this action in good part, fulfilling legal requirements by advertising a reward of one cent for the boy's return. His notice in the Franklin *Missouri Intelligencer*, Oct. 12, 1826, described Carson as "a boy about 16 years old, small of his age but thick-set, light hair." According to Carson, he arrived at Santa Fe in November and spent several years in New Mexico as a teamster and cook before joining Ewing Young to trap the country west of the Rio Grande.

This party left Taos in August 1829, going north to the San Luis Valley, then southwest past Zuñi to Salt River and the Verde. Here Young sent half his men back to Taos and headed for California with the rest. They crossed the Colorado apparently at the Mohave villages and went on to Mission San Gabriel via the Mohave River. After trading for beef, Young and his men turned north and spent the spring of 1830 trapping California's Central Valley. Winning the favor of the local authorities by helping to return some runaway Indians to Mission San José, Young was able to trade his furs to the captain of a schooner, and with means thus acquired to buy more horses at the mission. Carson was one of the small party that accompanied Young to Mission San José in July 1830, and was also one of a detachment that pursued "upwards of one hundred miles into the Sierra Nevada Mountains" some Indians who ran off most of the horse herd. "We surprised the Indians while they were feasting off some of our animals they had killed," Carson says. "We charged their camp, killed eight Indians, took three children prisoners, and recovered all of our animals, with the exception of six that were eaten." Thus early, Carson was blooded.

About the beginning of September 1830, Young's party turned south again, going as they had come via the San Joaquin to Mission San Fernando, thence to Pueblo de Los Angeles. It had been Young's intention to trap the lower Colorado and return to the coast in December to sell his beaver and buy mules, but he got into difficulties with the Frenchmen in his company. As he says in a letter of Oct. 10, 1830: "If it was not for some young Americans that is Men of confidence I would not be able to get back to New Mexico therefore I must drop all Idea of the Mule speculation for this year I am going down Red River [the Colorado] to the Mouth of the Hela and from there up the Hela to New Mexico. . . ."

Carson was one of the young "Men of confidence," and his decisive measures with Indians of the Colorado during the course of the fall hunt got Young's trappers out of several tight scrapes. They ascended the Gila, then crossed over to the copper mines in what is now Grant County, N.M. "We could not bring our beaver in to the settlements to dispose of, on account of not having a license to trap in Mexican territory," Carson recalls. "So we left it with [Robert] McKnight, concealing it in one of the deep holes which had been dug by the miners. Young and I remained a few days at the mines, after the balance of the party had started for Taos. We then went to Santa Fe, where Young procured a license to trade with the Indians on the Gila. He sent a few men back to the mines to get the beaver he had concealed, and they returned with it to Santa Fe. Everyone considered we had made a fine trade in so short a period. They were not aware that we had been trapping for months. The beaver, some two thousand pounds in all, was disposed of to advantage at Santa Fe."

Such was Carson's initiation as trapper and mountain man. He says the party was back in Taos by April 1831. Ewing Young returned to California later that year, but Carson entered the service of Thomas Fitzpatrick after the latter reached Taos in July. "We traveled north till we struck the Platte River and then journeyed up the Sweetwater, a branch of the Platte," Carson relates, not mentioning that Fraeb took charge of the party after it reached the North Platte. "We trapped to the head of the Sweetwater, then on to Green River, and then to Jackson's Hole, on a fork of the Columbia River, and from there on to the head of Salmon River." Here he wintered with the parties of the Rocky Mountain Fur Company.

"In April, 1832, we commenced our hunt again. We trapped back on to Bear River . . . then on to the Green River, where we found a party of trappers in charge of Mr. [Alexander] Sinclair. They had left Taos shortly after we had, and had wintered on Little Bear [Yampa] River, a branch of Green." Learning that John Gantt had wintered near the Laramie and was in North Park, Carson and three others struck out in search of Gantt, coming up with him ten days later; Carson was now a free trapper. "We remained in the Park trapping for some time, and then moved through the plains of the Laramie and on to the south fork of the Platte, then to the Arkansas. On our arrival on the Arkansas Gaunt took the beaver we had caught to Taos. Meanwhile, the party remained on the Arkansas, trapping. The beaver was disposed of, the necessaries for our camp were purchased, and in the course of two months Gaunt rejoined us. We trapped on the waters of the Arkansas until the rivers began to freeze, and then went into winter quarters on the main stream." Winter quarters became the post known as Gantt's Fort or Fort Cass, on the north side of the Arkansas below the mouth of Fountain Creek.

In the spring of 1833 Gantt headed north to trap the Laramie River again. On the South Fork of the Platte two of the party deserted with three of the best animals. Carson and another man were sent in pursuit but failed to overtake the deserters, who had lifted a beaver cache and set out down the Arkansas by canoe; the men were never heard of again. Having recovered the animals, Carson and his companion holed up at the embryo Fort Cass till Gantt's partner, Jefferson Blackwell, arrived from the states with fresh suppplies a month or so later. Afterward they joined Gantt in South Park. Beaver were scarce, "so many trappers having been there before us" (that would have included Bridger and Fraeb, who had made a summer hunt in the area). Accordingly Carson and two others "concluded to leave the party and hunt on our own hook. We trapped nearly all the streams within the mountains, keeping away from the plains from fear of danger. We had very good luck, and having caught a great amount of beaver we started for Taos to dispose of it and have the pleasure of spending the money that had caused us so much danger and hardship to earn. We arrived at Taos in October, 1833, where we disposed of our beaver for a good sum."

In Taos was Capt. Richard Bland Lee on leave from the U.S. Army. Following Bonneville's example, Lee procured an outfit from Bent & St. Vrain and set out to make his fortune. With Lee, Carson left Abiquiu Nov. 19, 1833, and made a forty-three-day march to the confluence of the White and the Green. As Carson says: "We followed the Spanish Trail that leads to California till we struck White River, went down it till we struck Green River, and crossed from Green to the Winty [Uinta], one of its tributaries, where we found Mr. [Antoine] Robidoux. He had a party of some twenty men that were trapping and trading."

During the winter, in an exploit typical of many that must be passed over, Carson went in pursuit of a "California Indian" of Robidoux's party who had run off with six animals. Having killed the thief when he "showed fight," Carson succeeded in bringing back the horses. Carson then says: "Some trappers came to our camp and informed us that Fitzpatrick and Bridger were encamped on the Snake River. In March, 1834, we struck out for the purpose of finding their camp, and in fifteen days succeeded." Lee himself declares that they set out February 22 and reached Fitzpatrick's camp in twenty days. Lee sold his goods to Fitzpatrick and took his pay in beaver, Carson adds, after which Lee started for Taos—that is, in Bridger's party. Carson says he himself "joined Fitzpatrick [Bridger?] and remained with him one month. He had a great many men in his employ and I thought it best to take three of them and go on a hunt by ourselves. We passed the summer [i.e., the spring] trapping on the head of the Laramie and its tributaries, keeping to the mountains, our party being too weak to venture on the plains."

Carson "rejoined" Bridger's party, en route to the rendezvous, after the latter's summer hunt in the Parks. Anderson must first have laid eyes on Kit when Bridger's men reached Hams Fork on June 25. Carson had maintained himself as a free trapper during the spring, for on July 8 at "Blackfork of Green River" Lucien Fontenelle gave him an order on Pratte, Chouteau & Co. for seventy dollars, clearly the purchase price of part of his spring hunt (say, twenty skins). Concerning the rendezvous, the first he had attended, Carson says only: "I think there were two hundred trappers encamped, awaiting the arrival of supplies from St. Louis. We had to dispose of our beaver to procure the necessities of life. Coffee and sugar were two dollars a pint, powder the same, lead one dollar a bar, and common blankets from fifteen to twenty-five dollars apiece."

As seen in the sketch of Bridger, Carson joined the party led to the Blackfoot country in the fall of 1834, which after a poor hunt came back to winter on the Snake. A transaction with Carson is recorded in the Fort Hall Account Books, Feb. 2, 1835. Later in the month, Blackfeet stole eighteen of the R. M. F. Co. horses. Carson and eleven others pursued some fifty miles and parleyed with the Indians, but obtained only five animals. In a fight Carson was shot through the shoulder. A few days later, he says, "we set out on our spring hunt. We trapped the waters of the Snake and the Green rivers, made a very good hunt, and then went into summer quarters on Green River. Shortly after we reached the rendezvous our equipment arrived. We disposed of our beaver to the traders that came up with it, remaining in summer quarters till September, 1835."

At the 1835 rendezvous Carson had his celebrated duel with "a large Frenchman in the party of Captain Drips, an overbearing kind of man, and very strong." They both fired at the same time, "and all present said that but one report was heard. I shot him through the arm and his ball passed my head, cutting my hair and the powder burning my eye, the muzzle of his gun being near my head when he fired. During the remainder of our stay in camp we had no more bother with this French bully." That Carson's antagonist, one Shunar (Joseph Shuno?), was not killed seems certain; David L. Brown, who came to the mountains in 1837, tells of the encounter and says that the man survived.

Concerning the fall hunt of 1835, Carson (in Bridger's party) relates: "We trapped the Yellowstone and Big Horn rivers, and then crossed over to the Three Forks of the Missouri, went up the North Fork, and wintered on Big Snake River and its tributaries." (Carson gives a more detailed account of this hunt in a mistaken context of 1839.) On the Snake, he says, they encountered Thomas McKay, one of the Hudson's Bay Company traders. "With Antoine Godey and four men, I joined McCoy, having heard that beaver were abundant on Mary's River [the Humboldt]. We trapped down the river until it lost itself in the Great Basin, but found few beaver. We then went back up the river some sixty miles and struck across to the waters of Big Snake River, where we separated, McCoy going to Fort Walla Walla and the rest of us to Fort Hall. On our march we found no game. The country was barren, and for many days we had nothing to eat but roots, and blood which we drew from our horses and cooked. On the fourth day before we got to the fort we met a party of Indians, and I traded with them for a fat horse. We killed it, feasted for a couple of days, and then concluded our journey to the fort in safety." At Fort Hall the clerk recorded, on June 26, 1836, the sale of $185.17½ in merchandise to Carson, which dates his return from the trapping tour to the Humboldt. The hard times experienced he mentioned to Frémont in 1843.

After a month at the fort Carson went on to the Green River rendezvous with Thomas McKay. In the fall he joined Bridger's brigade, bound for the Blackfoot country. His autobiography scrambles the chronology so as to give no very clear picture of the hunt, but the itinerary is recoverable from Osborne Russell's journal. Carson wintered with Bridger's party on the Yellowstone, and engaged in a fight with the Blackfeet in February 1837 (described by Carson, but with details of a similar fight in September 1836 mixed in).

Transactions with Carson at Fort Hall are recorded on April 10, May 27, June 6, and July 5, 1837; so he was speaking of this spring when he says that he and five others went to Fort Hall, joined a party attached to "the Northwest Fur Company," and "trapped to the head of Salmon River, then to the Malade, and down this stream to Big Snake River and up Big Snake. We then trapped Goose Creek and Raft River, and returning to Fort Hall, disposed of the beaver we had caught."

For the fall hunt of 1837 Carson joined the combined party led by Fontenelle and Bridger, of which Russell, Newell, and Meek were also members. "We trapped the Yellowstone, Otter, and Musselshell rivers and then went up the Big Horn and on to Powder River, where we wintered. During our hunt we had no fights with the Blackfeet, and we could not surmise the reason. Near our encampment was a Crow Indian village. The inmates were friendly and remained near us throughout the winter. They told us the reason we had not been harassed by the Blackfeet during our hunt was that the smallpox had broken out among them and they had gone north of the Missouri to escape it, so that none remained on our hunting ground." After an extremely cold winter, the spring hunt began in April 1838, as set forth in the sketch of Bridger. On reaching Horse Creek, they learned that the place of rendezvous had been changed to Wind River, and accordingly made their way to the appointed site.

"In twenty days," Carson recalls, "the rendezvous broke up, and I and seven men went to Brown's Hole, a trading post, where I joined [Philip] Thompson and [Prewitt] Sinclair's party on a trading expedition to the Navajo Indians. We procured thirty mules from them and returned to Brown's Hole. After our arrival Thompson took the mules to the South Fork of the Platte, where he disposed of them to Sublette and Vasques and returned with goods suitable for trading with the Indians. I was now employed as a hunter for the fort and I continued in this service during the winter, having to keep twenty men supplied with meat." Thus Carson describes the genesis of Fort Davy Crockett in Browns Hole.

Next spring (1839), Carson "joined Bridger. Besides myself, the party included Dick Owens and three Canadians. We five men started for the Black Hills [Laramie Mountains] to hunt. After we had trapped the streams in the vicinity of the hills we separated, Owens and myself taking one course, and the Canadians another. We made a good hunt for three months and then started to find the main camp, which was on a tributary of Green River."

After the rendezvous, on Aug. 23, 1839, Robert Newell met Carson and Owens on "Muddy of Blacks Fork" and went on to Browns Hole with them, arriving September 1. E. Willard Smith encountered Carson there October 2, and was given details of a fight with the Sioux on the Little Snake River a few days earlier, a fight mentioned by Carson to Frémont in June 1844, and more fully described to James F. Meline many years later.

In his autobiography Carson passes over these matters, saying only (in a mistaken context of 1840-1841): "in the fall, six of us went to Grand River and there made our hunt, passing the winter at Brown's Hole on Green River. In the following spring [1840] we went back to the Utah country and into the New Park, where we made our spring hunt. We then returned to Robidou's fort and disposed of our beaver and remained there till September. . . ." Carson mixes events of the spring of 1839 with those of 1840 when he elsewhere says: "In the spring of 1840 [when Bridger was not in the mountains], Bridger and his party started for the rendezvous on Green River, while Jack Robinson and myself went to Robidoux's fort in the Utah country, and there disposed of the furs we had caught on our march." Carson continues: "Beaver was getting very scarce, and finding that it was necessary to try our hand at something else, Bill Williams [but this seems to be a mistake; Williams had headed for southern California on a horse-stealing enterprise with the break-up of Fort Davy Crockett in the summer of 1840], Bill New, Mitchell, Frederick, a Frenchman, and myself concluded to start for Bent's Fort on the Arkansas. . . . I was kindly received at the fort by Messrs. Bent and St. Vrain, and was offered employment to hunt for the fort at one dollar per day. I accepted this offer and remained in their employ until 1842."

Hard dates are lacking for Carson from Oct. 2, 1839, to Jan. 28, 1842, when he was baptized at Taos, but clearly he entered the service of Bent & St. Vrain in 1840; F. X. Matthieu later recalled his being at Bent's Fort that fall. Carson continued with Bent & St. Vrain until the spring of 1842, when he made his first visit home since 1826. His object was to place with relatives in Missouri a five- or six-year-old daughter, Adaline, borne him by an Arapaho girl, said to have died before he went to Bent's Fort. He might have acquired this wife about 1835-1836, though she is not mentioned in the contemporary narratives. It has been related, though denied on Carson's authority, that while at Bent's Fort in 1840-1842 he married a Cheyenne woman, Making Out Road, who bore him a short-lived son and divorced him by throwing his belongings out of her lodge.

So ended Carson's years in the fur trade. On his 1842 visit to the states, he encountered the young Charles Frémont and made such an impression as to be hired as Frémont's guide. He went to South Pass and back to Fort Laramie with Frémont in the summer of 1842, then south to what was becoming his home, Taos. There on Feb. 6, 1843, he married young Josefa Jaramillo. In the spring he set out for the states as hunter for a Bent & St. Vrain train, but at Walnut Creek fell in with Philip St. George Cooke and a detachment of Dragoons sent to protect some Mexican traders from Texas freebooters. These traders offered Carson three hundred dollars to carry a letter to Governor Armijo in Santa Fe, so that troops might be sent to escort them on the last stage of the journey. He carried the letter via Bent's Fort to Taos, whence the alcalde sent it on to the governor. After carrying more dispatches back to Bent's, Carson learned that Frémont had returned to the mountains and that his services were wanted. Accordingly he journeyed with Frémont to Oregon and California, returning to Bent's Fort in July 1844.

On leaving Frémont, Carson went to Taos, remaining till the following March, when he and Dick Owens, concluding "that we had rambled enough . . . decided to settle down on some good stream and make a farm." They selected a site on the Little Cimarron, about fifty-eight miles east of Taos, but later in the year, learning that Frémont was on the Arkansas at the head of a Third Expedition, sold out their improvements for about half their worth and joined up again. Thus Carson accompanied Frémont to California, participated in the conquest, and in September 1846 was sent east via the southern route with official dispatches intended for Washington. On the Rio Grande he encountered Stephen W. Kearny, who ordered him to hand over his dispatches to Fitzpatrick and turn about as guide for his own command. Reluctantly complying, Carson had a part in the battle of San Pasqual, and afterward, with Lt. Edward Beale of the Navy, carried word to San Diego of Kearny's dire straits. On Feb. 25, 1847, Carson and Beale were started off to Washington with dispatches, traveling the Gila route and reaching the capital in June. Carson had two interviews with President Polk, who tendered him a commission in the Regiment of Mounted Riflemen (not confirmed by the Senate). He was sent back to California with more dispatches. This time he traveled via the Spanish Trail. Arriving in October, he was assigned to guard duty at Tejon Pass to discourage Indian horse stealing. In May 1848 he was ordered east, once more as a dispatch-bearer. Lieutenant George Brewerton traveled with him over the Spanish Trail and afterward published a celebrated account of their experiences. Carson got back to New Mexico from Washington in October 1848.

He remained in the Southwest most of the rest of his life. The first few years were spent guiding troops on forays against the Indians, beginning (with Lucien Maxwell) a settlement at the Rayado, some fifty miles east of Taos, trading with the emigrants at Fort Laramie in 1850, and in general living an active frontiersman's life. He visited St. Louis in 1851 and in the spring of 1852 made a last trapping tour. "We went to the Balla Salado [South Park], and down the South Fork to the plains; through the plains of Laramie River to the New Park, trapped it to the Old Park, trapped it again, then again to the Balla Salado, then on to the Arkansas where it comes out of the mountain; we then followed it on under the mountain, thence home to the Rayado, through the Raton Mountains, having made a very good hunt."

In the spring of 1853 Carson drove a flock of 6,500 sheep to California, going by way of Fort Laramie and the emigrant road. "We arrived about the first of

August, having met with no serious loss." The speculation was successful. He got back to Taos by a southern route in December 1853.

During his absence Carson had been named Agent to the Ute Indians of New Mexico. Establishing his headquarters at Taos, he occupied himself with Indian duties and occasional military missions, until the outbreak of the Civil War. Carson resigned his agency in June 1861 to become lieutenant colonel of the New Mexico Volunteer Infantry, Ceran St. Vrain being the nominal colonel. Carson had now learned to sign his name but was not a lettered man. He soon became colonel of the regiment, and as such fought in the battle of Valverde, Feb. 21, 1862, against invading Texans. Though the battle was lost, Carson gained in reputation. When five regiments of volunteer infantry were consolidated in May as the First Regiment of New Mexico Volunteers, Carson was made colonel. Afterward he became the trusted right hand of Gen. James H. Carleton, carrying out famous campaigns against the Mescalero Apaches, the Navahos, and the Kiowas. For his services and conduct at Valverde he was breveted a brigadier general of volunteers, to date from March 13, 1865. Other details of his military career are brought out in E. L. Sabin's *Kit Carson Days*, the best of the Carson biographies. He was formally mustered out of service at Santa Fe Nov. 22, 1867. Suffering from a heart ailment, he spent much of his last year at Fort Lyon, on the Arkansas. He died there May 23, 1868, just a month after the death of his wife from puerperal fever. Seven children survived, in addition to the child of his Arapaho wife. Carson was small in stature, but tough and wiry, and unceasingly active. With Bridger and Fitzpatrick, he is regarded as the mountain man par excellence, and owing to his association with Frémont, is the most famous of them all.

MICHEL SYLVESTRE CERRÉ

Son of Pascal Léon Cerré and Louise Thérèse Lami, Michel Cerré was born in St. Louis May 6, 1802; the birth date usually given (April 17, 1803) is that of his baptism. His name is often found in contemporary documents as Lami Cerré. Washington Irving made him five years too young in saying as of the spring of 1832 that Cerré had "been in expeditions to Santa Fe, in which he endured much hardship. He was of the middle size, light complexioned, and though but about twenty-five years of age, was considered an experienced trader."

Documents in the Ritch Collection at the Huntington Library place Cerré at Santa Fe in the spring of 1825, when he declared goods valued at 362 pesos to the customs office. He set out for home apparently in July. Two years later, on July 23, 1827, William Clark gave Cerré and thirty-one others, including Paul Baillio, Louis Robidoux, and Manuel Alvarez, permission "to pass through the Indian country to the Province of Mexico." This passport was presented in Santa Fe November 12, when Cerré was identified as a "*commerciante*." From a letter written by Ceran St. Vrain, it would seem that Cerré left Santa Fe toward the end of September 1828.

These New Mexican ventures must have been fairly successful, for by the summer of 1829 Cerré had enough capital to join his elder brother Gabriel Pascal Cerré, his brother-in-law Pierre Didier Papin, and five others in organizing P. D. Papin & Co., popularly known as "the French Company." The eight partners each put up two thousand dollars and set up a vigorous opposition to the American Fur Company, trading from the Ponca to Bad River, near which they built their principal post. The A. F. Company's Fort Tecumseh journal mentions the presence of "L. Cerré" in the neighborhood between Jan. 20 and Oct. 13, 1830, the opposition post being called sometimes Papin's, sometimes Cerré's House. Negotiations began for buying out the rival company, and on October 14 the journal records: "Bought out P. D. Papin & Co., engaged Papin, Cerre and Picotte. The other two [partners then on hand] are to return to St. Louis." Gabriel Cerré stayed on in the service of the American Fur Company; Michel returned to St. Louis.

Cerré next turns up, with Joseph Reddeford Walker, as one of Bonneville's principal lieutenants when the Captain embarked on the Rocky Mountain fur trade, leaving Fort Osage, Missouri, on May 1, 1832. Various mentions of Cerré occur after Bonneville reached the mountains; on September 26 he was detached to accompany the Nez Percés on a hunting expedition and to trade for a winter supply of meat; he returned to the Salmon River some weeks later. In March 1833 Bonneville sent Cerré with a few men to purchase horses from the Indians, preliminary to leaving the Salmon. And in July, at Green River, he entrusted to Cerré the job of convoying to the states the furs thus far collected. Bonneville accompanied Cerré to the point of embarkation on the Big Horn, made three bullboats, and about the middle of August 1833 gave his peltries "in charge of Mr. Cerré, with a party of thirty-six men." (On November 17 Wyeth commented that he had seen thirty packs "brot home by Cerry" to Alfred Seton of New York.)

Cerré carried east Bonneville's report to the War Department, dated at Wind River, July 29, 1833, which anticipated a meeting with Cerré the following June. Wyeth originally thought he might travel to the Rockies with Cerré in the spring of 1834, but came ahead of him. Anderson mentions that Cerré and Etienne Provost (the latter in charge of the American Fur Company's "Rocky Mountain Expedition") were encamped together at Sapling Grove on May 6, and Townsend records Cerré's presence at the rendezvous by June 22, but no details of the journey are known. Bonneville did not come over to the Green River Valley this year, and Cerré, who seems to have had about forty men, rode on west to join the Captain on Bear River.

In a letter written at Washington on Sept. 30, 1835, Bonneville recalled that he "fell in with Mr Cerre 28 June 1834, the gentleman to whom I had eleven months before entrusted my communication to the General in Chief, which he informed me, he had delivered, and that the General appeared perfectly satisfied with my Report and also with my determination to persevere in the course I had adopted and persued, that owing to his remaining longer in New York, than he had originally contemplated, he was prevented returning to Washington and consequently had left the former city without bringing an extension of my furlough or any communication whatever from the Dept. of War." Bonneville then decided to remain in the mountains and carry out his enterprise at all hazards. "Previous to putting this intention into practice I had prevailed upon Mr Cerre to take charge of my letters and reports to the General in Chief General Eustes and other Gentlemen, which although he had now became attached to the American Fur Company, and felt some delicacy in doing, he did promise to forward them to their various addresses, upon his reaching Council Bluffs."

Nothing more is known about an understanding between Cerré and the American Fur Company in 1834. On July 4 Wyeth tells of meeting "Mr. Cerry and Mr. Walker who were returning to St. Louis with the furs collected by Mr. Bonnevilles company about 10 pack and men going down to whom there is due 10,000$" —this on the Muddy, an eastern affluent of Bear River. Zenas Leonard adds to the confusion in saying that Cerré took "a few men" back to St. Louis with 4,000 pounds (about 40 packs!) of beaver and instructions to meet Bonneville at the Great Salt Lake the following summer. On July 7, 1834, Fontenelle on Blacks Fork wrote an order on Pratte, Chouteau & Co. to pay Cerré $235.50. Three days later Cerré set out for the states with William L. Sublette and Edmund Christy, reaching Missouri in late August. He was in St. Louis by September 6.

Unless the references are to his brother, Cerré accompanied Fontenelle to Fort William in the spring of 1835 and afterward went up to the rendezvous with Fitzpatrick in the service of Pratte, Chouteau & Co. From December 1835, when he wrote to help Bonneville in his fight for reinstatement, until his death in 1860, Cerré's life is identified with St. Louis. In 1848 he was the only Whig representative elected from that city to the Missouri legislature. In May 1849 he was elected clerk of the St. Louis Circuit Court, serving through 1853. In August 1858 he was elected (as a Democrat) sheriff of St. Louis County, an office in which he was still serving when he died of pneumonia on Jan. 5, 1860. Cerré's obituary in the *Missouri Weekly Republican*, Jan. 10, 1860, comments: "He was one of the early fur traders here, and among the first of those who visited New Mexico from this quarter for purposes of trade." Helen Lebeau, whom he married in 1839, bore him four children. A portrait of Cerré is reproduced in W. F. Wagner's edition of Zenas Leonard's *Narrative*.

JEAN BAPTISTE CHARBONNEAU

The history of this eldest child of Toussaint Charbonneau, like that of his mother Sacagaweah, has been obscured by an elaborate canon developed by the late Grace Raymond Hebard, who worked out life histories for mother and son that would bring them to their deaths in the 1880's on the Wind River Reservation in Wyoming. Both histories seem to be erroneous.

The death of the Snake squaw whom we know as Sacagaweah was recorded by John C. Luttig at Manuel's Fort on the upper Missouri Dec. 20, 1812: "This evening the wife of Charbonneau, a Snake squaw, died of a putrid fever. She was the best woman in the fort, aged about twenty five years." Although Miss Hebard, and writers who followed her, rejected this record as applying to some other Snake squaw, William Clark, who of all persons should have known the facts, listed

Sacagaweah as dead in a memorandum written about 1825 concerning the personnel of the Lewis and Clark Expedition (*Letters of the Lewis and Clark Expedition,* pp. 638-640).

The Hebard canon appears to have made two persons, Toussaint, Jr., and Jean Baptiste, of the child born to Sacagaweah at the Mandan villages on Feb. 11, 1805. (The scant documentary references to a "Toussaint" seem to apply the father's name to Jean Baptiste; a later allusion to one "Tessou" at Bent's Fort probably refers to one of the numerous Tesson clan.) With his parents the Charbonneau infant made the journey to the Pacific and back. Pompeys Pillar in the Yellowstone Valley is understood to have been named by Clark out of affection for the child ("Pomp"—meaning head or leader—being a name often applied to the firstborn son in a Snake family). After parting from Charbonneau near the Mandan villages in August 1806, Clark offered to take Baptiste and "educate him and treat him as my own child." About 1810 Charbonneau came to St. Louis, bringing his Snake wife; and when the two set out up the Missouri in the spring of 1811, as recorded by H. M. Brackenridge (who explicitly says that the woman with Charbonneau had "accompanied Lewis and Clark to the Pacific"), the six-year-old boy was left behind to begin his schooling. In the fall of 1813, after Sacagaweah's death, John C. Luttig was named temporary guardian—later replaced by Clark—of "the infant children of Tousant Charbonneau deceased, to wit: Tousant [i.e., Jean Baptiste] Charbonneau, a boy about the age of ten [eight] years; and Lizette Charbonneau, a girl about one year old." It turned out that the elder Charbonneau was not dead, but Baptiste remained at school in St. Louis, as recalled later by one of his schoolmates, William Clark Kennerly; expenditures by William Clark in his behalf in 1820 are on record.

In 1821 or 1822 Baptiste may have entered into the service of the Missouri Fur Company, though the only evidence is a letter by Thomas Hempstead that tells of reaching St. Louis from the Kansas post on Jan. 19, 1823, in company with four others, including "little Baptiste." Baptiste Charbonneau was at the Kansas establishment by July 1823, for Prince Paul, Duke of Württemberg, encountered him in the course of a voyage up the Missouri. Impressed with the youth, he paused at the Kansas post to take him aboard when he came back down the river in October. Baptiste went to Germany and received an extensive education before returning to America with Prince Paul late in 1829.

It would appear that Baptiste first traveled to the mountains in the spring of 1830, in the party led by Drips and Fontenelle. He was one of the detachment with Michel Robidoux which in November 1830 undertook to trap various tributaries of the Snake. Ferris mentions "Charbineau" as having been lost for a time north of the Snake; after eleven days he made his way to the encampment of Drips and Fontenelle in Cache Valley.

In the summer of 1832, perhaps on July 13, Robert Campbell listed "Sharbona" among a group of mountain men who were to trap "by the skin." We next hear of Baptiste Charbonneau in the summer of 1833 as one of the party led by Bridger and Fraeb, which was trapping in the Laramie Mountains area and did not go to the Green River rendezvous. On July 31 Nathaniel Wyeth, en route to the Big Horn in company with Fitzpatrick and others, recorded at Beaver Creek, a few miles above its junction with the Popo Agie, an encounter with "a party of 4 whites who have lost their horses . . . one of them wounded in the head with a Ball and in the body with an arrow very badly. . . . The case was this. Mr. Bridger sent 4 men to this river to look for us viz Mr. [Jefferson?] Smith, [Philip?] Thomson, Charbonneau a half breed and [Robert] Evans. Two days before it happend 15 Inds came to them (Snakes) and after smoking departed the second day after they were gone Thompson [while out hunting was attacked and wounded]. . . . the Inds got 7 horses all there were. Charboneau pursued them on foot but wet his gun in crossing a little stream and only snapped twice."

Charbonneau went on to the Yellowstone in a bullboat with Robert Campbell or in the land party led by Louis Vasquez, in any case reaching the mouth of the river by September 3. On September 26, when Campbell started a small party under Vasquez to trade with the Crows, he observed in his diary, "I started Charboneau along to go on express to Fitzpatrick." On December 22 Campbell learned from Kenneth Mackenzie that "the crows who came to Tullocks fort had said Charbono had arrived at their village but said nothing of Vasques. . . ." Presumably Charbonneau continued south to find Fitzpatrick and remained with him until Anderson encountered him the next summer. Anderson records a striking appreciation of Charbonneau in Fitzpatrick's camp on June 24, and mentions him again on August 5, just too early for us to determine whether Charbonneau stayed in the mountains another year or went down to the states.

When Charbonneau reappears in the record, he has become associated with the fur trade of the Southwest. E. Willard Smith, who on Aug. 6, 1839, left Independence for the Arkansas with Louis Vasquez and Andrew Sublette, says that in the company were a "Mr. [Philip] Thompson who had a trading post on the Western side of the Mountains [Fort Davy Crockett in Browns Hole], and two Half Breeds employed as hunters. One of them was a son of Capt. Clarke the great Western traveller and companion of Lewis [an interesting echo of Anderson's Diary entry of June 24, 1834.]—he had received an education, in Europe, during seven years." On April 26, 1840, Smith tells of starting down the South Platte from Fort Vasquez in a mackinaw boat with seven men, including "the hunter, Mr. Shabenare." The boat reached St. Louis July 3, 1840.

On July 9, 1842, Frémont's First Expedition came upon "Chabonard's camp," on an island in the South Platte (a few miles above the mouth of Bijou Creek). "Mr. Chabonard was in the service of Bent and St. Vrain's company, and had left their fort some forty or fifty miles above, in the spring, with boats laden with the furs of the last year's trade . . . and, finding it impossible to proceed [owing to low water], had taken up his summer's residence on this island, which he had named St. Helena. . . ." With Charbonneau were James Beckwourth and his wife, "a young Spanish woman from Taos."

On August 30 Rufus Sage reached this same encampment, "under the direction of a half-breed, named Chabonard, who proved to be a gentleman of superior information. He had acquired a classic education and could converse quite fluently in German, Spanish, French, and English, as well as several Indian languages. His mind, also, was well stored with choice reading, and enriched by extensive travel and observation. Having visited most of the important places, both in England, France, and Germany, he knew how to turn his experience to good advantage. There was a quaint humor and shrewdness in his conversation, so garbed with intelligence and perspicuity, that he at once insinuated himself into the good graces of listeners, and commanded their admiration and respect."

Charbonneau was delivered from his exile on St. Helena in time to join Sir William Drummond Stewart's excursion party to the Rockies in the spring of 1843. Kennerly recalls that Charbonneau drove one of the two-wheeled charettes, drawn by two mules driven tandem, and tells of his refereeing a fight between Leonidas Walker and a Joseph Smith. However, Charbonneau must have been one of the thirteen who turned back on June 14 after reaching the South Fork of the Platte, for he was in St. Louis two months later. A note in the Sublette Papers, signed by Francis Pensoneau at St. Louis, Aug. 14, 1843, attests this fact and also shows that Toussaint Charbonneau came to the end of his long life sometime between 1839 (when he was reported still alive) and 1843: "I promise to pay to J. B. Charbonno the Sum of Three hundred and twenty dollars, as soon as I dispose of land Claimed by him said Chabonno from the estate of his Deceased Father." An endorsement dated Aug. 17, 1843, is signed J. B. Charbonneau: "To be paid W. A. [sic] Sublette."

Solomon Sublette, writing his brother William from Fort Lancaster (Lupton) on the South Platte, June 6, 1844, mentions being in company with "M S Vrain Ward & Shavano who are on the same business as my-self," which indicates that Charbonneau was then attempting to capture live bighorn sheep and antelope for sale in the states. Next winter he was a hunter for Bent's Fort. As recalled many years later by W. M. Boggs: "he wore his hair long—that hung down to his shoulders. It was said that Charbenau was the best man on foot on the plains or in the Rocky Mountains." On Aug. 9, 1845, Lt. James W. Abert alludes to him at Bent's: "Mr. Chabonard called for me to accompany him on a visit to 'Nah-co-men-si,' or the winged bear, more generally known as 'Old Bark,' " a ranking Cheyenne chief then at the fort. Alexander Barclay at the Hardscrabble fort on the upper Arkansas on March 18, 1846, mentions the arrival of Charbonneau from Bent's Fort. Later that year Charbonneau was pressed into service as a guide when Kearny marched to the conquest of New Mexico and California. W. H. Emory refers to him on the Rio Grande above Valverde, Oct. 6, 1846, the day Kit Carson arrived from California. Carson was turned about to guide Kearny to the Pacific, so that Charbonneau and others were left behind. When Philip St. George Cooke with the Mormon Battalion reached Albuquerque, he referred to Charbonneau as "one of the guides left for me," and his journal of the march to San Diego includes many allusions to Charbonneau, an "active and useful" man.

According to Miss Hebard, Charbonneau fell into obscurity, came to the Snake country about 1853, and until his death in 1885 dwelt passively among the Shoshoni, known only as Baptiste, having no interest in tribal affairs, and rarely speaking in council. However, clear record exists of an entirely different later life. Nine months after he reached California, in November 1847, Charbonneau was appointed alcalde for San Luis Rey in the San Diego district. He held this position until July 1848, when he resigned because "a halfbreed Indian of the U. S. is regarded by the people as favoring the Indians more than he should do, and hence there is much complaint against him." Soon after, Charbonneau made his way north to the gold fields. His old associate Beckwourth stayed with him at Murderers Bar on the Middle Fork of the American River from late spring of 1849 to the onset of the rainy season in November. The circumstance is recalled not only by Beckwourth but by Thompson and West's *History of Placer County* (Oakland, 1882), p. 71, and by the *Historical Souvenir of El Dorado County* (Oakland, 1883), p. 184. The original California census returns for 1860 (Placer County, Secret Ravine Postoffice, p. 63) have a listing for John B. Charbonneau, age 57, Male, a Miner, birthplace Missouri. (Secret Ravine was about five miles from Auburn.) The *Placer County Directory* (1861), p. 79, lists "Charbonneau, John B. clerk, Orleans Hotel, Auburn." The circumstances of his death are related in the Auburn *Placer Herald*, July 7, 1866:

"We are informed by Mr. Dana Perkins, that he has received a letter announcing the death of J. B. Charbonneau, who left this county some weeks ago, with two companions, for Montana Territory. The letter is from one of the party, who says Mr. C., was taken sick with mountain fever, on the Owyhee, and died after a short illness.

"Mr. Charbonneau was known to most of the pioneer citizens of this region of country, being himself one of the first adventurers (into the territory now known as Placer county) upon the discovery of gold; where he has remained with little intermission until his recent departure for the new gold field, Montana, which, strangely enough, was the land of his birth [a mistake; he was born in present North Dakota], whither he was returning in the evening of life, to spend the few remaining days that he felt was in store for him.

"Mr. Charbonneau was born in the western wilds, and grew up a hunter, trapper, and pioneer, among that class of men of which Bridger, Beckwourth, and other noted trampers of the woods were the representatives. He was born in the country of the Crow [Hidatsa] Indians, and his mother a half breed of the Crow [Shoshoni] tribe. He had, however, better opportunities than most of the rough spirits, who followed the calling of trapper, as when a young man he went to Europe and spent several years, where he learned to speak, as well as write several languages. At the breaking out of the Mexican war he was on the frontiers, and upon the organization of the Mormon battalion he was engaged as a guide and came with them to California.

"Subsequently upon the discovery of gold, he, in company with Jim Beckworth, came upon the North Fork of the American river, and for a time it is said were mining partners.

"Our acquaintance with Charbonneau dates back to '52, when we found him a resident of this county, where he has continued to reside almost continuously since—having given up frontier life. The reported discoveries of gold in Montana, and the rapid peopleing of the Territory, excited the imagination of the old trapper, and he determined to return to the scenes of his youth.—Though strong of purpose, the weight of years was too much for the hardships of the trip undertaken, and he now sleeps along by the bright waters of the Owyhee.

"Our information is very meager of the history of the deceased—a fact we much regret, as he was of a class that for years lived among stirring and eventful scenes.

"The old man, on departing for Montana gave us a call, and said he was going to leave California, probably for good, as he was about returning to familiar scenes. We felt then as if we met him for the last time.

"Mr. Charbonneau was of pleasant manners, intelligent, well read in the topics of the day, and was generally esteemed in the community in which he lived, as a good meaning and inoffensive man."

Another notice appeared in the Ruby City, Idaho, *Owyhee Avalanche*, June 2, 1866:

"DIED.—We have received a note (don't know who from) dated May 16, '66, requesting the publication of the following:

"'At Inskip's Ranche, Cow Creek, in Jordan Valley [eastern Oregon, 70 miles west of Ruby City, Idaho], I. B. CHARBONNEAU, aged sixty-three years—of pneumonia. Was born at St. Louis, Mo.; one of the oldest trappers and pioneers; he piloted the Mormon Brigade through from Lower Mexico in '46; came to [northern] California in '49; and has resided since that time mostly in Placer County; was en route to Montana."

It appears that Charbonneau took a wife among the Cheyennes before going to California, but all that is known of this comes from an entry of Dec. 28, 1847, in Alexander Barclay's diary. At Pueblo Barclay encountered a mountain man who had "met Rufine and Charbonneaus child Louise at the Whirlwinds camp going down to Bents fort alone and afoot."

EDMUND TAYLOR CHRISTY

Born in St. Louis in 1810, Edmund Christy was the eldest son of Maj. William Christy (1764-1837), a prominent early resident of St. Louis. One sister, Matilda, married Dr. David Walker, by whom she had a son Leonidas, q.v.; another sister, Eliza, was the second wife of William H. Ashley, q.v.; and others were married to various Missouri notables. Young Christy was associated with William L. Sublette as early as November 1831 in renting a slave belonging to the estate of Jedediah Smith. Christy accompanied Robert Campbell to the mountains in 1833. At the rendezvous on July 20 he entered into a one-year copartnership agreement with the Rocky Mountain Fur Company, by which that firm furnished an outfit of $6,607.82½ "besides Twelve Men hired whose wages are to be paid Jointly," to be repaid in beaver at $3.25 per pound. All returns over that amount were to be equally divided, and any losses were to be equally sustained. Christy was to devote his personal services in conducting the business, and a member of the R. M. F. Co. was to accompany him. The illiterate Jean Baptiste Gervais was the partner assigned to this venture; for details, see the sketch of Gervais. Dr. John McLoughlin, in a Fort Vancouver letter of Sept. 30, 1835, mentions that the previous year "Mr. Christie of the American Rocky Mountain Company came here to purchase Goods," and other details are reported in the *Missouri Republican*, Aug. 26, 1834 (see note for July 10). Anderson records Christy's arrival at the rendezvous on June 18. He continued east with William L. Sublette on July 10. Like most mountain enterprises of 1833-1834, the trapping venture toward the Columbia was a failure. From documents in the Sublette Papers, it appears that on July 9, 1834, Christy gave Fitzpatrick, Sublette & Bridger a note for $2,355, due four months after date, no doubt representing his share of the losses. This note was not finally settled until Nov. 2, 1836. After his return to St. Louis Christy seems to have entered into a business with Henry Fraeb that turned out badly (see the sketch of Fraeb). Christy died unmarried in St. Louis on Nov. 21, 1839, aged twenty-nine.

MARSTON GREENE CLARK

A first cousin of George Rogers Clark and William Clark and also of the first wife of Anderson's father, Marston G. Clark was born at Lunenburg, Virginia, Dec. 12, 1771. He had a long and distinguished career in the Army and in Indiana public life, where he was Territorial Governor. (For details, see Warder W. Stevens, *Centennial History of Washington County, Indiana*, pp. 232-238; Daniel McDonald, *History of Freemasonry in Indiana, 1806-1898*, pp. 335-336; and W. H. English, *Conquest of the Country Northwest of the River Ohio*, pp. 34, 50, 830-832, 978.) When the Kansas subagency became vacant through the death of A. F. (Baronet) Vasquez, Clark was named to the office, having been recommended by the Indiana delegation in Congress.

As one justification for his appointment, the Indianans stated: "He has been in good circumstances but owing to his suretiship for an officer of the United States has a few years since been reduced to a state of almost poverty. His property all having been sold by the marshal of the U.S. We hope that it may be in your power to confer on him this office for which he is well qualified and which at present w[d] be very important to him." The appointment was made on Feb. 19, 1829, and Clark journeyed to his post the following May. Many interesting reports exhibit Clark's impartiality to fur traders and missionaries alike. He was made a full agent July 12, 1832. On July 3, 1834, the Commissioner of Indian Affairs wrote Clark that in consequence of an Act of Congress reorganizing the Bureau, his agency had been abolished; but five days later Clark was notified of a new appointment as subagent for the Shawnees, Ottawas, and other emigrating tribes. He was given another such appointment March 4, 1835, but he had written from Salem on February 27 proffering his resignation, which was accepted, effective at the end of March. On July 25, 1846, Clark died on his farm near Salem.

Perhaps the most graphic reference to Clark at the Kansas Agency is that by

John Treat Irving in *Indian Sketches* (first published in 1835, new edition edited by John Francis McDermott, Norman, Okla., 1955, p. 239). Irving pictured Clark as "a tall, thin, soldier-like man, arrayed in an Indian hunting shirt, and an old fox-skin cap." He elaborated on this description in a novel, *The Hunters of the Prairie*, published in 1837: "He was a tall thin man, of that hardened appearance which rather denotes extreme toughness, than great muscular strength. His hair was snowy white. His forehead was high and narrow, and his nose aquiline. His light blue eyes, half extinguished by two heavy lids, betokened calm reflection. His mouth was large, firmly set, and surmounted by two or three deeply-furrowed wrinkles. There was something in his look that betokened a man of resolution, bordering on obstinacy." A silhouette portrait of Clark is reproduced in William H. English, *Conquest of the Country Northwest of the River Ohio, 1778-1783*, II, 866.

CONMARROWAP (Ute Chief)

This Indian is first mentioned in a letter written by the Mexican secretary of state to the American minister on April 12, 1828, reflecting events at the Bear Lake rendezvous in 1827. According to reports received from New Mexico, "the Yuta Timpanago Indian, called Quimanuapa" had been appointed "captain general [of his tribe] by the North Americans" (25th Cong., 2nd Sess., *House Executive Document 351*, Serial 332, pp. 228-230). Warren Ferris, as of 1834-1835, speaks of him as "a celebrated Chief . . . a Eutaw by birth [who] forsook his own people and joined the Py-Euts, after he became a man, and by his prowess and bravery, acquired such an ascendency over the tribe of his adoption, as to become their principal chief. He has rendered himself an object of terror to them, by an atrocious custom of taking their lives, for the most trivial offences. He is the subject of conversation every where among the Eutaws, by whom he is universally detested; all agreeing, that he deserves death, but none can be found daring enough to attempt its accomplishment. He is the only Indian in the country, who ever dared to chastise a white man. . . ."

By "Py-Euts," Ferris refers not to the Paiute Indians of modern ethnology but to a division of the Utes, the Wiminuche, known as "Pautes" on the New Mexican frontier. They roamed much of the country crossed by the Spanish Trail in New Mexico, Colorado, and southeastern Utah. Conmarrowap may have been dead before 1841, by which time the Ute chief Wakara or Walker had risen to prominence. However, in the summer of 1855, when the Mormons sent a colonizing mission to what they termed the Elk Mountain Utes (the Wiminuches living in the vicinity of the La Sal Mountains), they baptized under the name Nephi a head man they called Conmarrowap. Was this the Conmarrowap known earlier to the trappers? (A photograph purportedly of "Conmarrowap" reproduced in *Utah Historical Quarterly*, IX, opp. p. 96, is not authentic, the name being applied by the whim of Herbert S. Auerbach to a photograph of an unidentified Ute.)

With regard to the events of 1834 involving Conmarrowap, Anderson and Ferris are the only real sources of information. Ferris says: "The Snakes declared war against the Eutaws last fall [1833], for killing several of their tribe, who were caught in the act of stealing their horses." In consequence Conmarrowap lost all his horses to the Snakes in the summer of 1834, his wife being carried off at the same time. Anderson picks up the story with his entries for July 19 and August 1. Ferris attributes the ransom of the Ute women to Joseph Reddeford Walker, but very likely he was mistaken, for Joe Meek preserved some memory of William O. Fallon in this connection (see the sketch of Fallon). Ferris, who rode south from the Hams Fork rendezvous in an American Fur Company party, tells of being overtaken on August 24 by Conmarrowap's squaw and child, with "a young, unmarried girl, of the same nation. . . . They had followed our camp twenty days, living upon roots and berries, and had avoided the trails and most frequented places, for fear of again falling into the hands of their enemies." On Nov. 23, 1834, after Ferris and his companions set up a winter camp on the Green near the mouth of the White River, Conmarrowap came into camp with his wife and ten horses. As Ferris tells the story: "Conmarrowap's wife and her companion, after leaving us last Summer, fell in with the relations of the latter, who unhesitatingly killed and devoured the horse, we had given to the former. Leaving the inhospitable relations of her companion, she proceded on, and reached her husband some days after. He had been sick during several weeks, and for some time was considered past recovery; but survived, and as soon as sufficient strength returned, set out to visit those who had robbed his wife. An altercation ensued, which resulted in the death of the man who was at the head of the family that had injured him, though not until he had received a slight wound from an arrow himself. He lost all his horses last summer, when his wife was taken prisoner, yet he now had ten of the finest we have ever seen among the Indians. He says they were presented to him, by the passing traders from Toas [Taos] to California; but it is much more probable that he took them by force, as he has already done to our knowledge in many instances. All the hunting parties from Toas look upon him as a terrible fellow, and submit to his insults, which they dare not resent; although I have seen one or two individuals, who have sworn to take his life, the first opportunity that occurs, when they may not endanger themselves. . . . There is nothing uncommon in the appearance of this Indian, save a stern and determined look; he is now slender, of a middle stature, and has a dark, keen and restless eye; but before his sickness, was quite corpulent, a rare circumstance among Indians. There is less in his dress and manners, to distinguish him from his fellows, on ordinary occasions. He appears to be about forty years of age."

HENRY DODGE

Henry Dodge was born in 1782 at Vincennes, Indiana. His family settled in Spanish Louisiana in the Ste. Genevieve District, where Dodge grew up, succeeded his father as sheriff, and became marshal of Missouri Territory and a major general of militia. He commanded a force of mounted volunteers in the Winnebago War of 1827 and had a conspicuous part in the Black Hawk War of 1832, which led President Jackson to appoint him major of a battalion of mounted rangers. When this body was replaced in 1833 by the First Regiment of U.S. Dragoons, Dodge was commissioned its colonel. He led the regiment to the Red River in 1834 and to the Rocky Mountains in 1835. According to Marcus Whitman, who talked with him at Fort Leavenworth on Oct. 26, 1835, he intended to go to the Pacific the following summer if the government would permit. Instead, in 1836 he was named first governor of Wisconsin Territory, comprising Wisconsin, Minnesota, Iowa, and parts of Dakota; he continued as governor of a diminished Wisconsin after Iowa was set off in 1838. Though replaced by a Whig in 1841, he was elected to Congress as delegate and was again made governor of Wisconsin Territory when the Democrats returned to power in 1845. Dodge became one of Wisconsin's first U. S. Senators. He retired in 1857 and died ten years later. See Louis Pelzer, *Henry Dodge*, and the sketch in *Dictionary of American Biography*.

ANDREW DRIPS

Drips was born in Westmoreland County, Pennsylvania, perhaps near Laughlinstown. The date has been given sometimes as 1790, sometimes as 1789; if the latter is correct, he was born late in the year, for on Nov. 29, 1852, he gave his age as sixty-two. His ancestors are said originally to have been Highland Scots by the name of Seldon, who migrated to northern Ireland rather than give up their religion and who at some place of refuge adopted the name Drips, suggested by water trickling from a spring. During the War of 1812 Drips volunteered for service at Cincinnati on Aug. 11, 1812, and was honorably discharged at Fort Barber on Feb. 17, 1813, after serving as private and first sergeant in the First Regiment, Ohio Militia. He again served from July 5 to Aug. 18, 1814.

After the war Drips came to St. Louis, where on Oct. 2, 1817, he was appointed ensign in the First Regiment, Missouri Militia. In St. Louis he became associated with Joseph Perkins & Co. On Aug. 11, 1819, this firm announced in the St. Louis *Enquirer* that business had been closed and that Drips would settle its affairs. Subsequently, on December 4, Drips as Acting Partner published a notice in behalf of Perkins & Drips and Joseph Perkins & Co. stating that business compelled him to be absent, and creditors must settle with Charles Wahrendorff. Perkins became a partner in the Missouri Fur Company when it was reorganized in September 1820, but Frederic Billon may have been mistaken in listing Drips as also a partner. He perhaps entered the company's service as a clerk. Drips was met descending the Missouri in the spring of 1822 with William H. Vanderburgh; so he was associated with the company by that year.

Until 1830 Drips traded in the Council Bluffs area, first at Fort Lisa, later at Bellevue. During this time he took as wife an Oto woman named Mary, who bore his son Charles A. on March 27, 1824, and his daughter Mary Jane on Nov. 15, 1827. James Kennerly's diary occasionally mentions him at Bellevue from May 1824 to April 1827; and a letter written by Fontenelle in 1829 tells of his having traded at the Pawnee villages from Feb. 14 to May 9, 1825. After the downfall of the Missouri Fur Company in 1824, Drips was among the partners who carried on, licensed to trade with the Indians on July 4, 1825, and on Aug. 15, 1826. He may have gone to the mountains with Joshua Pilcher in September 1827, but more probably he was left in charge of the Bellevue establishment. After Fontenelle returned from the mountains in the summer of 1828, he and Drips carried on at Bellevue; in February 1829 Fontenelle speaks of Drips as having done some trading among the Pawnees that winter. Next summer Drips was again among the Pawnees, but he was back at Bellevue by August 9.

In December 1829 Drips was sent to the Niobrara on business involving J. P. Cabanné of the American Fur Company. The second week of January 1830 he went down the Missouri to St. Louis to confirm with the A. F. Company partners the agreement that Fontenelle had reached with Cabanné, by which he and Drips should take an expedition to the Rockies.

Accompanied by Michel Robidoux, Drips set out by land from St. Louis in February, reached Bellevue March 31, and launched out into the West May 1. This party, led by Fontenelle, included Warren Ferris, who wrote a celebrated narrative of their experiences. On July 16, having reached Bear River, Drips started off to find the free men in Cache Valley. Returning unsuccessful, he moved with his partners to Hams Fork, where on August 23 the party divided. The detachment under Drips hunted northwesterly on the sources of Green River, then went to Cache Valley to winter. After an exceptionally severe winter, the partners opened their spring hunt at the forks of the Snake. Afterward, on June 19, 1831, Fontenelle and Drips set out for St. Louis from present Medicine Lodge Creek, going via Cache Valley.

Drips was to have brought an outfit back to the mountains that autumn. According to Ferris, he set out from Council Bluffs about October 1, but "want of grass, and the jaded state of his horses" compelled him to winter "at the foot of the Black Hills." He reached Bear River in late April 1832 and was at Pierres Hole by mid-June. On this journey Drips was accompanied by his wife Mary; and their third child, Catherine, was born at Pierres Hole July 12. At the battle of Pierres Hole six days later, Drips was shot through his hat, losing a lock of hair.

Fontenelle not having arrived with the supply caravan, on August 2 Drips and Vanderburgh set out to meet him; they encountered him near Horse Creek August 8 and entered into a new arrangement by which the separate ventures of Vanderburgh and Fontenelle, Drips & Co. were combined. Drips and Vanderburgh were made joint heads of the fall expedition into the Blackfoot country, with Drips doing the bookkeeping. The hunters ranged through Jackson and Pierres holes and on to Henrys Fork, the Big Hole, Deer Lodge, and other northern areas. They came up with Fitzpatrick's R. M. F. Co. party September 10 on the Missouri above the mouth of Dearborn River. Six days later Drips separated from Vanderburgh to make for the Three Forks of the Missouri in company with Fitzpatrick's party. On arriving at the Three Forks, Drips started up the Jefferson. He had not yet rejoined Vanderburgh when the latter was killed by Blackfeet on the Madison October 14. Six days later Drips was in the Big Hole. Ferris says that on the twenty-fourth "Mr. Dripps and company set out for Snake river, where he intended to pass the winter." In December 1832 Ferris found him at the Forks of the Snake, a favorite wintering ground thereafter.

Now in sole charge, Drips launched his spring hunt April 19, 1833, going to Grays Creek, Grays Hole, Salt River, the Snake, Pierres Hole, Jackson Hole, and finally the Horse Creek rendezvous, where he arrived June 7. In a letter written on July 31, Fontenelle spoke of Drips's disadvantage at the rendezvous, the opposition having large supplies of liquor: "however Mr Drips after some difficulty has made more than either [Bonneville or Campbell] and to his praise I can say that with about thirty four trappers who were with him he has made this spring what goes down now [except for what was got from William Fallon and James Vanderburgh] .... Drips has become very popular with the people in this country since last year and I had hard work to detain him with me." Fontenelle added that he had to give Drips fifteen hundred dollars a year to get him to remain in the mountains.

Where Drips made his next hunt is not stated, but Ferris says he reached his wintering ground on the Snake, "having been quite fortunate during the fall, and caught many beaver, losing neither men nor horses. He had seen no Indians, with the exception of a party of Snakes." Drips began his spring hunt sometime after March 20. On May 29, 1834, Ferris found him encamped on a lake described as "the source of the Western branch of the New Fork" of Green River in the Wind River Mountains. Soon after, Drips began moving south toward a rendezvous with Fontenelle. Anderson mentions their joint camp at the confluence of Blacks and Hams forks on June 29.

Anderson supplies the date, Aug. 3, 1834, when Fontenelle, Drips & Co. was merged in the new concern Fontenelle, Fitzpatrick & Co. On August 6, as Anderson further records, Bridger started off on his fall hunt. It would appear that Drips led a party in a different direction, possibly the one Ferris accompanied, which spent the fall and winter in northeastern Utah and northwestern Colorado. Drips is not again mentioned until the summer rendezvous on Green River, where Kit Carson had his celebrated duel with "a large Frenchman in the party of Captain Drips." Drips's wife Mary had remained with him, for on Aug. 12, 1834, she bore her fourth child, William F., the last before her death on June 1, 1846.

There is even less information on the movements of Drips in 1835-1836 than the previous year. Matthew Field's 1843 notes concerning Mark Head and John Robertson picture both as having got far south in 1836, and this may be a clue to the locale of Drips's hunt. (Robertson is represented as having trapped as far as the Mohave country, but that may have been in 1836-1837, when by his own statement he was at the head of a party trapping "the Mexican provinces.") On May 8, 1836, Osborne Russell found Bridger's camp at Thomas Fork of Bear River and with it "Mr A Dripps and his party consisting of about 60 whites and nearly as many half breeds." The combined camp moved over to Hams Fork "excepting Mr Dripps and a small party who went round to Blacks fork of Green river to get some furs and other articles deposited there in the ground"—another indication of a southerly hunt the previous fall. The trappers waited on the branches of Green River until June 28, 1836, when they gathered at Horse Creek. Rumors had become prevalent that Drips had taken to drink, but Joshua Pilcher had a good report of him in October after meeting him at the rendezvous.

That summer Pilcher acquired for Pratte, Chouteau & Co. the interests of Fontenelle, Fitzpatrick & Co. Drips remained in the Rockies under an arrangement with the new "Rocky Mountain Outfit." Nothing is known of his fall hunt, but the Fort Hall Account Books record transactions with him on March 11, April 29, and May 4, 1837, which would indicate that his spring hunt was on Snake waters. After the 1837 rendezvous on Horse Creek, Fontenelle took the place of Drips with the principal brigade, and Drips carried down the returns, making his first visit home in six years.

He returned to the mountains in 1838 in charge of the caravan. The year's missionary contingent traveled with him to the rendezvous, held this time on the Popo Agie. Drips by now, it appears, Indian-fashion had taken two wives, one or both of whom had remained at Fort Laramie the previous winter. The missionary Sarah Smith on June 1, 1838, "Received a call from some Indian females, wives of Capt. Dripps & Fontenelle, also a son of Fontenelle, a fine lad of 12 years." On June 9, a week after resuming the journey to the mountains, Mrs. Smith remarked: "Several female Indians are journeying with us. The two wives of Captain Dripps. They are trimmed off in high style, I assure you. The oldest wife rides a beautiful white horse, her saddle ornamented with beads and many little gingles a beautiful white sheepskin covering for the horse, cut in fringes ½ a yd deep, ornamented with collars like little bells, making a fine gingle as she rides along. Then comes the rider with her scarlet blanket, painted face & hankerchief on her head, sitting astride. This is the fashion of the country. The second wife acts as an attendant." (For a possible reference to views of Drips on Indian marriage, see the sketch of Fontenelle.)

After the usual business connected with the annual rendezvous, it was again Drips's turn for a mountain year, with Bridger as guide. Stewart did not think well of his prospects, saying, "his people are daily deserting him." Russell mentions the subsequent presence of the company in Jackson Hole, and Newell tells of joining it in Pierres Hole. Since later, at a camp near the head of Green River, Newell wrote, "Capt. Drips left in Dec. for wind river with his camp," we assume that Drips made his spring hunt in the Crow country, coming back to Green River to meet Joseph Reddeford Walker at the rendezvous of July 1839.

Drips took the returns down to the states, accompanied by Bridger, and in the spring of 1840 came back in charge of the caravan sent to the final rendezvous. Father De Smet said they left Westport April 30 and reached Green River June 30.

After leaving the mountains in 1840, Drips settled with his family at the village called Kansas, near the mouth of the Kaw. He seems to have been associated in 1841 with the Chouteaus' Osage outfit. He was living at Kansas next year when Frémont set out on his First Expedition.

Frémont expected to hire Drips as guide, but en route up the Missouri fell in with Kit Carson and employed him instead. Drips accepted a commission as Special Indian Agent for the Upper Missouri in August 1842. His labors as Indian Agent, and his travels up the Missouri and into the interior, which in the winters of 1844-1845 and 1845-1846 took him as far west as the posts on the Laramie, will not be described here. In 1846 he was removed from office on the representations of opposition traders that he favored the Chouteau interests; the termination was effective June 2. On July 21 P. Chouteau Jr. & Co. offered him a new job as trader on the Missouri. After that tour of duty he came down from Fort Pierre to the mouth of the Kansas by land, setting out on February 27 and arriving March 19, 1847, but he soon went back to Fort Pierre to take charge in the absence of Honoré Picotte. He came down to St. Louis early in 1848, but by April was at Kansas preparing to return. That summer Chouteau reorganized the fur business on the upper Missouri, reserving six shares for himself and giving one each to six traders, including Drips. In the fall of 1848 the veteran was sent to take charge of Fort Laramie. In mid-March 1849 he set out for Kansas, arriving by April 18.

That summer Fort Laramie, which had been formally known since 1841 as Fort John, was sold to the U.S. Army. Subsequently Chouteau directed the establishment of a new post at Scotts Bluffs, also known as Fort John. Drips was in charge through 1851 and a part of 1852, superintending the fur trade in the Platte Valley. He returned to the states in 1852 and may have spent the next five years in the Kansas City area. By the summer of 1857 he was back in the fur trade, stationed at Ash Point in the Platte Valley. Drips died at Kansas City on a visit home, Sept. 1, 1860. He was survived by his third (?) wife, Louise Geroux (or Terrien), who had married him as a Sioux girl of sixteen; she bore him five children between Oct. 14, 1850, and Oct. 21, 1857.

WILLIAM O. FALLON

According to Robert Campbell, Fallon was the son of a St. Louis wagonmaker (perhaps the "Wesley Fallon, jour. carriage maker, c. Locust & Fifth," listed in the 1842 *St. Louis City Directory*). Campbell describes Fallon as "a strong, athletic man, as spry as a cat, and a great horseman. His weight was 200 pounds. He could mount a horse on the run and pick up a sixpence from the ground while on the gallop." In *Edward Warren* Stewart calls him "the finest looking man in the mountains," with a "noble figure." Frances Fuller Victor terms him "a big, bullying Irishman," and later he was viewed in that light in California. His name appears in the literature as Fallon, Fallen, Fellun, O'Fallon, O'Fallen, O'Felon, etc. At times he has been confused with Maj. Benjamin O'Fallon, U.S. Indian Agent for the Upper Missouri during the 1820's, and with Thomas Fallon, who came to California with Frémont in 1844.

Fallon first appears in the record of the fur trade in Campbell's recollections. Relating experiences of Ashley's mountain-bound party in the spring of 1826, Campbell says: "At O'Fallon's Bluff, the expedition was joined by Bill Fallon, after whom the Bluffs were named. His name was Fallon, not O'Fallon. He had wintered there." Fallon may have been one of those free trappers who traveled from the mountains in the fall of 1828 to solicit competitive trading by Kenneth Mackenzie's Upper Missouri Outfit. He was operating out of Fort Union by the spring of 1829, for Mackenzie wrote on May 5, 1830: "Fallon ordered a Riffle last spring from St Louis, he is very anxious to get it and will be much disappointed if he don't." Moreover, the Chouteau account books on Aug. 19, 1829, note as due W. Fallon the sum of $1,086.30. In the summer of 1830 he accompanied Mackenzie to St. Louis and back; the Fort Tecumseh (Pierre) journal records their arrival from Fort Union on July 15, and their return from St. Louis on October 9. There are further accounts with Fallon from Nov. 2, 1830, to April 15, 1831.

He returned to the Rockies with the party Etienne Provost and William Gordon took out to William Henry Vanderburgh in the spring of 1831. On Sept. 30, 1831, Vanderburgh gave him an order on the American Fur Company for $491.75. This he endorsed to Bent & St. Vrain, which implies that he headed south after reaching Green River. George Nidever in the spring of 1832 encountered on the Platte "a trader by the name of O'Felon, an Irishman, who with a half doz. mules had brought liquor and a few articles such as blankets, &c., to trade with the trappers. He was accompanied by a trapper by the name of [Black?] Harris, and had 6 or 7 Mexicans to attend to his mules and packs. He was bound for . . . the appointed rendezvous." Nidever set out with "O'Felon," and reached Pierres Hole "just before the 4th of July."

Campbell says that this year he himself brought up a small outfit, which after the battle of Pierres Hole he sold to "Fallon and Vanderburgh." Fallon and this partner, James Vanderburgh, sought southerly trapping grounds, for next year Warren Ferris remarks: "one of the partisans, Fallen, went to Teos last winter for supplies, and on his return lost two Spaniards, 'Engages', who were frozen to death on their horses. He also suffered greatly from cold and fatigue." Nevertheless, Fallon and Vanderburgh made a good hunt. When Ferris reached the Horse Creek rendezvous on June 7, 1833, he found the two partners there ahead of him, and on July 23 Fontenelle issued an order on the American Fur Company in Fallon's favor. Fallon and James Vanderburgh made another southerly hunt in the fall of 1833, for Ferris mentions troubles which the partners had while encamped on Mary's (Yampa) River. Like other trappers, in 1833-1834 Fallon and Vanderburgh made a poor hunt, which broke them up.

Anderson records Fallon's presence on Hams Fork July 19, 1834, and mentions him August 1 in connection with the ransom of Conmarrowap's wife. Joe Meek told Frances Victor a less agreeable story, saying that "a big, bullying Irishman named O'Fallen . . . had purchased two prisoners from the Snake Indians, to be kept in a state of slavery. . . . The prisoners were Utes, or Utahs, who soon contrived to escape. O'Fallen, imagining that Umentucken [Meek's Snake squaw] had liberated them, threatened to whip her, and armed himself with a horsewhip for that purpose." She was prepared to defend herself in Meek's absence and presented a pistol to Fallon's head. "O'Fallen taken by surprise, and having every reason to believe she would keep her word, and kill him on the spot, was obliged not only to apologize, but to beg to have his life spared." As related by Anderson, Fallon left the mountains this summer, though Vanderburgh stayed on another year. After reaching Bellevue, Fontenelle wrote Fallon two orders on the American Fur Company, one dated Sept. 19, the other Oct. 22, 1834. Another account indicates that in January 1835 Fallon lent Fontenelle $201.95 at Liberty, Missouri.

In the summer of 1835 Fallon and Samuel P. Winter accompanied the U.S. Dragoons to the Platte. Apparently they were outfitted by A. G. Morgan, the sutler at Fort Leavenworth. Sergeant Hugh Evans mentions on July 3 this "party of traders under the command of Mr Winter formerly of Lexington, Ky"; and Captain Lemuel Ford says on July 8, when forty-one miles above the Forks of the Platte, "our traders Winters & Fallon left us and returned with the Richorees for trading." The two men next appear in William L. Sublette's letter of Nov. 2, 1835, to Robert Campbell from Columbia, Missouri. "Winters & [John] Gant[t] is Starting Out for the Mountens and Falon Passt here a few days Since."

Over the next seven years the record is meager. The Chouteau accounts show that on Oct. 16, 1835, Fallon bought some blankets; and cash was paid or lent him on Feb. 24, Oct. 16 and 29, Nov. 17, and Dec. 5 and 6, 1836. He seems to have been in Liberty in January 1836 and to have advanced funds to Fontenelle at that time. On March 11, 1839, Fallon was credited with $163 "for Chs. Primeau's note due 30th May 1837," and mention is made on Oct. 1, 1839, of $10, "Cash paid Wm. Fallon for his note."

Fallon returns to the record more definitely in connection with Dr. Elijah White's Oregon-bound party of 1842. Medorem Crawford on June 4, when beyond the Big Blue, speaks of "O'Fallen" as having come up with a Mr. Burns. On June 15, when White was voted out as captain in favor of Lansford W. Hastings, Crawford notes that two wagons and thirteen men remained with "Capt. Fallen." After other references to him, on June 22, near Ash Hollow, Crawford remarks that "Capt. Fallen & Esq. Crocker went on to Fort L[aramie]." At the fort on July 1, "Difficulty between Doct. White and Capt. Fallen. Fallen refused to go with us." It may have been intended that Fallon should guide the company to Fort Hall, a job Thomas Fitzpatrick took on next day.

Andrew Sublette, writing from Westport, May 13, 1844, concerning his engagement to guide a party of invalids and Catholic priests for seventy-five dollars per month, said he could have got more, "but Mr. Fallon and Steal offered to go for there board." Two days later James Clyman, about to leave for Oregon, made note of having lent "Wm Fallon 2.00." If Fallon set out for Oregon this year, he must have separated from the emigrants en route, perhaps after reaching Fort Laramie, for he turned up at Los Angeles in February 1845, having come by a southern route. (In a letter of Feb. 7, 1884, to H. H. Bancroft, John Bidwell recalled that Fallon arrived at Los Angeles with a party of about thirty men "from the Rocky Mountains via New Mexico.") Fallon participated in the Michceltorena War, a bloodless affray in which the Californians defeated a Mexican governor. In his Bancroft Library dictation, "California, 1841-8," Bidwell says that they received a timely addition in the shape of "some forty Americans mostly experienced mountaineers under the leadership of Wᵐ O. Fallon, a veteran Rocky Mountaineer"; in Bidwell's view, the fraternizing of these Americans with those who accompanied Micheltorena, to the detriment of the business at hand, led to Micheltorena's downfall. (On July 31, 1845, Sutter recalled to Thomas Larkin that "O'Fallon . . . marched against us with his gang for the sake of getting some horses.")

After the Micheltorena War Fallon came north, and in April 1845 participated in a campaign against the Tuolumne Indians. According to recollections by one of the company in the San Jose *Pioneer*, Aug. 9, 1881, "big Fallen or mountain Fallen" was shot through the cheek with an arrow during this campaign. Sutter's letter to Larkin says, "In a few days, O Fallen . . . with two other Men are going to the U.S. via fort Hall," but if Fallon went out to Fort Hall he soon returned. On Jan. 28, 1846, Sutter's *New Helvetia Diary* records the arrival of "W. O. Fallon from feather River." Soon after, on Feb. 6, 1846, Edward M. Kern, in the detachment of Frémont's Third Expedition guided by Joseph R. Walker, encountered on Calaveras Creek "Big Fallen, an old mountaineer, known more commonly by the sobriquet of 'Le Gros.'" From him they learned that Frémont was at Pueblo de San José. Next day "Fallen and Walker" set off for the pueblo to give "intelligence of our whereabouts."

On March 8, 1846, the *New Helvetia Diary* records the arrival of "Ofallon from the Upper Pueblo," and on the twentieth notes the departure of Fallon, with others, for Bear Creek. These two entries are possibly mistaken as applying to William Fallon, for the *New Helvetia Diary* on March 30 remarks the coming of "T. Fallon from up the Valley." The allusion is to Thomas Fallon, a Canadian born in 1819, who entered the service of Bent & St. Vrain, killed a man in an 1843 Fourth of July brawl on the South Platte, joined Frémont, and thus came to California, being released from service at Sutter's on March 14, 1844. In December 1845 Thomas Fallon was recorded in a census at Branciforte (Santa Cruz), but he had now come back to the vicinity of Sutter's. Thus there is every opportunity for confusion between Thomas and William Fallon during 1846-1847. Thomas Fallon became a wealthy resident of San Jose, where he died in 1887.

William Fallon was at Sonoma in June 1846, one of the moving figures in the Bear Flag Rebellion, and a signer of the declaration of principles issued by the "Bears" on June 14. Subsequently he recruited for Frémont's California Battalion and himself served in it. He was back in northern California by the spring of 1847, a principal figure in the Donner Fourth Relief, which left the settlements for the High Sierra on April 12 and returned about two weeks later. His diary of that venture was printed in the *California Star*, June 5, 1847. Fallon traveled again into the Sierra, and on May 29 the *New Helvetia Diary* recorded his return. Fallon then joined Gen. S. W. Kearny's command in marching back to the states —according to Edwin Bryant in the capacity of guide. Kearny left Sutter's June 16 and reached Fort Leavenworth Aug. 22, 1847. Soon after Fallon's return to the states, the St. Louis *Reveille*, Sept. 4, 1847, printed a "memorandum" or table of distances he supplied for the "Route between California and Fort Leavenworth." Fallon turned back to California in the spring of 1848, as recorded in Bruce Cornwall, *Life Sketch of Pierre Barlow Cornwall*, pp. 15-26, which erroneously gives his name as Tom. En route "Fallon became restless. With a Scotchman named Guthrie, who had joined them at Fort Hall, he left them to proceed more quickly to California. The two were attacked for their supplies by the Hill [sic] Indians, and some weeks later the main party came upon their mutilated bodies by the trail." The *Californian*, Sept. 2, 1848, reporting the arrival of the first "packers from the United States," notes that "Capt. O'Fallon, the brave soldier and well known recruiting officer under Col. Fremont, during the war in California, left Fort Hall alone for this territory" a few days prior to the departure of the packers, "and from the appearance of the Indians and his non arrival here, they express the belief that he has been murdered by the Indians on his way hither. . . ."

O'Fallons Bluffs, the first highlands that rise on the South Fork of the Platte above its confluence with the North Fork, commemorate Fallon; and it may be that his name is also reflected by O'Fallon Creek, a tributary of the Yellowstone in eastern Montana.

THOMAS FITZPATRICK

Fitzpatrick is said to have been born in County Cavan, Ireland, in 1799 and to have come to the United States before his seventeenth birthday. Out of total obscurity he emerges as a member of Ashley's second expedition in 1823. He survived the defeat at the Arikara villages in June 1823, and during the Arikara Campaign that followed served as quartermaster for Ashley's detachment of Leavenworth's "Missouri Legion."

Afterward, with Jedediah Smith, Fitzpatrick set out from Fort Kiowa for the Crow country. (An account in the Jedediah Smith Estate Papers of money owed to "Smith & Fitzpatrick" by one Chorate implies an actual partnership with Smith then or thereafter.) After wintering on Wind River, the party of eleven made its way to the Sweetwater, then crossed South Pass to the waters of the Green. Seven of the company including Smith trapped to the south, while Fitzpatrick, James Clyman, and two others hunted on the upper tributaries of the Green. In June 1824 Fitzpatrick rendezvoused with Smith on the Sweetwater, presumably at the "cache" noted by Anderson ten years later. He attempted to transport some of the furs down by bullboat, but the craft was wrecked in the North Platte below the mouth of the Sweetwater. Fitzpatrick cached the furs, and with his two men hiked down the Platte to Fort Atkinson, arriving in sorry condition early in September. Lucien Fontenelle bought his furs and hired mules to retrieve them, enabling Fitzpatrick to make delivery at Bellevue on October 26. He had written Ashley of the rich country found beyond South Pass, and by the time Fitzpatrick returned, Ashley had reached Council Bluffs with an expedition destined for the mountains.

Fitzpatrick joined Ashley's party, which left Fort Atkinson early in November 1824, and continued with it to Green River. When in April 1825 Ashley divided his party, Fitzpatrick led one detachment south to hunt Henrys Fork of the Green. His spring hunt seems to have amounted to eighty-five beaver.

Possibly Fitzpatrick was with William L. Sublette from July 1825 to January 1827. With Jackson and Campbell he may have hunted in the Green River Valley in the spring of 1827. From Beckwourth's narrative it would seem that he was at one of the winter camps near the Great Salt Lake in 1827-1828, and that next spring he hunted on the Portneuf and the Bear. From the Bear Lake rendezvous in July 1828 Fitzpatrick went as David E. Jackson's clerk to the Flathead country. He wintered with Jackson at Flathead Lake and presumably accompanied him on his spring hunt of 1829 into the Kutenai country, the most northerly penetration ever made by American trappers—an attempt to carry the fight for furs into Hudson's Bay Company terrain. Later in the spring Fitzpatrick was sent on express to Robert Campbell's party in the Crow country; Anderson's record gives us a glimpse of Fitzpatrick on June 20, 1829, waiting at the junction of Wind River and the Popo Agie. After William L. Sublette arrived from the states with the caravan, Fitzpatrick recrossed the Wind River Mountains as an express to Jackson, joining him and Jedediah Smith in Pierres Hole July 16.

If Fitzpatrick continued as Jackson's clerk, he made a fall hunt in the Snake country, wintered in the Crow country with the other parties, and in the spring of 1830 again hunted in the Snake region. By July 28 he was back on Wind River, settling accounts for Smith, Jackson & Sublette, and a few days later he joined Milton G. Sublette, James Bridger, Henry Fraeb, and Jean Baptiste Gervais in organizing the Rocky Mountain Fur Company, the successor firm. With the best head for business and the most drive, he was the dominant figure in the new concern.

After the 1830 rendezvous, in company with Milton Sublette and Bridger, Fitzpatrick took a sizable party north; Meek says they went "from the Wind River to the Yellowstone; crossing thence to Smith's River, the Falls of the Missouri, three forks of the Missouri, and to the Big Blackfoot River," ending up at a winter camp on Powder River. (Accounts by Fitzpatrick and Robert Newell place the winter camp on the Yellowstone.)

In March 1831, according to his own statement (February, according to Newell and Warren Ferris), Fitzpatrick set out for the states with a single companion to arrange for supplies. Ferris says the journey was performed on foot, much of the way on snowshoes. Fitzpatrick reached Cabanné's post at Council Bluffs on April 15 and set out for St. Louis four days later. He seems to have reached Lexington the first week of May. Smith, Jackson, and Sublette had just departed on a trading venture to Santa Fe; so Fitzpatrick set out in pursuit. His friends, Ferris says, "persuaded him to go on with them to New Mexico, promising to give him an equipment at Toas [Taos], which would not be more than twenty days march from Cache Valley, whither he could arrive in time to meet his companions in the month of July."

Thus Fitzpatrick was close by when Jedediah Smith was killed on the Cimarron, May 27, 1831. That same day he found on the plains the Arapaho waif he named Friday, who shared many of his journeys over the next seven years. The company reached Santa Fe July 4. Soon after, with forty men including the young Kit Carson and John Robertson, Fitzpatrick rode north from Taos. He may have had some idea of cutting through the mountains to Cache Valley, and he had the evident intention of making delivery of the R. M. F. Co. furs near Taos. But Fitzpatrick ended by taking his party to the Laramie River, thence up the North Platte.

He met Fraeb, as seen in the sketch of the latter, turned over his supply train, and with three companions set out for St. Louis. At the mouth of the Laramie he encountered the party John Gantt and Jefferson Blackwell had brought to the Rockies (including Zenas Leonard) and on September 3 continued on to the states, joined by Blackwell and two others. He and Blackwell both hoped to bring new outfits to the mountains next spring.

By his circuitous route Fitzpatrick reached Lexington, Missouri, before William L. Sublette got there from Santa Fe on October 16, and at Lexington he found Robert Campbell, just returned from Ireland. By November 20 he was in St. Louis. Sublette undertook to supply the new outfit, and on Sublette's responsibility and at his risk the caravan set out from Independence the following May.

After the party reached the crossing of the North Platte, June 18, Fitzpatrick rode ahead as an express to his partners. In the Green River Valley he ran into Gros Ventres and narrowly escaped with his life. The accident that crippled his left hand (so that he became known to the Indians as "Broken Hand" or "Bad Hand") may have occurred while he was trying to cross the Snake in Jackson Hole afterward; and his experiences are said to have prematurely whitened his hair (he also became known to the Indians as "White Hair"). He did not get to Pierres Hole until after Sublette himself arrived on July 8.

At the rendezvous Fitzpatrick proposed to Drips and William H. Vanderburgh that they divide the fur country with the R. M. F. Co., but the two men were not prepared to commit themselves. When the rendezvous broke up, Fitzpatrick took the R. M. F. Co's main brigade, by his own account, "to Salmon river and there made a deposit of all our goods &c. from thence to the Blackfoot country and further north in it than a company of whites ever has been before in search of beaver but found them much scarcer than I had any idea of." Vanderburgh, he added, "overtook us with a party of 112 men on Dearburn river which was a great disadvantage to us altho in all they caught but about 5 packs of fur while we got 20 they remained and camped with us until we arrived at the three forks of the missouri w[h]ere we separated." (Compare the sketch of Drips.) Irving overdramatized this fall hunt, implying that the exasperated Fitzpatrick led Vanderburgh to his death. As Fitzpatrick notes, "we both had a fight with the blackfeet." Vanderburgh was killed, but in his own party "Bridger was shot in 2 places with arrows," and a squaw was slain.

In November 1832 Fitzpatrick came back to the Salmon, establishing a winter camp in the Pahsimeroi Valley. In December he traveled to the Forks of the Snake to transact some business with Drips. At this time Bonneville was wintering on the

Salmon, and Joe Walker with most of Bonneville's party had settled in below Drips's camp.

The opposition accounts do not mention Fitzpatrick's spring hunt of 1833, though Irving implies that Walker's group and an unidentified R. M. F. Co. party (necessarily Fitzpatrick's) spent the season annoying each other. That may have been dressing up the facts. It appears that Walker mostly hunted in the Green River Valley, doing fairly well (see the sketch of Walker), while Fitzpatrick, Bridger, and Fraeb did very well indeed farther to the southeast with their party of sixty men; in his quoted letter dated "River [North] Platte," June 4, 1833, Fitzpatrick wrote that he had found "beaver much more plenty than I have in any part last fall   we have done very well so far this hunt   I put in cache a few days ago about 40 packs of good fur."

Fraeb was to have gone down to the states for a new outfit while Fitzpatrick and Bridger made a summer hunt in the Black Hills and the Three Parks of the Rockies, but this was changed when Fraeb fell in with Robert Campbell at the Laramie River. Louis Vasquez rode in search of Fitzpatrick and brought him to the Laramie. After purchasing Campbell's outfit, Fitzpatrick sent Fraeb to join Bridger, while he himself went on with Campbell to Green River, digging out his cached furs en route. According to Charles Larpenteur, the united party crossed South Pass July 2 and reached the Green near Bonneville's fort three days later.

After the breaking up of the rendezvous on July 24, Campbell and Fitzpatrick (accompanied by Wyeth, and followed on the twenty-fifth by Bonneville and Cerré) moved off toward the Big Horn, which they reached August 12. By the fourteenth Fitzpatrick and Milton G. Sublette signed a contract with Wyeth for an 1834 outfit, and next day Wyeth and Milton set out down the Big Horn.

According to Irving, Fitzpatrick now had between twenty and thirty men and about a hundred horses. Accompanied by Captain Stewart, q.v., he struck off to the east, intending to trap the Little Horn, Powder, and Tongue rivers. On September 5 he was robbed by the Crows. Robert Campbell learned in December from an American Fur Company man that "the Crows took all his animals but returned inferor ones in their stead and returned 2 sacks Coffee and some Chocolate—About half their Traps and all the Guns but one—that Fitz immediately started off for to join Bridger." On October 26 Bonneville found Fitzpatrick on Hams Fork, encamped with a Snake village. About this time he got together with Bridger and Fraeb. He was still on Hams Fork November 13 when he wrote Ashley to complain of the Crow robbery, instigated as he believed by the American Fur Company. He also wrote Milton Sublette that he would winter "here and here aboutes," and that he would "hunt nearly in the Same Section where I did last Spring," adding with regard to the rendezvous, "dont gou so high up on Seekkedde as horse Creek   strike Some where about the mouth of Sandy and remain until we come."

During the winter Fitzpatrick moved over to the Snake; at the end of March 1834 Kit Carson and Capt. Richard Bland Lee found him on Snake waters, probably near the Forks. Bridger seems to have wintered with him. It was Bridger, not Fitzpatrick, who led a spring brigade toward the Black Hills. From mid-April when, as we infer from Carson, he was still on the Snake, Fitzpatrick drops from sight until Anderson encounters him June 15 on the Green above the mouth of the Sandy. Five days later Fitzpatrick and William L. Sublette negotiated the Rocky Mountain Fur Company out of existence after four troubled years. On August 3, as Anderson again records, the new firm, Fitzpatrick, Sublette & Bridger, was merged with Fontenelle, Drips & Co. as Fontenelle, Fitzpatrick & Co. In consequence, Fitzpatrick did not remain in the mountains. While Bridger and Drips took brigades off in quest of beaver, Fitzpatrick and Fontenelle set out for the states with Fontenelle's returns. Anderson stayed with Fitzpatrick all the way to St. Louis, where they arrived Sept. 29, 1834. Friday came with them.

A document in the Sublette Papers places Fitzpatrick in St. Louis as late as Nov. 17, 1834, but by the spring of 1835 he and Friday returned to the mountains. Possibly he went up with Campbell to receive for Fontenelle, Fitzpatrick & Co. the Fort William property sold by Sublette & Campbell. If so, he left St. Louis April 9, 1835. Fitzpatrick was at Fort William when the annual caravan reached there July 26. Samuel Parker notes on the resumption of his journey to the rendezvous, Aug. 1, 1835, "Mr. Fontenelle stopped at the fort, and Mr. Fitz Patrick took his place in charge of the caravan." Neither Parker nor Marcus Whitman refers to Fitzpatrick thereafter, but Whitman says the returning caravan got back to the fort September 8. Fontenelle took it the rest of the way to the states.

In charge of Fort William through the fall of 1835, Fitzpatrick made a winter journey to St. Louis, leaving his post January 3 and arriving via Fort Pierre on Feb. 27, 1836. Friday accompanied him. Fitzpatrick did not remain below very long. He was aboard on March 11 when the *Diana* left St. Louis with the year's supplies. Three hundred miles up the Missouri, the steamboat snagged and had to unload in the woods; Fitzpatrick wrote Pierre Chouteau, Jr., on March 18, probably from near Liberty: "I need not undertake to give you a written account of our misfortunes as you will too soon have a verbal one however I will proceed on up to Council bluffs and accomplish (as far as practible) the affairs left in my Charge after which I will return to liberty and there await your advice. . . ."

With the outfit for Fontenelle, Fitzpatrick & Co. he got off from Council Bluffs May 16. William Drummond Stewart was again along, and on May 27 Whitman and his missionary party caught up at the Pawnee Tapage village. They arrived at Fort William June 14. Joshua Pilcher appeared on express six days later, and on June 29 the clerk, L. Crawford, wrote Pierre Chouteau that "Messrs Fitzpatrick and [Milton] Sublette left this seven days ago (& with them Mr Pilcher) for the mountains. . . . Mr Fitzpatrick with the Mountain party was met [by one lately arrived at the fort] at the crossing of the Platte and getting on well. . . ."

Nothing is said of Fitzpatrick at the rendezvous, where Pilcher had come to transfer control from Fontenelle, Fitzpatrick & Co. to their erstwhile backers. Fitzpatrick was back at Fort William by August 15, when he signed two documents. He went down to the states with Pilcher and the returns and was in St. Louis Nov. 2, 1836, when he signed a document now in the Sublette Papers. By this time his partnership with Milton Sublette had soured. However, Fitzpatrick made a winter journey to the fort on the Laramie; Robert Newell, trading on the South Platte for Bent & St. Vrain, jotted in his notebook, "Fitzpatrick back from the States March 17ᵗʰ." Thus he was on hand during the last three weeks of Milton's life.

Osborne Russell is the last to mention Fitzpatrick in connection with the fur trade of the northern Rockies, saying that the 1837 supply caravan arrived at Green River July 5 (properly, July 18), "consisting of 45 men and 20 Carts drawn by Mules under the direction of Mr. Thomas Fitzpatrick [not a mistake for Fontenelle?] accompanied by Capt. Wm. Stewart on another tour to the Rocky Mountains."

During the next two years Fitzpatrick is not located for certain anywhere. James P. Beckwourth, who entered the service of Vasquez & Sublette in the summer of 1838, speaks so familiarly of Fitzpatrick in connection with the trade on the South Platte that Fitzpatrick must have been associated with Vasquez & Sublette during 1838-1839. When F. A. Wislizenus rode in from Browns Hole on Sept. 3, 1839, he found at Fort Vasquez "the well-known Fitzpatrick.... He has a spare, bony figure, a face full of expression, and white hair; his whole demeanor reveals strong passions." Beckwourth says that Andrew Sublette and Fitzpatrick took a collection of furs to St. Louis, but if Beckwourth was referring to the summer of 1839, he was mistaken.

Fitzpatrick is next found in St. Louis preparing to take Father De Smet to the Rockies. The *Missouri Republican*, April 20, 1841, understands "that a portion of a party under the command of Mr. Fitzpatrick leaves to-day for the Rocky Mountains and the mouth of the Columbia, the remainder of the party will leave in a few days, and the whole expedition will rendezvous at Independence on the 10th of May next, immediately after which they will take up their march for the Mountains. . . ." De Smet reached Westport April 30 and set off ten days later. His accounts of the journey scarcely mention Fitzpatrick, though in a letter of 1849 De Smet speaks of "the pleasure and happiness" afforded by Fitzpatrick's company. Fitzpatrick is given abundant attention in the diaries and reminiscences of the California-bound Bartleson party, which benefited from Fitzpatrick's guidance as far as Soda Springs on Bear River.

Fitzpatrick himself stayed with De Smet and his companions until they reached the Bitterroot Valley on Sept. 24, 1841. Narcissa Whitman, writing from Waiilatpu on October 1, remarked that "Fitzpatrick is expected here when he has accomplished his piloting for that company, and is said to return to St. Louis this fall; if so, I hope to send this by him." However, her letter was eventually taken east by other hands. Fitzpatrick reappears in July 1842 traveling east from Fort Bridger with a company of trappers led by Jim Bridger. On arrival at Fort Laramie July 2, he was hired as guide by Elijah White, en route to Oregon as Indian subagent, and his services to the emigrants as far as Fort Hall, where they arrived August 14, were many and various.

In parting with him on August 15, White wrote the Secretary of War to ask that Fitzpatrick be paid $250 for "Pilotage," adding that Fitzpatrick intended returning West next year "and proffers to pilot another party. . . . He intends to start a month earlier so as to take the wagons through to the Wallamet. . . ." Fitzpatrick set out from Fort Hall August 20 with a single companion, Van Dusen. To avoid the Sioux and Cheyennes, who at this time were very hostile, he took a route via Bent's Fort. About 300 miles from Independence, on October 28, he fell in with a war party of Pawnees who robbed him of nearly everything but his horses, to the value of $207.50. (Some years later, the Pawnees having acknowledged their fault, this sum was deducted from their annuities and handed over to Fitzpatrick.) Rufus Sage had met Fitzpatrick and Van Dusen September 18 on an affluent of the Fontaine qui Bouit, indicating that they had traveled via Fort Laramie.

Fitzpatrick reached St. Louis by November 20. In February 1843 he went on to Washington. There the government concluded that White's effort to compensate Fitzpatrick for "Pilotage" was illegal, but a modus vivendi was found by giving him a nominal appointment as "Interpreter to the sub-agency for the Indians West of the Rocky Mountains," dated as of Jan. 1, 1843. In this capacity he stayed on the Indian Office payroll till Sept. 6, 1844, receiving a total of $503.35. No one objected that most of this time he was with Frémont's Second Expedition to Oregon and California. The Frémont accounts show that Fitzpatrick served as principal guide at the rate of $3.33⅓ per day from April 1, 1843, to Sept. 6, 1844 (twenty-seven days after his return to St. Louis), totaling $1,750 for 525 days. Fitzpatrick's labors on this expedition are well known, being recorded in Frémont's official report and in the diaries of Theodore Talbot and Charles Preuss. (The latter credits Fitzpatrick with the conception of returning home from the Columbia "via so-called California.")

In 1845 Fitzpatrick was guide for Col. S. W. Kearny's U.S. Dragoons in their march from Fort Leavenworth to South Pass, then back to Fort Laramie and down to Bent's Fort. This march is almost as well known as the Frémont expeditions, but interesting are comments on Fitzpatrick in the journal of Lt. J. H. Carleton, published as *The Prairie Logbooks*, including references to Fitzpatrick's early experiences among the Crows.

Fitzpatrick left the Dragoons after they reached Bent's on July 29, becoming guide for Lt. James W. Abert, who had been detached from Frémont's Third Expedition for a reconnaissance via the Canadian River to Fort Gibson. Abert disbanded his party in St. Louis November 12. For services rendered, Aug. 4-Nov. 26, 1845, Fitzpatrick was paid $373.33.

As shown by letters he wrote Abert, Fitzpatrick was in St. Louis in February, and again in May, after attending a Democratic convention in southern Missouri. He had found guide service more profitable than the fur trade, and war with Mexico brought another such job. On June 6, 1846, Capt. Benjamin Moore and a force of Dragoons left Fort Leavenworth on orders from Col. (soon General) Kearny to stop a company of Santa Fe traders that had set out for New Mexico with a supply of ammunition. Fitzpatrick went along as guide. The traders could not be overtaken; so Moore's command halted upon reaching Bent's Fort July 21-22 until Kearny's main force arrived on July 29. To Andrew Sublette on July 31,

Fitzpatrick wrote that he had been informed by Robert Campbell that he was about to receive appointment as Indian Agent for the Platte and Arkansas Indians, but with permission to remain with Kearny "should he stand in want of my services which I have concluded to do and will join his staff tomorrow morning."

Thus he marched with Kearny to occupy Santa Fe and with him set out for California on September 25. Near Socorro, Kearny met Kit Carson, eastbound from California, and since Carson knew the road and Fitzpatrick did not, Kearny switched their jobs, sending Fitzpatrick east with the military dispatches. Fitzpatrick reached Santa Fe October 11, arrived in St. Louis November 15, and was off to Washington two days later.

Meanwhile, he had been appointed to the new Indian Agency for the Upper Platte and Arkansas, his commission being dated August 6. Fitzpatrick accepted the appointment, and this work engaged him the rest of his life. The record is too full to be summarized here. Reference may be made to LeRoy R. Hafen and W. J. Ghent, *Broken Hand*, though the documentary record has been signally extended since that work appeared. Called to Washington on government business, Fitzpatrick died there Feb. 7, 1854, survived by his widow, a son, and a posthumously born daughter. He had been married about November 1849 to Margaret, daughter of a French-Canadian trapper named John Poisal who had taken an Arapaho wife.

In 1834 Anderson described Fitzpatrick as a "warm-hearted, gentlemanly Hibernian." He made a quite different impression on Wislizenus in 1839. F. X. Matthieu, who journeyed from Fort Laramie to Fort Hall with him in 1842, remembered him as "tall and spare with abundant gray hair; an Irishman of good common education, and even gentlemanly bearing. . . . Unlike the most of his race, however, he was very taciturn." W. H. Emory observed in 1846 that Fitzpatrick rarely laughed, though he could be convulsed by a grotesque spectacle. It seems doubtful that Fitzpatrick's contemporaries called him "Tom," as modern historians are inclined to do; they may have ventured no greater familiarity than "Fitz."

LUCIEN FONTENELLE

Lucien Fontenelle was born Oct. 9, 1800, probably in New Orleans. The baptismal records of St. Louis Cathedral there (Book 4, p. 36, Act 296) show that his parents were François and Maria Louise (Burat) Fontenelle, his paternal grandparents "Juan Baptista Martin Fontenelle and Marie Mayeux." He and a younger sister Amélie, whose name appears in the record as Juana Emelita, were baptized Nov. 16, 1803. The parents are said to have come originally from Marseilles, and to have settled at the Burat Settlement, near Pointe a la Hache, some miles below New Orleans, where they were drowned in a hurricane. The children at the time were living with an aunt, Amélie's godmother, Madame Mercier, so that they might be educated. According to the story told by one of Amélie's daughters, about 1816 Lucien, then a clerk in a New Orleans banking house, left home after being struck by his aunt, a harsh woman. He soon made his way up the Mississippi to St. Louis. Amélie remained in New Orleans and eventually married Henry Lockett, an eminent young lawyer, nephew of Judge Henry Carleton, who for many years was judge of the supreme court of New Orleans. See Nebraska State Historical Society, *Transactions*, I (1885), 89-93; IV (1892), 95-98.

By his own statement, Fontenelle's career in the Missouri fur trade began in 1819. In that year he traded for the Missouri Fur Company in the Council Bluffs area. He is mentioned at Fort Atkinson in January 1820 and four months later at the "Maha Portage." In the fall of 1820 he witnessed the signature of two partners to the articles of association of the reorganized Missouri Fur Company. In May 1821 he came down to St. Louis to assist Michael Immell in preparations for the company's first mountain expedition, and he was aboard the keelboat under Capt. Joseph Perkins that left St. Louis only to sink in the Mississippi early in August 1821. Fontenelle went up the river later in the year and returned in the spring of 1822 to take up yet another keelboat.

During the next five years Fontenelle operated in the Council Bluffs area, first at Fort Lisa, then at Bellevue, where the Missouri Fur Company established its headquarters in 1823. In August 1823 he was in St. Louis engaging new hands, and therefore had no part in the Arikara Campaign. James Kennerly's diary at Fort Atkinson mentions him at various times between Dec. 24, 1823, and Jan. 2, 1826. He may have become Joshua Pilcher's partner when the Missouri Fur Company expired in 1824, though the new license issued October 27 of that year was in Pilcher's name. Another license, on July 4, 1825, was issued to "Joshua Pilcher, L. Fontainelle Wm. Vandeburg, Chs. Brent [Bent] and A. Dripps." A third license, Aug. 15, 1826, lists "Fontainelle Brent Drips & Vandeburg" as partners. (Pilcher's name was apparently omitted by clerical error.) In September 1827 Pilcher took a company to the Rockies, and Fontenelle went along; the name of Fontenelle Creek may reflect the hunt he made in the spring of 1828. He returned to Bellevue in September 1828 with Pilcher's scanty beaver catch. (According to Matthew Field's observation in 1843, Independence Rock bore the inscription "*Fontenelle 27-28-30-37-38*," and Townsend saw his name on the Rock in 1834.)

Probably in the wake of Pilcher's downfall in 1828, Fontenelle and Drips became owners of the post at Bellevue. In 1833 Maximilian wrote that it "was formerly a trading post of the Missouri Fur Company, on the dissolution of which it was bought by M. Fontenelle, who parted with it to the government . . . [at which time] M. Fontenelle settled . . . 600 or 800 paces further down the river." After Fontenelle's death, his interest in the relocated Bellevue post may have constituted most of his estate.

Fontenelle was at Bellevue in February 1829, and again in August, when he wrote Robert Campbell to propose a partnership with Drips and himself. Early in January 1830 he reached an agreement with J. P. Cabanné by which he and Drips should go to the Rockies with the backing of the American Fur Company. They were accompanied by Michel Robidoux. According to Warren Ferris, when they set out from Bellevue on May 1, Fontenelle had the general superintendence of the party. On Green River, Aug. 23, 1830, the company split up into three detachments; that under Fontenelle hunted unsuccessfully on the sources of Blacks and

Henrys forks, then joined the Drips contingent for a winter camp in Cache Valley. After the spring hunt of 1831, which was on Snake waters, Drips and Fontenelle set out for St. Louis. With them went the famous first party of Nez Percés and Flatheads, seeking information about Christianity.

Fontenelle returned to the mountains in the summer of 1832. It had been anticipated that he would bring up one party from Council Bluffs to supply Drips while Etienne Provost led another from Fort Union in support of William Henry Vanderburgh, who had been sent independently into the Rockies by Kenneth Mackenzie. The two supply parties were combined under Fontenelle and started from Fort Union so late (about June 19) that the Pierres Hole rendezvous broke up before Fontenelle arrived. Drips and Vanderburgh came east to meet the expected caravans, and according to Ferris encountered Fontenelle and Provost near Horse Creek on August 8. Four days later Fontenelle took the back track for Fort Union, having combined the operations of Drips and Vanderburgh, with himself as directing head "when present." Fontenelle reached Fort Union by September 11, and nineteen days later the Fort Pierre journal recorded his arrival in company with Mackenzie. On October 15 the two men went on down the Missouri to St. Louis.

Early in May 1833 Maximilian encountered Fontenelle near Bellevue; and on reaching Fort Pierre by steamboat May 29, he found Fontenelle already there, "having performed the journey, on horseback, in eleven days." (The Fort Pierre journal had recorded Fontenelle's arrival May 21.) On June 8 Maximilian observed the departure of "Mr. Fontenelle's party, consisting of sixty men and 185 horses." They reached the Rockies in thirty days, as reported in letters Fontenelle wrote Mackenzie and Chouteau from the Green River rendezvous, July 23 and 31, 1833.

Both Drips and Fontenelle stayed in the mountains in 1833-1834. Where Fontenelle made his fall hunt is not definitely known. When Drips set up his winter camp on the Snake in November, Ferris observed that no intelligence had been received from "Mr. Fontenelle, and some others, since they left rendezvous"; but in the spring of 1834 he heard belatedly "that Dripps had received last fall an express from Fontenelle; stating that two of his men had been killed during the fall hunt, supposed by the Blackfeet." Fontenelle's spring hunt was made in the Utah country, as shown by an order drawn April 12, 1834, on Pratte, Chouteau, & Co. at "Eutah Lake"; Ferris speaks of him as having been in the Utah (Uinta) Mountains and on Bear River during the spring. By June 29, as recorded by Anderson, Fontenelle and Drips were encamped at the junction of Blacks and Hams forks.

The American Fur Company's "Rocky Mountain expedition" of 1834 was brought to the mountains by Provost. Fontenelle went back with it, as recorded by Anderson's journal and by Fontenelle's letter written at Bellevue on Sept. 17, 1834 (see pp. 214-215). On August 3, Fontenelle, Drips & Co. had combined with Fitzpatrick, Sublette & Bridger as a new concern styled Fontenelle, Fitzpatrick & Co. In the spring of 1835 this outfit purchased Fort William (Laramie) from

Sublette & Campbell, and as a result through 1840 this post occasionally appears in the record as Fort Lucien.

Fontenelle remained in the states to settle details of the year's outfit while Fitzpatrick went up to take possession of Fort William from Robert Campbell. Owing to cholera on the Missouri, Fontenelle himself being stricken, the caravan of 1835 was slow getting off, but with the missionaries Samuel Parker and Marcus Whitman it left Liberty May 15, arrived at Council Bluffs May 30, set out again June 22, and reached Fort William July 26. Fontenelle stopped at the fort while Fitzpatrick took the trading goods up to the rendezvous and brought back the furs. Thereafter Fontenelle took the caravan down to Bellevue, as recorded by Ferris and Whitman and mentioned in a letter which William L. Sublette wrote Campbell on Nov. 2, 1835. As an item of mountain gossip, Sublette remarked, "Fontenell they say leads near about the Same life as usual"—a reference to his increasingly notorious proclivity for the bottle. Fontenelle after many delays came down to St. Louis in late February 1836. Sublette describes the difficulty of getting his mind on business when he did arrive; he preferred to spend his time sleighriding out in the country.

Apparently it was in the spring of 1836 after an absence of twenty years that Fontenelle visited his sister in New Orleans. (Sublette wrote Campbell on April 30 that Fontenelle had not yet returned to St. Louis.) According to her daughter: "Mrs. Lockett one day was at home when the servant came up and told her that there was a gentleman in the parlor who desired to see her. On entering, the gentleman clasped her in his arms and called her sister, but she recoiled, absolutely denying she was his sister, as her brother was a white man, and he was an Indian in appearance. He insisted that he was Lucien Fontenelle, and asked if Sophie [an old colored nurse] was still living. She had never left Mrs. Lockett from her childhood, and of course was called in to identify him. She hardly recognized him, but asked him to let her see his foot upon which was a mark she distinctly remembered. Upon taking off his boot the mark was there. He was a thorough Indian in looks." This account says that Fontenelle could speak fifteen different Indian dialects, was intimately acquainted with the Chouteau family of St. Louis, and had once expected to marry into it. He seemed wealthy and said his home was at Bellevue. His sister was indignant that he had married an Indian. Fontenelle remained in New Orleans about six weeks, then left, promising to return.

Fontenelle's movements, after he got back from New Orleans, are obscure. The 1836 caravan was taken to the mountains by Thomas Fitzpatrick. According to a letter Whitman wrote from Fort Vancouver the following September, "Capt. Fantanell had become so intemperate that the Company had disposed of [deposed] him. Major Pilcher joined us at Fort Williams and came on to Rendezvoux, as agent of Pratt, Choteau & Co., in whose behalf he bought out the 'mountain partners', so that the whole business now belongs to them." (Thereafter it was conducted as the "Rocky Mountain Outfit.")

Fontenelle returned to Fort William prior to the spring of 1837, as shown by

Alfred Jacob Miller. When the young painter reached the fort with the annual caravan, he found in command "Fontnell [who] . . . received us with kindness and hospitality. We noticed around his apartment some large first-class engravings, from which we drew conclusions most favorable to Mr̲ F." Miller adds: "This gentleman afterward accompanied us to the Rocky Mountains, where he distinguished himself for speed of foot in running from a grizzly bear; he having no gun with him at the time."

The caravan seems to have gone on from Fort William June 27. William H. Gray recorded its arrival at Green River on July 18, and next day "Capt. Fontenelle called and took dinner with me, Mr. Miller at supper." (Twelve days earlier, as an apparent reference to Fontenelle, Gray had written in his journal: "The principal White trader from the East of the Mountains, I am told, has taken three wives. He tells the Indians to take as many as they can—thus setting at defiance every principle of right, justice and humanity, and law of God and man." It is possible that Gray has reference here to Drips instead, for Drips had two wives as of 1838.)

Fontenelle remained in the mountains next year while Drips took a vacation. John McLoughlin wrote on Oct. 31, 1837, of reports reaching Fort Vancouver from the American rendezvous that "the main party headed by Fountenelle is to endeavour to go to the Blackfoot Country, remainder of these men are dispersed to hunt South of the Colorado, except a few who are in the Youta Country, between the Salt Lake and the Colorado. . . ." Osborne Russell says that the party he joined, consisting of 110 men, "was destined for the Blackfoot country, under the direction of L. B. Fontenelle as commander and James Bridger pilot." Russell gives a few details of Fontenelle's movements in the Yellowstone country, and others are provided by Robert Newell. In November Fontenelle left his party on Powder River and came in to Fort William. According to Russell, on Jan. 28, 1838, a supply party started off for Powder River, "leaving Mr. Fontanell at the fort." Perhaps reflecting the prevalent idea of Fontenelle, Meek says he committed suicide "in a fit of *mania a potu*." That is an idle tale, for Fontenelle was at the fort, hale and hearty, when the Oregon-bound missionaries of 1838 reached there with the annual caravan on May 30. Both Mary Richardson Walker and Asa Bowen Smith speak of Fontenelle and of Fontenelle's Indian wife "& his son, a bright lad of about 12 years." When the caravan left the fort on July 2, Fontenelle and his son Logan accompanied it.

The only further record of Fontenelle in the high country is a letter he wrote Peter A. Sarpy Aug. 5, 1838, after coming back to Fort William from Wind River. He then left the mountains for good, taking down the returns and settling at Bellevue. In a letter of Oct. 11, 1867, Father De Smet, who had taken up his labors among the Pottawatomies at Council Bluffs in 1838, recalled that he had been very intimate with Fontenelle, and "gave him the last sacraments at the hour of his death." De Smet's biographer, Rev. W. L. Davis, sends us an extract from the missionary's letter of Feb. 5, 1840, to J. N. Nicollet from Council Bluffs. As translated from the French: "Mr. Fontenelle of Bellevue, died a few days ago. I assisted him in the last moments; he died in my arms, and I have every reason to believe as a good Christian." Thus Fontenelle died in late January or early February 1840, and not as a suicide. In his letter of 1867 De Smet said further: "In 1838 I baptized his four children together with their mother, the daughter of the chief of the Omahas, Ongpatongha, or Big Elk. Logan, the oldest of the children, was my godson."

Logan became a principal chief of the Omahas, but was killed by Sioux raiders in 1855. Another son, Henry, became a well-known Indian interpreter. It is related that after Fontenelle's death De Smet called on his sister in New Orleans, saying "he had been with Lucien during his last moments, and that he had requested him to come and see her and ask if she would take his only daughter, and that his fortune be appropriated for the education, by this priest, of his children, three sons and one daughter." Wealthy and socially ambitious, Mrs. Lockett refused to take the child. In view of the state of the fur trade during Fontenelle's last years, it is unlikely he left much in the way of a fortune.

HENRY FRAEB

Nothing is known concerning the antecedents of Henry Fraeb. He talked with a heavy "Dutch" accent and has been described as a German from St. Louis. His name was pronounced in such a way that it was usually spelled "Frapp." A letter written by Warren Ferris about 1850 gives us to believe that Fraeb was one of the mountain men who circumnavigated Great Salt Lake in the spring of 1826. The next account of him is Meek's, relating that in July 1829 William L. Sublette launched down the Big Horn a large trapping party headed by Milton G. Sublette, Jean Baptiste Gervais, and Fraeb. After the fall hunt this party was encountered in the Big Horn Basin and wintered with Jedediah Smith and David E. Jackson, first on Wind River, later on Powder River.

Where Fraeb trapped in the spring of 1830 is not known. By the first of August 1830 he was back at Wind River, where he joined Milton Sublette, Bridger, Fitzpatrick, and Gervais in founding the Rocky Mountain Fur Company. After the rendezvous, as Robert Newell says, "Fraab & Garvie went to the Snake Country and hunters in different directions for Beever." The two men, often associated from 1829 to 1835, set up a winter camp in Cache Valley, as described by Ferris. Their spring hunt of 1831 was perhaps in the Utah country, though a document in the Sublette Papers places Fraeb on Green River July 9. The R. M. F. Co. partners rendezvoused that summer in Cache Valley to meet Fitzpatrick, who was expected back from St. Louis with supplies. When Fitzpatrick failed to appear, Fraeb was named to go in search of him (even to St. Louis, to arrange a new outfit, if Fitzpatrick had been killed); other than Milton Sublette, he was the only partner able to read and write. Meek says that he and three others went with Fraeb, getting as far as the Black Hills before falling in with Fitzpatrick and the pack train brought from Taos. This was late August 1831. Fraeb took over the goods and most of the employees, while Fitzpatrick turned back to the states to arrange for the next year's outfit. Ferris records Fraeb's arrival at the winter camp on the Salmon River toward the end of October, and as of January 1832 places this camp on the east fork of the Salmon (the Lemhi River). Newell also mentions Fraeb at this winter camp among the Flatheads and Nez Percés. Possibly Newell reflects Fraeb's later movements in saying that in the spring of 1832 he himself "hunted from Psalmon River to hennrys fork to Lewises fort [fork] up Salt River Round to Piers hole."

When Nathaniel Wyeth reached Pierres Hole on July 8, 1832, he mentioned "Mr. Frapp" as present. On July 17 Wyeth set out with Milton Sublette and Fraeb. Their party encountered Gros Ventres, leading to the celebrated battle of Pierres Hole next day. On July 24 the party made a new start, down the Snake, up Raft River, over to Goose Creek, and on west into the rough, barren country south of the Idaho-Nevada boundary. On August 29 Wyeth separated from the R. M. F. Co. men to descend the Bruneau. Next month, rejoining his men on the Malheur after a nine-day absence, Wyeth learned that "Mr. Sublette with Mr. Frapp & party [had] joined our camp and crossed [the Snake] . . . intending to divide into 3 parties and trap up three streams coming in opposite the upper one of which proves to be Big Woody [Boise]. . . . They attempted to come down [the Owyhee] . . . but after toiling long and wearing down their horses in a cruel manner they crossed to the one that we decended. . . ." For the further adventures of this party, see the sketch of Milton G. Sublette. After an extensive tour of the lower Snake country, the company turned east to a winter camp at the forks of the Salmon. Warren Ferris, then at Bonneville's camp, tells of their arrival on November 7 and their departure up the Salmon preliminary to wintering in Little Salmon (Pahsimeroi) Valley.

The R. M. F. Co. divided into two detachments in February 1833, Sublette and Gervais heading for the Snake country again, while a larger party including Fitzpatrick, Bridger, and Fraeb hunted in the opposite direction. On June 4, by then on the North Platte above the Black Hills, Fitzpatrick wrote Robert Campbell: "Fraeb starts for St Louis this morning for the purpose of finding out our situation in that place [i.e., what the proceeds had been from the beaver taken down in the summer of 1832 by William L. Sublette] and should matters stand as we expect he will mount another equipment in time to send in our furs this fall. . . . Should this letter meet with you in St Louis I am in hopes you will be no more backward in assisting Freab than you have me last year. . . . I shall depend much on you; you are well aware of the incapacity of our agent." (Not a flattering view of Fraeb.)

A few days later Fraeb fell in with Campbell, coming up from St. Louis. According to Larpenteur, Campbell encountered Fraeb and two men just after crossing the Laramie. It was agreed that Fraeb should purchase most of Campbell's goods, and Louis Vasquez was sent to summon Fitzpatrick. Afterward the latter accompanied Campbell to the Green River rendezvous, while Fraeb with ten men set out to join Bridger. The two partners occupied themselves through the summer trapping in the Black Hills and the Parks. A notable incident was the loss of sixty horses, run off by Arikaras while Fraeb was encamped at the mouth of a tributary of the East Fork of the Medicine Bow River, thereafter known to the mountain men as "Frappe's Creek." (Jim Bridger pointed out the site to Capt. Howard Stansbury on Sept. 24, 1850.) This catastrophe occurred early enough for Wyeth to mention it in a letter written from Green River on July 18.

In the fall Bridger and Fraeb rejoined Fitzpatrick on Hams Fork, their summer hunt having produced about twenty-three packs of beaver. On November 13 Fitzpatrick commented: "Fraeb with about 20 men is Gone down the Seekeedee with Bil Williams for pilot and intends not to return before March 1st I think they may do well. . . . Mr Guthery was killed last fall by lightning and [Thomas] Biggs since suppl[i]ed his place." (The death of Guthrie by lightning in Fraeb's camp is described by Meek in a mistaken context of 1834; the event is said to have occurred in South Park, and the probability is that it happened in the late summer of 1833.)

Meek indicates that Fraeb got very far south on his fall hunt of 1833, for he claims to have met the next spring "a company of sixty men under Frapp and Jervais" on Bill Williams Fork of the Colorado. (This may be as erroneous with regard to Fraeb as with regard to Gervais, who had gone to the Columbia with Christy; the size of the party is doubled for good measure.) According to Meek's story, on his return Fraeb crossed over to the Little Colorado, went on to the Hopi villages, over to the headwaters of the Rio Grande and New Park, where he fell in with Bridger, then came back to Green River via North Park, the Little Snake, and Pilot Butte. But Bridger did not reach the rendezvous until June 25, and Fraeb was there by June 20, when he sold his interest in the R. M. F. Co. "for and in consideration of Forty head of horse beast, forty beaver traps, eight guns and one thousand dollars worth of merchandise, all to me in hand paid."

Anderson's entry implies that Fraeb was still on hand July 13. It appears from the Fort Hall Account Books that he trapped in the Snake country the next year; transactions with him are recorded Oct. 15, 1834, and Jan. 4, March 11, 26, and June 24, with a settlement July 16, 1835. These transactions totaled $571.19. Gervais must have been with Fraeb during these months, for transactions with "Captⁿ Batiste Jervey" are recorded at Fort Hall on Oct. 13, 15, and Nov. 17, 1834, and on Feb. 10 and March 11. These were similarly settled on July 16, 1835, as a total of $112. Both Fraeb and Gervais came down to Missouri that fall. William Sublette wrote Robert Campbell from Fulton on November 2 that three days earlier he had been "Overtaken by Fraeb & Jarvey from the Mountains they Came in with fontinell as fair as his place." Having ridden on to Columbia with the two, Sublette noted that on November 1 "Fraeb & Jarvey started for Sᵗ Louis," but as late as Feb. 9, 1836, Sublette in St. Louis was mentioning that Milton and Fraeb were in Fulton; "there is no doubt but they will be here in a fiew days." (See the sketch of Milton Sublette.) This year, or a little later, Fraeb entered into a partnership with Edmund Christy in St. Louis.

In the summer of 1837 Fraeb formed a partnership with Peter A. Sarpy, obtained a stock of goods from the Chouteaus, and went out to the South Platte to found Fort Jackson near present Ione, Colorado. From this post Fraeb set out about April 23, 1838, for St. Louis, where during the summer he sold out to Bent & St. Vrain. According to John E. Sunder, *Bill Sublette, Mountain Man*, p. 158, in 1839 Sublette & Campbell brought an action for debt against Fraeb and Edmund Christy. Fraeb consistently refused to appear in court, and when a judgment against him was given, "no good[s] chattels land or tenements" of his could be located in St. Louis County. On October 15 the Chouteau account books record of Fraeb, "By Cash ($2.75) rec'd of his Negro woman." In the spring of 1840 Fraeb formed a new partnership with Bridger. With thirty men they departed St. Louis in April, reportedly intending to trade and trap on the waters of the Columbia, but in February of the next year Fraeb turned up in southern California in company with Joseph R. Walker. As shown by several transactions recorded in the Abel Stearns Papers, Huntington Library, between February 10 and April 7, 1841, Fraeb and Walker made purchases with 417 pounds of beaver sold for $1,147. Bridger may have been with them at this time. (See the sketch of Walker.)

Fraeb returned from southern California in time to encounter the Bartleson party near Green River on July 22, 1841. He then had with him, according to John Bidwell, about twenty men. The two parties remained together, trafficking and trading, for three days. Shortly thereafter, Fraeb and Bridger began building the first Fort Bridger, on the west bank of Green River. Fraeb, sent out to "make meat," was attacked on the Little Snake by a large party of Cheyennes, Arapahos, and Sioux, and after a bitter fight he and several others were killed. Since Joseph Williams had news of Fraeb's death before leaving Fort Hall for the Columbia August 21, the battle doubtless occurred early in August. For an account of this finale to Fraeb's life, see LeRoy R. Hafen, "Fraeb's Last Fight and How Battle Creek Got Its Name," *Colorado Magazine*, VII (May 1930), 97-101.

It does not appear that Fraeb ever married, even to the extent of taking an Indian wife. John Ball's *Autobiography*, in speaking of the post-rendezvous events of 1832, says that "Mr Frapp had an Indian wife," who gave birth to a child, but Ball's memory here identified with Fraeb the woman and events associated with Milton Sublette in his more contemporary journal; see the sketch of Milton Sublette.

FRIDAY (Arapaho Chief)

The Arapaho waif adopted by Thomas Fitzpatrick who grew up to be a chief of his tribe is generally known by the name Fitzpatrick applied to the boy on the day he was found. According to Anderson, his Arapaho name was Warshinun, "which he tells me means 'black' spot." This can be compared with the name "Vash" attributed to him in 1851.

In the spring of 1831 Fitzpatrick was en route to Santa Fe with Smith, Jackson, and Sublette. On the day Jedediah Smith was killed, Friday, May 27, 1831, Fitzpatrick found the small boy alone (or with two other children; the accounts vary) hidden in some bushes, his people having been scattered by an enemy attack. Theodore Talbot heard in 1843 that Fitzpatrick "drew him forth more dead than alive, but soon succeeded in calming his groundless fears. On looking farther the other children were brought to light. Their wan faces too plainly told their pitiable situation. Taking compassion on them Fitzpatrick relieved all their wants and carried them to a place of safety. He was so much pleased with the one first found that he resolved to carry him to St. Louis. . . ."

Fitzpatrick took Friday to St. Louis by way of Santa Fe, Taos, and the Laramie region. Robert Campbell, who was at Lexington, Missouri, in October 1831, recalled in 1870 that Fitzpatrick came in from the plains with an Indian boy named Friday, who did not know what nation he belonged to. On reaching St. Louis, Talbot says: "Friday was sent to school and soon acquired a knowledge of the English language. He remained several years among the whites, occasionally making a trip into the Indian country with his patron."

Friday must have remained in school from the fall of 1831 to the spring of 1833, when Robert Campbell took him out to the mountains. He presumably remained with Fitzpatrick until the summer of 1834, when he came down to the states, as related by Anderson. Doubtless he returned to the mountains with Fitzpatrick early in 1835, for William L. Sublette wrote Robert Campbell in late February 1836 that Fitzpatrick had arrived in St. Louis from the Laramie on the night of the twenty-seventh, Friday coming with him.

Talbot relates that on one of Friday's excursions into the Indian country with Fitzpatrick "he accidentally entered an Arapahoe village. He had not been there long when a woman rushing up clasped him fervently in her arms, claiming him as her lost son. An explanation ensued and what she said was proved true, great therefore were the rejoicings among his family on recovery of the promising boy, whose untimely fate they had long deplored. Although delighted to again meet his friends and relations, Friday was still loathe to leave his ever kind friend and protector. It was only after oft repeated importunities & in fact vi et armis that he could be induced to remain with them."

Rufus Sage declares that Friday returned to his people after a seven-year absence—that is, in 1838. Since Fitzpatrick seems to have been in Arapaho country that year in the service of Vasquez & Sublette, the date may be correct. Talbot adds: "Once a denizen of the village he became enamored of that mode of life, nor has he since desired to forsake it. Now and then he pays a visit to the states, but always returns to his savage haunts." Talbot hints at an unrequited love for a white girl living near St. Louis.

The next encounter with Friday is recorded by Talbot himself, as a member of Frémont's party of 1843. On July 13 on the South Platte above Bijou Creek, "a handsome young indian came dashing up to Fitz. and cordially shaking his hand expressed in the best English kind interrogatories, as to his health, purpose, & &c. We were much surprised at this unusual Indian salutation until we heard its cause explained." Two days later Talbot says: "Friday, the starved little hero of the Cimarron, came to bid us good bye, as he accompanies the war party against the Youta Indians, now just about leaving."

Sage, returning to the states via the Arkansas in April 1844, was joined below the Big Timbers "by a young Arapaho Indian, named Friday, who was desirous of visiting the States. He had formerly lived in St. Louis, where he had acquired a knowledge of the English language, and still maintains a reputation for honesty, intelligence, and sobriety." Sage devoted most of a chapter to the young man. He also said: "Few Indians or whites can compete with Friday as a buffalo-hunter, either in the use of the bow or rifle. I have seen him kill five of these animals at a single chase, and am informed that he has not unfrequently exceeded that number. . . . But it is not in hunting exploits alone that he excels; his deeds of war equally command the respect and admiration of his tribe, among whom he is known as the 'Arapaho American.'" As a traveling companion Sage said he found Friday "agreeable and interesting. I am indebted to him for much valuable information relative to the habits and peculiarities of his own and various other Indian tribes, while his vast fund of ready anecdotes and amusing stories serves to beguile the weariness of camp hours." The two men separated near Council Grove when their routes led in different directions, "his for Independence, Mo., and mine for Van Buren, Ark."

On July 18, 1845, the U. S. Dragoons, guided by Fitzpatrick, encountered Friday with a small Arapaho band on Lodgepole Creek, south of Fort Laramie; Philip St. George Cooke tells of the reunion. A reasonably full account of Friday's last years is provided by Hafen and Ghent in their *Broken Hand*, with a photograph of him taken by W. H. Jackson about 1874. Friday was one of the Arapaho delegates at the great council with the Plains Indians at Horse Creek in the summer of 1851, and subsequently he revisited the states with Fitzpatrick. Numerous references to Friday between 1858 and May 13, 1881, when he died of heart disease on the Wind River Reservation in Wyoming, show him always a friend of the whites —and perhaps for that reason never head chief of his people.

JEAN BAPTISTE GERVAIS

Information respecting Gervais' birth is contradictory. When the belated 1850 Oregon census was taken, the Canadian-born Gervais gave his age as sixty-eight, indicating that his birthdate was 1782 or 1783. When he applied for a Donation Land Claim, he gave the year of his birth as 1790. But a list of Hudson's Bay Company personnel for 1824-1825 gives his age as twenty-seven, which would make the year about 1798.

Nearly all that is known of his early life is printed in King G. Davies, ed., *Ogden's Snake Country Journal, 1826-27*. Gervais entered the service of the North West Company before 1811, was employed in the Red River district until 1817, and was again in that district in 1818-1819. He was employed by the Hudson's Bay Company in the Ile-à-la-Crosse area during 1820-1821 and 1821-1822, and came out to the Columbia with the following outfit. As a free man, he set out from Flathead Post on Dec. 20, 1824, with Peter Skene Ogden's first Snake Country Expedition. After the wholesale desertion of Ogden's men at the Weber River, May 24-25, 1825, Gervais left the party on the twenty-ninth, one of the few who paid his debt. The fact of desertion is confirmed by two Hudson's Bay Company records of Servants' Accounts, one of which lists him as a bowsman from St. Philip, twenty-seven years of age, with ten (!) years' experience in the fur trade. The desertion is nevertheless puzzling, for Gervais was a member of Ogden's second Snake Country Expedition, which left Fort Nez Percés on Nov. 21, 1825. How and when he rejoined Ogden is not known. Ogden mentioned him in his party on Feb. 14, 1826, and a week later detached him with Finan McDonald for a separate hunt. He returned to Fort Nez Percés sometime after July 16.

Gervais was also a member of Ogden's third expedition, which left Fort Nez Percés Sept. 18, 1826. Eleven days later Ogden noted that Gervais and several others had overtaken him on this trapping tour to central and southern Oregon. On March 26, 1827, Ogden detached Gervais with a small party to trap a river, since called the Rogue, and open a communication between that quarter and Fort Vancouver. There he delivered his furs at the close of the spring hunt.

Sometime in the next year Gervais joined the Americans in the Snake country. Beckwourth refers to him as "Jarvey" in recounting events at the Bear Lake rendezvous of 1828. In the fall of 1828 Gervais probably accompanied the party which Robert Campbell and Jim Bridger took to the Crow country. Meek relates that after William L. Sublette rendezvoused with Campbell on Wind River in July 1829 Sublette started a company under his brother Milton "and two other free trappers and traders, Frapp and Jervais, to traverse the country down along the Bighorn River."

At the Wind River rendezvous in August 1830, Gervais associated himself with Fitzpatrick, Bridger, Milton Sublette, and Fraeb in organizing the Rocky Mountain Fur Company. He and Fraeb made a hunt in the Snake country, ending up at a winter camp in Cache Valley. He was back in Cache Valley in the summer of 1831. In the fall he and his partners hunted toward the Flathead country; Ferris encountered him on the Ruby River toward the end of September and at Horse Prairie with the Flathead camp on October 7. Presumably Gervais wintered with his partners on the Salmon and in the spring of 1832 trapped in the Snake country. He participated in the battle of Pierres Hole, then hunted westerly into the Snake country, as described in the sketches of Fraeb and Milton Sublette. After wintering at the forks of the Salmon, in February 1833 Gervais and Milton Sublette took another party to the Snake lands; Bonneville encountered them near the mouth of the Big Lost River on April 6 and remained in company with them much of the spring. (See the sketches of Bonneville and Sublette.)

Gervais was at Horse Creek when Robert Campbell arrived on July 5, and as seen in the sketch of Edmund T. Christy, went off as the R. M. F. Co.'s representative in a venture with Christy. Larpenteur records the departure: "On the 22nd of July Mr Jarvais started with a company of thirty men to trap in the root digers country." Very few details of this tour are known. A sketch of Franklin Bedwell printed in *History of Sonoma County*, pp. 614-617, helps out by saying that Bedwell "joined a party taking a south-westerly course to Bear river, where they camped a few days preparing buffalo meat. Going as far south as Humboldt river, the party again divided, part resolving to go to California; but some of the men becoming intoxicated, a quarrel ensued, and one man was killed. The whole party returned to Snake river. In the Spring of 1834 they went a hundred miles down Snake river, and, taking some Indians with the party, went as far west as Fort Walla Walla. Dividing into small parties, they passed several weeks in trapping. While returning, they met men coming from California with horses. . . ." (This last reference was probably to Walker's party, but compare Joe Meek's narrative, and the account owing to Stephen Meek printed in *Niles' Register*, March 25, 1837, LII, 50.) It may be supposed that Gervais reached the rendezvous with Christy June 18, 1834. Two days later Fraeb and Gervais sold out their interest in the R. M. F. Co., Gervais receiving "twenty head of horse beast, thirty beaver traps, and five hundred dollars' worth of merchandise," for which he signed by mark. Gervais and Fraeb continued in informal association through the next year in the Snake country and in the fall of 1835 came down to the states together (see the sketch of Fraeb).

When Gervais returned to the mountains is not known, but he had a child born in "Oregon" about 1838. There seems to be no record of him until the autumn of 1840. Archibald McDonald informed Dr. John McLoughlin from Fort Colvile on Jan. 5, 1841, that a Hudson's Bay Company party under Donald McLean "Near the head of the Muscell-Shell river . . . [had] the good luck to fall in with Big Jervais & 7 or 8 of his associates, of whom he obtained a good few Beaver; & for Rum, Sugar & Coffee could have got more . . ." (Letter in Provincial Archives of British Columbia). Gervais next emerges out of obscurity in the summer of 1843, when the missionary to the Flatheads, Father Gregory Mengarini, mentions encountering "a Frenchman named Gervais with his family," apparently on the sources of the Missouri. Gervais gave Mengarini information on early Christianity among the Flatheads; see Gilbert J. Garraghan, *The Jesuits of the Middle United States*, II, 238, 241.

Gervais probably remained among the Flatheads and Nez Percés until after the Whitman massacre. Robert Newell's memorandum respecting the Cayuse War relates that on March 4, 1848, "Jarvis and Some Nezperces with the Yellow Serpent come to camp," and next day, "The Indians with Mesrs. [William] Craig & Jarvis left for the Nezpece Camp . . . and is to return tomorrow with all the warriors 250 men." These events were crucial in the resolution of the war. Gervais settled on a claim at Oregon City in November 1850 and became a naturalized citizen Sept. 8, 1851. The documents supporting his Donation Land Claim recite that he married Mary Gervais in 1846 (sic), "Flat Head Country of Oregon," and that she died Jan. 7, 1851, leaving five children. The 1850 census return for Marion County, Oregon, reports the family to consist of J. B. Gervais, aged sixty-eight, born in Canada; Celestine Gervais, aged seventeen, born in Oregon Territory; Fresine Gervais, aged twelve, born in Oregon; Rosalie, aged ten, born in Oregon; Abraham, aged six, born in Oregon; Lizette, aged three, born in Oregon.

Jean Baptiste Gervais probably died in 1859 or 1860. He appears on the Marion County assessment roll in 1858, and as a signer of a petition to allow half-breeds to vote dated Jan. 7, 1859. He should not be confused with Joseph Gervais, a settler on "French Prairie" in the Willamette Valley, who came out to Oregon with the overland Astorians of 1811-1812 and remained there the rest of his life.

WILLIAM GORDON

Several William Gordons figure in Western history, and it is difficult to disentangle them. One man of this name, an Ohioan who became a trapper, established himself in New Mexico in the 1830's, came to California in 1841, and settled north of San Pablo Bay, where he died in 1876 at the age of seventy-five. The William Gordon who concerns us is thought to have been born in Virginia, but in selling a Negro boy to Kenneth Mackenzie on Dec. 27, 1828, he described himself as "of St Louis, Missouri (formerly of Tennessee)." In 1823 Joshua Pilcher spoke of him as "a young gentleman." His first documentary record is provided by Stella M. Drumm, who says that he was in St. Louis in 1818, when he joined John C. Sullivan, surveyor, in running the northern Indian boundary in Illinois. In November of the same year, she adds, Gordon and two other traders were arrested for committing "an affray" on a night watchman.

According to his own statement in 1831, Gordon first went to the Rockies to engage in the fur trade in 1822 as a clerk with Immell and Jones. He survived the Immell-Jones massacre on the Yellowstone in May 1823, participated in the Arikara Campaign during July and August, joined Angus McDonald in burning the Arikara villages, and in the fall of 1823 went with Charles Keemle from Fort Recovery to the Crow country to press the Missouri Fur Company's claim to a share in the trade, in rivalry with Jedediah Smith. With Keemle, in the summer of 1824, Gordon returned to the settlements by way of the Big Horn, Yellowstone, and Missouri, robbed by the Crows en route. Next year, in connection with the Atkinson-O'Fallon expedition, he witnessed the Ponca treaty on June 9 and the Sioux treaty on June 22. Afterward he carried an express from Fort Kiowa to the Mandan villages, then continued with the expedition until it reached Fort Kiowa on its return, September 9. He disembarked there, "intending to stay." James Kennerly at Fort Atkinson has a reference to him on March 27, 1826: "Mr Gordon & Pilcher started down today Gordon goes to St. Louis." In October 1826 Benjamin O'Fallon unavailingly recommended that he be appointed subagent for the Sioux on the Missouri after George H. Kennerly resigned.

Gordon entered the service of the American Fur Company, trading mostly in the Sioux country. To judge from a letter Kenneth Mackenzie wrote Pierre Chouteau on Jan. 2, 1829, he was at Fort Tecumseh (Pierre) at the beginning of the year, but on May 5, 1830, Mackenzie reported him trapping with four or five men on Powder River. On Aug. 23, 1830, his presence at Fort Tecumseh with "other clerks of the company" was recorded. Soon after, on September 8, he set out for St. Louis with the subagent, Maj. Jonathan L. Bean, and a party of twenty-one Indians, mostly Yankton Sioux. On Jan. 18, 1831, the Fort Tecumseh journal notes the return from St. Louis of "Mr. Gordon and lady," and their departure on February 10 "for Mr. Laidlaw's establishment on the Grand Cheyenne river." His father-in-law, a Yankton, is mentioned on March 1. (According to Doane Robinson, Gordon was known in his time as Pegleg Gordon, and in 1918 "Joseph Gordon, a mixed blood grandson," was "a respected citizen of Burke, South Dakota.") The Fort Tecumseh journal on March 26, 1831, remarks Gordon's arrival from above with horses for the party being sent to the Rockies under Etienne Provost to supply William H. Vanderburgh; and on April 2 notes further: "Gordon left us to join the men who left here yesterday with horses. He conducts them to Cherry river, where it is expected they will fall in with Provost."

If we have the right Gordon, as indicated by Anderson's giving his name in the Journal as "W. Gordon," we might infer that it was in 1831 that Gordon had the long wait with one Brown near Willow Spring. But in a letter to the Secretary of War, St. Louis, Oct. 3, 1831, Gordon says: "I left the head of the Colorado of the West where it issues from the Rocky Mountains on the 18th of July last and arrived at St. Louis the last of August." There could have been no long pause when homeward bound, and time for misadventure on the outbound journey is narrowed by a document in the Sublette Papers, an order for $32.25 given Gordon by Henry Fraeb on Green River July 9, 1831.

In St. Louis on Oct. 29, 1831, William Clark gave Gordon a two-year license to trade at various localities on the Missouri and its tributaries, from the Niobrara to Cherry River. According to the license, he had twenty men employed and a capital of $1,145.61. If he went up the Missouri this autumn, he did not remain. We assume that he was the William Gordon who commanded in the Black Hawk War in the summer of 1832 what is variously described as a "company of spies" and a "company of mounted volunteers—part of the 1st Regiment of the 3rd Brigade, Illinois Militia."

Later in 1832 Gordon bought an interest in the fur trading venture of J. B. D. Valois and P. N. Leclerc. When J. P. Cabanné made a "citizen's arrest" of Leclerc for carrying liquor into the Indian country, Gordon joined his partners in writing bitter protests to the government, dated St. Louis, Jan. 11 and March 2, Jefferson City, May 19, and St. Louis, Aug. 12, 1833. In the spring of 1833 Clark hired Gordon to carry out certain duties relating to the Indians, and this work preoccupied him for several years. On April 14, 1835, the Commissioner approved Clark's arrangement "with Major William Gordon for the Survey of the Sac & Fox lands" under the treaty of September 1832. A year later, on May 4, 1836, Clark wrote the Secretary: "Maj. Gordon having declined the appointment of Sub Agent for the Chippeways, I have . . . appointed him on behalf of the U. States to lay off and divide the land reserved by the treaty of 1824 for the use of the half breeds of the Sacs & Foxes. . . ." The day before this letter was written, Clark had granted W. R. McPherson a license to trade "at the Dirt Lodge on the Desmoines river, with the Sacs & Foxes." One man was employed, with a capital of $558.55. Since Gordon was the surety, obviously McPherson was his employee, hired to carry on trade while Gordon engaged in government work nearby.

We have found no record of Gordon during the next few years. The last definite mention of him might indicate that he had acquired a white wife. T. H. Harvey, Superintendent of Indian Affairs at St. Louis, wrote Agent Andrew Drips on Feb. 21, 1844: "Mrs Gordon the wife of Capt William Gordon has applied at this office to know if she could obtain any information in regard to her husband who went on a traping trip to the upper Missouri about eighteen months ago" (Drips Papers, Bancroft Library). Frank Triplett says that Gordon, "the laughing philosopher of the trappers," was killed by lightning while crossing the Yellowstone, but we have small faith in this story. A trapper named Madison Gordon was in the mountains in 1839; so far as we have ascertained, he is first mentioned in the Chouteau account books in 1834.

JOHN GRAY

John Gray (or Grey), whose name appears in Hudson's Bay Company records of 1824-1825 alternatively as Ignace Hatchioraquasha, is characterized as an Iroquois half-breed of American ancestry. Investigations by Mr. James Anderson present the possibility that his father was William L. Gray, a Revolutionary soldier from Cambridge, New York, one of the deputies of the Seven Nations and interpreter under the treaty of May 31, 1796, who settled at St. Regis with an Iroquois wife. Since in 1840 Gray's age was given as between forty and fifty, he must have been born in the 1790's. It has not been established when he traveled to western Canada. He took along his Iroquois wife, Marianne Naketiehou of St. Regis.

Gray first appears in the Rocky Mountain fur trade as one of Alexander Ross's Snake Country Expedition, which left Flathead Post Feb. 10, 1824. He was already something of a leader, and Ross found him difficult. Ross provides the interesting detail that Gray could play the fiddle. After many vicissitudes, he got back to Flathead Post with Ross on Nov. 26, 1824. Next month, with his wife and children, Gray joined the new Snake Country Expedition, led by Peter Skene Ogden. The brigade made its way south to the Weber River in present Utah, where on May 24-25, 1825, twenty-three of the British party deserted. Both Ogden and his assistant William Kittson viewed Gray as the ringleader.

Unlike some of the French Canadians, Gray never went back to the British service. At Ashley's rendezvous with his men near Henrys Fork of the Green on July 1, 1825, he mentions Gray in association with the American trapper Johnson Gardner. On April 9, 1826, on the Snake below the mouth of the Portneuf, Ogden met "a Party of Americans and some of our deserters of last Year 28 in all"; and next day Ogden wrote: "From what I could observe our deserters are already tired of their New Masters and from their manner I am of opinion will soon return to their old employers they promise to reach the Flat Heads this Fall. . . ." John Work, trading for the Hudson's Bay Company in the Flathead country the ensuing summer, heard that a party of Americans had been there, and on Aug. 24, 1826, had more direct information: "A party of the F. Heads had fallen in with some of the Snake deserters and some Americans, two of the deserters, J. Grey and Jacques accompanied them to some of the Camps and Grey presented the two chief Gros Pied and Grand Visage with some tobacco and a little scarlet as from the chief of the American party Ashly, whom they said wished to see the Indians, and that he was off for a large quantity of supplies.—A few F. Heads, Nezperces and 2 Snakes in all 22 have gone off to see them." This might indicate that Gray was among the Flatheads during the spring and induced an Indian delegation to accompany him to the summer rendezvous of Ashley and his men in Cache Valley.

Gray is lost to view for a while, but was doubtless among the Iroquois who accompanied William L. Sublette and David E. Jackson on the fall hunt of 1826 to Yellowstone Lake and the sources of the Missouri, ending up at the winter camp in Cache Valley. No information appears respecting the spring hunt of 1827, but after the summer rendezvous Campbell "took charge of the Iroquois, and others of the party" and made a hunt in the Flathead country. On the sources of the Jefferson the principal Iroquois chief, "Old Pierre" Tivanitagon, was killed by Blackfeet, in consequence of which most of Campbell's party, including the Iroquois, wintered with the Flatheads. However, they probably accompanied Campbell to the rendezvous at Bear Lake next summer.

By the summer of 1830 Gray may have become the acknowledged leader of the Iroquois trappers. Warren Ferris records that in September 1830 one of Drips and Fontenelle's detachments encountered on Smiths Fork of the Bear "a party of Iroquois," who informed them that Smith, Jackson & Sublette had sold out to the new Rocky Mountain Fur Company in July at Wind River. "From that place parties were sent out in various directions, amongst which was one led by Fraeb and Jarvis, consisting of twenty two hired men, and ten free Iroquois, with their wives and children—which departed to hunt on the waters of the Columbia. The Iroquois, however, became dissatisfied with some of the measures adopted by the leaders of the party, and separated from them to hunt the tributaries of Bear River. . . . [Michel] Robidoux engaged three of them, and the others promised to meet us in Cache Valley, after the hunting season."

Apparently Gray and his Iroquois again hunted in the Snake country in the spring and fall of 1831. On March 5, 1832, Ferris, encamped on the Snake near the mouth of the Blackfoot, says that John Gray and David Montgomery set out for Cache Valley to learn whether Drips had got back from the states with supplies. Five days later "two of our hunters brought in Gray . . . whom they found half dead in the cedars, near Portneuf." Montgomery had been killed and Gray wounded, when the two were attacked by Blackfeet near the head of the south fork of the Portneuf. "When Gray reached his own lodge," Ferris relates, "his mangled frozen feet were examined; they were swollen to twice their natural size, and were quite black; however, at the expiration of two months, he was quite well, and the circumstances of his so narrow escape almost forgotten."

An episode said to have occurred in the spring of 1832, which would have been after the above affair, is related by Joe Meek. He tells of Bridger and Milton Sublette going with the R. M. F. Co. brigade to Bear River. "A Rockway Chief, named Gray, and seven of his people, had accompanied the camp . . . in the capacity of trappers. But during the sojourn on Bear River, there was a quarrel in camp on account of some indignity, real or fancied, which had been offered to the chief's daughter, and in the affray Gray stabbed Sublette so severely that it was thought he must die." Milton had to be left behind, Meek looking after him through a forty-five-day convalescence. This tale is documented by a footnote in William Drummond Stewart's *Edward Warren* regarding one of the plot turns in that novel: "John Gray stabbed Milton Sublette in the back, in a similar scene got up on purpose, the blow happily was not fatal." Elsewhere Stewart says of Gray: "This Iroquois was a most successful trapper, but a drunken and treacherous man; who, however, had this vast merit in the eyes of a trading company, that he drank almost all the price of his beaver in brandy, at thirty-two dollars a gallon."

According to Ferris, Gray's Hole was called "after John Gray, a half breed Iroquois, who discovered it some years since." Grays River was also named for him, as was the stream now called Willow Creek. Ferris provides the only clues to Gray's movements during the hunt of 1832-1833 when he says on June 7, 1833, that he went ahead of his camp "to ascertain if any of our long absent friends, who left us at 'Pierre's Hole,' with John Gray nearly a year since, had arrived at 'Horse creek.' . . ." Ferris found Gray, along with Joseph R. Walker, at Fort Bonneville. Ferris describes Gray as "a herculean trapper [who] has fought several duels with [grizzly bears], in which he has thus far been victorious, though generally at the expense of a gun, which he usually manages to break in the conflict."

Anderson mentions Gray at the 1834 rendezvous. The next reference to him is by Fontenelle in a letter sent up to Drips from Fort William, August 1, 1835: "John Gray & myself have not settled any of our affairs—it is left to you & him   his outfit is to be paid half by him & the other half belongs to the company   the outfit is to be charged at cost adding one hundred per cent on the same—If there has been any Horses lost by him or his Party (that is the Horses which we furnished) he is to loose the one half also   as regards his arrangement with [Michel?] Robidoux, I do not know any thing about, I leave it to you to fix—He takes up [to the rendezvous] some *Beans Corn Meal* & Pumpkins—which are sent up by my woman for yours. . . ."

Notwithstanding the intimation in Fontenelle's letter, Gray came down from the mountains in the fall of 1835, along with Fraeb, Gervais, Newell, Ferris, and other experienced trappers, as mentioned by William L. Sublette in a letter to Robert Campbell. Gray now established himself among the small colony of French Canadians and half-breed Indians near the mouth of the Kansas River. The earliest reference to him at this place is the confirmation of marriage of his daughter Charlotte to Benjamin Legauthière on July 18, 1836. On March 19, 1837, his daughter Agnes was baptized at the same place, being then twelve years old. The 1840 census found the household of John Gray to consist of two males under five, one aged five to ten, two aged ten to fifteen, and one aged forty to fifty (Gray himself). Females included one aged five to ten, one aged ten to fifteen, one aged fifteen to twenty, one aged forty to fifty.

In 1841 Gray traveled out to Green River as a hunter for a young Englishman named Romaine, who accompanied the party of Father De Smet. A number of references to Gray occur in the diaries and reminiscences of the Bartleson party, as well as in De Smet's letters. Gray's name, seen on Independence Rock by Matthew Field in 1843, may have been carved there July 6, 1841. That day Bidwell says: "John Gray and Romaine were sent on to Green river to see if there were any Trappers at the rendezvous, and then return to the company with the intelligence." A week later, farther up the Sweetwater, the emigrants "met John Gray and Romaine returning from Green river, they found no person at the rendezvous, on Green river, nor any game ahead, it was therefore thought best to lay in more meat, while we were in the vicinity of the Buffalo." On July 15 Bidwell adds: "As many of the company had articles of traffic which they wished to dispose of at Green river, a subscription was raised to recompense any who would go and find the trappers. John Gray started in pursuit of them, while the company marched on slowly waiting his return. . . ." On the evening of July 22, by which time the Bartleson party had reached the Big Sandy Gray returned, "having found Trapp's [Fraeb's] company . . . now encamped on Green river about 8 miles distant. Gray had suffered much in overtaking the Trappers, his mule gave out, there being no water for a great distance, and he, himself, was so much reduced by hunger and thirst that he was unable to walk, he was therefore compelled to crawl upon his hands and feet, and at last came up with the Company in the most forlorn situation imaginable—if they had been another half mile farther, he never could have reached them."

The emigrants went on to Green River and traded with the mountain men for two days. On July 25 Bidwell records: "Left the rendezvous this morning, 6 of the company, viz. John Gray, Peyton, Frye, Rogers, Jones and Romaine, started to return to the United States." Their arrival is recorded in an Independence letter of Sept. 21, 1841, printed in *Niles' Register*, Oct. 16, 1841, which mentions that the returning party was attacked "six or eight times, but not seriously injured." A remark by Father De Smet indicates that Gray had been accompanied this summer by his wife and "a little girl but one year old."

Mr. James Anderson, who has gathered considerable information respecting Gray's children, quotes John Calvin McCoy to the effect that Gray, a "half-breed Scotch and Iroquois," was killed by the wife of Pierre Perrault, one of the settlers at Kansas. This was prior to 1845. Gray's wife is pictured as a woman of strong religious inclinations who "spoke English imperfectly, but had a good command of French and her own dialect. She was strong and fearless and at the approach of strangers carried a large stick which she held hoisted in a threatening manner until she was sure of the friendly intentions of the invaders."

MOSES ("BLACK") HARRIS

According to the St. Louis *Democrat*, June 12, 1844, Harris was a native of Union County, South Carolina. Apparently he first ascended the Missouri River in 1822, for James Clyman referred in 1844 to his twenty-two years of experience.

It seems probable that he was one of two men named Harris who left Major Henry's party on the Yellowstone to descend the Missouri late in 1823, arriving at Fort Atkinson December 18. Possibly he went to the Rockies and back with William H. Ashley in 1824-1825, though the only evidence of this is the confused account by Beckwourth. He may instead have been with the Atkinson-O'Fallon expedition. Beckwourth more convincingly identifies him as one of the party (led by Jedediah Smith) that left St. Louis for the Rockies at the end of October 1825 but had to winter at the Pawnee villages on the Republican River and on the Platte. Apparently Harris and Beckwourth carried the word to Ashley that Smith required more pack animals.

In the spring of 1826 Harris was one of Ashley's party that joined Smith on the Platte. According to Campbell, Ashley then "sent off Smith and Harris to the trappers in the Mountains, to arrange in advance for a rendezvous." He remained in the mountains, accompanied Sublette and Jackson on the fall hunt of 1826, then made a winter journey to the states with William L. Sublette, as described in the sketch of the latter. Harris may have kept in company with Sublette, all the next year. Beckwourth tells of his arrival at Bear River, ahead of the caravan, in company with "my old friend Portuleuse," but one cannot be sure whether Beckwourth is referring to the spring of 1828, which is his context, or that of 1827.

Black Harris is next definitely mentioned in the fall of 1829 as one of the brigade Smith and Sublette led in a large circuit around the present Yellowstone Park. From Wind River on Christmas Day Harris set out with Sublette on another winter journey to the states, reaching St. Louis February 11. After this he is lost to sight for a while. He appears to have been in the Fort Union area in 1831 and may have returned to the mountains that spring with William O. Fallon in the supply party which Etienne Provost took out to William Henry Vanderburgh. George Nidever tells of encountering on the Platte in May 1832 "a trader by the name of O'Felon, an Irishman, who . . . was accompanied by a trapper by the name of Harris, and had 6 or 7 Mexicans to attend to his mules and packs." As seen in the sketch of Fallon, this little party had visited the New Mexican settlements during the winter.

From the Pierres Hole rendezvous of 1832, sixteen free trappers, including Harris, Zenas Leonard, and George Nidever, started out with the party of Fraeb and Milton Sublette, but according to John Ball they diverged west of the Portneuf on August 12. They made a fall hunt into the Humboldt area, north to the Snake, east to the Bear, south to the Great Salt Lake, and east to Green River. Here they prepared to winter, but Crows ran off some of their horses. They regained the horses at the Crow camp on Stinking Fork of the Big Horn and wintered there. In the spring of 1833 the party hunted in the direction of the Platte and the Laramie, but ran afoul of the Arikaras, who ran off their horses as well as those of Bridger and Fraeb. The free trappers footed it to the rendezvous on Green River. Wyeth says in a letter of July 18, 1833: "Harris party now in hand 7 packs Beaver and are now on foot."

Thus Harris was present when George Holmes was bitten by a rabid wolf, one of the memorable events of the 1833 rendezvous. It appears that in the fall of 1833 Harris and other free trappers made an independent hunt in the Crow country, for at the mouth of the Yellowstone on October 5 Robert Campbell speaks of the arrival from Fort Cass on the Big Horn of two men "who had started on a hunting expedition with Harris but the party broke up without doing anything." By November 13 Harris was in Fitzpatrick's camp on Hams Fork, preparing to set out for the states in company with Dr. Benjamin Harrison. (Holmes is supposed to have gone along and to have died during the journey.) In his letter of November 13 to Milton Sublette, Fitzpatrick said that Harris was "going after a small Equipmt you will, if you alow him to take up make terms with him about it he will be Owing us Considerable." However, Harris came back to the mountains with William L. Sublette, presumably in an engaged capacity. Anderson refers to him on May 29 and again on July 23, the latter entry showing that he did not go back to the states with Sublette in 1834 but leaving it uncertain whether he remained in the mountains with Bridger or came back with Fontenelle.

Harris is next recorded as one of the caravan of 1836 with which the Whitmans traveled; Narcissa mentions having had for tea on May 30 "Capts. Fitzpatrick, Stewart, [and] Major Harris." In a letter written after reaching the Columbia, Marcus Whitman said, "Major Harris is to go to St. Louis and return to Fort Hall this fall," apparently in connection with some project by which the Hudson's Bay Company would supply the mountain men.

Whenever Harris may have come back to Missouri, he was one of the caravan of 1837, and thus attracted the attention of Alfred Jacob Miller. One of Miller's sketches purports to represent Harris, and Miller relates several anecdotes about him: "Harris (nicknamed Black) told us at the camp fire that . . . he carried with him a supply of dried meat so as to avoid making fires, which would have infallibly betrayed him. On being asked if he had not felt lonesome sometimes on these solitary excursions?—he laughed as if it was a good joke—'never knew in his life what it was to feel lonesome, or low spirited'. . . . This Black Harris always created a sensation at the camp fire, being a capital *raconteur*, and having had as many perilous adventures as any man probably in the mountains. He was of wiry form, made up of bone and muscle, with a face apparently composed of tan leather and whip cord, finished off with a peculiar blue-black tint, as if gunpowder had been burnt into his face. In riding expresses for the Fur Co^y, in which he had no equal;—he told us that in running the gauntlet among hostile Indians, he laid by in the day for sleep, and rode hard all night. At times, he would raise the envy of the Trappers by recounting a discovery he had made somewhere in the Black hills of a 'putrified' (petrified) Forest, and wind up with some horrible stories of butcheries among the Indians in which he bore a hand."

From Fort William, Harris rode ahead of the caravan on express. William H. Gray noted his arrival at the rendezvous on June 30, 1837. On July 13 Harris gave Gray an interesting list of "names of streams on the East and West sides of the mountains" from Independence to beyond the Red Buttes.

Harris again accompanied the caravan of 1838, captained by Andrew Drips;

Myra Eells mentions "Major Harris" as one of the company at the crossing of the Kansas River April 28, again on approaching Fort William May 26 (Harris having proceeded to the fort "some days" before), and at the rendezvous July 4. He had gone on express from Wind River to leave word at Green River that the rendezvous would be on Wind River instead. ("Come to Popoazua . . . . you will find plenty trade, whiskey, and white women.") Myra Eells says: "Major Harris comes to us again; says that nine days out of eleven it rained and snowed constantly since he left us, and that the snow was twelve or fourteen inches deep in the mountains."

In 1839 Harris was commander of the caravan, as recorded in the diaries of Asahel Munger and F. A. Wislizenus; the latter speaks of Harris as "a mountaineer without special education, but with five sound senses, that he well knew how to use." The company arrived at Fort William June 14. Apparently Harris continued in charge all the way to the rendezvous near Horse Creek, which was reached July 4. He was back in St. Louis by October 31.

Harris accompanied the caravan of 1840 to the final rendezvous on Green River. Robert Newell says that some missionaries came along, whom he engaged to pilot with their wagons to Fort Hall, as a result of which Harris "shot at me about 70 or 80 yards but done no damage only to him self." In a letter written in 1867, Newell explained that one of the missionaries "had made a partial bargain with a man who came up with Captain Dripps . . . who was known in the mountains as Black Harris, to pilot them to Fort Hall." Enraged when Newell undercut his extortionate price, Harris took a shot at him, which "was close but a miss. I wheeled and galloped toward Harris who ran and hid in a thicket, and was denounced by all in camp—and Captain Drips told him that had the ball struck me he would have hung him." The incident reflects the demoralization of the fur trade referred to in the sketch of Newell.

Harris is next heard of in Independence on June 4, 1841, when he wrote a letter to Thornton Grimsley evincing interest in a filibustering scheme to take California; possibly he had intended to go to California with the Bartleson party but had changed his mind. In this letter Harris spoke of having been "20 years in the mountains." He was in St. Louis March 18 and Nov. 1, 1842, between which dates he was on the Missouri in the service of the Upper Missouri Outfit. The Chouteau account books mention him between January and July 25, 1843, but yield no information as to his whereabouts, except that he was in St. Louis on the latter date. The New Orleans *Picayune* of Jan. 7, 1844, reports him at Independence, "preparing for a great expedition to Oregon next spring," and in March alludes to a rebuttal to Thomas Farnham he had published in an Independence paper. James Clyman's journal places him at Westport on May 15, 1844, and thereafter mentions his service as guide to the Oregon emigrants who started that month from Independence, captained by Nathaniel Ford.

The last five years of Harris' life are comparatively well documented. In July 1845 he joined Elijah White and others in the Willamette Valley in an unsuccessful effort to find a pass across the Cascade Mountains. The following month he set out with White for the states, but left the party near The Dalles. In October 1845 Harris participated in relief efforts in behalf of the emigrants who had attempted the disastrous Malheur River cutoff. Early in 1846, with six others, he sought unsuccessfully to find a good pass at the head of the Willamette Valley, then joined the party of road-hunters who worked out the Applegate Cutoff to the Humboldt River. In December, back in Oregon, he assisted in relief activities for emigrants who had taken the new cutoff.

On May 5, 1847, Harris headed east, again via the Applegate Cutoff. The westbound Mormon pioneers encountered him at Pacific Spring on June 26, 1847, and Orson Pratt noted that "from here he intended to act as a guide to some of the emigrant companies, if they wished to employ him." Harris continued in the Mormon camp until June 28, selling "many of his peltries." A few days later John E. Howell, eastbound from Oregon, encountered him in the Bear River Valley near the mouth of Smiths Fork. It was in this area, on July 20, that he fell in with the party of Gen. S. W. Kearny, eastbound from California. Apparently Harris was employed as guide, for Capt. H. S. Turner writes: "Left the valley of Bear River and the Oregon road at starting this morning—being conducted by 'Black Harris', an old mountaineer who promised to take us a better and nearer route—fell in the emigrant road again at Ham's fork of Green river, having had a most laborious days march and gained but little in distance—25 miles—cool."

As Kearny already had a guide in William Fallon, he had no need of Harris' services east of South Pass. Harris offered himself to the party of Com. Robert F. Stockton, which came east from California later in the summer. The St. Joseph (Mo.) *Gazette*, Dec. 3, 1847, in remarking that Harris would remain there during the winter, said he had acted as pilot "to the company that escorted Commodore Stockton across the plains, and arrived at St. Joseph with that company." The *Gazette* understood that Harris intended returning to Oregon in the spring of 1848 and recommended that emigrants employ him as guide. One way or another, sometime in the next year Harris got as far west as Fort Laramie. He accompanied an express to Fort Pierre, which set out from Fort Laramie about March 10, 1849. On April 1, with two others, he started down the Missouri in a canoe, arriving at St. Joseph on April 18, as reported in the *Gazette* of April 20. Harris went on to Independence and was employed as pilot by the Turner & Allen "Pioneer Line," which hoped to establish a sort of overland stage to California in the midst of the gold rush. While preparing to depart, Harris was stricken with cholera and died at Independence on May 6, 1849.

INSILLAH (Flathead Chief)

The name of this Flathead (Salish) chief is given by Anderson as Insillah, by others Insulá, Insala, Incilla, Ensyla, etc. His name signifies "the war eagle's plume," or "the war cap, with the war eagle's feathers in it," as Anderson variously says (by others rendered "Red Feather"). He was also known to the whites as the Little Chief, and in the literature of the fur trade he is sometimes confused with Ma-wo-ma, the Little Chief of the Snakes.

Gustavus Sohon, who made a portrait of Insillah on April 28, 1854 (now in the Smithsonian Institution and reproduced in the American Heritage *Book of Indians*, p. 326), estimated his age at that time as seventy; so he may have been born about 1784. Under the name Red Feather he can be traced back as far as 1825; on July 1 of that year, on the sources of the Missouri, William Kittson of Ogden's Snake Country Expedition referred to him as a good-looking Indian who commanded the camp of seventy lodges in the absence of the Flathead chief La Breche. A year later John Work commented on the presence of three Flathead chiefs, La Breche, Gros Pied, and Grand Visage at Flathead Post, and mentioned that Grune and Red Feather were in the Bitterroot Valley. A work attributed to Peter Skene Ogden, *Traits of American-Indian Life and Character*, devotes a chapter to "The Red Feather, Flathead Chief." After describing the character and exploits of the Red Feather (a portrait agreeing in all respects except height with what is known of Insillah), the narrative ends with an account of his being burned to death in a prairie fire set by Blackfeet. Since such an event in Ogden's context would necessarily have occurred in 1825 and Red Feather was alive after that date, it may be that the narrative in the *Traits* is in some part fictional.

In August 1833 Warren A. Ferris gives a considerable account of "a little hardy old veteran, the Chief," whom Ferris' editor, Paul C. Phillips, identifies with "Insula," but since Ferris lays stress on the man's age, calling him "the old chief," and "the venerable chief," the identification is doubtful. Insillah first appears in American annals of the fur trade in Anderson's Diary and Narrative; see entries for June 17, 1834, et seq. Insillah is next mentioned at the Green River rendezvous of August 1835. In a council with Samuel Parker and Marcus Whitman, he related how he had come with some of his people to meet the "man near to God." Afterward he furnished Parker a horse to help him reach the Columbia.

L. B. Palladino, *Indian and White in the Northwest*, pp. 22-24, mistakenly says that the Flatheads and their "'Little Chief and Great Warrior,' Insulá," were not satisfied with the looks or message of the Protestant missionaries of 1835, wanting Black Robes instead, and did not come to the rendezvous in 1836. Flatheads were present there, but whether Insillah was among them has not been established.

By 1834 Insillah had developed a warm relationship with some of the principal mountain men, in particular Robert Campbell and Thomas Fitzpatrick. Some fur trader provided the account of Insillah published in Thomas L. McKenney and James Hall, *The Indian Tribes of North America*, II, 278: "A friend of the writer saw [a] feat performed by Incilla, the present chief of the tribe, on the plains east of the Rocky Mountains. The chief threw himself upon the back of a wild horse recently taken, holding in one hand a small flag, and in the other a hoop covered with a skin, after the fashion of a tambourine. On being turned loose, the animal dashed off, rearing and pitching, and using the most violent exertions to disengage himself from his fearless rider, who clinging with his heels, maintained his seat, in spite of the efforts of the horse to throw him. When he wished to check the speed of the animal, he blinded him by throwing the flag across his face; while he guided him, by striking him with the tambourine, on the one side or the other of the head. This exercise he continued, scouring the plain at full speed, and directing the course of the furious steed at will, until the latter was wearied out and subdued."

In the summer of 1840, told that Father De Smet was coming to the mountains, Insillah journeyed with a band of Flatheads to meet the priest at Green River, afterward escorting him to the Flathead country. As Anderson says: "Insillah was the first convert to Christianity, by Father De Smet and called 'Michael.'" This name was given "on account of his fidelity and courage." When Father De Smet journeyed to the Flathead country again in 1841, he was met on the sources of the Missouri by the principal chiefs, including "Insula." "Long before," De Smet writes, "the Flathead warrior who is surnamed the Bravest of the Brave sent me his finest horse to Fort Hall, having strongly recommended that no one should mount him before he was presented to me. Soon after the warrior himself appeared, distinguished by his superior skill in horsemanship, and by a large red scarf, which he wore after the fashion of the Marshals of France. He is the handsomest Indian warrior of my acquaintance."

Terming Insillah the most influential among the Flatheads, "surnamed 'The Little Chief,' from the smallness of his stature," De Smet tells of marvelous exploits, and says that the Nez Percés, a nation far more numerous, "came to offer him the dignity of being their head chief," only to have him reply, "By the will of the Great Master of Life I was born among the Flatheads, and if such be his will, among the Flatheads I am determined to die." One of De Smet's fellow missionaries, Father Nicholas Point, drew a striking portrait of "Insula or Red Feather. Michel. Great Chief and brave among the Flat-heads"; it is reproduced in De Smet's *Oregon Missions and Travels over the Rocky Mountains, in 1845-46,* opp. p. 273; Insillah is depicted wearing a cross, but no headdress.

In his reminiscences Granville Stuart recalls that in 1855 when Gov. Isaac Stevens proposed to treat with the Flatheads for cession of their land, they were divided into three groups. "Chief Michael lived with the Kootenais on the head-waters of the Columbia and north of Flathead lake, Alexander with the Pend d'Oreilles were south of the lake and in the Jocko valley while Victor, chief of the Flatheads and hereditary chief over all, claimed for his home the beautiful valley of the Bitter Root." None of the chiefs was willing to leave his home, though agreeable to ceding the lands of the others.

Father Adrian Hoecken wrote Father De Smet from "Flathead Camp in the Blackfeet Country," Oct. 18, 1855: "Among our dear Flatheads, Michael Insula, or Red Feather, or as he is commonly called on account of his small stature, 'The Little Chief,' is a remarkable instance of the power which the Church has of developing the most amiable virtues in the fierce Indian. He united in his person the greatest bravery with the tenderest piety and gentlest manners. Known amid his warriors by the red feather which he wears, his approach is enough to put to flight the prowling bands of Crows and Blackfeet, that have frequently infested the Flathead territory. He is well known and much beloved by the whites, who have had occasion to deal with him, as a man of sound judgment, strict integrity, and one on whose fidelity they can implicitly rely. A keen discerner of the characters of men, he loves to speak especially of those whites, distinguished for their fine qualities, that have visited him, and often mentions with pleasure the sojourn among them of Colonel Robert Campbell, of St. Louis, and of Major Fitzpatrick, whom he adopted, in accordance with Indian ideas of courtesy, as his brothers. He has preserved all his first fervor of devotion, and now, as when you knew him, one can hardly ever enter his wigwam in the morning or evening without finding him with his rosary in his hands, absorbed in prayer. He cherishes a most affectionate remembrance of you and of the day he was baptized. . . . The Kalispel chief Alexander, Michael Insula and the other Flathead chieftains, the leaders of the Kootenai and Flat-Bow bands, and all our neophytes, beg to be remembered in your good prayers—they, on their part, never forget to pray for you."

Father Hoecken again wrote to De Smet from "Mission of the Flatheads," April 15, 1857: "The package destined for Michael Insula, the '*Little Chief*,' lies here for the present. . . . The good man is abroad on a hunting excursion; but we expect him back in a few days. I doubt not that he will be very sensible to these marks of friendship, or, as he usually expresses it, 'these marks of fraternity.' He set out from here, when he had harvested the grain he had sowed. Always equally good, equally happy, a fervent Christian, he is daily advancing in virtue and in perfection. He has a young son, Louis Michael, whom he teaches to call me *papa*. It is a real pleasure to him to be able to speak of your Reverence and of his two adopted brothers, Messrs. Campbell and Fitzpatrick [the latter now three years dead]. I will give him the packet directly after his return. . . ." Father Hoecken added as a postscript to this letter: "Michael, the Little Chief, has arrived. I presented him the gracious gift of Colonel Campbell. He was astonished that the colonel should think of him, and was much moved at this mark of attachment. Then he cited a long list of kindred, dead since his last interview with Colonel Campbell [in 1832 or 1833], and entertained me at length with the great number of Americans that he had seen annually passing Fort Hall. He told me with what solicitude and anxiety he sought his friends among these successive multitudes, and when at length he could not discover him, he believed that he was dead." (These letters of Father Hoecken are quoted from *Life, Letters and Travels of Father Pierre Jean De Smet, S. J. 1801-1873*, ed. Hiram Martin Chittenden and Alfred Talbot Richardson, IV, 1231-1232, 1236, 1245.)

Major John Owen recounts in his diary on April 13, 1861, a talk with Victor, head chief of the Flatheads, then adds: "The Kootenay [Indians] I have not Yet been able to see. The Chief Michelle has been over in the Kootenay Country the past two Years It is the impression that he does not intend locating with his people on the Jocko reservation." In footnoting this entry, Paul C. Phillips says: "Chief Michelle was probably the Flathead chief variously known as Insula, Red Feather, and Little Chief; christened Michael by Father De Smet. . . . According to Duncan McDonald he was one half Nez Percé and one half Flathead. He lived part of the time with the Flatheads and part of the time with the Pend O'reilles. He was killed near Milk River in October, 1860, by Crees and Assiniboines. At the time he was killed he was living with the Kootenais and Pend O'Reilles." If Insillah was killed in October 1860, it is singular that the news had not reached his tribesmen by April 1861.

KENTUCK (Nez Percé Indian)

Anderson introduces this Nez Percé to history and provides most of our personal data concerning him, including the information that his nickname resulted from "his continual endeavours to sing 'the hunters of Kentucky.'" He was known as Kentuck even among his own people, Anderson says, though called The Bull's Head in his own language. Anderson does not include him in his lists of Nez Percé chiefs.

In August 1835, when Samuel Parker and Marcus Whitman counciled with the Nez Percés at the Green River rendezvous, they agreed that Parker should go with the Indians to Fort Walla Walla. In consequence, Parker says: "They selected one of their principal young men for my particular assistant, as long as I should have need of him, who was called Kentuc." After reaching Fort Walla Walla, Oct. 6, 1835, Parker separated from the Nez Percés to visit the lower Columbia. He came back up the river next spring, and on May 15, 1836, commented: "Kentuc, the Indian who attended me so faithfully on my outward route, came to me anxious to describe the different manner in which he regarded the worship of the two chiefs, Charlie and Teutàcus. He said Charlie prayed with his lips, but Teutàcus prayed with his heart." Parker gave Kentuck letters to be carried to the rendezvous, having decided to return home by sea.

Marcus Whitman picks up the story in a letter written to Parker Sept. 18, 1836, after reaching Fort Vancouver: "On our arrival at Big Sandy we met the Nez Pierces ready to receive us, and learned that you were not at Rendezvoux. Kentuck gave us a letter from you. 'Rotten-bellie' (the Indian Chief) came all the way with us, and was very faithful. We employed Kentuc (your favorite Indian) but he did not do well. He was offended with Mr. [John] McLeod [Hudson's Bay Company trader], about some beaver trading which he made with a Diggar Indian, and gave him his old robe, for five beaver skins; the Diggar complained and McLeod interfered; at which Kentuc left us. . . ."

In the aftermath of the Whitman massacre, Kentuck participated with many other Nez Percés in a council at Waiilatpu, March 7, 1848. The *Oregon Spectator*, April 20, 1848, quotes him as follows: "The chiefs have all spoken; I have listened, and now I wish to speak a little. I had been much with the Americans and French— they know my heart, can any one tell any thing bad of me? In war with the Blackfeet, I and my father fought with the Americans, and my father was killed there— he (pointing to Mr. [Robert] Newell) knows it. Last year I was in California, at Captain Sutter's [evidently having accompanied a party of Walla Walla Indians there in 1846], and helped Captain Fremont—not for pay, but from a good heart. I came home, and heard the Doctor was killed! We heard that the whites were told, we were with the Cayuses [who killed Whitman]. We have not such hearts. I and my people are from the farthest part of our country. We had heard there, that you

333

were coming to kill off the last Indian west of the mountains. We have never shed the blood of the Americans. We are glad to hear that you want none but the murderers."

W. H. Gray, who reprinted this speech in his *A History of Oregon*, p. 564, prefaced it with a characterization of Kentuck as "a good-natured, sensible, and yet apparently crazy Indian."

CHARLES LAJEUNESSE

Doubtless a member of the well-known Missouri family that included such names as Basil, Baptiste, François, Joseph, and Louis, Charles Lajeunesse appears in the records of the Missouri Historical Society as "Lajeunesse, Charles dit Simond (Simono)." In 1827 he contracted with P. Chouteau, Jr., as a winterer, and in 1830 was a voyageur attached to the Yanktonais establishment of the American Fur Company at a wage of $135 per year. In 1831 he engaged with Chouteau as boatman on the upper Missouri, and on March 26, 1832, was one of those the American Fur Company sought to retain in the Indian country under U. S. license. He probably went to the Rockies in Fontenelle's supply party that summer; next spring Warren Ferris mentions him as a member of Andrew Drips's party, involved with the hunter Emanuel Martin in a bear-killing exploit. (The same story was related in 1843 by Matthew Field, with the embellishment that Lajeunesse was killed by the bear.) Lajeunesse left the mountains in the summer of 1833 with Provost, as shown by an order drawn by Fontenelle upon William Laidlaw and P. Chouteau, Jr. Thus he was at liberty to return next year in the employ of William L. Sublette. It would seem that he was one of the men detailed to remain at Fort William, help Patton in the construction of the fort, and bring the Sioux in for trade; Anderson met him Aug. 24, 1834, returning from a profitless search after the Sioux and Cheyennes. Earlier in Anderson's text he appears as a Pawnee interpreter. On Sept. 6, 1839, the Upper Missouri Outfit paid "Simono Lajeunesse" the sum of $96.82. It is likely that the entry for Charles Simony in these accounts for 1841 also refers to him; he was paid $66 on April 1, 1841.

The last reference we have seen to Charles Lajeunesse is an ambiguous allusion in connection with a survey of Fort Bridger made for Bridger in November 1853, which includes the remark, "Lewis Vasquez, Charles LaJunesse, and James Bridger, settled upon the land within site of Fort, as stated by Mr. Bridger." This would bring Lajeunesse's story forward to the 1840's. We have not ascertained anything as to his later life; a story that he was killed by the Sioux in 1862 seems mistaken.

LONG HAIR (Crow Chief)

Long Hair is alternatively called by Anderson "old Burns," a name also used by Robert Campbell in 1833. His name was given as E-she-huns-ka when he signed the treaty with Atkinson and O'Fallon at the Mandan villages, Aug. 4, 1825. (He signed first among the sixteen Crow chiefs; another signer mentioned by Anderson was Har-rar-shash, "One that Rains.") Zenas Leonard in the fall of 1834 judged him to be "75 or 80 years of age"; Osborne Russell in March 1837 thought him to be about eighty; and Isaac P. Rose, probably in 1836-1837, estimated his age at about seventy. He was chief of the more numerous Mountain Crows, as distinguished from the River Crows, whose principal chief, until killed by Blackfeet in the summer of 1834, was Arapooish (Rotten Belly; not to be confused with the Nez Percé chief bearing this name). William Drummond Stewart in *Edward Warren*, p. 340, commented: "Long Hair was the name of one of the great chiefs of the Crows, his hair was upwards of eleven feet long; he was very old, but retained his influence till his death, though hardly able to walk; he was miserably poor, but had the means of bestowing riches upon others, and his had all been expended in furnishing arms and horses to an army of braves, who enforced his authority when he thought it right to interfere." Russell in 1837 noted that Long Hair appeared to be afflicted with dropsy, the only case of the kind he had ever known among the mountain Indians. Long Hair was probably dead before Stewart made his last visit to the mountains in 1843; Edwin Thompson Denig, writing in 1856, said "he died a few years since."

What made him a marvel was his hair. Maximilian, after visiting the upper Missouri in 1833-1834, observed that long hair was considered a great beauty among the Crows. "The hair of one of their chiefs, called Long Hair, was ten feet long, some feet of which trailed on the ground when he stood upright." George Catlin, who visited the upper Missouri in 1832, heard that Long Hair had "received his name as well as his office from the circumstance of having the longest hair of any man in the nation." Sublette and Campbell, Catlin added, "told me they had lived in his hospitable lodge for months together, and assured me that they had measured his hair by a correct means, and found it to be ten feet and seven inches in length; closely inspecting every part of it at the same time, and satisfying themselves that it was the natural growth." Zenas Leonard, as of 1834, reported the hair "no less than nine feet eleven inches long." Other estimates were more extensive. Anderson on Aug. 31, 1834, said that when Campbell had measured the hair a year or two before, it was 11 feet 4 inches long. "Now it measures 11 feet, 8 inches according to Mr Vasques rule." Osborne Russell in 1837 gave the length as "eleven feet six inches," and Isaac Rose attests to Bridger's claim that it was fourteen feet long. Denig in 1856 reported that the hair had been "36 feet in length."

Denig explained: "Encouraged by a dream when a young man, that he would become great in proportion to the growth of his hair, he tied weight to it, which aided in its growth, and every few months separated the locks into small parcels which were stuck together with the gum of the pine tree. In this way none of his hair could be lost. If any fell out the gum prevented it from dropping. At the age of 50 his hair was the length mentioned, 'tho no single stalk was longer than usual among females of our own color. This cumbersome bunch of hair he rolled up into two large balls and carried them in front of his saddle while riding. When on foot, the rolls were attached to his girdle. On great festivals he mounted on horseback, unrolled his hair, and rode slowly round the camp with his scalplocks trailing some distance behind him on the ground."

Others mentioned Long Hair's management of his tresses. Catlin reported: "On ordinary occasions it is wound with a broad leather strap, from its head to its extreme end, and then folded up into a budget or block, of some ten or twelve inches in length, and of some pounds weight; which when he walks is carried under his arm, or placed in his bosom, within the folds of his robe; but on any great parade or similar occasion, his pride is to unfold it, oil it with bear's grease and let it drag behind him, some three or four feet of it spread out upon the grass, and black and shining like a raven's wing." Zenas Leonard declared that Long Hair worshiped "nothing but his hair, which is regularly combed and carefully folded up every morning into a roll about three feet long by the principal warriors of his tribe." Osborne Russell said the hair was "done up in an enormous queue about eighteen inches long and six inches thick hanging down his back." According to Isaac P. Rose: "It hung down his back nearly to his heels in a thick roll, stuck together at intervals of about a foot and a half with pitch, and tied with a buckstring whang. From his heels his hair was again turned up to the back of his neck and again fell nearly to his heels, making three lengths of between four and five feet each. . . ." James P. Beckwourth remarked that after Rotten Belly's death, in token of mourning, "Long Hair cut off a large roll of his hair, a thing he was never known to do before."

These contemporary accounts are supplemented by the modern investigations of Dr. Edward F. Corson of Philadelphia, whose interest was aroused by remarks made by Gen. Hugh L. Scott at a dinner in 1934. In an article, "Long Hair, Chief of the Crows," *Archives of Dermatology and Syphilology*, LVI (October 1947), 443-447, Dr. Corson writes that General Scott had seen strands of Long Hair's locks, preserved as "medicine" after his death, in the possession of "Plenty Coups" at the Crow Agency. The strands, as shown in 1930 to General Scott and to Scott Leavitt, a member of the House of Representatives, were wrapped in the form of an open circle in cloths of many colors and, finally, in buckskin. Each layer was peeled off until the lock was exposed. It was measured by Max Bigman as it was unrolled, hand over hand, for seventy-six hands one finger (about 792 cm.). Many Coups was incensed when General Scott asked whether the hair was spliced. Leavitt wrote Dr. Corson in 1941 that he had no doubt the hair was all one strand. "There was some reddish ceremonial paint in the hair, which was itself black or dark brown." The interpreter told Leavitt and Scott they were the only white men to whom the hair had ever been shown. "The Indians considered the length to have been 99 hands (about 1,006 cm.) and that most of it had been given to Plenty Coups but some to others." Dr. Corson comments: "Comparison of this length with that reported by the travelers and traders presented a gap. Even the lesser dimension was freakish, while the greater one was almost incredible. If the average rate of growth of scalp hair is put at 6 inches (15.24 cm.) a year it would require fifty years to arrive at such a length. There would probably be less growth in infancy and old age, illness might check it and privation (a not infrequent experience among the Indians of that era) could interfere with the normal production. . . . Even the shortest length estimated constituted a record in growth as far as I have been able to discover."

In June 1958 Dr. Corson was able to examine the specimen in the Many Coups Museum at Pryor, Montana. In a letter of July 29, 1958, to Dale L. Morgan, he remarked that at the time of his visit the lock of hair could not be stretched, owing to its fragility, but in its lax state measured about 22½ feet in length. "I judged that there were about 100 hairs on the average although it varied, sometimes containing no more than 25. It was my idea to thread one hair through a wire loop and carry the latter along as far as it would go and measure it and then try others the same way—but it couldn't be done. Every so often I came to a block of dried material about like putty through which the hair either continued or was spliced to other shafts at those places. These blocks were at irregular intervals—from 3 to 4½ feet apart. The hair could not have been combed except between the masses. Scott spoke of them as areas of 'red ceremonial paint.' There is no color now."

EMANUEL MARTIN

This famous hunter is said to have been of Spanish blood. Accounts with him are recorded in the Chouteau Papers, Missouri Historical Society, from April 11, 1827. Warren Ferris refers to him as "a well known one eyed Spaniard by the name of Manuel," who was on Snake waters in the company led by Andrew Drips in the spring of 1833. At this time he saved a companion who had been attacked by a grizzly. Matthew Field in 1843 heard the same story, with the incorrect twist that his companion, Charles Lajeunesse, q.v., had been killed by the bear.

A narrative by a girl of mixed Nez Percé ancestry, printed in *The Frontier*, May 1930, as "An Indian Girl's Story of a Trading Expedition to the Southwest about 1841," indicates that Emanuel was one of the mountain men, including Pegleg Smith,who descended on the horse herds of the southern California ranchos in 1840; the girl recalled Emanuel as "a half Spanish Indian, a sound, well-formed, muscular man of one eye," who guided the party much of the way, evincing considerable familiarity with the arid country of the lower Colorado River.

Something of his later life is recorded by George F. Weisel, *Men and Trade on the Northwest Frontier As Shown by the Fort Owen Ledger*, p. 38. In connection with accounts of Emanuel and John Owen from Oct. 27, 1851, to Nov. 24, 1854, Weisel writes: "Emanuel Martin, generally known as 'Old Manwell the Spaniard,' was a Mexican trapper who had spent a lifetime in the Rockies and knew the country perfectly from Mexico to Canada. Somewhere between 1850 and '54 he guided the first wagons into the Bitterroot Valley, leaving from Salt Lake or Fort Hall and traveling through the Big Hole Valley and over Gibbon's Pass.

"The ledger shows that he was in the Bitterroot in 1851. He was employed in making the first adobe bricks for Fort Owen in the spring of 1852, and also in that year he made a trip to Salmon River for Major Owen. The following spring he was making adobes again. Emanuel accompanied Owen as guide and interpreter on another expedition to the Salmon River on October 26, 1854, to trade with the Snake Indians. On the return the party had a number of scares by the Blackfeet, but they arrived safely at Fort Owen on the 22nd of November. . . . By 1858 Emanuel gave up his roving and settled on a farm in the Bitterroot [Valley].

"He comes to notice again in 1865, for on the eve of that New Year a man named Watson was murdered in his cabin. The culprit responsible for the crime, 'Fogerdy', was apprehended at Skalkahol Creek and tried before a people's jury at Fort Owen on January 7. '[It] was proved Satisfactory to the People that he was gilty and was hung by the People of the Valley today'.

"Around 1873 'Old Manwell' died near Fort Owen."

ROBERT NEWELL

Born at Putnam, Ohio, March 30, 1807, Newell is said to have been apprenticed as a saddler at Cincinnati before coming to the mountains as one of William L. Sublette's party in 1829. With him came Joseph L. Meek, on whose authority William H. Gray, *History of Oregon*, pp. 125-126, explains how Newell picked up his nickname. On reaching Independence, Newell said to Meek: "Titles are very necessary here in Missouri, what title shall we take?" "Well," said Meek, "I will take *Major*." Newell replied, "I will take *Doctor*." Accordingly they rode up to the best hotel and called for lodgings. "Well, Doctor, what shall we have for supper?" asked Meek. "I don't care, Major, so as we get something to eat," rejoined Newell. The Major and the Doctor enjoyed their supper—and, Gray adds, "have borne their titles to the present time."

During Newell's first mountain year, he was associated with Smith, Jackson & Sublette, trapping in the party led by Jedediah Smith. His account of the next two years is largely quoted in the sketch of Milton Sublette. After the battle of Pierres Hole in July 1832, he accompanied Fitzpatrick north: "from Piers hole to Psalmon River crossed the mountain to the 3 forks of Missourie (a scrimmage with Black feet) Up to the head of the galiton fork met craig and some of our hunters we parted with at the Rendezvous (met Some black feet 60 warriors made piece with them and the next day fought another party) Returned to Psalmon River and took up winter quarters." Newell left Fitzpatrick's service on Jan. 25, 1833, to join Bonneville (perhaps meaning Walker's party), but he says only, "Broke up winter quarters and hunted on to green River where all opposition Companies met I left Capt Boniville and engagied to Messers Fontinell and Drips Rondezvous held broke up I was Sent to [by] fontinell & Drips to the flat heads to trade with 7 men after 31 days travel I found them on Bitter Root River (near a place called hellsgates) on a large fork of the Columbia I returned to Snake River whare I joined my employer Mr Drips and took up winter quarters

"In the Spring of 1834 I was Sent again to the flat heads left in March the 20th and arived at the village by the way of the head of Missourie on account of Snow on Deer lodge River nears its mouth in April with 9 men (a Scrimmage with the black feet) went with the indians up deer lodge on to the head of Missourie then on to Psalmon River on to a fork of Snake River called Commerce [Camas] Creek (a party of hundred black feet c[h]arged on our village) left there for green River accompanied by 25 indians for Suplies met the company held Rondezvous at hams fork."

It was at this time that Anderson met Newell and admired his Indian wife. Newell does not mention that Warren Ferris had started with him from the rendezvous to the Flathead country in July 1833, continuing in his company till they reached Drips's camp on the Snake. Nor is anything said about his wife. She was a daughter of the Nez Percé chief Kowsoter (or Cowsotum, as Anderson renders the name), and her sisters became the wives of Joseph L. Meek and Caleb Wilkins. We are informed by Alvin M. Josephy, Jr., that a family record apparently in Newell's own hand shows that he married Kittie M. on July 27, 1833. When in later years Newell applied for a Donation Land Claim in Oregon, he gave the year as 1834 and the place of marriage as "on Green River, Oregon." Their first child, Francis Ermatinger Newell, is stated in the family record to have been born on "Green River, South Pass, June 14, 1835." Kittie bore Newell five sons altogether.

After the 1834 rendezvous, Newell says he "Returned with goods to the flat head indians after 51 days travel came to the Village on Bitter root river from thare up Deer loge River on to the head of Missouri Bridger came to us on piers fork near horse prairie from thare to Snake River and wintered

"In the Spring of 1835 went up lewises fork in to Greys hole (a Scrimmage with Black feet on lewises fork) from thare to Salt River on to bear River up it and on to green River whare we met our Supplies from St. Louis Rondezvoux over I Started from My home to go to St Louis as it appeared went to the Council Bluffs and to St Louis from thare to Kentuck and to Ohio Cincinnati my former Residence."

Like many other trappers, Newell came down from the mountains in 1835 with Fontenelle's party. He does not mention spending January 1836 on William L. Sublette's farm near St. Louis, though Sublette several times wrote Robert Campbell that "Dr Newell" was with him. In the spring of 1836 he made his way to Independence, where he engaged with Bent & St. Vrain, and set out for the Arkansas May 25, arriving at Bent's Fort July 11. Until the spring of 1837 he traded for Bent & St. Vrain among the Arapahos and Cheyennes on the Fontaine qui Bouille and the South Platte. Then, on May 19, 1837, in company with Philip Thompson and an *engagé* he set out for the rendezvous, going by way of the Laramie Plains and the Little Snake to the Green River and Horse Creek.

Kittie remained among her people during Newell's two-year absence, for William H. Gray, present at the 1837 rendezvous, says that "Dr. Newell, as he is called . . . won a woman on a wager. On hearing that his old Flat Head wife was coming with McLeod's party, he said he must get rid of the [newly acquired] woman. Accordingly, he went and sold her to her previous owner for One Hundred Dollars." The reunion with Kittie was a warm one, for a second son was born March 30, 1838. (The other three sons were born between 1840 and 1843.)

Newell engaged for 1837-1838 with "Drips & fontinelle," and had a dangerous time in the Crow country. At the winter camp on Powder River he noted that "times is getting hard all over this part of the Country beever Scarce and low all peltries are on the decline." In the spring, as seen in the sketch of Bridger, he hunted beaver and fought Blackfeet on the Yellowstone and in the Snake country, distressed by the increasing lawlessness of the mountain men. After the Wind River rendezvous, in August 1838 he began trapping out of Fort Hall, at this time first mentioning in his "memorandum" the family he had acquired, "my woman and two little boys." He was at the rendezvous in the summer of 1839, and the following winter traded in Browns Hole with goods brought from Fort Hall. Newell attended the final rendezvous of 1840 in the Green River Valley, and agreed to guide several missionaries to the Columbia. The two wagons he took along were the first to reach the Columbia across the Blue Mountains. Meek and Wilkins came with him to the Willamette, all settling on the Tualatin plains.

A few years later Newell moved to Champoeg, where he prospered modestly as a farmer and entrepreneur. He helped organize the Oregon provisional government and became a member of the legislature, twice serving as speaker. He had a hand in many local affairs, and with Joel Palmer served on the peace commission following the Cayuse War of 1848. Later he went to California for gold, and acted as subagent for the Indians south of the Columbia. He had a store at Champoeg, as well as other business interests, and was elected to the first state legislature in 1860. The last years of Newell's life were mainly devoted to his old friends, the Nez Percés, especially after a flood in the winter of 1861-1862 largely destroyed his properties at Champoeg. His wife Kittie died in 1845, and in 1846 he married Rebecca Newman. When Rebecca died in 1867, he married a Mrs. Ward, who survived him. Newell died at Lapwai, Idaho, in November 1869. See Dorothy O. Johansen, ed., *Robert Newell's Memoranda*.

(EDWIN L.?) PATTON

William Marshall Anderson is almost the only source of information on the Patton who was William L. Sublette's clerk in 1834, builder of and first bourgeois at Fort William (Laramie). In the Diary and Journal Anderson does not give Patton's first name but in his Narrative of 1871 he says that "Fort William . . . contained the triad prenames of clerk, leader, and friend." There is no mention of a William Patton, but definite record exists of an Edwin L. Patton in the Chouteau account books of 1832-1833.

When Maximilian came up the Missouri in 1833, he was greeted on arrival August 9 at Fort McKenzie, the post at the mouth of the Marias, by "Mr. Patton, clerk of the Company, and hitherto director of Fort MacKenzie." Five days later Maximilian says: "Mr. Patton . . . a man well known in the Rocky Mountains, and thoroughly acquainted with the business of the fur trade, left us . . . with eleven *engagés*, in a strong pirogue, to return to Fort Union and thence to Fort St. Louis." Wyeth met him at Fort Union Aug. 27, 1833. Kenneth Mackenzie wrote D. D. Mitchell from Fort Union on Jan. 21, 1834: "I regret the loss of Mr. Pattons services, he remained with me a month & improved upon acquaintance, he was firmly resolved on visiting his brother &c. in Alabama & has almost promised to return next Spring but I fear he will not, we went down stream together as far as Fort Pierre leaving this place 19 Sept. & he took charge of the mountain beaver from thence [to St. Louis] 60 packs...."

In view of the responsibility of the job, Edwin L. Patton almost certainly was Sublette's clerk at Fort William. Patton continued in charge during the winter of 1834-1835, and after Sublette & Campbell sold out to Fontenelle, Fitzpatrick & Co. in the spring of 1835, Patton no doubt helped to bring down the furs and robes he had traded. He might have brought with him the first journal kept at Fort William; conceivably it was taken to Alabama and exists there to this day.

JOSHUA PILCHER

According to Frederic L. Billon, Pilcher was born in Culpepper County, Virginia, March 15, 1790, and came to St. Louis during the War of 1812. "Originally a hatter by occupation, being a gentleman of intelligence and enterprise, he engaged in mercantile pursuits, associated for some time with Col. Thos. F. Riddick, who was a relative." Prior to this association, he had another connection, for the St. Louis *Missouri Gazette*, Aug. 17, 1816, has a notice of the dissolution of the partnership Joshua Pilcher & N. S. Anderson, owing to the death of the latter. Riddick & Pilcher was in business by the following November and continued until 1819, when Pilcher entered the Missouri Fur Company. On Dec. 8, 1817, he was elected one of the new directors of the Bank of St. Louis, but as a result of a disagreement resigned Feb. 11, 1818.

Pilcher went up the Missouri in the fall of 1819. He is mentioned in the narrative of the Long Expedition as trading with the Omahas. When the Missouri Fur Company was reorganized in September 1820, Pilcher emerged as its dominant figure, "Acting Partner on the Missouri" in charge of field operations. He made Fort Lisa his base until he built a new post at Bellevue in 1823, meanwhile establishing many other posts on the Missouri. In 1822 Pilcher ascended the river as high as the Mandans, and in 1823 had a controversial part in Leavenworth's Arikara Campaign. After the Missouri Fur Company expired by limitation in the fall of 1824, he organized a new concern, Joshua Pilcher & Company, which traded on the Missouri for three years. Meanwhile he began angling for government appointments. On hearing that Atkinson and O'Fallon had been made commissioners to treat with the Indians of the upper Missouri, in 1824 he vainly sought appointment as their secretary. Early in 1825 he was confirmed as U. S. Consul at Chihuahua, but declined the appointment. After Benjamin O'Fallon resigned as Indian Agent for the Upper Missouri in December 1826, Pilcher unsuccessfully applied for the office.

In September 1827 Pilcher took a brigade to the Rocky Mountains, but his horses were run off by the Crows and his cached goods were ruined by seeping water. From the Bear Lake rendezvous in July 1828 he set out on a trapping tour of the Northwest. Governor Simpson rebuffed proposals he sent from Flathead Lake on Dec. 30, 1828, for the Hudson's Bay Company to back him in operations on American territory. In February 1829 Pilcher launched a bootless trapping tour into the Kutenai country. He finally sold his traps and other gear to David E. Jackson, and made his way to Fort Colvile, where he arrived Sept. 1, 1829.

Three weeks later Pilcher started east with the annual H. B. C. express, going via Boat Encampment, Jasper House, Fort Assiniboine, Edmonton House, Carlton House, Cumberland House, Moose Lake, and the Red River settlement to Brandon House, which he reached April 4, 1830. With a half-breed guide, Pilcher then set out for the Mandan villages, arriving April 22. He got back to St. Louis via the Missouri in June 1830.

On October 12 following, from Bellevue, Pilcher applied unsuccessfully for an Indian agency. He was in St. Louis in November 1831, and soon after went to Washington with an Assiniboine delegation but had returned to St. Louis by April 10. Late the following month, upon the murder of the Sac and Fox agent Felix St. Vrain—an incident that precipitated the Black Hawk War—Gen. William Clark appointed Pilcher acting agent. He served at the Rock Island agency until the new agent, M. S. Davenport, arrived late in 1832. Benton had vainly sought this appointment for Pilcher.

On March 26, 1833, Clark urged that Pilcher be made special or provisional subagent to carry out certain duties, and the Indian Office sanctioned the step on April 8. Clark could not make the appointment, for Pilcher had entered the service of the American Fur Company to conduct trade at Council Bluffs in the place of J. P. Cabanné. Hence the job was given to William Gordon. Pilcher ascended the Missouri on the same steamboat with Maximilian, reaching Council Bluffs May 4, 1833. He greeted Maximilian when the German prince passed down the Missouri in May 1834, and was on hand when Anderson came in from the mountains with Fontenelle in September.

Following the resignation of Jonathan L. Bean in March 1835, Pilcher was made subagent for the Sioux of the Missouri. Holding such an office did not prevent his going to the Rockies for Pratte, Chouteau & Co. in the spring of 1836 to effect a transfer of the mountain business from Fontenelle, Fitzpatrick & Co. He reached Fort William (or Fort Lucien, as he called it) June 20, six days after Fitzpatrick got there with the annual caravan. Afterward he accompanied Fitzpatrick to the rendezvous; Marcus Whitman commented in a letter of Sept. 18, 1836: "Major Pilcher joined us at Fort Williams and came on to Rendezvoux, as agent of Pratt, Choteau & Co., in whose behalf he bought out the 'mountain partners,' so that the whole business now belongs to them. A change which will not be for the worse, if Major Pilcher continues to be their agent." William H. Gray, in Whitman's party, recalled in 1870 that Pilcher "usually rode a fine white mule, and was dressed in the top of hunting or mountain style, such as a fine buckskin coat trimmed with red cloth and porcupine quills, fine red shirt, nice buckskin pants, and moccasins tinged and nicely trimmed; he was, in fact, very much of a gentleman in all his conversation and bearing."

On his return from the mountains Pilcher was met at Fort Leavenworth by General Clark, who, as Pilcher wrote from Bellevue on October 10, "done me the *favour* to order me back in Company with Majr. Dougherty on some very important business." This business was the negotiation of the Platte Purchase, which became northwestern Missouri. In the summer of 1837 Pilcher conducted a Sioux delegation to Washington.

After William Clark's death in September 1838, Pilcher was named Superintendent of Indian Affairs at St. Louis. A Democratic partisan, he was due for the chopping block when the Harrison administration came to power; and even the Tyler administration, in June 1841, saw fit to nominate Charles Keemle, another Democrat, to the office. After a week's reflection, Keemle declined, and David D. Mitchell was named Superintendent.

Pilcher died in St. Louis on June 5, 1843, never having married. Chittenden says Pilcher was "represented as a man of good ability, strict integrity of character, and high standing in business and social circles." Of rather small stature, he was termed by Indians "the little chief."

ÉTIENNE PROVOST

Provost was born in Canada about 1782, the son of Albert and Marianne (Menard) Provost. Nothing is known of his early life, but Audubon in 1843 said he had "been in the trade for 29 years," or from 1814. He first appears in the fur trade in connection with the Chouteau–De Mun party, which set out from St. Louis in September 1815 to trap the headwaters of the Arkansas and extended its operations to the South Platte and other mountain streams. This party was arrested on a southern branch of the Arkansas on May 24, 1817, and taken to Santa Fe. After forty-eight days in jail, the men were released, but their furs, trade goods, and best horses were confiscated. On returning to St. Louis, Provost joined in signing (by mark) an official protest to the U. S. government dated Sept. 25, 1817. (Many years later, not long before his death, Provost furnished another affidavit concerning this affair, enabling the estates of the complainants to collect damages from the Mexican government.)

When news came in 1822 of the opening up of New Mexico to American trade, Provost was among the earliest to go out to Santa Fe. He went in association with (François?) Leclerc, possibly with backing from Joseph Robidoux. On Aug. 1, 1823, Benjamin O'Fallon at Fort Atkinson wrote the Governor of New Mexico regarding news received from "Messrs Provot, Leclere, and several other Americans"; and the Chouteau account books in the Missouri Historical Society have a single entry under the name "Provost," July 8, 1823, intimating that Provost returned to St. Louis that summer.

He soon went back to New Mexico, and by the summer of 1824, with his partner Leclerc, had penetrated as far north and west as the Uinta Basin of Utah.

343

That fall Provost led a party across the Wasatch Mountains, seemingly as far as the Valley of the Great Salt Lake. He may well have been the first trapper to see the lake, anticipating Jim Bridger by a few weeks or months. In October, probably on the Jordan River, a Shoshoni band treacherously attacked his party, killing eight of the ten-man party and forcing Provost to flee to the base camp on the Green, near the mouth of the White. In the spring of 1825 Provost recrossed the Wasatch, and by May 23 had reached the vicinity of Mountain Green in the canyon of the Weber, where on May 23 Peter Skene Ogden encountered him at the head of "a party of 15 men Canadians & Spaniards," accompanied by some Utes. Provost soon turned back to the Green River but on June 7, near present Fruitland, met William H. Ashley, fresh from his exploration down the Green. Provost agreed to transport Ashley's cached goods to his place of rendezvous. After raising the cache, he rejoined Ashley on June 14 at the junction of the Duchesne and the Strawberry (possibly bringing all his men with him), guided Ashley across the Wasatch to the Weber, and afterward accompanied him to the July rendezvous on the Green, at or near the mouth of Henrys Fork. Provost was never associated with Ashley except in this narrow transport arrangement, terminated at the rendezvous.

Presumably Provost eventually returned to New Mexico. He may have obtained supplies from Ceran St. Vrain, who in a letter written from Taos on April 27, 1825, expressed hope "that when the hunters come in from there hunt that I well Sell out to Provoe & Leclere." He lost a man to the Snakes on the Weber in 1825, but whether before or after the meeting with Ashley is not known. Apparently the association with Leclerc expired with poor returns, and Provost came back to St. Louis in the late summer of 1826.

The Chouteau account books record transactions with him on September 22 and October 1, when sundries were sold him to the considerable total of $1,770. About this time Ashley made a proposition to the Chouteaus to join him in supplying Smith, Jackson & Sublette with an outfit in the spring of 1827. It would seem that Provost was seeking backing, for Bartholomew Berthold, the partner in charge of Fort Lookout, wrote on Dec. 9, 1826, to J. P. Cabanné: "I dare not advise anything about the project with Ashley. However, it seems to me that it would be well for us to assure ourselves of Provost, who is the soul of the trappers of the Mountains. It will hurt us. Even if it was only to hinder the meeting [reunion] between him and the Robidoux [brothers] I would say it seems that he should be made sure of, unless you have other plans."

What was done is not clear, though in March 1827 Chouteau and his associates went ahead with the limited undertaking broached by Ashley. Provost may have remained in St. Louis much of this year. On Feb. 1, 1827, he was sold $32.30 in sundries, and on July 21, 1827, was sold more sundries, valued at $28 and $376.70. (The account indicates some involvement of "Gra[tiot] Ch[outeau] & Co.") On Aug. 20, 1827, Provost was sold such items as a saddle, bridle, linen bag, saddle bag, and surcingle, indications that he was going somewhere; and next day he was given a hundred dollars "Cash to you on account," besides a red flannel shirt.

These transactions were incommunicatively settled November 28, "By Office for and of the above accts."

From the summer of 1827 to the fall of 1828 there is no clear record of Provost. It may be that the American Fur Company employed him for field service. But he may have gone out to the Rockies in the party which Jackson and Sublette led out of Lexington in October 1827—or, though the time factor would be tighter, as one of the forty-five-man party Joshua Pilcher took up from Council Bluffs in September 1827. The principal reason to think he may have gone to the mountains, at a time when he is otherwise out of sight, is that Beckwourth seems to have preserved some memory of Provost at the Bear Lake rendezvous of July 1828. After that rendezvous some of the mountain men, dissatisfied with the high prices Smith, Jackson & Sublette had placed on their merchandise, sent Hugh Glass to Kenneth Mackenzie at the mouth of the Yellowstone, asking that Mackenzie send goods to the mountains next year. Conceivably Provost accompanied Glass on this mission. The one clue is that H. M. Chittenden, possibly misunderstanding a document now lost, says: "In the fall of 1828 he [Mackenzie] sent Etienne Provost to look up the trappers . . . with a view to bringing them in to Fort Floyd [Fort Union, as it was soon renamed] . . . to trade. . . ."

Mackenzie himself next brings Provost into view, writing Pierre Chouteau, Jr., from Fort Tecumseh on July 7, 1829: "Provost is just arrived from his spring hunt, he is bound for St. Louis he will not give me five minutes to write you. . . . Provost goes down to St. Louis in order to get equiped & come up immediately to trade with the Crows & trap at the same time. . . . I forgot to say that Provost would not give me his spring hunt, but he owes me nothing." (It would seem that Provost as well as Robert Campbell had made a successful hunt in the Crow country.) He reached St. Louis by July 27, when he was paid a hundred dollars by William Renshaw. On August 4 the sum of $1,145.71 was credited to his account, "By Cash received of Wᵐ Renshaw for balance on Beaver." Provost was able to equip himself as Mackenzie anticipated, for on August 13 the American Fur Company opened the books on "E. Proveau's advanture." He and the company each put up half of a total initial capital of $835.42.

Before leaving for the mountains, Provost took a wife. On Aug. 14, 1829, he married Marie Rose Sallé, dit Lajoie, daughter of Lambert and Madeleine (Delor) Sallé, dit Lajoie. This was a late marriage, Provost presumably being in his forty-seventh year. He spruced up for the occasion, as shown by the purchase on his wedding day of a razor, shaving box, brush, razor hone—and with these items a pair of "Blankets Green 3 pts." A day later he purchased from Pierre Chouteau, Sr., a large piece of ground on which in the course of time he and his wife erected a building to be used as a lodging house, in consequence of which he eventually shows in the Chouteau accounts as a "tavern keeper."

The date of Provost's departure for the Crow country does not appear, but by October 2 he had reached the Kansas post, where he was furnished with various supplies. Engagés included A. Mathieu (is this the otherwise unknown Matthieu who was with Bonneville in 1832-1833?), one "Cotté noir," and possibly one

Labonbardi. Advances were made him at Fort Union in February 1830, and on May 5 Kenneth Mackenzie summed up the news at that post by saying: "Mʳ Vanderburgh and his party will be in I think about the last of June. Gordon with four or five men is trapping on powder River Provost is with the Crows." In June 1830 "Etienne Provost & Co" was advanced or credited with $627.67 at Fort Union.

Provost would have had plenty of competition in the Crow country in 1829-1830, with Smith, Jackson & Sublette and many free trappers ranging the area, to say nothing of Vanderburgh. It may be that the "advanture" was not very successful. Provost seems to have entered the service of the Upper Missouri Outfit on an engaged basis; indeed, the enterprise of 1829-1830 is the last independent trading and trapping operation Provost is known to have had any part in. He is recorded as a hunter at Fort Union in the American Fur Company lists for 1830, and may have gone to the Yellowstone and upper Missouri with William Henry Vanderburgh for the fall hunt. If so, he came in to Fort Union during the winter, leaving the party at its winter camp on the Powder River. Eight cash advances were "paid his lady" in St. Louis between Sept. 13, 1830, and July 30, 1831, showing his sustained absence from home.

In the spring of 1831 Provost had the job of resupplying Vanderburgh. The record of this work begins on February 21, when the Fort Tecumseh journal mentions the arrival of Provost from Fort Union with dispatches from Mackenzie. Three days later "Mr. Provost with 10 men and 9 horses laden with merchandise left us for Powder River where he expects to meet Mr. Vanderberg with a party of trappers." Other men set out April 1-2 with more horses, under William Gordon, who "conducts them to Cherry river, where it is expected they will fall in with Provost." Provost evidently got together with Vanderburgh (a second time?) at Green River early in July and turned east again July 18. Gordon tells of having reached St. Louis from the mountains about the last of August 1831, and this may apply to Provost as well; on Aug. 21, 1831, the Chouteau account books credit him with $1,000 for "services ending this Sumʳ."

Provost was again to have supplied Vanderburgh in 1832, leaving from Fort Union while Lucien Fontenelle supplied Drips from Bellevue. As that was obviously illogical, the parties were combined under Fontenelle's command, Provost acting as boss of the pack train. Much delayed, the caravan did not get away from Fort Union until about June 19 and did not come up with Vanderburgh and Drips until August 8, as seen in the sketch of Fontenelle. Warren Ferris says that Fontenelle "had about fifty men, and three times that number of horses, and was aided by Mr. Provean in conducting the expedition." On August 12 the two men began their journey back to Fort Union with thirty men and the year's returns. The party reached Mackenzie's post by September 11, and Provost came down to the states with the furs. On October 6, 8, and 13 in St. Louis he was sold such furnishings as flannel shirt, pantaloons, and whisky.

Provost had a large part in the expedition of 1833; on June 30 he is credited with $1,400 for "Services ending" in the fall of 1833. In February he had gone to

Cahokia, St. Charles, and Portage des Sioux to hire men. Fontenelle was again in charge of the mountain party. Maximilian observed its departure from Fort Pierre on June 8, and Fontenelle wrote from the rendezvous that the party had suffered "a tedious journey of thirty days." As Fontenelle remained in the mountains, the returns were taken down by Provost; he left the rendezvous about August 1, and his arrival at Fort Pierre is recorded on August 29 by William Laidlaw. The date of his return to St. Louis is not stated, but there seems to have been a settlement of accounts on September 21.

Sundries sold and advances made to Provost between Oct. 10, 1833, and March 10, 1834, indicate that during this winter the transformation of his home into a lodging house was accomplished. By March he was probably satisfied to leave this job to his wife and give his attention to the "Rocky Mountain expedition," of which he had sole charge. Owing to the "arrangement" reached in New York by the American Fur Company and William L. Sublette, this was to have been the last caravan taken up to Fontenelle, Drips & Co. Some accounts charged to Provost on March 13 and 25 supply a list of his *engagés*, all but two of the thirty-one men being French Canadians: James Daugherty, Vincent Baudin, Benito Garcia, Ch. Duroché, Baptiste Desilay, Michel Rocheford, Joseph Pin'yeau, Amable Deroin, Joseph Parisien, Jr., John Wright, Baptiste Catalane, Etienne Papin, Amable Franceur, J. Bte. Lefaire, Michel Deroin, Bte. Coté, Augte Lucier, Jean Lesage, Joseph Poirier, Louis Tellier, Martin Jourtias, J. Bte. Lusier, L. Papin, Frans. Pangolle, J. Molland, Bte. Grand Louis, Pierre Lafleure, Antonio Gravelle, Paul Vilneuf, Bte. Perrin, and (added April 12), Fr. Maugrin. (Charles Duroché and Michel Rocheford subsequently deserted.)

Provost left St. Louis about April 12, going via the Kansas, Little Blue, and the Platte. This particular route had never been used by the American Fur Company, which had tried to carry its goods by steamboat to some upper post, thence overland; this cut costs but rarely got goods to the mountains in time to compete for the trade of the free trappers. Both Sublette and Wyeth beat the company again this year, after Anderson on May 6 noted the presence of Provost and Cerré at Sapling Grove with "the same destination as ourselves." Townsend records Cerré's presence at the rendezvous on June 22, and Provost doubtless had reached Hams Fork by then. As shown by Anderson, Fontenelle took over the party, including Provost, and led it back to Council Bluffs, arriving at Bellevue September 14. He afterward sent his furs downriver under "the superintendence of Etienne Provost."

When Provost reached St. Louis is not certain. He was advanced some cash on Nov. 26, 1834. Further advances were made on Dec. 1 and 27, and on Jan. 25 and 30, 1835. The record of the fur trade is confused after this year by the appearance of other Provosts. One is referred to by Fontenelle on August 1 as "Young Provost." This may have been Constant Provost, probably a nephew. (Perhaps all the others were nephews, too, from Canada.)

Etienne was absent from St. Louis in the summer of 1835, various cash sums being paid to his wife by the Chouteaus. He went out to Fort William (or Lucien, as it was now sometimes called) and remained until late autumn, for on Jan. 31,

1836, William L. Sublette in St. Louis heard "that the two Prevoes has Got in this Laist Evening and that they left Fontenell at St. Charles who Is Expected here to day. . . . Report Say Fontinell Intends Quiting the Company and Joining Prevo & Some Others & gouing Out   that he has purchaised Some goods in Liberty &c." On February 9 Sublette had more correct information: "The two Prevoes left him at liberty Sending whiskey up to the Black Snake hills." Sublette then related "Old Prevoes tale" with regard to recent developments at Fort William and the doings of Thomas Fitzpatrick during the autumn.

The Chouteau account books on July 20, 1836, credit Provost with $225 "for his trip this Spring to fort Lucien." Since there was a general settlement of accounts with Provost that day, it is evident he made an express journey out to the Laramie River in advance of the annual caravan taken out by Fitzpatrick. (He was accompanied by Toussaint Racine, who was paid $150 for the job.) Other accounts with Provost from July 20 to Oct. 11, 1836, relate mainly to his boarding house, but a cash payment was made him September 24. In December 1836 and on Feb. 2, 1837, his absence from St. Louis is attested by cash payments made his wife. This absence evidently involved a fifty-one-day journey to and from Council Bluffs, the charge for which (a hundred dollars) was assessed against the Upper Missouri Outfit and the Sioux Outfit.

In the spring of 1837 Provost went to the mountains with the celebrated party in which William Drummond Stewart and the painter Alfred Jacob Miller traveled. Miller drew the stout trail boss into one of his sketches, and supplied a verbal description: "Mo'sieur P. adipose & rotonde—'larding the lean earth as he walks along,'—now raises both hands to his mouth and with stentorian lungs bawls out something like '*Attrapez des Chevaux*'—the men immediately rise and run towards a cloud of dust from which the horses are seen emerging—these are being driven in by the horse-guards from their range. . . ." Stewart himself described Provost in *Edward Warren*, though in a context of 1833, when Provost was one of Fontenelle's party. Stewart pictured "Old Provost the burly Bacchus" as "a large heavy man, with a ruddy face, bearing more the appearance of a mate of a French merchantman than the scourer of the dusty plains." These are the only portraits of Provost. (One many times reproduced, first represented as a likeness of Provost in W. R. Harris, *The Catholic Church in Utah*, is fictitious; it was also published in *Ontario Archeological Report*, 1917, p. 10, as a purported representation of Jean Nicollet.)

Provost came down from the mountains with the caravan in the late summer of 1837, being paid six hundred dollars for the season's work. On December 29 James Archdale Hamilton wrote Pierre Chouteau, Jr., from St. Louis: "Provost started yesterday morning with letters and papers for the Upper posts," his destination Council Bluffs. On Feb. 25, 1838, Hamilton wrote again: "Late last evening Provost arrived and this morning (Sunday) we have been all occupied in perusing the melancholy details of plague pestilence and devastation, ruined hopes and blasted expectation" consequent upon the smallpox epidemic raging upon the upper Missouri.

The Chouteau books indicate that Provost again traveled out to the rendezvous in 1838, for which he was paid $450. That would have been his last journey to the Rocky Mountains; henceforth his job consisted of rounding up men each spring and delivering them to the Missouri River posts. There were some interludes. On Dec. 19, 1838, he was advanced forty dollars "for travelling Expenses to Arkansas," and on Jan. 16, 1839, handed back six dollars. More important, in the spring of 1839 Provost was in the company taken by Jean Nicolas Nicollet and John Charles Frémont to map the plateau country between the upper Missouri and upper Mississippi. The party set out from St. Louis by steamboat, and after crossing over from Fort Union reached Prairie du Chien early in November. For seven and a half months' service, on November 21 Provost was paid through the Chouteaus $750. During his absence, one interesting account is that of June 1, for twenty-five dollars "Cash Sent his wife per Nephew." Four other payments were made her, up to November 20.

Provost was in St. Louis through Feb. 5, 1840, but information is scant on his activities the rest of this year; perhaps he was concerned with the procurement of labor. Accounts of August 25 and November 23 indicate his presence in St. Louis on those dates. This year he formed a partnership with Clement Lambert. "Proveau & Lambert, Tavern Keeper" was credited with various sums to Feb. 15, 1841. The business no doubt was operated by Provost's wife.

Cash payments made to Provost on Feb. 15, March 15 and 23, and April 11 and 14, 1841, point to his presence in St. Louis. On April 7 no less than twenty-seven names are listed of men to whom small advances had been made, including "C. Prevost" and "M. Prevost." Doubtless these were men hired for a steamboat voyage up the Missouri. Provost was back in St. Louis by July 21, when a cash settlement was made. He was given further payments on August 18 and September 20. On Nov. 23, 1841, cash was "paid him per his wife"; he may then have been absent on the thirty-eight-day trip to Council Bluffs for which the Upper Missouri Outfit was debited in February. He received payments in St. Louis on Feb. 20, March 20, and April 1, 1842. From April 11 to September 29 of the same year he was in the service of the Upper Missouri Outfit, being paid $50 per month, or $280 in all. This was less money than he had once made, but he was no longer young, and times were hard. He was placed in charge of a barge loaded with 240 packs of robes, sent down from Fort Pierre in August 1842. The barge sank near Weston, with an estimated loss of eight hundred dollars, and Provost continued on to reach St. Louis by steamboat, the latter part of September.

Provost had a gift for managing men. Chittenden's history of early steamboat navigation on the Missouri tells of contests for physical supremacy among the *engagés*: "It was a favorite pastime with that veteran mountaineer, Etienne Provost, who was often sent up in charge of recruits, to compel an early settlement which would determine all blustering and quarreling. He would form a ring on the forecastle and compel every braggart to make good his claims before the assembled passengers and crew. One after another would succumb, until one man would emerge from the contest victorious over all the others. He would then be awarded the championship, and receive a red belt in token thereof."

In 1843 Provost set out with the usual contingent of recruits on the *Omega*, leaving St. Louis April 25. John James Audubon went up the Missouri on the steamboat, and after reaching Fort Union, on June 13, hired Provost. This had been Audubon's desire before setting out; in his letter of April 2 from St. Louis, Audubon wrote respecting the pending voyage of the *Omega*: "We will have from 80 to 90 Trappers and Hunters going to the Mountains for the Chouteau Concern, they have the Deck-floor and live in messes of 12 each. They are fed on corn unground boiled in lard or Pork, and have their rations every morning.—We may per chance have an old Voyager who has been in the trade for 29 years, and in the employ of the Chouteaux. he may however go with Lieut^t Fremont U. S. A. with whom he made a partial engagement. If not succeeding in that quarter, when he has disposed of the Trappers, we may have him to return with us in a Mackinaw Boat, built expressly for us 25 feet long and 12 beam. This Mr Provost is an excellent waterman &^{c} and is known by all the Indians as being in the employ of the Company.—We therefore sincerely hope that he may go with us." Edward Harris, in Audubon's party, recorded at Fort Union: "old Mr. Provost, the captain of the Trappers up to this place is now one of our party, and will take Command of our barge and pilot us down the river." On the voyage up the river Audubon commented: "At Belle Vue we found the brother-in-law of old Provost, who acts as clerk in the absence of Mr. Sarpy." The journals of Audubon and Harris exhibit Provost's skill as a hunter while the naturalists were working in the vicinity of Fort Union. On August 16 the fourteen-man party started down the Missouri in a mackinaw boat. According to Audubon, on their arrival at St. Charles October 18 Provost got "extremely drunk," and left the boat to go by land to St. Louis. On settlement, he received $214 for his services from June 13 to October 19.

Provost was upriver again in 1844, for A. R. Bouis wrote Alex Culbertson from Fort Pierre on Oct. 9, 1845, to complain that J. B. Moncrave in June 1844, "while going up with a keel boat to the Blackfeet got drunk several times and gave upwards of 20 gallons of liquor to the men. . . . The informers are Messrs. Chardon, Harvey, Champagne, and Etienne Provost." A Fort Union account shows the presence of Provost there on Oct. 14, 1844, this account settled by cash at St. Louis, Feb. 13, 1845.

So far as known, Provost's last voyage up the Missouri was in 1848, aboard the steamboat *Martha*, commanded by Joseph LaBarge. Chittenden tells of an incident that occurred June 9, when Yankton Sioux forcibly prevented the hands from loading wood. Provost roared at the discomfiture of his men, "then went out himself onto the bank where the Indians were, and said, 'Now, men, come out here and get this wood.' They came and loaded up. 'Now go on board,' he said, and they went entirely unmolested. Provost went last, and before descending the bank, turned toward the Indians and asked them: 'Why don't you stop them? Are you afraid of *me*?' The truth is they were afraid of him, and understood that he would stand no foolishness." Nevertheless, the Yanktons attacked the boat soon after, getting possession of the forward part and flooding the boiler grates with water, so as to put out the fires. LaBarge forced the Indians off with the aid of a light-wheeled cannon. One deckhand was killed.

Provost died in St. Louis July 3, 1850. His will, filed for probate July 24, had been drawn up on April 1, 1839, just before he set out with Nicollet. Since Provost had never learned to write, the document was signed by mark, witnessed by Alphonso Wetmore and two others. All property, consisting mainly of two lots in St. Louis and a tract in the halfbreed Sac and Fox lands in Iowa, was left to his wife, Marie Rose Provost. On July 29 she swore that Provost's only heirs were Mary, widow, and Mary, daughter; she too signed by mark. In the writing out of the will, Provost's name was rendered Provôt, and this circumstance, ascertained by Judge Walter B. Douglas in 1909 for the benefit of W. R. Harris, led historians for a number of years to insist upon such a spelling. Researches by Stella M. Drumm indicate that "Provost," as introduced to the literature of the fur trade, is correct. The name is pronounced phonetically "Provo," the spelling adopted for Provo River and Provo City in Utah.

The St. Louis census returns of 1830 show that the Provosts then had one child; the household of "Elean Provo" consisted of one female under five and one between thirty and forty. Collet's Index to St. Louis Church Registers records as children of the Provosts Marie Provot, born May 1 [1830?] to Etienne Provot and Marie Salé Lajoie, baptized Sept. 12, 1831; also a second daughter, Marianne Provot, born Sept. 21, 1833, baptized March 2, 1834. Marianne was dead by 1850.

ROTTENBELLY (Nez Percé Chief)

This distinguished Nez Percé chief, according to Anderson's account, was wounded by the Gros Ventres in the battle of Pierres Hole, July 18, 1832, "at the time that Sublette was shot." Anderson first encountered Rottenbelly on June 18, 1834, when he had an uproarious reunion with Sublette. Rottenbelly has some-times been confused with the Crow chief, Arapooish, also styled Rotten Belly, who was killed in the summer of 1834. His Nez Percé name, given by Anderson as Ta-kin-shwai-tish, by later writers is rendered Tai-quin-su-wâtish, Tack-en-su-a-tis, Takansuatis, etc. (We are informed by Alvin M. Josephy, Jr., that modern Nez Percés make nothing of this name, except that "suatis" means cloud.) Toward the end of his life H. H. Spalding gave the Indian the baptismal name Samuel.

Rottenbelly was one of the Nez Percé and Flathead chiefs who counciled with Samuel Parker and Marcus Whitman at the Green River rendezvous in August 1835. Both missionaries call him "the first chief of the Nez Perces," which is more than Anderson was prepared to say (see p. 232); indeed, Parker's account of his travels from the rendezvous to the Columbia records an eventual encounter with another band whose chief, Charlie, is identified as "the first chief of the Nez Percé nation."

Rottenbelly met the Whitmans and Spaldings at the Green River rendezvous of 1836, and afterward escorted them to Fort Walla Walla; as Whitman wrote

Parker from Fort Vancouver, "'Rottenbellie' (the Indian Chief) came all the way with us, and was very faithful." In another letter to Parker written from Fort Walla Walla in October 1836, Whitman related that he and Spalding had just returned from the Nez Percé country, where they had selected the mission station subsequently famous as Lapwai; he added: "'Rottenbelly' (the chief) spares no pains, says he will rove no more, go no more to hunt buffalo; but will work and grow grain and potatoes."

In these pioneer years of the Oregon mission, Spalding wrote much in favor of Rottenbelly. In a letter of Sept. 20, 1836, printed in the *Missionary Herald*, October 1837, he said that Tack-en-su-a-tis "gave us a horse at the rendezvous, and said he would stick by us. He came with us to Wallawalla, and we found him as good as his word. . . . He is very strict in his observance of morning and evening prayers, and in the observance of the Sabbath. I do believe if there is one in the darkness of heathenism that wishes to do right it is this chief. He is always ready and anxious to hear something about God and the Bible; says he is but a little boy in knowledge, is liable to do wrong; but wants to know how to please God. His conduct to his Flat Head wife has undergone a material change since being with us and observing how we treat our wives." In another letter of Feb. 16, 1837, Spalding told of his efforts and those of William H. Gray to establish themselves at Lapwai: "Chief Tack-en-su-a-tis was most cooperative. Although the Indians were not accustomed to manual labor as were the white men, the Chief took an ax and set the example for his men to aid in cutting logs for a cabin."

This spiritual honeymoon could not last. On April 22, 1839, Spalding wrote in his diary of a talk the previous day with Rottenbelly and another Nez Percé: "Today they leave. I do not know that I ever felt discouraged in the least before in relation to this people. Really I fear they will all prove to be a selfish, deceptive race of beings. . . ." There was trouble afterward, for Asa Bowen Smith commented in a letter from Kamiah, Feb. 6, 1840: "People at home may think . . . that he [Takansuatis] is a christian, but he is far from it. Instead of being settled with Mr. S. he has become his enemy & proves to be a very wicked man & now spends much of his time in the buffalo country. It is now very evident what his motives were in being so kind & obliging [in 1836], & when his selfish expectations were not gratified, he showed out his wickedness. . . ." Again, in a letter of Sept. 3, 1840, Smith wrote that "'Takansuatis', when he fell out with Mr. Spalding, accused him of 'selling the body of Christ for a horse,'" an allusion to the sale of some religious paintings made by Mrs. Spalding. Yet on Feb. 21, 1842, Spalding mentioned in his diary setting out at Lapwai sixteen apple trees "belonging to old Tackensuatas."

The mission at Lapwai was broken up in 1847. Toward the end of his life, Spalding came back to institute a great revival among the Nez Percés. C. M. Drury writes: "Heading the list of those received [in baptism] on November 12th [1871] was old Lawyer, once Head Chief of the Nez Perces [mentioned by Anderson in the end pages of his Diary]. The second name on the list of men was Samuel, which was the baptismal name Spalding gave to Tack-en-su-a-tis." These baptisms led to such an increase in enrollment that by Feb. 1, 1872, the local church had 246 new members, and the revival had lasting effects.

We have not ascertained when Rottenbelly died. In *Henry Harmon Spalding*, Drury says: "It is reported that one of Samuel's sons and two of his daughters are still living (1935) in the vicinity of Stites, Idaho."

WILLIAM GEORGE DRUMMOND STEWART

This second son of Sir George Stewart and Catherine (Drummond) was born Dec. 26, 1795, at Murthly Castle, Perthshire, Scotland. At the age of seventeen he was appointed cornet in the Sixth Dragoon Guards, saw service the following year, then was commissioned a lieutenant in the Fifteenth King's Hussars. With his regiment he went through the Hundred Days and fought at Waterloo. He was promoted to captain in 1820, but was placed on half pay the following year, when his battalion of the Hussars was mustered out. In 1830 he married Christian (or Christina) Mary Stewart, and one son was born to them.

Stewart had money from his mother's estate as well as his miniscule army pay, and he traveled widely before sailing to the United States in April 1832. Going on to St. Louis, Stewart became acquainted with several prominent fur traders, including Kenneth Mackenzie, William L. Sublette, and Robert Campbell. With the latter he journeyed to the Rockies in 1833. Stewart's novel, *Edward Warren*, published anonymously in 1854 (a copy with emendations in Stewart's own hand is in the Huntington Library), reflects his experiences on the trail and in the mountains afterward.

The Captain figured in incidents at the rendezvous, including attacks on the various camps by rabid wolves. When the rendezvous broke up on July 24, he accompanied Campbell and Fitzpatrick to the Big Horn. Afterward he joined Fitzpatrick on a hunt in the Crow country. On reaching Tongue River September 5, as Irving relates, a large body of Crows "got possession of the camp, and soon made booty of everything—carrying off all the horses." Stewart, in charge of the camp during the absence of Fitzpatrick, is represented as having "behaved with great spirit; but the Crows were too numerous and active." As seen in the sketch of Fitzpatrick, many of the horses were restored by the Crows, but Fitzpatrick found it expedient to get out of their country. Indeed, Stewart says in *Edward Warren*: "We . . . recovered our horses from the Crows, on condition of leaving their hunting grounds." Thus by October 26 Fitzpatrick was domiciled with a Snake village on Hams Fork.

The Captain's movements during the next five months are not definitely known. He may have wintered with Fitzpatrick and Bridger, first on Hams Fork, then on Bear River, finally on the Snake. Or he may have headed for the Ute country with Fraeb and Old Bill Williams; if so, he set out before November 13, when Fitzpatrick mentions the recent departure of the latter and their anticipated return in March. A passage in *Edward Warren* may be literal autobiography: "I . . . left the main body to make a hunt with a party, of whom old Williams was the head, towards the Utewa country, and from there across Snake river to the Titons, and the horse plains. . . . I was an expert beaver hunter by the spring. Bill had not the reputation of being rash, and we avoided a great deal of danger by a great deal of caution. We had been a part of the winter with the Snakes at the little lake [Bear Lake], and passed on from thence by the Black-foot river, to cross Lewis' Fork towards the Titons. . . ."

As seen in the sketch of Fraeb, there is some doubt where Fraeb went this winter, and no information whether at some point a small group under Bill Williams separated from the main party. (Fraeb's party numbered only twenty men on setting out, but with them went a company of "Spanish" free trappers—men originally outfitted at Taos.) The record clarifies in March 1834. Captain Richard Bland Lee, on leave from the Army, had set out from Abiquiu Nov. 19, 1833, with an outfit furnished by Bent & St. Vrain; and with twelve men including Kit Carson, q.v., Lee made a laborious forty-three-day march to a winter camp at the confluence of the White and Green rivers. There, as he reported later, he "remained until the 22^d of February exposed to many hardships and great suffering for the want of provisions," so that he "determined to force my way to the head of the Snake river, a country generally abounding with game, which I reached after twenty days excessive toil [arriving March 13, 1834?], and the loss of several animals—Here I had the satisfaction to find a plenty of game. . . ."

Lee represented all this travel to the War Department as serving a military purpose, saying nothing of vulgar commerce. Carson says rather more frankly that some trappers came to the winter camp on the White "and informed us that Fitzpatrick and Bridger were encamped on the Snake River. In March, 1834, we struck out for the purpose of finding their camp, and in fifteen days succeeded. Captain Lee sold his goods to Fitzpatrick and agreed to accept his pay in beaver. Lee then started for Taos. . . ."

When Lee left Fitzpatrick's camp for the New Mexican settlements, he traveled in the party Jim Bridger took back to his hunting grounds of the previous summer, the Black Hills and the Three Parks of the Rockies. Lee's summation, ignoring all these details, says: "after a few days rest [I] proceeded slowly in the direction of the North fork of the river Platte—Thence to the Black Hills, thence to the several heads of the different forks of the Platte, thence to the head of the Arkansas, and thence to Santa Fe which place I reached in safety on the 12th June—"

Stewart places himself in this party, for a footnote in *Edward Warren*, pp. 288-289, relates that in the spring of 1834 he "was with Jem Bridger and one of the bravest and most dashing hunters of the day, Captain Lee, of the U. S. A., in a range of mountains whose western slopes give birth to the waters of California, and near the city of Taos." (This range might have been the San Juan Mountains.) Here, Stewart tells us, occurred the celebrated episode involving Mark Head and the five-hundred-dollar scalp. So notorious is this affair that Stewart's account is given in full:

"We had in camp a young Ioway Indian, who had been brought up in a French village near St. Louis, and had hired as a camp follower to the company of which

Jem Bridger was chief. This youth, whose name was [Charles?] Marshall, had become so lazy and disobedient, that Bridger and Fitzpatrick had discharged him, and he was (without an animal) obliged to follow the camp on foot. I took compassion on him and hired him, giving him traps and a mule to ride, but having found that he was perfectly unwilling to do any thing, had recourse to frequent lectures, and at last threatened to turn him adrift also. Seeing that his love of idleness, inherent in all Indians, was likely to bring him again into trouble, he determined to abscond, and one night went off with a favourite rifle, my best running horse (Otholoho) and another; this was announced to me at the turn out, and I got up, scarcely believing in such ingratitude. The rifle was a serious loss, a most accurate-shooting gun; the horse, which was the swiftest in the West, beat the Snake nation, and would, had there not been unfair play on the part of the man who took charge of him the night before the race, have beaten all the horses of the whites. I was in great trouble, and rushed out of my lodge; the greatest part of the camp were assembled to examine the pickets, no rope had been cut, and the rifle had been taken from beside the fire, and Marshall was missing: there was therefore no doubt in the group of who was the thief, and I exclaimed in my wrath, for they laughed a little at my having thought to get any good out of such a scamp, 'I'd give five hundred dollars for his scalp.'

"After breakfast, upon reflection we saw that, not knowing the country, he would probably miss his way, and not be out of reach, I organized two or three parties to go in search of him, cautioning them, however, that he was armed with bow and arrow as well as a rifle, both of which would be dangerous in the hands of a cunning and desperate man. The result proved how much I was mistaken in this Indian from first to last, Mark Head and a Spaniard found him not far off, unable to resist the desire of killing a bison on the fastest horse in the plains; after having dropped two bulls with his arrows, he had dismounted to take the meat of one; while thus engaged, these two came upon him unperceived, and accosting him, asked 'What he was about?' 'He was,' he stated, 'sent out for meat by the Captain, but thought perhaps the meat of the other bull was better, and would ride over to it to see.' His drift was evident, the Spaniard hung back, Mark thought there might be some technical difficulty about the reward if he did not bring the scalp, or he was afraid of the Spaniard joining the other, Marshall was putting the cord to rights as he was about to mount, when Mark shot him dead under the horse's neck. In the evening, between us and the sun, the loiterers of the camp saw two men leading two horses making their way towards camp, and on a rifle was displayed the scalp of the horse-thief. This was a little more than I looked for, and I tore the bloody trophy from the gun and flung it away. The horse returned to my hands, but I never afterwards crossed his back,—he was a year after taken by the Blackfeet, and beat every thing in their country."

(Mark Head, described by Matthew Field in 1843 as a Virginian, "bred in Missouri," is mentioned by Joe Meek in the mountains as early as 1829. If that is correct, he returned to the states and came back to the mountains as one of William L. Sublette's party in 1832; he is listed in Sublette's license of that year. Stewart says that he "had come early in the spring of life to the mountains, and was considered one of the most successful beaver hunters of the West; though rather under the usual scale of intellect, he had contrived to get through difficulties and dangers, such as had checked or baffled men who considered themselves as possessing more intelligence and experience than himself." Field provides an account of his life through most of the 1830's. Head was killed in the Taos massacre, January 1847.)

According to Meek, Bridger's party made its way home via the Rio Grande (San Luis Valley), South Park, North Park, "thence to the Little Snake, a branch of Bear [Yampa] River; thence to Pilot Butte; and finally to Green River to rendezvous. . . ." Anderson notes the arrival of Stewart from the south on June 24, and of Bridger with the main party next day. It is curious that Anderson should not have recorded the tale of Mark Head and the scalp, beloved of mountain yarn-spinners ever after.

When Wyeth took the trail on July 2, Townsend wrote: "We were joined . . . by a Captain Stewart, an English gentleman of noble family, who is travelling for amusement, and in search of adventure. He has already been a year in the mountains, and is now desirous of visiting the lower country, from which he may probably take passage to England by sea." Townsend entertainingly recounts a call made by Wyeth and Stewart on overtaking Captain Bonneville beyond Soda Springs, the "bald chief's" supply of metheglin (diluted alcohol sweetened with honey) being sadly depleted before the visit ended.

On July 14 Wyeth reached the site of Fort Hall. Stewart and the missionaries waited while Wyeth began construction. On July 30 they were able to go on with a small Hudson's Bay brigade led by Thomas McKay, from which they separated at Fort Boise on August 16. Turning northwesterly across the mountains, the travelers fell in with Bonneville again in the Grande Ronde Valley August 29, and it appears that Stewart reached Fort Walla Walla two days later, a little ahead of the missionaries. Wyeth in turn arrived on September 2. Jason Lee documents an allergy, for he writes at Fort Walla Walla, "Capt. Stewart killed a horse for meat, being the only kind he could get here, as he could not eat fish."

Townsend, who had accompanied Wyeth, says: "The missionaries informed us that they had engaged a large barge to convey themselves and baggage to Fort Vancouver, and that Captain Stewart . . . [was] to be of the party." Wyeth himself writes on September 4, "In morning left Walla Walla in a boat hired by Capt. Stewart. . . ." Wyeth left this craft at The Dalles on September 8 to make arrangements for his party coming along behind. Hampered by adverse winds, the others reached Fort Vancouver September 15.

On October 6, Wyeth wrote several letters of introduction for Stewart, anticipating that the Captain would present them to friends and relatives after a voyage around the Horn. Stewart must have changed his mind, for Dr. McLoughlin wrote on Nov. 18, 1834: "Captain Stewart is an Officer of the British army and shewed me a letter of introduction from the Right Honble. Edwd. Ellice addressed to 'John Allen Esquire York, Samuel Gerrard Montreal, Governor Simpson and

356

The Chief Factors & Chief Traders Hudsons Bay Co? and he says he intends (according to the means of conveyance he may find) to go to Canada or St. Louis on the Mississippi next spring."

Stewart joined Francis Ermatinger when the latter set out from Fort Vancouver on Feb. 11, 1835, with a "brigade of 3 boats taking up the outfits for the upper forts." Wyeth, who met this flotilla below The Dalles the same day, says that with Ermatinger traveled "Capt. Stewart Mr Ray [William Glen Rae] and one more gentleman." It may be assumed that during the late winter and spring Stewart visited the various Hudson's Bay posts on the upper Columbia, probably happy in proportion to the distance he attained from a staple diet of salmon, but there is no record of him until Osborne Russell writes at Fort Hall: "On the 10th of June a small party belonging to the Hudsons Bay Company arrived from Fort Vancouver on the Columbia River under the direction of Mr F. Ermatinger accompanied by Capt. Wm. Stewart an English half pay Officer who had passed the winter at Vancouver and was on a tour of pleasure in the Rocky Mountains. On the 12th they left Fort Hall and started for the grand rendezvous on Green River."

Stewart had a long wait at Horse Creek, for the 1835 caravan did not reach the rendezvous until August 12. Parker and Whitman came along, and the day after their arrival Stewart pocketed the Blackfoot arrowhead "which had been for years," as he writes in *Edward Warren*, "wandering about Jim Bridger's back and hip." This souvenir came to him through the operation performed by Dr. Whitman.

Stewart evidently left the rendezvous with the returning caravan on August 27, arrived at Fort William September 8, and reached Cabanné's post Oct. 10. Six days later he wrote William L. Sublette from Council Bluffs: "I am thus far on my way to St. Louis & take the opportunity of some boats going down to write to you to beg you would keep any letters that may arrive for me. . . ." He may have descended the Missouri with Cabanné and Whitman, leaving Bellevue October 20 and reaching St. Louis November 4.

St. Louis did not detain him long. Charles Augustus Murray, who had spent the summer in the Pawnee country, tells of joining a party that embarked on *The Far West* November 29. The party consisted of "Captain S——, a cousin and old acquaintance of mine in Scotland, who had been above two years among the Indians, in and beyond the Rocky Mountains; my friend V——, and a Dr. W——, also from Scotland, a lively and well-informed companion." Ice was running in the Mississippi, so thick and hazardous that the steamboat was forced to return to St. Louis, not able to start again till December 2, and making slow work of the voyage. Still, the travelers reached New Orleans on December 14.

From the Crescent City Stewart went to Cuba, thence to Charleston, South Carolina, where he wrote William L. Sublette on Feb. 28, 1836. He then intended "proceeding to the West" via Washington and Philadelphia. He reached St. Louis in time to take passage on a Missouri River steamboat that sailed April 24. This boat was probably the *Diana*, repaired after the damage described in the sketch of Fitzpatrick. It was the *Diana* that disappointed Marcus Whitman and his fellow

357

missionaries of 1836 for transportation to Council Bluffs, so that they caught up with Fitzpatrick's caravan only by dint of great energy and perseverance.

Stewart was accompanied to the mountains this year by a "German Gentleman" named Sellem, encountered somewhere between New Orleans and Charleston. With Fitzpatrick the two set out from Council Bluffs May 16, arrived at Fort William June 13, and went on again on June 22, and reached the Green River rendezvous July 6. By Osborne Russell's account, the rendezvous broke up on July 16. Stewart's arrival at Council Bluffs with the returning caravan has not been dated, but he had descended the Missouri to Fort Leavenworth by September 28. On that day Col. Stephen W. Kearny wrote in his diary: "Capt Stewart dined with me today, an intelligent man—in speaking of the Rocky Mountains & the Indians between there & us, he remarked that Col. Dodge's expedition with the Dragoons in 1835, to the mountains, had had a bad effect with the Indians—that the course he pursued towards those he met led them to believe he & the Whites were afraid of the Indians."

As he had done the previous year, Stewart took a steamboat from St. Louis to New Orleans. There, probably in March 1837, he engaged the young painter Alfred Jacob Miller to go to the rendezvous with him next summer. The caravan set out from Independence, permanently breaking with the tradition that the point of departure should be north of the Platte. Only once before, in 1834, had this southerly route been employed by the Chouteau interests. Perhaps Stewart was technically in command of the caravan, but Etienne Provost was plainly the trail boss. Fontenelle (and perhaps Fitzpatrick, if Russell's comment at the rendezvous can be trusted) joined the caravan on its departure from Fort William June 27. They reached the rendezvous July 18.

In *Across the Wide Missouri* Bernard DeVoto postulated some post-rendezvous travels by Stewart on the basis of certain scenery depicted in Miller's sketches and a few vague allusions in the literature. No such travels have been substantiated, nor has the date of Stewart's return to the states been established. But Stewart was in St. Louis Nov. 25, 1837, when he was baptized a Catholic, having "returned to the faith of his illustrious ancestors." He remained a Catholic to the end of his life.

Presumably Stewart wintered again in New Orleans. He came back to St. Louis in time to leave with the caravan of 1838, conducted by Andrew Drips; see the sketch of the latter. Stewart's dismay over mountain conditions is shown by a letter he wrote William L. Sublette on the homeward journey, dated "Head of the [Little] Blue Fork," August 27, 1838: "We have about 38 packs of beaver   the American Co. are about wound up in the Mts. The Hudson Bay people [who the previous year had taken over Fort Hall] have got the whole country, Drips makes a hunt in the Blackfoot country but his people are daily deserting him   there will not be twenty packs brought down next year   The H. B. Co. have established a fort on the Wintey [a mistaken reference to Antoine Robidoux' new post?] & Andy's [Andrew Sublette's] people will be driven from there [i.e., from Browns Hole]—if the Government does not take some steps there will not be a mule load of goods taken up on the platte in two years." Having revealed that his sentiments lay with the American traders, rather than with his compatriots, Stewart went on to say he expected to reach Westport in eighteen days. "I shall need to draw [on Sublette & Campbell] for my expenses down & shall probably go by land. . . . I trust you will be able to give me a room if you have not rented the upper part of the house we are suffering from heat you must be boiling below."

So Stewart bade farewell to the Rockies in the era of the fur trade. By September 28 he was in St. Louis, and soon after he received the anticipated news that his brother was dead; since May 20, Stewart learned, he had been Sir William, nineteenth of Grandtully and seventh baronet. Stewart went on to New Orleans to look into his investments and see how Miller was getting on with the paintings commissioned for Murthly Castle; he wrote William L. Sublette from the Crescent City December 17. Later he went to New York, whence he sailed for London in May 1839.

The West retained its grip on this extraordinary man who had seen the last six rendezvous of the fur trade. In November 1839, about to leave London for Constantinople and Egypt, Stewart wrote William L. Sublette: "I have not yet done with the United States & if it pleases God shall be in New York in the fall of 1840 with a view of going to the mountains in Spring following if I can get a party to join me sufficiently strong—pray let Dripps or any of my friends in the mountains know that if I am in life & health I shall be on the Susquadee in July 1841 & you can so arrange it that Ande's equipment may go up & meet a party at Larames fork & notice to Braclet de fer & the Little Chief to meet us at the rendezvous. . . . try & pick up some tall strong mules to be ready I am very anxious to be well equipped if I can make it out so do what you can for me by buying young animals & I think I shall take carts instead of a waggon." These plans he could not carry out, even had swift change in the West awaited his pleasure. Not until the autumn of 1842 was Stewart able to reach New York. He spent the winter in New Orleans and came to St. Louis in the spring of 1843. Now possessed of a considerable fortune, he was happy to finance an excursion to the Rockies.

Audubon has several striking references to Stewart this spring. In a letter of April 2 the artist commented: "Sir Wam Stewart arrived here [St. Louis] last night on board the Julia Chouteau, having being [sic] himself on the point of losing his Life and that of all on Board the Steamer L. [J.] M. *White* who struck a rock on the 'Grand Chain' about 40 Miles above the mouth of the Ohio in the Mississippi, and sunk to the roof of the Hurricane Deck in *4 minutes*. . . . [Edward] Harris and I called on Sir Wam last evening and spent about one hour with him, he was engaged in Drying his effects by the fire.—he is a rather tall, very slender person and talks with the lisping humbug of some of the English nobles.—He is most anxious that we should join his party and offered us every kind of promises &c but it wont do for us. he has just [?] too many people of too many sorts. he takes 16 days provisions only, and then depend[s] on dried Buffaloe Meat for the rest of the Journey, excepting when they have opportunities of procuring fresh.—he gave us a most flourishing a/c of the Country he intends visiting &c and would almost have assured us that we would see nothing, procure nothing &c &c &c [unless Stewart's route were adopted] but this he did not quite dare.—He had the most superb Uniforms for Cavaliers that I have seen since We left England, Scarlet Blue &c covered with *Gold lace* and truly Splendid.—These he probably takes to present to the Great Chiefs he may have to encounter. he speaks of the Dangers of his trip, and I have no doubt on that a/c would like to add our 5 bodies, guns &c to augment his Cavalcade." In another letter of April 8 Audubon commented: "Sir W^am Stewart is so desirous that we should accompany him & party, that he offered me 5 Mules and a Waggon for ourselves; but I will not change my plans!—No one knows his views, and he may *Winter* in the mountains. . . ." Again on April 17: "Sir W^am Stewart and his gang cannot . . . go off until about the 10th or 15th of May.—No one *here* can understand that man, and I must say that in my opinion he is a very curious character. I am told that he would give a great deal that we should join him. If so why does he not proffer some $10,000; who knows but that in such a case I might venture to leap on a Mule's back and trot on some 7 or 8 thousand miles." Audubon voyaged up the Missouri instead, and no artist of stature accompanied Stewart's 1843 safari.

William L. Sublette went along, as did many others, "doctors Lawyers botanists Bugg Ketchers Hunters & men of nearly all professions," in Sublette's phrase. Among them was the New Orleans journalist Matthew Field, who had previously made a journey to Santa Fe. To Field's diaries, and the letters and sketches he published in the New Orleans *Picayune*, we are indebted for most of what we know about the "hunting frolic." Stewart's party left Westport in the midst of the Oregon emigration in late May 1843 and reached the Green River Valley the first week of August. On August 17 Stewart turned his back on the scenes of rendezvous, to return only in the memories that pervade his novels, *Altowan* and *Edward Warren*. He died in his lodge near Murthly Castle April 28, 1871, as related by his biographers, Mae Reed Porter and Odessa Davenport, *Scotsman in Buckskin*.

It has been speculated that William Drummond Stewart, as a half-pay British army officer, was obligated to report to his government what he saw in the American West. Inquiries made for us in the Public Record Office of Great Britain have developed no support for these speculations.

ANDREW WHITLEY SUBLETTE

To judge by his own statement in the 1850 census, which gives his age as forty-two, Andrew Sublette was born about 1808. His birthplace was Crab Orchard, Kentucky. Andrew was fourth among the five sons of Phillip Allen Sublette and Isabella Whitley (see the sketch of William L. Sublette). Little is known of Andrew's life at St. Charles, Missouri, where the family settled about 1817. He may have gone to the Rockies with William in 1827, as did his brother Pinckney. If so, he came back to Missouri in the summer of 1828, for some accounts of William H. Ashley with Smith, Jackson, & Sublette include the item, "Octr 1828 Cash sent p^r

Andrew Sublette (to Lexington) 150 00." This errand would have been from St. Louis, but whether Andrew had just arrived from the mountains with William and had been sent on ahead to St. Louis is conjectural. (Pinckney was killed by Blackfeet in the spring of 1828.)

Supposedly Andrew accompanied William to Wind River and back in 1830, but that is inference from a story printed at the time of his death that he first went to the mountains at so early an age that William took along a milk cow for his benefit. A cow did go to the Rockies in William's caravan of 1830—but by then Andrew had reached voting age.

In 1831 Andrew accompanied Jackson & Sublette on their trading venture to and from Santa Fe, being paid wages for seven and a half months at twenty dollars a month. Another account for the following winter shows that Andrew received a month's wages, twenty-five dollars, for attending mules. This was prior to his departure for the mountains in William's company of 1832. Robert Campbell's letter of July 18, 1832, refers to his participation in the battle of Pierres Hole, July 18, 1832. Ten days after the battle, he witnessed with Louis Vasquez the will of the Iroquois Martin Sword before turning homeward. On the return journey John B. Wyeth described the skill at creasing horses of that "admirable marksman, young Andrew Sublet." And after his return to St. Louis, accounts of the R. M. F. Co. include small payments to A. W. Sublette for "bill at Town's" and "work at Beaver."

It would appear from Robert Campbell's diary that Andrew accompanied his brother William in the keelboat voyage to the Yellowstone and back in the summer of 1833. Andrew was in Missouri in the spring of 1834. Sublette & Campbell having concluded their "arrangement" with the American Fur Company for a division of the fur country, he was sent up to the Yellowstone on the *Assiniboine*, carrying the necessary papers for Campbell to transfer the property. F. A. Chardon at the Mandan post, Fort Clark, recorded the arrival of the steamboat June 18 and its departure next day. On July 7 Kenneth Mackenzie at Fort Union wrote Justin Grosclaude at Fort Cass (the Crow post established in 1832 about three miles below the mouth of the Big Horn): "Having bought out Sublett & Co. and understanding they have some articles of Merchandise in cache near your fort, I hereby instruct you to receive the same on my acc^t from Mr Andrew Sublett or such other Agent as Messrs. Sublett & Co may appoint to deliver them to you. . . ."

After transacting the business at Fort Cass, Andrew crossed from the mouth of the Big Horn to the North Platte, then down to the new fort on the Laramie. (At Fort Union Charles Larpenteur tells of a Sublette & Campbell trapper, Isaac Vancourt, having become so indebted to the company that he was obliged to accompany "A. Sublette and several others" from Fort William on the Yellowstone to serve out his time at the new Fort William on the Laramie.) Andrew must have arrived there too late to see William on the latter's homeward journey. During the fall of 1834 Andrew spent some time with Louis Vasquez. When Vasquez wrote his brother from "Fort Convenience" on Dec. 30, 1834, he mentioned that Andrew was about to leave for the states. However, it seems unlikely that Andrew returned at this time, for on Feb. 10, 1835, Robert Campbell wrote from St. Louis that "A Brother of Mr Sublette" was out in the mountains. Campbell left St. Louis for Fort William in April to transfer the post to its new owners, Fontenelle, Fitzpatrick & Co. Andrew returned to the states from the Laramie with him, and the two with a company of twelve were encountered by Samuel Parker and Marcus Whitman on June 27, 1835, at the Elkhorn River, just short of Bellevue.

Andrew now entered into a formal partnership with Louis Vasquez. They took out their first license at St. Louis on July 29, were at Independence by August 19, then made for the mountains, where they began the construction of Fort Vasquez, the first known post on the South Platte. The firm was energetic but unsuccessful. During its six-year existence occasional mention is found of Andrew, who was known to the Plains Indians, according to Beckwourth, as "Left Hand." Robert Newell shows that Andrew was in Independence on April 14, 1836, having just arrived from the mountains, perhaps. He soon returned to the South Platte, for on October 9 Vasquez wrote his brother that Andrew was about to take down some robes, urging him to "treat Sublette as you would me for my sake. He is a good youngster." Vasquez indicated that Andrew planned to return to the mountains the ensuing winter. Doubtless he did, for it was Vasquez who came down to the states next in June 1837. On July 15 Vasquez obtained a new license for the partners. Vasquez & Sublette took out yet another license on June 30, 1838. To judge from Beckwourth, Andrew was the one who applied for it.

Both Andrew and Vasquez were in the states in 1839. When they left Independence for the mountains on August 6, they were accompanied by E. Willard Smith, who kept a journal of his experiences. The company reached Fort Vasquez on September 13. On April 26, 1840, Smith set out from Fort Vasquez in a mackinaw boat carrying a cargo of buffalo robes and tongues, but of his six companions only (Jean Baptiste) Charbonneau is named, and it is not known whether Andrew was one of the party that reached St. Louis on July 3.

After the downfall of Vasquez & Sublette in 1841, Andrew lived for several years on William's farm near St. Louis. In December 1842 William vainly sought of Thomas H. Benton appointments as Indian agents for Andrew and Thomas Fitzpatrick. Andrew stayed behind when William and Solomon Sublette visited the mountains in the summer of 1843. In 1844 he traveled out to Fort Laramie as guide for a party of invalids and Catholic missionaries, concerned to rid himself of a cough. With Solomon he wintered in the Colorado Rockies and New Mexico. On March 3, 1845, he wrote William from the South Fork of the Platte that he and Solomon proposed leaving for Taos or Santa Fe next day, but intended returning to the North Fork of the Platte in April or May, with the object of guiding an emigrant company to California. Solomon went to California, but Andrew did not. He encountered Antoine Robidoux at Fort Laramie on July 4, 1845, and was at the "Lower Pueblo" on the Arkansas by August 23, when Frémont bought two mules from him. Sometime before December 1 he returned to St. Louis.

After the outbreak of war with Mexico, Andrew unsuccessfully sought a commission in the First Missouri Mounted Volunteers. He had better luck when a special "Oregon Battalion" was organized in the summer of 1847, being elected captain of a St. Louis company. He served at (Old) Fort Kearny on the Missouri, in the fall of 1847 was in charge of the escort when (New) Fort Kearny was laid out on the Platte near the head of Grand Island, and was stationed at that fort during the summer of 1848. He was discharged from service in time to join the express being carried to California by Lt. Edward Fitzgerald Beale. During the summer of 1849 Andrew occupied himself at Sonora in the southern mines. Soon after, he was made sheriff of the District of San Francisco. In June 1850 he was living in San Jose, but left for southern California. Unsuccessful in a Mohave Desert mining venture, for a time Andrew made a living as a market hunter. In the spring of 1853 he entered into a partnership with James Thompson as a contractor for the Fort Tejon Indian Reservation, but was badly mauled by a bear in May 1853, and fatally wounded in another such encounter the following winter, dying December 18.

Bayard Taylor, who met Andrew Sublette in the fall of 1849, said that "from his bravery and daring [he] has obtained among the Indians the name of Kee-ta-tah-ve-sak, or One-who-walks-in-fire." Taylor described him as "a man of about thirty-seven, of fair complexion, long brown hair & beard, and a countenance expressing the extreme of manly frankness and integrity." A photograph of him in uniform is reproduced in Doyce Blackman Nunis, Jr., *Andrew Sublette, Rocky Mountain Prince*. Another portrait is reproduced in *Colorado Magazine*, XLI (Summer 1964), 202.

MILTON GREEN SUBLETTE

Second of the Sublette sons, born at Somerset, Pulaski County, Kentucky, in 1801, Milton may have been the first to seek opportunity in the wilderness. At the time of his death an obituary said he "embarked in the Indian trade as early as 1822," which would have been a year ahead of William; and Nathaniel Wyeth's journal of 1833 implies that Milton had descended the upper Missouri at least once. It is possible Milton first entered the fur trade with the Ashley-Henry venture of 1822.

Nothing is definitely recorded of Milton until he went out to New Mexico. In the fall of 1826 he appears as one of a company attempting to trap the Gila and its tributaries. The party was organized by Ewing Young, who in late August 1826 obtained a license from the New Mexican authorities. Young fell ill and stayed behind, but some of his men, including Milton, William Wolfskill, and Thomas L. Smith, made a hunt west of the Rio Grande. They were driven back by Apaches. According to Wolfskill, "Smith and Sublette determined to take up their traps, and in attempting to do so were fired upon, a perfect shower of arrows falling about them. Sublette was hit in the leg, and it was only by the aid of Smith he managed to escape; the party lost their traps, but saved their scalps."

Young organized a second expedition and "chastised the Indians, killing several chiefs, etc., so that his party was enabled to trap unmolested." James Ohio Pattie, a member of this party, gives a confused and inflated account of its wanderings, down the Gila to its mouth and up the Colorado at least as high as the Virgin. The troubles of this party at the Mohave villages led to the massacre of Jedediah Smith's second California expedition, in August 1827. Apparently the party split up into several detachments, one returning to New Mexico by what became known later as the "Spanish Trail." Which party Sublette accompanied has not been determined.

He and Young were back in New Mexico by late May 1827. As there had been a change in administration in Santa Fe, Young concealed his furs at a house in Peña Blanca north of the capital. The furs were nevertheless seized by the Mexican authorities early in June. On July 11 Governor Armijo permitted three of Young's men to air and dust the confiscated pelts, but when they were laid out on the plaza in Santa Fe, Milton (referred to by the governor as "the alien Soblet" and "the thief Soblet") made off with two packs that bore his personal brand. An uproar followed, heard all the way to Mexico City, but neither Sublette nor his furs could be found. In the late summer of 1827 Milton joined the expedition into the northern Rockies led initially by Sylvestre Pratte, and after Pratte's death in North Park on October 1, by Ceran St. Vrain.

Subsequently Thomas L. Smith was shot in the leg by an Indian, the arrow shattering the bone above the ankle. Since no one in the party had the hardihood or surgical knowledge to amputate his foot, Smith operated on himself, using a butcher knife. According to the story told in *Hutchings' California Magazine*, February 1861: "Milton Soublette, compassionating his condition, took the knife from his hand and completed the operation by severing the tendon achilles, and bound it up with an old dirty shirt."

Except for creating a Pegleg Smith, Pratte & St. Vrain's expedition was not successful. It seems to have wintered on or near Green River, possibly in Browns Hole, and got back to Taos about May 23. Milton himself profited to the extent of earning "919.07½" in wages (whether for this one venture is not clear). He had made his peace with the authorities or was able to keep out of their way until he set out for the states in the summer of 1828 with the party of M. M. Marmaduke. This company had several brushes with Indians. William Waldo recalled in 1880 that "Gov. Marmaduke, in company with Milton Sublette, the 'Thunderbolt of the Rocky Mountains,' and five others, seven in all, had a deathly conflict with one hundred and fifty Comanches, west of the Arkansas River, fifty-two years ago," and that the little party, out hunting, "were only saved from certain death by the skill and long experience of Milton Sublette in Indian warfare."

Milton returned to the Rockies with his brother William, leaving St. Louis in March 1829 and reaching Wind River early in July. There, Meek says, William detached Milton, Fraeb, and Gervais to take a considerable party through "the country down along the Bighorn River." They were in the Big Horn Basin in December and accompanied Jedediah Smith and William L. Sublette to the first winter camp, on Wind River. Doubtless Milton went along when, after Christmas, a new camp was made on the Powder. It is not clear whether in the spring of 1830 he trapped with Smith on Yellowstone waters, with Jackson in the Snake country, or independently.

In August 1830 at the Wind River rendezvous Milton joined with Fitzpatrick, Bridger, Fraeb, and Gervais to found the Rocky Mountain Fur Company. Thereafter Fraeb and Gervais headed for the Snake country while Sublette, Fitzpatrick, and Bridger made for the Three Forks of the Missouri (see the sketch of Fitzpatrick). From the winter camp on the Yellowstone, in March 1831 Fitzpatrick set out for the states. Milton and Bridger, as Robert Newell says, "proceded from the yellow Stone River South   Came to Tongue River   lost 57 head of animals by the Crows indians . . . . went from there to powder River   there Bridger & Sublette Separated   Sublette went to the [North] Park on the Platte   I being one of Bridgers number went with him to the head of the Laramas fork   met Sublette in the Park   from there to the Snake Country on Bear River near the Big Lake [Cache Valley]   took up Summer quarters to wait the arival of Mr. Fitzpatrick with Supplies but in vain   left for fall hunt from Bear River to Greys fork of Snake River (a Scrimmge with Black feet) from thare to Snake River and on to Psalmon River a fork of the Columbia   on to deer lodge River and on to the head of flat hed River at that time was called a fork of the River Missourie by our heds, Bridger and Sublette but Since I traveled [I have come] to [k]now Better   from thare we Returned to Psalmon River and met Mr Freab with Supplies from Mr Fitzpatrick and took up winter quarters with the flat heds and napercies   Spring of 1832 hunted from Psalmon River to hennrys fork to Lewises fort [fork] up Salt River Round to Piers hole   Met all hunters of these parts."

This chronicle, covering nearly two years of Milton Sublette's life, is paralleled in Meek's narrative, though with some discrepancies and errors. Meek relates that in the spring of 1832, on Bear River (Kit Carson agrees that one R. M. F. Co. party was on the Bear this spring), Milton was involved in a quarrel as a result of some real or fancied indignity offered John Gray's daughter, "and in the affray Gray stabbed Sublette so severely that it was thought he must die." (Stewart tells of this occurrence in *Edward Warren* but as a deliberate attempt to do away with Milton.) Milton had to be left behind, Meek remaining with him to take care of him while he lived and bury him if he died, "which trouble Sublette saved him, however, by getting well." The convalescence took forty days. The two came near being put to death by a Snake band, but were saved by the intercession of the chief with the help of a girl Meek calls Umentucken Tukutsey Undewatsey, the Mountain Lamb. Meek says that the beautiful Snake girl became the wife of Milton; and after Milton's return to the states, the spirited wife of Meek himself. As seen below, Milton's marital affairs may require untangling.

Following the 1832 rendezvous, the battle of Pierres Hole was brought on by an encounter of Gros Ventres with the R. M. F. Co. party led by Milton, Fraeb, and Gervais. Afterward, the journals of Wyeth and John Ball enable us to follow Milton from the time of leaving Pierres Hole, July 24, until August 28. During those weeks Milton acquired a stepson or a son—if the latter, his intimacy with Umentucken was of longer duration than Meek would give us to think. John Ball writes in his journal under date of August 1: "Mrs. Milton Sublette (a squaw) had a child, and the next day she mounted her horse, the babe was put in a basket feet down and hung on the pommel of her saddle, and she rode fifteen miles that day. Mrs. Sublette also had a child about three years of age who rode a gentle pony. The child was so fastened on by blankets as to keep it upright, and the pony followed the train with loose horses, never straying far from its charge." (Wyeth mentions the birth of the baby on July [30] without saying to whom the squaw belonged.) During this last week of July and the first four weeks of August, Milton and Fraeb descended the Snake to the Raft, ascended that stream to its head, and went on west, across the northern sources of the Humboldt and some southern sources of the Snake, to the head of the Bruneau. Afterward they attempted to descend the Owyhee, but had to make their way to the Snake by way of the Bruneau, crossing over to the north bank of the Snake opposite the mouth of the Malheur about September 20. Wyeth says it was then the intention of Milton and Fraeb "to divide into 3 parties and trap up three streams coming in opposite the upper one of which proves to be the Big Woody [Boise]."

Meek, as one of Milton's party, relates that the company "kept on to the north, coursing along up Payette's River to Payette Lake," where Milton camped while his men went out trapping. Meek and three others "proceeded to the north as far as the Salmon river and beyond, to the head of one of its tributaries, where the present city of Florence is located." There they were joined "by the remaining portion of Sublette's command, when the whole company started south again. Passing Payette's lake to the east, traversing the Boise Basin, going to the headwaters of that river, thence to the Malade, thence to God[d]in's river, and finally to the forks of the Salmon, where they found the main camp [Fitzpatrick, Bridger, et al.]." On November 7 Ferris met a detachment of the company and heard "that they had been down near the Walla Walla trading house of the Hudson Bay Co., but had made a *'bad hunt'* owing to the scarcity of Beaver in that quarter."

From the winter camp on the Pahsimeroi, in February 1833 Milton and Gervais took a thirty-man party back to the Snake country. Bonneville encountered this company, "twenty-two prime trappers, all well appointed, with excellent horses in capital condition" at the south end of Goddin's Defile (canyon of the Big Lost River) about April 6, "in full march for the Malade hunting ground." The snow being too deep for crossing by "the usual pass" to the Malade (now Big Wood River), the rival companies camped together until April 25. Irving's vague summary is the only direct information about the subsequent spring hunt of Milton and Gervais: "We shall not follow the captain throughout his trapping campaign, which lasted until the beginning of June; nor detail all the manoeuvres of the rival trapping parties, and their various schemes to outwit and out-trap each other. Suffice it to say, that after having visited and camped about various streams with various success, Captain Bonneville set forward early in June for the appointed rendezvous"—that is, Horse Creek in the Green River Valley. Bonneville's letter of July 29, 1833, descriptive of his spring hunt, shows more concretely that he attempted to trap the same country Milton, Fraeb, and Gervais had trapped the previous fall (see the sketch of Bonneville).

Milton and Gervais seem to have been at the rendezvous by the time Campbell got there July 5. On July 24 Fitzpatrick, Campbell, and Milton began their march for the Big Horn, Wyeth traveling with them. They reached a navigable point on the Big Horn August 12, and on the fourteenth Milton signed a contract with Wyeth for supplies to be furnished the R. M. F. Co. next year. On August 15 Milton and Wyeth set out down the Big Horn and Yellowstone by bullboat, and on the twenty-seventh they encountered William L. Sublette just below Fort Union. As Milton chose to continue down to the states with his elder brother, Wyeth descended the Missouri without him.

Milton had reached St. Louis by November 20; Dr. Bernard Farrar attended him from that date to December 4. Soon after, he set out for the east, joining Wyeth in Boston Jan. 8, 1834. The two men remained together till the second week of February, separating in New York on the twelfth. On February 14 Milton briefly visited Philadelphia with Hugh Campbell, then continued on to St. Louis, which he reached by March 13. All this time his leg had been bothering him, as well it might in view of the conclusion of Dr. R. W. Gaul ("Death of the Thunderbolt," *Bulletin of the Missouri Historical Society*, XVIII [October 1961], 33-36) that he was suffering from bone cancer. Still he persisted in his plans for going to the mountains with Wyeth.

The young naturalist John K. Townsend, also accompanying Wyeth, reached Independence April 14 and wrote six days later: "We were joined here by Mr. Milton Sublette, a trader and trapper of some ten or twelve years' standing.... He appears to be a man of strong sense and courteous manners, and his men are enthusiastically attached to him." Townsend noted that when the caravan took the trail April 28, "Captain Wyeth and Milton Sublette took the lead," but his intimation that Milton had hired twenty men on his own account is a misunderstanding; they were Wyeth's men.

It turned out that Milton's leg would not serve him. On May 8, at the Little or Red Vermilion, the diarists in Wyeth's party chorused their regret that Milton could go no farther. Wyeth himself said merely: "In the morning Mr Sublette finding that his leg would not bear travelling turned back." In a letter to his backers Wyeth commented: "I am sorry to say that Mr. M. G. Sublettes leg has grown so troublesome that he is to day obliged to turn back and by him I write this. He has given me an order on his partner for the amt. of advances made him payable in furs. I regret this circumstance much but it was unavoidable as he was perfectly unable to go on." Among the missionaries, Jason Lee wrote: "Milton Sublet returned this morning on account of lameness which detained us till 10 o'clock.... Was very sorry to have him leave us for he is a clever man and far better acquainted with the route and with Indians' character than any man in company." Cyrus Shepard observed that Milton was "afflicted with an inflamtory swelling in his leg which has for several days been growing worse and has finally become so bad that he can proceed no further—he will probably either have to lose his leg or his life." And Townsend commented: "He has been suffering for a considerable time with a fungus in one of his legs, and it has become so much worse since we started, in consequence of irritation caused by riding, that he finds it impossible to proceed. His departure has thrown a gloom over the whole camp. We all admired him for his amiable qualities, and his kind and obliging disposition."

Next day Anderson tells of meeting Milton on the back trail; and ten days later, returning down the Missouri, Maximilian encountered him at "Portage d'Independence" (Independence Landing). Confusing Milton with William, the prince said: "He has always been engaged in the fur trade; in the first instance, in opposition to the American Fur company; subsequently, however, in connection with it; he was now waiting for the steam-boat, *Oto*, intending to go by it to St. Louis." Milton reached St. Louis by May 27, when his leg was treated by Dr. Farrar. There proved to be no alternative to amputation, performed on Feb. 4, 1835. For three months thereafter Dr. Farrar dressed the stump. When Townsend published his narrative in 1839, he added a footnote: "I have since learned that his limb was twice amputated; but notwithstanding this, the disease lingered in the system, and about a year ago, terminated his life." No other source speaks of more than one amputation.

Hugh Campbell in Philadelphia had a "*left* cork leg" manufactured for Milton. On Nov. 6, 1835, he wrote William Sublette that it was not yet finished but would be sent on as soon as received. This leg carried Milton on a tour into central Missouri that winter. William wrote Robert Campbell from St. Louis on January 4: "Milton & Fraeb is still at Mr. Cooks [in Callaway County]   I look for them here in a month." Again on February 9, "I have been informed Milton & Fraeb is in Fulton waiting for Fontinell   there is no doubt but they will be here in a fiew days as I have Written Milton to Come down Imedeately as [John B.] Sarpey requested." By February 24 Milton was in St. Louis, requesting Pratte, Chouteau & Co. to pay Dr. Farrar $150 for the amputation, which they did. Three days later William Sublette, writing Robert Campbell concerning his efforts to promote a settlement with Fontenelle, Fitzpatrick & Co., commented: "Milton apears anxious to have Every thing Setled and keeps Verry Steady him & Fraeb." (This evidently refers to the Demon Rum rather than to ambulation on the cork leg.)

Milton traveled out to Fort William with Fitzpatrick in the spring of 1836. Narcissa Whitman refers to him in a letter written from above the Forks of the Platte on June 3: "The Fur Company have seven wagons drawn by six mules each, heavily loaded, and one cart drawn by two mules, which carries a lame man, one of the proprietors of the Company." Milton may not have been so amiable as in 1834, for Narcissa does not mention having him to tea.

The party reached Fort William (or Lucien) on June 14. Afterward Milton accompanied Fontenelle, Fitzpatrick, and Pilcher up to the Green River rendezvous, where Pilcher bought out Fontenelle, Fitzpatrick & Co. for Pratte, Chouteau & Co. When the returns were taken down in the late summer, Milton remained at Fort William. On December 13 he wrote Pratte, Chouteau & Co. that Fitzpatrick had not sent up supplies as promised, in consequence of which the fall trade had been lost. It had been reported to him that Fitzpatrick wanted nothing more to do with him—"that is A thing I neaver craved from the gentleman, though it leavs me in an awkward situation as I am at A loss how to draw on the Company. . . . pleas rite me at cantoonment Levensworth as that will be the first place I shal Call how I shal procede."

The chronicle of Milton G. Sublette ends with an obituary in the *Missouri Republican* June 16, 1837: "Died—On 5th of April last, at Fort William, River Platte, Milton G. Sublette, long known as one of the most enterprising Indian traders of the Rocky Mountains. The deceased first embarked in the Indian trade as early as 1822, & by his intrepid bravery soon acquired an influence amongst his associates which he retained until the hour of his death. The hardy pioneers of the Rocky Mountains, in his death, have met an irreparable loss, which they will long mourn." Dr. Gaul concludes that he was destroyed by cancer, which had spread to his liver and lungs. When William and Solomon Sublette visited the fort in the summer of 1843, they found Milton's grave marked only by a "rude cross, prostrate and broken." Solomon erected upon the grave what Matthew Field called "a monument built somewhat in Christian fashion." Milton seems never to have taken a white wife. Meek volunteers no information as to what might have become of any children borne Milton by Umentucken. She herself, Meek says, was killed by the Bannocks. That would have been the affray at Green River in June 1837.

WILLIAM LEWIS SUBLETTE

William L. Sublette was the eldest of the five sons (Milton Green, Pinckney W., Andrew Whitley, and Solomon Perry) born to Phillip Allen Sublette and Isabella Whitley, a family of Huguenot descent. William was born in Lincoln County, Kentucky, on Sept. 21, 1799. As related in John E. Sunder's biography, *Bill Sublette, Mountain Man*, the family moved to Somerset, Pulaski County, back to Lincoln County, where they lived at Crab Orchard, and eventually, in 1817, to St. Charles, Missouri. Here William served as deputy constable in 1820 and township constable in 1821. Both parents died between December 1820 and January 1822. William administered their estates, a business that preoccupied him till March 3, 1823, and occasionally thereafter.

If Milton went to the Yellowstone with an Ashley-Henry party in 1822, that may have influenced William to sign up with Ashley's second expedition, which set out from St. Louis on March 10, 1823. He shared in the Arikara Defeat on June 2, reportedly as a member of the shore party with Jedediah Smith, and later participated in Leavenworth's Arikara Campaign, being named sergeant major in Ashley's detachment of the "Missouri Legion" prior to the fighting at the Arikara villages on August 9-14. Afterward with Ashley's men he dropped down the Missouri to Fort Kiowa, then late in September set out for the Crow country in Jedediah Smith's little party, which also included Thomas Fitzpatrick and James Clyman. With Smith he wintered among the Crows on Wind River, in February 1824 struck south to the Sweetwater, and in March crossed South Pass to the Green River. Later in the spring he trapped beaver with Smith in the southern reaches of the Green River Valley, probably on Blacks Fork, then in June rode east to the appointed place of rendezvous with Fitzpatrick on the Sweetwater.

With Jedediah Smith and five others, William next made for the Snake country. In the late summer, near the lower Blackfoot River, the Americans came upon some of Alexander Ross's Iroquois, who had been looted by Bannocks, and accompanied these free men to Ross's camp on the Salmon, arriving October 14. Smith and Sublette (identified next summer by Ashley as Smith's assistant) with their companions followed Ross to Flathead Post, which they reached on November 26. They remained at the fort nearly a month, while Peter Skene Ogden was outfitting the new Snake Country Expedition. Ogden started on December 20, and nine days later the little American party came up with him. They went up the Bitterroot, over to the Big Hole, across to the Lemhi, and finally in April 1825 south to the Snake and the Bear.

On April 26 the party of Smith and Sublette started up the Bear while Ogden moved down it, but they soon learned of the presence of John Weber's party in the country and came back down the Bear, overtaking Weber in the valley of the Great Salt Lake. It does not appear that Smith or Sublette had any part in the desertion of Ogden's free men, procured by members of Weber's party on May 24-25, but they all went on together to Ashley's appointed rendezvous on Henrys Fork of the Green at the end of June.

William remained in the mountains the next year, but no definite information as to his movements has come to light, particularly during the fall of 1825. He must have escorted Ashley and Smith to the Big Horn, then trapped his way back to the winter camp on Bear River. When the spring hunt was launched, apparently in late February 1826, one sizable party headed into the country northwest of Great Salt Lake searching for a rumored river rich in beaver, and there is reason to believe that William L. Sublette and David E. Jackson led this party. It was forced, in a starving condition, to swing north to the Snake; and after a circuit of the lower Snake country, made its way back to the Bear in July. Robert Campbell recalled in 1870 that the rendezvous was over before Jackson and Sublette appeared: "After we left Cache Valley, Jackson and Sublette met us on Bear river. Ashley then sold out his interest in the fur trade to Smith, his partner, and to Jackson and Sublette, the new firm being known as Smith, Jackson & Sublette." On July 18, 1826, the new partners signed a provisional contract with Ashley for goods to be sent to the mountains next year, provided confirmation reached St. Louis by March 1.

Ashley set off for the states, and Jedediah Smith launched the "South West Expedition" that took him to California. Jackson and Sublette headed for the Snake. As described in a famous letter by Daniel T. Potts, they reached Yellowstone Lake (thereafter for some years known as Sublette Lake). Afterward they hunted on the sources of the Missouri and finally made their way back to Cache Valley.

Their prospects were now such that on Jan. 1, 1827, William set out for St. Louis with a single companion, "Black" Harris, to confirm the contract with

Ashley. After a notably hard journey the two reached their destination March 4. Within a month Sublette was off for the mountains again with the outfit Ashley had got together. The party left Lexington, Missouri, about April 11, 1827. After their arrival at Bear Lake sometime in June, the trappers had a skirmish with Blackfeet, in which William conducted himself valiantly.

When the rendezvous broke up on July 13, 1827, Jackson and Sublette made for the states. An agreement had been reached by which Ashley should meet them with a new outfit at Lexington, also selling them the pack animals used during the summer. This accomplished to their satisfaction, they set out for the mountains again early in October. An early and severe winter prevented them from getting back to Bear River, and no information has appeared as to where they wintered. There is some indication that Sublette made a spring hunt north of the Snake.

From the Bear Lake rendezvous of 1828 William took down the returns of Smith, Jackson & Sublette, reaching St. Louis toward the end of September. With a new outfit he set out for the mountains again in March 1829. After rendezvousing with Robert Campbell on Wind River and starting a trapping party down the Big Horn, he moved along to Pierres Hole to join Jackson and Smith about August 5. When the fall hunt opened, Jackson turned his attention to the Snake country, while Sublette and Smith took a strong brigade toward the Blackfoot lands. After circling present Yellowstone Park, they established a winter camp on Wind River. So successful was the fall hunt that the partners agreed on a new outfit for 1830. Accordingly, on Christmas Day, Sublette and Black Harris set out for the states. Except for Meek's statement that they traveled on snowshoes with a train of pack dogs, Anderson's Diary for Aug. 27, 1834, is the only source that reflects their experiences. They reached St. Louis Feb. 11, 1830.

Possibly Ashley had given attention to their probable need of a spring outfit, for on April 5 Sublette was able to leave St. Louis with a caravan of ten wagons drawn by five mules each, and two dearborns drawn by one mule each. These were the first wagons ever taken to the northern Rockies, though Ashley had sent out a cannon on a carriage in 1827; Anderson's journals have occasional interesting reflections of these historic wagons. With his caravan Sublette reached Wind River July 16. At the rendezvous Smith, Jackson & Sublette sold out to the newly organized Rocky Mountain Fur Company, after which the partners set out for home. They left Wind River on August 4 and got back to St. Louis about Oct. 10, 1830.

Jackson & Sublette organized a new partnership, and with Jedediah Smith co-operating set out for Santa Fe. They left St. Louis in April 1831, got away from Independence about May 4, and on May 27 reached the Cimarron, where Smith was killed by Comanches while hunting for water. At Santa Fe, reached July 4, Jackson decided to enter into a California mule-buying speculation with David Waldo and Ewing Young. Sublette set out for Missouri about the end of August, to reach Lexington October 16 and St. Louis two weeks later.

As usual—Sublette was probably the most consistently fortunate man ever to enter the Western fur trade—the Santa Fe venture had been successful; and on his return he found Thomas Fitzpatrick at hand, anxious to arrange a spring outfit for the R. M. F. Co. With Robert Campbell helping, Sublette busied himself during the winter and on May 13, 1832, left Independence for the mountains with a party that included Campbell and Nathaniel Wyeth. On the Little Blue Sublette passed Bonneville's company, which had started nearly two weeks earlier. In a journey marred only by a night raid in the Green River Valley July 2, when Gros Ventres ran off a few horses, Sublette reached Pierres Hole July 8.

Ten days later he was wounded while leading the trappers in the battle of Pierres Hole. Robert Campbell took charge of the party on its homeward journey, which commenced July 30. The company rode into Lexington on September 21, and Sublette was in St. Louis soon after. He intimated that he intended to retire from the fur trade (two years earlier he had purchased from J. P. Cabanné a farm at Sulphur Springs in St. Louis County), but as his wound mended he changed his mind, entering into a partnership with Robert Campbell, as seen in the sketch of the latter. Sublette started up the Missouri in mid-April 1833, establishing trading posts as he went, and getting to the Yellowstone August 29, one day before Campbell arrived via the Rockies. He was so ill that for two weeks he lay at the point of death, but he began to mend on September 12, and a few days later left for St. Louis. He did not reach there until mid-November.

Sublette had discussed with his partner a prime object, getting the American Fur Company to agree to a division of the fur country. Campbell had no success with Kenneth Mackenzie at Fort Union, but Sublette did better on a New York visit in January 1834; insofar as the two parties were concerned, the American Fur Company agreed to divide the West with Sublette & Campbell. To Sublette and his partner fell most of the mountain territory, while the Missouri River trade was reserved to the older company. The A. F. Co. bought out all the Sublette & Campbell establishments on the Missouri.

The partners needed a new base, and Sublette had in mind building a new fort on the Laramie even before leaving St. Louis on April 20, 1834, as shown by the license he obtained from General Clark. Anderson's journal depicts what followed, up to the time Sublette left the rendezvous on July 10. Sublette was back in the settlements by the end of August. In July he may have had some expectation that he or Campbell would come out to winter at the new post on the Laramie (see the sketch of Vasquez), but this was not carried out.

The partners had big things in mind for 1835, but instead came to an understanding with the new mountain firm, Fontenelle, Fitzpatrick & Co., to dispose of Fort William, Campbell going up to the Laramie in the spring of 1835 to transfer the property. Dissatisfied with the way Fontenelle and his associates carried out their part of the bargain, Sublette and Campbell through the early months of 1836 were threatening to return to the mountains and make their money on the spot, but this was smoothed out, and the two settled down to a mercantile life in St. Louis.

In 1843 Sublette revisited the Rockies as a member of the excursion party organized by his old friend, Sir William Drummond Stewart. He was by this time politically and socially active in the St. Louis community and angling for an appointment as Superintendent of Indian Affairs. Also he had married Frances Hereford on March 21, 1844. No children were born before his death from consumption, at Pittsburgh, while en route to the East Coast on July 23, 1845. Robert Campbell brought his body back for burial in St. Louis.

Alfred Waugh made a bust of Sublette, based on a death mask, which unfortunately has been lost. Beckwourth says the mountain Indians knew Sublette as "Fate" and as "Cut Face"; Anderson and Matthew Field join in preserving Sublette's Crow name, given by one as "Straight Walking Cane" and by the other as "Straight Walking Rain"; see notes for May 16. Anderson has also left us our most memorable descriptions of Sublette; see p. 237. A description, more prosaic but revealing in its details, is afforded by the passport he carried to Santa Fe in 1831. This presents a picture of William L. Sublette as six feet two, forehead straight and open, eyes blue, nose Roman, mouth and chin common, hair light or sandy, complexion fair, face long and expressive, and "scar on left of chin"—hence Beckwourth's "Cut Face."

LOUIS VASQUEZ

Pierre Louis Vasquez was born in St. Louis Oct. 3, 1798, son of Benito and Julie (Papin) Vasquez. His father died when he was twelve years old, and Louis was reared by his eldest brother, Benito, long active as a Missouri River trader. Thus Louis may have seen the Indian country in his teens. He went to the upper Missouri in 1822 with the Ashley-Henry parties, for Scharf's *History of Saint Louis City and County*, I, 192, says that "Francis Yosti . . . with his friend Luis Basquez (son of Benito Basquez) joined Henry and Ashley's trading expedition to the upper Missouri in 1822, and were in the fight with the Arickaree Indians in 1823."

A letter from his mother to Benito, dated St. Louis, Feb. 27, 1823, speaks of the arrival of a man "who said he had seen Vasquez who was in good health, hunting beaver with several other hunters   according to his story he thinks that they will return this spring if he has a load." Presumably Vasquez participated in the Arikara Campaign as one of the contingent which Andrew Henry brought down from the Yellowstone after Ashley's defeat by the Arikaras. Vasquez then returned to St. Louis, for on Sept. 24, 1823, he was given by Richard Graham a one-year license to trade with "Paunis Republic Fork." He evidently came out of the Pawnee country in the spring of 1824 via Fort Atkinson, the bearer of news concerning fresh Arikara outrages on the Platte. This news was printed in the St. Louis *Enquirer* of June 7, 1824, as having been brought by "Mr. Vasques, just from the Upper Missouri."

Vasquez was still in St. Louis on Dec. 8, 1824, as shown by a letter in the Vasquez Papers, Missouri Historical Society, and thus he could not have accompanied Ashley on the latter's first expedition to the Rockies. Apparently he first journeyed to the mountains in the party of Jedediah Smith, which left St. Louis at the end of October 1825, and wintered along the Republican. Smith's party was joined by

Ashley in the Platte Valley in the spring of 1826 and traveled with the General to Cache Valley, arriving in June.

Vasquez was probably in the Rockies most of the next six years, but he cannot be followed until 1832. On July 28, in Pierres Hole, he witnessed the will of the Iroquois Martin Sword, then set out for the states with William L. Sublette and Robert Campbell. En route, on August 15, he joined Campbell in certifying the contents of caches opened in behalf of the Rocky Mountain Fur Company on the Sweetwater and the Platte. An account of the R. M. F. Co. with William L. Sublette includes an entry dated Oct. 3, 1832, showing a payment to Vasquez of $1,333, doubtless for furs bought at different times since 1830; beaver recently caught he would have brought down from the mountains himself and marketed in St. Louis.

On Dec. 10, 1832, Vasquez drew up his will in St. Louis, in view of his intention of returning to the mountains. In the spring of 1833 he journeyed back to the Rockies with Robert Campbell. Many details of his activities on this expedition are related by Charles Larpenteur. On leaving the Green River rendezvous, Vasquez accompanied Campbell to the head of navigation on the Big Horn, then took charge of the land party when Campbell embarked with his furs in bullboats about August 15. Larpenteur says Vasquez arrived at the mouth of the Yellowstone on September 3. According to Robert Campbell's diary, Vasquez with eight men was started back to the Crow country on September 26. He returned sometime in January or February, having by Larpenteur's account traded thirty packs of robes and one of beaver. About March 1 Vasquez again set off for the Crows, bearing a letter from Campbell to Bridger. Anderson indicates that he made his way south to the Sweetwater and on to Green River, where he joined Fitzpatrick prior to June 15.

From Hams Fork, on July 9, 1834, Vasquez wrote his brother Benito: "I had two men killed this Spring by the Blackfeet, the litte Bourdon from St. Charles and Pierre Hebert of Cahokia. I traded with the Crows last Fall and Spring. I am not going down this year. . . . Mr. Sublette or Campbell are going up again this Fall. . . . If you could find me some novels, Mr. Campbell would be glad to bring them to me." Next day Anderson records the departure of Vasquez and ten men, their objective probably the Laramie Mountains. On Dec. 30, 1834, Vasquez wrote Benito from "Fort Convenience" to say he was in good health. (This fort has not been identified, but conjecturally is a precursor of Fort Vasquez on the South Platte.)

In the summer of 1835, after Sublette & Campbell sold out, Vasquez revisited St. Louis. At that time he leased to Benito seventy-seven and a half acres he owned in St. Louis County and also entered into a formal fur trading association with Andrew W. Sublette. Their first license was dated at St. Louis July 29, 1835. They had reached Independence by August 19, when they swore to the truth of the will witnessed in 1832. They went on out to the South Fork of the Platte and during the autumn of 1835 built the first of the numerous trading posts that sprang up on that river. Fort Vasquez was situated a mile south of present Platteville, Colorado.

A dominant peak in the neighborhood, presumably Longs Peak, thereafter became known to the mountain men as Vasquez Peak.

On Oct. 9, 1836, Vasquez wrote Benito from the Platte to say he was well. He journeyed to the states again next spring; the missionary Moses Merrill recorded his arrival at Bellevue June 3, 1837. In St. Louis, on July 15, Vasquez took out a new license for Vasquez & Sublette, their capital stated to be $2,199, with twenty-two men employed. Another license was issued in 1838. The partners did not confine their business to the Colorado area, ranging north into present Wyoming, Nebraska, and South Dakota. In the summer of 1839 both Vasquez and Sublette were in St. Louis. They left Independence with a new outfit August 6 and got back to their fort September 13.

First and last, they made what William L. Sublette called a "rather sinking business of it," and in 1841 sold out to Locke & Randolph, a firm that soon went broke. Vasquez, who had stayed in the mountains on business connected with the transfer, came in to St. Louis in the summer of 1842, apparently in company with Jim Bridger. This same year Vasquez & Sublette was sued by Sublette & Campbell for the value of goods sold the firm, and the court judgment for $2,751.77 plus costs was met in part by Vasquez' giving up his land in St. Louis County.

Vasquez now entered into a partnership with Bridger. He wrote his brother on Aug. 18, 1842: "I am about to return [to the mountains], we leave Saturday [August 20]. The company offers me advantages by which I am profiting. They advance me merchandise, delivered in the mountains, at 50% advance on the New York prices, and I consider this a great advantage when the freight from here to there is so high &c.... I am leaving to make money or die."

Thus backed by P. Chouteau Jr. & Co., Bridger & Vasquez established a new Fort Bridger on Blacks Fork of the Green, and from this post they traded until Bridger was run out by the Mormons in 1853 (see the sketch of Bridger). Much of the time, Vasquez acted as resident partner. The first word of him after his return to the mountains occurs in a letter from W. D. Hodgkiss to Andrew Drips, dated Platte River, March 25, 1843: "Mr. [P. D.] Papin [at Fort Laramie] received an express from Bridger & Vasques in the winter. They had not done much. The body of traders equipped by H. B. Coy was a strong opposition to them."

As seen in the sketch of Walker, Vasquez brought the year's returns down to Fort Laramie in July 1843. According to Joseph Bissonette, these returns were "very poor." A letter from Bissonette in the David Adams Papers notes that on July 25 Vasquez turned back to Fort Bridger. He arrived there with the Oregon and California emigrants on August 13. With Walker and some of the emigrants, he made an elk hunt on the upper Bear River, then on August 30 returned to the fort with a band of Ute Indians, as recorded by Theodore Talbot. There is no mention of him during the next year, except by his partner (see again the sketch of Bridger), but it is a reasonable certainty that Vasquez was at Fort Bridger when the 1844 emigration passed at the end of August.

Residence at Fort Bridger when Sioux, Cheyennes, and Arapahos were raiding into the area was no sinecure, and for months at a time Vasquez abandoned the fort. In late January 1845 David Adams recorded at Fort Platte that "Bridgrs and waska traping party . . . is in the mountins on litl snak rivr." Overton Johnson, returning from Oregon in the spring of 1845, told of arriving at Fort Hall on June 17, and of seeing a letter written from the camp of "Messrs. Vasques and Smith, (Peg Leg,) . . . addressed to any Company, returning from Oregon to the United States, stating that there were several persons there [probably including Joe Walker], who wished to go down by the first opportunity, and requesting us to come that way. We were informed that they had probably gone, but our anxiety to receive any addition to our numbers, urged us to leave nothing doubtful." Johnson's party from Oregon having been joined at Fort Hall by that in which William Winter had come from California, the combined party started on June 22, and soon arrived at "the camp of Vasques and Peg Leg; the former of whom, had left his trading house, for fear of the Sioux and Shians. We found them several miles from the emigrant's trail, on one of the branches of Green River. . . . We found, upon arriving at this place, that those persons who wrote the letter, which we received at Fort Hall, had met with a company of traders [Antoine Robidoux' party?], and had been gone about twenty days. . . . We passed here, the 4th of July, and on the 5th, again proceeded."

Vasquez was at Fort Bridger when the 1845 emigration passed by; he is mentioned on July 28 by Jacob R. Snyder. He had meanwhile sent—probably through the Johnson and Winter party—a letter to the clerk in charge at Fort Laramie. As relayed to Fort Pierre: "Vasquez writes from Black's fork that in consequence of Bridgers party not having been heard from, he will not come to Fort John this season. He had traded 5 Packs Beaver 600 Do Deer Skins &c. he is very sanguine in his expectations & thinks Bridger will make a first rate hunt." On the heels of this news Bridger reached Fort Laramie on September 2 with his California returns and word that "Vasquez has gone with ten men to hunt on Wind River Mountains."

Next spring Vasquez and Bridger came into Fort Laramie together, arriving about May 29. Vasquez was still on the Laramie as late as June 15, when Francis Parkman mentions him, but he got back to his fort in advance of the emigration, which passed in July. Reportedly it had been the intention of Bridger and Vasquez to visit St. Louis in the fall of 1846, but perhaps only Vasquez did so.

The Oregon-bound party of Elizabeth Dixon Smith Geer traveled with Vasquez from Fort Laramie to Fort Bridger (July 13-Aug. 9, 1847). She calls Vasquez a good and intelligent man who had a white wife. This is the first mention of Mrs. Vasquez, an American woman from Kentucky, Narcissa Burdette Land Ashcroft. She had two children, including a son Hiram, when she married Vasquez in 1846, possibly at Fort Laramie. She bore him a son, "Louis Vasquez, Jr.," at Fort Bridger on July 7, 1847.

No effort can be made here to follow Vasquez after 1847. He traded with forty-niners and is said to have run a ferry on Green River for a time. In 1855 he took the initiative in selling to the Mormons the post from which they had driven Bridger two years before, and the transaction thus begun was completed when he visited Great Salt Lake City in October 1858. Next year Vasquez had business interests in Denver, though he had settled at Westport, Missouri. His last years were mainly spent in St. Louis and Westport and on a farm near that of Bridger south of Westport. Vasquez died at Westport in September 1868.

JOSEPH REDDEFORD WALKER

Walker was born near Knoxville, Tennessee, on Dec. 13, 1798, one of a family of five brothers and three sisters. It is said that the family moved to Bedford County, Tennessee, in 1801, and that Joe spent part of his boyhood in Louisiana and Alabama. In 1818 or 1819 the Walkers moved to Missouri, settling near Fort Osage. According to Irving, Joe was "among the earliest adventurers to Santa Fe, where he went to trap beaver and was taken by the Spaniards. Being liberated, he engaged with the Spaniards and Sioux Indians in a war against the Pawnees; then returned to Missouri, and had acted by turns as sheriff, trader, trapper, until he was enlisted as a leader by Captain Bonneville." Walker's tombstone has the information: "Emigrated to Mo. 1819. To New Mexico, 1820. Rocky Mountains 1832...."

Before embarking on this New Mexico venture, Walker became a stock raiser at Fort Osage. John C. McPherson, writing as "Juanita" in the Oakland *Daily Transcript*, Jan. 15, 1873, says on the basis of an interview with Walker that he "had been on a trip to New Mexico, where he remained for two years, having left a younger brother in charge of his stock. On his return he found himself the owner of a large band of cattle." Joel P. Walker's narrative supplies some dates; Joel tells of going to Santa Fe in May 1822 with a party raised by Stephen Cooper and himself. En route, near the Great Bend of the Arkansas, Joel "saw as I supposed, an Indian with his hair flying up and down. He came up and to my immense astonishment I saw he was my brother, Capt. Joe Walker, who had started the year before trapping.... My brother had a Camanche Indian named Francisco Largo as guide. (My brother had returned to the Arkansas river for goods *cached* there the previous year when on his way to Santa Fe. He had already got them and was returning to Santa Fe when we accidentally met him.)" Apparently Joe stayed with Joel the rest of the way to Santa Fe and returned to Missouri with him in the fall.

On his return home, McPherson writes, Walker "built a distillery for the manufacture of whiskey.... Cattle and hogs, of the latter he had a very large number, and whisky were at that time of little cash value." In July 1825 Walker joined the Reeves-Sibley party sent by the government to survey and mark the Santa Fe Trail to the Arkansas River, and he was concerned in the affairs of this commission until October. On May 23, 1827, George C. Sibley again hired Walker for trail work, but three days later his brother Joel replaced him. Jackson County having just been organized, Joe had been appointed its first sheriff. He was elected sheriff at the first general election in August 1828, but did not stand for reelection in 1830. Walker's markets for his livestock were primarily the Harmony and Union missions in the Osage country, and Fort Gibson in the Indian Territory, where he also sold his whisky. At the fort he became acquainted with Captain Bonneville. According to an obituary in the Sonoma *Democrat*, Nov. 25, 1876: "Bonneville told him of his proposed expedition and wished Walker to join it as a partner; he had not money enough and was engaged as one of the captains of the 240 [110] men which composed the company when it rendezvoused at Fort Osage in 1832." McPherson states somewhat differently: "Bonneville intimated a great desire to form a company for the purpose of trading with the Indian tribes in the Rocky Mountains, if he (Walker) would become a member. After a while, Walker consented and Bonneville obtaining a furlough for two years, proceeded to New York and did form a large company, with a capital of almost unlimited amount. It was determined that Bonneville, Walker and a young man named Sera [Cerré], belonging to St. Louis, would be partners to the extent of one third of the profits arising from trading with the Indians and trapping." This account seems exaggerated, but it is possible that Walker, like Bonneville, did have a financial stake in the enterprise.

For the movements of the company following its departure from Fort Osage on May 1, 1832, see the sketch of Bonneville. After reaching the Salmon River on Sept. 26, 1832, Bonneville sent off three brigades, Irving says, to subsist by hunting buffalo. That is an evident misunderstanding; Walker's party went trapping in the Flathead country as part of a general plan (see again the sketch of Bonneville), the only one sent out at this time. Walker's detachment rode north to the Little Hole northwest of Horse Prairie, fought with Blackfeet, and returned to the Salmon early in November. Soon after, says Irving, Bonneville "detached fifty men towards the south, to winter upon Snake river, and to trap about its waters in the spring, with orders to rejoin him in the month of July [1833], at Horse creek...." Warren Ferris, who went with this party to the Snake, says it numbered forty men, with Walker in charge. They reached the Snake via the Three Buttes on December 11 and set up a winter camp at the mouth of the Blackfoot River. Ferris, who settled in with Drips at the Forks of the Snake a few miles above, speaks of visitors from Walker's camp in February. The spring was late, and it may be that Walker, like Drips, did not open his spring hunt until mid-April 1833.

McPherson's account says: "Mr. Walker with his men wintered on Lewis' Fork, and then went to Green River, which he had left the summer before. Scattering all but six men in different parties to trap, he, with these six persons went towards the cache [at Horse Creek]. On his way he fell in with a large encampment of Snake Indians (two hundred lodges). The chief manifested a very friendly disposition, and offered to accompany Walker and his men as the Blackfeet Indians might be around and massacre them. The Chief and his party went along and remained with Walker till the last of July. This was in 1833." When Ferris reached Bonneville's fort on June 7, he found there "Capt. Walker [who earlier had been reported on Bear River] with some of his men, also John Gray, and a small party headed by Fallen and Vanderburgh.... These different parties had made good hunts, without being molested by unfriendly Indians.... One of Capt. Walker's men had been attacked by a brown bear, but escaped with a broken arm. Some fifty or sixty lodges of Snakes lay encamped about the fort. . . ." Most of the beaver sent down by Bonneville in the summer of 1833 must have been taken by Walker's parties.

Walker now set out on the famous expedition to California, leaving the rendezvous July 24, 1833, with a party of some forty men. This episode is too well known to require detailed discussion here, though much remains to be learned about it. Walker made for the Great Salt Lake, thence for the Humboldt, or "Barren River" as Zenas Leonard of his party termed it, followed that stream to its Sink, kept south along the east foot of the Sierra Nevada to Walker Lake, then made a difficult crossing of the Sierra, in the course of which Walker became (as he afterward contended) the first white man to see Yosemite. After wintering in California, he took his party south through the San Joaquin Valley, recrossed the Sierra by Walker Pass, traveled north to regain his outbound trail, and got back to Bear River in June. He had battles with the Indians near the Sink of the Humboldt coming and going.

After the rendezvous with Bonneville and Cerré on Bear River in late June 1834, the Walker record falls into confusion, Wyeth met Cerré and Walker en route to Green River on July 4 and wrote in his journal that they were "returning to St. Louis with the furs collected by Mr. Bonnevilles company." Irving makes essentially the same statement, after which he never again mentions Walker. Irving further relates that Bonneville at the same time sent a brigade under (Antonio) Montero to hunt in the Crow country with the intention of setting up a winter camp on the Arkansas (this had to be changed, and a summer rendezvous on Wind River was decided upon). The operations of Montero in the Crow country are attested by two letters Zenas Leonard wrote him from Wind River in January 1835, when Montero was on Powder River. Oddly, in his *Narrative*, published as early as 1839, Leonard makes no mention of Montero, assigning the command of the party in the Crow region to Walker and giving many details of Walker's movements with his "55 men."

Leonard further relates that "we"—and he mentions Walker in March—spent April, May, and part of June trapping on the headwaters of various tributaries of the Yellowstone and the Missouri before rendezvousing with Bonneville at the confluence of Wind River and the Popo Agie. However, the Fort Hall Account Books record various transactions with Walker from Dec. 22, 1834, to April 4, 1835, which implies that he joined Bonneville at his winter camp on Bear River. It may be that Walker did hunt on the Crow lands in the fall of 1834 (but see the sketch of Bonneville), then left that country to Montero, operating farther west until June 1835.

Leonard will not leave the record in peace. After mentioning the June rendezvous with Bonneville, he says: "Captain Walker, with 59 men, was to continue trapping in this country for one year from this time, and Captain Bonneville, with the remainder, taking all the peltries we had collected, was to go to the States, and return in the summer of 1836, with as strong a force as he could collect, and a large supply of merchandize, and meet Capt. Walker in this neighborhood." The Captain did revisit the mountains in the summer of 1836, but there is no recorded association between Bonneville and Walker after the summer of 1835. One obituary account of Walker states that he spent four years in the service of the American Fur Company, which would have been from the summer of 1835 to that of 1839, but until 1837 only two ambiguous allusions to him appear in the documents. Fontenelle writes from Fort William, Aug. 1, 1835, in a letter taken up to Drips at the rendezvous: "N. B. you will receive a bridle from Capt Walker which I send up to you." Had Walker gone down to the states and left this bridle at the fort as he passed? The implication is that Walker was not present at the rendezvous of 1835. The Fort Hall Account Books on Nov. 28, 1836, include a transaction with one M. Sorrill that in some way involved Walker, from which we infer that he was then in the mountains, but no more can be made of it.

Alfred Jacob Miller, who made both a portrait and a sketch of Walker on horseback, places Walker at the Green River rendezvous of 1837, after which he disappears until the rendezvous of 1838. Mary Richardson Walker, one of the Oregon missionaries, says when two days above Independence Rock, June 17, 1838: "Met some of Capt. Walker's company." Myra Eells writes in turn on June 25, two days after reaching Wind River with Drips: "Mr. Walker, an American trader in the mountains, comes to our camp with a large company, perhaps 200 or 300 horses." This was ten days before Bridger's company came in, showing that the two had made separate hunts. McLoughlin's remark of Oct. 31, 1837, quoted in the sketch of Fontenelle, might indicate that Walker had hunted "South of the Colorado," and the size of his *caballada* may be significant. On June 29 Mrs. Eells writes: "Mrs. Drips, [Mrs.] Walker and [Mrs.] Robinson [John Robertson] call on us. Wish me to cut a dress for Mrs. R." Then on July 4, "Captain Drips, Walker and Robbins [Robertson] take dinner with us."

Robert Newell says that after the rendezvous (which broke up on July 15, according to Jason Lee): "Mr. J Walker went to the Snake Country with a part of Drips camp 30 or 40 men   Drips took with him 80 or 90." Newell also relates that Walker wintered with a small party on Green River and Hams Fork, part of the time with a group of Bannocks and Snakes. Newell adds: "The Spring commenced to open first of march 1839   on to Blacks fork Green River . . . we arrived there on the 10th of march and now the 21   our horses are mending fast but poor yet   we had a verry hard winter   lost severel horses and mu[les]   snow 2 & 3 feet verry cold   Tedious   from Blacks fork out to Bear River   left Walker on to hams fork to Green River   met Drips [i.e., Harris] with 4 carts of Supplies from below   held randezvous."

The missionary Asahel Munger, who had come to the mountains with the caravan, tells of reaching the Big Sandy on July 4, 1839, and of coming upon Drips there: "Capt. Walker with him," to the joy of all the camp. F. A. Wislizenus similarly tells of the appearance of "Trips and Walker . . . accompanied by their Indian wives and a lot of dogs. The two squaws, quite passable as to their features, appeared in highest state. Their red blankets, with the silk kerchiefs on their heads, and their gaudy embroideries, gave them quite an Oriental appearance. Like themselves, their horses were bedight with embroideries, beads, corals, ribbons and little bells. . . . The squaws . . . took care of the horses, pitched a tent, and were alert for every word of their wedded lords."

Both Munger and Wislizenus describe the low state to which the fur trade had fallen; Munger says: "The American Fur Co. have made a poor collection of furs this year—are brin[g]ing their business to a close." In these circumstances Walker left the service of the company. He went to Fort Davy Crockett in Browns Hole, for Wislizenus, who had gone west as far as Fort Hall and then circled back, ran into him August 23 on the Little Snake River, a few days' travel east of Browns Hole. Walker's little party, Wislizenus observed, consisted of himself "and some trappers and Indians, who had come here some days ago to get dried [buffalo] meat." Walker was "an original among mountain loafers," Wislizenus decided, having "taken such a fancy to this life that it is unlikely that he ever returns to civilization. We found him with a pipe in mouth and clad in nothing but a blanket, for which he excused himself, because his shirt was in the wash."

E. Willard Smith, who visited Browns Hole between Oct. 1, 1839, and Jan. 1, 1840, remarked while at Fort Davy Crockett: "There is a party going in boats from this valley in the Spring, down Grand River of the Colorado of the West, to California. They will be led by Mr. Walker, who was with Bonneville in the mountains. They intend trapping for Beaver on the way." It turned out that Walker could get no one to join in this attempt to trap the canyons of the Colorado by water. A party of mountain men went to California to steal horses, but there is every reason to think that Walker did not go along. (According to Joe Meek, during the winter of 1839-1840 Walker commanded a party of some thirty mountain men who went down the Green River from Fort Davy Crockett as far as the mouth of the Uinta to recapture a herd of horses stolen from the Snakes by "renegade" trappers under Philip F. Thompson; it was these latter who subsequently carried out the celebrated raid on the southern California ranchos.)

He may have visited the states early in 1840 and obtained a passport that would permit him to visit California on legitimate business. Walker next turns up at Los Angeles on Feb. 10, 1841. According to the prefect, Walker and two other Americans (Bridger and Fraeb?), "in charge of twelve individuals of the same nationality," presented a passport viséed by the Mexican chargé d'affaires at Washington, having come "with the object of purchasing horses and remaining in the area two months." Walker offered to convey information to the American government of the horse raids by mountain men the year before. Having established a credit with Abel Stearns, who agreed to buy his beaver at three pesos per pound, he purchased horses from Juan Bandini and others. His presence in the Los Angeles area, with that of Henry Fraeb, is documented (Stearns Papers, Huntington Library) from Feb. 10 to April 7, 1841, when he doubtless set out for Green River (see the sketch of Fraeb).

The next definite mention of Walker is by Matthew Field on July 18, 1843. At the upper crossing of the North Platte, W. D. Stewart's excursion party met some mountain men under Louis Vasquez bringing down the returns of Bridger & Vasquez. With Vasquez, says Field, was Walker, "a fine old mountaineer—hale, stout-built and eagled-eyed, with gray hair." Stewart's men ferried Vasquez and Walker across the North Platte on the morning of the nineteenth, and they went on together toward Fort Laramie. On the twentieth they encountered the Oregon emigration. After delivering their furs at the fort, they overtook the Oregonians at Independence Rock on August 1 and traveled with them to Fort Bridger, reached August 13. Among the Oregon emigrants were some intending Californians led by Joseph C. Chiles. No California trail yet existed, and since Walker had traveled there ten years before, Chiles hired Walker on August 15 to guide the wagon company to its destination.

When he left Fort Bridger two days later, Walker detoured toward the head of Bear River, hoping to procure enough elk meat to last the company to California. On September 14, the evening before Walker left Fort Hall with his emigrants, Theodore Talbot talked with him. "Walker says that he has often endeavored to raise a party to descent Green River, but with no success. . . . He calls it thirty days to California with pack animals, sixty with wagons. He intends to go by way of Mary's River and Lake."

With his charges, Walker established for wagons much of what became the California Trail, going up Raft River, over to Goose Creek, on to Thousand Springs Valley and the Humboldt ("Marys") River, and down that river to its Sink. He then traversed his eastbound trail of 1834, south to Owens Valley, and across Walker Pass to the San Joaquin Valley. By Jan. 1, 1844, he had brought his charges to the site of Gilroy, south of Pueblo de San José.

Walker now went to Monterey, where on Feb. 24, 1844, he applied for a passport authorizing him and three companions to proceed by way of Los Angeles in returning to the states. Obviously he had not been stealing horses and had no reason to fear the authorities. Walker left Los Angeles late in April with the annual caravan to New Mexico. Hearing that Frémont was on the trail, he rode ahead to overtake the young topographical engineer. On May 14, 1844, the day after leaving Mountain Meadows, in the southwestern corner of present Utah, Charles Preuss wrote in his diary: "A small party of eight Americans who come from Pueblo [de los Angeles] have caught up with us and will travel with us. Five of them all the way and three to the Colorado. Among the latter is Captain Walker, a well-known character in this part of the country, who will be most welcome as a guide after we leave the Spanish Trail." Frémont said that Walker had run "the gauntlet of the desert robbers, killing two [Indians], and getting some of the horses wounded." After reaching Utah Lake on May 26, 1844, Preuss observed: "Captain Walker has decided to travel with us to the Arkansas. This is very gratifying because he knows the country very well." The Frémont accounts show that J. R. Walker receipted at Fort William (Bent's Fort), Arkansas River, July 3, 1844, "For services rendered to United States in a journey of Capt Fremont's Expedition, as guide from The Lesser Youta Lake" to "Ft William Arkansas R— at Two Dollars and Fifty cents per diem for Forty-two Days from May 25th to July

5th 1844 inclusive 105 00." (He was given another fifty dollars as an allowance of twenty days' pay to return to the "Snake District.")

After his discharge at Bent's, Walker turned north to Fort Laramie. E. E. Parrish, an 1844 Oregon emigrant who reached Fort Laramie July 31, relates that the emigrants waited briefly after leaving the fort "for Walker's party who wish to join us." Parrish tells of Walker's guide service, appreciated and otherwise, until the arrival at Fort Bridger on August 30, when he says: "Captain Walker kindly conducted us to the place of encampment and then returned to his own wigwam among his own Indians of the Snake nation. It is said he has several squaws, whether servants, concubines or wives, I know not. Mr. Walker has taken some pains to pilot this company from Fort Larimo to Fort Bridger."

Walker may have remained with the Snakes or Vasquez over the winter, or he may have trapped independently. He appears to have come down from the mountains with Antoine Robidoux, who was abandoning the fur trade in consequence of Ute hostility. Lieutenant J. H. Carleton, bound for South Pass with the Dragoons, tells of meeting Robidoux' small company on June 23 near the upper crossing of the North Platte; and Jacob R. Snyder, who left Fort Laramie June 26, three days later encountered "Antoine Robidoux from the Spanish Country," saying that he was obliged to come through this way "on account of the Indians, 8 of his men having been killed."

It appears that Walker turned back from Fort Laramie, overtaking the leading companies of the 1845 emigration at the crossing of the North Platte. On July 8 Philip St. George Cooke, with the returning Dragoons, wrote: "This afternoon Mr. Walker, whom we met at Independence Rock, and who is now on his way to California, visited our camp: he has picked up a small party at Fort Laramie; and wild-looking creatures they are—white and red. This man has abandoned civilization,—married a squaw or squaws, and prefers to pass his life wandering in these deserts carrying on, perhaps, an almost nominal business of hunting, trapping, and trading—but quite sufficient to the wants of a chief of savages. He is a man of much natural ability, and apparently of prowess and ready resource."

On July 17, high on the Sweetwater, the Oregon-bound Joel Palmer fell in with "the celebrated mountaineer Walker, who was traveling to Bridge[r]'s fort," and perhaps traveled the rest of the way to the fort with him. Palmer reached Fort Bridger July 25, as did Jacob Snyder, who decided to pack from that point. When Snyder resumed his journey July 28, he voiced appreciation "to Capt. Walker & Mr. Vascus for their kind attention & assistance, this mode of travel being entirely novel to us."

After the emigration passed, Walker headed south toward White River. Here again the Frémont accounts pick him up; Walker was hired as a member of Frémont's Third Expedition on September 22 (about two days before Frémont reached the Green River down the valley of the White); at the rate of $3.33⅓ per day (a total of $546.066⅔) he continued in Frémont's employ until March 4, 1846. During that time the Expedition made its way to Great Salt Lake, crossed the Salt Desert, and went in two detachments to Walker Lake, Walker guiding the group that traveled via the Humboldt. From Walker Lake, Frémont's party again went on in two divisions, Walker taking one detachment across the Sierra by Walker Pass, with minor variation using his route of 1843. After various delays, described in Edward M. Kern's journal, Walker and Frémont got together again at or near Pueblo de San José early in February 1846. The date Walker left Frémont's service, March 4, shows that this separation occurred at William Hartnell's rancho in the Salinas Valley east of Monterey, just before Frémont got involved with the California authorities.

John McPherson, writing in the Oakland *Daily Transcript*, Jan. 26 and 29, 1873, relates that Walker's nephew, D. F. McClellan, an 1843 California emigrant, made up his mind in 1846 to drive a herd of horses to Missouri with a party announced to return east from Sutter's Fort. In March young McClellan, with one Monro, "drove his animals to Gilroy and there met with his uncle, Capt. Jo. Walker and some of his men. He was induced by his uncle to abandon his intention of returning to Missouri from Sutter's Fort, and to accompany him by the way of Los Angeles on a southern route." Under Walker's guidance they drove the herd south to Isaac Williams' Chino Ranch, beyond Los Angeles, then late in May started on, Solomon P. Sublette making one of this company. "On they journeyed through the Cajon Pass, then over to the Mohave, down that river to a point at which they struck the Santa Fe trail, Capt. Walker, of course, guiding the party. . . . Continuing on the trail, they passed several streams—the Muddy, Virgin river, etc., and at last reached Utah Lake. Passing by the southern extremity of this, they traveled up the Provo, one of the tributaries of the lake, and thence over a range of the Bear River mountains, ultimately arrived in safety at Fort Bridger, on Black's fork of Green river. Every one here was well acquainted with Capt. Jo, and here the party remained for some time."

Walker probably reached Fort Bridger with his horse herd about July 4. He was there on July 9 when W. E. Taylor, with the leading emigrant company, reached the fort, and he was still there on July 24 when Heinrich Lienhard arrived. From these emigrants Walker and his nephew learned of the outbreak of the Mexican War and of the impending march of Kearny's Army of the West to Santa Fe. Accordingly they drove their horses toward the Arkansas. Alexander Barclay at the Hardscrabble fort west of Pueblo on August 20 noted the arrival of "Tim Goodale and party & Cap Walker from Blacks fork" and the departure for Pueblo two days later of "Walker Goodale & party." On August 26 Walker called on Lt. James W. Abert at Bent's Fort. "He has a party encamped on the bank of the river about 8 miles north of the fort," Abert wrote in his journal, "and is there awaiting the arrival of Colonel Price's regiment, for which he has a supply of mules. As the antelope and deer were quite abundant in the vicinity of his camp, Mr. Marcellus St. Vrain went off with him, intending to spend a week in hunting. . . ." Abert recorded other comings and goings, and finally on September 8: "Captain Walker came down the river, having received information of the approach of a large body of volunteer's [Price's Missouri regiment]. He had some sixty head of mules, and will, doubtless, dispose of them to the volunteers with great advantage, both to himself and to the troops, as their horses are completely broken down by the march. . . ."

McPherson says that from Bent's Fort, Walker started with a number of animals for Santa Fe, while McClellan made for Missouri, with the understanding that they would meet at Fort Laramie in the summer of 1847. The nephew went to St. Louis next spring to buy goods and provisions, and on his return was surprised to find Walker at his father's home. Walker had come in with Solomon P. Sublette, who in a letter dated St. Louis, May 4, 1847, relates that, having left Santa Fe with the mail on March 26 with two men and six mules, next day he "was joined by Capt Walker and two men and we traveled together to Ft. Leavenworth where I arrived on 21st April. . . ."

Toward the end of August 1847, McPherson continues: "Frank [McClellan], accompanied by his cousin James T. Walker and seven other persons, including Captain Jo, started for California." That family recollection is documented by a series of letters written by Andrew Goodyear, who had come west this summer seeking his brother Miles. Writing from Independence, Aug. 29, 1847, Andrew refers to a recent conversation with Walker; and in a second letter from Fort Laramie on October 18 relates that he left Independence September 1 in company with four others, mounted on mules and taking along a wagon and four yoke of oxen. "On the 15th of September Captain Walker and two others came up to us, as we were encamped on a branch of the Little Vermillion. His arrival cheered up every one of us, as heretofore we had had neither captain nor guide." Soon after they fell in with P. D. Papin en route to Fort Laramie with six men. On September 26 they reached the Platte; on October 6, a little east of Ash Hollow, encountered Brigham Young returning from the Valley of the Great Salt Lake; and on October 16 arrived at Fort Laramie. The little company resumed its journey October 19 and reached Green River about Nov. 8, 1847. Andrew rode on to his brother's fort on the Weber River, while Walker prepared to winter on Henrys Fork.

Sometime in the winter Walker took the trail to southern California. Lorenzo D. Young, in the infant Great Salt Lake City, remarked in his diary on Jan. 23, 1848, that the presiding authority among the Saints "wants a compney to go to Calafornia to look for a new Rout with Mr. Marke [Walker]," but nothing more appears with regard to the southbound journey. About the middle of May, Kit Carson and Lieutenant Brewerton, en route to New Mexico as a military express, reached the Amargosa River and according to Brewerton came upon "a new party, with a large drove of horses and mules. . . . These new-comers proved to be a small band of Americans, who were driving their cattle [sic] into the Eutaw country, with the view of trading with that tribe of Indians. The owner of the animals and leader of the party was a Mr. Walker, an old acquaintance of Carson's." McPherson does not mention this trip to southern California, saying only that James T. Walker and his cousin Frank McClellan "remained in the Rocky Mountains with their uncle, Captain Jo. till July, 1848, when they left for California." That departure is said to have occurred about the middle of the month.

Richard May, in the rearmost company of the 1848 California emigration, traveled the Greenwood Cutoff, bypassing Fort Bridger. On this route, west of the Green River, May wrote in his diary on July 26: ". . . at our noon halt Joseph Walker, the noted mountaineer met us   he is a very fine looking man   the very picture of health and discourses well on most topics. he continued with the train through the evening. He conducted us through a pass in these mountains by which means we avoided a very steep hill both up & down. Mr. Walker appears to be about 45 years of age and steps off with the alacrity of a youth, but this much may be said of any one that has lived in these mountains a few years. . . ."

How and when Walker moved along to California is not clear. In November 1849 Jacob Grewell reported him living about thirty miles below Sacramento. Grewell said also: "Walker intends to examine the route this spring from the bend of the Joaquin,—Tulare valley—to the Eutaw valley, which can be travelled with pack animals in 17 or 20 days." The Death Valley party of late 1849, traveling west, had no luck with such a route, and Walker did not seriously attempt to work it out. In February 1850, as recounted in the San Francisco *Daily Herald*, Nov. 28 and 30, 1853, he set out from San Francisco "with a party of eight men, and the necessary complement of mules and supplies . . . pushed rapidly down the Coast Range to its junction with the Sierra Nevada, in the neighborhood of the Tejon Pass . . . crossed the Sierra, and turned his face eastwards." The account goes on to say that Walker "struck due east over the inhospitable desert," fell upon the Mohave River, traveled down it 200 miles, "until its course inclined to the south," then "turned off, and left the river to his right," suffering much for water till he reached the Colorado. Crossing that river, he made "across the table land nearly due east, for the Rio Grande. In his journey he followed the course of the Little Red River, or Rio Colorado Chiquito. . . . Capt. Walker crossed the Little Red about sixty miles south of the Moquis villages, and continued his journey, without further adventure, through the Pass in the Rocky Mountains. He struck the Rio Grande, as he had intended, at Albuquerque."

Whether or not it reflects Walker's return from the above trip, a news report in the Los Angeles *Star*, Dec. 13, 1851, tells of his arrival at the Chino Ranch. Having left New Mexico on November 1, "Capt. Walker went to N.M. with the intention of procuring sheep for the California market, but finding they sustained too high a price to render the speculation profitable, he returned without them. . . . [He] had a slight skirmish with the Apaches, but saving that he had no trouble with the Indians."

During most of the next ten years Walker remained in California, spending much of this time on a ranch east of Soledad Mission in Monterey County. In April 1856 Walker's sight was reported affected "by the hardships of his mountain campaigns," but this did not prevent his acting as guide in a campaign against the Yuma Indians in January 1859, or as head of famous prospecting parties in Arizona, 1861-1863 and 1866-1867. When he returned to California, he settled on the ranch of his nephew, James T. Walker, in the Ygnacio Valley, Contra Costa County, where he lived until his death on Oct. 27, 1876. Walker never married in civilization, so far as is known. No children by Indian wives are recorded.

LEONIDAS D. WALKER

According to Frederic L. Billon, *Annals of St. Louis, 1804-1821*, p. 276, Walker was born Aug. 16, 1817, and died Aug. 4, 1866. He was the son of Dr. David Walker, who settled at St. Louis in 1812. Dr. Walker's first wife was Matilda, daughter of Maj. William Christy, who moved to St. Louis from Kentucky in 1804 and occupied various positions until his death in 1837. (Another daughter of Major Christy was the second wife of William H. Ashley; a sketch of his eldest son, Edmund Christy, may be found on an earlier page.) Walker became a post-office clerk in St. Louis. In March 1843 he was tried for the murder of Bethel S. Farr but found not guilty. He revisited the Rockies that summer as one of Stewart's excursion party; Matthew Field recorded among the inscriptions on Independence Rock "L. D. Walker (Susan) 43" and "L. D. Walker 34." (The latter was the only 1834 inscription Field noted.) During the Mexican War Walker served with Battery A from Missouri. Walker was only sixteen years old when he had the adventure Anderson describes in the Diary on June 11.

JOHN H. WEBER

According to his son William, John H. Weber was born in 1779 in the town of Altona, near Hamburg, then part of the Kingdom of Denmark. At an early age he ran away to sea, eventually becoming master of a sailing vessel. The Napoleonic wars forced him to come to America, and by July 29, 1807, he was living at Ste. Genevieve, Missouri. He is presumably the Weber mentioned in the narrative of Solomon Zumwalt, one of four soldiers who during the War of 1812 survived an Indian attack at Fort Cap-au-Gris on the Mississippi about Cuivre River—"a grate swimer" who came off victorious in an underwater knife fight.

In the Missouri mining district, as at Ste. Genevieve, Weber was thrown into intimate association with William H. Ashley and Andrew Henry. In September 1814 he was at Mine à Breton and three years later signed a petition (also signed by Ashley and Henry) asking statehood for Missouri. In 1822 he became associated with the Ashley-Henry fur trading enterprise. His son, in an account published about 1908, reprinted in Charles L. Camp, "The D. T. P. Letters," *Essays for Henry R. Wagner*, pp. 24-25, declared him to have been an actual partner. J. C. Hughey of Bellevue, Iowa, published a similar statement in the Salt Lake *Tribune*, July 24, 1897, p. 31. Both accounts say that after reaching the Yellowstone in 1822, Weber and Henry took charge of separate thirteen-man parties. Since Henry is known to have conducted a group up the Missouri that fall, and another is known to have set out up the Yellowstone, this assertion as to Weber may be correct.

Nothing is definitely known of Weber's experiences until Ashley mentions him on June 7, 1825, as having wintered west of the continental divide. It is apparent, however, that he was at the head of the party that set out from the Big Horn in July 1824, and with Daniel T. Potts, Jim Bridger, Ephraim Logan, Samuel Tulloch, Caleb Greenwood, and some twenty others crossed South Pass and the Green River Valley, made a fall hunt on Bear River, and set up a winter camp in Cache

Valley just north of the Utah-Idaho line. Jim Bridger in 1861 named him as heading this party, and James P. Beckwourth's autobiography consistently applies the name Weaver's Lake to Bear Lake, indicating another connection with events of 1824. In the spring of 1825 Weber took his party down into the Valley of the Great Salt Lake; the name of the Weber River no doubt dates from this time. Anderson's suggestion that Weber might, with better warrant than Ashley, be considered a discoverer of Great Salt Lake reflects the circumstance that Jim Bridger was one of his party when Bridger undertook the reconnaissance in the late fall or winter of 1824-1825 that made the lake known to American trappers (see the sketch of Bridger).

According to his son William, Captain Weber left the mountains in 1827; perhaps the year should be 1825 or 1826, for another son, Stephen Decatur Weber, is reported to have been born in Missouri Nov. 2, 1827. From St. Louis the Captain moved to Galena, Illinois, in the spring of 1832, and twelve years later crossed the Mississippi to Bellevue, Iowa, where he supported himself by various clerical jobs. Census returns in the National Archives show the captain living at Galena in 1840 as head of a family, and at Bellevue in 1850 in his son William's household, his age in the latter year given as seventy and the place of his birth as Denmark. A sufferer from neuralgia, he put an end to his life in the winter of 1859 by cutting his own throat, dying in a few minutes. Weber is described as having been "a man of large and powerful frame, of erect carriage and graceful manner; his face indicated the superior intelligence behind it, he had a nose like a Roman Emperor and an eye as regal and piercing as that of an American eagle, the courage of a hero, and the staying qualities of a martyr. . . , but he was impetuous and peculiar in many ways and at times disagreeable and unhappy."

NATHANIEL JARVIS WYETH

Wyeth was born at Cambridge, Massachusetts, on Jan. 29, 1802. By the time he was twenty-two he had married a cousin, Elizabeth Jarvis Stone, and become manager of an ice company at Fresh Pond owned by Frederic Tudor. Having an inventive turn of mind, Wyeth devised many of the implements used in the ice business, and with Tudor succeeded in establishing an ice export business to the tropics.

In 1831 Wyeth was attracted by the proposals of Hall Jackson Kelley for the colonization of Oregon. A man of action and of a practical bent, he soon gave up any idea of cooperating with Kelley. Instead he launched a serious effort to exploit the resources of the Columbia River basin, especially its furs and fish. Having organized a joint stock company of which he was the sole director and business agent, Wyeth obtained backing and sailed from Boston March 10, 1832. He reached Baltimore March 23 and soon after was off for the West, arriving in St. Louis April 18. William L. Sublette gave him a friendly reception, regarding Wyeth not so much a competitor as a babe in the woods. Thus he and his company tagged along when Sublette left Independence May 13. Some of the party turned back during the ten-day stopover at Independence; three more quit after traveling 170 miles; and thus the "Oregonians" were reduced to twenty-one by the time they reached Pierres Hole.

Because Wyeth declined to submit to "democratical" procedures, knowing the need for a controlling authority, nine of his men left him in the shadow of the Tetons. With the other eleven he was leaving Pierres Hole with the R. M. F. Co. brigade led by Milton Sublette and Henry Fraeb when the collision with the Gros Ventres brought on the battle of Pierres Hole. Six days later, on July 24, he started anew in company with Milton, remaining close to him in a trapping tour south and west until August 29, when he started down the Bruneau. Wyeth reached the Snake September 10 and the Malheur a week later. After a foray up that stream, he continued on across the Blue Mountains, to arrive at Fort Nez Percés (Walla Walla) on October 14. Wyeth then descended the Columbia in a Hudson's Bay Company barge, to reach Fort Vancouver October 29. Eight days later he went on down the Columbia. After looking over the country at its mouth, he returned to Fort Vancouver November 15.

Wyeth's men asked to be released, and he did release most of them, the ship on which he had depended for supplies having been lost at sea. He remained at Fort Vancouver till November 29, then made a ten-day tour up the Willamette, examining its valley for seventy-five miles. The rest of December and January he passed the time as a guest at Fort Vancouver, enjoying the company of Dr. McLoughlin and his people.

Francis Ermatinger left Fort Vancouver for the interior on February 3, carrying up goods for the Hudson's Bay Company's interior posts. Wyeth went along, remaining with Ermatinger until July 7. The itinerary took him to Fort Walla Walla, old Spokane House, Fort Colvile, and Flathead Post, then to the Salmon River by the usual route via the Bitterroot and the sources of the Missouri. He reached the Salmon on May 29, having traveled with the Flathead village for some weeks. On July 2 he camped with Captain Bonneville in the basin of the Snake. He and the Captain came to an agreement by which Wyeth should lead a trapping party to California, but this fell through—the project was alive July 4 and dead the next day. (Perhaps Bonneville had decided on his own account to send Joe Walker on such an expedition.) After separating from Ermatinger, Wyeth rode on to Pierres Hole, over to Jackson Hole, on again to Fort Bonneville at Horse Creek, which he reached July 15; he then settled in at the R. M. F. Co. camp ten miles farther down the Green.

When the rendezvous broke up on July 24, Wyeth took the trail to the Big Horn with Fitzpatrick and Campbell; most of the companies were sending returns down by water this summer, because the Arikaras were acting up on the Platte. The combined party reached the Popo Agie July 31 and the Big Horn August 12. Two days later Wyeth and Milton Sublette started down the Big Horn in a bullboat.

Wyeth had reached a tentative agreement with Fitzpatrick and Milton Sublette to provide the R. M. F. Co. with goods, a three-thousand-dollar outfit (at first cost), to be paid for in beaver at four dollars a pound in the mountains. Since he was uncertain whether he could find backing, and there were uncertainties on the part of Milton and Fitzpatrick, the contract provided for abrogation by either side on payment of a five-hundred-dollar forfeit. Wyeth and Milton reached Fort Union August 27, and next day encountered William Sublette, ascending the Missouri for his appointed meeting with Robert Campbell. Milton delayed to go back to the states with his brother, but Wyeth went right on, reaching Fort Leavenworth September 27 and St. Louis October 9. A month later he was back in Cambridge. By November 19 he was writing Milton that he was prepared to go ahead with the contract. He did not regard this contract as big business, amounting to "little more than carrying me into the Indian country free of expense and procuring the buisness of a very efficient concern." He had learned much during his two years in the West, so that he was anything but a greenhorn now, and he thought he could put the fur trade on a sounder basis: goods might be sent to the Columbia by sea and furs shipped home the same way, with costs cut all along the line. He had in mind a mutually advantageous arrangement with the Hudson's Bay Company, and also believed a salmon-packing business could be established on the Columbia, the salted salmon to be carried home in the same vessel that transported his furs. To carry out these plans, he organized a "Columbia River Fishing and Trading Company," fitted out a brig to sail around Cape Horn, and himself left Boston Feb. 7, 1834, with Milton Sublette.

This overland expedition of 1834 is more fully described in the Introduction and the notes. Milton had to turn back soon after leaving the frontier, and when Wyeth reached the rendezvous Fitzpatrick paid the forfeit in preference to accepting Wyeth's goods. Angered, Wyeth continued on to establish the trading post on the Snake envisioned before leaving home (it is a mistake to suppose that this project originated in pique). Thus was founded Fort Hall July 15, 1834. Wyeth contemplated that two dependent posts should be built later, one near the Great Salt Lake, another on the Salmon River. Leaving Robert Evans in charge of Fort Hall, Wyeth resumed his journey on August 6, going via Big Lost River, Camas Prairie, and Boise River to the Snake. He then took the familiar road across the Blue Mountains to arrive at Fort Walla Walla September 2. Twelve days later he was paying his respects to Dr. McLoughlin.

The day after he reached Fort Vancouver, Wyeth's brig arrived in the Columbia. She had been struck by lightning at sea, requiring her to put into Valparaiso for repairs. In consequence of the delay, she had missed the salmon fishing season. Undiscouraged, Wyeth located a base, Fort William, on Wappatoo Island at the mouth of the Willamette, also selecting a farm site some distance up the Willamette. He remained on the lower Columbia until the fall of 1835, during that time ascending no higher than Fort Walla Walla, from whence in November 1834 he sent Capt. Joseph Thing to relieve Robert Evans in charge of Fort Hall.

His enterprise and energy availed nothing. On Sept. 6, 1835, he wrote Tudor: "This buisness has not been successful in any of its branches therefore it will terminate soon. I shall not order another equipment to this country until I see again those concerned with me, and if I know the people they will be the last to go very far in any buisness that commences unprofitably." He anticipated that he would be back in Boston by Nov. 1, 1836, coming by way of Santa Fe and New Orleans, and he made no bones of saying he might be glad to reenter Tudor's ice business. To his brother Charles he wrote: "Our salmon fishing has not succeeded. Half a cargo only obtained. Our people are sick and dying off like rotten sheep of billious disorders. I shall be off by the first next month to the mountains and winter at Fort Hall. In the Spring I shall return here, then again to Fort Hall and start about June to see all in the States, lucky if I get through with all this without accident."

He did not reach Fort Hall until about Dec. 9, 1835. Osborne Russell, who gives the date as December 20, says he brought a contingent of sailors and Kanakas to replace men whose time had expired. Wyeth turned back to the Columbia about the end of February 1836. He had not entirely given up hope as late as May 5, when he sought from the Hudson's Bay Company an agreement he might present to his partners. He was prepared to abandon Fort Hall if necessary, and carry out his part of the trade "on the waters of the Salt Lake, the Colorado del Norte, and the Rivers of the Atlantic." A biographical statement Wyeth prepared in 1847 passes over this fruitless project, saying merely that in the autumn of 1835 he "proceeded to Fort Hall with supplies, having sent some previous to that time. During the winter of 1836 I resided at my post of Fort Hall, and in the Spring of that year returned to Fort William of Wappatoo Island whence I carried more supplies to Fort Hall arriving there the 18th June, and on the 25th left for the U. S. by way of Taos and the Arkansas river and arrived home early in the Autumn of 1836." He visited the rendezvous site of 1836 before wending his way homeward, arriving July 1 and leaving two days later, before the caravan arrived. After his long journey by way of New Mexico, he reached Liberty, Missouri, on Sept. 2, 1836, bringing with him 1,100 beaver and a small quantity of castoreum.

Wyeth remained in the ice business until he died on Aug. 31, 1856. On leaving Fort Hall, he had placed Joseph Thing in charge. A year later Thing as agent for the Columbia River Fishing and Trading Company disposed of the fort to the Hudson's Bay Company, and himself returned to Boston in 1839.

Bibliography

MANUSCRIPTS

Adams, David. Papers. Missouri Historical Society. Includes his fragmentary papers with Bonneville, 1832-1837; fragmentary diaries, 1841-1845; and letters by Zenas Leonard, 1835.

American Board of Commissioners for Foreign Missions. Archives deposited in Houghton Library, Harvard University. Includes correspondence with various missionaries who traveled overland to Kansas, Nebraska, and Oregon beginning in 1834, including Samuel Allis, John Dunbar, William H. Gray, Samuel Parker, Asa Bowen Smith, Henry Harmon Spalding, Elkanah Walker, and Marcus Whitman. The reports of some of these men amounted to diaries and have been published as such.

Anderson, Kitty. A Historical House and Its Famous People. Typescript in Huntington Library.

Anderson, Richard Clough. Papers. University of Illinois Library. From 7,000 to 8,000 letters, 1785-1881, to and from Richard Clough Anderson and members of his family, including some dozen items concerning William Marshall Anderson, 1839-1854, relating to land entries, surveys, warrants, etc.

Anderson, William Marshall. Anderson-Latham Papers, 1771-1911. The Filson Club, Louisville, Ky. Includes 30 letters from William Marshall Anderson to Allen Latham, 1826-1843.

———. Letters, 1824-1891. Draper Collection, State Historical Society of Wisconsin.

———. Papers. Huntington Library. Includes Rocky Mountain diaries, March 13-Sept. 29, 1834, and journal, 3 vols.; Mexican diaries, 1865-1866, 7 vols.; and family correspondence, scrapbooks, newspaper clippings, and ephemera, 1868-1936.

Archives of California, 1767-1846. Notes and transcripts. Bancroft Library.

Ashley, William H. Letter (draft copy) to Gen. Henry Atkinson, December 1825. State Historical Society of Missouri.

———. Papers. Missouri Historical Society.

Atkinson, Henry. Journal, 1818-1820. Kept in large part by Lt. Thomas Kavanaugh. Coe Collection, Yale University Library.

Ayer Collection, Newberry Library. Includes various fur trade papers.

Ball, John. Itinerary from Independence, Missouri, to Fort Walla Walla, May 12-Oct. 18, 1832. Typescript in Oregon Historical Society.

———. Papers. Private collection of Fred A. Rosenstock, Denver, Colo.

Barclay, Alexander. Papers. Bancroft Library.

Bidwell, John. California, 1841-8: An Immigrant's Recollections. Bancroft Library.

———. Letter to H. H. Bancroft, Feb. 7, 1884. Bancroft Library.

BIBLIOGRAPHY

Bonneville, Benjamin Louis Eulalie de. Letters relating to his venture in the fur trade, 1831-1836. National Archives, Records of the War Department. Printed in whole or in part in A. H. Abel-Henderson, "General B. L. E. Bonneville" (1927); J. Neilson Barry, "Captain Bonneville" (1932); and Washington Irving, *The Adventures of Captain Bonneville U.S.A.* (1961).

Campbell, Robert. Dictation, 1870. Missouri Historical Society.

——. Estate Papers. Missouri Historical Society.

Census Records. National Archives, Records of the Bureau of the Census.

Chouteau Collection, Missouri Historical Society. Includes Chouteau Account Books, Fort Tecumseh and Fort Pierre journals, Fort Union Letterbook, and cited letters by Bartholomew Berthold, A. R. Bouis, James Bridger, J. P. Cabanné, L. Crawford, E. T. Denig, Andrew Drips, Lucien Fontenelle, James Archdale Hamilton, William Laidlaw, Kenneth Mackenzie, Joshua Pilcher, Ceran St. Vrain, Milton G. Sublette, and William Henry Vanderburgh.

Collet's Index to St. Louis Church Registers. Missouri Historical Society.

Drips, Andrew. Papers. Bancroft Library. Includes cited letters by Lucien Fontenelle and T. H. Harvey, and Joseph Perkins memoranda.

——. Papers. Missouri Historical Society. Includes cited letters by Lucien Fontenelle, W. D. Hodgkiss, and Joseph Perkins memoranda, as well as data on Drips family history.

Ellison, Robert H. Notes respecting William Marshall Anderson and his diary of 1834. Huntington Library.

Field, Matthew. Papers. Missouri Historical Society.

Fontenelle, Lucien. Letter to Kenneth Mackenzie, Fort Union, Sept. 11, 1832. Beinecke Collection, Yale University Library.

Fort Hall Account Books. Oregon Historical Society.

Frémont, John Charles. Accounts relating to his Western expeditions, 1842-1847. National Archives, Legislative and Fiscal Branch, Records of the General Accounting Office.

Gantt, John. See Ritch Collection and McCoy, Isaac.

Gauld, Charles Anderson. Biography of William Marshall Anderson, dated Vancouver, Wash., Dec. 12, 1954. Typescript in Anderson Collection, Huntington Library.

Gordon, William. Correspondence with the Secretary of War and officials of the Office of Indian Affairs, 1831-1836. National Archives, Records of the Bureau of Indian Affairs.

Gray, William Henry. Diary, Dec. 28, 1836-Oct. 15, 1837. Original in Oregon Historical Society, paginated 92-[182]. Gray's missing overland diary for 1836 once formed part of this manuscript.

——. Memories of 1848-1849 written for the *Oregon American*. Photocopy in Bancroft Library.

Grewell, Jacob. Notes of interview by Benjamin Hayes, 1850. Bancroft Library (C-E 92).

Hempstead, Stephen. Letterbook kept as Acting Partner at St. Louis for Missouri Fur Company, 1821-1823. Coe Collection, Yale University Library.

Kearny, Stephen W. Diaries, 1820-1841. Missouri Historical Society.

Kennerly, James. Diaries, 1823-1840. Missouri Historical Society.

Larpenteur, Charles. Papers. Minnesota Historical Society. Includes diaries, 1833-1872, and autobiography, 1833-1871.

Lee, Jason. Correspondence with the Board of Home Missions, Oct. 1835-Oct. 1843 (26 letters). Office of Board of Home Missions and Church Extension, Methodist Episcopal Church, Philadelphia.

———. Letters to Dr. Wilbur Fisk, May 2-3, June 29, 1834; Feb. 6, 1835; March 15, 1836. Wesleyan University, Middletown, Conn. Printed in Brosnan, *Jason Lee*, q.v.

———. Overland diary, April 20, 1834-July 17, 1838. Lee Papers, Oregon Historical Society.

———. Typescripts by Cornelius James Brosnan of material relating to Jason Lee et al., in Methodist publications (2 vols.). Bancroft Library.

Lee, Richard Bland. Letters relating to his travels in New Mexico and the Rocky Mountains, 1833-1834. National Archives, Records of the Adjutant General's Office.

Lewis, John F. Diary, May 12-Dec. 31, 1849. Yale University Library.

Lorton, William B. Overland diary of 1849. Bancroft Library.

McCoy, Isaac. Papers. Kansas State Historical Society. Include a letter from John Gantt, Fort Cass, Arkansas River, March 10, 1835.

McDonald, Archibald. Papers. Provincial Archives of British Columbia. Include a letter to Dr. John McLoughlin, June 5, 1841.

Mann, Henry R. Incomplete diary, June 21-Sept. 18, 1849. Photocopy in Bancroft Library.

Maximilian-Bodmer Collection. Deposited in the Joslyn Museum and Art Gallery, Omaha, by the Northern Natural Gas Company. Includes Maximilian's diaries, 1833-1834, correspondence, and numerous original sketches by Charles Bodmer.

May, Richard. Diary, May 7-Oct. 10, 1848. Bancroft Library.

Miller, Alfred Jacob. Rough Draughts for Notes to Indian Sketches. Gilcrease Institute, Tulsa, Okla.

Miner, C. C. History of Fort Bridger, Fort Bridger, Wyo., 1884. Bancroft Library.

Munger, Asahel. Diary, May 4-Sept. 4, 1839. Draper Collection, State Historical Society of Wisconsin.

O'Fallon, Benjamin. Letterbook, 1823-1829. Coe Collection, Yale University Library; photocopy in Bancroft Library.

Oregon Donation Claim Records. Oregon Historical Society.

Potts, Daniel Trotter. Letters respecting his experiences in the Rocky Mountains, 1824-1828. Yellowstone National Park Museum; photocopies in Bancroft Library.

Parker, Samuel. Letter to his family, Aug. 19, 1835. Photocopy in Oregon Historical Society.

Parkman, Samuel (Pablo). Papers. Bancroft Library.

Risvold, Floyd E. Private collection, Minneapolis, Minn. Includes correspondence of William H. Ashley, Robert Campbell, Andrew Drips, Thomas Fitzpatrick, Lucien Fontenelle, Jedediah S. Smith, William Drummond Stewart, William L. Sublette, and John Kirk Townsend, 1829-1836, and deposition of Arthur Black, 1832.

Ritch Collection. Huntington Library. Includes cited New Mexico customs records respecting Michel Cerré and Spanish copies of documents relating to John Gantt, 1831-1832.

Robertson, John. Letter to his mother, Green River, Aug. 5, 1837. Union Pacific Historical Museum, Omaha; photocopies in Missouri Historical Society and Bancroft Library.

St. Louis Cathedral, New Orleans. Baptismal records.

Shepard, Cyrus. Diary, March 3, 1834-Dec. 20, 1835. Coe Collection, Yale University Library.

Smith, Jedediah S. Estate Papers. St. Louis Probate Court, File 930; film in Bancroft Library.

———. Family Papers. Bancroft Library.

Spalding, Henry Harmon. Narrative of an overland journey to Fort Vancouver and Lapwai in 1836. Typescript in Miller Collection, Yale University Library.

Stearns, Abel. Papers. Huntington Library.

Stuart, Robert. Diary, June 29, 1812-April 30, 1813, and rewrite known as "travelling memoranda" written between June 1813 and April 1821. Coe Collection, Yale University Library.

Sublette Papers. Missouri Historical Society. Letters and accounts of William H. Sublette and Solomon Sublette; includes cited letters by Hugh Campbell, Robert Campbell, Thomas Fitzpatrick, William Drummond Stewart, and Andrew Sublette; and William L. Sublette's fragmentary diary of 1843.

Talbot, Theodore. Papers. Library of Congress.

Thing, Joseph. Papers. Yale University Library.

Townsend, John Kirk. Papers, 1834-1846. Academy of Natural Sciences of Philadelphia. Includes copy of his journal, 1834-1836, as sent his family, and fifteen letters sent his family during the same period.

Turner, Henry S. Journal of Gen. Kearny's Return from California in 1847. National Archives, Records of War Department, Adjutant General's Office, 249K/1847; photocopy in Missouri Historical Society.

Vasquez, Louis. Papers. Missouri Historical Society.

Walker, Elkanah. Diary, March 7-May 15, 1838. Huntington Library.

Walker, Mary Richardson. Diary, May 9, 1837-Nov. 11, 1848. Huntington Library.

White, Elijah. Letter from Fort Hall, Aug. 15, 1842, to the Secretary of War. National Archives, Records of the Bureau of Indian Affairs, Letters Received, Oregon Superintendency.

Whitman, Marcus, and Narcissa Whitman. Papers. Bancroft Library. Includes copy of her diary, July 18-Oct. 18, 1836, made by Narcissa Whitman for her mother-in-law; a fragmentary diary, May 14-July 13, 1835, of Whitman's first journey to the Rocky Mountains with Samuel Parker; letter by Whitman to his stepfather and mother, June 3, 1836; and letters by Mrs. Whitman to her brother-in-law, June 27 and July 16, 1836.

———. Papers. Whitman College Library, Walla Walla, Wash. Includes the version of Narcissa Whitman's diary, July 18-Nov. 1, 1836, sent her parents.

Work, John. Diaries, July 1823-Oct. 1835. Provincial Archives of British Columbia, Victoria, B. C.

Wyeth, Nathaniel Jarvis. Papers. Oregon Historical Society.

PRINTED SOURCES

Abel-Henderson, Annie Héloise. "General B. L. E. Bonneville," *Washington Historical Quarterly*, XVI (July 1927), 207-230.

Abert, James W. *Journal . . . from Bent's Fort to St. Louis in 1845.* 29th Cong., 1st Sess., Sen. Doc. 438 (Serial 477). [Washington, D.C., 1846].

———. . . . *Report and Map of the Examination of New Mexico* [1846-1847]. 30th Cong., 1st Sess., Sen. Ex. Doc. 23 (Serial 506). [Washington, D.C., 1848].

———. *Western Americana in 1846-1847,* ed. John Galvin. San Francisco, 1966.

Allen, A. J. *Ten Years in Oregon. Travels . . . of Dr. E. White and Lady West of the Rocky Mountains....* Ithaca, N.Y., 1848.

Allis, Samuel. "Forty Years among the Indians and on the Eastern Borders of Nebraska," Nebraska State Historical Society, *Transactions*, II (1887), 133-166.

———. "Letters to the American Board Relating to the Pawnee Mission," Kansas State Historical Society, *Collections*, XIV (1915-1918), 690-699.

Alter, J. Cecil. *James Bridger, Trapper, Frontiersman, Scout and Guide. . . .* Salt Lake City, 1925. Expanded ed., Columbus, Ohio, 1951. Recast as *Jim Bridger*, Norman, Okla., 1962.

American Heritage. *Book of Indians.* New York, 1961.

[Anderson, Charles]. *Ye Andersons of Virginia and Some of Their Descendants.* [1908].

Anderson, Edward Lowell. *Soldier and Pioneer: A Biographical Sketch of Lt.-Col. Richard C. Anderson of the Continental Army.* New York, 1879.

Anderson, Richard Clough, Jr. "Cartagena to Bogotá, 1825-1826 . . . ," ed. E. Taylor Parks and Alfred Tischendorf, *Hispanic American Historical Review*, XLII (May 1962), 217-231.

———. *Diary and Journal, 1814-1826,* ed. Alfred Tischendorf and E. Taylor Parks. Durham, N.C., 1964.

Anderson, Thomas McArthur. *A Monograph of the Andersons, Clark, Marshall and McArthur Connection.* [Portland, Oregon, 1908].

Anderson, William Marshall. "Adventures in the Rocky Mountains," *American Turf Register*, VIII (May 1837), 409-412.

———. *Adventures in the Rocky Mountains in 1834.* Reprinted from *American Turf Register*, 1837. [New York, 1951].

————. *An American in Maximilian's Mexico, 1865-1866* . . . , ed. Ramón Eduardo Ruiz. San Marino, Calif., 1959.

————. "Anderson's Narrative of a Ride to the Rocky Mountains in 1834," ed. Albert J. Partoll, *Frontier and Midland*, XIX (Autumn 1938), 54-62. Contains entries for May 27 to June 19, derived from last two installments of the Narrative as printed in the Circleville, Ohio, *Democrat and Watchman*, 1871. Reprinted as *Sources of Northwest History*, No. 27, Missoula, 1938; and in John W. Hakola, ed., *Frontier Omnibus*, Missoula and Helena, 1962.

————. "A Horseback Ride to the Rocky Mountains in 1834," Circleville, Ohio, *Democrat and Watchman*, Sept. 15, 22, 29, Oct. 13, 1871.

————. "Letter to the National Intelligencer February 16, 1860" [published Feb. 25, 1860]. Reprinted in J. H. Simpson, . . . *Report of Explorations across the Great Basin of the Territory of Utah*, Washington, D.C., 1876.

————. "Scenes and Things in the West," *American Turf Register*, VIII (Nov. 1837), 549-552.

————. "Scenes in the West—The Platte, &c.," *American Turf Register*, VIII (July 1837), 454-457.

Anderson, William Pope. *Anderson Family Records*. Cincinnati, Ohio, 1936.

Ashley, William Henry. "The Diary of William H. Ashley, March 25-June 27, 1825," ed. Dale L. Morgan, *Bulletin of the Missouri Historical Society*, XI (Oct. 1954- April 1955), 9-40, 158-186, 279-302. See also under Morgan.

Atkinson, Henry. "Journal of the Atkinson-O'Fallon Expedition," ed. Russell Reid and Clell G. Gannon, *North Dakota Historical Quarterly*, IV (Oct. 1929), 5-56.

————, and Benjamin O'Fallon. [Report "respecting the movements of the expedition which lately ascended the Missouri River," Louisville, Ky., Nov. 23, 1825]. 19th Cong., 1st Sess., H. R. Doc. 117 (Serial 136). [Washington, D.C., 1826].

Audubon, John James. *Audubon and His Journals*, ed. Maria R. Audubon and Elliott Coues. 2 vols. New York, 1897.

————. *Audubon in the West*, ed. John Francis McDermott. Norman, Okla., 1965. Letters of 1843.

Aull, James, and Robert Aull. "Letters . . . ," ed. Ralph P. Bieber, Missouri Historical Society, *Collections*, V (June 1928), 267-310.

Ball, John. "Across the Continent Seventy Years Ago," ed. Kate N. B. Powers, *Oregon Historical Quarterly*, III (March 1902), 82-106.

————. *Autobiography* . . . , ed. by his daughters, Kate Ball Powers, Flora Ball Hopkins, and Lucy Ball. Grand Rapids, Mich., 1925.

————. [Letter to the Montana Historical Society, from Grand Rapids, Mich., Oct. 14, 1874], Montana Historical Society, *Contributions*, I (1876), 111-112.

————. [Letters to Dr. T. C. Brinsmade, April 29, July 15, 1832; Jan. 1, Feb. 22, 1833]. *Daily Troy* (N.Y.) *Press*, Aug. 23-24, 27-28, 1833; reprinted in *Zion's Herald*, Dec. 18, 1833; Jan. 1, 8, 15, 1834; and again in A. B. Hulbert, *The Call of the Columbia*, q.v.

Barrows, H. D. "The Story of an Old Pioneer [William Wolfskill]," *Wilmington* [Calif.] *Journal*, Oct. 20, 1866.

398

Barry, J. Neilson. "Captain Bonneville," *Annals of Wyoming*, VIII (April 1932), 610-633.

Barry, Louise. "Kansas before 1854: A Revised Annals," *Kansas Historical Quarterly*, (series beginning Vol. XXVII, Spring 1961).

Becknell, William. [Article], Franklin *Missouri Intelligencer*, June 25, 1825.

Beckwourth, James P. See Bonner, T. D.

Beidleman, Richard G. "Nathaniel Wyeth's Fort Hall," *Oregon Historical Quarterly*, LVIII (Sept. 1957), 197-250.

Bell, John R. *Journal . . . to the Rocky Mountains, 1820*, ed. Harlin M. Fuller and LeRoy R. Hafen. Glendale, Calif., 1957.

Berry, Don. *A Majority of Scoundrels: An Informal History of the Rocky Mountain Fur Company*. New York, 1961.

Bidwell, John. *Echoes of the Past. . . .* Chico, Calif., n.d.

———. *A Journey to California* [1841]. San Francisco, 1937. First printed Weston, Mo.? 1843? Again reprinted, Berkeley, 1964.

Billon, Frederic L. *Annals of St. Louis [1764-1804] and 1804-1821*. 2 vols. St. Louis, 1886, 1888.

Boardman, John. "The Journal of . . . from Kansas to Oregon in 1843," ed. J. Cecil Alter, *Utah Historical Quarterly*, II (Oct. 1929), 99-121.

Boggs, William Montgomery. "The W. M. Boggs Manuscript about Bent's Fort, Kit Carson, the Far West and Life among the Indians," ed. LeRoy R. Hafen, *Colorado Magazine*, VII (March 1930), 46-69.

Bonner, T. D. *The Life and Adventures of James P. Beckwourth. . . .* New York, 1856. New ed. by Bernard DeVoto, New York, 1931.

Bonneville, Benjamin Louis Eulalie de. [Letter to the Montana Historical Society, from Fort Smith, Arkansas, n.d.], Montana Historical Society, *Contributions*, I (1876), 105-110.

———. See Irving, Washington.

Brackenridge, Henry Marie. *Views of Louisiana: Together with a Journal of a Voyage up the Missouri River, in 1811*. Pittsburgh, 1814. Journal separately printed, 1815 and 1816.

Bradbury, John. *Travels in the Interior of America in the Years 1809, 1810, and 1811*. Liverpool, Eng., 1817.

Bradley, James H. [Journals and papers], Montana Historical Society, *Contributions*, II (1896), 140-228; III (1900), 201-287; VIII (1917), 105-250; IX (1923), 29-140, 226-351. The 1896 publication has been republished by Edgar I. Stewart as *The March of the Montana Column*, Norman, Okla., 1961.

Bray, Lauren C. "Louis Vasquez, Mountain Man," in Kansas City Westerners, *The Trail Guide*, III (Dec. 1958), 1-19. Also printed in Denver Westerners, *Monthly Roundup*, XV (July-Aug. 1959), 7-20.

Brewerton, George Douglas. *Overland with Kit Carson . . .*, ed. Stallo Vinton. New York, 1930.

[Bridger, James]. [Items concerning], San Francisco *Daily Herald*, Oct. 9, 1853; Denver Weekly *Rocky Mountain News*, May 15, 1861; *Oregon Spectator*, March 23, 1847.

Bright, Verne. "Black Harris, Mountain Man, Teller of Tales," *Oregon Historical Quarterly*, LII (March 1951), 3-20.

Brosnan, Cornelius James. *Jason Lee, Prophet of the New Oregon.* . . . New York, 1932.

Brown, David L. "Kit Carson, the Rob Roy of the Rocky Mountains," *The Spirit of the Times*, Jan. 23, 1847. Reprinted from the *Cincinnati Chronicle*.

———. "Recollections of Rocky Mountain Life," *The Spirit of the Times*, April 17, 1847. Reprinted from the *Cincinnati Chronicle*.

———. *Three Years in the Rocky Mountains.* New York, 1950. Reprinted from the Cincinnati *Atlas*, 1845.

Bryant, Edwin. *What I Saw in California* . . . [in 1846-1847]. New York, 1848.

Caesar, Gene. *King of the Mountain Men: The Life of Jim Bridger.* New York, 1961.

Camp, Charles L. (ed.). *George C. Yount and His Chronicles of the West.* Denver, Colo., 1966.

———. "The D. T. P. Letters," in *Essays for Henry R. Wagner*, San Francisco, 1947.

———. "Kit Carson in California," California Historical Society *Quarterly*, I (Oct. 1922), 111-151.

Campbell, Robert. "Correspondence of . . . 1834-1845," ed. Stella M. Drumm, *Glimpses of the Past*, VIII (Jan.-June 1941), 1-65.

———. "The Private Journal of Robert Campbell," ed. George R. Brooks, *Bulletin of the Missouri Historical Society*, XX (Oct. 1963-Jan. 1964), 3-24, 107-118.

———. *The Rocky Mountain Letters of.* . . . New York, 1955. Reprinted from the Philadelphia *National Atlas*, 1836.

Carleton, James Henry. *The Prairie Logbooks* [journals of 1844-1845], ed. Louis Pelzer. Chicago, 1943.

Carson, Christopher. *Kit Carson's Own Story of His Life*, ed. Blanche C. Grant. Taos, N. M., 1926. Also ed. Milo M. Quaife as *Kit Carson's Autobiography*, Chicago, 1935.

Catlin, George. *Letters and Notes on the* . . . *North American Indians.* 2 vols. London, 1841.

[Cerré, Michel Sylvestre]. [Obituary], *Missouri Weekly Republican*, Jan. 10, 1860.

[Charbonneau, Jean Baptiste]. [Obituaries], Ruby City, Idaho, *Owyhee Avalanche*, June 2, 1866; and Auburn, Calif., *Placer Herald*, July 7, 1866.

Chardon, Francis A. *Chardon's Journal at Fort Clark, 1834-1839* . . . , ed. Annie Héloise Abel. Pierre, S. D., 1932.

Chittenden, Hiram Martin. *The American Fur Trade of the Far West.* . . . 3 vols. New York, 1902. Reprinted in 2 vols., New York, 1935.

———. *History of Early Steamboat Navigation on the Missouri River.* 2 vols. New York, 1903.

[Christy, Edmund T.]. [Item emanating from], St. Louis *Missouri Republican*, Aug. 26, 1834.

Clayton, H. J. [Recollections of James Bridger], San Francisco *Daily Alta California*, April 21, 1872.

Clayton, William. . . . *Journal* . . . [1846-1847]. Salt Lake City, 1921.

BIBLIOGRAPHY

Cleland, Robert Glass. *This Reckless Breed of Men.* . . . New York, 1950.

Cline, Gloria Griffen. *Exploring the Great Basin.* Norman, Okla., 1963.

Clyman, James. *James Clyman, American Frontiersman* . . . , ed. Charles L. Camp. San Francisco, 1928. Expanded ed., Portland, Oregon, 1960.

Connor, Daniel Ellis. *Joseph Reddeford Walker and the Arizona Adventure,* ed. Donald J. Berthrong and Odessa Davenport. Norman, Okla., 1956.

Cooke, Philip St. George. [Journal 1846-1847], in *Exploring Southwestern Trails,* ed. Ralph P. Bieber, Glendale, Calif., 1938.

———. *Scenes and Adventures in the Army.* . . . Philadelphia, 1857.

Cornwall, Bruce. *Life Sketch of Pierre Barlow Cornwall.* . . . San Francisco, 1906.

Corson, Edward F. "Long Hair, Chief of the Crows," *Archives of Dermatology and Syphilology,* LVI (Oct. 1947), 443-447.

Coutant, C. G. *The History of Wyoming.* . . . Laramie, Wyo., 1899.

Crawford, Medorem. *Journal of Medorem Crawford: An Account of His Trip across the Plains with the Oregon Pioneers of 1842,* ed. F. G. Young, in *Sources of the History of Oregon,* I, No. 1, Eugene, Oregon, 1897.

Dale, Harrison C. *The Ashley-Smith Explorations.* . . . Cleveland, 1918. Revised ed., Glendale, Calif., 1941.

Dawson, Nicholas. *Narrative of Nicholas "Cheyenne" Dawson (Overland to California in '41 . . .)* . . . , ed. Charles L. Camp. San Francisco, 1933. First published ca. 1901.

Day, Mrs. F. H. "Sketches of the Early Settlers of California. Jacob P. Leese," *The Hesperian,* II (June 1859), 145-156.

Deland, Charles E. "Basil Clement (Claymore)," *South Dakota Historical Collections,* XI (1922), 245-389.

Dellenbaugh, Frederick S. *Frémont and '49.* New York and London, 1914.

Denig, Edwin Thompson. *Five Indian Tribes of the Upper Missouri* . . . , ed. John C. Ewers. Norman, Okla., 1961.

DeVoto, Bernard. *Across the Wide Missouri.* Boston, Mass., 1947.

Drumm, Stella M. (ed.). "Reports of the Fur Trade and Inland Trade to Mexico, 1831," *Glimpses of the Past,* IX (Jan.-June and July-Sept. 1941), 1-86. Important for the notes; see under Jackson, Andrew, for original publication.

Drury, Clifford Merrill. *Elkanah and Mary Walker: Pioneers among the Spokanes.* Caldwell, Idaho, 1940.

———. *First White Women over the Rockies.* 3 vols. Glendale, Calif., 1963, 1966. Includes letters and diaries of Narcissa Whitman and Eliza Spalding (1836), Myra Eells, Mary Walker, and Sarah Smith (1838). (Reprint of Eells and Walker diaries consists of extended excerpts, with occasional omission of entries pertinent to fur trade history; Vol. III includes 1838 journals of William H. Gray and Elkanah Walker, and letters of Cornelius Rogers and Asa Bowen Smith.)

———. *Henry Harmon Spalding.* Caldwell, Idaho, 1936.

———. *I, the Lawyer, Head Chief of the Nez Percé.* New York, 1960.

———. *Marcus Whitman, M.D.: Pioneer and Martyr.* Caldwell, Idaho, 1937.

Dunbar, John. "Letters to the American Board Relating to the Pawnee Mission," Kansas State Historical Society, *Collections*, XIV (1915-1918), 570-689.

Dye, Job Francis. *Recollections of a Pioneer, 1830-1852. Rocky Mountains, New Mexico, California.* Los Angeles, 1951.

Eaton, W. Clement. "Nathaniel Wyeth's Oregon Expeditions," *Pacific Historical Review*, IV (June 1935), 101-113.

Ebbert, George Wood. "Joe Meek Trip to Washington, 1847-8," *Oregon Historical Quarterly*, XIX (Sept. 1918), 263-267.

Edwards, Philip Leget. Letter to the (Liberty) *Missouri Enquirer*, "Waters of the Colorado of the West, June 23, 1834," reprinted in *Niles' Register*, XLVII (Oct. 11, 1834), 92.

———. *Sketch of the Oregon Territory: Or, Emigrants' Guide.* Liberty, Mo., 1842.

Eells, Myra F. "Journal . . . Kept While Passing through the United States and over the Rocky Mountains in the Spring and Summer of 1838," Oregon Pioneer Association, *Transactions*, XVII (1889), 54-88a. Extended excerpts reprinted in Drury, *First White Women over the Rockies*.

Eells, Myron. *Marcus Whitman, Pathfinder and Patriot.* Seattle, Wash., 1909.

Egan, William M. *Pioneering the West, 1846 to 1878. Major Howard Egan's Diary. . . .* Richmond, Utah, 1917.

Eldridge, William E. "Major John Dougherty, Pioneer," Kansas City Westerners, *The Trail Guide*, VII (Dec. 1962), 1-15.

Eliot, W. G., Jr. *An Address on the Life and Character of the Late Hon. Wm. H. Ashley: Delivered in St. Louis, Mo., June 6th, 1838, at the Request of the Committee of Arrangements.* St. Louis, [1838].

Elliott, T. C. "The Coming of the White Women," *Oregon Historical Quarterly*, XXXVII (June-Dec. 1936), 87-101, 171-191, 275-290.

———. "'Doctor' Robert Newell, Mountain Man," *Washington Historical Quarterly*, XVIII (July 1927), 181-186.

———. "'Doctor' Robert Newell, Pioneer," *Oregon Historical Quarterly*, IX (June 1908), 103-126.

Emory, William Hemsley. *Notes of a Military Reconnaissance, from Fort Leavenworth, in Missouri, to San Diego, in California . . . in 1846-7. . . .* 30th Cong., 1st Sess., H. R. Ex. Doc. 41 (Serial 517). Washington, D.C., 1848.

English, William Hayden. *Conquest of the Country Northwest of the River Ohio, 1778-1783; and Life of Gen. George Rogers Clark. . . .* 2 vols. Indianapolis and Kansas City, 1896.

Estergreen, M. Morgan. *Kit Carson: A Portrait in Courage.* Norman, Okla., 1962.

Evans, Hugh. ". . . Journal of Colonel Henry Dodge's Expedition to the Rocky Mountains in 1835," ed. Fred S. Perrine, *Mississippi Valley Historical Review*, XIV (Sept. 1927), 192-214.

———. "The Journal of Hugh Evans, Covering the First and Second Campaigns of the United States Dragoon Regiment in 1834 and 1835," ed. Fred S. Perrine and Grant Foreman, *Chronicles of Oklahoma*, III (Sept. 1925), 175-215.

Everett, Horace. *Regulating the Indian Department.* 23rd Cong., 1st Sess., H. R. Report 474 (Serial 263). Washington, D.C., 1834.

Ewers, John C. *The Blackfeet, Raiders on the Northwestern Plains.* Norman, Okla., 1958.

———. "The Indian Trade of the Upper Missouri before Lewis and Clark: An Interpretation," *Bulletin of the Missouri Historical Society*, X (July 1954), 429-446.

[Fallon, William O.]. [Account of], San Francisco *Californian*, Sept. 2, 1848.

———. [Diary], San Francisco *California Star*, June 5, 1847. Reprinted in Morgan, *Overland in 1846.*

Favour, Alpheus. *Old Bill Williams, Mountain Man.* Chapel Hill, N. C., 1936. New ed., Norman, Okla., 1962.

Ferris, Warren A. *Life in the Rocky Mountains . . .* , ed. Paul C. Phillips. Denver, Colo., 1940.

Field, Matthew C. *Prairie and Mountain Sketches*, ed. Kate L. Gregg and John Francis McDermott. Norman, Okla., 1957. Includes his diary of 1843 and sketches written for the New Orleans *Picayune*, 1843-1844.

[Fitzpatrick, Thomas]. [Item concerning], *Missouri Republican*, April 20, 1841.

———. [Letter, St. Louis, Nov. 28, 1842]. Published as "Robbery on the Santa Fe Trail in 1842," *Kansas Historical Quarterly*, XIX (Feb. 1951), 50-51.

Ford, Lemuel. "Captain Ford's Journal of an Expedition to the Rocky Mountains [1835]," ed. Louis Pelzer, *Mississippi Valley Historical Review*, XII (March 1926), 550-579. Republished as *March of the First Dragoons to the Rocky Mountains in 1835*, ed. Nolie Mumey, Denver, Colo., 1957.

"Fort Boise: From Imperial Outpost to Historic Site," *Idaho Yesterdays*, VI (Spring 1962), 14-16, 33-39.

"Fort Tecumseh and Fort Pierre Journal and Letter Books," ed. Doane Robinson, *South Dakota Historical Collections*, IX (1918), 69-239.

Frémont, John Charles. *Report of the Exploring Expedition to the Rocky Mountains in the Year 1842, and to Oregon and North California in the Years 1843-'44.* 28th Cong., 2nd Sess., Sen. Ex. Doc. 174 (Serial 461). Washington, D.C., 1845.

Frost, Donald McKay. *Notes on General Ashley, the Overland Trail, and South Pass.* Worcester, Mass., 1945.

Garraghan, Gilbert J. *Catholic Beginnings in Kansas City, Missouri.* Chicago, 1920.

———. *The Jesuits of the Middle United States.* 3 vols. New York, 1938.

Gaul, R. W. "Death of the Thunderbolt," *Bulletin of the Missouri Historical Society*, XVIII (Oct. 1961), 33-36.

Gauld, Charles, III. "A Trip to Yellowstone and the Oregon Country in 1834," *Washington Historical Quarterly*, XXVI (Jan. 1935), 28-29. Reprinted in *Annals of Wyoming*, XII (Jan. 1940), 62-64.

Geer, Elizabeth Dixon Smith. "Diary [1847] . . . ," *Oregon Pioneer Association, Transactions*, XXXV (1907), 153-179.

Graham, R. H., and Sidney Smith. "Report of Journey to the Rocky Mountains [1843]," ed. John E. Sunder, *Bulletin of the Missouri Historical Society*, XI (Oct. 1954), 41-53.

BIBLIOGRAPHY

Grant, Louis S. "Fort Hall under the Hudson's Bay Company, 1837-1856," *Oregon Historical Quarterly*, XLI (March 1940), 34-39.

Gray, William Henry. "Gray's Journal of 1838," ed. Clifford M. Drury, *Pacific Northwest Quarterly*, XXIX (July 1938), 277-282. Reprinted in Drury, *First White Women over the Rockies*.

———. *A History of Oregon, 1792-1849....* Portland, Oregon, 1870.

———. [Letter to David H. Ambler and Family, Sept 9, 1836], ed. A. B. and D. P. Hulbert, *Marcus Whitman, Crusader*, I, 216-229, and T. C. Elliott, "From Rendezvous to the Columbia," *Oregon Historical Quarterly*, XXXVIII (Sept. 1937), 355-369.

———. "The Unpublished Journal of . . . from December, 1836, to October, 1837," *Whitman College Quarterly*, XVI (June 1913), [70 pp.].

Greenburg, Dan W. "How Fort William Now Fort Laramie Was Named," *Annals of Wyoming*, XII (Jan. 1940), 56-62.

Gregg, Josiah. *Commerce of the Prairies....* 2 vols. New York, 1844.

Grinnell, George Bird. "Bent's Old Fort and Its Builders," Kansas State Historical Society, *Collections*, XV (1919-1922), 28-91.

Hafen, Ann Woodbury. "Baptiste Charbonneau, Son of Bird Woman," in Denver Westerners *Brand Book*, Denver, Colo., 1949, pp. 39-66.

Hafen, LeRoy Reuben. "The Bean-Sinclair Party of Rocky Mountain Trappers, 1830-32," *Colorado Magazine*, XXXI (July 1954), 161-171.

———. "Colorado Mountain Men," *Colorado Magazine*, XXX (Jan. 1953), 14-28.

———. "Fort Davy Crockett, Its Fur Men and Visitors," *Colorado Magazine*, XXVIII (Jan. 1952), 17-33.

———. "Fort Jackson and the Early Fur Trade on the South Platte," *Colorado Magazine*, V (Feb. 1928), 9-17.

———. "Fort St. Vrain," *Colorado Magazine*, XXIX (Oct. 1957), 241-255.

———. "Fort Vasquez," *Colorado Magazine*, XLI (Summer 1964), 198-212.

———. "Fraeb's Last Fight and How Battle Creek Got Its Name," *Colorado Magazine*, VII (May 1930), 97-101.

———. "Mountain Men—Andrew W. Sublette," *Colorado Magazine*, X (Sept. 1933), 179-184.

———(ed.). *The Mountain Men and the Fur Trade of the Far West.* Glendale, Calif., 1965-1966. (First 3 vols. of a continuing series.)

———. "Mountain Men—Louis Vasquez," *Colorado Magazine*, X (Jan. 1933), 14-21.

———. "Mountain Men—William Craig," *Colorado Magazine*, XI (Sept. 1934), 171-176.

———. "Old Fort Lupton and Its Founder," *Colorado Magazine*, VI (Nov. 1929), 220-226.

———. "Thomas Fitzpatrick and the First Indian Agency in Colorado," *Colorado Magazine*, VI (March 1929), 53-62.

———. "When Was Bent's Fort Built?" *Colorado Magazine*, XXXI (April 1954), 105-119.

———, and Ann W. Hafen. *Old Spanish Trail.* Glendale, Calif., 1954.

—— (eds.). *To the Rockies and Oregon, 1839-1842.* Glendale, Calif., 1955. Includes diaries of Sidney Smith, Obadiah Oakley, E. Willard Smith, and narrative of Joseph Williams.

Hafen, LeRoy Reuben, and Francis Marion Young. *Fort Laramie and the Pageant of the West, 1834-1890.* Glendale, Calif., 1938.

Hafen, LeRoy Reuben, and W. J. Ghent. *Broken Hand: The Life Story of Thomas Fitzpatrick....* Denver, Colo., 1931.

Haines, Francis. "Pioneer Portrait: Robert Newell," *Idaho Yesterdays,* IX (Spring, 1965), 2-9.

Harmon, Appleton. *Appleton Milo Harmon Goes West* [1847], ed. Maybelle Harmon Anderson. Berkeley, Calif., 1946.

Harris, Earl R. "Courthouse and Jail Rocks: Landmarks on the Oregon Trail," *Nebraska History,* XLIII (March 1962), 29-51.

Harris, Edward. *Up the Missouri with Audubon* [1843].... Norman, Okla., 1951.

Harris, Moses (Black). [Articles about], *St. Louis Democrat,* June 12, 1844; St. Joseph *Gazette,* Dec. 3, 1847, April 20, 1849.

Harris, William Richard. *The Catholic Church in Utah....* [Salt Lake City, 1909].

Hayden, F. V. *Preliminary Report of the U.S. Geological Survey of Wyoming.* Washington, D.C., 1872.

Hebard, Grace Raymond. "Jacques Laramie," *Midwest Review,* VII (March 1926), 32-34, 69-70.

———. *Sacajawea....* Glendale, Calif., 1933.

[Hildreth, James]. *Dragoon Campaigns to the Rocky Mountains . . .* [in 1834]. New York, 1836.

Hill, Joseph J. "Ewing Young in the Fur Trade of the Far Southwest, 1822-1834," *Oregon Historical Quarterly,* XXIV (March 1923), 1-35.

Historical Souvenir of El Dorado County. Oakland, Calif., 1833.

History of Cole, Moniteau, Morgan, Benton, Miller, Maries and Osage Counties, Missouri. Chicago, 1889.

History of Jackson County, Missouri. Chicago, 1881.

History of Placer County. Oakland, Calif., 1882.

History of Sonoma County. San Francisco, 1880.

Hodge, Frederick W. (ed.). *Handbook of American Indians North of Mexico.* 2 vols. Bureau of American Ethnology, *Bulletin 30,* Washington, D.C., 1907-1910.

Hopewell, Menra. [Article], *Missouri Republican,* July 25, 1858.

Houck, Louis. *A History of Missouri....* 3 vols. Chicago, 1908.

Howell, John E. "Diary of an Emigrant of 1845," *Washington Historical Quarterly,* I (April 1907), 138-158.

Hughey, J. C. [Statement on John H. Weber], *Salt Lake Tribune,* July 24, 1897.

Hulbert, Archer Butler (ed.). *The Call of the Columbia . . . 1830-1835.* Colorado Springs and Denver, Colo., 1934.

———. *Southwest on the Turquoise Trail: The First Diaries on the Road to Santa Fe....* Colorado Springs and Denver, Colo., 1933.

———. *Where Rolls the Oregon . . . 1825-1830.* . . . Colorado Springs and Denver, Colo., 1933.

———, and Dorothy Printup Hulbert (eds.). *Marcus Whitman, Crusader.* 3 vols. Colorado Springs and Denver, Colo., 1936-1941. Contains letters of Marcus Whitman, Samuel Parker, et al.

———. *The Oregon Crusade . . . 1830-1840.* Colorado Springs and Denver, Colo., 1935.

Hunt, Wilson Price. [Diary], in *Nouvelles Annales des Voyages*, Paris, 1821, X, 31-38. Translated in Stuart, *Discovery of the Oregon Trail*, 1935.

Hunter, John Dunn. *Manners and Customs of Several Indian Tribes Located West of the Mississippi.* . . . Philadelphia, 1823. Reprinted in London, 1823, as *Memoirs of a Captivity among the Indians of North America.* . . .

Hyde, George E. *Indians of the High Plains: From the Prehistoric Period to the Coming of Europeans.* Norman, Okla., 1959.

———. *Pawnee Indians.* Denver, Colo., 1951.

———. *Red Cloud's Folk.* Norman, Okla., 1937.

"An Indian Girl's Story of a Trading Expedition to the Southwest about 1841," ed. Winona Adams, *The Frontier*, X (May 1930), 338-351.

"An Indian Skirmish on the Tuolumne River in 1845," San Jose *Pioneer*, Aug. 9, 1881.

Irving, John Treat. *Indian Sketches.* 2 vols. Philadelphia, 1835. New ed. by John Francis McDermott, Norman, Okla., 1955.

Irving, Washington. *Astoria.* . . . 2 vols. Philadelphia, 1836.

———. *The Rocky Mountains.* 2 vols. Philadelphia, 1837. Annotated ed. with supplementary documents, ed. Edgeley W. Todd as *The Adventures of Captain Bonneville U.S.A.*, Norman, Okla., 1961.

[Jackson, Andrew]. *Message from the President of the United States . . . concerning the Fur Trade, and Inland Trade to Mexico.* 22nd Cong., 1st Sess., Sen. Ex. Doc. 90 (Serial 213). Washington, D.C., 1832.

———. *Message from the President of the United States . . . Relative to the British Establishments on the Columbia, and the State of the Fur Trade, &c.* 21st Cong., 2nd Sess., [Sen.] Doc. 39 (Serial 203). Washington, D.C., 1831. Contains letters by Joshua Pilcher, William H. Ashley, and Smith, Jackson & Sublette, 1829-1830.

Jacob, Norton. *The Record of . . .* [1844-1851], ed. C. Edward Jacob and Ruth S. Jacob. Salt Lake City, 1949.

James, Edwin. *Account of an Expedition from Pittsburgh to the Rocky Mountains, Performed in the Years 1819 and '20 . . . under the Command of Major Stephen H. Long.* 2 vols. Philadelphia, 1822-1823.

James, Thomas. *Three Years among the Indians and Mexicans*, ed. Walter B. Douglas. St. Louis, 1916. First ed. Waterloo, Ill., 1846. New ed. by A. P. Nasatir, Philadelphia and New York, 1962.

Jefferson, T. H. *Map of the Emigrant Road from Independence to St. Francisco, Cal.* [in 1846]. New York, 1849. Reprinted San Francisco, 1945.

Johnson, Sally A. "Fort Atkinson at Council Bluffs," *Nebraska History*, XXXVIII (Sept. 1957), 229-236.

———. "The Sixth's Elysian Fields—Fort Atkinson on the Council Bluffs," *Nebraska History*, XL (March 1959), 1-38.

Johnson, Overton, and William H. Winter. *Route across the Rocky Mountains. . . .* Lafayette, Ind., 1846. Reprinted Princeton, N.J., 1932.

Josephy, Alvin M., Jr. *The Nez Perce Indians and the Opening of the Northwest.* New Haven, 1965.

Kearny, S. W. *Report of a Summer Campaign to the Rocky Mountains, &c., in 1845.* St. Louis, Mo., Sept. 15, 1845. 29th Cong., 1st Sess., H.R. Doc. 2 (Serial 480). Washington, D.C., 1845. Pp. 210-220.

Kelly, Charles, and Maurice L. Howe. *Miles Goodyear. . . .* Salt Lake City, 1937.

Kennerly, James. "Diary of . . . 1823-1826," ed. Edgar B. Wesley, Missouri Historical Society, *Collections*, VI (Oct. 1928), 41-97.

Kennerly, William Clark. "My Hunting Trip to the Rockies in 1843," ed. Bessie K. Russell, *Colorado Magazine*, XXII (Jan. 1945), 23-38.

———. *Persimmon Hill: A Narrative of Old St. Louis and Far West . . .*, ed. Elizabeth Russell. Norman, Okla., 1949.

Kern, Edward Meyer. [Journal, Nov. 5, 1845-Feb. 15, 1846]. Printed as Appendix Q, pp. 477-486, in J. H. Simpson, *Report of Explorations*, q.v. See also *Life* Magazine, April 6, 1959.

Kingsbury, Gaines Pease. *Journal of the March of a Detachment of Dragoons under the Command of Colonel Dodge, during the Summer of 1835.* 24th Cong., 1st Sess., H. R. Ex. Doc. 181 (Serial 289). Washington, D.C., 1835.

Kittson, William. [Diary, 1824-1825]. Printed in Ogden, *Snake Country Journals*, q.v.

Kivett, Marvin F. "Excavations at Fort Atkinson, Nebraska: A Preliminary Report," *Nebraska History*, XL (March 1959), 39-66.

Larkin, Thomas. *The Larkin Papers*, ed. George P. Hammond. 10 vols. Berkeley, Calif., 1951-1964.

Larpenteur, Charles. *Forty Years a Fur Trader on the Upper Missouri . . . 1833-1872 . . .*, ed. Elliott Coues. 2 vols. New York, 1898. New ed. by M. M. Quaife, Chicago, 1933.

Lavender, David S. *Bent's Fort.* Garden City, N. Y., 1954.

Lecompte, Janet. "Gantt's Fort and Bent's Picket Post," *Colorado Magazine*, XLI (Spring 1964), 111-125.

Lee, Daniel, and J. H. Frost. *Ten Years in Oregon.* New York, 1844.

Lee, Jason. [Abstract of his overland journal, April 28-June 29, 1834; July 2, 1834-Feb. 6, 1835]. Printed in New York *Christian Advocate and Journal*, Oct. 3, 1834, Oct. 30, 1835. Reprinted in A. B. Hulbert, *The Oregon Crusade*, q.v.

———. "Diary . . . [1834-1838]," *Oregon Historical Quarterly*, XVII (June-Dec. 1916), 116-146, 240-266, 397-430.

———. [Letters relating to his overland journeys in 1834 and 1838, dated Feb. 5, April 29, May 2, and July 1, 1834, Nov. 12, 1838]. Printed in New York *Christian Advocate and Journal*, Feb. 21, June 13, Sept. 26, 1834, Nov. 23, 1838.

———. "The Mission Record Book of the Methodist Episcopal Church, Willamette Station, Oregon Territory, North America, Commenced 1834," ed. Charles Henry Carey, *Oregon Historical Quarterly*, XXIII (Sept. 1922), 230-266.

Leonard, Zenas. *Narrative* [1831-1835]. ... Clearfield, Pa., 1839. Reprinted, ed. W. F. Wagner, Cleveland, 1904. New ed. by John C. Ewers, Norman, Okla., 1959.

Lewis, Meriwether, and William Clark. *Letters of the Lewis and Clark Expedition* ..., ed. Donald Jackson. Urbana, Ill., 1962.

———. *Original Journals of the Lewis and Clark Expedition 1804-1806* ..., ed. Reuben Gold Thwaites. 8 vols. New York, 1904-1905.

Lienhard, Heinrich. *From St. Louis to Sutter's Fort, 1846*, ed. Erwin G. Gudde and Elisabeth K. Gudde. Norman, Okla., 1961.

Long, Stephen H. See James, Edwin.

Lowie, Robert H. *The Crow Indians*. New York, 1935.

Luttig, John C. *Journal of a Fur-Trading Expedition on the Upper Missouri, 1812-1813*, ed. Stella M. Drumm. St. Louis, 1920. New ed. by A. P. Nasatir, New York, 1964.

Lyman, H. S. "Reminiscences of F. X. Matthieu," *Oregon Historical Quarterly*, I (March 1900), 73-104.

McCoy, Isaac. "Journal of ... for the Exploring Expedition of 1830," ed. Lela Barnes, *Kansas Historical Quarterly*, V (Dec. 1936), 339-377.

McDermott, John Dishon. "The Search for Jacques Laramee: A Study in Frustration," *Annals of Wyoming*, XXXVI (Oct. 1964), 169-174.

McDonald, Daniel. *History of Freemasonry in Indiana, 1806-1898*. Indianapolis, 1898.

McKee, Ruth Karr. ... *Mary Richardson Walker: Her Book*. Caldwell, Idaho, 1945.

McKenney, Thomas Loraine, and James Hall. *The Indian Tribes of North America* ..., ed. Frederick Webb Hodge and David I. Bushnell, Jr. 3 vols. Edinburgh, 1933-1934.

McLoughlin, John. *Letters of Dr. John McLoughlin Written at Fort Vancouver 1829-1832*, ed. Burt Brown Barker. Portland, Oregon, 1948.

———. *The Letters of John McLoughlin from Fort Vancouver to the Governor and Committee, First Series, 1825-38*, ed. E. E. Rich. London and Toronto, 1941.

[McPherson, John C.]. "Juanita," pseud. [Articles in] *Oakland* [Calif.] *Daily Transcript*, Jan. 4, 15, 26, 29, 1873.

McWhorter, Lucullus Virgil. *Hear Me, My Chiefs! Nez Perce History and Legend* ..., ed. Ruth Bordin. Caldwell, Idaho, 1952.

Madsen, Brigham Dwaine. *The Bannock of Idaho*. Caldwell, Idaho, 1958.

Marsh, James B. *Four Years in the Rockies: or, The Adventures of Isaac P. Rose*. ... New Castle, Pa., 1884.

Marshall, T. M. "St. Vrain's Expedition to the Gila in 1826 ...," in H. Morse Stephens and Herbert E. Bolton, *The Pacific Ocean in History*, New York, 1917. Also in *Southwestern Historical Quarterly*, XIX (Jan. 1916), 251-260.

Mattes, Merrill J. "Chimney Rock on the Oregon Trail," *Nebraska History*, XXXVI (March 1955), 1-26.

———. "Hiram Scott, Fur Trader," *Nebraska History*, XXVI (July-Sept. 1945), 127-162.

Matthieu, F. X.   See Lyman, H. S.

Maximilian, Prince of Wied-Neuwied.   *Travels in the Interior of North America.* London, 1843.

Meek, Joseph L.   See Victor, Frances Fuller.

Meline, James F.   *Two Thousand Miles on Horseback.* . . .   New York, 1867.

Mengarini, Gregory.   "Mengarini's Narrative of the Rockies . . . [1841-1850]," ed. Albert J. Partoll, *Frontier and Midland*, XVIII (Spring and Summer 1938), 193-202, 258-266.

Merrill, Moses.   "Extracts from the Diary of Rev. Moses Merrill, a Missionary to the Otoe Indians from 1832 to 1840," Nebraska State Historical Society, *Transactions*, IV (1892), 160-191.

Miller, Alfred Jacob.   *The West of Alfred Jacob Miller (1837)* . . . , ed. Marvin G. Ross.   Norman, Okla., 1951.

———. "West to the Rendezvous," *Fortune*, XXIX (Jan. 1944), 111-121.

Moody, Marshall D.   "Kit Carson, Agent to the Indians in New Mexico," *New Mexico Historical Review*, XXVIII (Jan. 1953), 1-20.

Morehouse, George P.   "History of the Kansa or Kaw Indians," Kansas State Historical Society, *Collections*, X (1907-1908), 327-368.

Morgan, Dale L.   *Jedediah Smith and the Opening of the West.*   Indianapolis and New York, 1953.

———. *Overland in 1846.*   2 vols.   Georgetown, Calif., 1963.   Includes diaries of William E. Taylor, Nicholas Carriger, Virgil Pringle, Thomas Holt, George McKinstry, James Mathers, Hiram Miller, James Frazier Reed, Patrick Breen, and William Fallon, besides letters and newspaper accounts.

———. *The West of William H. Ashley, 1822-1838.*   Denver, Colo., 1964.   Includes Ashley's diary of 1825.   See also under Ashley.

———, and Carl I. Wheat.   *Jedediah Smith and His Maps of the American West.*   San Francisco, 1954.

Mudge, Zachariah Atwell.   *The Missionary Teacher: A Memoir of Cyrus Shepard.* . . .   New York, 1848.

Mumey, Nolie.   . . . *Bent's Old Fort and Bent's New Fort on the Arkansas River.*   Denver, Colo., 1956.

Munger, Asahel.   "Diary of Asahel Munger and Wife [1839]," *Oregon Historical Quarterly*, VIII (Dec. 1907), 387-405.

Murray, Charles Augustus.   *Travels in North America during the Years 1834, 1835, & 1836.* . . .   2 vols.   New York, 1839.

Nasatir, A. P.   *Before Lewis and Clark.*   2 vols.   St. Louis, 1952.

Newell, Robert.   *Robert Newell's Memoranda* . . . , ed. Dorothy O. Johansen.   Portland, Oregon, 1959.

Nichols, Roger.   *General Henry Atkinson: A Western Military Career.*   Norman, Okla., 1965.

Nicollet, Joseph Nicolas. *Report Intended To Illustrate a Map of the Hydrographical Basin of the Upper Mississippi River....* 26th Cong., 2nd Sess., Sen. Doc. 237 (Serial 380). Washington, D.C., 1843.

Nidever, George. *The Life and Adventures of . . . ,* ed. William Henry Ellison. Berkeley, Calif., 1937.

Nunis, Doyce Blackman, Jr. *Andrew Sublette, Rocky Mountain Prince. . . .* Los Angeles, 1960.

———. "Milton Sublette: Thunderbolt of the Rockies," *Montana, the Magazine of Western History,* XIII (Summer 1963), 52-63.

Nuttall, Thomas. *A Journal of Travels.* Philadelphia, 1821.

Ogden, Peter Skene. [Abridgments of his *Snake Country Journals,* 1825-1826, 1826-1827, 1827-1828, 1828-1829], ed. T. C. Elliott, *Oregon Historical Quarterly,* X (Dec. 1909), 331-365; XI (June, Dec. 1910), 201-222, 355-396.

———. *Snake Country Journals, 1824-25 and 1825-26,* ed. E. E. Rich. London, 1950.

———. *Snake Country Journal, 1826-27,* ed. K. G. Davies. London, 1961.

[———, supposed author]. *Traits of American-Indian Life and Character. By a Fur Trader.* London, 1853.

Oglesby, Richard Edward. *Manuel Lisa and the Opening of the Missouri Fur Trade.* Norman, Okla., 1963.

O'Meara, James. "Captain Joseph R. Walker," *Oregon Historical Quarterly,* XVI (Dec. 1915), 350-363.

Ontario Provincial Museum. *Annual Archaeological Report, 1917.* Toronto, 1917.

Overmeyer, Philip Henry. "Members of First Wyeth Expedition," *Oregon Historical Quarterly,* XXXVI (March 1935), 95-101.

Owen, John. *The Journals and Letters of Major John Owen . . . 1850-1871 . . . ,* ed. Paul C. Phillips. 2 vols. New York, 1927.

Palladino, Rev. L. B. *Indian and White in the Northwest....* Baltimore, Md., 1894. New ed., Lancaster, Pa., 1922.

Palmer, Joel. *Journal of Travels over the Rocky Mountains . . . during the Years 1845 and 1846.* Cincinnati, Ohio, 1847.

Parker, Samuel. *Journal of an Exploring Tour beyond the Rocky Mountains . . . in the Years 1835, '36 and '37....* Ithaca, N. Y., 1838.

———. "Letter, Green River, Aug. 17, 1835," *Missionary Herald,* XXXII (Feb. 1836), 70-72.

———. "Letters to the American Board Relating to the Pawnee Mission," Kansas State Historical Society, *Collections,* XIV (1915-1918), 742-746.

———. [Report to the American Board on his tour to Oregon and back, 1835-1837]. Boston, June 25, 1837. Printed in A. B. and D. P. Hulbert, *Marcus Whitman, Crusader,* I, q.v.

Parkman, Francis. *Journals of . . . ,* ed. Mason Wade. 2 vols. New York, 1947.

Parrish, E. E. "Crossing the Plains in 1844," Oregon Pioneer Association, *Transactions,* XVI (1888), 82-122.

Pattie, James Ohio. *The Personal Narrative of . . . during Journeyings of Six Years* . . . , ed. Timothy Flint. Cincinnati, Ohio, 1831.

Pelzer, Louis. *Henry Dodge.* Iowa City, Iowa, 1911.

———. *Marches of the Dragoons in the Mississippi Valley. . . .* Iowa City, Iowa, 1917.

Phillips, Paul Chrisler. "William Henry Vanderburgh: Fur Trader," *Mississippi Valley Historical Review,* XXX (Sept. 1943), 377-394.

———, and J. W. Smurr. *The Fur Trade.* 2 vols. Norman, Okla., 1961.

Placer County Directory. . . . San Francisco, 1861.

[Porter, Clyde H.]. "Jean Baptiste Charbonneau, Son of Sacajawea," *Idaho Yesterdays,* V (Fall 1961), 7-9.

Porter, Kenneth Wiggins. *John Jacob Astor, Business Man.* 2 vols. Cambridge, Mass., 1931.

Porter, Mae Reed, and Odessa Davenport. *Scotsman in Buckskin: Sir William Drummond Stewart and the Rocky Mountain Fur Trade.* New York, 1963.

Pratt, Orson. "Interesting Items concerning the Journeying of the Latter-Day Saints from the City of Nauvoo, until Their Location in the Valley of the Great Salt Lake [journal, 1846-1847]," *L.D.S. Millennial Star,* XI-XII (1849-1850), passim.

Preuss, Charles. *Exploring with Frémont . . . ,* ed. Erwin G. and Elisabeth K. Gudde. Norman, Okla., 1958.

Raynolds, William Franklin. *Report on the Exploration of the Yellowstone River. . . .* 40th Cong., 1st Sess., Sen. Ex. Doc. 77 (Serial 1317). Washington, D.C., 1868.

Reading, Pierson Barton. "Journal . . . [1843]," ed. Philip B. Bekeart, Society of California Pioneers, *Quarterly,* VII (Sept. 1930), 148-198.

Reed, James Frazier. "Letter from Fort Bridger, July 31, 1846, Springfield, Ill.," Springfield *Sangamo Journal,* Nov. 5, 1846. Reprinted in *Utah Historical Quarterly,* XIX (1951), 192-194.

[Riley, Bennet]. [Report on the Santa Fe Escort, 1829, Cantonment Leavenworth, Nov. 22, 1829]. 21st Cong., 1st Sess., [Sen.] Doc. 46 (Serial 192). Washington, D.C., 1830.

Robinson, Doane (ed.). "Official Correspondence of the Leavenworth Expedition into South Dakota for the Conquest of the Ree Indians in 1823 . . . ," *South Dakota Historical Collections,* I (1902), 179-256.

Rogers, Cornelius. "The Journey to the Rocky Mountains [letter dated at rendezvous, July 3, 1838]," *The Oregonian, and Indian's Advocate,* I (Dec. 1838), 75-78. Reprinted from the *Cincinnati Journal.* Again reprinted in Drury, *First White Women over the Rockies.*

Ross, Alexander. *The Fur Hunters of the Far West. . . .* 2 vols. London, 1855. Revised ed., Kenneth A. Spaulding, Norman, Okla., 1956.

———. "Journal of . . . Snake Country Expedition, 1824," ed. T. C. Elliott, *Oregon Historical Quarterly,* XIV (Dec. 1913), 366-388. An abridgment of the MS in the Hudson's Bay Company Archives, London.

Russell, Carl P. "Trapper Trails to the Sisk-ke-dee," *Annals of Wyoming,* XVII (July 1945), 89-105.

BIBLIOGRAPHY

———. "Wilderness Rendezvous Period of the American Fur Trade," *Oregon Historical Quarterly*, XLII (March 1941), 1-47.

Russell, Osborne. *Journal of a Trapper . . .*, ed. Aubrey L. Haines. Portland, Oregon, 1955. Earlier eds., Boise, Idaho, 1914 and 1921.

Ruxton, George F. *Life in the Far West*. Edinburgh, 1849. First published in *Blackwood's Magazine*, June-Nov. 1848.

Sabin, Edwin Legrand. *Kit Carson Days (1809-1868). . . .* Chicago, 1914. Revised ed., 2 vols., New York, 1935.

Sage, Rufus. *Scenes in the Rocky Mountains. . . .* Philadelphia, 1846. New ed., 2 vols., by LeRoy R. and Ann W. Hafen, Glendale, Calif., 1956.

[Santa Fe prisoners, 1818]. 15th Cong., 1st Sess., H. R. Doc. 197 (Serial 12). Washington, D.C., 1818.

Satterlee, Benedict. "Letters to the American Board Relating to the Pawnee Mission," Kansas State Historical Society, *Collections*, XIV (1915-1918), 746-750.

Scharf, John Thomas. *History of Saint Louis City and County. . . .* 2 vols. Philadelphia, 1883.

Shepard, Cyrus. [Abstract of his overland journal, April 27-June 20, 1834, with letter, June 28, 1834], *Zion's Herald*, Sept. 24, 1834.

———. [Letters relating to his overland journey in 1834], April 10, 23, 1834, Nov. 8, 1834, in New York *Christian Advocate and Journal*, June 20, 1834, Oct. 2, 1835; Jan. 1, 10, 1835, in *Zion's Herald*, Nov. 4, Oct. 28, 1835.

Sibley, George Champlin. *The Road to Santa Fe . . . 1825-1827 . . .*, ed. Kate L. Gregg. Albuquerque, N. M., 1952.

Simpson, George. *Part of Dispatch from . . .* [1829], ed. E. E. Rich. London and Toronto, 1947.

Simpson, James Harvey. *. . . Report of Explorations across the Great Basin of the Territory of Utah . . . in 1859. . . .* Washington, D.C., 1876.

De Smet, Pierre Jean. *Letters and Sketches. . . .* Philadelphia, 1843.

———. *Life, Letters and Travels . . .*, ed. H. M. Chittenden and Alfred Talbot Richardson. 4 vols. New York, 1905.

———. *Oregon Missions and Travels over the Rocky Mountains, in 1845-46.* New York, 1847.

Smith, Asa Bowen. See Spalding, Henry Harmon, and Drury, *First White Women*.

Smith, E. Willard. [Journal, 1839-1840]. Printed in LeRoy and Ann W. Hafen, *To the Rockies and Oregon, 1839-1842*, q.v.

Smith, Jedediah. *The Travels of . . .*, ed. Maurice Sullivan. Santa Ana, Calif., 1934.

Smith, Joseph. *History of the Church of Jesus Christ of Latter-Day Saints*, ed. Brigham H. Roberts. 7 vols. Salt Lake City, 1902-1932.

[Smith, Thomas L.]. "Sketches from the Life of Peg Leg Smith," *Hutchings' Illustrated California Magazine*, V (Oct. 1860-March 1861), 147-155, 198-206, 318-321, 334-336, 420-421.

Snyder, Jacob R. "[Diary] of . . . 1845," Society of California Pioneers, *Quarterly*, VIII (Dec. 1931), 224-260.

Spalding, Eliza. See C. M. Drury, *First White Women over the Rockies.*

Spalding, Henry Harmon. *The Diaries and Letters of Henry H. Spalding and Asa Bowen Smith . . . 1838-1842*, ed. Clifford Merrill Drury. Glendale, Calif., 1958.

———. "Letter from the Rocky Mountains," July 11-16, 1836, *New York Evangelist,* Oct. 22, 1836. Reprinted, ed. J. Orin Oliphant, in *Oregon Historical Quarterly,* LI (June 1950), 127-133.

———. [Letters, July 8, Sept. 20, 1836, Feb. 16, 1837], *Missionary Herald,* XXXIII (March, Oct., Dec. 1837), 122-123, 421-428, 497-501.

Stansbury, Howard. *Exploration and Survey of the Valley of the Great Salt Lake of Utah. . . .* 32nd Cong., Spec. Sess., Sen. Ex. Doc. 3 (Serial 608). Philadelphia, 1852.

Stevens, Warder W. *Centennial History of Washington County, Indiana.* Indianapolis, Ind., 1916.

[Stewart, Sir William George Drummond]. *Altowan . . .* , ed. J. Watson Webb. 2 vols. New York, 1846.

[———]. *Edward Warren.* London, 1854.

Stuart, Granville. *Forty Years on the Frontier . . .* , ed. Paul C. Phillips. 2 vols. Cleveland, Ohio, 1925.

Stuart, Robert. *The Discovery of the Oregon Trail; Robert Stuart's Narratives of His Overland Trip Eastward from Astoria in 1812-13 . . .* , ed. Philip Ashton Rollins. New York, 1935.

———. *On the Oregon Trail*, ed. Kenneth A. Spaulding. Norman, Okla., 1953.

Sublette, Milton Green. [Obituary], *Missouri Republican,* June 16, 1837.

Sublette, William L. "A Fragmentary Journal of . . . [1843]," ed. Harrison C. Dale, *Mississippi Valley Historical Review,* VI (June 1919), 99-110.

"A Summer upon the Prairie," *Army and Navy Chronicle,* II-III (1836), passim. (This narrative of the Dragoon Expedition to the Rocky Mountains in 1835 signed "F" has been attributed to Lemuel Ford, but the possibility should be investigated that the author was the Assistant Surgeon B. F. Fellowes.) Reprinted in A. B. Hulbert, *The Call of the Columbia*, q.v.

Sunder, John Edward. *Bill Sublette, Mountain Man.* Norman, Okla., 1959.

———. *The Fur Trade on the Upper Missouri, 1840-1865.* Norman, Okla., 1965.

———. "Solomon Perry Sublette, Mountain Man of the Forties," *New Mexico Historical Review,* XXXVI (Jan. 1961), 49-61.

Sutter, John Augustus. *The Diary of Johann August Sutter . . .* , ed. Douglas S. Watson. San Francisco, 1932.

———. *New Helvetia Diary: A Record of Events . . .* [1845-1848]. San Francisco, 1939.

Swanton, John R. *The Indian Tribes of North America.* Bureau of American Ethnology, *Bulletin 145*, Washington, D.C., 1952.

Talbot, Theodore. *The Journals of . . . 1843, and 1849-52 . . .* , ed. Charles H. Carey. Portland, Oregon, 1931.

Taylor, Bayard. *Eldorado, or, Adventures in the Path of Empire. . . .* 2 vols. New York, 1850.

Taylor, Creswell. "Charles Bent Has Built a Fort," *Bulletin of the Missouri Historical Society*, XI (Oct. 1954), 82-84.

Teit, James A. *The Salishan Tribes of the Western Plateaus*, ed. Franz Boas. Bureau of American Ethnology, *45th Annual Report*, Washington, D.C., 1930.

Territorial Papers of the United States, ed. Clarence Edwin Carter. Louisiana-Missouri Territory, 1803-1821. 3 vols. Washington, D.C., 1948-1951.

[Thompson, Mrs. A. L.]. "Interesting Historical Notes Relating to the Fontenelle Family . . . ," Nebraska State Historical Society, *Transactions*, I (1885), 89-93.

[———]. "The Romantic History of a Man Well Known to Nebraskans [Lucien Fontenelle]," Nebraska State Historical Society, *Transactions*, IV (1892), 95-98.

Thornton, J. Quinn. *Oregon and California in 1848*. 2 vols. New York, 1849.

Tobie, Harvey Elmer. "Joseph L. Meek, a Conspicuous Personality," *Oregon Historical Quarterly*, XXXIX (1938), 123-146, 286-306, 410-424; XL (1939), 19-39, 243-264; XLI (1940), 74-90.

———. *No Man Like Joe: The Life and Times of Joseph L. Meek. . . .* Portland, Oregon, 1949.

Townsend, John Kirk. [Journal, July 10-Oct. 6, 1834], in *Waldies' Select Circulating Library*, Part II (1835), 427-432. Reprinted in A. B. Hulbert, *The Call of the Columbia*, q.v.

———. *Narrative of a Journey across the Rocky Mountains, to the Columbia River . . . .* Philadelphia, 1839. Reprinted as *Sporting Excursion in the Rocky Mountains . . . ,* London, 1840.

Triplett, Frank. *Conquering the Wilderness. . . .* New York and St. Louis, 1883.

Ulibarri, George S. "The Chouteau-DeMun Expedition to New Mexico, 1815-17," *New Mexico Historical Review*, XXXVI (Oct. 1961), 263-273.

Victor, Frances Fuller. *The River of the West* [biography of Joseph L. Meek]. Hartford, Conn., 1870.

"Visitors from Oregon [Jason Lee's party]," *Peoria Register and North-Western Gazetteer*. Reprinted in New York *Christian Advocate and Journal*, Nov. 16, 1838.

Waldo, William. "Recollections of a Septuagenarian [1880]," ed. Stella M. Drumm, *Glimpses of the Past*, V (April-June 1938), 59-94.

Walker, Joel P. *A Pioneer of Pioneers: Narrative of Adventures thro' Alabama, Florida, New Mexico, Oregon, California, &c.* Los Angeles, 1953.

Walker, Joseph Reddeford. [Accounts of], San Francisco *Daily Herald*, Nov. 28, 30, 1853; Los Angeles *Star*, Dec. 13, 1851; [obituary], Sonoma *Democrat*, Nov. 25, 1876.

Walker, Mary Richardson. "The Diary of . . . June 10-December 21, 1838," ed. Rufus A. Coleman, *The Frontier*, XI (March 1931), 284-300. Extended excerpts reprinted in C. M. Drury, *First White Women over the Rockies*.

Warren, Eliza Spalding. *Memoirs of the West: The Spaldings. . . .* Portland, Oregon, 1916? Includes Eliza Spalding's diary, 1836-1838. See also C. M. Drury, *First White Women over the Rockies*.

Warren, Gouverneur K. *Memoir To Accompany the Map of the Territory of the United States from the Mississippi River to the Pacific Ocean. . . . Reports of Explorations for Pacific Railroads*, Vol. XI. Washington, D.C., 1859.

Watson, Douglas Sloane. *West Wind: The Life Story of Joseph Reddeford Walker....* Los Angeles, 1934.

Weisel, George Ferdinand. *Men and Trade on the Northwest Frontier As Shown by the Fort Owen Ledger.* Missoula, Mont., 1955.

Wells, Eugene T. "The Growth of Independence, Missouri, 1827-1850," *Bulletin of the Missouri Historical Society*, XVI (Oct. 1959), 33-46.

Wetmore, Alphonso. *Gazetteer of the State of Missouri.* St. Louis, 1837.

Wharton, Clifton. "Report, Fort Gibson, July 21, 1834," in Fred S. Perrine, "Military Escorts on the Santa Fe Trail," *New Mexico Historical Review*, II (July 1927), 269-304.

Wheat, Carl I. *Mapping the Transmississippi West.* 5 vols. in 6. San Francisco, 1957-1963.

Wheeler, Olin Dunbar. *The Trail of Lewis and Clark....* 2 vols. New York, 1904.

Wheelock, Thompson B. [Journal of Colonel Dodge's expedition from Fort Gibson to the Pawnee Pic village, 1834]. 23rd Cong., 2nd Sess., Sen. Ex. Doc. 1 (Serial 266). Washington, D.C., 1834.

Whitman, Marcus. "Journal and Report . . . [1835]," ed. F. G. Young, *Oregon Historical Quarterly*, XXVIII (Sept. 1927), 239-257. Also printed in A. B. and D. P. Hulbert, *Marcus Whitman, Crusader*, I, q.v.

Whitman, Narcissa. "A Journey across the Plains in 1836: Journal of Mrs. Marcus Whitman," Oregon Pioneer Association, *Transactions*, XIX (1891), 40-68. Also printed in Myron Eells, *Marcus Whitman*, Seattle, Wash., 1909, and in C. M. Drury, *First White Women over the Rockies.*

———. "Letters . . . ," Oregon Pioneer Association, *Transactions*, XIX (1891), 79-179; XXI (1893), 53-219.

Williams, Joseph. *Narrative of a Tour from the State of Indiana to the Oregon Territory, in the Years 1841-2.* Cincinnati, Ohio, 1843. Reprinted in LeRoy and Ann W. Hafen, *To the Rockies and Oregon*, q.v.

[Wilson, Richard L.]. *Short Ravelings from a Long Yarn....* Chicago, 1847.

Wislizenus, Frederick Adolphus. *A Journey to the Rocky Mountains in the Year 1839.* St. Louis, 1912. Originally published as *Ein Ausflug nach den Felsen-Gebirgen im Jahre 1839*, St. Louis, 1840.

Work, John. *Fur Brigade to the Bonaventura . . . 1832-1833 . . .* , ed. Alice Bay Maloney. San Francisco, 1945.

———. "The Journal of . . . July 5-September 5, 1826," ed. T. C. Elliott, *Washington Historical Quarterly*, VI (Jan. 1915), 26-49.

———. "Journal of . . . [Aug. 22, 1830-March 18, 1831]," ed. T. C. Elliott, *Oregon Historical Quarterly*, XIII (Dec. 1912), 361-371.

———. "Journal of . . . [April 21-July 21, 1831]," ed. T. C. Elliott, *Oregon Historical Quarterly*, XIV (Sept. 1913), 280-314.

———. *The Journal of . . .* [1831-1832], ed. William S. Lewis and Paul C. Phillips. Cleveland, 1923.

Wyeth, John B. *Oregon: or A Short History of a Long Journey....* Cambridge, Mass., 1833. Written from Wyeth's notes by Dr. Benjamin P. Waterhouse.

Wyeth, Nathaniel Jarvis. *The Correspondence and Journals of Captain Nathaniel J. Wyeth, 1831-6 . . .* , ed. F. G. Young, in *Sources of the History of Oregon*, I, Nos. 3-6, Eugene, Oregon, 1899.

————. "Indian Tribes of the South Pass of the Rocky Mountains; the Salt Lake Basin; the Valley of the Great Säaptin, or Lewis' River, and the Pacific Coasts of Oregon," in H. R. Schoolcraft, *Historical and Statistical Information Respecting . . . the Indian Tribes . . .* , Philadelphia, 1851, I, 204-228.

Young, Lorenzo Dow. "Diary . . . 1846-7-8," ed. Robert J. Dwyer, *Utah Historical Quarterly*, XIV (1946), 133-171.

Young, Otis E. *The First Military Escort on the Santa Fe Trail, 1829. . . .* Glendale, Calif., 1952.

————. "The United States Mounted Ranger Battalion, 1832-1833," *Mississippi Valley Historical Review*, XLI (Dec. 1954), 452-470.

————. *The West of Philip St. George Cooke, 1809-1895.* Glendale, Calif., 1955.

[Zumwalt, Solomon]. "Three Generations in the Span of a Continent: The Zumwalt Family," ed. Eugenia Learned James and Vivian K. McLarty, *Missouri Historical Review*, XLVIII (April 1954), 249-263.

Index

417

INDEX